The German Invasion of Norway

To my father

'In Norwegen kreuzen sich drei große Kraftlinien:
Die deutsche, die russische und die englische.'

In Norway, three great power lines cross:
the German, the Russian and the British.

Dr Heinrich Sahm,
German minister to Norway, 1938

The German Invasion of Norway

— *April 1940* —

Geirr H Haarr

Seaforth

PUBLISHING

Copyright © Geirr H Haarr 2009

First published in Great Britain in 2009 by
Seaforth Publishing,
Pen & Sword Books Ltd,
47 Church Street,
Barnsley S70 2AS

www.seaforthpublishing.com

British Library Cataloguing in Publication Data
A catalogue record for this book is available from the British Library

ISBN 978 1 84832 032 1

Typeset and designed by JCS Publishing Services Ltd, www.jcs-publishing.co.uk
Printed and bound in Great Britain by the MPG Books Group

Contents

Acknowledgements

MANY PEOPLE HAVE CONTRIBUTED to this book, some from a lifetime of their own research, others with a small but important detail. Their contributions are highly appreciated.

Above all, the altruistic help and support from Robert Pearson of Ipswich, England, is gratefully acknowledged. Were it not for him, this project would have been shelved a long time ago. David Goodey, Reinhard Hoheisel-Huxmann, Erling Skjold and Andrew Smith are also thanked sincerely. Without their help and support nothing would have been achieved.

John Ballam, Ronald Crocker, Albert Goodey, Bernhard Hallis, Vic Hiscock, Dagfinn Kjeholt, Derek Morris, Jan Reimers and Wilfred 'Robbie' Robinson were all there in 1940 and some sixty years later gave me the privilege of taking part in their thoughts and memories. Often sad, sometimes troubled, but inevitably low-key and with an understatement I could not fully fathom, they spoke of the little things that are not in the reports. Many have crossed the bar since and precious few are left. Let us never forget them or their mates.

The efficient staff at Sola Folkebibliotek, my local library, deserve great thanks. There is not a single book or document I have asked for they have not been able to find. Also the nameless staffs of the National Archives at Kew, Bundesarchiv in Koblenz and Freiburg, and Riksarkivet in Oslo deserve thanks for patience and professional dedication. The Naval Museum in Horten and Nordland Røde Kors Krigsminnemuseum (War Museum) in Narvik are thanked for enthusiastic support.

Julian Mannering at Seaforth Publishing deserves great thanks for believing in me and giving me the deadlines I needed. Without his support the project might never have seen completion.

Frank Abelsen, Dag-Jostein Andressen, John Asmussen, Bill Bartholomew, Keith Batchelor, Øystein Berge, Jostein Berglyd, Alexander Dietzsch, Tore Eggan, Ivar Enoksen, Nicole Granholt, Peter Harrison, Pamela Jacobsen, Tor Jevanord, Svein Aage Knudsen, Ernst Knutson, Sonia Law, George Malcomson, Oddvar Naas, Finn Nesvold, Tor Ødemotland, Simon Partridge, Paul Sedal, Halvor Sperbund, Ian Thomas, Ulf Eirik Torgersen, Trond Erik Tveit, John Warburton-Lee, Alister Williams, Ingrid Willoch, Ellen Margrete Willoch, Kåre Willoch and Atle Wilmar all deserve acknowledgement.

Last, but not least, thanks to my beloved wife Gro, for allowing me to share my passion for her with that for history; listening patiently when I needed to discuss some detail and skilfully distracting me when I needed to relax.

Geirr H Haarr
Sola, Stavanger, May 2009

— 1 —

Introduction

THIS BOOK DOCUMENTS THE German invasion of Norway in April 1940 (Operation Weserübung), focusing on the events at sea.[1] The objective is to give a balanced and factual account; readable but without compromising the demand for research and accurate detail.

As far as possible, the narrative has been based on primary sources. There is still an overwhelming amount of detail and anybody having information that would lead to modifications or improvements are more than welcome to contact me. The research material has come in many languages: Norwegian, German, English, Swedish, Danish and French. All translations into English are my own responsibility and where necessary I have striven to maintain the significance of what was said or written rather than create a word-by-word translation.

The military impact of Operation Weserübung has largely been overshadowed by the events on the Western Front and the fall of France, but there is no doubt that the invasion of Norway and the subsequent campaign had a significant influence on WWII in Europe. On paper, Germany had made a move of great strategic significance, breaking the British blockade of the North Sea and opening a potential to strike out towards the Atlantic. Lacking the resources to capitalise on the gains though, the conquest instead became a burden. The surface arm of the German Navy was small before the operation; afterwards it was crippled virtually beyond recovery. There were insufficient resources available to develop the full potential of the Norwegian bases and through the loss of many large surface ships the Kriegsmarine was, in reality, converted to a navy of small ships, incapable of even considering reaping any strategic gains from the venture. The Norwegian U-boat bases were of limited value compared to those on the French coast that became available very shortly after the Norwegian ones.

Nevertheless, Hitler and his senior staff were strengthened by Operation Weserübung and in spite of grave losses, the Führer consolidated his grip on the armed forces, paving the way for the campaigns in the West and in Russia.

The true strategic value of Norwegian territory appeared after the invasion of Russia in 1941, when northern Norway was used as a springboard for the polar front and the air and naval attacks on the supply route to Murmansk – neither of which were considered at all in 1940. Even after the attack on Russia it was difficult for the German Navy to find the resources to utilise the Norwegian ports and seaways to their full potential.

The loss of Norway and her territorial waters was in itself not catastrophic for the Allies but it took away an option to outflank Germany at the start of the campaign in France. Ironically, the most persuasive asset for either side prior to the events, the Swedish iron ore, was almost irrelevant afterwards. The supply to Germany continued virtually unaffected through the Baltic, and its strategic value diminished as the iron-ore mines in Lorraine were seized shortly after.

— 2 —

Wheels Within Wheels

Operation Weserübung

THERE WERE NO GERMAN plans whatsoever for an attack on Scandinavia in September 1939. The rationale for Hitler to unleash his dogs of war on Norway and Denmark seven months later developed during the winter through a series of intertwined incidents and processes involving the German fear of being outflanked, Norwegian neutrality policy, and Allied aspirations to sever German iron-ore supplies and to establish an alternative front in Scandinavia.

The first of several catalysts for the development was a visit to Berlin by the Norwegian National Socialist leader Vidkun Quisling in December 1939. He arrived on the 10th to keep abreast of political issues and to try to activate German support for his minority party. Instead, he was willingly entangled in an impromptu plan – the consequences of which were out of all proportion – staged by Quisling's man in Germany, Albert Hagelin.[1] The morning after his arrival, Quisling was taken by Hagelin to see Reichsleiter Alfred Rosenberg, head of the Nazi Party's internal 'Foreign Policy Office and Propaganda Section'.[2] The two men, who had met before, discussed the situation in Norway, which Quisling held had become very anti-German after the alliance with Russia and that country's attack on Finland.

Hagelin was also friendly with Fregattenkapitän Erich Schulte-Mönting, the navy Chief of Staff, and in the afternoon Quisling was brought to the naval headquarters at Tirpizufer. Here, Schulte-Mönting introduced the Norwegians to Grossadmiral Erich Raeder, the C-in-C of the German Navy. Quisling presented himself (correctly) as an ex-major who had served in the Norwegian General Staff and as a former defence minister. Raeder was impressed and gave him his attention, all the more so because Hagelin (falsely) managed to give the impression that Quisling was the leader of a significant political party with strong military and ministerial connections. Raeder had for some time argued in favour of an expansion of the Kriegsmarine's operating base into Scandinavia and saw an opportunity for support.[3] At the Führer conference on 12 December, the admiral recounted his conversation with the Norwegian, referring to Quisling as 'well informed and giving a trustworthy impression'. He also took the opportunity to recount the threat that a British landing in Norway – which Quisling held to be very likely – would create for the iron-ore traffic and the Kriegsmarine's ability to maintain an effective merchant war against England. Cautioning that the Norwegian might be playing a political game of his own, he nevertheless recommended that Hitler meet him and make up his own mind. Raeder suggested that if the Führer was left with a positive impression, the High Command of the armed forces (Oberkommando der Wehrmacht – OKW) should be allowed to work out provisional plans for an occupation of Norway, peacefully or with to Scheidt, Hitler made it clear that 'Any sign of English intervention in Norway would be met with appropriate means'. It would be preferable to use the troops elsewhere, but 'Should the danger of a British violation of Norwegian neutrality ever become acute . . .', he would land in Norway with six, eight, twelve divisions, and even more if necessary'. Quisling wrote that 'Upon mentioning the eventuality of a violation of [Norwegian] neutrality, Hitler worked himself into a frenzy'.

When Quisling had left, Generalmajor Alfred Jodl, chief of the operations office at OKW, was instructed to start a low-key investigation 'with the smallest of staffs' into how Norway could be occupied 'should it become necessary'. Several meetings were held over the next few days regarding Norway. Quisling, Hagelin and Scheidt participated in some and apparently received repeated promise of support. Unprecedentedly, Quisling was invited back to the Reichskanzlei on the 18th. This time, Hitler was virtually the only one to speak. He restated his absolute preference for a neutral Norway, but stressed that unless the neutrality was strictly enforced, he would be required to take appropriate measures, securing German interests. British landings in Norway were totally unacceptable and would have to be pre-empted. Finally, Hitler underlined the confidentiality of their meetings but indicated that Quisling would be consulted should a pre-emptive intervention become necessary. There was no mention of any plans for a coup.[9]

Quisling's skewed description of the situation in Norway was at best a product of his imagination, but his assessment of the alleged political situation in Norway made an impression in the Reichskanzlei. Hitler was already frustrated by the growing anti-German sentiment in Scandinavia, and the Norwegian's account of a Jewish-influenced Anglo-Norwegian alliance conspiring for offensive operations made sense to him; it was far from reality, but it had the right ingredients. Used by internal German forces protecting their own interests, Quisling had authenticated previous warnings of Allied intentions in Scandinavia and events were about to take a new direction.[10]

Neither the German Embassy in Oslo nor the Foreign Office in Berlin had been involved in Quisling's visit to Germany and when Foreign Minister Joachim von Ribbentrop learned that Quisling had met with Hitler he became rather disturbed. The German minister in Oslo, Curt Bräuer, confirmed that Quisling had exaggerated his leverage in Norway and vastly overstated the number of his followers and their political and military influence. Bräuer affirmed that Quisling's sympathies were national-socialistic and pro-German enough, but his politics could not be taken seriously. In Bräuer's opinion, openly siding with Quisling and his party would at best be a waste of resources and could very well harm German interests. 'Nasjonal Samling has no influence in this country and probably never will,' he concluded, adding that there were no indications that Quisling had support among Norwegian officers. As far as could be judged by the embassy, the officers were loyal to the government, which was really making an effort to enforce the country's neutrality. The OKW frowned on the prospect of an operation that would depend on support from Norwegian confidants – not to mention the difficulties of maintaining security.[11] 'Quisling has no one behind him,' army Chief of Staff Generaloberst Halder remarked laconically in his diary. Hitler listened for once and it was decided that even if Scheidt went to Oslo, he should keep the Norwegian 'Führer' at arm's length and, above all, not involve him in any planning.[12]

Hence, Quisling would have no further involvement in the ensuing preparations for the invasion of Norway, although he took all he had been promised at face value and went home, trusting plans were being developed in Germany that would eventually put him in power in Norway. It is doubtful if Quisling realised he had been sidelined, and that neither he nor his coup figured in the German plans. He stood alone in his treachery and nobody except Hagelin was fully involved.[13]

After attending a Führer conference on 1 January 1940, Halder wrote in his diary: 'It is in our interest that Norway remains neutral. We must be prepared to change our view on this, however, should England threaten Norway's neutrality. The Führer has instructed Jodl to have a report made on the issue.'[14] The plan for an intervention in Scandinavia was but a contingency at this stage, only to be activated against a clear British threat. As no such threat was substantiated, focus remained in the West, but wheels had been set in motion.

The initial sketch of the plan, 'Studie Nord', was completed by OKW during the second week of January. The Luftwaffe and army staffs were preoccupied with the attack on France and showed little interest when asked to comment. Raeder, on the other hand, ordered the Naval High Command (Seekriegsleitung – SKL), to assess Studie Nord properly and prepare constructive feedback. This they did, concluding that continued Norwegian neutrality was to the advantage of Germany and a British presence could not be tolerated. Still, pre-emptive plans would have to be developed – just in case. On 27 January, Hitler instructed the OKW to set up a special staff – Sonderstab Weserübung – to develop plans for such an operation. Kapitän zur See Theodor Krancke was given the task of leading the work, which commenced on 5 February, based largely on an updated version of SKL's comments and feedback to Studie Nord.[15] Knowledge of Weserübung was to be restricted and the 'issue of Norway should not leave the hands of the OKW'. Two basic principles emerged when the Sonderstab set down to work. First, an occupation of bases in southern Norway alone was pointless and would be difficult to uphold; Trondheim and Narvik would have to be occupied, as well as the sea lanes along the coast, to secure the transport of iron ore. Secondly, occupation of at least parts of Denmark would be necessary in order to secure sustainable connections to Norway across the Skagerrak and to prevent Allied access to the Baltic. Air bases in northern Jylland would also facilitate anti-shipping operations and reconnaissance in the North Sea.[16]

Shortly before midnight on 16 February 1940, Captain Philip Vian, on Churchill's orders, took the British destroyer Cossack into Norwegian territorial waters at Jøssingfjord, south of Stavanger. In spite of protests from Norwegian naval vessels, he attacked and boarded the German tanker Altmark. During the ensuing skirmish, 299 British sailors captured in the South Atlantic by the raider Admiral Graf Spee were liberated from Altmark while eight German sailors were killed. This was at the height of the 'phoney war' and the incident created headlines all over the world. General Jodl wrote in his diary that Hitler was furious about the lack of opposition from Germans and Norwegians alike: 'No opposition, no British losses!' The Royal Navy had humiliated Germany and the Norwegians had been unable – or unwilling – to defend their neutrality against the British intruders. Rosenberg wrote: 'Downright stupid of Churchill. This confirms

Commissioned in 1938, the 10,698-GRT *Altmark* belonged to a class of fleet auxiliaries, an integral part of the Kriegsmarine's merchant warfare. On her way home from the South Atlantic, where she had supported the *Graf Spee*, she was driven into Jøssingfjord south of Stavanger by British destroyers in the afternoon of 16 February 1940. During the night, Captain(D) Philip Vian of the 4th Destroyer Flotilla took *Cossack* into the fjord in spite of Norwegian protests and after a short gunfight liberated 299 British sailors, captured by *Graf Spee*. Eight German sailors were killed. (Author's collection)

Quisling was right. I saw the Führer today and . . . there is nothing left of his determination to preserve Nordic neutrality.'

The day after the boarding of *Altmark*, Admiral Raeder was told by an angry Hitler that as Norway 'was no longer able to maintain its neutrality,' the planning of Operation Weserübung was to be intensified immediately. The time had come to take control of events rather than just prepare for an eventuality. Raeder, uncomfortable with the sudden hurry, advised caution. In another meeting with Hitler a few days later, he argued that maintaining Norwegian neutrality was probably the best way to protect the vital ore transport along the Norwegian Leads. A German intervention would inevitably result in the traffic being threatened by the Royal Navy, and protecting the 1,400-mile coastline would be very difficult, requiring U-boats, aircraft and surface vessels not readily available. On the other hand, a British occupation of Norway would be totally unacceptable, all the more so as Allied forces in Norway, in Raeder's opinion, would put pressure on Sweden and threaten the main ore traffic through the Baltic. Hitler agreed: Norway must not fall into British hands. Germany would have to act, whatever the cost. A sense of urgency pulsed through the OKW. 'The Führer is pushing the preparations for Operation Weserübung. Ships must be fitted out, troops must be ready,' Jodl noted in his diary.'

The 55-year-old General der Infanterie Nicolaus von Falkenhorst (right) (1885–1968), C-in-C of XXI Army Corps, was chosen to lead Operation Weserübung. (Author's collection)

Jodl suggested giving responsibility for the planning to one of the corps commanders with experience from Poland and an established staff. The Führer agreed, and the 55-year-old General der Infanterie Nicolaus von Falkenhorst, C-in-C of XXI Army Corps, was called to Berlin at midday on 21 February. Von Falkenhorst had been a staff officer during the brief German intervention on the 'white' side in Finland in 1918 and was one of the very few German generals with some experience in overseas operations. Hitler told the general that a similar expedition was being considered as a pre-emptive strike to forestall British intervention in Norway to secure the supply of iron ore and other produce from Scandinavia. British forces in Norway would change the whole strategic situation, and the northern flank had to be secured prior to opening the campaign in the West. In addition, the German Navy needed freedom to operate in the North Sea and unhindered access to the Atlantic. Britain was already preparing landings in Norway, Hitler said, and had, according to reliable sources, reached an agreement with the Norwegian government to this effect. The recent *Altmark* episode demonstrated this beyond all doubt.

Stressing the need for absolute secrecy, Hitler invited von Falkenhorst to leave for a while, to think through how he would occupy Norway, and to come back in the afternoon. Somewhat shaken, von Falkenhorst went into a bookshop, bought a Bädeker tourist guide to Norway and sat down to find out how to conquer the country he had barely been aware of a few hours earlier. Returning at 5pm with some ideas and sketches, von Falkenhorst realised that his whole career was at stake. His ideas were to Hitler's liking, though, and the Führer decided he was the right man for the job. Von Falkenhorst was ordered to gather members of his staff and to start preparations immediately. Jodl noted in his diary that von Falkenhorst 'accepted with enthusiasm'.[18]

Generaloberst Walter von Brauchitsch, C-in-C of the German Army was less enthusiastic. He called von Falkenhorst to his office and told him in no uncertain language that he disapproved of Hitler's decision and saw the whole operation as 'unnecessary'. Besides, he had not been consulted and the Führer was 'doing all of this only with the advice of Raeder'. It probably did not help von Brauchitsch's opinion of the operation that von Falkenhorst was to report directly to the OKW and not to him – an unprecedented break with procedure. Generaloberst Halder, the army Chief of Staff, also expressed discontent with the operation and the fact that army command was largely kept out of the planning.[19]

Meanwhile, Krancke's group had produced a workable base-plan for the invasion. Spending a day reading this and other material available from Norway, von Falkenhorst and his staff took up work in some discreet back-offices of the OKW building in Berlin on Monday 26 February. Initially, only some fifteen officers were directly involved. To maintain secrecy there were no secretaries, which meant work from seven in the morning until late at night, seven days a week. Kapitän Krancke remained a member of the group, representing the Kriegsmarine. Oberst Robert Knauss from the Luftwaffe and Major Strecker from Abwehr handled liaison with their respective services and Oberst Walter Warlimont, deputy chief of the Operations Office, would secure a close connection to the OKW – although he did not become involved in the details of the planning. Hitler, on the other hand, kept a keen interest in the operation and influenced the planning on several occasions.[20]

The knowledge of Norwegian infrastructure, administration and armed forces was at best meagre and outdated. An invasion had been so far off the table that methodical intelligence had hardly been gathered. Maps were scarce and it was often necessary to rely on travel guides and tourist brochures. The embassy in Oslo had sent a fair amount of information regarding military installations, ports and harbours over the past years, but it was found to be unsystematic with limited verification. An intense programme of intelligence gathering was initiated under Major Pruck of the OKW, partly involving the embassy. In addition, a discreet search was initiated for merchant sailors and business people who had been to Norway as well as those who had been there as part of the children's aid programmes after WWI. On the day of the invasion, the German commanders would have a surprising amount of detailed information available to them, a credit to the efforts of the German intelligence. There were significant gaps, though, and in many cases the information was available centrally, but had not reached the operational end in time.

Concerning the Norwegian Army, von Falkenhorst's intelligence officer, Hauptmann Egelhaaf, could provide only a sketchy picture. Public sources indicated the existence of six army divisions, but details of mobilisation and deployment in case of an emergency were not available. Egelhaaf reckoned that centralised depots, inexperienced officers and an inadequate number of NCOs would slow the mobilisation process down and concluded that 'The Norwegian Army cannot offer sustained opposition against an attack from the major powers'. Oberst Erich Buschenhagen, Chief of Staff for XXI Corps, agreed, provided the attack came as a surprise, applying 'all means at hand'. The Norwegian Navy and Air Force were for all practical purposes disregarded at this stage, as were the coastal forts.[21]

* * *

In late February, less than two weeks after the *Altmark* episode, German naval attaché Korvettenkapitän Richard Schreiber made a visit to the Norwegian Admiral Staff, accompanied by his colleague, air attaché Hauptmann Eberhart Spiller. The Germans asked to meet the head of Naval Intelligence, Kaptein Erik Steen, and told him that they had secure information from Berlin regarding an imminent British action against Norway. This would certainly draw Norway into the war, and the Norwegians would have to make a choice in due course on which side they would join. The warning was clear and would not have been made without instructions from Berlin. Steen made a report of the meeting to the Admiral Staff and commanding admiral. The report was forwarded to the Norwegian Foreign Office, but apparently not to the commanding general or the Ministry of Defence.

On 4 March, Schreiber was back at the Admiral Staff again. This time he informed Steen that he had been called to Berlin to give an update on the general situation in Norway. In particular, he had been asked to comment on whether the country would oppose British forces occupying parts of the Norwegian coast and now asked for Steen's advice on what to say. A somewhat perplexed Steen referred to the prime minister's speech in January, where he clearly said that Norway would defend itself as best it could against any intruder.

Schreiber and Spiller went to Berlin a few days later. In separate meetings, they were asked to give their view of the general situation in Norway, the attitudes of the military and civilian administration and in particular their views on what opposition the Norwegians would put up against an invasion, German or Allied. They were both of the opinion that resistance against Allied intruders would be symbolic at best, as the *Altmark* episode had demonstrated. How a German invader would be met was more uncertain, but also in this case they apparently both assumed that opposition would be limited. It is unlikely that Spiller and Schreiber were given the full details of Operation Weserübung, but both returned to Norway with instructions to report as much as they could find on the Norwegian armed forces, airfields and harbours. Neither could travel freely in Norway, and the information they provided was mostly taken from public sources and largely limited to the Oslo area, adding little to the information from the professional intelligence officers.[22]

In the afternoon of 29 February, von Falkenhorst and his staff met with Hitler and presented their first sketch of Operation Weserübung. The Führer liked what he heard and, on head of OKW, Generalmajor Wilhelm Keitel's recommendation, approved the overall concept. He gave a few instructions and asked to be updated every other day. Jodl proposed to have Weserübung developed independently from Operation Gelb, the campaign in the West, and this was accepted even if the two operations needed to be synchronised; Gelb tentatively starting three days after Weserübung.

Hitler signed the formal directive for Weserübung on 1 March. This was the first official acknowledgement of the operation to the services from the OKW. The rationale for the operation was listed as threefold: to pre-empt British intervention in Scandinavia and the Baltic, to secure the iron-ore supply from Sweden and to extend the operational basis for the navy and air force against Britain. The available forces were limited and if at all possible, the operation should be carried out as a 'peaceful occupation' under the pretext of giving 'armed support to Nordic neutrality'. Maximum surprise and swiftness would have to compensate for low numerical strength, and secrecy was vital. Opposition could not be tolerated and should be met 'with all necessary force'. There was no mention at all of Quisling and his NS Party.

The Army High Command objected immediately against diverting forces to what they considered a secondary operation. Presumably there was also some resentment for being kept out of the planning and the troops having been assigned without their consulation. Generaloberst Halder held that Hitler had not 'exchanged a single word with the Commander-in-Chief of the Army on the subject of Norway'. Protests were futile, and the next day Jodl noted laconically in his diary: 'The Army agrees [to Operation Weserübung].'[23]

Weserübung Süd, the invasion of Denmark, would primarily secure Copenhagen and the airfield at Aalborg in northern Jylland, the latter to be captured by paratroopers followed by an airlifted battalion. Mechanised units would cross the border in the south and push north on the Jylland peninsular, while groups of smaller warships and requisitioned civilian vessels would land troops on the west coast and the islands. Command in Denmark was given to XXXI Corps under General der Flieger Leonard Kaupisch; subordinated to von Falkenhorst during the invasion phase.

In Norway, Weserübung Nord would see regimental-strength landings from warships at Narvik, Trondheim, Bergen and Kristiansand, while the wireless stations at Egersund and Arendal were assigned one company each. The equivalent of two regiments would head for Oslo, plus the support functions. Parts of the Oslo force would secure the naval base at Horten en route. Fornebu airport outside Oslo and Sola airport outside Stavanger were to be captured in airlift operations spearheaded by paratroopers. By securing the key coastal cities and ports between Oslo and Trondheim, a thin ring would be closed around southern Norway, within which most of the country's population, administration and armed forces could be controlled, and barracks and depots secured to prevent mobilisation and subsequent build-up of resistance.

Officers would be instructed to try a soft approach first, in particular towards the civilians; the soldiers should behave as friends and protectors, not aggressors. Bombers and long-distance fighters would be over the cities, ports and military installations to enforce the order, but without bombing or strafing unless deemed necessary by those on the ground. Von Falkenhorst later held that he hoped a 'peaceful occupation' could be achieved through a non-aggressive but 'firm, soldierly behaviour', but feared the Norwegians would resist.[24] It would have to be left to the man in charge of each group to decide which actions to take, when to bluff and when to open fire. Tasks would inevitably be solved differently, with different outcomes.

The bridgeheads in the west would have supply lines at the mercy of the Royal Navy. Hence, there would be no means of reinforcement other than by air until overland contact had been established. It would be necessary to bring sufficient troops and supplies in the initial landing phase to secure control and to initiate break-out operations towards the main force, which would move out from the Oslo region. Narvik would remain isolated until superiority in the south had been secured. On the positive side, the Allies would have few places left to land, should they attempt to intervene.[25]

The warships could not carry sufficient supplies to sustain the invasion forces and a carefully timed supply operation was set up whereby a handful of tankers and transport vessels would arrive at the invasion ports after the warships.[26] There was grave concern in the SKL over the safety of these ships, as they would have to leave Germany several days ahead of the naval ships and travel through Norwegian waters with no protection other than camouflage. Additionally, as the ports in western Germany could not accommodate the entire invasion and support fleet, some ships would have to pass through the Danish Belts, where they would undoubtedly be observed.[27]

After some debate between the OKW and the army, six divisions were eventually assigned to occupy Norway: 3rd Mountain Division and 69th, 163rd, 181st, 196th and 214th Infantry Divisions (ID). None of the units had combat experience, except for the 3rd Mountain Division, which had been partly used in Poland, and officers and NCOs who had transferred from other units. The 170th and 198th ID were assigned to Denmark, together with the 11th (motorised) Rifle Brigade. All units had a lower than usual complement of artillery and motor vehicles, but this was considered acceptable for operations in Scandinavia.

Around 8,850 men would be on board the warships heading for Norway in the first attack wave, while the airborne contingent would be some 3,500 men. The transport ships would land an additional 3,900 men, 742 horses, 942 vehicles and four tanks on the invasion day. Altogether there would be less than sixteen thousand men in the first wave, roughly the size of a regular German division. Not much to seize a whole country, but reinforcements of men and matériel would follow by air and sea as fast as possible. Most of these would go to Oslo in the ships of the sea transport echelons. The route east of Denmark to the Oslofjord would be the shortest and furthest away from the Royal Navy and the RAF. Weather was also less hazardous here than in the North Sea. Within three days, eight thousand troops were to be transported by air and sea, and an additional 16,700 during the subsequent week. In all a hundred thousand men would be brought to Norway in a continuous shuttle.

The British Navy was seen as the main threat to the operation, not only at sea but also in terms of counter-attacks. The guns of the Norwegian coastal fortifications were needed for defence against such an attack, and naval gunners would be onboard the ships of the first wave to man them as soon as possible. Raeder knew there was reason to fear the guns of the coastal forts during the invasion even if there was a good chance they might not be able to open fire in time unless they were pre-warned. He believed that few Norwegian officers would open fire on British ships; in the initial operation order, signed on 6 March, the warships were instructed to fly British flags until just before disembarkation commenced. All challenges from patrol vessels or coastguard stations should be answered in English. The exception was Narvik, where the local commander, Oberst Sundlo, was known to be German-friendly and was expected to react positively to German flags. According to international conventions, the use of false flag is permitted as a ruse of war until fire is opened, when own flag shall be flying. The order nevertheless created massive protests from some of the commanders, among them Oberst Buschenhagen and Generalmajor Tittel of the 69th ID. The order was eventually recalled by radio in the afternoon of 8 March and the German ships did not use British flags when entering Norwegian ports.[28]

Virtually the entire Kriegsmarine would be directly involved and all other naval operations were suspended, including U-boat sorties and preparations for the offensive in the West. Not everybody appreciated this and on 28 March, General Jodl noted in his diary that 'Some naval officers are lukewarm concerning Weserübung and need a stimulus . . . Falkenhorst's three chiefs of staff are having thoughts that are not their business. Krancke sees more drawbacks than advantages,' without elaborating. Von Falkenhorst commented later that Krancke 'at times did not agree with the plans of the Führer, criticising his decisions with sharp words.'[29]

Once the invasion had started, the Royal Navy would be alerted, whatever the security, and the SKL wished for the warships to return as soon as possible to try to avoid interception. The army argued that they would need the guns of the warships for support in case of opposition or Allied countermeasures and demanded that the navy stayed. Hitler agreed with the army and insisted that destroyers should be left behind in Narvik and a cruiser in Trondheim. Raeder held it was more important to have the ships available at sea rather then locked up in the fjords, and promises from Göring that the Luftwaffe would secure their stay inshore were dismissed as uncertain and weather-dependent. On 29 March Raeder discussed the issue with Hitler in private. He must have had some good arguments, as the Führer accepted that all destroyers could return from Narvik. At Trondheim he was firm: some destroyers should remain. A couple of days later, the SKL obliged, concluding that 'The Kriegsmarine has a commitment to protect the troops also after disembarkation and it may become necessary to leave some ships behind . . . until the army can no longer be hindered by Norwegian naval forces from fulfilling their task.'

After the invasion, the iron-ore traffic from Narvik would no longer be protected by Norwegian neutrality and a sustainable defence of the Norwegian coast would require a significant reorganisation of the Kriegsmarine's resources. The larger ships would be needed elsewhere and available forces would be limited to smaller vessels and U-boats. As many of the Norwegian ships as possible would have to be captured intact and pressed into service, however obsolete. It was to be expected that transit of ore through Narvik would cease until the Norwegian sea lanes had been secured by minefields, coastal batteries and air patrols. This would take time, perhaps several months. To handle matters after the invasion, Admiral Hermann Boehm was designated 'commanding admiral Norway': Raeder's direct representative, with headquarters in Oslo. Reporting to him, would be 'admiral south coast' in Kristiansand, Konteradmiral Otto Schenk, and 'admiral west coast' in Bergen, Vizeadmiral Otto von Schrader; the port commanders in Trondheim, Narvik and Stavanger reporting to the latter. These officers and their staffs were to become involved in the final stages of the planning and would be onboard the invasion vessels to take charge from day one.[30]

Göring and his Chief of Staff, General Jeschonneck, were annoyed over the downgrading of the Luftwaffe in Operation Weserübung, claiming they had been kept in the dark.[31] Never one for co-operation or sharing of influence, Göring feared that the subordination of Luftwaffe units to an overall operational command would threaten his authority. Anti-aircraft (A/A) units, airfield engineers, staff and maintenance personnel would be flown into Norway and Denmark as soon as the airfields were secured and there was no way the Luftwaffe could accept losing control over these, he argued. Hitler eventually gave in and on 4 March accepted the placing of all aircraft and personnel under the operational control of the X Fliegerkorps, which remained under Luftwaffe command.

Commander of X Fliegerkorps, the 48-year-old Generalleutnant Hans Ferdinand Geisler, and his Chief of Staff, Major Martin Harlinghausen, were called to Berlin on 5 March and, in a meeting with Göring and Jeschonneck, informed of their involvement in Weserübung. In addition to transport of troops and equipment, X Fliegerkorps was to provide direct support for the landings as well as reconnaissance and offensive capacity against intervening Allied naval forces. Geisler was instructed to co-operate with von Falkenhorst and the Kriegsmarine, but he should not report to any of them. To meet its tasks, the X Fliegerkorps would be temporarily strengthened with additional bomber, long-distance fighter and reconnaissance units, supplementing the two permanent bomber wings, KG 26 and KG 30, so far mainly tasked with anti-shipping operations in the North Sea.[32] During March, 500 Junkers Ju52/3m aircraft were gathered for the sole purpose of Operation Weserübung. Oberst Carl-August von Gablenz, a former Lufthansa manager and transport specialist was appointed to oversee the establishment and tactical operation of the transport units. The aircraft and pilots were assembled at airfields in the north while Geisler and his staff moved into Hotel Esplanade in Hamburg. The top floor of the six-storey building was discreetly emptied of all guests, but otherwise the hotel was run as usual to avoid drawing any attention to the arrangement. Maps, communication equipment and files were brought in and Geisler, Harlinghausen, von Gablenz and their staffs settled down to plan the huge task.[33]

The greatest weakness of Operation Weserübung, besides the lack of enforced co-operation between the services, was the absence of contingencies. There was no indepth assessment of the accuracy of the assumption of Norwegian acceptance of the invasion. Neither was there any fallback if things did not evolve as planned – other than application of brute force. The political and administrative aspects of the invasion and subsequent occupation were nowhere near as well considered as the military, largely because few outside the OKW and the Weserübung staff had knowledge of the operation being planned at all.[34] Apart from the initial XXI Corps staff, the OKW and parts of the SKL, knowledge of Operation Weserübung was kept on a strictly need-to-know basis. Division commanders, staff officers and naval and air group commanders were informed individually at the latest possible moment – and with details only of the part of the operation they were to be involved in.[35] This would benefit security but was detrimental to any joint doctrine or training prior to the operation.

A draft note on the administration of the occupied areas was issued by Oberst Warlimont in late February and appears to have been accepted without much discussion. A key element in the draft was to secure military control of Norway with minimal disturbance of the existing administration. Hitler believed King Haakon could be persuaded to legalise the occupation through a convincing show of force and it was considered particularly important that he remained in Oslo. Government, civil administration and police should continue as unaffected as possible, provided there was collaboration. The radio would be taken over by German personnel, while press loyal to the new regime could continue as before; the people should be won over through propaganda. Political parties and the Parliament – the Storting – would be ignored and eliminated as soon as possible. If the government would not co-operate, they would be removed and replaced with ministers open to accept the new situation. The same would apply to local authorities outside Oslo.

All communication with the Norwegian government should be through Curt Bräuer, the German minister in Oslo. Von Falkenhorst and his men should focus on the military tasks of the occupation and suppress any activity directed against Germany. When Raeder queried the political development in Norway following the occupation, von Falkenhorst and Keitel reassured him that the Führer would handle this and they, as soldiers, need not worry. Von Falkenhorst assured Raeder it would be feasible to collaborate with Foreign Minister Koht, a statement Raeder later referred to as 'politically naive'.[36]

Neutrality Watch

The news of the German attack on Poland was received with anxious apprehension in Norway. The empathy with Poland and anger with Germany was virtually unanimous, but there was also a general feeling that this was not Norway's war. During the afternoon of 1 September, the Norwegian government issued a declaration of neutrality. When Britain and France declared war on Germany two days later, the neutrality was extended to cover this conflict as well. An immediate freeze of all prices was decided while petrol, coal and some imported provisions were rationed. The government advised that people followed a careful lifestyle and asserted there would be no shortage of basic goods as long as nobody started hoarding. Private use of cars, motorcycles and boats was limited for a while, and the demand for horses and bicycles rose sharply. During September the situation stabilised and the war seemed far away, even if the newspapers often carried stories of death and dramatic rescues at sea. Between September 1939 and April 1940, fifty-five Norwegian merchant ships were sunk outside Norwegian territory, almost exclusively the result of German activities; 393 Norwegian sailors perished in these actions.

There was broad political agreement to limit the mobilisation of the Norwegian defences. The cost had been astronomical during 1914–18 and it was felt it would be better to keep a reasonable coastal defence and only mobilise fully if a crisis developed. Last time, no real threat to Norwegian territory had developed and few believed it would be different now. Consequently, the navy was given the first-line task of maintaining a Neutrality Watch, focusing on escort and patrol duties. The neutrality was to be vigilant but passive; prepared to handle 'occasional violations'. Force should be used with discretion except in the case of alien warships seeking to enter a restricted area or krigshavn, where all means should be applied after due warning.[37] In support, the air forces of the army and navy were mobilised whereas only a limited part of the coastal artillery was set up.[38]

The Royal Norwegian Navy (RNN) of 1939 was by no standards an instrument of deterrence. Originally a symbol of the Norwegian quest for independence at the beginning of the twentieth century, general disarmament and political development had reduced the once-imposing naval force almost to insignificance, with a severe lack of qualified officers and NCOs. Nevertheless, Commanding Admiral Henry Diesen on 28 August 1939, with the consent of the government, issued orders to prepare for recommissioning

The pansership *Eidsvold* passing Stavanger in the autumn of 1939 on her way to northern Norway. *Norge* and *Eidsvold* were armoured cruisers or coast defence ships of some 4,200-ton displacement. They were elegant, well-designed vessels with good sea-keeping abilities – and obsolete in every conceivable manner. (Ingrid Willoch)

the ships of the naval reserve.[39] Staff officers were drafted and coastguard stations, naval air bases and communication centres were manned. By the end of September, all ships fit for commissioning were in service, including two panserships and nine submarines; the only vessels that could be considered anything like a tactical reserve. The ships had been well looked after during storage and most were found to be in acceptable condition.

By 8 April 1940, 121 vessels were in commission by the RNN, of which fifty-three were chartered auxiliaries and nine unarmed support vessels.[40] Of the fifty-nine naval ships, nineteen had been launched after WWI, while seventeen were of pre-1900 vintage. Some 5,200 naval officers and men were in service onboard or onshore. Of these, 3,565 were sailors and 237 drafted officers, the rest professional officers and NCOs from the pre-war navy. The latter was a highly qualified cadre with much experience at sea; there were just not enough of them. Some NCOs were given temporary rank after brief officer courses and sent to serve on the auxiliaries, thus leaving holes in the ranks and disrupting well-exercised routines and relationships onboard the more modern ships.

During the 1933 reorganisation of the armed forces, the Naval Defence Force (Sjøforsvaret) was established, consisting of the Navy (Marinen), the Coastal Artillery (Kystartilleriet), the Naval Air Arm (Marinens Flyvevåben) and the Coastguard (Kystvakten). The coast was subdivided into three sea defence districts (SDD), in turn sub-divided into sea defence sectors (SDS). Each district was led by a sea defence commander based in Horten, Bergen or Tromsø respectively, reporting to the commanding admiral. The commanders of the coastal forts were subordinate to the relevant sea defence commander, as were the aircraft of the Naval Air Arm. Only the staff functions of commanding admiral and the supreme sea defence command were left in Oslo. The navy had advocated this organisation for a long time as it was considered critical to have an efficient co-ordination between the forts and the ships at sea. The practical side of the co-ordination was never tested, though, leading to a serious neglect of the landside defence of the forts.

The British Legation in Oslo summed up the situation of the RNN in the annual report on Norway in 1936: 'Promotion is extremely slow; material is largely out of date, money is very scarce.'[41] It was undoubtedly correct at the time, but progress had been made since, and ten new ships were launched between 1936 and 1939.

The coastal forts were among the most potent weapons of the Norwegian defences – if adequately manned. When designed in the 1890s, the coastal artillery was state of the art with concentrated firepower through strategically placed guns, larger than those on most ships, supplemented by lighter guns, mines and torpedoes. By 1940 they were obsolete, in spite of having been well maintained. Accuracy was fair if a reasonably trained crew handled the guns as fire control and range-finding systems had been modernised, but rate of fire was slow and upgraded ammunition in limited supply.

From 1900 to 1940, the speed of the naval ships had almost doubled and an intruder, originally expected to be in the firing zone for fifteen to twenty minutes, would be through in five to ten minutes. With reloading taking up to three minutes for the heavy guns, it would require optimum conditions for more than a few shots to be fired – unless mines or torpedoes could slow down the intruder. Early warning was essential and the commanders had to be determined to open fire at first sight. Plans for moving some of the batteries to a more forward position and to establish additional minefields existed, but had not been initiated.[42]

Commanding Admiral Diesen considered the navy more important than the coastal artillery for the Neutrality Watch and the latter was given low priority during the mobilisation. Stationary guns were of little use for escort purposes, and since both parties appeared to respect Norwegian neutrality, aggressive intrusions in force were not anticipated. Less than three thousand officers and ratings were drafted to the coastal artillery, around one-third of the full roll. There was a general shortage of officers, in particular sergeants and sub-lieutenants, which meant there had to be a strict prioritisation of which guns and batteries to man. Test firing of the larger guns with full-calibre ammunition was usually not allowed and neither guns nor men were prepared for extended firing, all the more so as the technical personnel needed for sustained live firing were no longer available. With an unfortunate short-sightedness, all the youngest and most recently trained ratings were drafted first. Thus, by the spring of 1940, a good number of the gunners had done their tour and been replaced, either by older men, trained up to twenty years earlier, or by youngsters, totally new to military life. At some forts, the crew had only been at their guns for a few days when the alarm sounded in the small hours of 9 April. A large number of guns, searchlights, torpedo batteries and A/A defences remained unmanned. No minefields were laid.

The Norwegian Army was subdivided into six 'district commands' or divisions. Each division had one field-brigade with one artillery and two or three infantry regiments to be mobilised in an emergency. In September 1939, four battalions were drafted in

Johan Nygaardsvold (1879–1952). Norwegian prime minister from 1935. Nygaardsvold focused on economic and social progress for the majority of the population and there is little doubt that Norway was a better society for most of its inhabitants by 1939. He was affectionately known as 'Gubben' or the Old Man. (Billedsentralen/ Scanpix)

any other member of the government made any serious efforts to grasp the state of the Norwegian defences and what an appropriate preparedness would mean in operational terms – far less how it could be achieved, what it would cost or how long it would take.[46]

Koht's distaste of Nazism was indisputable, but it was paralleled by a rejection of imperialism in general, which would not favour him to either side. He later wrote:

> In September 1939, the most challenging and difficult time of my life started. The seven months [before the German invasion] was every hour filled by a restless struggle to keep the country out of the war and secure its freedom. I was on duty day and night, weekdays and weekends – like on a tightrope between the belligerents. There is no doubt that the relationship with Britain – and thereby France – was the most difficult during this period and wore hard on my nerves. Politically, ideologically, nationally and personally my affinity, as well as that of the nation, rested with the Allies. Still, the British had a demanding attitude that was difficult to accept and continuously forced their issues onto us instead of negotiating affably.[47]

The constant responsibility took its toll and in April, Koht was tired and worn out.

The Labour government took power in 1935 with a negative attitude towards the armed forces and, although reality prevailed, the defence budgets increased unhurriedly through 1936–37 in spite of the threatening situation. Typically funds were made available in the form of extraordinary grants, special grants, grants for one-off purchases and eventually for the Neutrality Watch instead of a long-term dedicated budgetary commitment. As the international situation hardened through the 1930s the politicians, who almost universally

Halvdan Koht, Norwegian foreign minister from 1935. The photo is taken in Molde in late April and Koht (left) is in a meeting with his secretary, Tostrup. (Krigsarkivet/Scanpix)

lacked experience and competence in military matters, failed to initiate a constructive dialogue with the appointed leaders of the army and navy on how best to organise an effective and credible defence. From the memoirs of Koht and other ministers it appears that the government, to a large extent, believed that the extraordinary grants to the armed forces actually put things right. As late as September 1939, a new special grant was voted down, as funds already set aside for the Neutrality Watch were considered adequate. In practical terms, the fundamental conceptual difference between the government and the staffs resulted in disagreement on how to apply the extraordinary grants and on the prioritisations of the modification of the armed forces. In particular this would affect the navy, where the government's wish for quantity of ships overruled the Admiral Staff's wish for firepower.[48]

Minister of Church and Education Nils Hjelmtveit later wrote that he often 'had the impression the military administration worked efficiently, but very slowly [and] often took a very long time to prepare purchase of new equipment'.[49] Chief of the General Staff Oberst Rasmus Hatledal, however, held that prioritised lists of needed equipment and supplies were submitted on several occasions to the Ministry of Defence, but never responded to. It appears that at least part of the confusion can be explained by the unfortunate lack of co-ordinated management between the services and the inability of the Ministry of Defence to secure a proper dialogue between the military and the government. On the other hand, years of political neglect could not be restored overnight, irrespective of the increased funds available. The lack of experienced officers, NCOs and technical personnel would take considerable time to amend. Above all, the purchase of high-quality weapon systems from abroad was rapidly becoming virtually impossible, while Norway's own armament industry had been all but decimated. Specialised naval vessels could only be built at the naval yard in Horten and building of the *Sleipner*-class destroyers there, for all practical purposes, took up the available capacity – these would be the only RNN vessels with genuine combat value launched after 1936.[50]

By the spring of 1940, the Army and Navy Air Arms jointly had some 150 aircraft under order from Britain, the USA, Italy and Germany – sixty of them fighters. All of these had been delayed several times and in some cases purchases had been cancelled just before delivery. Nineteen Curtiss Hawk 75A-6 fighter aircraft from the USA had actually been delivered, but not yet made operational.[51] Around 150 20–40-mm guns were ordered from wherever they could be found, but none was delivered before 9 April. Last but not least, eight modern motor torpedo boats (MTBs) were ordered from Britain in early 1939. Two officers and four engineers went to Britain in February to oversee the completion of the boats, but none had been delivered before the invasion.[52]

In London it was recognised that Norway might be important for Germany as a source of vital supplies. To prevent this and tie the country as close as possible to the Allies with the smallest of means, the British minister to Norway, Sir Cecil Dormer, was instructed to assure Koht in a 'confidential but formal' manner that Britain would give Norway support against potential German aggression and would consider 'a German attack on Norway as tantamount to an attack on this country'. This he did on the 11 September 1939. Koht later wrote that the assurance pleased him and, as it was given to him in strict confidence, he considered it a trustworthy commitment. As he 'did not wish to tie [Norway] closer to Britain than it already was', he replied curtly that he did not believe Germany 'would do anything like that as there was nothing to gain'. Dormer reported to London that Koht made few remarks, but it probably 'had a good effect'.

On the 22 September the British minister was back. This time he confirmed that Britain would respect the declared Norwegian neutrality, but added that this would only apply as long as Germany did the same.[53] Again Koht did not respond much, but later wrote that this visit caused him concern as it made British respect for Norwegian sovereignty depend on London's interpretation of third-party action, not Norway's own handling of affairs.[54] Still, there was no doubt in Koht's mind as to which was the 'right side', should Norway be drawn into the war. In an interview with Reuters in early April, he said with clear reference to London:

> . . . We understand very well the difference between the goals of the warring parties, but it is part of our neutrality not to take sides. Neutrality is the only possible policy for us. . . . The harm done by Germany to Norwegian life and property has created great anger in this country and we do what we can to make it stop. British acts against our neutrality are of a different character, often affecting our honour and independence as much as our material interests [and] it may come to a point when also small nations must defend their honour.[55]

On 22 December, Koht told the Foreign Affairs Committee that he believed 'England and France would very much like to drive Norway out of its neutrality and into the war.' Koht realised that circles in London saw a direct interest in undermining Norwegian neutrality and provoking retaliatory German actions, which would force Norway into the war on the Allied side. He mistakenly believed that Berlin would find the reasons for maintaining Norwegian neutrality more compelling than those for military actions and therefore would not rise to the Allied lures. In all his rationality, Koht failed to grasp that the leadership in Berlin had a logic of its own and was not hindered by international boundaries and declarations of neutrality, even after Austria, Czechoslovakia and Poland had been overrun.

For personal and political reasons, Koht declined several invitations to go to Berlin and Rome. He never travelled to London either, but later alleged this to be coincidental and largely due to lack of a good opportunity. In his memoirs, he wrote that a planned visit to England in early 1939 was cancelled on the advice of the Norwegian minister in London, Erik Colban, as a recent visit from the Polish foreign minister had been portrayed in British media as the building of an alliance. Had Koht and Colban found an opportunity to develop relations and perhaps a better understanding of intentions in both London and Oslo, things might have been very different. Koht played a hard hand with both the German and British ministers in Oslo, being very conscious not to let them know what he really believed or expected. That the politicians in London were offended by his apparent lack of distinction between the aggressive German warfare and what they considered defensive measures did not occur to Koht. 'My impression was that both the Germans and the Allies were uncertain of me . . . I think this was to the benefit of my country,' he wrote.[56]

In December 1939, Oberst Birger Ljungberg was appointed defence minister, replacing the ageing Fredrik Monsen. The appointment was somewhat surprising as Ljungberg was a professional officer, unknown outside the army and not a member of the Labour Party. If anything, he was a Conservative. The appointment of a professional military man was well received in the Parliament, where it was believed that the government would now be guided in the right direction.[57] For many, Oberst Otto Ruge, the inspector general of the army, would have been the natural choice. Nygaardsvold and Koht agreed, however, that he was too obstinate for them and would never accept a passive role in the government. Thus, when Monsen suggested Ljungberg as his successor, Nygaardsvold eagerly concurred.[58] Welcoming his new minister to the government, Nygaardsvold bluntly advised him to 'concentrate on the administration of the defence [as] the political side would be handled by the other ministers'. That this reinforced Ljungberg's position as an outsider seems not to have bothered Nygaardsvold. The communication between the military and the government was unsatisfactory during the neutrality period in general and in early April in particular. The responsibility for this cannot be put anywhere but on the defence minister. What might have happened, had a stronger, more influential personality like Ruge, Fleischer or Hatledal been chosen, remains conjecture.[59]

Commanding general, Generalmajor Kristian Laake (from 1933), and commanding admiral, Kontreadmiral Henry Diesen (from April 1938), both of whom reported directly to the defence minister, were largely political appointments having been given

Birger Ljungberg, Norwegian defence minister from 1940. (NTB/Scanpix)

their offices because the government knew it could trust their loyalty and subordination to political decisions.[60] Before becoming commanding general, Laake had led the preparatory work for the Defence Act of 1933, and there would be no better man to carry it through, cutting the Norwegian defence forces to the bone. Laake and Diesen must take responsibility for the failure of the armed forces to optimise the use of the resources made available to them and for not taking a more active role towards the politicians when it became clear that not even the minimum obligations of the Defence Act would be followed. Both accepted that the government had to take 'economic considerations' and expressed their opinions through budget proposals and occasional reports, but neither man was prepared to take individual initiatives on a scale required to rock the boat. They believed the 'prescient Foreign Office' would initiate necessary precautions in due time, if needed. Neither man ascertained whether the time it would take and the resources needed to increase the strength of the Norwegian defences were appreciated by the government. In 1945, Laake told the Investigating Committee that he believed the 'initiatives taken during the autumn of 1939 were adequate [as] the government counted on England and assumed it would never come to actions of war on Norwegian soil. Should a German attack occur, England would help reject it – and versus the British, one should not fight.'

Commanding General Laake was nearing retirement. His health had started to fail and the 55-year-old Oberst Hatledal, Chief of the General Staff, troubled by the situation, took on more and more of the tasks and responsibilities of the general. It appears that Ljungberg did not appreciate this and a fatal gap in communication opened up between the General Staff and the minister.

Between the army and the navy, there was a fundamental disagreement on the assessment of threats and tactics to be applied. Hatledal as well as Oberst Otto Ruge, inspector general of the army, assumed a potential attacker would have clear military objectives – naval and air bases or iron ore. Contrary to Koht and the Foreign Office, Hatledal and Ruge believed that the main threat to Norway would come from Germany (and Russia in the north). Britain would, in all likelihood, respect Norwegian neutrality, but attempt to tie the country as close as possible to their economic warfare and not accept any of the other powers utilising the neutrality for its own purposes. A full-scale occupation of the country was not envisaged, as Ruge later openly admitted. When the grants for the military did start to rise, large-scale combined field exercises were organised in south-west Norway in 1937, 1938 and 1939. The exercises were intended to test the defence against an expeditionary corps that had landed between Kristiansand and Stavanger, moving towards Sola airfield. Naturally, numerous flaws and inadequacies emerged and it was clear that it would take years before the Norwegian defences could adequately meet a real threat. Above all, tactics and mobility needed to be improved and new weapon systems against aircraft and armoured vehicles were desperately needed. Demonstrating such shortcomings had undoubtedly been part of the exercises, but there is no record of this being explicitly presented to and understood by the government.

The navy was involved in the exercises, scouting, protecting convoys and acting as opponents. Chief of the Admiral Staff Kommandør Elias Corneliussen argued, with support from fellow naval officers, that the scenario for the exercises was unrealistic as long as the Royal Navy dominated the North Sea. In a newspaper interview in January 1939, Commanding Admiral Diesen held that he considered a war between Britain and Norway improbable, and hence a German intervention in Norway unlikely. 'To attack Norway one needs supremacy in the North Sea – but if one has, there is no need to,' he argued – tacitly implying that the threat to Norway indeed was from Germany, but held in check by Britain's naval strength.

Ruge, on the other hand, predicted that under certain conditions Britain could become engaged elsewhere, creating a situation where Germany might seek to improve its position. The modernised Luftwaffe was a far greater threat to British naval power than before and might achieve at least temporary supremacy, covering the transport and landing of German troops on the Norwegian south coast. This would eventually provoke a British response, he wrote, but '. . . British intelligence may fail, or British hesitation may miss the moment of opportunity. In any case, we must be aware that the powers at war will not assist us out of mere sympathy, bur consider their own interests. We shall have to bear the brunt of the first attack alone.'[61]

The commanders expected the government to keep them informed of the development of the international situation. The government, however, expected the commanders to keep them informed of the military situation and of any shortcomings in the ability of the armed forces to sustain the neutrality. Neither happened. Diesen and Laake never had adequate insight into the government's thinking regarding the international situation and the threats to Norwegian neutrality. The politicians never understood the mobilisation apparatus, its terminology or inevitable disruption of everyday life. Important intelligence and assessments were not disseminated, far less discussed between the military and civilian authorities. After 1 September 1939, the commanders were not called to the government on a single occasion to discuss the political and military situation – before 8 April – and there is no evidence to suggest the Ministry of Defence sought to improve the situation. The threat analysis from the General Staff, later shown to be very accurate, was ignored.

Nygaardsvold and Koht most probably believed that the already mobilised forces were adequate to handle the neutrality and that the defence minister was taking care of military matters in a satisfactory manner. Koht later admitted his poor knowledge of the armed forces, but claimed that it did not matter much as he left this to the defence minister. His actions do not always support this claim, though, and on several occasions there was direct contact between Commanding Admiral Diesen and him, sidelining Ljungberg. Koht believed that his communication with the ministry of defence was good, as 'all kinds of information' was forwarded and 'the members of the government met at least three times a week,' but there is no record of interaction, joint analysis or assessment of the information; far less of ascertaining that the actual state of the defences matched the situation. 'Neither of the powers have any unsettled business with Norway', said Defence Minister Monsen in the Parliament in March 1939. At the same time, Koht argued that the purpose of the army and navy was 'not to wage war, but through all possible means keep us out of it'. Neither position was revised until it was too late.[62]

Winston is Back[63]

In September 1939, Norway was given little consideration in the British War Cabinet for the conduct of the coming war. The sympathies of that country's government and people would, according to Minister Dormer in Oslo, 'favour the British cause, to a greater extent perhaps than in any other neutral country'. The only real concern was that the Scandinavian states might not actively join the blockade of Germany.[64] For First Lord of the Admiralty Winston Churchill, the 'thousand-mile-long peninsula stretching from the mouth of the Baltic to the Arctic Circle had an immense strategic significance', and severing the import of iron ore to Germany from Scandinavia, particularly the portion that went through Narvik, became a focus soon after his arrival at the Admiralty. Some of the senior staff there advocated 'a division of destroyers in Vestfjorden' as a convenient tool, even if this would challenge Norwegian authorities and naval forces. Others, like C-in-C Nore Admiral Drax, argued repeatedly for minefields. Churchill was at first against 'any drastic operations like landing forces or stationing ships in Norwegian waters', and instructed his staff to assess the option of severing the Leads by laying minefields 'at some lonely spots on the coast, as far north as convenient'.

On 19 September, Churchill for the first time drew the attention of the War Cabinet to the issue of Swedish iron ore to Germany. He fully supported the recently initiated negotiations for chartering the Norwegian merchant fleet, but urged diplomatic pressure be applied to halt German ore traffic inside the Norwegian Leads. Failing this, Churchill said, he would be compelled to propose more drastic measures such as 'the laying of mines inside Norwegian territorial waters [to] drive the ore-carrying vessels outside the three-mile limit'. The Cabinet accepted the importance of the ore import for Germany, but would give no support to try to sever it, beyond diplomatic means. First of all, German ore ships leaving Narvik had virtually ceased after the outbreak of war. Secondly, the Chiefs of Staff Committee (CoS) had two weeks earlier stated in a note to the War Cabinet that in view of Norway's economic importance to Germany, Berlin was unlikely to violate Norwegian neutrality, unless provoked by an Allied intervention or an interference with the iron-ore supplies. Last but not least, there was fear of negative reactions from the USA and other neutral countries if Britain were to violate Scandinavian neutrality.

By mid-November, the Admiralty had developed plans for how and where the Royal Navy could '. . . control the approaches to Narvik by naval forces in order to divert German iron ore imports to Great Britain.' On 30 November, Churchill brought to the War Cabinet a report he had received a few days earlier from the Ministry of Economic Warfare (MEW), concluding that 'complete stoppage of Swedish exports of iron ore to Germany would, barring unpredictable developments, end the war in a few months' – a conclusion based on the complete and sustained severing of the whole Swedish ore supply, not only that through Narvik. Churchill asserted that during the coming winter the Baltic would be closed by ice and the export confined to the Leads, where even small minefields would force the ore ships into international waters where the Royal Navy could intercept those bound for Germany.

The Chief of the Imperial General Staff, General Edmund Ironside, agreed that Swedish iron ore was a significant strategic objective and there were advantages in taking the war to Scandinavia, 'seizing the initiative from Hitler'. He argued that laying mines would only annoy the Norwegians, at little gain, and favoured a more sustained operation – securing control of the entire Lapland deposits with well-equipped troops and careful planning. Germany would certainly be provoked, but not able to react before May, giving ample time to establish a proper defence. All the more so, Ironside held, as in 'such a remote and forbidding country a very small force could hold up a large one'. Not quite convinced either way, the War Cabinet 'invited the CoS to prepare an appreciation of the military factors involved . . . to stop the import of iron ore to Germany by the sea route from Narvik, either by stationing a naval force in the Vest Fjord or by laying a minefield on the Norwegian coast'. At the same time, the MEW was 'invited to consider, in consultation with other Ministries, the effect this might have on Germany's economic position'. Both reports should also address the potential counter-measures Germany might take by military or economic means. Wheels had been set in motion.[65]

At dawn of that same day, 30 November, more than 450,000 Soviet troops with over 1,000 tanks crossed the borders to Finland after the Finnish government had refused to allow Russian bases around Leningrad. Led by Field Marshal Carl Gustav Mannerheim, the Suomi soldiers, contrary to all expectations, put up a spirited resistance, making full use of terrain and the coldest winter of the century. The Russians, seriously underestimating the Finnish will to resist, were not equipped for winter and suffered grievously. The Russian advance was stalled by Finnish tenacity, and the 'Winter War' ground to a halt.

From 1935 to 1939, the overall German iron-ore import rose from fourteen to nearly twenty-two million tons, of which the high-grade Swedish ore accounted for around nine million tons.[66] Mined in the Kiruna–Gällivare district of Lapland, just north of the Arctic Circle, the ore was exported through Luleå in the Gulf of Bothnia or Narvik in Norway. Purpose-built railway lines connected the mines with both ports. In the winter, when the Gulf of Bothnia froze and Luleå became icebound, normally from late November to mid-April, the export went solely through Narvik. Of the 6.5 million tons of Swedish ore shipped through Narvik during the winter of 1938/39, some 4.5 million tons went to Germany, in addition to some 1.2 million tons of Norwegian ore, mainly from Kirkenes. After the outbreak of war, the export through Narvik to Germany dropped rapidly. During the first seven months, 763,000 tons went to Germany, as opposed to 798,000 tons to Britain. In late March, after a visit to Oslo, Minister Colban presented a memorandum to British Foreign Secretary Halifax from Koht, where it was pointed out that of the six hundred thousand tons of iron ore waiting to be loaded in Narvik harbour, 400,000 were destined for Britain and only 200,000 for Germany. This information was confirmed by Swedish sources, adding that 'non-cooperation' at the railways delayed the German iron-ore traffic significantly while pressure on the Norwegian Pilot Association for a boycott was beginning to take effect, forcing German ships into open waters. No ore ships were sent from Germany to Narvik between 3 September and 25 October. By early November, some ten ships were involved in the German traffic to Norway, increasing to over twenty by the year end and to fifty by early March. On 18 December, the last ore transport of the year left Luleå and from then on, until the ice broke in the gulf again, German off-take of Swedish iron ore would be stockpiled or go via Narvik.

The export facilities in Narvik were thus useful, but not indispensable for the German ore import. Severing the traffic through Narvik without halting that through Luleå would at best have limited consequences, and would only have any effect at all during the winter. This was clearly spelled out by the MEW to the British War Cabinet in early December in their report, which concluded that 'The principal argument therefore put forward by the First Lord in favour of action in Norwegian waters [is] invalid.'[67]

Between 7 and 13 December 1939, the Greek freighter *Garoufalia* and the British *Deptford* and *Thomas Walton* were sunk off the Norwegian coast. Investigations by the RNN could not exclude drifting mines as the causes of the shipwrecks, but circumstantial evidence indicated that they had been torpedoed. Commanding Admiral Diesen stated it could not be said with absolute certainty the *Thomas Walton* had been inside the three-mile limit, whereas *Garoufalia* most likely and *Deptford* definitely had been. Actually, the culprit in all three cases was the German submarine *U38* under the command of Kapitänleutnant Heinrich Liebe.[68]

Seizing the moment, Churchill submitted a new memorandum to the War Cabinet on the 16th, arguing that,

. . . the effectual stoppage of the Norwegian ore supplies to Germany ranks as a major offensive operation of war . . . If Germany can be cut from all Swedish ore supplies from now onwards till the end of 1940 a blow will have been struck at her war-making capacity equal to a first-class victory in the field or from the air, and without any serious sacrifice of life . . . British control of the Norwegian coast-line is a strategic objective of first-class importance.[69]

Internal pressure in France made the Daladier government almost desperate for diversionary measures away from a potentially new Western Front and on 19 December, the French delegation to the Allied Supreme War Council proposed to send a *corps d'expedition* to Norway, officially to help Finland, but also to take control of the Swedish ore deposits as well as the export sites in Narvik and Luleå. Daladier argued that depriving Germany of the ore might lead to a swift victory; failing to act might prolong the war by several years.

The French proposal was discussed in the War Cabinet on the 22nd, by which time the CoS had also submitted their report on stoppage of Swedish iron ore. The CoS had found the question complicated. Stationing a naval force in Vestfjorden would be most effective, but run a high risk of clashing with the Norwegian navy. Laying of mines would have fewer risks, but supposedly be less effective. Churchill enthusiastically reiterated the proposed naval intervention from his memorandum of the week before and urged 'taking the first step of interrupting supplies from Narvik after such preliminary diplomatic negotiations as might be necessary'. Foreign Secretary Halifax, rather less excited, felt the consequences of limited actions in Norwegian waters were unpredictable; isolated landings in the Narvik area would be welcomed by neither Norway nor Sweden and could compromise the larger project of stopping all Nordic supplies to Germany. Severing the iron ore from Narvik alone was of 'little importance', he held; 'the key to the whole problem [being] the stoppage of supplies from Luleå'. Prime Minister Chamberlain concluded there were two distinct projects for Scandinavia: the 'smaller scheme', halting the traffic from Narvik, through mines or naval patrols, and the 'larger project', securing the ore-fields proper, severing all supplies of ore to Germany. The latter, which undoubtedly had French support, would require 'the good will of both Norway and Sweden', and diplomatic pressure was the most he was prepared to apply at the moment. Still, the CoS was 'invited to give further consideration to all the military implications of a policy aimed at stopping the export of Swedish iron ore to Germany'.

On 27 December, the War Cabinet discussed the Scandinavian issue again, now with firm conclusions from the Admiralty that the three merchant ships had been torpedoed inside Norwegian territory. Norwegian authorities, though not directly to blame in the opinion of the Admiralty, had been unable to prevent this, and 'steps to stop the German traffic from Narvik down the Norwegian coast' were advised. This time the War Cabinet concurred. Before any operations were initiated, though, Oslo and Stockholm should be informed that they could count on Allied help, should they undertake to assist Finland, followed by a notice to Norway that Britain was planning to send warships to intercept the German traffic. Meanwhile, the CoS was instructed to finish their report on the military implications of severing the iron ore from Sweden to Germany, while the War Office should 'continue preparations with a view to the ultimate despatch of a force to Narvik'.[70]

The Swedish and Norwegian ministers in London were that same day called to the Foreign Office and given aide-mémoires informing them that His Majesty's and the French government were disposed to give 'all the indirect assistance in their power' to Finland and were at present assessing how this could be done in the most efficient manner. The two countries were requested to grant consent for the transit of equipment and 'technicians', in return the Allies would be willing to discuss protection against the consequences of such permission. The Norwegian answer came over New Year: Norway would be pleased to assist in any aid to Finland, including transit of material '. . . without any military attendance' and transit of a 'technical mission to Finland . . . granted that such *technicists* will travel . . . in their private capacity'. The note concluded that 'the Norwegian government was grateful for the offer of an assurance for the preservation of the integrity and independence of Norway', but did not 'at the present moment wish to have this assurance more precisely defined'.[71] The Swedish answer was identical.

In the meantime, on 31 December, the CoS reported to the War Cabinet that – provided it was ascertained that Germany would be adversely affected by an interruption of the Lapland ore – despatching an expedition to Scandinavia could be worthwhile. It was underlined that this would represent a 'fundamental change' in British policy and a shift to 'offensive operations, which might well prove decisive'. Provided the security of France was not compromised, the strategy of operating in Scandinavia was considered 'sound', but an expedition inland from Narvik, in the face of Norwegian and Swedish opposition, would not be feasible. Concluding, the CoS advised against any minor naval projects until the larger project was ready in March, as this might trigger a major German offensive, which could not be forestalled.

Initial plans for the expedition, assuming Norwegian and Swedish co-operation, were presented to the War Cabinet and their advisers on 2 January and discussed thoroughly in the following days. The significance of the Swedish iron ore for the long-term German ability to wage war was generally agreed and few doubted that severing the supply through Narvik would provoke a response from Berlin. What kind of response was unclear, but besides direct action in Sweden, a likely retaliation would be to seize bases in southern Norway, probably between Kristiansand and Stavanger. A move on Oslo was considered less probable, as this would be a much larger operation and most likely to be met with Norwegian opposition. German bases on the Norwegian west coast would be a most serious threat to British control of the North Sea and it might be difficult to dislodge them once established. Hence, forestalling a German intervention in Norway would be essential. Norwegian reactions to an unprovoked Allied intrusion were largely expected to be symbolic.

Churchill was not convinced the Germans would react in force at all and repeatedly urged immediate action to 'see what happened', adding that British naval forces were standing by and ready to seize German ore ships coming out of Narvik. Chamberlain wished to gauge the Norwegian reactions through political means, and the delivery of a second, stronger memorandum to the Norwegian government was agreed. Meanwhile, the CoS should give further consideration to the consequences of a German occupation of southern Norway and how this could be avoided – including pre-emptive occupation of Stavanger, Bergen and Trondheim.[72]

Eric Colban, Norwegian
ambassador in London.
(Topfoto/Scanpix)

On Saturday 6 January, Halifax called Minister Colban to his office again, handing him a memorandum expressing dire concern by His Majesty's government over the recent 'flagrant violation of Norwegian territorial waters by German naval forces'. The British government, Halifax said, would in the near future be obliged to take 'appropriate dispositions to prevent the use of Norwegian territorial waters by German ships and trade', if necessary by operating inside those waters. The Norwegian government was taken aback by the British note. 'Colban's report from his meeting with Halifax shocked me,' Koht wrote, 'it was the most serious scare and I really felt the war looming. Not for a second did I doubt the Germans would see this as a provocation and turn their war-machine against Norway.' The memorandum and its implications were discussed at length in the Norwegian government over the next few days. Koht held that, should a situation arise where there was no choice left, it was vital Norway was not brought into the war on the German side. It was equally important, he said, that this was not publicly known as it might in itself compromise the neutrality.

The reply from Oslo eventually took the form of an emphatic letter from King Haakon to King George, delivered by Colban on 9 January. The king's letter, no doubt endorsed by the government, underlined his 'great surprise and consternation' over the plans to 'make Norwegian territorial waters a basis for British naval action' and 'appealed to [His Britannic Majesty] to prevent such steps, which inevitably would bring Norway into the war and imply the greatest danger for her existence as a Sovereign State'. Embarrassed by this approach and fearing Norwegian reactions might harm the 'larger project', Chamberlain and Halifax decided to abandon any operations against the Narvik traffic for the time being. As the Swedish reactions were also very negative, the War Cabinet accepted this on the 12th. The CoS was nevertheless 'invited to consider the possibility of capturing the Gällivare ore fields in the face of Norwegian and Swedish opposition'.[73] No indication of the decision to stand down should be given to the Scandinavian governments, but Laurence Collier of the Foreign Office remarked sourly to Colban a few days later: 'You have won – so far.'[74]

Scandinavia was not long off the agenda of the War Cabinet, however. Minister Colban was called to Halifax again on 18 January and learned that:

> . . . the real question at issue was not one of law, and it was for that very reason [Halifax] regarded the case of His Majesty's Government as stronger than the Norwegian Government seemed willing to admit. Not only was it a case in broad equity for equalising the treatment of the two parties in respect of the conduct of war so that the Germans could no longer be permitted to break all the rules and commit inhumanities of every sort, not only in Norwegian waters but everywhere on the high seas while His Majesty's Government were expected to refrain from even the smallest technical violation of international law.[75]

To this, Colban answered that after the incidents in mid-December, the Norwegian Navy had started escorting convoys along the exposed parts of the coast and nothing more had happened. As for supporting the Allied cause, the charter agreement for merchant tonnage had just been signed and the negotiations for a war trade agreement were making progress.

Meanwhile, the planning of the 'larger project' progressed unfalteringly and had by late January grown to three parallel, complementary operations; one in northern Norway–Lapland, one in southern Norway and one in southern Sweden. It was underlined by the CoS to the War Cabinet on 28 January that the stakes of such an operation would be high, but the prize of success would be 'great' and should be seized 'with both hands' should an opportunity arise. Breaking through determined resistance would be costly and the co-operation of both countries was 'essential'. Even with the consent of the Scandinavian governments, the operation would draw heavily on the navy for transport and protection; two divisions intended for France would have to be diverted. In order to be 'ready to act in April', the CoS concluded it would be necessary to make a decision to launch the operation 'in the near future'. Chamberlain, however, was still smarting from the defeat in January and not prepared to make any firm decisions. The troops, naval forces and transports earmarked for the operation were to be released even if the CoS was allowed to continue the detailed planning for Scandinavia, including the 'purchase of specialised stores and clothing required for Arctic conditions'.[76]

*   *   *

brigades were all that would end up in Finland, where they would remain near the railway in the north to avoid getting too close to the Russians or being cut off by a likely German intervention when the Gulf of Bothnia unfroze. The ultimate goal for the Allied planners was the Norwegian west coast and the Swedish iron ore, not aid to Finland. The secretary of state for war, Oliver Stanley, warned the Cabinet on 18 February that the 'whole affair was in danger of becoming unmanageable', as with a commitment of this scale Britain would 'not be able to send any more troops to France until well into the summer'. Chamberlain expressed concern over this 'new and somewhat disturbing [information], which had not before been brought to the notice of the War Cabinet', but left it at that.

Churchill also had second thoughts for a while; partly on moral grounds, partly from seeing the size of the Scandinavian operation. He wished for a 'pretext for getting a footing in Scandinavia' and within a fortnight got this from the *Altmark* incident, which he to a large extent orchestrated himself. Following this, he argued emphatically that the alleged Norwegian inability to protect its own waters from German trespassing should be used to lay one or more minefields in Norwegian territorial water forthwith, 'to prevent similar episodes'. This would not 'prejudice the larger operation', he held, but might – quite to the contrary – 'succeed in provoking Germany into imprudent action, which would open the door for us'. Invading Norway on a large scale against Norwegian acceptance, Churchill warned, would be a 'grave error'. Even a few shots between Norwegian and British forces 'would be a most unfortunate affair', but minor violations at carefully selected sites could be performed without confrontations with the Norwegian Navy. His arguments were not accepted by the Cabinet this time either, but he did receive support to start preparations for mining, should it be decided later. Hence the Admiralty was ordered to be prepared for operations in Norwegian waters, which, 'being minor and innocent may be called Wilfred'.

According to General Ironside, the army was not ready for a 'hurried action' and would not be so until mid-March. 'This [mining] project of the First Lord will accelerate any contemplated German actions in Scandinavia,' he held with some frustration. 'We must be absolutely clear that once we land a Force in Scandinavia, we are committed to a war there. . . . The expedition itself may be small to begin with, but will grow to be a major effort.' On 29 February Chamberlain concluded that, in spite of *Altmark*, he could 'not advise the War Cabinet to take action in Norwegian territorial waters for the present'. Any mining would have to be deferred 'and its execution reconsidered as the situation developed'. In a letter to Ambassador Corbin on the same day, it was explained that the War Cabinet did not think mining or any other minor naval actions offered 'advantages sufficient to offset the disadvantages on moral ground . . . but rather to make difficult . . . the plan for sending help to Finland' as it would inevitably make Norway and Sweden hostile to the Allies.[80]

By the beginning of February the Russians had renewed their attacks on the Finnish defences on the Karelian Isthmus with new units and improved tactics. The brave Finns were tiring and could not hope to sustain the resistance for long. After a few weeks, the Russians were approaching the 'Mannerheim Line', the final defences before Helsinki. In an attempt to avoid a disaster, Field Marshal Carl Gustav Mannerheim advised his government to opt for peace while still maintaining an impression in the Kremlin that an Allied intervention was an option.[81]

French impatience with what was considered British indecision was made well known through the embassy in London. Admiral Auphan later wrote: 'It's a little cynical to say so, but no one really hoped to stop the Soviet army and save Finland. The idea was to use the pretext of such an operation to lay our hands on the Swedish iron ore, and thus deny it to Germany.' Paul Reynaud also goes a long way in his memoirs to say that an expeditionary force might never reach Finland, but still attain a major goal should it occupy the Swedish ore fields and halt the export to Germany. Seen from Paris, there were few reasons why the Allies should respect Norwegian and Swedish neutrality if this could avert a German attack on France.[82]

The British Cabinet eventually agreed to submit yet another memorandum to Oslo and Stockholm, informing that Allied forces were all set for despatch to Finland, requesting co-operation during the transit through Narvik and Kiruna-Gällivare. Should this co-operation lead to hostilities with Germany, other Allied forces were being prepared for 'extensive military assistance'. The Norwegian government would be informed when British forces were prepared to land at Trondheim, Bergen and Stavanger to pre-empt German intervention in western Norway. The memorandum arrived on 2 March, and when discussed by the Norwegian government that same afternoon, there were for the first time voices speaking in favour of accepting the Allied request. Nygaardsvold made it clear however, that as long as he was prime minister, 'Norway would not voluntarily join the war'. Nevertheless, there was a clear attitude between his ministers from this point on, that if the Allies would come, it would be vital not to end up in an open fight with British soldiers, driving Norway onto the 'wrong side' of the conflict. Koht tried to co-ordinate the official answer with Stockholm, but the Swedish government had already categorically rejected the request and the Norwegian refusal followed on 4 March.[83]

The Allied military hardly registered the rejections. Général Sylvestre-Gérard Audet and his expeditionary force were standing by in France and most things were also ready in Britain. Major-General Pierce J. Mackesy, commander of the 49th Division, was confirmed as overall land commander and Admiral Edward R. Evans as commander of the naval force.

Chamberlain made it clear to the War Cabinet on the 11th that 'it would be fatal to abandon the expedition altogether merely because we had received diplomatic refusal from the Scandinavians to our demand for passage'. Churchill, with fewer reservations than he had two weeks earlier, did not think the landings would be vigorously opposed' by the Norwegians, but rather 'a matter for persuasion and cajolery'. The reward was high in his opinion:

Once ashore we should have secured a valuable prize not only in the possession of about a million and a half tons of iron ore, but also in our occupation of the harbour which would be of the greatest use for naval purposes. Even if the railway had been sabotaged, our forces should install themselves securely in the port in the hope that ultimately we might persuade the Scandinavians to give us railway facilities for a further advance.

General Edmund
Ironside, the Chief of the
Imperial General Staff.
(Author's collection)

Things suddenly accelerated. Ambassador Corbin had earlier in the day told Halifax that Prime Minister Daladier would have to consider resigning unless the issue of aid to Finland was decided positively very soon. At the end of the meeting, the War Cabinet invited the CoS to consider the details of landing in Norway and to report the next day for a final review. Also the instructions to be given to the naval and military commanders were to be presented for approval by the Cabinet. Next day, caution prevailed and the Cabinet decided that Operation Avonmouth should be confined to landings at Narvik at first. Departure should be the next day, 13 March, and if things developed satisfactorily at Narvik 'without any appreciable use of force', landings at Trondheim could follow immediately, the ships standing by offshore. The forces for Bergen and Stavanger were not to be despatched until further decisions by the Cabinet, in order to avoid the impression of 'a general attack'. In Oslo, Dormer was instructed to deliver a formal and urgent request' to the Norwegian government for the passage of 'a force of Allied troops across Norwegian territory to Finland' as soon as the news of landings at Narvik was confirmed.[84]

The British commanders were informed in a meeting with the CoS and parts of the Cabinet later in the day that their objectives were to establish a force at Narvik and to render assistance to Finland, while ensuring that 'north Swedish ore fields were denied to Germany and Russia for the longest possible period.' The Norwegian reaction was uncertain, they were told, and the War Cabinet only wished the force to land 'provided it could do so without serious fighting'. 'Minor opposition' could be accepted, even if it involved casualties; the British soldiers were only to fire back 'as an ultimate measure of self-defence should their forces be in jeopardy'. How to recognise 'minor opposition' was not detailed. When the first ships reached Narvik the turn of events would depend on the reactions of the local Norwegian commanders and the Allied commanders' interpretation of their intentions. General Ironside was certain it would be handled well:

> We are now working away at this plan, which means we must be prepared for some sort of an opposed landing. I can see our great big Scots Guards shouldering the sleepy Norwegians out of the way at 5 a.m. in the morning. It seems inconceivable the Norwegians should put up any opposition if they are in anyway surprised.[85]

In spite of Ironside's optimism, Major-General Mackesy, who would be C-in-C in the field, was concerned that a dangerous situation might develop. It would take weeks before his largely untrained troops were at full strength. No roads existed into the mountains and the only connection from the coast to Lapland was the single-track railway. This was electrified and there were few if any diesel or steam engines if the electricity was cut. Destruction of rolling stock and demolition of tunnels and overhangs would further hamper transportation eastwards. German retaliation could easily escalate beyond Allied capacity. The operation had all the prospects of becoming a dismal failure by having to turn back in the face of Norwegian opposition or worse, a quagmire of growing liability. Still, the embarkation of the British expeditionary force began in the morning of the 13th.

Meanwhile, the Finnish government decided the Allied offer of large-scale support was unrealistic and authorised its negotiators in Moscow to sign an armistice on 12 March 1940, to become effective the following day. Around midday on the 13th the news of the ceasefire in Finland broke and Chamberlain issued orders to suspend the expedition that afternoon.

In the War Cabinet the next day, the expedition was officially cancelled and orders for disembarkation of the soldiers issued. Churchill argued that the primary goal of the expedition, the Lapland ore fields, remained and insisted the landings at Narvik should still go ahead, lest Russia should seize the opportunity and 'make her way to the Atlantic'. Ironside urged the Cabinet to keep the force assembled. Both were overruled by an obviously relieved Chamberlain. The majority of the troops were disbanded and sent to France, against the protests of the Daladier government, who still hoped for a second front. The French warships and transports, which had been ready in Brest and Cherbourg, were released and sent to the Mediterranean, while the legionnaires and Alpine troops returned to their billets. Only some twelve thousand special forces – British, French and Polish – were retained in northern Britain, 'in case minor actions against the ore-transport should become necessary'.[86]

Operation Wilfred and Plan R4

In France, there was great bitterness over the Winter War and the governments' inability to help the Finns. On 19 March, Daladier lost a vote in the Parliament and his administration folded. The new government, formed two days later by the 62-year-old Paul Reynaud, predictably took an aggressive stance, eagerly supported by Général Gamelin. Reynaud wrote to the British Cabinet, stressing the need for a military initiative and proposed to intercept German shipping in Norwegian territorial waters, if necessary through occupation of strategic points on the coast. It was also suggested that a 'decisive operation' was launched in the Baltic, the Caspian or the Black Sea, with the aim of cutting Germany's petroleum supplies and 'paralysing the whole Soviet economy'. The note arrived in London on 26 March and created a storm of frustration, not least with Chamberlain, who read it as a direct criticism of his conduct of the war. In the Cabinet on the following day, there was broad agreement that the war should be fought neither in the Balkans nor in the Black Sea. On the other hand, a continued crisis in the French government would be disruptive and was to be avoided, even at the cost of Norwegian neutrality.[87]

In early March, preparations for Operation Royal Marine – the laying of floating mines in German rivers and estuaries to disrupt commercial traffic – were reported to be near completion. The War Cabinet found the concept interesting, but it had, so far, been rejected by the French government for fear of retribution. In London on 28 March, at the first meeting of the Supreme War Council since Reynaud took over, Chamberlain strongly advocated Royal Marine, while brushing lightly over Reynaud's repeated proposals for the Balkans. During the ensuing debate, which at times was quite heated, the British delegation vetoed any actions that could draw Russia into the war. The French were still sceptical about Royal Marine, but after some bargaining agreed to consider the concept – provided it was tied to a simultaneous mining of the Norwegian Leads. Chamberlain accepted this, as he expected it might draw attention away from the infringement of Norwegian neutrality. He did insist, though, that the Norwegian government should receive a warning a few days ahead of any mining.

It was agreed that by 1 April, diplomatic warnings should be submitted to Norway and Sweden, stating the Allies reserved the right to stop the German iron-ore traffic. Three days later, mining in German waterways would commence, followed by Norwegian waters on the 5th. One minefield would be laid in the approaches to Vestfjorden north of Bodø and one off Stadlandet, south of Ålesund. A third area off Bud between Molde and Kristiansund would be declared dangerous, but no mines would be laid. Confrontation with Norwegian naval forces was to be avoided, but if the mines were swept they should be relaid. Parts of the Home Fleet would be available for protection of the minelayers, just in case. Churchill's Operation Wilfred was finally on. Lawrence Collier wrote after the war that the intention was to 'stop German misuse of Norwegian neutrality'. Before the meeting, however, Halifax told Ambassador Corbin that in British opinion, German violations of Norwegian territory had been neither numerous nor well documented lately and now that spring was approaching and opening the Baltic, actions in Norway would only have a 'small interference with Germany's import'.[88]

The British decision-making process at this stage became imprecise and ambiguous. General Ironside and Général Gamelin met after the meeting, and the next day the British War Cabinet almost casually added 'a British brigade and a French contingent [to be] sent to Narvik to clear the port and advance to the Swedish frontier in case of German countermeasures to the mining'. Plan R4, as the operation was called, would be activated when the Germans took the bait and 'set foot on Norwegian soil, or there was clear evidence they intend to do so' – although what evidence of German action was needed was not specified. Landings at Narvik alone made little sense to the CoS and part of the plans from two weeks earlier were put forward again while efforts were initiated to try to reassemble as much as possible of the dispersed Stratford and Avonmouth forces. Troops for southern Sweden were no longer available. This operation would be confined to Norway and, if necessary, Lapland.

Two separate but linked interventions were thus being prepared: the mining and the landing of Allied soldiers in Narvik, Trondheim, Bergen and Stavanger. The laying of mines was not subject to Norwegian consent and when the landings were added so casually, the political safety valve, which had been a prerequisite for the War Cabinet so far, was lost. The CoS concluded that 'All preparations should be made for the despatch of at least one British battalion at the same time as the laying of the minefield, to be followed by the remainder of the force at the earliest possible date.' Within parts of the military it appears Plan R4 was expected to go ahead without waiting for the Germans. Churchill told the War Cabinet on 29 March that it was necessary 'to continue in a state of readiness to despatch a light force to Narvik and possibly . . . Stavanger', but added that he 'personally doubted whether the Germans would land a force in Scandinavia'. He probably kept the issue low-key on purpose so as not to raise objections and postpone Operation Wilfred once more. It is noteworthy that in the early morning of 31 March Vice Admiral Cunningham of 1st Cruiser Squadron was notified by the Admiralty that Plan R4 would be 'put into operation [and] also Stratford, probably 3rd April'. Less than two weeks after they had been saved by the Finnish capitulation, Chamberlain and Halifax had lost control of events again. This time, they would not regain it.

General Ironside commented in a note to the CoS and the War Cabinet that 'The projected operation in Scandinavia [has] a different political background from that . . . in early March when similar operations were contemplated.' Apprehensively, he added: 'From this beginning, we cannot foresee what may develop,' and advised them to 'have in hand a reserve', pending German reactions, including plans for 'the withdrawal of two to three divisions from France'.

On the request of the War Cabinet, the CoS issued a memorandum on 31 March, assessing various German reactions. The most that could be envisaged by the CoS was that Berlin might establish air and naval bases in southern Norway in order to take control of the minefields and attack British naval and air bases. Increased intelligence to detect German countermoves would be initiated, even if it were recognised that this might not be so easy.[89]

On 8 April, the British Military Intelligence Branch (MI) issued a paper entitled: 'The Possibilities of German Action against Scandinavia'. Based on the information available in the service departments and the Foreign Office, it concluded that the known disposition of German forces did not 'support any probability of a Scandinavian invasion'. Limited operations on the Norwegian coast were to be expected to counter any Allied mining, but there was little advantage to be gained by Germany from occupying Denmark.[90]

The French and British press printed, with remarkable indiscretion, reports of the Council's meeting on 28 March, including stories of imminent Allied intervention in Norway. For once, Koht asked the envoys in London and Paris to investigate. Colban reported back on the 29th, after meeting Halifax, that he did not believe 'the British Government had made any decision regarding actions in Norwegian territory'. Similarly, Minister Bachke in Paris reported that he could not see that any concrete actions had been decided, but a 'test-campaign might be launched to observe reactions'.

On 2 April, Chamberlain gave a speech in the House of Commons, but avoided any mention of concrete actions emerging from the Supreme War Council.

> [The] most important . . . weapon of our economic warfare is the employment of our sea power, and the Allies are determined to continue and intensify the use of this weapon to the full. His Majesty's ships have already taken certain practical steps to interfere with the unimpeded passage of the German cargo ships from Scandinavia. These operations have been carried out in close proximity to German naval bases, showing once again how empty are the German boasts the control of the North Sea has passed into their hands . . . The House may be assured that we have not yet reached the limit of our effective operations in this region.[91]

Colban commented to Oslo that the prime minister had 'carefully circumvented any revelation of the intentions of the government'. Other less diplomatic commentators concluded that Chamberlain's words actually signified that an intervention was already being prepared.

Reynaud, who felt that accepting mining of the German waterways was but a 'minor concession' compared to swaying the British Cabinet into offensive actions in Scandinavia, went home after the meeting on the 28th to discuss the plans with his Comité de Guerre Français. The French War Committee, under the influence of Daladier, strongly supported the actions in Norway, but rejected any execution of Operation Royal Marine, and Reynaud had to inform London accordingly on 31 March. Frustrated over what he considered French manipulation, Chamberlain told Ambassador Corbin, 'no mines, no Narvik', and both operations were postponed.[92]

On 3 April, Chamberlain discussed the status of the Norwegian issue with the Military Coordination Committee – of which Churchill had just taken over the chairmanship.[93] Intelligence of troop concentrations in the Baltic were given, but dismissed as German preparations to counter Allied moves. The French refusal of Royal Marine had stalled momentum but Chamberlain was acutely aware that a line had been crossed and ' . . matters had now gone too far for us not to take action.' If the French eventually turned down Royal Marine altogether, it would be necessary to 'proceed with the Norwegian Territorial Waters Operation alone'. Churchill was asked to go to Paris to try to change their minds, while a personal letter was sent from Chamberlain to Daladier. It appears the persuasion worked better the other way and on 5 April Churchill reported back to Halifax that Reynaud needed room to manoeuvre and the French may be 'right in wanting to postpone the mining of the Rhine until the French Air Force is strong enough to meet German retaliation'. To avoid a renewed political crisis in Paris, the War Cabinet later in the day gave in and accepted to 'proceed with the Norwegian plans'. The date for Operation Wilfred was confirmed as 8 April. That this was close to Reynaud's intentions all the time is difficult to ascertain, but easy to believe.[94]

Available units were hastily assembled: the 24th Infantry (Guards) Brigade supported by French troops for Narvik and the incomplete 49th Division for Trondheim, Bergen and Stavanger. Norwegian-speaking officers were transferred from wherever they could be found and information on conditions in Norway was distributed to officers and NCOs. Though not officially acknowledged, there was little doubt among the men where they were going. The troops for the Narvik part of Plan R4 were assembled on the Clyde and instructed to commence embarkation of the transport ships in the morning of 8 April. They would leave later in the day, escorted by the cruisers *Penelope* and *Aurora* with Admiral Evans and Major-General Mackesy onboard the latter. Brigadier CG Phillips and two battalions each for Bergen and Stavanger were to embark the cruisers *Devonshire*, *Berwick*, *York* and *Glasgow* of the 1st Cruiser Squadron in Rosyth on 7 April. A single battalion for Trondheim would follow two days later. It was assumed these forces would be able to forestall potential German reactions until reinforced, even if they were short of A/A defences. Chamberlain demanded that if faced with other than token opposition, the landing forces should withdraw and the operation be called off. Mackesy's revised instructions, dated 5 April, state that:

> . . . It is the intention of His Majesty's Government that your force should land only with the general cooperation of the Norwegian Government . . . It is not the intention that your force should fight its way through Norway. If Norwegian troops or civilians open fire on your troops, a certain number of casualties must be accepted. Fire in retaliation is only to be opened as a last resort. Subject to this, you are given discretion to use such force as may be required to ensure the safety of your command, but not more . . . You are to obtain further instructions from the War Office before entering Sweden.[95]

The 2nd and 18th Cruiser Squadrons were to be kept ready as a 'striking force', at Rosyth and Scapa Flow respectively, and the Home Fleet would be ready 'to deal with any sea borne expeditions the Germans may send against Norway'. None of the covering force would be at sea and all reactions depended on a timely recognition of German intentions.

On 4 April, the CoS submitted another memorandum to the War Cabinet informing that 'Special arrangements have been made for obtaining from Scandinavia the earliest possible authentic information of a German move against Norway or Sweden. We have been informed of the details of these arrangements and are satisfied they should prove adequate.' It is not detailed what the arrangements were, but as soon as information of German action was received in London, it would be forwarded to the War Cabinet, the Foreign Office and the service departments, including their sources in order to ascertain authority. Timing would be all important, and it was suggested that the Admiralty was empowered to initiate the departure of the troopships as soon as the first news of a move against Scandinavia was rumoured, however vague. It would take some twenty hours until the ships were off their Norwegian targets and they could be recalled at any time during this period should the War Cabinet decide the information was false or inadequate. Such pragmatism, which the Cabinet endorsed, makes the decisions made by the Admiralty a few days later to disembark the troops even more curious.

Part of the 'arrangements' referred to by the CoS in all likelihood included a handful of Military Intelligence Research (MIR) officers, clandestinely arriving at the legation in Oslo during 2 and 3 April. Nominally, they were to supervise the transit of remaining equipment for Finland. Actually they were to report status in Norway and to liaise with the Norwegian forces when R4 arrived. Captains Croft and Munthe came via Sweden, while Major Palmer flew in via Perth. The legation was instructed to give them all necessary assistance. Within a few days, Munthe continued to Stavanger, Croft to Bergen and Palmer to Trondheim. A fourth officer, Captain Torrance, went directly to Narvik via Stockholm. How these men were to detect German intentions regarding Norway before anybody else is not obvious.

The willingness of the British decision makers to engage in complicated and far-reaching operations with so limited preparations and so little knowledge of things Norwegian is startling – as is their lack of realistic analysis of German intentions. The degree of provocation necessary for Berlin to react seems never to have been debated properly, far less realistic scenarios of how the Germans might respond. All British (and French) thinking was based on traditional suppositions of moves and countermoves within given 'rules' of strength and mobility. That the new German war machine was operating under its own dynamics was yet to be revealed.[96]

At Sullom Voe, the C-in-C of 2nd Destroyer Flotilla, Captain (D)2 Bernard Warburton-Lee wrote in a letter to his wife Elisabeth dated 4 April, after learning that he was to escort the minelayers to Vestfjorden: '. . . the war is going to start quite soon – I am going to start it.'[97] Not even he could imagine that German naval units were already preparing to take to sea.

Rubicon

During March, intelligence mounted in Berlin, indicating consistent Allied pressure on the Norwegian government to allow transit of troops to Finland and the establishment of bases in Norway. There would be protests, said the reports, but only nominal and no opposition would be offered. One report for instance, arriving via Scheidt, held that 'a person close to both the King and Commanding Admiral' considered a British intervention 'unavoidable' – and it would come 'very soon'. Another agent reported with certainty that 'England had requested right of passage through Narvik and a naval base in Kristiansand.' Further reports alleged that Allied officers were surveying Norwegian ports with tacit Norwegian acceptance. In an unsigned report to SKL dated 5 March, it is stated that the Norwegian government had given in to French and British pressure and accepted 'transit of Allied troops and the establishment of points of support' on the Norwegian coast. It was part of the alleged agreement that the Norwegian government should deny the existence of any accord and should protest verbally against the Allied intrusions, as it had done during the *Altmark* episode.[98] Further reports of increased British air reconnaissance, agent activity in Norway, troopship concentrations in Scotland, French Alpine troops embarking ships in the Channel ports, the return of the British Home Fleet to Scapa Flow and heavy cruisers withdrawn from the Northern Patrol, augmented the picture: large-scale Allied landings in Norway were under development.

There was little doubt in Berlin that, in spite of the expressed grief over Finland, the real objective of the Allied landings was to sever the iron-ore traffic to Germany and capture bases in Norway. Hitler decided Germany would have to act 'quickly and decisively'.

'Full speed ahead for Weserübung,' Halder noted in his diary on 4 March and the next day Hitler for the first time discussed Weserübung with all three service commanders present. Two days later, he declared that the occupation of Norway and France should be planned independently and that the disposition of forces, as suggested by von Falkenhorst, was final and no longer subject to change. To avoid any provocation, it would be necessary to inform the Russians prior to the attack and let them know that the occupation of northern Norway was only for the duration of the war with Britain.[99]

'Operations Order No. 1 for the Occupation of Norway' was issued by von Falkenhorst on 5 March. Weserübung was ready to be launched, but the persistent severe ice conditions in the Baltic meant a number of the warships and transports were confined to port and there was growing concern that the Allied intervention in Scandinavia could be initiated any day. On the 6th, General Halder noted in his diary that it had been ascertained that the Allies had requested free transit of troops for Finland through Sweden and Norway, adding 'the Führer will now act.'[100]

In a status meeting with Hitler and von Falkenhorst on 9 March, Admiral Raeder held that in his opinion the current development of the situation in Finland made Weserübung 'urgently necessary'. If the Allies were to use the pretext of helping Finland, as intelligence indicated, they would certainly occupy Norway and Sweden en route, completely severing the supply of iron ore and establishing offensive bases. Raeder added that it was his duty to point out that Weserübung contradicted all principles of naval warfare, as it would have to be carried out in the face of a superior British fleet. He was convinced, though, that the operation would succeed, if complete surprise could be obtained.

On 10 March, it was noted in the SKL War Diary that '. . . the totality of the reports point in a compelling manner towards the possibility of immediate action by the Allies in Norway.' Radio intercepts during the 13th tracked no less than thirteen British submarines deployed in the North Sea and at the entrance to the Skagerrak, with two more underway from Rosyth. This was more than twice the usual number and a clear signal that something was going on. Most likely, the boats were covering the flank of an Allied landing operation in Norway that appeared from other intelligence to be developing. Nothing was ready on the German side and as news was coming in from Moscow that Finland had capitulated, it was decided to do nothing, other then alerting U-boats in the area to be extra vigilant.[101]

On the 15th, further intercepted signals ordering the submarines to disperse revealed that the Soviet–Finnish ceasefire had indeed upset the Allied plans. Interpretation of the signals indicated the operation was not cancelled, just put on hold with forty-eight to ninety-six hours' notice. Oberst Warlimont concluded in a memorandum to Jodl that he believed the pretext for an Allied intervention in Norway had gone and that Operation Weserübung should be cancelled and the forces released. The SKL took a more conditional stance:

The consequence of the Finnish–Russian ceasefire for Germany's warfare is as yet unclear. The Allied plans for an immediate landing in Norway . . . seem to have been deferred for the moment. The SKL believes England's strategic goals in the north have not changed and the planned action will be initiated when another favourable occasion has been found.[102]

At the Führer conference on 26 March, intelligence was presented showing how close an Allied intervention in Norway had been when the Finnish–Russian ceasefire was announced. Raeder added that even if the imminent danger of such an operation had been reduced, the ultimate objective of the Allies to sever the iron-ore supplies to Germany remained and an intensified effort against German merchant traffic in neutral waters was to be expected. Sooner or later, Allied plans for an intervention in Norway would re-emerge and Germany would have to carry out Weserübung. The operation had originated from the premise that Germany could not accept British control of Norwegian territory and that only a pre-emptive occupation could avert that. Therefore, Raeder suggested, Weserübung should be initiated in the next new-moon period and no later than 15 April. Everything was ready and the dark nights needed to cover the transit would soon become too short, increasing the overall risk to the operation. Virtually all operational U-boats had been deployed along the Norwegian coast or in the North Sea during March and would start running low on fuel and provisions in mid-April, thus closing the current window of opportunity. Sooner or later it would also be noted in London that other naval operations had been suspended. Earlier in the day, Raeder said, he had met with Hagelin and learned that the Norwegian Admiral Staff expected British naval forces to take control of the Norwegian Leads soon in a 'staged provocation', followed by seizure of naval and air bases in southern Norway. Hagelin believed that the Norwegian government would, at the most, offer only symbolic opposition. Careful as always, Raeder added that in spite of intelligence reports to the contrary, he personally was not sure an Allied intervention in Norway was imminent.[103] Hitler concluded that it was not to be expected that the Allies had abandoned their strategy in the north; threats of a German attack in France could trigger an Allied intervention in Norway. Hence, a preliminary date for Weserübung was set for between 8 and 10 April. The SKL, on Raeder's instruction, issued orders that all ships should remain on stand-by and arrangements for embarkation of troops and equipment continued until further notice – as should all security measures.[104]

In the evening of 26 March, Kapitänleutnant Wolf-Harro Stiebler lost his bearings during a snowstorm in the Skagerrak and ran his boat U21 firmly onto Oddskjæret, one of the southernmost rocks of the Norwegian coast, well inside territorial waters. The Norwegian government wished to make a stand and decided to intern the boat and its crew. A minor diplomatic crisis ensued, but Germany could not afford a disturbance at that moment and Kapitänleutnant Stiebler and U21 were sacrificed for the greater cause. He was ordered to escape if possible and that was it.[105]

The news from the Supreme War Council meeting on 28 March was taken as evidence that it had been correct to assume that Allied interest in Norway had not lessened. In the evening of the 28th, the Naval Chief of Staff Fregattenkapitän Schulte-Mönting told the Swedish naval attaché in Berlin Kommendörkapten Anders Forshell over dinner that the political and military development in the north was 'highly disturbing'. Germany feared Allied interventions on the Norwegian coast, in particular against Narvik, and with the Russians now having concluded the campaign in Finland, there was no knowing what they would do next. An 'Anglo-Russian race' for Narvik could not be accepted, and Germany would have to initiate countermeasures should this appear to become reality. A pre-emptive strike was far better than a belated reaction. The challenge according to Schulte-Mönting was where to strike and when.[106]

The plans for Operation Weserübung were formally approved by Hitler on the afternoon of 1 April after a five-hour, detailed review of the operation in the Reichskanzlei, starting at 13:00 with 'breakfast'. Von Falkenhorst and all senior navy, army and Luftwaffe commanders involved in the operation were present and Hitler talked to each one of the officers. According to von Falkenhorst, 'He cross-examined every man, who had to explain very precisely the nature of his task. He even discussed with the ship commanders whether they would land their men on the right or on the left side of a given objective. He left nothing to chance; it was his idea, it was his plan, it was his war.' Satisfied with what he heard, the Führer ended the meeting with a commanding appeal, underlining the importance of the operation for the conduct of the war.[107]

The following day, 2 April, Hitler asked for assurance by Raeder, Göring, Keitel and von Falkenhorst that all preparations were completed and neither ice nor weather could create adverse conditions. This they all confirmed. Hitler then asked Oberst Erich Buschenhagen, Chief of Staff for Group XXI, as the corps had temporarily been renamed, what would be the latest possible date to cancel the operation. The baffled Buschenhagen, who had worked day and night for five weeks preparing the operation, had not given this much thought, but after some deliberation answered 'Wesertag minus five'. The operation could be cancelled or postponed without risk until five days before the designated day of the invasion; after that, wheels would be rolling and the number of involved personnel with knowledge of what was happening would rise sharply.[108] Hitler gave the answer some consideration and decided the invasion should commence at 05:15, German time, on 9 April. The first supply ships would be at sea within less than forty-eight hours. At 19:17 on 2 April a signal was sent from the SKL to Groups East and West, C-in-C U-boats and C-in-C Fleet: 'Wesertag ist der 9. April.'[109] A note was made in the SKL War Diary:

> With the order from the Führer . . ., Weserübung has been initiated, commencing one of the boldest operations in the history of modern warfare. Its implementation has become necessary in order to defend vital German interests and supply of raw materials, which the enemy is attempting to sever . . . The outcome of the venture will to a large degree depend on the quality and the readiness of the naval forces as well as the determination of the individual officers in command. The landing operation will predominantly take place in an area where England rather than Germany has naval supremacy. Surprising the enemy . . . is important for success, and will depend on the extent to which, in the coming days, secrecy can be maintained . . .

And on 5 April:

The at times limited operational options of the German sea and air forces will improve significantly through an occupation of southern Norway. Germany now has the capacity to implement such an incursion swiftly. The basis for the operation will obviously be the loss of Norwegian neutrality to England and the total inability of the Norwegians to resist this loss.[110]

Acting Commander-in-Chief for Group West Generaladmiral Rolf Carls wrote in his war diary on 6 April as he was handing the command of the group back to Generaladmiral Alfred Saalwächter, returning to his own command in Group East:

> The significance of this operation is not only to secure the ore supplies and to sever British trade with Norway, but to include the whole of Scandinavia in the German power-sphere . . . The British have to a large extent influenced the timing of the operation. A massive attempt from their side to forestall our seizing of the Norwegian harbours is to be expected . . . The risks associated with this task for the deployed surface units of the navy are well known to the SKL as well as to the Führer; [Raeder] has seen to that, in the same way as all group commanders have been made aware that the success of this operation, contrary to conventional, operative considerations, is based on secrecy, surprise, lack of Norwegian opposition and ruthless use of force to overcome all difficulties.[111]

The multiple set of motives behind Operation Weserübung is evident. Quisling set the scenario of a British intervention in Norway firmly on the agenda of the OKW in December 1939 and the decision to launch the operation matured over time, pushed by Raeder and Rosenberg and fuelled by a number of seemingly minor incidents. Gradually the question changed from *if* it should be initiated to *when*. After the *Altmark* incident, there was hardly any question other than when. Whether German intentions were aggressive or defensive has been argued at length since 1940. In fact it was both, or rather a complicated, multidimensional combination of several factors, some of which had aggressive and strategic rationale, independent of Allied dispositions, some defensive and tactical, intended to forestall perceived Allied intentions. Berlin had no direct knowledge of Operation Wilfred, but the German intelligence organisation Abwehr could partly decipher British naval codes and during the winter the build-up of an expeditionary force to Finland was duly registered. In addition, French and British press reported freely on plans for Scandinavia and both Churchill and Reynaud were rather loose-lipped about their intensions.[112]

In the war diary of the SKL, there is a note on 4 April, stating that in spite of official British assurances that no operations in the north are being planned, the SKL believe there is and conclude that 'a race between England and Germany towards Scandinavia' has developed.[113]

Information was forwarded to the Ministries of Defence and Foreign Affairs 'when of interest'. Similarly, information came to the intelligence offices from the ministries, but rarely with any comments or analysis. Between the Nordic countries, there was a close, but unofficial and informal co-operation regarding military intelligence, largely unknown to the politicians.[3]

The threat from Germany was recognised by the military, but, as the analysis of strategic intelligence rested with the Foreign Office, the Ministry of Defence and the army and navy staffs lacked the necessary political perspective on their part of the intelligence. Tactical intelligence was not recognised as a concept and neither was the need for such information to be gathered, shared and systematically assessed between the political and military administrations. Defence Minister Ljungberg did not systematically forward the assessments given to him by the military staffs to the government; nor did the military themselves forward all information they possessed to their minister.

In the report of the post-war Commission of Inquiry, Prime Minister Nygaardsvold was criticised for not having taken charge of the information flow, analysis and decision-making process after the outbreak of war. Instead, he was sidelined and remained passive, leaving assessments and decisions to others.[4] This criticism can easily be extended to Koht, Ljungberg, Diesen and Laake – at least.[5]

Error of Judgement

In the early part of the war, British intelligence was no less fragmented than in Norway. Co-ordinated acquisition of intelligence from reliable sources was rare and the exchange of analysis and interpretations almost non-existent. Hence, the disregard of the mounting evidence that Germany was preparing to invade Norway and Denmark is almost a textbook example of lack of co-ordination and inability to conceive that the opponent could actually do something unexpected. The German readiness to face British supremacy at sea, landing troops around the coast from Oslo to Narvik, ran counter to all predictions made to the British government by its military advisers.

On 28 December, two weeks after Quisling set the wheels moving in Berlin, the British War Office sent a summary note to the Foreign Office indicating signs of possible German plans for Scandinavia, picked up by the Secret Intelligence Service (SIS). Two weeks later, on 8 January, the War Cabinet received a memorandum from the Foreign Office, concluding from compiled intelligence that Germany was contemplating an invasion of southern Scandinavia. Nobody pursued the issue and when a month later the German section of military intelligence concluded that the preparations probably had other purposes, as some twenty-five to thirty divisions would be needed for such a venture and only six could be recognised in north-west Germany, few eyebrows were raised.[6]

During the spring, several reports arrived at the Naval Intelligence Staff in Whitehall, detailing amphibious exercises in the Baltic and the gathering of paratroopers, transport aircraft and troopships in northern Germany. In the middle of March the Luftwaffe bombed Hatston in the Orkneys for the first time, whereas mine-laying sorties and U-boat attacks in the Atlantic ceased altogether. Simultaneously, signals were intercepted from a German intelligence vessel operating in Norwegian waters, reporting in

Loading transport ships in Stettin. From right: *Westsee, Antares, Ionia*. This photograph was probably taken in late March. (E Skjold collection)

Abwehr code. Had information such as this been processed collectively by a group of trained intelligence analysts, supported by evidence from signals intelligence (sigint) and photographic reconnaissance, it might have created a different picture. The Joint Intelligence Committee (JIC) and the Operational Intelligence Centre (OIC) had been set up to ensure just such collation of assessments, but the procedures for submitting information to these was as yet in its infancy and poorly adhered to.[7]

On 17 March, the British military attaché in Stockholm, Lieutenant Colonel Sutton-Pratt, reported visiting German officers having told Swedish colleagues that Norway 'would be taken care of in a very short time'. A week later, on 26 March, the British Embassy in Stockholm reported an increased concentration of aircraft in northern Germany and ships in Baltic ports, which were now rapidly becoming ice free. It was added that a 'senior naval officer in the Ministry of Defence' had disclosed that 'Swedish staff believe Germans are concentrating aircraft and shipping for operation which Swedish intelligence consider might consist of seizure of Norwegian aerodromes and ports. Pretext being disclosure of Allied plans of occupation of Norwegian territory, thus compelling German intervention.'[8] Several reports followed in the coming days confirming the build-up of tension in Germany over Allied intentions in Scandinavia. On 31 March, newspaper clippings reported sources 'in close touch with German government' saying there was an 'immense danger for [the] neutrals and particularly for Scandinavian countries'. The British 'policing of Scandinavia, [with] the British Fleet controlling the Kattegat and neutral waters, through which Germany obtained her supplies from the north', had reached a critical level and Germany now found itself 'compelled to protect her interest, by all means at its command'.[9]

On 3 April, the War Cabinet was notified that the War Office had received reports of troop concentrations in the Rostock area and there were several troopships in Stettin and Swinemünde, believed to be ready for an intervention in Scandinavia. The deputy chief of naval staff, Vice Admiral Tom Phillips, compiled a memorandum to Churchill and First Sea Lord Admiral Pound where he concluded: 'The Germans are all ready for some operation against southern Scandinavia, and they may be planning to carry one out in the near future.' It was not clear 'whether the action is taken independently by the Germans or as a result of action we may take vis-à-vis the Norwegians'. To be on the safe side, Phillips advised that the army 'should be instructed . . . to be prepared to improvise an expedition at the shortest notice'. It appears however, that the two lords were of the opinion that the Germans were waiting for the Allies to strike first and no recommendations were made to the War Cabinet or the CoS.[10]

In an appendix to the orders issued on 5 April to the commanders of the R4 forces, copied to the War Cabinet, the CoS discusses 'possible German operations in Norway'. It is concluded that at least four divisions were available in northern Germany, with some training in combined operations, and others could quickly be moved to the coast. Sea and air transport for these troops were abundantly available. The most likely German targets were considered to be Stavanger and Kristiansand, because of their airfields. An attack in Oslofjord was considered 'most hazardous', and, should the Germans decide to go for the capital, it would most likely be through the landing of troops on each side of the outer fjord. No German landings were considered at all north of Stavanger.[11]

In the small hours of 6 April the British vice-consul in Copenhagen, Charles Howard-Smith, reported to London that he had been informed the previous evening by the US minister, who had a well-placed neutral source, that Hitler had given 'definite orders to send one division of ten ships to land at Narvik on 8 April, occupying Jutland on the very same day, but leaving Sweden [alone]'. In the afternoon of the same day, a supplementary telegram said the troops had actually embarked on 4 April, but there was disagreement in the military as to the prudence of the operation and they 'hoped to have the order rescinded'.[12]

The naval section of the Government Code and Cypher School (GC&CS) at Bletchley Park informed the Admiralty's OIC on 7 April of a significant increase in German naval radio activity indicating several ships at sea in the Baltic and west of Denmark. The OIC had limited experience with the novel science of sigint – it was mainly run by civilian academics with little knowledge of naval matters – and, not being informed of other warning signals, did not sound the alarm.[13]

At the RAF, an increased Luftwaffe reconnaissance activity was registered in the North Sea and Skagerrak after a period of relative inactivity. By chance, the first aerial photos of Kiel harbour were taken on the 7 April, showing numerous ships and significant activity. As there were no previous photos to compare it with, and as *Scharnhorst* and *Gneisenau* were reported in Wilhelmshaven, nothing appeared urgent to the RAF analysts – not even when subsequent reconnaissance flights in the evening reported 'intense shipping activity and brilliantly lit wharves' at Eckernförde, Kiel, Hamburg and Lübeck.[14]

* * *

In Denmark, the British naval attaché Henry Denham heard rumours of German minesweepers off the Danish coast, and in the morning of Sunday 7 April drove south from Copenhagen to investigate. To his immense excitement he twice observed large warships heading west. Added to other information of recent German fleet movements, Denham had no doubt that this was serious and rushed back to Copenhagen. At 14:35 he reported to the Admiralty: 'German warships *Gneisenau* or *Blücher* with two cruisers and three destroyers passed Langeland [in the] Great Belt northbound daylight today. Similar force now passing northward, off Møen. Through Sound at 11:00. Large concentration of trawlers in Kattegat'. At 17:42, a second report from Denham stated he had had the report confirmed by the Danish Admiralty, but as the ships had not been sighted since midday, it was unclear if they had continued northwards.

Some months later in London, Denham met his friend Captain Ralph Edwards,

. . . who had been Duty Captain at Admiralty the evening of 7th April when my telegram, reporting enemy ships and their probable Norwegian destination, had been received. He told me he had taken it straight across to Winston Churchill who, after studying the contents, had merely remarked 'I don't think so'. Months later when the two men happened to be together at sea, crossing to a Washington conference, Churchill, recognising Edwards and remembering their earlier meeting about my telegram, generously admitted his error of judgement.[15]

The last entry of the Admiralty War Diary on 7 April, at 23:58, notes the naval attaché in Copenhagen having reported personally sighting the cruiser *Blücher* and other German warships south of Gedser on a westerly course at 14:00 and again at 17:00. The report was dismissed however, with the comment 'evidently doing exercise with ship out of sight'.[16]

Harry Hinsley, a historian and cryptanalyst who worked at Bletchley Park during WWII, concludes: '. . . given the organisation of intelligence and the state of its sources, . . . we can scarcely be surprised that the significance of the many indications Germany was preparing the invasion of Norway and Denmark eluded the individual intelligence bodies and the interdepartmental authorities'.[17] Possibly, but a significant responsibility rests with the decision makers who failed to collate the growing information into a pertinent picture of German intentions while maintaining necessary flexibility to realise and act upon a strategic concept, differing from what they had expected. It was all the more puzzling as Plan R4 was to be initiated as soon as the Germans 'set foot on Norwegian soil', or there was clear evidence they intend to do so'.

Major-General Ismay, secretary of the Military Coordination Committee later wrote:

We had suspected, that some mischief was brewing in Norwegian waters, for there had been reliable information two nights previously that a sizeable, German naval force was on the move northwards, and at the War Cabinet meeting the next morning the First Lord had reported that a few hours previously the destroyer *Glowworm* had signalled that she was in action against a superior force, that her signals had suddenly ceased, and that she had evidently been overwhelmed. This was confirmation that a German force was at sea, but it was thought their objective was probably limited to forestalling any action that we might take at Narvik.[18]

Occupied Next Week

On 31 March, the Swedish minister in Berlin, Arvid Richert, sent a note to Foreign Minister Christian Günther in Stockholm. The note said reliable sources had informed the embassy that troops, horses, vehicles and equipment had been embarked in fifteen to twenty-five large ships in Stettin and Swinemünde. The troops might be intended for a preventive seizure of key areas in Sweden to secure the supply of iron ore. Supplementary information over the next days confirmed the embarkation, but shifted the potential target of the operation to Norway, and held it would not be initiated without Allied provocation. Richert argued, though, that as troops and equipment were actually being loaded, the Germans most likely knew or expected that an Allied intervention was being planned. The embarkation, which was confirmed from several sources, took place behind guarded fences, but there was little doubt the ships were under military command. Bars and restaurants in the Stettin docks had been invaded by a large number of 'new officers of all kinds', unfamiliar to the regulars. It does not appear that this information was forwarded from Stockholm to Oslo in any form, but Richert discussed the news with the Norwegian minister in Berlin, Arne Scheel. Meanwhile, German disinformation had been spread that the troops and equipment were intended for east Prussia, where flooding had caused an emergency. Both envoys therefore concluded there was no reason for alarm. In a letter written on 1 April, Scheel reported to Oslo that Richert had told him the Reichskanzlei was concerned regarding imminent British actions to sever the German ore transport through Narvik, but ended the letter assuring him that the troops embarking in the Baltic ports were most likely 'to be sent east'. Neither Koht nor Nygaardsvold saw 'any reason for concern' from the content of this letter.[19]

In the morning of 31 March, British naval attaché, Rear Admiral Boyes, called the navy Chief of Staff Corneliussen, asking about the rumours of German preparations in the Baltic. Corneliussen admitted he had received the reports, but was 'not perturbed', believing the activity to be related to 'proposed Allied assistance to Finland'.[20]

For a number of reasons, including earlier warnings of German naval operations against Norway that never materialised, Koht had limited faith in the Norwegian representatives in Berlin. Minister Arne Scheel, a diplomat of the old school, was of the opinion that in order to act as neutral as possible, it was best to attend host country arrangements as invited. Koht, however, believed attendance at official Nazi Party arrangements should be minimised. Furthermore, in March, Ambassador Scheel dispatched a rather concerned letter to the Foreign Office in Oslo claiming that Norway had come to German attention as a result of threats to the iron-ore transport through Narvik. He recommended that Norwegian neutrality be 'upheld as strong as our utmost abilities permit' – words Koht partly interpreted as reflecting the German point of view and partly as a criticism of him and his policy.[21] Stortingspresident Hambro later wrote that Scheel and Koht 'could not understand – far less appreciate each other'. To make matters worse, the vice-consul at the embassy, Ulrich Stang, had during his assignment developed Nazi sympathies. Neither Koht nor Scheel were happy with this and had discussed having him removed. Stang was still in Berlin in April 1940.[22]

*   *   *

Arne Scheel, Norwegian ambassador in
Berlin.
(Aufn. Scherl/NTB/Scanpix)

In a meeting with OKM Chief of Staff Schulte-Mönting on 2 April, the Swedish naval
attaché in Berlin, Anders Forshell, brought up the subject of the embarkations in Stettin.
Fregattenkapitän Schulte-Mönting brushed it aside; nothing was happening in Stettin
and there were no German threats towards Sweden. Still, Forshell concluded in his report
to the Chiefs of Staff and Foreign Office in Stockholm that in his opinion, based on other
things Schulte-Mönting had said earlier, Germany was preparing to forestall a British
intervention in western Norway. The report was copied to the Swedish embassies in Oslo
and Copenhagen on 4 April 'for information', but its content appears not to have been
forwarded to the government or military authorities of the two countries, except for a
brief, informal telephone call from the Swedish Naval Intelligence Office to its Norwegian
counterpart.[23]

In the afternoon of 3 April, Minister Colban in London sent a telegram to the Foreign
Office in Oslo informing them that Noel Baker, a Labour MP in the House of Commons
had 'let him understand the British government was preparing a direct action against
the ore traffic inside Norwegian sea territory, very soon'. This telegram was copied to
Nygaardsvold and Ljungberg and very much focused the attention of the Norwegian
government and military in the days to come. Foreign Minister Koht later wrote that the
telegram from Colban made him more uneasy than any of the information that came
from Berlin in the following days.[24]

Oberst Hans Oster was one of Admiral Wilhelm Canaris's closest associates in the
German Abwehr. He was a convinced anti-Nazi and when he learned of the plans for

Oberst Hans Oster of the Abwehr.
(Bundesarchiv Koblenz)

Weserübung, it appears he saw an opportunity to cause a military defeat large enough to provide the occasion for a coup against Hitler. It has not been possible to ascertain whether Canaris endorsed Oster's actions, but the two men had a close personal and professional relationship and it is unlikely Canaris was unaware of what was happening. Oster asked his old friend the Dutch military attaché in Berlin, Major Gijsbertus Jacobus 'Bert' Sas, to see him in the afternoon of 3 April. The details of what exactly was passed from Oster to Sas are lost, but Sas later insisted Oster told him that imminent German operations would be directed simultaneously at Denmark and Norway and the offensive in the west would follow shortly after. Whether this is correct and the subsequent distortions were made inadvertently when forwarding the information or remembered differently by one or more of those involved, we shall never know. Oster was treading a fine line and may deliberately have tainted the information to protect himself and to avoid unnecessary loss of German lives, or perhaps he tried to make what he did less treasonous in his own eyes by not revealing the plans correctly. Meeting briefly again next morning, Oster confirmed to Sas that the operation was set for 9 April and encouraged his friend to forward the information to the embassies of the countries involved.[25]

During the morning of the 4th, Sas contacted Swedish Naval Attaché Forshell, informing him of the information he had received from Oster. Forshell, who was already aware of German planning against Norway from his conversations with Schulte-Mönting, realised the seriousness of the information brought by the Dutchman. He briefly informed his minister, Arvid Richert, of the news and hurried across to the Danish Embassy, asking to meet Kommandørkaptajn Frits Hammer Kjølsen. The stunned Danish naval attaché listened with growing unease as Forshell told him his country would be the subject of

German aggression within a week, followed by an occupation of Norway and later most likely an attack on the Low Countries. Troopships had been made ready in the Baltic and soldiers, including Alpine troops, were embarking at that very moment. Unaware that Forshell had already been to the Danish Embassy, Major Sas came shortly after to share the information from Oster, asserting it came from 'reliable sources inside the OKW dissatisfied with Hitler'. Sas later insisted he told Kjølsen both Denmark and southern Norway would be invaded simultaneously on the morning of 9 April. Kjølsen, however, categorically denied having been given any dates for the invasion other than 'next week', claiming the accounts of Sas and Forshell were 'near identical'.[26]

The Norwegian representation in Berlin was one of the few without a military attaché and Vice-Consul Stang would be Major Sas's natural level of contact. Sas was aware of Stang's friendly relations with a number of high-ranking German officials, and chose to 'bump into him by chance' at the Hotel Adlon, where he knew he would most likely have his lunch, rather than ask for a meeting. Later, Sas claimed he had emphasised in a few brief sentences that both Denmark and Norway would be attacked simultaneously on the 9 April. Stang, however, denied this, claiming Norway had not been mentioned at all and that he had forwarded exactly what he had been told (or at least what he thought he had been told). Based on what Sas told Forshell and Kjølsen, it is hard to believe he did not mention Norway to Stang.[27]

Kjølsen informed Minister Herluf Zahle of the information he had received from Forshell and Sas and called the Norwegian Embassy, asking to be received in the afternoon to discuss 'matters of utmost political consequence'. Unknown to Kjølsen, his telephone was tapped and his calls to Zahle and the Norwegian Embassy were intercepted by German intelligence. The information ended up in the OKW and eventually in the SKL on the 7th, where it was concluded it was possible that the Danish naval attaché 'somehow had obtained information on the forthcoming Operation Weserübung!'[28]

At the Norwegian Embassy, Kjølsen informed Minister Scheel. Understandably, the old diplomat was 'very upset to learn of the serious threats to his country'. Later in the evening, Stang, who had not been present at the meeting, came to the Danish Embassy to discuss matters. Kjølsen and Undersecretary Steensen-Leth presented all the information they had to Stang. He responded that he had been informed of German plans from a 'neutral civilian source' without elaborating, but claimed, to the surprise of the Danes, that the attack would not be directed north, but south and west towards Holland and France.[29]

During the afternoon, Minister Zahle at the Danish Embassy signed a memorandum to the Foreign Office in Copenhagen written by Kjølsen, and had it couriered home by one of his staff on the afternoon flight. The next day Kjølsen sent a supplementary report to the Naval Ministry, copied to Zahle and the Foreign Office, stating that he believed Major Sas's information to be reliable. Indeed, troop concentrations and loading of transport vessels in Stettin and Swinemünde indicated something was going on. Kjølsen concluded that 'contrary to the Norwegian Embassy' (i.e. Stang), he believed Norway would be attacked and the possible attack in the west would be limited to Holland.[30]

What discussion took place between Stang and Scheel in the Norwegian Embassy after Kjølsen left is not known, but Stang's view must have won the day, as next morning, 5 April, a telegram was received in Oslo informing the Foreign Office that the embassy had 'been informed from an attaché at one of the neutral embassies – in strict confidence –

of German plans to invade Holland in the near future'. Denmark was also threatened as Germany might be seeking 'air and U-boat bases on Jylland's west coast'. Norway was not mentioned at all. The embassy forwarded the information cautiously, it was stressed, as it could not be verified, even though the attaché who had brought the information was 'usually reliable and well informed'. The telegram was composed by Stang and signed by Scheel in spite of the somewhat different information he had received from Kjølsen. It must have occurred to Scheel that the message could be misleading; some hours later, a second telegram followed adding that information from Danish diplomats indicated that places on the Norwegian south coast might be threatened as well 'to increase the speed of the war and pre-empt Allied actions'.[31]

Koht rated both telegrams as rumour and took little notice of either. They were copied to Ljungberg the next day, but not to any other member of the government. No initiatives were taken by the Foreign Office to discuss the information internally in the government or with the other Nordic foreign offices. The telegrams were forwarded to the Admiral Staff and the General Staff during the 5th and shown to relevant officers who came in the next day (Saturday), including the army Chief of Staff Oberst Hatledal.[32]

Swedish Minister Richert found the information from Sas highly disturbing, even if Sweden was not directly threatened, and asked Forshell for a meeting, to which Kjølsen was also invited. In the meeting a memorandum to the Swedish Foreign Office was compiled, detailing the information received over the last couple of days. This and a similar memorandum from Forshell to the Swedish Naval Intelligence Staff were couriered to Stockholm on the first available flight. The Swedish government, Foreign Office and military intelligence were thus informed of Operation Weserübung in the evening of 4 April. Richert added information from other sources indicating that on 2 April Hitler appeared to have made 'some important decision', and persons in the German Foreign Office seemed 'nervous and pre-occupied'. Forshell in his short military style summarised: 'Denmark will be occupied next week,' whereafter Norway would be attacked from the Oslofjord to Bergen while no aggression towards Sweden was planned. Observations of mountain troops in northern Germany confirmed in his opinion that Norway was on the list of targets.[33] Both Richert and Forshell concluded that the operation was imminent, as all the foreign military attachés in Berlin had been invited on a tour of the Western Front, starting in the evening of Sunday 7 April. Forshell had decided not to attend this tour, with his minister's approval, believing it to be a pretext to have the attachés out of the way.[34]

Later that same day, an official but discreet message was passed from the German Ministry of Propaganda to the Swedish Embassy stating that there was no acute danger to Sweden from Germany in the near future. Richert sent a brief update to the Foreign Office in Stockholm: 'I have the firm impression that far-reaching actions towards Denmark and Norway are to be expected shortly; most likely within days.' For reasons difficult to comprehend, none of this detailed and exact information was forwarded to the Norwegian or Danish governments.[35]

On Friday 5 April, around 11:40, Minister August Esmarch at the Norwegian Embassy in Copenhagen telephoned Undersecretary Jens Bull at the Foreign Office in Oslo. The minister had been called to the Danish Foreign Office earlier in the morning, as had Swedish Minister Hamilton. Both had been questioned by Undersecretary Mohr as to their respective countries' reactions to the recent information from Berlin of a German offensive on the Low Countries, western Denmark and southern Norway. Esmarch had no knowledge of this and made the call to Bull requesting advice on what to tell the Danes. Being careful on the open telephone line and assuming Oslo had actually received the information referred to, he just forwarded the request without going into the background he had been given by Mohr, other than to mention the danger of a German attack on Denmark and southern Norway. 'Copenhagen was nervous,' according to Esmarch and wanted to know as soon as possible the considerations from Oslo.

Bull did not question Esmarch in any detail, as he apparently assumed Koht would know what this was all about. When learning of the telephone conversation with Esmarch, Koht dismissed the issue as the same rumours Scheel had mentioned and took no initiatives to ascertain what the Danish request referred to. Bull returned a call to Esmarch just before 14:00, informing him that Oslo would do nothing 'based on rumours' – and he could say so to the Danish Foreign Office. No information of Esmarch's conversation with Mohr and the request for a Norwegian reaction went beyond the inner circles of the Foreign Office.[36] Esmarch on his side reported back to the Danes that Oslo did not give the report 'any significance at all'. The Swedish Minister Hamilton reported back, according to Mohr, that this was 'old news' and Stockholm had information the rumours were exaggerated.[37] Satisfied, the Danish Foreign Office forwarded a summary of the information to the British Embassy and did little else.[38]

During the evening of the 5th, Oberst Carlos Adlercreutz, head of intelligence at the Swedish defence staff, called his Norwegian counterpart at the General Staff in Oslo, Oberstløytnant Wrede-Holm, informing him that Sweden had reliable information from Berlin of an imminent German attack on Denmark, followed by a similar attack on Norway.[39] Shortly after, an almost identical message arrived from the Danish General Staff. Reports of these communications were sent to the commanding general, the Admiral Staff and the Ministry of Defence, though Ljungberg later had 'no positive recollection of the issue' and could not remember having seen any of Scheel's letters. Nobody in the Foreign Office or the government appears to have been informed. Likewise, neither the commanders nor their intelligence officers were informed of similar information coming from the embassies.[40]

The Norwegian journalist Theo Findahl, stationed in Berlin for the Norwegian newspaper *Aftenposten*, somehow got hold of the rumours of an imminent attack on southern Norway. He was subject to strong restrictions, but managed to submit an article to Oslo over the weekend. Unfortunately Findahl stated the number of Germans to be landed in Norway to be in the order of '1.5 million'. The editor, while preparing a dramatic front page for Monday's edition, contacted the office of the commanding admiral in the evening for comments, speaking to Kaptein Håkon Willoch, the duty officer at the Admiral Staff. Willoch referred the enquiry to the commanding admiral, who found the story of 1.5 million men 'too fantastic' and, to his dismay, the editor received a call from the Foreign Office shortly after with instructions to halt the publication of the report.[41]

*   *   *

Meanwhile, another telegram from Scheel in Berlin arrived in the Foreign Office in Oslo. It stated that according to reliable sources, fifteen to twenty large ships loaded with troops and equipment had left Stettin on the night of 4/5 April, heading west. An unknown destination would be reached on 11 April. Ulrich Stang later told the Commission of Inquiry that this new information came from Kjølsen, adding that the reference to a westerly course should have indicated to Oslo that Norway was at risk.[42] The cipher secretary on duty, Gudrun Martius, considered the message serious enough to call Koht at home as no senior political staff were present in the office. Having the telegram referred to him, Koht reassured Miss Martius that the ships were not heading for a destination in Norway, but 'into the Atlantic'. How Koht knew this, and what a large fleet of German transport ships loaded with troops was hoping to achieve there, was not discussed. A copy of the report was couriered to the Admiral and General Staff that evening, but no further measures were taken, as Koht had given no instructions. The next day, a copy of the signal was sent to the Ministry of Defence, but whether it reached Ljungberg or not is unclear. It appears the mentioning of the 11th, which was several days away, to a large extent affected Koht's dismissal of Norway as the target. Miss Martius was confused after the conversation with Koht, but could only conclude that, as the foreign minister took the telegram so calmly, he had other information that put the situation in a different light. A copy of the signal reached Kaptein Willoch at the Naval Staff around 22:00 on the 7th. He called the commanding admiral and, quoting it, asked if he should initiate any measures: for example alert the districts and prepare for mines to be laid. Diesen answered no,

Kaptein Håkon Willoch (1896–1955), the brother of Odd Willoch in Narvik and Gunnar Willoch in Bergen – and father of Kåre Willoch, prime minister of Norway from 1981 to 1986. (Kåre Willoch)

and assured Willoch he himself would make sure those who needed to know would be informed. Willoch's frustration was marked, all the more so as he never heard back on the issue. According to Steen, the commanding admiral and his Chief of Staff agreed the troopships were most probably related to an attack on Holland.[43]

Thus, the information from Oster reached Oslo during 5 April through circuitous routes while there was still time to prepare the Norwegian armed forces to meet an invasion on the 9th. Neither Koht nor Ljungberg or his commanders, however, considered the signals from Berlin to indicate a 'clear and present danger' towards Norway and none of them initiated investigations to have the signals verified. There are independent accounts of Koht having commented on the reports from Germany with something like, 'Either the rumours are false, in which case there is no cause for alarm, or they are correct, in which case we will not have any useful answers.' That might be true, but no attempts were made to compile the signals and assess them jointly. Neither was the government or the prime minister made accurately aware of the incoming warnings. No initiatives were taken to discuss the situation with the commanders or their staff and no contact was made with the other Nordic governments to hear their views on the development. Indeed, the initiative from Copenhagen to do just that was dismissed. Why this was so is less obvious. Arguably, the telegrams to Oslo were less precise than those received in Stockholm and Copenhagen, partly due to the omissions and distortion of the original message by Stang, but this cannot explain it all. Perhaps it was personal issues that made the warnings from Scheel and Stang less believable. Perhaps it was cognitive priming. Whatever the reason, the information lost its significance somewhere between Berlin and Oslo and no initiatives were taken to have it verified or assess its consequences, should it be correct.

In the meeting of the Foreign Affairs Committee on 8 April, Koht said: 'There have been several reports in the last couple of days from Germany regarding planned actions against Norway. These are reports without any official foundation and we cannot know what they are based on or how serious they are . . .' Koht later denied using the word 'official', but the stenographer asserted the minutes were correct. Either way, Foreign Minister Koht in this meeting, some eighteen hours before Weserzeit, told his government colleagues that he doubted the validity of the warnings and saw no reason to act upon them.[44]

Mobilisation needed a political decision, but none was taken. How much this was affected by the relationship between Ambassador Scheel and Koht, Stang's corruption of the initial information or Ljungberg's incompetence in political matters, we shall never know. Neither shall we know what might have happened had Danish Foreign Minister Munch advised his government to mobilise the Danish armed forces based on the reports from Berlin. He at least had the full, undistorted information from Oster and Sas. Partly due to the rather firm dismissal of the 'rumours' from Oslo, however, and partly due to a subsequent telegram from Minister Zahle toning down the threat somewhat, Munch decided not to take action 'in order not to create panic'.[45] How the Norwegian government would have reacted to a Danish mobilisation remains hypothetical, but it would certainly have brought the reasons for such a development to the surface.

— 4 —

The Dogs of War

Implementation

'WESERTAG IST DER 9. April' – 'Weser-day is 9 April', was the laconic entry in the war diary of Vizeadmiral Lütjens, acting C-in-C of the Western Fleet at 19:50 on 2 April. Hitler had taken his final decision a few hours earlier and the SKL in Berlin had just forwarded the information to key officers. Operation Weserübung was being implemented.[1]

On 3 April, the head of Abwehr Group I, Oberst Hans Piekenbrock, met in utmost secrecy with Vidkun Quisling in Room 343 at Hotel d'Angleterre in Copenhagen. Questioning Quisling on the status of the Norwegian defences and their willingness to fight, a disappointed Piekenbrock got the impression that he had limited knowledge and was largely out of touch. Quisling was taciturn, almost sulky, and on this occasion apparently more so than usual. Two things the Norwegian was absolutely certain of: there were no minefields in the Oslofjord and the coastal forts would not open fire on their own initiative without explicit orders from the government. Large proportions of the senior officers, Quisling claimed, were members or sympathisers of his NS Party and would offer only token resistance once it was clear the intruders were German. He also (falsely) confirmed there were guns covering the entry to Narvik.

Piekenbrock did not reveal anything about Operation Weserübung, but it must have been clear to Quisling that something was afoot, all the more so as, two weeks earlier, Major Walter de Laporte of the Abwehr had contacted him clandestinely in Oslo, asking to what extent the Norwegians would oppose an Allied invasion.[2] Judging from his actions in the days to come, or rather lack of action, it is unlikely that Quisling realised his answers to both men would be tested within a week. He went back to Oslo by train over the weekend, unaware that the first of the supply ships were already at sea.

Quisling had been ill most of the winter and had been out of the public eye since his return from Berlin just before Christmas.[3] He had played no role whatsoever in the German preparations for Weserübung. In Jodl's diary for 4 April, there is a comment on the meeting and of an increased unease in the OKW that the defences in Norway might have been alerted. The SKL noted in its diary that there was little news of relevance to the navy in Piekenbrock's report.[4]

On the same day, 4 April, a much better source of information would come to Berlin. The head of the Abwehr, Admiral Wilhelm Canaris, had unexpectedly shown up at the embassy in Oslo on 31 March, disguised as 'Oberregierungsrat Fuchs', partly to solve difficulties between the naval and Abwehr staff at the embassy, partly to inform his staff what was happening and to get a last minute update in person. Erich Pruck, the main Abwehr agent in Norway was in Narvik and could not get back in time. It seems therefore that Canaris focused on the personnel issues and did not discuss Operation Weserübung

0 | 200 miles
0 | 300 km

N

British routes
German routes
Airborne troops
British minefields
Laid 8th April
Alleged

NORTH SEA

Gneisenau
Scharnhorst

Alta

Tromsø

Renown

Narvik
Kiruna

Gr I

Malmberget

Mo

Luleå

Repulse

Mosjoen

SWEDEN

Gr II

Namsos

Glowworm
sunk

Kristiansund

Trondheim

Ålesund

Tynset

Dombås

Lillehammer

Hamar

18th CS

NORWAY

Bergen

Fornebu

Oslo

Stockholm

Home
Fleet

Drøbak

Shetlands

1st CS

Stavanger

Gotland

Egersund

Mjölby

Arendal

2nd CS

Groups
I, II

Gr
III

Gr
IV

Kristiansand

Alvesta

Öland

Aalborg

Gr
V

Gr
VI

DENMARK

Copenhagen

Esbjerg

Malmö

Bornholm

GREAT
BRITAIN

Sylt

Kiel

Lübeck

Wilhelmshaven

Cuxhaven

GERMANY

Wesermünde

Hamburg

Rittmeister Friedrich 'Rudi' Eickhorn, acting commander of the Radfahrschwadron of the Aufklärungs Abteilung 169 of the 69th Infantry Division. (Dalane Folkemuseum)

When Oberleutnant Hans Taraba, commander of 7th Company IR 193 was ordered to march towards the railway station at Neustettin with all his men and equipment, he was sure it was serious and not another exercise. At the station, the C-in-C of the regiment, Oberst Karl von Beeren was waiting and asked jovially:

'Well, Taraba, where do you think we are going?'

'Scandinavia, Herr Oberst,' answered the lieutenant willingly.

Von Beeren, who knew the regiment would be heading for Stavanger and Bergen, laughed although he must have shocked at the clear-sightedness of his young officer: 'Why do you think so?'

'The *Altmark* affair,' he replied, to which the oberst answered, 'Ah well, it could just as likely be Scotland, could it not?' Taraba was not so sure, but held his tongue.[8]

'Weserübung is being implemented according to plan,' General Jodl wrote in his diary on 5 April.[9]

For most Norwegians, a quiet weekend lay ahead. Heavy snowfall in the south had slowed the country down more than on a normal Friday afternoon and the weather forecast was not particularly good. For Foreign Minister Halvdan Koht, however, there would be no rest at all. The British and French embassies had jointly asked Koht to receive their respective ministers the same evening. Arriving around 19:00, the British

Minister Cecil Dormer and the French Minister Comte de Dampierre handed Koht a joint memorandum from their governments.[10] It was a harsh note, claiming that events over the last few months had shown that the Norwegian government was under pressure from Berlin and unable to act independently. Furthermore, Britain and France could no longer accept the continuous flow of supplies to Germany from the Scandinavian countries. It was therefore necessary to 'notify the Norwegian government frankly of certain vital interests and requirements, which the Allies intend to assert and defend by whatever measures they may think necessary'. Five points followed. The first four were of general character. The last held that the Allied governments were waging war on behalf of the smaller, neutral states and could not accept any advantages for Germany whatsoever. There was no reference to iron ore or any specific demands, but the note concluded that the Allies considered it within their rights,

> . . . to take such measures as they may think necessary to hinder or prevent Germany from obtaining from those countries' resources or facilities which for the prosecution of the war would be to her advantage or the disadvantage of the Allies. . . . The shipping of Norway, Sweden and other neutral countries is attacked and destroyed almost daily by German submarines, mines and aircraft, in defiance of international law and with deliberate disregard for the loss of life involved. The Allies will certainly never follow this example of inhumanity and violence, and when the successful prosecution of the war requires them to take special measures, the Norwegian Government will realise why they do so . . . and the Allied Governments feel confident that this fact will be duly appreciated in Norway.[11]

Koht was shaken. He had little doubt that this was a warning of imminent naval intervention in Norwegian waters, most likely to provoke a German response. Most of the content of the note was 'uncalled for' he told the ministers angrily, particularly the allegations that Norway was commercially and politically under German control and he found the language 'disdainful, unworthy of His Majesty's government'. Himself distressed by the note and by Koht's reaction, Dormer meekly defended his government by claiming the words were directed towards Germany more than Norway.

Koht did not think so. Colban commented from London that he 'believed the note to be directed mainly at the internal criticism against the Allied governments and their lack of initiatives in the war' and 'considered the matter with some ease', but this did not help much. The Allies had given themselves carte blanche to proceed at will in Norwegian waters and from this point on, Koht was preoccupied with the threat of Allied aggression. The uncertainty of what actions the Allies had in mind and what timetable they worked to only increased the anxiety. Mounting evidence of a parallel threat developing on the German side was dismissed.[12]

After seeing the Allied ambassadors off, Koht left his office to dine in the US Legation. It does not appear that he even considered informing the prime minister or the other members of the government, far less the Foreign Affairs Committee. Koht arrived late and excused himself to Mrs Harriman, saying that the day 'had been the most nerve-racking of his official life'. He did not go into any detail, but the American envoy noticed that 'his face was drawn' and 'sensed that the day really had been more tense than usual'.[13]

On that same evening, the German minister Dr Curt Bräuer entertained a large number of Norwegian politicians, civil servants and officers at an official reception in the German Embassy. The invitation was at short notice and some of the invitees (among them Koht), excused themselves. More than 200 guests came, including Commanding General Laake and several officers of the General Staff. Ministers and officials were present too, as well as a large press corps. Nobody knew why they were there, but after a rich supply of snacks and drinks, the surprise was revealed: there was a film to be shown! Titled 'Feuertaufe' or 'Baptism of Fire', the reel had come from Berlin that same day with orders for it to be shown as soon as possible to a selected audience. To everybody's embarrassment it turned out to be a propaganda film from the conquest of Poland, covering the bombing of Warsaw in particular. Accompanied by Wagner's music it showed in ghastly detail what happened to the Polish capital – according to the commentator 'thanks to the intervention of their English and French friends'. The concluding scene was a map of Britain going up in flames. After the show there was a long silence, before quiet conversations began on any topic other than what they had just seen. Most of the guests excused themselves and left as soon as they could.[14] It had been an unpleasant and tactless demonstration of power that few believed had been unintentional.

Next morning, Saturday 6 April, Koht gave an account to the Parliament of the political situation. There was a great public interest for the meeting and the public galleries were crowded. For over an hour the foreign minister elaborated the international situation, concluding that the Norwegian will to remain neutral had not faltered and, surprisingly, added that 'None of the belligerents had attempted to drive Norway away from this policy.' He ended his speech by stating that 'Employing all available resources to defend Norway's national independence is a duty to our country and to the future.' Nobody in the Parliament disagreed and the customary debate was not prompted. Koht mentioned neither the warnings from Berlin nor the Allied note nor any of the other threats received during the week. Later he wrote that he had believed it would be 'inappropriate' to reveal 'what had been given to him in confidence' as he did not wish to 'frighten the public'. Unknown to Koht, several European papers reported the contents of the Allied note that morning and the news was in the Norwegian newspapers by lunchtime.[15]

After the orientation, Koht at last informed the government of the note he had received the night before, but made it clear that he would handle this alone, as usual, and there was no need for the others to worry. Minister of Finance Oscar Torp did worry and insisted the Neutrality Watch should be strengthened around the Oslofjord immediately. Nygaardsvold asked him to discuss the matter with Ljungberg to see what could be done. Eventually nothing was. Unbelievably, neither Koht nor Ljungberg brought up the reports from Berlin and Copenhagen and when Carl Hambro, the president of the Parliament and chairman of the Foreign Affairs Committee, called Koht in the afternoon to ask what was going on and why he had not been informed of the Allied notes, he was curtly assured that everything was under control and the Foreign Office would handle matters.[16] Nobody in the government or the Parliament had the slightest notion that Operations Weserübung and Wilfred were both already under way.

*   *   *

At Tirpitzufer in Berlin, the SKL officer on duty over the weekend entered in the war diary that Koht had stated in the Norwegian Parliament that the goal of his policy was 'sustained Norwegian neutrality'.

[There is] heightened tension in most countries over the development of the Norway issue . . . [but] there is no evidence that the Allies have recognised Germany's strategic intentions. At least, they do *not* grasp the dimensions of the operation. The measures of the enemy indicate . . . that he himself is very close to initiating his own actions in Norwegian waters. As he is undoubtedly aware of German preparations of some kind and will anticipate immediate German reactions, we must expect him to be well prepared to defend his own forces. How far in its preparations the enemy is, or if this operation has already been initiated, is *not* known. The SKL is, however, of the opinion that the launch of Weserübung is now *highly urgent*. 9 April appears to be the last possible date for the operation.[17]

How right he was – and how wrong. Operation Wilfred was indeed underway. Commander King-Hartman had taken the minelayer *Teviot Bank* to sea from Scapa Flow in the morning of 5 April, before the warning note was delivered in Oslo. Escorted by the 3rd Destroyer Flotilla led by Captain (D)3 Percy Todd onboard *Inglefield* with *Isis*, *Imogen* and *Ilex* in company, Force WS was heading for Stadtlandet to lay the southernmost of the two real Wilfred minefields.

Later that same day, Vice Admiral Commanding Battlecruiser Squadron William 'Jock' Whitworth took to sea from Scapa Flow onboard *Renown* (Captain CEB Simeon), screened by the destroyers *Greyhound*, *Glowworm*, *Hero* and *Hyperion*. The intention was to meet up with *Birmingham*, *Fearless* and *Hostile*, who were hunting German fishing vessels, off Lofoten on the evening of the 7th. British intelligence believed all four Norwegian panserships were at Narvik and it was hoped the presence of a deterrent force might prevent a confrontation with the minelayers. In the morning of the 6th, Captain J Bickford of the 20th Destroyer Flotilla fell in with his four mine-laying destroyers *Esk*, *Ivanhoe*, *Icarus* and *Impulsive* (Force WV), carrying sixty mines each for the Vestfjorden minefield, escorted by *Hardy*, *Hunter*, *Havock* and *Hotspur* of the 2nd Destroyer Flotilla under the command of Captain (D)2 Bernard Warburton-Lee.[18]

In view of the potential situation that might arise from swift German reaction to the mine-laying, it is difficult to understand why the Admiralty did not order at least parts of the Home Fleet to sea. From a central position north of the Bergen–Shetland Narrows, both mine-laying operations could have been covered against German reactions without exposing the ships to the Luftwaffe.

In the early morning of 6 April, Lieutenant Commander Gerard Broadmead Roope of *Glowworm* reported losing a man overboard, asking for permission to search for him in spite of the worsening weather.[19] Permission was given and *Glowworm* turned back, rapidly losing sight of the rest of the force, which shortly after changed course further to the north. After several hours searching, Roope decided there was no hope of finding the sailor and attempted to rejoin *Renown*. Being under strict radio silence, this turned out to be an impossible task. Eventually, Roope realised he was on his own and set course back towards Scapa Flow to receive new orders.

HMS *Glowworm*. 1,350 BRT, overall length 323 feet (98.5 metres) and a normal complement of 145 men. Her maximum speed was thirty-six knots. Armament was four single 4.7-inch guns and two quadruple 0.5-inch A/A guns. She was in addition fitted with two experimental five-tube torpedo mountings. (Wright and Logan)

Hyperion and *Hero* were both low on oil and were sent back to Sullom Voe for refuelling when the minelayers had joined up. Admiral Whitworth expected *Glowworm* to catch up and counted on his screen to have been enhanced by *Birmingham* and consorts by the time the mine-laying force would be detached. *Hyperion* and *Hero* were instructed to look for *Glowworm* and give her an update on *Renown's* last position and course, should they come upon her. On midday of the 5th, *Birmingham* received instructions for a rendezvous with *Renown* off Vestfjorden in the evening of the 7th. Delay in the transfer of prize crews to several captured trawlers and a heavy head-sea, however, prevented Captain Madden from complying.[20]

Meanwhile, *Glowworm* was close enough to Scapa Flow for Roope to break radio silence and ask for orders. At 11:43, a signal was received from C-in-C Home Fleet with *Renown's* estimated position and orders to turn back and look for her. During the evening, a supplementary signal was received from *Renown* with her anticipated position next morning.[21]

Departures

Having a long way to go, the German transport ships destined for Narvik, *Rauenfels*, *Bärenfels* and *Alster*, departed Brunsbüttel at 02:00 on 3 April. In the afternoon, the tanker *Kattegat* followed. Over the next several days, the freighters *Main*, *Sao Paulo*, *Levante*

Transport group 'Karl' leaving Stettin in the afternoon of 6 April heading for Kristiansand. Photo is taken from *Kreta* with *Westsee*, *August Leonhardt* and *Wiegand* following. (Author's collection)

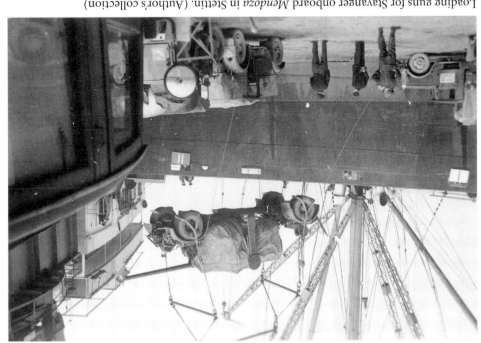

Loading guns for Stavanger onboard *Mendoza* in Stettin. (Author's collection)

and the tanker *Skagerrak* departed for Trondheim, followed by *Roda* for Stavanger. Some fifteen other vessels departed Lübeck and Stettin, heading for the southern Weserübung ports, packed with soldiers of the 69th and 163rd IDs and a large amount of provisions and heavy military equipment. Officially these ships brought supplies to east Prussia, which had been isolated by floods, but once out of sight from land they turned west for the Danish Belts. At the German supply base Basis Nord near Murmansk, the 12,000-ton tanker *Jan Wellem* received orders to leave during the evening of 6 April and relocate to Narvik where further orders from the German consul would be received.[22]

In the morning of 7 April a further eleven ships left Gotenhafen, scheduled to arrive in Oslo in the days following the invasion with further provisions and soldiers of the 196th ID. None of the vessels except *Jan Wellem* were to enter Norwegian ports prior to Weserday. The transport ships were a constant source of worry for the SKL. Security was not properly maintained during their loading and any incident they might become involved in at sea could potentially compromise the operation. Originally, the ships were to carry equipment and provisions with a minimum of troops onboard. During the last few days before departure, however, to the surprise of the navy, a large number of soldiers arrived to be transported to the invasion ports on orders from Group XXI.

On the evening of the 7th, Kontreadmiral Carsten Tank-Nielsen, commander of SDD2 in Bergen, called the Admiral Staff in Oslo, informing Chief of Staff Corneliussen that during the last few days an unusual number of German ships had entered the Leads south of Haugesund asking for pilots in Kopervik. German ships – in particular ore ships – were normal, but these were different. They had all been inspected, but most carried deck-loads of coal concealing the hatch-covers and the holds could not be accessed. The captains claimed to be heading for Murmansk, but what the coal should be used for there, nobody knew. Papers looked simplified or defective. No guns, ammunition or other military equipment had been found, but in the rooms inspected, the ships carried large amounts of food and supplies in crates marked Wehrmacht. In some cases captains and cargo-masters refused inspection of rooms, referring to 'orders'. Tank-Nielsen found the activity suspicious and told the Chief of Staff he feared it might be an indication that the Germans 'were up to something'. Corneliussen did not share his worries, but told him to 'keep an eye on things'. Not very reassured, Tank-Nielsen ordered his officers to track the movements of the German ships and observe 'increased preparedness until further notice'. It was left to each captain to interpret what this meant.

Bärenfels and *Main* were among the last ships of the first wave to arrive at Kopervik on 6 April asking for clearance and a pilot. By now, there were no pilots left and they had to wait, against the protests of their captains. The tankers *Skagerrak* and *Kattegat* for Trondheim and Narvik respectively, were also delayed and it seemed unlikely they would be in place in time to refuel the destroyers, causing deep concern in Group West. On 6 April, Naval Attaché Schreiber paid a visit to the Admiral Staff, complaining about recent delays to German merchant ships caused by extensive inspections. They were all in perfect order, he claimed, and there was no reason not to let them pass, but he offered no explanation as to why they were in such a hurry. Kontreadmiral Tank-Nielsen was not informed of Schreiber's visit and it seems nobody in Oslo drew any conclusions worth mentioning.[23]

* * *

Befehlshaber der Unterseeboote (Commader of the Submarine Fleet), Konteradmiral Karl Dönitz had forty-eight U-boats in commission in April 1940; nine less than on the day hostilities commenced. During the first week of March, most U-boats had been withdrawn from the Atlantic. As soon as service, replenishment and rest for the crews had been completed, they were sent into the North Sea with orders to observe absolute radio silence and attack only warships or obvious troop convoys. Few results were obtained and four of the boats were lost, including the grounded *U21*. At the confirmation of Operation Weserübung on the 2nd, a total of thirty-two boats were at sea; fourteen Type VII and Type IX boats from Stadt and northwards and eighteen Type II boats in the Skagerrak and the North Sea. At 20:30 on the 6th, a signal from Dönitz to all U-boats contained the codeword 'Hartmut', indicating that sealed envelopes with orders written on water-soluble paper should be opened. The envelopes contained detailed orders for all boats to move into new positions along the Norwegian coast, taking care not to reveal their new positions. Allied warships and troop transports could still be attacked, but Norwegian or Danish ships should be left alone.[24]

From London, Vice Admiral (Submarines) Max Horton issued similar orders to his boats in the Skagerrak and Kattegat. German warships could be attacked but otherwise the boats should conceal their presence as much as possible. Merchant ships should be left alone – unless German warships and transports were encountered together, in which case it would be most important to attack the transports. Lieutenant Commander Bryant of *Sealion* found this order challenging and wrote in his diary on the 7th:

> Some 25 merchant vessels were sighted during the day, mostly northbound. Some were suspicious, but none that I could say definitely were German transports . . . One small ship marked Estonia had a funnel corresponding to that of Saaberk Co of Hamburg. Five ships had no flags or markings, three being greyish. It was not possible to surface and investigate them so no action was taken. I was much concerned that I might be letting enemy ships by owing to taking no action. On the other hand, orders received conveyed the impression that it was essential not to compromise my position. The definition of a 'transport' was not clear in my mind.[25]

Due to improved signal discipline, German sigint had problems tracking the submarines compared to a few weeks earlier and was largely unaware of their number and whereabouts. Except for *Trident*, who had already stopped and examined several neutral merchant ships off Lista on the 4th and 5th, and *Unity*, who had made an unsuccessful attack on a U-boat in the Helgoland Bight on the 5th, there had been few indications of where the submarines were hiding. Based on the amount of land-based radio traffic, however, the B-Dienst estimated that some fifteen to twenty submarines were at sea.[26] This number worried the SKL, as it might indicate that the Allies were aware of Operation Weserübung and preparing a trap. On the other hand, it might be that the large number of submarines was a defensive measure for their own operation against Norway, as in March. Either way, the submarine alert was heightened and preparation for increased air and sea protection of the transfer convoys was ordered.[27]

* * *

Hellmuth Guido Alexander Heye (1895–1970), captain of the heavy cruiser *Admiral Hipper*. (Author's collection)

The 45-year-old Kapitän zur See Hellmuth Heye of the heavy cruiser *Admiral Hipper* was in charge of Kampfgruppe II, the warships for Trondheim. The 18,200-ton *Hipper* was the first of her class and extensive trials and modifications followed her entry into service a year earlier. Except for an uneventful sortie together with *Scharnhorst* and *Gneisenau* in February, *Hipper* had largely spent the winter in Wilhelmshaven until 20 March, when ordered to Cuxhaven in preparation for Weserübung. Also assigned to Group II were the destroyers of the 2nd Destroyer Flotilla: *Paul Jacobi*, *Theodor Riedel*, *Bruno Heinemann* and *Friedrich Eckholdt* under the command of Fregattenkapitän Rudolf von Pufendorf onboard *Jacobi*.[28] Heye wrote:

> I was, as the other group commanders, well aware of the magnitude of the task and the risk for the Kriegsmarine associated with this mission. In order to maintain security, it would be difficult to obtain intelligence and thus ample opportunities to end up in an unexpected situation, such as encountering the enemy at the start of the operation, running into a parallel enemy operation at the target, weather complications, missing resupplies etc. I compiled my considerations in an order for the ships of Group II . . . so that if something unexpected should happen, it would be possible to initiate swift countermeasures without long orders . . . The targets were ranked according to their priority, and the captains made aware of their priorities.[29]

During the afternoon of 6 April, the embarkation of soldiers commenced under the supervision of *Hipper*'s first officer, Korvettenkapitän Wegener, and his assistant, Kapitänleutnant Piontek. The troop trains were shunted into the closed-off Amerika-Kai and 1st and 3rd Battalions of the 138th Mountain Regiment, most of 83rd Pioneer Unit, a battery of mountain artillery as well as regimental staff, intelligence and communication personnel, naval artillerymen and anti-aircraft gunners climbed the gangways. In all there were seventeen hundred men: nine hundred onboard *Hipper* and two hundred onboard each destroyer.[30] The commander of the 138th Regiment, Oberst Weiss, was welcomed onboard *Hipper* by Heye, but he would have no say in the operation until back on dry land in Trondheim. Heye was very careful that all explosives, ammunition, fuel and other dangerous items were stored below deck. Extra space was made in the magazines by storing as much as possible of the ammunition for the ship's guns in ready lockers. Explosives that could not be stored below the armoured deck were spread throughout the ship in small crates and boxes to minimise the risk from incoming fire. The troops were confined below deck with orders to remain there until permission to come on deck was given. Engine rooms and turrets would be off-limits at all times. No smoking would be allowed outside or in the doorways after dark. On Heye's insistence, every soldier, few of whom had ever been onboard a ship before, was issued with a personal lifebelt. The medical staff of the cruiser was ordered to prepare as much as possible to assist the soldiers in fighting the inevitable seasickness.

The cruiser was ready at 22:00 GeT (German Time) and cast off while the tide was still high, waiting at anchor in the river Elbe for the destroyers. Some hours later, Fregattenkapitän von Pufendorf's destroyers joined and at 01:30 on 7 April the five ships commenced navigating the narrow channel towards the sea. Shortly after passing the river mouth, *Eckholdt* reported overheating in the port propeller shaft and had to slow down. She was left behind with *Riedel* and ordered to initiate transfer of her troops to the backup destroyer unless the problem could be repaired in time for her to rejoin the fleet

Gebirgsjägers of the 138th Mountain Regiment onboard *Hipper*. (Author's collection)

German destroyer *Z21 Wilhelm Heidkamp*. 1,811 BRT and overall length 123 metres, and a normal complement of 325 men. Her maximum speed was over forty knots. Armament consisted of five single 12.7-cm guns, four 37-mm guns and four 20-mm guns. In addition, she carried 8 torpedoes and up to sixty mines. (Author's collection)

during the morning. *Hipper* and the remaining destroyers continued westward across the Bight towards the Schillig-Reede off Wilhelmshaven to join Group I. From this time onwards, until at anchor in Trondheim, the crew of *Hipper* would be at their stations – for reasons of battle readiness, but also to make room below deck. Secrecy had been absolute, and very few people onboard knew what was happening and where the ships were heading.[31]

The ships of Group I for Narvik assembled in Wesermünde during the first week of April.[32] The group consisted of the ten destroyers: *Wilhelm Heidkamp, Erich Koellner, Wolfgang Zenker, Georg Thiele, Bernd von Arnim, Hermann Künne, Erich Giese, Anton Schmitt, Hans Lüdemann* and *Dieter von Roeder* with C-in-C Destroyers Kapitän zur See Kommodore Friedrich Bonte onboard *Heidkamp*.[33] He would be subordinated to Vizeadmiral Lütjens at first and when detached would report to Admiral Saalwächter at Group West in Wilhelmshaven.[34] The commander of the landing troops, Generalmajor Eduard Dietl, also on *Heidkamp*, reported to General von Falkenhorst at Group XXI and would, in theory, not have any say during the transfer.

Bonte called a meeting at 09:00 on the morning of 5 April for his destroyer captains and their senior officers. For most of them, it would be the first time they received official information of Weserübung. The Kommodore referred to the orders he had received from Admiral Raeder, where it was said that the landing operations would take place under British naval supremacy and depended on secrecy, swiftness and determination to succeed. He added that when issuing the orders, Raeder had underlined to him that the German Supreme Command had known for some time that the Allies were planning an intervention in Norway. This was totally unacceptable and had to be pre-empted. The outcome of the operation was vital for the future of Germany as well as for the honour of the navy. The rest of the meeting was spent discussing operational details, including intelligence of the Norwegian forces and expected opposition. From Wesermünde to Narvik is more than 1,200 sea miles – 2,000 kilometres. Maintaining a constant speed of over twenty knots to reach the target at the designated time would put a severe strain on ships and men. Korvettenkapitän Hans Erdmenger, captain of the flagship *Heidkamp* must have been particularly uncomfortable. Not only did he have the Kommodore on his bridge, but also the general of the landing troops. His every move would be observed.

By midday on the 6th, Wesermünde harbour was closed off. Embarkation of the troops was to commence in the early evening and the captains were advised of their berthing places on the Columbuskai docks. All sailors were restricted to their ships and no communication with the outside was allowed. Dietl and his mountain rangers of the 3rd Gebirgsdivision had left their temporary barracks outside Berlin the evening before with only a few hours' notice. In total secrecy they had been loaded onto trains that would take them northwards across the Lüneburger Heide during the night. The 138th Regiment went to Cuxhaven to embark on the ships of Group II, whereas Dietl stayed with the 139th Regiment, which went to Wesermünde. Arriving between 13:00 and 17:00, the three trains were shunted into the harbour area, where the soldiers were let into large warehouses to be out of sight. Later they were joined by small units of naval gunners, propaganda staff and intelligence personnel, arriving in covered trucks. Police troops kept all eyes away from the docks. It was obvious that something big was on and rumours flourished. A raid on English or French Channel ports seemed likely, as did attacks on Iceland and the Shetlands. The officers knew nothing and shrugged their shoulders when asked; 'I hob kei Ahnung!'– 'I have no idea!' Few if any guessed Norway. Nobody mentioned Narvik.

Loading of the equipment started immediately. Ammunition was stowed in the magazines of the destroyers, as much as they could take, and the rest wherever there was room below decks. Large items, motorcycles, guns and crates were lashed on deck; the consequence of which would be deeply felt in the weeks to come. Around 20:30, as darkness fell, the troops started embarking with their personal equipment, two hundred men to each ship. To the surprise of the sailors, the soldiers had Edelweiss symbols on their caps and cuffs. The Gebirgsjägers were Austrians from the provinces of Vorarlberg, Kärnten, Steiermark and Tyrol – a rare sight onboard a ship of the Kriegsmarine. Including their general, few of the soldiers had seen the sea before, far less been onboard a ship, and they felt utterly lost. It would be a trip the survivors would remember for the rest of their lives.[35] The men were onboard within two hours and Bonte gave the order to cast off. By 23:00 the destroyers were moving down the channel from Wesermünde towards the Bight.[36]

Kapitän zur See August 'Curry' Thiele had in early March received orders to prepare the heavy cruiser *Lützow* for a raid into the South Atlantic. Thus, in late March, *Lützow* lay fully stored and fuelled in Wilhelmshaven waiting for a suitable combination of moon and weather to depart when Hitler decided she should take part in Weserübung. Before

Gneisenau and her sister ship *Scharnhorst* were the first capital ships of the new German Navy. They should have been armed with 35-cm guns, but the turrets could not be completed in time and three upgraded triple 28-cm turrets were mounted as a temporary solution. (Author's collection)

against even light opposition. Should British cruisers meet with the battleships, so much the better as this would mean a certain German victory. Holding the battleships back in the North Sea would increase the chances of encountering superior British forces: to be avoided at all costs. The risk of alerting the Allies to Operation Weserübung two days before its implementation by allowing the battleships to take to sea was worth taking. Should they be sighted, it was even possible that the Admiralty would conclude it was another Atlantic breakout and concentrate their forces between Iceland and Shetland, an advantage for Group III following behind. For the 51-year-old Acting Fleet Commander Vizeadmiral Günther Lütjens onboard the flagship *Gneisenau* this would be a unique chance to show his abilities at sea.

Reaching Lightship F at 03:00, the battleships were joined by Kommodore Bonte and his ten destroyers and, not long after, the compact shadows of *Hipper* and two destroyers could be distinguished. A few signals were sent and acknowledged from darkened lamps and the newcomers fell in. The most powerful fleet the German Navy had mustered in over twenty years headed northwards at twenty-two knots.[39]

'No disturbing news,' wrote General Jodl in his diary.[40]

Gathering Storm

Dawn on Sunday 7 April found the fleet in calm sea between the Danish peninsular of Jutland and the German Westwall minefield. 'Daylight Formation' was ordered at 05:50 and the destroyers spread out in front of and around the larger ships steaming abreast some two thousand metres apart. Speed was increased to twenty-three knots. *Eckholdt* and *Riedel* rejoined the fleet during the morning, reporting everything in order.[41] The soldiers were allowed on deck in the sunshine and marvelled at the ships and the sea. They were warned that in case of alarm they would have to hurry below, lest anybody (not even neutral ships or fishing vessels) should see there were soldiers onboard. The sea was exceptionally calm and few paid much attention to the ominous advice given over the tannoys on how to avoid seasickness. Everybody listened very carefully, though, when it was announced that their target was Narvik in northern Norway, to be reached at dawn on 9 April. Few had any idea where this was, and a scramble for maps ensued. Anticipating this, some of the destroyer captains had large-scale plastic-covered maps ready for the sailors to show the Jägers, and discussions continued throughout the day. Few had given much thought to the necessity of invading Norway and there was genuine relief when it was explained that they were coming as friends to 'assist the Norwegians to deter Allied plans to establish bases in the north'.[42]

Vizeadmiral Lütjens was worried about the calm weather and good visibility, which increased the risk of being sighted. British reconnaissance over Wilhelmshaven the previous afternoon had found the battleships and several cruisers in harbour and their departure during the night had been unnoticed. At 11:31, Group West informed Lütjens that some two hours earlier a British air-reconnaissance report had been intercepted, reporting 'one cruiser and six destroyers with eight aircraft on course 350° at 55°30'N'. Luftwaffe fighters ahead of the fleet had chased off two Hudsons during the morning, but apparently not before some of the ships had been observed. Subsequent signals from Group West reported (correctly) that most of the heavy ships of the Home Fleet were in port or far to the south, and there appeared no imminent threat to the operation. Still, Lütjens ordered an increase of speed to twenty-five knots at 12:13 and an hour later to twenty-seven in order to get into the overcast weather ahead.

At 14:20, off northern Jutland, the alarm was sounded and the Jägers rushed below decks. Twelve Blenheims of 107 Sqn approached from cloud bands in the east at about two thousand metres. *Hipper* was easternmost in the line-abreast and received most of the attention. Dense flak kept the Blenheims at a respectful height and the forty-five 125-kg bombs dropped hit the water well away from the ships, making little impression on the Germans.[43] Action stations were stood down after less than half an hour, even if most ships kept the crews at their guns. A signal from one of the aircraft, intercepted by *Gneisenau*'s B-Dienst, read 'Three battleships steering north accompanied by destroyers', and Lütjens took it for granted that the British now knew that a large German force was at sea. It was later confirmed from Group West that the Admiralty believed at least one *Scharnhorst*-class battleship was at sea. Increased signal traffic to and within the Home Fleet was registered, as was the departure of at least one cruiser squadron, but Group West – and Lütjens – remained unaware that British capital ships took to sea during 7 April. At 22:05, the SKL informed them that they believed, 'The enemy has now recognised a northward-directed operation and will initiate countermeasures.' Kapitän zur See Heye of *Hipper* commented in his diary that, based on the incoming signals, he expected British 'counter-operations' during the night from destroyers and submarines, but trusted the deteriorating weather would be to their advantage.[44]

During the afternoon of 7 April a strong low-pressure system moved in from the Atlantic as predicted by the German meteorologists and the fine weather gave way to low clouds and showers.[45] Visibility was reduced to less than a mile and the sea started to grow under a mounting gale from south-south-west. Towards midnight the wind reached Force 8 to 9 and a heavy swell from aft developed. The destroyers were ordered to leave their anti-submarine stations and form two lines en-échelon to port behind the battleships, preparing for heavy weather. This formation would give the larger ships room to manoeuvre and open fire should an attack come during the night. Lütjens wanted to be well north of Trondheim by dawn and speed was set at twenty-six knots. All doors and hatches were battened shut, while traffic on deck was restricted. The German destroyers, never known for their sea-keeping abilities, began to feel the effects of the stern waves quite badly. The following sea gave the Type-34 Zerstörers weather helm, turning them port broadside onto the sea.[46] The helmsmen worked hard, trying to maintain course and position and often had to be assisted by engine manoeuvring. The Type-36 Zerstörers faired somewhat better, but onboard these too conditions became quite appalling. Pitching and rolling with a tireless malice, the bows dug deep into the seas, throwing tons of water over the low forecastle and open bridge, where everyone was soaked to the skin. As the storm increased, there was a real danger that the bow might actually cut under, and radical course and speed alterations became necessary, straining bridge and engine personnel to the limits. In the engine and boiler rooms, water was coming through the ventilator intakes, adding to steam leaking from flanges and connections. Damage and technical defects developed and as lighting-circuits often tripped out, repairs had to be carried out in semi-darkness or aided by unsteady torches. In particular, the electrically driven rudder engines were vulnerable and created constant emergencies when breaking down. *Heidkamp* had one particularly heavy sea crash into the no.1 boiler room through

Increasing winds during 7 April made the sea rise towards the afternoon. (Author's collection)

the fan intakes, temporarily extinguishing the burners and darkening parts of the ship. Onboard *Hipper* the chief engineer reported the rudder engine overheating because of the continuous adjustments, and requested less use of the rudder.

The larger ships were also affected by the heavy seas from astern. Speed was temporarily reduced to fifteen knots around 21:00 but this created problems for the fuel pumps of *Scharnhorst* and had to be increased again. Speed was thereafter kept between twenty-two and twenty-six knots during the night. As darkness approached, stern lights were rigged to help keep contact and avoid collisions. The destroyers were instructed over USW radio to do their best and to try to regain contact at first light if they could not keep up. It was imperative that the fleet was as far north as possible by dawn and it was better for some of the destroyers to find their way alone than for the landings to be delayed. On the positive side, the chance of being sighted by British aircraft was negligible.

The Jägers felt as if they had been thrown into hell. Trapped in a crowded, alien environment below deck, with an unbearable atmosphere, they sank into apathy, paralysed by seasickness and fear. The noise was infernal as the shrieking of the storm added to the racket of the fans and engines and the never-ending seas crashing over the forecastle. Everything loose was thrown about by the violent rolls. 'Hold di fast!'– 'Hold tight!' – was the call. The next sea could be fatal if sleep or exhaustion relaxed attention. Arms and legs were broken, heads smashed and the medical personnel worked overtime.

General Dietl was one of the very few not affected by the storm, it was said. He stayed on the bridge of *Heidkamp*, next to Bonte and Erdmenger, virtually the whole journey, except for a few short naps. A feat that added nicely to the already long list of legends and anecdotes associated with his name. 'We would never have risked this speed under such conditions in peacetime,' commented Bonte. 'Well,' answered Dietl, 'just get me there in time, that's all I care about.'

Around midnight, the German fleet passed the latitude of Bergen. The wind increased further and some of the destroyers started to lose touch with the flagship. Rolls of over forty-five degrees were experienced during the night and most army equipment lashed on deck, as well as the ships' own boats and depth charges, went overboard. Some of the latter exploded in the wake of the ships, creating yet another unwanted danger and tension onboard the larger ships – where it was at first believed the explosions were incoming shells. Moving about on deck was hazardous and, in spite of ropes strung on all decks, at least ten men went overboard from the destroyers between the evening of the 7th and the morning of the 9th. 'Keine Rettungsversuche' – 'no rescue attempts' – was the laconic order given. It would have been virtually impossible to rescue anybody from the corkscrewing ships anyway, even if they, against all odds, survived more than a few minutes in the icy water.[47]

Back in Wilhelmshaven, Konteradmiral Hubert Schmundt, acting flag officer scouting forces in charge of Group III, considered Bergen the most dangerous objective of the whole invasion.[48] Groups I and II would be very exposed indeed, but unless the Royal Navy was already at sea, they would have a fair chance of escaping interception even though they most likely would be sighted. Group III would leave Germany some twenty-four hours behind Groups I and II and Schmundt expected to be confronted by fully alerted British forces. Bergen was only eight to nine hours' steaming from Scapa Flow

Konteradmiral Hubert Schmundt,
acting flag officer scouting forces in
charge of Group III.
(Bundesarchiv Koblenz)

and securing the Bergen–Shetland Narrows would, in Schmundt's opinion, become a British priority once it was clear that German ships were at large. It did not ease his worries either that all the large, modern units of the navy had been allocated to Narvik, Trondheim and Oslo. In particular, the disposition of several heavy ships in the Oslo group annoyed Schmundt, as he believed this to be for prestige reasons. Group III, on the other hand, in addition to the light cruisers *Köln* and *Königsberg*, had been left with *Bremse*, a gunnery training ship, the torpedo boats *Leopard* and *Wolf* and the depot ship *Carl Peters* with six S-boats (motor torpedo boats).

Bremse and *Carl Peters* both had cruising speeds of less than twenty knots, meaning the crossing would take about twenty-four hours, including a full day in the North Sea, increasing chances of interception and submarine attacks. Schmundt appealed to the SKL, requesting a swap of the two for *Karlsruhe* from the Kristiansand group in order to have a homogeneous force with a higher transit speed. His request was denied and he had to make do with what he had; Krancke at one stage remarked to Buschenhagen that Schmundt seemed to have lost his nerve. Schmundt contacted Generalmajor Hermann Tittel, C-in-C of 69th ID, to ensure that *Bremse* and *Carl Peters* carried as few as possible of the men absolutely needed on the invasion day. In case of problems, the slower ships could turn east and seek shelter in Norwegian waters or in the Skagerrak, while the cruisers and torpedo boats attempted a high-speed breakthrough towards Bergen after darkness, supported by the S-boats.

On 7 April, *Köln*, *Königsberg* and *Bremse* were at Wilhelmshaven, *Carl Peters* and the torpedo boats in Cuxhaven and the S-boat Flotilla at Helgoland.[49] It was forbidden to leave the ships from early morning, and telephone lines were barred. In the afternoon, the senior officers were informed of the operation and soon after the first troops started to arrive in small groups. The main embarkation started when a troop train was shunted into the enclosed area of the Hipperhafen docks as darkness fell. All men were onboard by 23:00, *Köln* having embarked 640 officers and men, mostly from I and II/IR 159 in addition to Generalmajor Tittel and his staff. *Königsberg* embarked a further 735 men, including Oberst Graf von Stolberg, commanding officer of IR 159, Vizeadmiral von Schrader, the designated commanding admiral for the Norwegian West Coast and their staffs. Onboard *Bremse* were 207 men , mostly from 8th Company IR 159, but also some police and guard units. Korvettenkapitän Hans Marks, commander of 6th Torpedo Boat Flotilla, was in charge in Cuxhaven, where the remainder of the two battalions embarked on *Carl Peters*, *Leopard* and *Wolf*. In all, some 1,900 soldiers were onboard the ships of Group III. Support personnel, field guns, heavy matériel, horses, vehicles, A/A guns and

Light cruiser *Köln*. The 6,650-ton K-class cruisers were capable of well over thirty knots and armed with nine 15-cm guns, six 88-mms and twelve torpedo tubes. (Author's collection)

further provisions were onboard the transports *Rio de Janeiro*, *Marie Leonhardt* and *Curityba*, already at sea.

Confined below decks, the soldiers were given a meal, followed by brief instructions of what to do and what not to do while onboard and advised to go to sleep. The cruisers and *Bremse* cast off at 23:10 and after passing through the locks headed down the Jade towards the open sea. Shortly after, Admiral Schmundt received information from Group West that the British had sighted Groups I and II, but it appeared that only light enemy forces had taken to sea so far. *Carl Peters* and the torpedo boats, having left Cuxhaven an hour earlier, had orders to join the flag in the forenoon of 8 April, west of Ringkøbing.[50] Meanwhile, the cruisers zigzagged northwards at twenty-three knots. By daylight, a handful of escort aircraft arrived overhead. There were (false) torpedo alerts on a few occasions, but after some quick turns the ships were back on main course again.[51] To Schmundt's great relief, the weather closed in during the morning with low clouds and rain, reducing visibility. Around 10:45, fog set in and visibility was reduced. The air cover had to give up and turned for home, but that meant little as no British aircraft or submarines could find them either. USW-radio contact was made with Korvettenkapitän Marks onboard the torpedo boat *Leopard*, but there was no visual contact. By 11:00, the end of the mine barrage was reached and course was set for Utsira at eighteen knots with *Königsberg* and *Bremse* in line-astern behind *Köln*. At one stage, *Königsberg* ventured too close to *Köln* and, evading to port, lost sight of the flagship in the dense fog. Contact was maintained by USW radio and Group III continued northwards. Twice, aircraft engines were heard overhead, but the German ships were safe inside the fog and not sighted. No further signals were received from Group West and there was little knowledge of what lay ahead.[52]

Just after 05:00 on 8 April, the third K-class cruiser, *Karlsruhe*, under the command of Kapitän zur See Friedrich Rieve, left Wesermünde heading for Kristiansand, accompanied by the torpedo boats *Luchs*, *Seeadler*, *Greif* and the depot ship *Tsingtau*. Onboard were I/IR 310 plus staff, support personnel and naval gunners to take over the coastal forts – in all some 1,070 men. Konteradmiral Schenk, the designated commanding admiral for the Norwegian South Coast, and his staffs were also onboard. Passing Lightship D later in the morning, Group IV split up: *Karlsruhe*, *Luchs* and *Seeadler* taking a westerly route, zigzagging at twenty-one knots, while *Tsingtau* and *Greif* hugged the Danish coast at sixteen knots, the best the depot ship could do. C-in-C Torpedo Boats Kapitän zur See Hans Bütow was onboard *Luchs* and Korvettenkapitän Wolf Henne, commander of 5th Torpedo Boat Flotilla, was onboard *Greif*. They were prepared to take independent action if the flag faltered. Kapitänleutnant Rudolf Petersen's 2nd S-boat Flotilla, also assigned to Group IV, was a mix of boats of different designs, which gave him operational challenges. He and his crews were among the most experienced 'torpedomänner' of the German Navy though, and would run independently towards the Skagerrak.[53]

The last of the western groups to leave for Norway was Group VI. The 600-ton minesweepers *M1*, *M2*, *M9* and *M13* carried the 150 men of Rittmeister Eickhorn's Radfahrschwadron, tasked with securing Egersund. Eickhorn and his unit had arrived at the port of Cuxhaven by train from their barracks near Stettin in the late morning of

Kapitän zur See Friedrich Rieve of *Karlsruhe* leading Group IV. Behind him is the intelligence officer Düwal and von Schroeder, Rieve's adjutant. (Kapitän Rieve's photo collection via K Mæsel)

Sunday 7 April, were shunted directly into the closed-off harbour area, and loading onto the minesweepers commenced. No transport vessels were assigned to Group VI so all the equipment needed for the unit to survive until reinforcements could be brought in from Stavanger, had to be carried onboard the minesweepers. The tiny flotilla under the command of Korvettenkapitän Kurt Thoma of *M9* left Cuxhaven at 20:30 and anchored off the island of Neuwerk, waiting for the appropriate time to head north. With forty to fifty additional soldiers onboard and bicycles, motorcycles, machine guns, crates and other equipment in every available space on and below deck, conditions were cramped indeed. While waiting, the sailors and soldiers were briefed on the task ahead. It was a huge surprise that Egersund and Norway turned out to be their target. The information that they would come as friends was encouraging, but few dared to hope the Royal Navy would stay at home. At 05:45 on the 8th, anchors were weighed again and course resumed on a flat sea with a light south-easterly wind. Later, Group VI met up with the minesweepers and minelayers of Groups X and XI, heading for Denmark, and the small ships travelled north together.[54]

* * *

Blücher, the second of the *Hipper*-class cruisers, had been commissioned in September 1939. The subsequent harsh winter with heavy ice in the Baltic delayed her working-up, as did additional post-launch alterations and only on 30 March was she released from the yard in Kiel. Altogether, *Blücher* had only spent some twenty days at sea. Neither the torpedo batteries nor the 20.3-cm guns had ever been fired. The young crew had been assembled while she was still in the yard and they knew each other well, but few had experience from other ships – far less from war. The officers were also inexperienced and only a handful had been in battle. Emergency training, damage control and action-station drill were deficient or at best incomplete. Manuals were being implemented, except for those of the engine room, which were still being drafted. Nevertheless, Raeder wanted to free *Lützow* for her Atlantic sortie, and decided *Blücher* should join Group V for Oslo. The SKL saw no particular risk in assigning the new cruiser to this presumably simple task and did not protest. Thus the 47-year-old Kapitän zur See Heinrich Woldag was ordered to prepare for exercises in the Baltic with the light cruiser *Emden* as soon as he was ready. *Emden* was the oldest and least battleworthy of the light cruisers, but was seen as fit for the Oslofjord.[55]

During the transfer to Oslo, Konteradmiral Kummetz would be in charge of Gruppe Oldenburg, reporting to Generaladmiral Carls of Group East in Kiel.[56] Kummetz embarked on *Blücher* with his staff in the afternoon of 5 April, heading into the Baltic in the company of *Emden*. Only Kummetz, Woldag and their senior staff officers knew what was going on. Docking in Swinemünde in the late morning of the 6th, preparations were immediately initiated with the staff of the 163rd ID for the embarkation of troops. A number of administrative, civilian and propaganda personnel came onboard during the day, as well as an advance party of von Falkenhorst's staff. The embarkation of the soldiers commenced as darkness fell. Most of the equipment was stored on deck while the men made themselves comfortable in the confined, unfamiliar environment below. Few of them received any information at all about what to do in case of alarm. Due to the haste of the preparations, *Blücher*'s magazines still contained practice ammunition of all calibres. Because of lack of time and to avoid any questions, it was decided not to land this, but merely to stow the live ammunition on top. Thus, there was no room for the ammunition brought onboard by the soldiers, which was left up top; partly on deck, partly in the torpedo workshop and aircraft hangar.[57] Ten to twelve Marks floats, with room for fifteen to forty men, arrived the day before sailing after much pressure from Woldag. Kapok lifejackets also arrived late and were for convenience strapped to the guardrails along the superstructure decks.

Blücher left Swinemünde accompanied by *Emden* and the torpedo boats *Albatros* and *Kondor* at 05:30 on 7 April. First they steered east, but as soon as they were out of sight from land, they turned west, heading for Kiel. During the day, *Blücher*'s main guns were fired for the first and, as it turned out, last time with live ammunition; one round for each gun. Other types of exercises were held all over the ship, particularly focusing on battle drill and damage control. The Landsers, under protest, were kept below deck practising disembarkation drills.[58]

Shortly before 21:00, the group dropped anchor in Strander Bucht off Kiel, alongside the heavy cruiser *Lützow*, which earlier in the day had come through the canal from

Group V at sea in the Kattegat. The photo was taken from *Emden*, with *Lützow* ahead and *Blücher* in the lead. (Bundesarchiv Koblenz)

Wilhelmshaven. During the stay off Kiel, the soldiers were only allowed on deck in small groups wearing navy garments borrowed from the sailors. Most of the men believed they were involved in some kind of exercise and found the masquerade quite funny. Waiting for departure time, Konteradmiral Kummetz invited captains, navigation officers and army commanders onboard *Blücher* to discuss the last details with Generalmajor Erwin Engelbrecht, commander of the 163rd ID. Engelbrecht would be in charge once the troops landed in Oslo and would be acting C-in-C until General von Falkenhorst arrived. For most of the officers this was the first they had learned of their mission.

At 03:00 on 8 April, the group weighed anchor in darkness and headed north through the Belts. *Blücher* was in the van; *Lützow, Emden, Kondor* and *Albatros* followed. At 05:30, the torpedo boat *Möwe* also fell in, having spent the night at anchor further offshore. Almost 2,200 Wehrmacht personnel were onboard the ships of Gruppe Oldenburg. *Blücher* had embarked 822 men, *Emden* 610, *Möwe* 114, *Albatros* and *Kondor* about 100 each. Most of the soldiers came from 1st and 2nd Battalion of IR 307 but there were also staff personnel from Group XXI and 163rd ID as well as naval artillerymen, communication personnel, pioneers, war correspondents and ground crew for the Luftwaffe units to be stationed at Oslo-Fornebu. *Lützow* had 400 Gebirgsjägers and some 50 Luftwaffe men originally intended for Trondheim.[59]

All ships were at sea and there was no way back.

Meanwhile, General von Falkenhorst and his staff moved from Berlin to Hamburg. Hotel Esplanade, where Generalleutnant Geisler of X Fliegerkorps had worked since December had been emptied of guests and on 7 April became the temporary headquarters for Operation Weserübung.[60]

War of Nerves

The first report of German warships at sea reached Whitehall at 06:37 on 7 April, when aircraft sightings from the night before of a large, unidentified ship heading north at fifteen to twenty knots off Helgoland were logged. At 08:48, a Hudson of 220 Sqn reported 'one cruiser and six destroyers escorted by aircraft' on a northerly course off Horns Reef. This report only reached C-in-C Home Fleet Admiral Forbes at Scapa Flow at 11:20. Half an hour later, he received a supplementary signal from C-in-C Rosyth that the cruiser was 'probably of the *Nürnberg*-class'. The shadowing Hudsons had been chased off, but bombers were on their way.

At 13:15, an entry in the Admiralty War Diary was made, stating air reconnaissance in the afternoon of the day before had confirmed *Scharnhorst* and *Gneisenau* to be at anchor off Wilhelmshaven while one pocket battleship, two K-class cruisers and one *Hipper*-class cruiser were moored at the various docks. *Lützow* was (falsely) reported to be in Stettin. German U-boats were operating near the Orkneys, while one was believed to be in the Bristol Channel and another in the Irish Sea. This outdated and partly incorrect information, together with the initial under-reporting of Groups I and II at sea, gave the Admiralty the impression that nothing untoward was going on.[61] At 14:00 there was another brief entry in the war diary noting that a heavy cruiser, probably *Blücher*, had been sighted off Gedser on a westerly course, while C-in-C Rosyth reported three destroyers off Horns Reef heading south, apparently back towards Germany. At about the same time, Admiral Forbes received another signal from the Admiralty, where it had been issued over an hour earlier:

> Recent reports suggest a German expedition is being prepared. Hitler is reported from Copenhagen to have ordered unostentatious movement of one division in ten ships by night to land at Narvik with simultaneous occupation of Jutland. Sweden to be left alone. Moderates said to be opposing the plan. Date given for arrival at Narvik was 8th April. All these reports are of doubtful value and may well be only a further move in the war of nerves.[62]

Forbes later remarked that in the light of subsequent events, 'It was unfortunate that the last paragraph was included.' First Sea Lord Admiral Pound was out of office at Mountbatten's estate near Romsey most of Sunday 7 April. The wording of the signal was that of the Deputy Chief of Naval Staff, Vice Admiral Tom Phillips – he had already warned Churchill and Pound a week earlier that the Germans appeared to be planning an operation of their own. Admiral Pound did not modify any of the actions taken or signals sent when he came to Whitehall around 20:00 that evening, so it must be assumed he concurred with what had been done. Nor did he take any initiatives to get an update of the situation or to verify the state of affairs with the other services or the CoS. Neither did Churchill initiate any modifications or initiatives when he came by later. It was incomprehensible to the Admiralty that Germany would try anything like invading western Norway – far less Narvik – across the North Sea. Such an operation would, it was believed, require ship concentrations well beyond the capacity of the Kriegsmarine. According to the diary of Captain Ralph Edwards, Director of Operations (Home),

'The Old Man [Pound] was away fishing for salmon and arrived back rather late in the evening dead beat. DCNS [Phillips] was tired and the First Lord well dined. The result was they all failed to come to any useful decision.'[63] The day of 7 April 1940 is not one to be remembered with pride in the history of the Admiralty.

Only when the report of the Blenheims having attacked heavy German forces in the Bight arrived at 17:35 did Admiral Forbes order his ships to raise steam and prepare for sea.[64] At 20:50, *Rodney* (flag), *Repulse* and *Valiant* cleared Hoxa Boom and half an hour later reached open water, where a north-easterly course was set. The cruisers *Sheffield* and *Penelope* were in company as were the destroyers *Codrington, Brazen, Bedouin, Electra, Eskimo, Escapade, Griffin, Jupiter, Punjabi* and *Kimberley*.[65]

About half an hour later, 2nd Cruiser Squadron under Vice Admiral GF Edward-Collins left Rosyth with orders to make a sweep into the North Sea and then join the Home Fleet. Besides the cruisers *Galatea* and *Arethusa* the force consisted of the destroyers *Afridi* D(4), *Cossack, Gurkha, Kashmir, Kelvin, Sikh, Mohawk, Zulu* and the Polish destroyers *Grom, Burza* and *Blyskawica*. Next morning they were joined by *Somali* D(6), *Mashona, Matabele* and *Tartar*.

The carrier *Furious* was at Clyde after a refit, and Forbes seems to have forgotten her in the general melee. It was not until 16:37 on 8 February that the Admiralty intervened, ordering *Furious* to re-embark her aircraft and prepare to join the fleet. It would be another twenty-four hours before her two Swordfish Squadrons (nos. 816 and 818) had been landed onboard and Captain Troubridge could take to sea. The carrier's Fighter Squadron (no. 801) was at Evanston, too far off to comply in time and *Furious* took to sea without fighter aircraft onboard.

Vice Admiral Geoffrey Layton, commander of 18th Cruiser Squadron, was at sea with *Manchester* and *Southampton*, covering outward-bound convoy ON25 to Norway. During the afternoon, he was ordered by the C-in-C to turn the convoy back to Scotland and join the Home Fleet. It appears that Admiral Layton missed or misread parts of the signal from the C-in-C and, considering his orders inadequate, he stood off to the south during the night intending to regain contact with the convoy and its escort in the morning.

Left behind at Rosyth for the time being was Admiral Cunningham's 1st Cruiser Squadron with *Devonshire, Berwick, York, Glasgow* and eight destroyers embarking troops and equipment for Bergen and Stavanger.[66] The cruisers *Penelope* and *Aurora* and six destroyers were at the Clyde, ready to provide cover and escort for the transports to Narvik and Trondheim.

Just before leaving, the German fleet was reported to consist of 'one battle-cruiser, one pocket battleship, three cruisers and twelve destroyers'. Admiral Forbes took it for granted that updates would reach him once at sea, but the weather deteriorated rapidly, hampering the Hudsons from Leuchars, and he would have no further information until next morning. The course set by the Home Fleet upon leaving Scapa Flow would enable the fleet to intercept ships attempting to break out into the Atlantic, but left the central North Sea and the Norwegian coast uncovered. At 22:00, the armed merchant cruisers of the Northern Patrol were ordered to withdraw southwards, out of harm's way. At 22:51, the minelayer *Teviot Bank* was recalled, and her destroyer escort instructed to rejoin the Home Fleet after refuelling. Admiral Forbes was preparing to meet an Atlantic breakout. During the night the fleet steered north-north-east at twenty knots and at dawn on 8 April passed 60° N, between Shetland and Bergen. By then the German fleet was some 200 miles further north-east, off Trondheim, widening the gap with every passing hour.[67]

British Mines

When Admiral Whitworth arrived off Vestfjorden in the evening of 7 April, the minelayers and their escorts were detached according to plan at 19:00. They headed for Landegode, north of Bodø, while *Renown*, with only *Greyhound* in company, hovered to the west, some thirty miles off Skomvær Lighthouse. A signal was sent to *Birmingham* and *Glowworm* with estimates of intended position during the night and next day with orders to join forthwith. The minelayers reached Vestfjorden without incident and by 05:26 on Monday 8 April, 234 mines were laid as planned.

The Norwegian auxiliary *Syrian* was at anchor on the landward side of Vestfjorden that morning. The weather was poor with large swells and patches of fog. At 04:20, eight destroyers were observed well inside Norwegian territory. A little later, some of them were seen to commence dropping what appeared to be mines from their sterns. Kaptein Bjarne Kaaveland sent a preliminary radio signal to SDD3 in Tromsø while weighing anchor and headed for the lead destroyer. The signal 'Neutral Territory' was hoisted at the masthead while the signal 'Protest. Leave Norwegian territory' was repeatedly flashed by lamp. The destroyer, already identified as the British HMS *Hunter* from the pennant H35 on her side, answered by hoisting 'Minefield ahead. Stop for instructions' and replied by lamp 'Will not leave territory'. Closing, a boat was lowered from *Hunter* and a British officer came across. He informed them that mines were being laid and handed Kaptein

HMS *Impulsive* of 20th Destroyer Flotilla. To facilitate the carrying of mines, the after deck of the mine-laying destroyers had to be cleared and the torpedoes and aft gun removed. (Goss/ Navpic)

Norwegian destroyer *Sleipner*. Four 735-ton *Sleipner*-class destroyers were in commission by the end of 1939. Capable of thirty-two knots, they were the fastest ships of the RNN, but were comparatively under-gunned, armed with only three 10-cm guns, one 40-mm Bofors L/60 and two torpedo tubes Asdic and a fair number of depth charges on the quarterdeck made the nimble destroyers potentially dangerous adversaries for submarines. (Marinemuseet)

been at sea for 35 years both in sail and steam'.[70] Lieutenant Egan presented Ullring with a copy of the Admiralty's signal giving the co-ordinates of all three alleged minefields off the Norwegian coast, adding that three hundred mines had been laid within the marked co-ordinates earlier that morning. The astonished Ullring repeatedly asked the British officers if the mines really had been laid and told them he now feared German reprisals out of all proportion. Having submitted a signal to the SDS in Trondheim, Ullring invited the British officers to join him for breakfast while he awaited instructions.[71]

It took several hours before the answer came, and during the extended breakfast the rapport between the Norwegian and British officers grew very friendly. Ullring suggested that *Sleipner* should take responsibility for guarding the minefield if *Hyperion* and *Hero* would leave Norwegian territorial waters. Lieutenant Egan – who knew there were no mines – answered that this was probably acceptable, and Kaptein Ullring asked to be taken onboard the British destroyer to make the final agreements with Commander Nicholson (and undoubtedly take a look at his ship). By now, the weather was deteriorating fast, though, and he eventually decided to stay where he was. The answer from the commanding admiral finally came via Trondheim after 10:30. It was short and not very helpful: '. . . Protest against violation of neutrality . . . ref paragraph 17 of neutrality procedures.' The British officers left *Sleipner*, having received a formal protest. Through some further signalling, Ullring accepted responsibility for guarding the 'minefield', whereafter *Hyperion* and *Hero* departed Norwegian territory at 11:38.[72]

At Stad, no British naval vessels had been observed and several ships had crossed the area after the minefield was supposed to have been laid. Receiving the information from the Admiral Staff that there was a minefield here too, Tank-Nielsen sent the torpedo boat *Snøgg* and two auxiliaries to patrol the area.

The first German knowledge of the British mine-laying was a signal picked up at 07:35 from the British radio station at Cleethorpes, announcing the three danger areas. Politically, this development could not have been timed better, as it underlined perfectly the need for a German 'rescue operation' in Norway. The minefields would not affect the landing operations, but they might disturb the supply and tanker traffic to the bridgeheads. The SKL believed the British warning might very well be a bluff, but during a telephone conference with Admiral Saalwächter, it was agreed that no chances should be taken and the danger areas avoided, if necessary by going outside the Leads.[73]

Meanwhile, events progressed at sea.

Glowworm *and* Hipper

The slow Nordic dawn became visible onboard the German battleships around 04:45 GeT in the morning of Monday 8 April. At this time, they were a hundred miles off Trondheim, steering 045° for Vestfjorden. Visibility was fair to good and once it was light enough to take a tally, most of the destroyers were found to be missing. It was expected that they were not far away and would soon catch up. During the morning, the wind began to veer north-westerly, increasing to Force 7, gusting to 9, with the sea still mounting.

At 04:30 BrT (British Time), *Glowworm* reported to *Renown* that she had been hove to during the night, but would shortly proceed to rendezvous as ordered. *Glowworm*'s gyrocompass had jumped off its mountings and it appears that Lieutenant Commander Roope had decided it was fruitless to try to locate the battlecruiser without. All the more so as no fix had been obtained for close to forty-eight hours and *Glowworm*'s position was uncertain. On deck, there was damage caused by the heavy seas and the whaler and motor dinghy had been washed away. A couple of hours after dawn, another destroyer was sighted, answering 'Swedish destroyer *Göteborg*' when challenged. Roope did not find this likely; when the other ship turned away he ordered steam, hoisted the battle ensign and opened fire. Rolling badly, the shots fell short, and the other ship vanished in the murk before *Glowworm* could follow.[74]

Far from being Swedish, the sighted ship was *Lüdemann* trying to catch up with the battleships.[75] The German lookouts sighted the British destroyer some time before it became obvious they had been sighted themselves and Korvettenkapitän Friedrichs, the captain of *Lüdemann*, was prepared to attack, believing he had a tactical advantage. Fregattenkapitän Hans-Joachim Gadow, C-in-C of 3rd Zerstörer Flotilla, however, decided their primary task was to bring the Jägers to Narvik and ordered him to turn away towards the north-west. The rest of the German fleet was expected to be to the north-east and it was important that the British destroyer did not find the battleships, should it succeed in following.

Vizeadmiral Lütjens was alerted to the British destroyer through two USW-radio signals from *Lüdemann* recorded at 08:58 and 08:59 GeT in his war diary. This means that the first sighting of *Glowworm* probably happened some five to ten minutes earlier, around 07:50 BrT.[76] German reports state that *Glowworm*, when sighted from *Lüdemann*, was at slow speed on a southerly course with unmanned guns and without steam on several boilers. Unless this is a misapprehension, it can only be explained by the repair of the gyrocompass taking longer than expected, and Lieutenant Commander Roope believing there was no danger this far north under the prevailing conditions.

Shortly after the first destroyer had vanished, *Arnim* appeared on *Glowworm*'s port bow, closing fast, and a running fight ensued. In the heavy seas neither destroyer scored any hits. In particular *Arnim* was rolling badly. Onboard *Lüdemann*, still speeding away, a USW-radio signal was received, believed to come from *Arnim*, briefly sighted through the murk: 'Am attacking enemy'. Fregattenkapitän Gadow replied as he had done to Friedrichs: 'Consider your main task'. Korvettenkapitän Curt Rechel of *Arnim* later denied that the 'Attack' signal had come from him. In his version, he had only received a fragmented USW signal from *Lüdemann* and was not sure what was going on.

The British destroyer suddenly emerged from a rainsquall, too fast for him to get out of harm's way. Rechel turned *Arnim* north-westwards behind a smokescreen. Roope gave chase and the German reports do not hide the fact that the British destroyer fared much better than the German in the heavy seas. At thirty-five knots, the foreship and bridge of *Arnim* were seriously damaged and two men lost overboard. Speed was reduced to twenty-seven knots. *Glowworm* could maintain a higher speed without taking damage and started to gain on *Arnim*, firing continuously. *Arnim*'s forward turrets could only bear at times and the theoretical superiority of the five German 12.7-cm guns versus the four British 12-cm came to naught. German reports claim three hits on their adversary, but none of the British survivors confirmed this. Rechel must have started to feel the situation getting out of hand; he now turned north-east, towards the fleet. What Lieutenant Commander Roope believed, we can never know, but he decided to follow the German destroyer even though it must have occurred to him that she was heading for company. German sources report British survivors to have said they never expected to find a cruiser coming at them, but few of the survivors were on the bridge. At 09:30, *Gneisenau* received a USW signal from *Arnim*, giving an assumed position, requesting support. A few minutes earlier, Lütjens had already signalled for *Hipper* to turn back and sort out the mess.

The Zerstörers of the 2nd Flotilla had managed to stay close during the night and when Flotilla Commander Fregattenkapitän von Pufendorf in *Jacobi* received copies of USW signals indicating enemy contact, he ordered the other ships of his group, *Riedel*, *Heinemann* and *Eckholdt* to close up and steered towards the scene of action. Not long after, gun flashes were seen to the north. Before they could get close, though, *Jacobi* tilted more than 55° during a particularly heavy sea, drenching the port boiler room intakes, shutting down the port engine temporarily and throwing five men overboard. Frustrated, von Pufendorf, who did not share Gadow's view on the priorities, had to slow down, but continued towards the encounter.[77]

At 07:59 BrT, Lieutenant Commander Roope sent a signal to Admiral Whitworth in *Renown*, reporting enemy contact at 65° 04' N, 6° 04' E, followed two minutes later by: 'Am engaging enemy destroyer'. Three hundred miles to the south-west, on the bridge of *Rodney*, Admiral Forbes received *Glowworm*'s signals shortly after. The reported position puzzled him. It either meant that the fleet sighted the day before had made over twenty knots during the night in spite of the atrocious weather, or there were two German fleets at large. Both cases were equally alarming. In the Admiralty War Diary, there is a scribble over the encoded position of the signal: 'wrongly coded'. German reports place the encounter at 64° N, 07° E, sixty miles further south. At 08:40, *Glowworm* reported 'Enemy making smoke', and five minutes later, 'Am endeavouring to draw enemy northwards'. Two more signals followed, reporting the German destroyer retiring north-eastward behind smoke, until at 08:55 came: 'One enemy vessel unknown identity bearing 000°, 6 miles, course 180°'. A position added to the signal was unintelligible except for 65° N. The last signal from *Glowworm* was made at 09:04, fading out and making a sinister indication of her fate.[78] *Renown* and *Greyhound* turned south shortly before 08:45, as did *Birmingham* and *Fearless*, which had still not caught up with the flag. At 10:00 Admiral Forbes detached *Repulse* and *Penelope* with *Eskimo*, *Bedouin*, *Punjabi* and *Kimberley* from the Home Fleet, ordering them to head north-east at maximum speed.[79]

Receiving the signal to search for the destroyer in trouble, Heye ordered all army personnel below deck and turned his cruiser south. Going against the sea, *Hipper* took heavy water and, to facilitate observation and keep the forward guns ready, speed was kept moderate. From *Lüdemann*, a fantastic sight was witnessed when *Hipper* appeared briefly, crashing majestically through the heavy waves. *Glowworm* was in for a nasty surprise.

At 09:50, *Hipper*'s foretop reported a masthead forward to port and shortly after another to starboard. The destroyer to port was shrouded in smoke, apparently from a deliberate attempt to hide. Both ships were rolling madly in the heavy seas. Neither foretop nor bridge could at first decide which of the two emerging destroyers was the

Glowworm laying smoke. This photograph was taken from *Hipper*. (Bundesarchiv Koblenz)

enemy and Kapitän Heye held his fire. The starboard destroyer started to flash 'A-A-A' repeatedly towards the cruiser. The signal did not make sense to the Germans, but one of the officers held it was English, meaning 'What ship?' Heye still hesitated, but finally gave permission to fire when the foretop reported the signalling destroyer to be flying a White Ensign. It was 09:58 GeT when *Admiral Hipper*'s 20.3-cm guns opened fire in anger for the first time. Range to target was 8,400 metres.

Heye kept the cruiser's bow at the destroyer to avoid torpedoes and only the 'A' and 'B' turrets could bear at first. After three salvoes, the after arcs opened and the 'D' turret could fire too. 'A' turret was at times troubled by seas washing over it and its fire had to be halted when the destroyer came inside maximum depression. Loading and aiming was difficult in the high seas and the interval between salvoes was irregular; all the more so as it was difficult for the main turrets to follow the fast-moving destroyer over the shortening distance.

The first hit on *Glowworm* was observed on the starboard side between the bridge and the funnel after the fourth salvo. Lieutenant Commander Roope ordered smoke and turned the destroyer back into it, attempting to gain a respite but *Hipper* followed her moves on the DeTe radar, firing into the smoke. Emerging again, *Glowworm* started to take hits from *Hipper*'s 10.5-cm guns, which had been allowed to shoot. The radio room and wireless aerial were destroyed, halting further signalling. Communication between engine room and bridge was severed, making emergency measures necessary. Further hits opened the hull to the sea. One 20.3-cm shell wrecked the captain's day cabin, temporarily in use as a first-aid station, killing the medics and most casualties. Another exploded deep in the engine room, fracturing steam pipes and starting multiple fires. Still, Engine-Room Artificer Henry Gregg somehow managed to maintain speed and manoeuvrability. On deck, *Glowworm*'s forward 4.7-inch gun vanished in a gust of fire while parts of the yardarm crashed onto the siren lanyards, starting a banshee wailing above the howl of the storm. The bridge of the destroyer was a mess of twisted plates and tubes, hit by at least one 10.5-cm shell.

Few shots were fired from *Glowworm* during the encounter according to the German reports, and there were no direct hits on the cruiser. Only one shell exploded near the foreship, sending shrapnel harmlessly over the deck. Using the cover of his smokescreen, Roope made a torpedo attack at 10:10 GeT. In spite of being close (some eight hundred metres), Heye's careful tactics of pointing the bow at his adversary paid off and he was able to avoid the torpedoes, even though the nearest was only metres away to port. Roope's attempts to swing the other mounting out to get off the rest of the torpedoes were hampered, being continuously raked from *Hipper*'s 3.7- and 2-cm guns.[80] *Glowworm* turned again, re-entering the smokescreen. Heye wanted a quick solution to the encounter before further torpedoes could be fired, and he steered the cruiser into the smoke. Coming out on the other side, the two ships were suddenly very close. Fearing that *Glowworm* might get another opportunity to launch torpedoes, Heye ordered 'hard-a-starboard' in order to close and, if necessary, ram the destroyer. The heavy seas delayed the rudder response, however, and *Hipper* turned slowly. Whether Roope also intended ramming the cruiser or if the ensuing collision happened fortuitously will never be ascertained, in spite of the legend. Torpedo Officer

Glowworm after the collision, with bow broken off. Both torpedo mountings are swung out and appear to be empty, so most likely all ten torpedoes were fired. (Bundesarchiv Koblenz)

Lieutenant Ramsey, the sole surviving British officer, later told his rescuers that neither the helm nor the emergency rudder were manned at the time, and so the destroyer's turn towards *Hipper* was probably accidental.[81]

Whatever the intentions of the two captains, *Glowworm* tore into *Hipper's* forward starboard side with sirens wailing, striking just abaft the anchor. The destroyer's bow was pressed under the side of the cruiser and broke off. The remains of the hull scraped along the starboard side-armour, making a thirty-five-metre crescent-shaped dent, tearing away a large part of the railings and wrecking the forward starboard torpedo mounting. Mechanikergefreiter Ritter, leading seaman on the forward 10.5-cm, was lost overboard. Several bulkheads were opened to the sea and some five hundred tons of water flooded the hull before the leaks could be isolated. The cruiser was not seriously damaged, in spite of the forecastle being low in the water and a starboard list.[82]

After the collision, *Glowworm* drifted clear with a devastating fire raging amidships and Heye ordered 'Cease fire' at 10:13. Thirty-one shells had been fired from the 20.3-cm guns, 130 from the 10.5-cm guns, 156 from the 3.7-cm guns and 132 from the 2-cm guns during the fourteen or fifteen minutes that the battle lasted. At first, it was Heye's intention to leave *Glowworm* as she was – incapable of shadowing the German fleet any more. There were other British ships nearby, he expected, and these would come to the rescue.[83]

Glowworm was going down quickly and Lieutenant Commander Roope gave the order to abandon ship. As she sank, men climbed onto her bow or jumped into the freezing, oil-covered water. Legend has it that at the last moment, Lieutenant Commander Roope shook the hand of every man around him. At 10:24 GeT, *Glowworm's* boilers exploded and she slipped under; the abrupt stop of the siren causing an eerie silence in spite of the storm.

Having searched briefly for Mechanikergefreiter Ritter and not yet fully under way, Kapitän Heye felt obliged to assist the British sailors struggling for their lives. He gave the unprecedented order for *Hipper* to heave to, downstream of the drifting survivors. In spite of the danger of British ships showing up at any time, he stayed for over an hour rescuing survivors. Lowering of boats was out of the question, but all personnel on deck, including some of the soldiers, helped to pull the frozen, oil-soaked British sailors up by ropes and ladders. The oily, icy water exhausted the British survivors. Many grabbed the ropes thrown at them but could not hold on and drifted away. Lieutenant Commander Roope was seen in the water helping his men to the ropes. Finally he took hold of a line himself and was pulled some distance up the side of the cruiser. To the horror of British and Germans alike, just before reaching safety, he let go and fell back into the water. From a crew of 149 onboard *Glowworm*, forty men were pulled out of the water. Several were wounded and at least two later died. The rescued men not in need of medical attention were given dry clothes, cigarettes and hot coffee. They were questioned, but only a few were willing to say much. Kapitän Heye learned little more than the name of the destroyer and that she had belonged to a squadron of three more destroyers and possibly one or two larger ships, bound for Lofoten. None of the survivors appeared to have any impression of the larger tactical picture and expressed surprise to have encountered a German cruiser at sea.[84]

Survivors being carried to safety onboard *Hipper*. (Bundesarchiv Koblenz)

Nothing more to do, Kapitän Heye ordered speed and signalled for the four destroyers of 2nd Flotilla, which had eventually arrived on the scene just as the battle was over, to gather on the cruiser. At 10:54, a laconic signal was sent to the fleet: 'Fühlungshalter versenkt' – 'Shadower has been sunk'. There was no point in trying to reunite with the flag. Group II was near the point where they would have been detached anyway and the five ships from now on proceeded independently. It was far too early to approach the coast and, after a sweep north-eastwards to acquire a bearing on the Halten Lighthouse, Heye steered back and forth offshore, waiting for the appropriate time to head for Trondheim. On request from the destroyers, a moderate speed was set to minimise sea effects.

It was only after the repatriation of the *Glowworm* survivors after the war, when Lieutenant Ramsey was interviewed by the Admiralty, that the full order of events came to be known in Britain. As a result Lieutenant Commander Roope was posthumously awarded the Victoria Cross, Lieutenant Ramsey received the Distinguished Service Order and Engine-Room Artificer Gregg, Petty Officer Scott and Able Seaman Merritt the Conspicuous Gallantry Medal.[85]

Ironically, the lost *Glowworm* was the only British surface ship to gain contact with the German invasion fleet on 8 April. It is possible that *Hostile* also brushed with *Hipper* that afternoon. *Glowworm*'s signals were picked up and, after ordering the captured trawler *Nordland* to proceed independently towards Kirkwall, Commander Wright turned to assist. At 15:45, a warship was sighted 'hull down to the North East, steering a North Westerly course'. Wright believed this to be *Renown* and steered to gain touch. Snow reduced visibility and the sighted ship, probably *Hipper*, vanished. At this time, *Renown* was well to the north, meeting up with the mine-laying force, and it is quite possible that *Hostile* might have shared *Glowworm*'s fate had it not been for the squall.[86]

On the same day, the German auxiliary cruiser *Orion* (*Schiff 36*) travelled along the Norwegian coast, independent from Weserübung. She was to have been escorted by *U64* into the Atlantic, but the two never met and Fregattenkapitän Weyher decided to proceed alone as the weather was closing in, favourable for a breakout. At 17:26, a 'steamer' was observed on a south-westerly course, accompanied by four destroyers. Course was changed away from the potential danger and the rest of the breakout went as planned.[87] The five ships *Orion* narrowly avoided were certainly *Teviot Bank* and her escort returning from the aborted mine-laying sortie. Had the destroyers sighted the auxiliary cruiser, she would have been a fine scalp from an otherwise futile sortie.

Lütjens was seriously concerned that the encounter with *Glowworm* had compromised the operation. He was certain that the British destroyer had submitted a report before going down; the Admiralty would understand that German destroyers this far north could only mean an operation against northern Norway. The apparent unpreparedness of the British destroyer, indicated in a signal from Fregattenkapitän Gadow at 12:03, on the other hand, was strong evidence that the Royal Navy had not been put on a general alert. Group I gathered on the battleships during the morning, except *Giese*, which remained missing. At one stage, Lütjens considered staying with Group II and letting Group I carry on alone, but eventually decided to follow the plan. The announcement of the minefield in Vestfjorden, which he was made aware of through Group West during the morning,

made it likely that British ships were in the vicinity. It was also known from Pruck's report that the Norwegian panserships were at Narvik and might be encountered. The fuel situation of the *Zerstörers* meant that they could not return to Trondheim should they run into trouble. *Hipper* and her consorts, on the other hand, would be better off as they could withdraw northwards if necessary. Splitting the battleships with one in each group was not an option. During the morning, the wind turned from south-south-west to north-west, increasing further. At midday, Bodø Radio forecast a full north-westerly storm in the Lofoten area by nightfall. At 13:50 Lütjens ordered second-degree readiness (half of the positions manned) and a general speed of twenty-five knots. An hour later, a signal from Group West forwarded an observation from a long-distance reconnaissance aircraft, which had sighted 'two battlecruisers, one heavy cruiser and six destroyers' on a northerly course north-west of Ålesund.[88]
The chase was on.

Orzel and Rio de Janeiro

In the morning of 8 April the Polish submarine *Orzel* (*Eagle*) of the 2nd Submarine Flotilla was cruising at periscope depth in the Skagerrak off Lillesand when Lieutenant Commander Jan Grudzinski sighted an approaching merchantman. She carried no flag, but with the periscope at maximum magnification he could read the name *Rio de Janeiro* on her bows. Unknown to the Polish captain, *Rio de Janeiro* was one of the transports assigned to Group III, heading for Bergen. Originally a 5,261-ton liner carrying cargo and passengers between Europe and Latin America, she was now loaded with large amounts

Rio de Janeiro in Stettin, just prior to departure. (Author's collection)

of military equipment including four 10.5-cm guns, six 20-mm A/A guns, seventy-three horses, seventy-one vehicles and 292 tons of provisions in her spacious hull. In addition there were 313 passengers, most of them wearing uniform.[89]

In spite of orders to the contrary, Grudzinski brought *Orzel* to the surface and flashed a challenge: 'Stop engines. The master with ship's papers is to report on board immediately.' Instead of stopping, Kapitän Voigt increased speed and turned shoreward. *Orzel* could do twenty knots on the surface and gave chase, firing bursts of warning shots from her Lewis gun. *Rio de Janeiro* halted and a boat was lowered, but stayed close to the liner in spite of a few sailors pretending to be rowing. Meanwhile, the radio operator of *Orzel* reported that the German was sending a coded radio signal and Grudzinski flashed by lamp to abandon ship as he was about to fire a torpedo. There was no reaction. While the torpedoes were prepared, the coaster *Lindebø* and the fishing vessel *Jenny* chanced to pass nearby. Grudzinski ordered fire at 11:45 and the torpedo struck amidships, after which he took his boat down. Steam and dense smoke poured from *Rio de Janeiro* and suddenly her deck came alive with men in field-grey uniforms, falling or jumping into the sea. Lifebelts and pieces of wood were thrown over the side as more men followed into the water. No one seemed to try to lower the lifeboats. *Rio de Janeiro* listed and turned slowly to starboard, but did not appear to be sinking. *Lindebø* and *Jenny* moved in to assist.

The Polish *Orzel*. On the surface, she could do over nineteen knots and, submerged, almost ten. Four torpedo tubes in the bow, four in the stern, four external amidships, one 105-mm gun and two 40-mms made her a welcome addition to the Allied submarine force. (Author's collection)

At 11:15, Kristiansand SDS received a signal from Justøy coastguard station that they could see the tower of a submarine on a westerly course just outside the territorial limit and a merchant ship, which appeared to be idle next to it. The nationalities of both vessels were unknown. An MF11 reconnaissance aircraft was ordered up from the naval air base at Marvika and took off shortly after, arriving just as the torpedo struck. Kvartermester Almton took his aircraft low over the listing ship and Lieutenant Hansen in the observer's seat could see chaotic conditions onboard with people running through flames and smoke, tumbling into the sea and trying to reach a few nearby floats. Several dead men were floating face down and horses were also in the water, adding to the horror. The submarine, which had dived as the aircraft arrived, was nowhere to be seen. A brief signal was sent to Marvika at 12:07 as Almton headed back towards Kristiansand to report.

Orzel, which had circled underwater, fired a second torpedo from periscope depth. It struck at 12:15 and the bow of the transport broke off and sank quickly. *Lindebø* had splinters flying over her deck from the explosion and several of the just rescued sailors were killed or wounded. The hull of *Rio de Janeiro* rolled over and sank minutes later, leaving hundreds of men to fight for their lives in the freezing sea.

The destroyer *Odin*, which had been sent to investigate, arrived at 12:45, joining the rescue work. Conditions were rough, though, and soon the surface was scattered with bodies. Eventually some 150 men were rescued by various Norwegian vessels while around 180 perished (19 crew and about 160 soldiers), plus all the horses.[90] An accurate cross-plot of the position made from Justøy and Høvåg coastguard stations concluded that *Rio de Janeiro* had been just outside the Norwegian three-mile territorial limit when torpedoed. Lieutenant Commander Grudzinski took *Orzel* away from the carnage and eventually surfaced to send a report.[91]

Odin headed for Kristiansand with seventeen wounded and eighteen dead under a tarpaulin on the deck, flying her flag at half-mast. Most of the others ended up in Lillesand. The dead were taken to the chapel at the local cemetery. The less wounded were treated by three local doctors in the harbour area while the serious casualties were sent to the hospital in Arendal. The Germans were wet and miserable and obviously shaken by their ordeal. Chief of Police Nils Onsrud arrived to take charge of the operation. He became very concerned when he discovered that virtually all of the survivors wore uniform and that some even had guns. What was obviously an officer tried to maintain some order and shouted 'Wehrmacht hier! Marine hier!'[92] These men were no ordinary sailors! Onsrud started questioning them and some answered openly that they were soldiers heading for Bergen to assist the Norwegian Army against an Allied invasion – at the government's request. The officer, presenting himself with a salute as Lieutenant Voss, held that *Rio de Janeiro* had been nothing but a merchantman loaded with general provisions. Onsrud was certain the man was lying and that he had stumbled onto something of great importance. He cordoned off the harbour area as best he could and organised dry clothes, food and cigarettes to keep the Germans busy, while he went looking for a telephone. His call to Kristiansand SDS came through at 14:30, but to Onsrud's astonishment, the naval officer he spoke to at Marvika doubted his observations and saw no need to initiate any actions other than the ongoing rescue operation. To take care of the survivors and guard them, Onsrud was advised to contact the army 'as the men were already on land . . .'. This he did, but at General Liljedahl's office they saw no reason to interfere either.

After nearly two hours of fruitless telephoning and discussions, Onsrud was tired of being pushed around and called Undersecretary of State Rognlien at the Lord Chancellor's Office in Oslo. Rognlien believed Onsrud and called both the General Staff and the Admiral Staff to inform them. His surprise was great when he learned that the Admiral Staff already knew about the Germans in uniform claiming they were heading for Bergen, having received the same information upon *Odin's* return to Kristiansand, but did not consider the matter much to worry about compared to the British mines. The defence minister had been informed but initiated no actions. Rognlien could only call Onsrud back and ask him to do his best.[93]

The reports from Lillesand and Kristiansand were forwarded to the Ministry of Defence and the Foreign Office at around 18:30 and referred by Defence Minister Ljungberg to the Storting shortly after 20:00. Nobody reacted and no precautions were taken.

In London, Grudzinski's report never reached the Admiralty. They only heard of the sinking of *Rio de Janeiro* through Reuters and apparently thought little of it.[94]

Meanwhile, further east, off Svenner Lighthouse, *Trident* intercepted the 8,036-ton tanker *Stedingen* intended for Sola-Stavanger airfield with aviation fuel. Lieutenant Commander Seale wrote:

> A large tanker, laden, with no national marks or name on her side was sighted steaming west outside territorial waters. This vessel appeared most suspicious and was thought to be a German Auxiliary. I decided to investigate and at 12:15 surfaced on her port quarter and fired a blank shot. She turned to starboard for territorial waters and increased speed. I then fired two rounds of SAP which fell just short in line with bridge. This caused her to stop engines. I closed on her quarter with 'Do not transmit' flying and made by lamp 'Abandon ship, I shall torpedo you in five minutes'.[95]

Stedingen, which was outside the territorial limit, was hastily abandoned by her crew after removing the valve covers in the pump rooms. Somebody also managed to send an SOS before leaving. The boats eventually pulled clear and made for shore. *Trident* intercepted them and the German master, Kapitän Schäfer, was detained. *Stedingen* was sinking slowly and Seale finished her off with a torpedo before heading away. The rest of the crew, some fifty men, continued towards land and the lifeboats were eventually towed into Stavern by a pilot vessel.[96] *Kreta*, one of the supply ships for Kristiansand, was also fired at by *Trident*, but escaped into Norwegian waters.[97]

A Day of Highest Tension

As dawn approached on 8 April, Kapitän Rieve, onboard *Karlsruhe* heading for Kristiansand, was every bit as concerned as Lütjens had been the day before. Leaving Helgoland aft, calm seas, clear skies and good visibility prevailed. Rieve knew that Groups I and II had been attacked the day before and it was inconceivable that British aircraft would not continue to search the area. *Luchs* and *Seeadler* were kept tirelessly skirting around looking for submarines while the cruiser's gunners and lookouts searched for aircraft. Unbelievably, nothing at all happened during the morning. The soldiers and sailors had been informed of their target around 09:30 and at midday the Landsers were allowed on deck to enjoy the sun. In the early afternoon, off Horns Reef, a few fog-patches fluttered by, the wind started to pick up and the weather closed in, much to Rieve's relief. By 16:30, the fog was so dense he ordered *Luchs* and *Seeadler* into line-astern to prevent losing touch. There was no contact with *Tsingtau*, *Greif* or the S-boats but no reason to assume they were not on course for the meeting point off Hanstholm. Arriving there around midnight, a searchlight was shone into the murk and soon most of the group was in touch over USW radio. Rieve ordered a north-easterly course towards Kristiansand, while *Greif*, assigned to secure Arendal further east, set an independent course.[98]

In the North Sea, Group III continued northwards through the fog during the day. Admiral Schmundt was quite comfortable with the low visibility, but the meteorologists onboard predicted the fog would lift towards the afternoon. A signal from Group West at 12:58 reported the British cruiser *Galatea* between Stavanger and Aberdeen, based on radio intercepts. She was probably not alone and an encounter might be likely. Schmundt considered turning south to remain inside the fog belt until nightfall, but decided against as he had only USW-radio contact with the ships of his group.

Around 17:00, the fog lifted sufficiently for the ships of Group III to gain visual contact and gather again. The cruisers formed line-abreast some 1,500 metres apart with *Bremse* and *Carl Peters* astern while *Leopard* and *Wolf* secured the flanks. At 17:45, Group West forwarded a radio interception report indicating a large number of enemy ships off western Norway. Schmundt found this information less than useful as the observation was six hours old and they could be anywhere by now – including in Bergen. In fact, danger was closer than was comfortable. Vice Admiral Edward-Collins's 2nd Cruiser Squadron was probably only some sixty to seventy miles away from the German force, between them and Korsfjorden, the entry to Bergen. Besides *Galatea* and *Arethusa* the British force consisted of fifteen destroyers and would have been a deadly threat to Schmundt's group. The two British cruisers had only three dual 15.2-cm turrets, compared to the three triple 15-cm turrets of the Germans, but *Köln* and *Königsberg* were loaded with troops and there is little doubt that the large number of destroyers in the group would have been a challenge to Group III, had they met. During the evening, however, the British force was instructed to join the Home Fleet further west, opening the passage for the Germans.

At 15:49, orders were issued from the SKL cancelling the use of the British flag during the entry of the invasion ports: 'Do not use British war flag.' Schmundt commented defiantly in his war diary that he had 'already decided to enter without flag'.[99]

At nightfall, Group III was some twenty miles west of Karmøy, zigzagging on a northerly main course at fifteen to seventeen knots. The fog had lifted, but the night was dark with rainsqualls and the ships closed up to remain in contact. Conditions were nothing like further north, but the wind had freshened and the sea was heavy. Utsira and later Slåtterøy Lighthouse came into sight and speed was reduced to arrive at the entry to the fjords on schedule. The news that the lighthouses were burning was received positively and Admiral Schmundt was becoming optimistic that they might make it after all.

The S-boats of the 1st Flotilla caught up as planned off Utsira, having left Helgoland in the early morning. Soon after falling in, *S21* and *S19* collided, the latter being holed aft above the water line. *S21* was able to keep up with the force, but *S19* was taking water

it was almost too much. The wind dropped after midnight, but the rain and fog remained and after a while the lookouts reported they could only see *M1*. Thoma had no choice other than to proceed as planned and hope for the other half of his flotilla to do the same. A searchlight was moved to the stern of *M9* pointing directly aft, giving *M1* a beacon to follow. The two ships continued towards Egersund.[102]

At 21:00 GeT, Group I had reached the latitude of Bodø, and Vizeadmiral Lütjens, giving the Zerstörers the latest estimate of their position, turned *Gneisenau* and *Scharnhorst* to port into the Norwegian Sea. The wind had turned to north-west and reached full storm. The sea was extreme and even experienced sailors were affected by seasickness. West of the Lofoten Islands, the course was set to 310°. Both battleships started to take damage and speed was reduced to twelve knots, later to nine and at 23:16 to seven knots. Lütjens could not know that he was following more or less in the wake of *Renown*, by now some twenty-five to thirty miles ahead.

Onboard the detached Zerstörers the rolling gradually started to lessen as around 23:00 they came under the lee of the Lofoten Islands, somewhere off to the north-west. Gradually, conditions became more bearable and parts of the crews who had been isolated in their positions because of the risk of moving about on deck and opening doors and hatches, could be relieved. For the Jägers below deck, the last part of the journey had been the worst. In the mounting wind, the destroyers, riding high due to empty bunker tanks, had been pressed towards the lee side. This limited the roll, but increased the pitch towards the limit of what the slender ships could take.

Nothing was heard from *Giese* and the nine Zerstörers continued in line-astern behind *Heidkamp*, leaving Korvettenkapitän Smidt to find his own way towards Narvik. Time was running short, and there was no question of waiting for him to catch up.[103] On Bonte's order, all ships were at action stations. Apart from an intermittent signal from the radio beacon at Skrova Island in Lofoten there were no landmarks and nothing even close to an exact position could be determined in the snowy darkness. Proceeding up Vestfjorden, the ships corkscrewed less and less and speed could gradually be increased to twenty-seven knots. At one point a few glimpses of light were seen to the starboard, most likely the auxiliary *Syrian*, still guarding the minefield off Landegode. Later, approaching the narrows off Barøy, *Heidkamp* turned sharply to port, signalling wildly as a rockface rose out of the sea ahead when the snow suddenly lifted. Another time, fire was almost opened when the shadow of a cliff was mistaken for a warship.[104]

It had been a busy day on the airfields in the north of Germany. Escort and reconnaissance missions had been flown in large numbers until the deteriorating weather forced most aircraft back to their bases. Only two Do26 flying boats of the Transozeanstaffel appear to have ventured beyond the North Sea on this day. It must have been hard even for these very experienced aircrews to fly into the storm and the war diary of Group West is complimentary regarding their work.

Major Lessing, commanding officer of KüFlGr 906, arrived in the morning at Hotel Esplanade in Hamburg, where he had been invited to a meeting with X Fliegerkorps. Somewhat to his surprise, a large number of other Luftwaffe commanders turned up and they were all sworn to secrecy. Geisler and Harlinghausen then arrived and informed them they had been chosen to lead the imminent occupation of Denmark and Norway.

After the meeting, the others hurried back to their respective bases to prepare the crews while Lessing was pulled aside by Lufttransportchef See Oberst Ernst Roth, and told to go directly to Norderney and take command of KGzbV 108, a special squadron being set up with Ju52 and He59 seaplanes. He was not to return to his original squadron and not to let them, or anybody else, know where he was going. Leaving Hamburg, Roth received written orders, which revealed that the target for his new unit would be Bergen and his cargo would be soldiers and equipment. At Norderney, the aircraft were already being fuelled and loaded. The pilots were assembled and briefed on technical matters for the mission to commence the following morning. Take-off times, weather forecast and emergency procedures were given, but few of the pilots had knowledge of where their targets really were. Later, all personnel were ordered to bed to get as much rest as possible. The base was sealed off by police troops during the afternoon and nobody was allowed to leave or make external telephone calls. 'Security measures were watertight,' according to Lessing.[105]

In Wilhelmshaven, Admiral Saalwächter sat down to summarise the situation around midnight. He was optimistic that the British mine-laying gave Germany the right to 'meet this act of violence with similar measures'. On the negative side, it probably meant that parts of the British fleet would be at sea. It was not yet clear if the Admiralty realised the German objectives or if they were reacting to what they believed to be an Atlantic breakout. Saalwächter feared that the sinking of *Rio de Janeiro* had given the German intentions away, but reckoned that even if this was the case, it was too late for London to initiate effective countermeasures against the invasion forces. The dousing of the outer lighthouses indicated the Norwegians had been warned and were preparing a defence, but Saalwächter believed nothing could stop the German warships at this stage.

The SKL arrived at the same conclusion: 'Operation Weserübung has left the stage of secrecy and camouflage . . . The element of surprise has been lost and we must expect resistance at all points.' Except for a single report of heavy warships sixty miles north-west of Ålesund, made by one of the Do26 of the Transozeanstaffel, no German sightings of British capital ships were made that day. Several cruiser groups were reported further south, in the North Sea, but none of these called for any change of plans.[106]

The 8th was 'a day of highest tension', Jodl wrote in his diary.[107]

In the morning of 8 April there were eight British destroyers in Vestfjorden between Kommodore Bonte's Zerstörers and their target, with *Renown* and *Greyhound* in support further west. At 10:07, the Admiralty instructed the destroyers to join *Renown*; the first of a series of unfortunate signals where the Admiralty would give tactical orders directly into the chain of command. Admiral Forbes, who had crossed the Bergen–Shetland line with the Home Fleet shortly after dawn, some six hours behind Vizeadmiral Lütjens, found the order bewildering, but assumed there was a good reason and did not wish to break radio silence for clarification. At 11:00 a signal to Forbes, copied to Whitworth, informed that the Admiralty now believed the intelligence regarding landings 'may be true and [that] German forces are on their way to Narvik'.[108] If so, the reason for moving the destroyers out of the way rather than order *Renown* to join them in blocking the entrance to Narvik has never been adequately explained.

Admiral Whitworth had steered south since receiving *Glowworm*'s emergency signals, but had to slow down from the initial twenty-four knots as *Renown* started to take damage in the heavy seas.[109] After the signal cut short at 09:04, nothing more was heard from *Glowworm* and Whitworth turned north again at 13:30, meeting up with the destroyers in the afternoon, some twenty miles south-west of Skomvær Lighthouse.

Meanwhile, a Sunderland flying boat of 204 Sqn had been diverted from convoy escort to scout the Norwegian coast. The aircraft hugged the coast to Kristiansund and continued northwards into the Norwegian Sea. Visibility was one to two miles with low clouds and constant rain. At 14:00 Flight Lieutenant EL Hyde and his crew sighted what they believed to be 'one battlecruiser, two cruisers and two destroyers' on a westerly course at 64° 12' N, 6° 25' E. This of course was *Hipper* and her four destroyers wasting time before heading for Trondheim. Visibility was poor and Lieutenant Hyde ventured too close to the German ships in order to verify their identity. *Hipper*'s A/A fire was accurate and with his Sunderland damaged Hyde was unable to stay in pursuit. Turning back, an initial sighting signal was sent, supplemented by a more comprehensive report upon landing about an hour later.[110] *Rodney*'s Walrus was flown off at 18:43 but sighted nothing and sent no reports.[111]

Admiral Forbes took the report from Hyde's Sunderland to mean that even if some German ships might be steering for Narvik, others were heading into the Atlantic. To intercept the latter, he ordered the Home Fleet to alter course to 000° at 15:30, modified to 340° at 16:15. The detached *Repulse, Penelope* and destroyers were also ordered to turn west, but this decision was revised and they were ordered to continue north-eastwards for a rendezvous with *Renown*.

Further north, Admiral Whitworth exercised his own judgement and decided Vestfjorden could wait. Screening westward from Skomvær Lighthouse during the afternoon, assisted by the destroyers, he intended to turn south at nightfall – leaving the entrance to Narvik open. Group I was at the time probably around two hours behind *Renown*. Discovering what was happening, the Admiralty countered his dispositions with a signal at 17:24 concluding that 'As Sunderland only sighted part of force . . . it is possible that the unlocated part is still making for Narvik.' This was followed by a 'Most Immediate' signal at 18:50: 'The force under your orders is to concentrate on preventing any German forces proceeding to Narvik.' It was too late. By 19:15, when Whitworth received this signal, the storm, after a brief lull, was worse than ever. He considered the prospect of taking his ships towards land in low visibility during a heavy storm too risky and decided to 'stand to seaward during the dark hours'. He expected the Germans to do the same. A later signal from the Admiralty, authorising all British ships off Norway to 'enter territorial waters as necessary', made no practical difference at this stage. The weather deteriorated further and at 20:00 Whitworth ordered his destroyers to gather on the battlecruiser, continuing: 'Our objective is to prevent German forces reaching Narvik. My present intention is to alter course at 21:00 to 280 degrees and to turn 180 degrees in succession at midnight. Enemy heavy ships and light forces have been reported off Norwegian coast. Position of *Birmingham* force is not known.'[112] At 21:30 Whitworth was informed that *Repulse* and *Penelope* were on their way to reinforce him, too far away to make any difference at the moment, but asking for his position. He gave this as sixty miles south-west of Skomvær Lighthouse, steering 310° at six to eight knots into a north-westerly Force 10 storm. At 21:40, Captain Warburton-Lee reported that the destroyers 'had become unmanageable in the seaway' and could do nothing but trail behind the battlecruiser, concentrating on staying afloat. Turning back at midnight as intended would not be possible.

By taking his ships into the Norwegian Sea, Whitworth lost his tactical manoeuvrability. He could have turned *Renown* back alone, but chose to stay with the destroyers. No further signals came from Forbes during the evening. Neither did the Admiralty follow up on the missing response to their orders, arguably the occasion when an interception would have been appropriate. In his report, Whitworth concluded: 'Hearing that the enemy forces had reached Narvik, I felt very strongly that I had made a mistake.'[113]

Further south, Admiral Forbes learned through a series of signals from the Admiralty during the afternoon that *Manchester* and *Southampton*, the four destroyers escorting the recalled *Teviot Bank* and the two destroyers pretending to lay mines off Bud were put at his disposal. To his surprise, he was also informed that Vice Admiral Cunningham had been ordered to disembark the troops he had just embarked at Rosyth, less their stores and equipment, and take 1st Cruiser Squadron to sea forthwith.[114] The French admiral Derrien in *Emile Bertin* and her two destroyers had been placed under Cunningham's command. Furthermore, *Aurora* and destroyers had been sent to Scapa Flow without troopships and would take to sea as soon as ready. Finally, Forbes was informed that unless he broke radio silence, the Admiralty would issue orders as they believed appropriate. The cancellation of Plan R4 came as a great surprise to Admiral Forbes. He had sufficient cruisers already at his disposal to chase the German fleet he believed to be heading into the Atlantic, and could see no reason why R4 should not go ahead as planned.[115]

Nothing more was heard of the ships reported by Flight Lieutenant Hyde but new reports arrived of a second German force consisting of *Gneisenau* or *Blücher* supported by several cruisers and destroyers having passed Skagen on a westerly course.[116] At 20:10 Forbes received a signal sent from the Admiralty an hour and a half earlier, outlining two objectives: to prevent the German northern force returning, and to deal with the force in Skagerrak, should they proceed further west 'to Stavanger or Bergen'. In consequence, the Home Fleet was ordered to 'sweep to south with light forces spread to northward, keeping east of 02° 35' E'. Meanwhile, 1st Cruiser Squadron (*Devonshire*, *Berwick*, *York*, *Glasgow* and *Emile Bertin*) was instructed to 'sweep to northward keeping west of 01° 50' E', while 2nd Cruiser Squadron (*Galatea*, *Arethusa* and fifteen destroyers) was ordered to 'act as striking force by night' between the two given longitudes. The 18th Cruiser Squadron (*Manchester* and *Southampton*) was ordered to patrol between 01° 50' E and 02° 35' E, north of 62° N, unless receiving alternative orders from C-in-C. Admiral Forbes immediately turned the Home Fleet to the south.

Later the Admiralty concluded there were two German fleets at sea and that it was possible they intended to meet up at dawn around 60° N. Fearing the cruiser squadrons might be caught between the two enemy forces, the previous search pattern was cancelled and the groups instructed to gather on the fleet. A night of confusion followed. Additional orders and counter-orders were issued by both the C-in-C and the Admiralty, few of which could be effected due to the atrocious weather. At midnight of 8/9 April, the

Home Fleet passed through 63° 15' N, 03° E, course 180° with a speed of eighteen knots. *Manchester* and *Southampton* joined the fleet at 06:30 on the 9th, just south of 62° N, while 1st and 2nd Cruiser Squadrons fell in at 09:30, by which time the British ships had been shadowed by German floatplanes for over an hour.[117]

The cancellation of Plan R4 and disembarkation of the troops destined for western Norway is arguably the decision with the direst consequences taken during 8 April. It was, according to General Ian Jacobs, assistant military secretary to the War Cabinet, made by Churchill without consulting the Chiefs of Staffs or the Cabinet. The order to disembark came by telephone from the First Sea Lord to Admiral Cunningham through C-in-C Rosyth around 11:30, confirmed by signal shortly after. During the subsequent Cabinet meeting the same morning, Chamberlain asked how far the cruisers had gone and when they would be able to put the troops ashore. Being informed by the First Lord that the soldiers had disembarked, 'so that the cruisers could join the fleet', he 'looked decidedly sheepish', answering with a surprised exclamation 'followed by a distinct silence'.[118]

Plan R4 was intended as an answer to German reactions provoked by the mine-laying. That the Germans came on their own accord should only have made things better, but Churchill and Pound believed they saw a naval operation develop and made a naval response. We shall never know what would have happened had Plan R4 gone ahead and Vice Admiral Cunningham's ships had arrived off western Norway with their troops during 9 April. The British soldiers would not have been in place before the German landings, but had they been at sea in fast cruisers, they could have made a significant difference in Stavanger, Bergen or Trondheim.[119] By chasing a tactical, naval victory the Admiralty lost the strategic overview and initiative. This was to cost many lives, eventually topple the Chamberlain government and make way for Churchill in Downing Street.

Increased Preparedness

On the morning of Monday 8 April, Norway woke up to a new reality. The newspapers had headlines: 'The Allies have blocked Norwegian territorial waters', and 'British minefields at Stadt, Hustavika and Vestfjorden'. Norway was practically cut in two. About halfway down the pages were less conspicuous articles reporting German 'minesweepers, destroyers and cruisers' heading north through Danish waters. Few realised what was happening, but most felt fear, uncertainty and frustration. There would inevitably be German reactions to the mine-laying and, unless the crisis could be countered, there might be actions of war on Norwegian territory.

Foreign Minister Halvdan Koht was up as usual shortly after 06:15. While he was having his breakfast, a courier from the Foreign Office arrived with a copy of the Allied note. Koht telephoned Prime Minister Nygaardsvold at his home and suggested the government should meet as soon as possible. Nygaardsvold wanted to include the Foreign Affairs Committee in the meeting as well. Koht disagreed, but was overruled, and the meeting was set for 10:00. While finishing his breakfast and waiting for Nygaardsvold to confirm the meeting, Koht received a call from Commanding Admiral Diesen. He feared that British ships guarding the minefield in Vestfjorden might enter Ofotfjorden and attack German ore ships at Narvik and sought Koht's approval to give the panserships orders to oppose, should this happen. Koht agreed and when Nygaardsvold called back shortly after, he had no objections either.[120] Most likely, neither Koht nor Nygaardsvold really believed the British ships would go to Narvik – if they did, they would certainly turn back if met by opposition before anything serious developed.

At 10:00 the government sat down with the Foreign Affairs Committee to discuss reactions to the mine-laying. Commanding Admiral Diesen and the Chief of the Admiral Staff Kommandør Corneliussen were also present. At first, Koht read parts of the Allied note of Friday 5 April and that of the same morning. For most it was the first time they had heard of either. While Commanding Admiral Diesen pointed out where the minefields allegedly were, Koht was called to the telephone to talk to Swedish Foreign Minister Günther in Stockholm. He returned with the information that there was no apparent action in Swedish waters. The rest of the meeting was spent discussing how to react and how others would react, Germany in particularly. A firm protest would have to be made to London and Paris, quickly, and the mines would have to be swept as soon as possible. The note said that British ships would guard the minefields for forty-eight hours, and the RNN should be ready to move in once the British were out of the way. There was widespread agreement in the meeting that events must not lead to Norway entering the war *against* Britain, and hostilities with the Royal Navy should be avoided, in spite of the anger over the mine-laying. Britain had been seen as the guarantor of Norwegian neutrality and now – for the second time this spring – the neutrality had been severely violated. Before the meeting, Commanding Admiral Diesen had suggested to Ljungberg that the planned mine barrages in the Oslofjord should be laid immediately. Ljungberg promised he would discuss the issue with the government, but it was not brought up in the meeting and, in spite of repeated requests, Diesen did not hear back from the minister during the day.[121]

The meeting with the Foreign Affairs Committee lasted until 12:30. There were many participants and most had something to say. Towards the end, Koht brought up Minister Esmarch's contact with the Danish Ministry of Foreign Affairs and the reports of German ships, but brushed lightly over both. At an impromptu press conference around 12:55 in one of the corridors of the Parliament, Koht informed the press of the situation, concluding that 'The Norwegian government can in no way accept that a belligerent country lays mines in Norwegian territorial waters. We demand that the mines are removed and that the foreign warships leave our territory immediately.'

After a short lunch, Koht met briefly with the assistant Swedish chargé d'affaires in Oslo, Carl Douglas. Curiously, Koht told Douglas that the government had initiated 'certain military security measures, notably the alarming of the coastal fortresses and the concentration of the Norwegian Navy on certain key points'.[122] It is not clear exactly what Koht referred to; most naval officers would probably contest that this was the case. Perhaps Koht and other members of the government believed that such precautions were obvious and would be initiated by the Ministry of Defence. When Douglas left, Koht sat down to fine-tune the protest and plan what to say in the Parliament.

At 15:00, while still working on the orientation to the Parliament, the foreign minister was interrupted by an urgent telephone call from the Norwegian Embassy in London. A few hours earlier, the embassy had been requested to send an envoy to the Admiralty regarding a matter of utmost importance. At the Admiralty, the Deputy Chief of Naval

Staff, Vice Admiral Phillips, had informed Vice-Consul Smith-Kielland that German naval forces had been sighted off the Norwegian coast heading north. 'It is strongly suspected that operations against Narvik are intended and that they could arrive at Narvik before midnight,' had been Phillips's conclusion. A telegram detailing the British warning would be sent from London as soon as possible. Koht acknowledged and went back to work. 'I was so absorbed that it needed a mental effort to gather my thoughts on what I had heard,' Koht later wrote. Narvik was so far north it was difficult to comprehend the significance of the information. Coming from the British Admiralty, Koht felt sure that whatever was going on, the British Navy would take care of it. Besides, there were Norwegian panserships in Narvik and significant army units that would handle the Norwegian side, he believed, should that become necessary.[123]

The Storting assembled at 17:15. Both the commanders and their Chiefs of Staff were asked by Ljungberg to attend (on the public balcony) and were thus put out of contact with their staffs for over three hours during the afternoon. Koht, visibly tired and distressed, opened by referring parts of the Allied note of 5 April, the note regarding the mine-laying and the Norwegian protest, which had by now been forwarded to the French and British Embassies in Oslo. There could be no justification, Koht said, for the Allies to 'bring the war to Norwegian territory'. Several of the representatives expressed concern and frustration over the mine-laying, but cautioned that this must not lead to Norway entering the war against Britain. Some of the speakers advised the time had come to increase the preparedness of the navy and the coastal forts, including the laying of their own minefields. Nobody suggested a mobilisation. When Defence Minister Ljungberg, towards the end of the meeting, reported the sinking of *Rio de Janeiro* and the subsequent rescue operation of German soldiers, the news was hardly discussed. Ljungberg later told the Commission of Inquiry that he assumed the German ships were heading somewhere else, or were part of a force showing off against Allied provocations. Carl Hambro, the president of the Parliament, who was to act very decisively once he understood what was going on, later wrote that the reports of the uniformed rescuees from *Rio de Janeiro* claiming they were heading for Bergen were taken as 'confirmation that German soldiers would believe anything they were told by their officers'.[124]

At 18:00, the telegram from the Norwegian Embassy in London arrived at the Foreign Office, confirming the warning given by Vice Admiral Phillips. It read:

> German naval forces were sighted in the North Sea yesterday accompanied by, it is believed, a merchantman, possibly a troop transport. This morning, the vanguard was observed off the Norwegian coast heading north. It is with certainty assumed their intention is to operate against Narvik and that they will arrive there before midnight. Admiral Phillips added the Germans might arrive at Narvik already at 10pm.[125]

After deciphering, the telegram was copied to the Admiral Staff, where it arrived at 19:05. It is unclear if Koht or Ljungberg actually read the telegram or just had it referred. It is certain that none of the other members of the government, including Nygaardsvold, saw it – or even heard of it. When the Storting eventually concluded its proceedings close to 21:00, most of the MPs were worried, but of the opinion that there was no imminent danger. Berlin would be provoked, but it was expected that the Germans, as before, would wait and see how the Norwegians handled the situation before they reacted.[126]

*　*　*

While the decision makers were in the Parliament or other meetings, several disturbing reports arrived at the Foreign Office from various sources. Most of the signals were forwarded to the Ministry of Defence and the Admiral and General Staffs according to standing procedures, but never with any comments as to their significance.

Around 14:00, Minister Esmarch in Copenhagen forwarded to Oslo information he had received directly from the Danish General Staff of 'two German battlecruisers, one battleship, three torpedo boats and several smaller vessels' passing the Belts. In addition, German troops were marching northwards (if still some distance away from the border) and the transport ships loading in the Baltic ports had departed. At about the same time, the embassy in Berlin submitted a brief signal to the Foreign Office, stating that the Danish Embassy had let them know that several troop transports had been observed on a northerly course through the Belts. These signals, as well as a confirmation from the embassy in Berlin that loaded troop transports had left Stettin on 5 April, were already in the Foreign Office and Ministry of Defence when the report of German soldiers being rescued from *Rio de Janeiro* arrived from the Admiral Staff between 17:30 and 18:30. Nobody saw the connection.[127]

The Intelligence Offices of the navy and army also received news of German ships passing through the Belts from their Danish and Swedish counterparts. Oberst Carlos Adlercreutz, head of intelligence at the Swedish Defence Staff, called the General Staff in Oslo at midday informing his friend Wrede-Holm of the German warships passing through the Belts during the morning. The Danish Naval Staff Commander Pontoppidan called his Norwegian colleagues at 10:43 with the information of cruisers, Räumboote and trawlers moving north, followed by a signal from the Danish naval intelligence at 18:20: 'At 17:15, a squadron passed Hirtsholm on a northerly course, consisting of *Gneisenau*, *Deutschland*, *Emden* and three torpedo boats of the *Möwe* class. At 17:00, two armed steamships of 600 tons passed Storebelt. Many people onboard (troops?), course north. Also seventeen trawlers.' The two intelligence offices forwarded the information to each other, and their commanders, but it is not clear if these reports reached the Ministry of Defence.

Around midday the British naval attaché in Oslo, Rear Admiral Boyes, came by the Admiral Staff and told the head of the Intelligence Office, Kaptein Steen that he had 'reason to believe' that a British fleet was on its way across the North Sea 'to meet the German forces taken to sea'. During the day, this statement was apparently distorted and at 15:40 the Admiral Staff, on Commanding Admiral Diesen's order, issued a signal to the SDDs stating that 'a British fleet is on its way towards Kattegat to intercept reported German warships'. It is inconceivable that Boyes had received such information from the Admiralty, at least this early in the day, and he later denied having made the statement at all. Regardless, the belief that a British fleet was on its way to Kattegat was to have wide-ranging consequences.

Two compiled signals were sent from the Naval Intelligence Staff in Oslo to the SDDs around 13:30:

Legation in Berlin informed 7 April . . . fifteen to twenty troopships left Stettin night of 5 April heading west. Unknown destination to be reached 11 April.

The Danish Naval Staff reported at 10:43 this morning forty-eight German Räumboote and thirty-eight armed trawlers . . . spread in northern Kattegat . . . *Gneisenau*, *Leipzig* and *Emden* have passed Langeland on northerly course between 06:00 and 07:00 today followed by three torpedo boats and six armed trawlers. Swedish Defence Staff has 12:15 today reported strong German naval forces passing through Storebelt. Parts of force have reached Kattegat . . . Other vessels have passed Mön. [German] infantry and artillery has been observed in region of Rendsborg heading north, but in Denmark nothing has been observed at border.

Somebody in the Naval Intelligence Staff saw the information in the right context, but apparently had no authority to draw any conclusions, far less suggest countermeasures on his own.[128]

The man who had the authority, Commanding Admiral Diesen, was oddly passive during this day – in spite of access to ample intelligence to create a comprehensive picture of the threats developing. Oberst Hammerstad, C-in-C of the coastal artillery, was asked to attend a meeting with Commanding Admiral Diesen during the morning. Arriving at 09:30, he was told by Diesen: 'The war is coming.' To his surprise, though, he was only instructed to be ready to draft further men to the forts – when orders were issued.[129] Kaptein Willoch of the Naval Intelligence Office overheard a telephone conversation between Diesen and Kommandørkaptein Askim in Narvik during the morning. Askim asked for instructions regarding the British mine-laying off Landegode; Diesen would give no orders, but referred to the instructions of the Neutrality Act. Askim argued that these instructions were too general to cover such a specific event where reactions (or lack of reaction) might have the most serious consequences. Orders would have to come from the commanding admiral or the government. Diesen repeatedly referred to the instructions and the lengthy conversation ended without Askim having received any orders. A similar hesitance can be found in the transcript of a telephone conversation between Diesen and Tank-Nielsen in Bergen, a few hours later, regarding what to do in case British destroyers arrived to lay real mines off Stadt. Diesen keeps referring to the 'instructions', in spite of Tank-Nielsen's request for 'permission to use force'. The most concrete initiatives from the commanding admiral during 8 April were the order to douse the lighthouses south of Bergen at 22:00 and the signal to the commanding general at 22:15 requesting infantry support for the forts at Bergen and Trondheim the following day. There are probably two main reasons for Diesen's reserve: his strong belief that the Royal Navy ruled supreme in the North Sea and, most important, his unfaltering loyalty to the government. When neither Ljungberg nor Koht nor Nygaardsvold gave any orders to change mode from Neutrality Watch to war, Diesen was not the man to cause ructions.[130]

Diesen later explained to the Commission of Inquiry that neither he nor Corneliussen believed a German attack on Norway was imminent at nightfall on the 8th. The information from the survivors from *Rio de Janeiro* that they were heading for Bergen was considered 'clever camouflage' and he expected the German ships were heading for Denmark, Shetland, the Faeroes or Iceland. His attention, and that of Corneliussen, was taken by the British mine-laying, and both were kept busy attending the drawn-out meetings of the Foreign Affairs Committee and the Parliament. There was no need for both men to attend all meetings and there were other men available to follow and assess

German movements. Before attending the meeting with the government, Diesen issued instructions to the SDDs for 'increased preparedness' (repeated at 20:00), but it was left to each local commander to interpret what it meant. Firm orders to the districts to prepare for war – even in the afternoon of the 8th after the telegram from London arrived – could have changed matters. Instead, except where local commanders exercised their own initiative, the naval ships remained where they were, ready for escort and patrol duties the next day.[131]

The General Staff, less preoccupied by the British mines, actually registered the increasing German activity both offshore and on land. On the maps held by the head of intelligence, Oberstløytnant Wrede-Holm, a disturbing picture emerged and during the day the General Staff discussed the situation several times as it became 'obvious the operations were directed at Norway'. The only person apparently not believing this was Commanding General Laake.[132]

The army Chief of Staff Oberst Hatledal recognised early that something was going on and in the morning of Friday 5 April, he had asked to see Defence Minister Ljungberg, asking if there were 'any notes to the government from the belligerents'. To this, Ljungberg answered 'no'. Hatledal pointed out the time that would be needed for an effective mobilisation, asking if the situation was not serious enough to consider taking the first steps, but he could get no permission from the minister to initiate anything. On Saturday 6 April Hatledal again approached Ljungberg, arguing for mobilisation

Army Chief of Staff
Oberst Rasmus Hatledal.
(Forsvarsmuseet)

of at least the field brigades in southern Norway. By this time, he had seen copies of the two telegrams from the embassy in Berlin referring to German attacks on Holland, Denmark and possibly Norway. Still there was no response. Ljungberg, who presumably had received the same information, did not believe there was any acute danger and saw no reason for bringing the issue of mobilisation to the government. To a direct question from Hatledal, Ljungberg again denied having received any signals of importance from the belligerents.[133]

In the morning of Monday 8 April, Hatledal returned to Defence Minister Ljungberg, advising a full mobilisation immediately, at least in the south. Ljungberg asked for an assessment of the cost of a mobilisation – including some lesser alternatives. Hatledal, hardly believing what he heard, protested, but Ljungberg dismissed the Chief of Staff and went to the meeting with the Foreign Affairs Committee. He later told the Commission of Inquiry that he reminded Hatledal to involve the commanding general and that a request for mobilisation should come through him, in writing. When Commanding General Laake arrived later in the morning, Hatledal informed him of the meetings he had had with Ljungberg, and they went to see the minister together at midday. Ljungberg asserted the government would not agree to anything but the mobilisation of a few battalions around Oslo, repeating the request for cost assessments. Hatledal, supported by Laake, insisted there was no time to lose and reiterated the recommendation to mobilise at least the four southern field brigades. Ljungberg was in a hurry, but said he would bring their recommendations to the government and dismissed the men, saying they would be informed as soon as a decision had been made. By not inviting them along to speak directly to the government, Ljungberg must take the full responsibility for the issue not receiving the attention he promised.

With the reports of the sinking of *Rio de Janeiro*, 'all doubt was removed' for Hatledal and the telegram from London with the message from the Admiralty only made it clear that all of Norway was threatened. He was certain that a mobilisation would be ordered during the afternoon and instructed the staffs to be ready to action the orders. Meanwhile, Laake and Hatledal were asked by Ljungberg to attend the meeting in the Storting in the afternoon. During the three-hour meeting, however, they heard nothing regarding mobilisation, and were not invited to speak. Commanding General Laake later said he could think of no other explanation than that the government had confidential information that there was no danger to Norway. Hatledal, in his own words, 'ran after the minister in the corridor after the meeting, asking for a decision. Ljungberg answered that no decision had been taken; the issue would be discussed in the government meeting, to which he was on his way, and the General Staff would be informed first thing next morning. Hearing this, Laake decided, against Hatledal's protest, to dismiss those of his staff not on duty. The divisions were informed at 21:00 that no further orders would be issued until next morning and that the staffs could be dismissed for the night. Only duty-personnel were to stay behind. Totally de-motivated, Oberst Hatledal told Kaptein Leif Rolstad, the duty officer at the General Staff, that his efforts to obtain a decision on mobilisation 'had come to naught', and he was now so exhausted that he asked not to be disturbed 'unless something very special happens'.[134]

* * *

The government convened at 21:00. By now, they were all tired, and the meeting was brief. No notes have been preserved and details of what was said or agreed have been difficult to ascertain. The issue of mobilisation was certainly on the agenda but it appears Ljungberg advised calling only the two line battalions around the Oslofjord, as proposed by Torp several days earlier and significantly less than advocated by Hatledal. Trygve Lie later held that this was agreed; Ljungberg insisted no concrete decisions were taken during the meeting. It appears that most ministers later believed that a positive decision for a limited mobilisation was taken in the evening of 8 April. Nothing was done, however, to follow up the decision and no written orders were issued. According to Prime Minister Nygaardsvold, it was decided to lay the defensive minefields in the Oslofjord. Trygve Lie later supported that this was the case, but none of the other ministers left with such an understanding and Commanding Admiral Diesen never received any orders to action such a decision.

What certainly *was* decided in the meeting was to sweep the British mines as soon as possible and not later than the morning of 10 April, unless the British started the removal themselves. Ljungberg had already dismissed the General Staff for the night and made no attempt to contact anybody there or in the Admiral Staff after the government meeting adjourned at 21:40.[135] Why he hesitated has never been explained. His inability to appreciate the situation probably played a role, as did diffidence in bringing drastic measures to the government, and the awkward relationship with his nominally senior officers in the General Staff. The ultimate accountability for the lack of clarity as to what was actually decided in the meeting, who was responsible and when the decision should be executed, rests with Nygaardsvold.

At Oslo Militære Samfund (the Military Club) a long-planned dinner was arranged, with King Haakon as guest of honour. It was known in advance that the king would come and attendance was high, including a large part of the General Staff, which had been dismissed just in time. King Haakon, otherwise highly vigilant and well aware of his country's vulnerability, later admitted he had not paid sufficient attention to the warnings from Berlin and Copenhagen, of which he had been informed.[136]

Prime Minister Nygaardsvold went home to spend some time with his family before going to bed, exhausted after a long day. Halvdan Koht was also tired when he left his office in the evening to join his lady-friend for supper. Expecting a quiet night, he did not even leave information as to where he could be reached.[137] Koht admits in his memoirs that he misinterpreted the situation that evening. His and many other's attention was focused on the threat from the Allies, and he saw the signals from Berlin as an indication of the coming of the long expected German offensive in the West. 'No one can suffer this miscalculation more bitterly than me,' he wrote, adding:

> Something must have failed in my brain that evening. I was unable to make the right connections, and could not see the fragments of information I had received in a proper context. Perhaps I was too tired. The truth is I could not give the government a complete and correct overview. I did not have it myself, which is why the subsequent events would come as such a shock to me.[138]

It was a cold night in Norway: windy, gusting to storm force, with frequent snow squalls in the north and dense fog in the south. Many families remained huddled around their fireplaces or in the kitchen throughout the evening. The day had been dramatic, with extra newspaper editions and news broadcasts. The last bulletin on the radio was at 22:00 and few missed it. In restaurants and cafés, those who had not already gone home asked for the radios to be turned on. Concerts halls and cinemas were empty; nobody wanted to go to places where they could not talk. Few believed there was a direct threat against Norway, but many expected encounters between German and British naval forces during the following days, leading to violations of Norwegian territory involving the navy and endangering civilian ships. Newspapers and news agencies established a duty roster, preparing for the morning editions. Towards midnight, everything was quiet in Oslo and few lights remained burning. At the British Embassy, Minister Dormer had an early night and slept well.

Twilight

Among the passengers on the train from Copenhagen via Sweden, arriving in Oslo on the morning of 8 April, were two Germans: Oberstleutnant Hartwig Pohlman, first officer (Ia) in General von Falkenhorst's staff and Herr Schumburg, a secretary from the Foreign Office. Pohlman travelled under his real name, but he was in civilian clothes and passed through immigration on a brand-new diplomatic passport giving his title as Ministerialrat (adviser) from the Ministry of the Interior.[139] The luggage, handled by the secretary, was protected by diplomatic immunity and thus not searched. Had it been, it would have created a major diplomatic crisis as it not only contained Pohlman's uniform, including his sidearm, but also several incriminating maps and sealed envelopes for the German minister in Oslo.

Pohlman was met at the station by the Abwehr agent Erich Pruck, and given a tour of the city to familiarise himself. Later, from his hotel room, Pohlman called the German air attaché in Oslo, Hauptmann Eberhard Spiller, instructing him to meet at Fornebu airfield next morning to receive the German forces, expected to land around 07:45. Excited, Spiller confirmed he would be there, but added that the fighters at Fornebu had been put on alert. Pohlman was not concerned; a handful of fighters would mean little against the German squadrons arriving next morning. Having concluded the talk with Spiller, Pohlman prepared for dinner with Minister Bräuer at the German Embassy.

Bräuer had been sidelined from the start of the planning and only that evening would he learn what was about to happen.[140] 'Pohlman had strict orders not to reveal anything about Operation Weserübung to the minister before 23:00. 'Rarely have I seen a man more surprised than [Bräuer] when I told him of the events to come and his designated role in them,' he later wrote. Two envelopes were given to the minister. The first contained a letter from his superior, Foreign Minister von Ribbentrop, outlining Bräuer's intended role vis-à-vis the Norwegian authorities. The second held a lengthy ultimatum for the Norwegian government, demanding surrender. This was to be delivered to Foreign Minister Koht at 04:20 precisely the next morning, a few minutes after the German landing operations had started, but while confusion still reigned. Bräuer was not to request the meeting or

Admiral Erich Raeder (right) at the launch of
the cruiser *Admiral Hipper* in February 1937.
(Author's collection)

force. Hitler consulted with Rosenberg, who recommended Quisling highly, and invited
the Norwegian to the Reichskanzlei on 13 December.[4]

Quisling came accompanied by Hagelin and Rosenberg's subordinate, Amtsleiter
Hans-Wilhelm Scheidt, head of the Nordic Office.[5] Scheidt later wrote that Hitler listened
'quietly and attentively' to Quisling, who spoke thoughtfully in halting German.[6] The
general Norwegian attitude had been firmly pro-British for a long time, Quisling said,
and in his opinion it was 'obvious that England did not intend to respect Norwegian
neutrality'. The president of the Parliament, Stortingspresident Carl Hambro, was of
Jewish descent and Quisling asserted he had close connections to the British secretary
of state, Leslie Hore-Belisha, also Jewish.[7] These two, he claimed, conspired to bring
Norway into the war on the Allied side and to secure British bases in Norway. Indeed,
there was evidence that the Norwegian government had already secretly agreed to Allied
occupation of parts of southern Norway, from which Germany's northern flank could
be threatened. Concluding, Quisling asserted that his party, the Nasjonal Samling (NS),
had a large and growing group of followers, many of whom were in key positions in the
civil administration and the armed forces. With the support of these people, he would be
prepared to intervene through a coup to avert 'Hambro's British plans' and, having seized
power, to 'invite German troops to take possession of key positions along the coast'.[8]

Hitler then delivered a twenty-minute monologue underlining that Germany had no
plans for an intervention in Norway while its neutrality was properly enforced. He had
always been a friend of England, he held, and was bitter about the declaration of war over
Poland. He now hoped to force England to her knees through a blockade rather than full-
scale war. A British occupation of Norway would be totally unacceptable and, according

southern Norway in addition to one artillery unit and half a dozen local companies. It was intended that the men should serve for two months before being replaced. This kept the division staffs preoccupied with the rotations and limited the time available to prepare for a full mobilisation. In mid-November, Commanding General Kristian Laake requested permission from the Ministry of Defence to draft cavalry, artillery and engineer units, totalling some 7,300 men, for extended training and exercises and to bolster the Neutrality Watch during the winter. This was declined, but after some argument, he was allowed to draft one battalion from each artillery regiment on a rotational basis. The post-war Parliamentary Investigating Committee found the Norwegian defences in 1939 'extremely weak [and] poorly equipped to protect our nation, to say nothing of making an efficient effort in open war'.[43] Still, it is worth noting that Brigadier Vale, the British military attaché to Norway in 1937, reported from observing a week of exercises with the 6th Division that the soldiers, in spite of limited number of training days, appeared 'competent in weapon handling and physically very fit'.[44]

In 1939 both the Naval Air Arm and the Army Air Force were small and neither was equipped to handle the demands of the Neutrality Watch. Disagreement on the organisation of the air forces and types of aircraft needed had seriously delayed necessary renewals, and only some thirty-five naval aircraft were available, spread in small groups around the coast. By 9 April, wear and tear had reduced the number of operational aircraft to twenty-eight, and of these, only the six He115s taken into service during the summer of 1939 had any real combat value. Apart from a handful of Gloster Gladiator bi-planes and small Caproni bombers, the Army Air Force faired no better. Only the airfields at Kjeller-Oslo and Værnes-Trondheim were properly staffed and equipped. Sola-Stavanger, Fornebu-Oslo and Kjevik-Kristiansand were civilian airfields where the air force at best was seen as a guest.

Contrary to Quisling's claims, an alliance between Norway and Britain was never even close to reality, in spite of the British chartering of the Norwegian merchant fleet and the signing of a war trade agreement in March.[45] The concept of war was repulsive to Norwegian Prime Minister Johan Nygaardsvold and for him it was an absolute that Norway should be neutral. International issues had for years been handled by Foreign Minister Halvdan Koht, who had masterminded Norwegian foreign policy since the coming to power of the Labour Party in 1935. Now he took it upon himself to steer Norway outside the war.

Koht was a complex individual. He had been professor of history at the University of Oslo and was very highly educated. He firmly believed that the rights and duties of neutral states were laid down in established principles and precedents of international law and saw no need for alternatives. A pacifist by his own definition, Koht considered the best defence for a nation to be 'informed and sober politics' rather than armed force and he believed neutrality, once declared, could be maintained without substantial armed forces. He realised a defensive war might become necessary, should all attempts at solving conflicts through diplomacy fail, and said '. . . we shall defend our neutrality, but if at all possible, not become entangled in a war.' Only if political means failed should the armed forces be alerted and prepared to fight. This relied on a 'prescient Foreign Office' being able to decide if the international situation demanded that it would be necessary to mobilise the defences. The problem was that neither Koht nor

In early February, the French ambassador to London, Charles Corbin, asked Foreign Secretary Halifax for 'the whole question of [the] policy in Scandinavia and Finland' to be discussed in the next meeting of the Supreme War Council. The meeting was convened in Paris on 5 February. Three days earlier, the British War Cabinet had decided, against cautioning from the Foreign Office, that it 'ought to do something, even if it were only to divert from ourselves the odium of having allowed Finland to be crushed'. Thus, Chamberlain, after having dismissed a French proposal to land troops at Petsamo in northern Finland, advocated the larger project. He did however, urge the Council not to lose sight of the principal aim, the defeat of Germany, in their determination to save Finland. The ideal operation would, according to Chamberlain, be one which, proceeding from Norwegian ports, combined assistance to Finland with control of the Lapland ore fields. Daladier was happy to comply and on this day, almost two weeks before the *Altmark* incident, the council agreed to set up an Anglo-French expeditionary force – to be ready by 20 March – ostensibly to help Finland but first and foremost to secure the Swedish iron ore, gain strategic control over the Norwegian coast and, with any luck, to divert substantial German forces from the Western Front. To overcome their unwillingness it was decided to exert 'vigorous moral pressure' on Norway and Sweden, while Finland would be asked to issue an official appeal for help to add moral pressure. According to Churchill, the issue of what to do if Norway and Sweden refused, as seemed probable, was never brought up. The risk of becoming entangled in a war with Russia appears also to have been pushed under the carpet; possibly few of the British delegation really expected that the soldiers would go beyond the Swedish ore fields. The Germans would respond, but this would take time and meanwhile any attack in the west would be postponed – it was assumed.[77]

General Ironside noted enthusiastically in his diary:

> If we bring this off, we shall have carried out a great *coup*, which will upset . . . German preparations. One is almost frightened at the boldness of the plan, knowing what slender means one has at the moment to carry it out. We must see we are politically strong, and remain quite cynical about anything except stopping the iron-ore.[78]

The plan was indeed bold. In spite of the setback in late January, military preparations had continued steadily and plans were now nearing completion. Operation Avonmouth would seize the Lapland fields, Operation Stratford would secure control of western Norway and Operation Plymouth would secure a defence of southern Sweden. Four to five divisions, including five French and one or two Polish battalions would be deployed in Narvik–Lapland–Luleå, while five additional battalions would occupy Trondheim and Bergen (from where railway lines necessary for transport of heavy material connected eastward) and would be prepared to protect these ports against German attacks.[79] A front line was envisaged from Bergen via Oslo to Stockholm, south of which German air attacks would be fierce. Stavanger would be occupied temporarily and in the event that superior German forces attempted to take control of the airfield and the city's port, both should be demolished before a withdrawal towards Bergen.

In all, a hundred thousand British and fifty thousand French/Polish troops with naval and air support would be deployed under overall British command. Two or three

— 3 —

Storm Warning

A Hundred Incidents

IN 1941, THE US minister to Norway, Florence Harriman, wrote: 'Hindsight is all we seem to have. But it is fantastic that none of the things which happened in the week preceding the fatal daybreak of April 9th awakened us to danger. A hundred incidents should have prepared us. Instead we were transfixed, still watching the war in Finland.'[1]

Indeed, the almost uniform inability to see and understand the warning signals, which were abundantly available in spite of tight security, is one of the great enigmas of Weserübung. Not only were the signals overlooked in Oslo, but equally so in London, Paris and Copenhagen. Swedish authorities in Stockholm realised what was going on, but did nothing.

In the early pre-electronic part of the war, identification of relevant information in the flow of often contradictory signals arriving was demanding. All the more so, as even the 'right' signals were rarely unambiguous and could, more often than not, justify several rational interpretations. Thus, the psychological concept of cognitive priming must be accounted for, where the appreciation of new information is influenced by the receiver's expectations and beliefs. Something that confirms an existing point of view is far more readily accepted than something pointing in an unfamiliar direction. This was certainly true for Norway in 1940.

Intelligence consists of four elements: acquisition, analysis, interpretation and distribution. If one is missing or weak, the others become meaningless. The Norwegian government of 1940 did not have any individuals or groups with access to all available intelligence material and tasked with assessing the threats to neutrality. The ministers would have to do this themselves, in addition to their many other tasks, without professional military analysis or management systems. Foreign Minister Koht in particular worked alone. He had a personal confidence that gave him strength, but also made him inaccessible to other people's advice and arguments. Koht believed himself to be the best man to interpret and understand the incoming information and decide how to act upon it – or not – in most cases without seeking a second opinion. He had no group of analysts established to try to help him see the larger picture and he never took any initiatives to have incoming signals systematically verified.

As with most tasks in the Norwegian military, intelligence was handled separately by the services. The Admiral Staff had an Intelligence Office led by Kaptein Erik Anker Steen and the General Staff a similar unit: Section IV (the 'Foreign Office') led by Oberstløytnant Harald Wrede-Holm.[2] Both offices were understaffed, but worked well together and shared most of the information they received. Communication between the military and the government was never made interactive – not even after September 1939 – and no systematic assessment of the incoming information in a political context existed.

with anybody. Sensing he had missed something important when he returned to Oslo, Pruck took the Lufthansa morning flight to Berlin on the 4th – on his own initiative. Canaris was at first upset that he had come and concerned that Pruck might not get back in time, but mellowed when he realised that the Abwehr, through Pruck, could pass on vital information. Hence, Pruck was informed of the imminent invasion and ordered to brief key officers before heading back to Oslo as fast as he could.

First, Pruck met with Oberst Erich Buschenhagen and Oberstleutnant Hartwig Pohlman of von Falkenhorst's staff. The two men were mainly interested in whether the Norwegians would fight or not, Pruck answered that in his opinion, based on extensive discussions with officers and politicians, they would. Their tactics would be to establish a defence with smaller units, utilising the terrain, pending mobilisation of the main forces and Allied help. A perturbed Pohlman claimed this contradicted other sources, but Pruck was firm; the Norwegians would defend their neutrality – also against the Allies, but with far less vigour and stamina. In particular there was, in Pruck's opinion, reason to fear the torpedoes and guns of the coastal forts. Though old, they had a considerable sting, and he was certain they would be used. The conversation ended with Pohlman informing Pruck he would come to Oslo in the afternoon of the 8th, ahead of the invasion forces. Pruck promised him all possible help and wished both men good luck. He than hastened to meet General Dietl, who was to lead the troops landing at Narvik. Having been to that city only a few days earlier, Pruck was a unique source of information for the general, adding details to the map of Narvik and its defences. In particular, the information that he had seen the two panserships *Norge* and *Eidsvold* at anchor in the harbour was important. Pruck had not met Oberst Sundlo, the Norwegian commander of the garrison in Narvik, but he could confirm that he was definitely pro-German and that Berthold Benecke, the other Abwehr agent in Oslo, held him in high esteem. Whether Sundlo would open fire on a German invasion force, Pruck could not tell.

Having completed his round of briefings, Pruck headed for Tempelhof airport to take the Lufthansa flight back to Oslo, while it was still possible.[5]

In the early afternoon of Friday 5 April 1940, Rittmeister Friedrich 'Rudi' Eickhorn of the 69th Infantry Division reported to his regiment in Stettin on the German Baltic coast. The captain was a reserve officer and acting commander of the Radfahrschwadron of the Aufklärungs Abteilung 169.[6] Arriving at the regiment, Eickhorn had to take an oath of secrecy before being given a short outline of Operation Weserübung and informed that he and his squadron would be landed less than four days later in Egersund on the south-western coast of Norway. They would come as friends, to assist the Norwegians against Allied aggression, but should nevertheless take control of the town and secure the landfall of the telegraph cable to Peterhead in Scotland. A briefcase, containing orders, a few maps and some intelligence information, was handed over with orders not to let it out of sight until the mission was accomplished. The astounded Eickhorn left the regiment with mixed feelings. He was pleased that something was happening, but not so sure the Norwegians would be overly enthusiastic about receiving assistance not asked for. Eickhorn went back to his barracks and, locking the door to his office, started studying the maps. His unit would be a tiny part of the invasion, but the success here was as important as the rest of the operation.[7]

going into the Atlantic the cruiser should lead Group V to Oslo. Raeder wanted *Lützow* in the Atlantic and did not like this at all. Hence, when the cruiser *Blücher* was released from the yard in late March he assigned her to Group V instead, making *Lützow's* sortie independent of the Norwegian operation. Hitler intervened again, and on a request from OKW, decided *Lützow* should accompany Group II to Trondheim. There, she should land some four hundred Gebirgsjägers at Stjørdal before slipping into the Atlantic in the expected confusion, covered by the battleships *Scharnhorst* and *Gneisenau.*

Thiele took *Lützow* from Cuxhaven to Wilhelmshaven on 5 April to embark the Jägers and their equipment. The Fleet Commander Vizeadmiral Lütjens was not enthusiastic. *Lützow's* cruising speed was twenty-one knots and her emergency speed would barely exceed twenty-four knots. If challenged by British forces, Lütjens would have to decide between leaving her behind or standing by, Kapitän Thiele was not much happier. Bringing the Weserübung troops to Trondheim would be a diversion and he was worried about having to join a large force of ships on a daylight passage of the Bergen–Shetland Narrows. In his opinion, it was bound to attract British attention and could easily compromise his breakout to the Atlantic. Should they manage to evade the Home Fleet, Thiele was still worried *Lützow* might not be able to keep up with the rest of the group entering the fjord and would receive the full attention of the alerted Norwegian coastal forts. Neither officer had any option, however, other than comply with orders.

At 15:00 on the 6th, only a few hours before departure, Group West was informed that cracks had been discovered in the base of *Lützow's* auxiliary motor no. 1. The cracks could be temporarily welded but she would be unable to exceed twenty-three knots. An Atlantic breakout was out of the question without dockyard repairs, as was a passage through the Bergen–Shetland Narrows, and at 17:00 on 6 April, Raeder reassigned *Lützow* to Group V, where she would be less exposed. To catch up with the new assignment, Thiele had to depart immediately and in the small hours of the 7th, after a hurried embarkation of four hundred Gebirgsjägers of II/GjR 138 and some fifty Luftwaffe men, *Lützow* cast off, heading for Kiel through the Kaiser Wilhelm Canal. There was no room for the troops onboard the other ships, and to compensate for the loss of the men now going to Oslo,it was decided that all four destroyers of Group II should go to Trondheim rather than two of them diverting to Andalsnes as originally planned. It was a small change, but one that would become significant a week later when British soldiers landed just there.[37]

Scharnhorst and *Gneisenau* weighed anchor from Wilhelmshaven at 00:45 on 7 April.[38] After clearing the river mouth, course was set for Lightship F. The battleships would act as cover for Groups I and II and carried no troops. Following the conference in the Reichskanzlei on 1 April, where all the group commanders had met, there had been discussion over how best to deploy the battleships. Arguments were put forward that it might be better to send the destroyers alone to Narvik and keep the battleships south of the Bergen–Shetland Narrows in order not to draw the attention of the British fleet to Weserübung too early. Others suggested letting the heavy units move out with Group III for Bergen and remain in the North Sea so that the Home Fleet, when alerted, would concentrate on them and leave the invasion groups alone. The SKL eventually decided *Scharnhorst* and *Gneisenau* would be best employed in support of the groups for Narvik and Trondheim. Loaded with troops and stores, the destroyers would need protection

Kaaveland a map with the co-ordinates. The officer added that two destroyers would stay with the minefield to warn approaching ships for forty-eight hours, and requested *Syrian* to assist. Several merchant vessels had already been stopped and the traffic along the coast was for all practical purposes severed. While the officer from *Hunter* was still onboard *Syrian*, one of the other destroyers moved to the north side of the alleged field while the rest headed south-westwards, out of sight in the mist.

Kaaveland reported the details of the incident in an updated radio signal to SDD3 at 05:30 and gave the co-ordinates he had received from the British officer, adding that the eastern side of Vestfjorden was closed to traffic. To pass the minefield, ships would have to leave undisputed Norwegian territory for several tens of nautical miles. From Tromsø, the signal was forwarded to Kommandørkaptein Askim in Narvik and to the Admiral Staff where it was registered at 05:58.[68]

While reading the signal, the duty officer at the Admiral Staff, Kaptein Håkon Willoch, was informed that the British and French naval attachés in Oslo were in the building, requesting an urgent meeting with him. Rear Admiral Hector Boyes and his French colleague Capitaine de Frégate d'Arzur wished Willoch a good morning and handed him a copy of a comprehensive memorandum, adding that at that very moment the original was being presented to the Foreign Office by their respective ministers, Dormer and de Dampierre. The memorandum, which Boyes insisted required 'immediate attention', argued at length how the deliberate increase in German violations of Norwegian neutrality and the Norwegian inability to prevent this, forced the Allied governments to take measures believed necessary. With reference to the memorandum of 5 April, of which Willoch had no knowledge, it had been decided to deny Germany the use of stretches of Norwegian territorial waters; three minefields had been laid that morning – off Stadlandet, at Bud and in Vestfjorden. The co-ordinates of the minefields were given and it was added that British warships would patrol the fields for forty-eight hours to stop merchant ships entering the danger zones.[69]

At 05:10, Vevang coastguard station, near Hustadvika, reported two destroyers', probably British, having entered Norwegian territory, and the destroyer *Sleipner* was ordered out from Kristiansund to investigate. The two destroyers were indeed British. After departing with *Renown* in the morning of the 6th, *Hyperion* and *Hero* proceeded to Sullom Voe for refuelling. They left again at 05:15 on the 7th with orders to head for Bud on the Norwegian west coast and pretend to be laying a minefield. By 03:15 on the 8th, Ona Lighthouse was sighted and an accurate position obtained. The dummy mine-laying was commenced a little after 05:00. The two destroyers ran at slow speed side by side, heading back and forth on parallel tracks. When three fishing boats were sighted, oil-drums filled with seawater were dropped at the inshore end of the lines to give the impression they were laying mines. After about an hour thus pretending, the destroyers took positions, one at each end of the 'minefield', to warn off approaching vessels.

Around 07:20 *Sleipner* approached *Hyperion* with the signals 'Protest', 'Violation' and 'Neutral waters' hoisted. *Hyperion* returned 'Minefield ahead. Stop for instructions', followed by 'Am sending boat.' A boat was lowered and Lieutenants Egan and Treseder came across, in spite of the adverse weather conditions. According to Egan, Kaptein Ulfing received them 'most courteously . . . and in perfect English' . . . a charming man, who had

Group III heading for Bergen. *Köln* seen from *Königsberg* with *Wolf* screening to port. The photo must have been taken after 17:00 on 8 April, when the fog lifted and the groups joined up. The swastika flag on the foredeck is for aircraft recognition purposes. (Sperbund/Sedal collection)

in the heavy sea and Kapitänleutnant Birnbacher ordered *S22* to escort her to sheltered waters near Selbjørnsfjorden. Admiral Schmundt detached *Wolf* to follow and they both stayed with *S19* until it was sure she could make it alone, before hastening to rejoin the group.[100]

By midnight, action stations were called onboard the ships and course set for Korsfjorden and the Bergen Leads. *Leopard* was in the lead, followed by *Köln*, *Königsberg*, *Bremse*, *Carl Peters* and the two remaining S-boats. Approaching the mouth of Korsfjorden, the main lighthouses were suddenly doused one by one. Tension rose. Did the Norwegians know they were coming?[101]

Meanwhile, the minesweepers of Group VI were alone again after having departed with the boats for the Danish ports at nightfall. It had been a peaceful transit and no incidents occurred. Rittmeister Eickhorn had spent the day discussing with his staff what to do in the crucial first hours after landing in Egersund. The ships would leave as soon as possible and he and his soldiers would be on their own, waiting for reinforcements. According to the information they had, there would be no Norwegian troops in the town, but they might be transferred from Stavanger or Kristiansand within hours and the torpedo boats usually in the harbour could become a challenge.

Towards the afternoon, the barometer fell sharply, clouds gathered and the wind picked up. The holiday mood among the soldiers gave way to seasickness and fear. After a while, rainsqualls and fog reduced visibility to fifty metres. At first Korvettenkapitän Thoma was relieved because it reduced the risk of being detected, but when darkness fell

The German minister to Norway, Dr Curt Bräuer. (Author's collection)

make any prearrangement before 04:00 so as not to raise any suspicion, and he was not to reveal the nature of the meeting when insisting upon being received. If Koht was not to be found, the memorandum should be presented to Prime Minister Nygaardsvold or the deputy foreign minister.

From midnight, Bräuer would be the 'authorised representative of the Reich',[141] the highest civilian German authority in Norway and the only political contact between Berlin and the Norwegian government. His objectives were clear: making Nygaardsvold and his government co-operate and ensuring King Haakon remained in Oslo under German protection. Troops would be made available if necessary. If things did not work out according to plan, Bräuer would have to improvise. Norwegian reactions should be reported to Berlin as soon as possible, using the radio at the embassy or public telephone via Sweden, using brief codes. These codes reveal which answers Berlin expected: four referred to situations where the Norwegian government accepted the terms, held back the orders to fire, negotiated or offered symbolic protests; only one referred to resistance being offered. The Norwegian government was not expected to stand against the mighty Wehrmacht.

Bräuer later said he was stunned by the news but, after talking to Pohlman, the two men agreed the Norwegian government was likely to comply with the German demands and to allow the German forces to land – provided the ultimatum was delivered with a powerful fleet of warships in Oslo harbour, before any widespread fighting had commenced.[142]

* * *

After the telephone conversation with Pohlman, Air Attaché Spiller turned his attention to the preparations of a private dinner party he was arranging. The invitees were senior Norwegian officers and their spouses. Spiller was one of the few at the embassy informed of Operation Weserübung and he probably planned the supper as a way of distracting key persons at a critical moment. Most of them were already alerted by the events, however, and Mrs Ursula Spiller received several regrets during the day. In the end only two junior Norwegian officers showed up, together with some embassy officials and two Lufthansa representatives. It was a pleasant evening, in spite of the circumstances, and the Norwegians left around midnight. Spiller left his house around 03:00 with the two Lufthansa representatives. He wore uniform but carried a civilian overcoat. The two cars halted near Fornebu outside the house of Alfred Kleinman, a German businessman living in Oslo with his Norwegian wife. The entourage was let into the house and shown to the living room, from where there was a good view towards the airfield. It would be a longer wait than expected.[143]

Naval Attaché Schreiber had been in Berlin a couple of times during the winter, presenting his views on Norway in general and naval matters in particular to Admiral Raeder and the SKL. On one occasion in February, just after the *Altmark* episode, the Grossadmiral had told him that preparations for a German attack on Norway would be initiated unless the country showed a significant improvement in the handling of Allied violations of the neutrality. On his last visit to Berlin in March, Schreiber repeated what he had said before: the Norwegians would not oppose a German occupation when it was made clear they came as friends. On 5 April, Schreiber was informed through a coded telegram from Berlin that Wesertag would be 9 April and that he, at 05:00 that morning, should be ready to receive Generalmajor Engelbrecht in Oslo harbour.

Schreiber was nervous on the 8th. With increasing frequency he kept calling the Norwegian Admiral Staff asking if there was any new information on German merchantmen being torpedoed off the coast. He was politely informed there was not, but his behaviour reinforced the feeling in the Admiral Staff that something was going on. In the afternoon, Schreiber was confronted with the reports of German warships moving north and asked what this signified. He answered carefully that he did not know, but assumed they had taken to sea as part of a strengthened German defence of the Belts, where a British operation was anticipated.[144] Later in the afternoon, Schreiber reported a certain 'anxiety' in the Norwegian Admiral Staff and Ministry of Defence in a telegram to Berlin, but ascribed it to the British mine-laying:

Have received the following information privately from the admiral staff. First, German fleet has been observed passing northwards through the Danish Belts during the night of the 8th. Secondly, minefields have, according to the British naval attaché, been laid at 05:00 on the 8th at specified locations. Further mine barrages are at the moment being laid at Halten, the northern entry to Trondheim. Thirdly, expect the coastal fortresses to be at increased preparedness.[145]

In the evening, the Abwehr agent Oberleutnant Hermann Kempf boarded the German freighter *Widar* at anchor in Oslo harbour some 1,500 metres west of Akershus. Kempf had no knowledge of Weserübung when he arrived from Berlin a few days earlier, but

Schreiber had briefed him in the morning and ordered him onboard *Widar* to supervise her radio transmissions until Group V arrived.[146] *Widar* had arrived in Oslo on 7 April; she was a regular merchantman loaded with coal but – as were many German freighters – equipped with a high-powered radio and a locked cabinet with codebooks and special orders. The captain knew nothing of Weserübung, but had been instructed to observe closely all traffic on sea and in the air and report to the Abwehrstelle in Hamburg.[147]

Vidkun Quisling must have guessed from his contacts with de Laporte and Piekenbrock that something was about to happen even if he had no concrete knowledge of what or when. A regular meeting of the 'NS council' was held in Oslo on 7 April with some twenty-five members present. The meeting had been postponed several times because of Quisling's illness and the final date had only been set a week earlier. In his review of the situation, Quisling did not indicate anything untoward, except the usual warnings of dangerous times.[148] After the meeting all council members returned home, including those who would be named as 'ministers' a few days later. Had Quisling known or suspected that a German invasion of Norway was already unfolding he would certainly have kept his closest associates in Oslo.

The mine-laying upset Quisling. In his opinion, the action put Norway at war with Britain and was only a prelude to widespread landings. Shortly after 18:00 on 8 April, NS members started issuing leaflets in Oslo condemning the mine-laying and the government, which in Quisling's opinion had provoked the situation. The text of the leaflet concluded that NS was the only party that could save Norway's 'freedom and independence' and it was Quisling's 'duty and right' to take over the government. As usual, hardly anyone paid attention to his pompous language.

Late in the evening NS propaganda manager Haldis Neegaard-Østbye and secretary Harald Knudsen persuaded Quisling to leave his home and check in at the Hotel Continental in central Oslo, as they feared for his safety. The mine-laying could indicate the British were on their way and if the Germans came first, as the sinking of *Rio de Janeiro* might indicate, 'Those who felt guilty [for the inability to protect Norway's neutrality], might wish to eliminate him,' Knudsen later wrote. Quisling alleged at his trial in 1945 that, 'upon hearing the news of the German transport sunk with horses and vehicles onboard', he believed the Germans were on their way to Norway as well, and that he had to go into hiding 'to avoid being detained'. It was probably no coincidence that Albert Hagelin, who had moved to Oslo during the winter, also stayed at the hotel – even if Knudsen later held he chose the Continental as it was the only hotel in Oslo with anything like a bombproof cellar. Knudsen booked a single room in his own name and smuggled Quisling in through the back stairs. The two men settled in for the night; Quisling in the bed, Knudsen on the couch.[149]

Intruders

Weather remained good in the Kattegat on 8 April with only a light breeze and a cloudless sky. As dawn broke, *Blücher* and her consorts steamed north at eighteen knots between the Danish islands Fyn and Sjelland. The Halskov Rev lightship was passed at 08:00 and entering open waters, the torpedo boats fanned out, flanking the cruisers, which took up a zigzag pattern. Overhead, aircraft arrived for escort. As long as they were inside the Belts, the Landsers were confined below deck in hiding from any observers, but later, after passing the Schultz-Grund lightship around 11:40, they were allowed up if they could find some navy clothing to cover their army uniforms. Onboard *Blücher*, off-duty crews were gathered on the afterdeck and informed by Kapitän Woldag of their mission. There was widespread excitement about going into action, but some puzzlement over Norway. Nothing much happened during the day, apart from a few false submarine alarms and, just after 13:00, a fishing buoy was riddled by machine-gun fire from *Blücher*, mistaking it for a periscope. A signal from the German merchantman *Kreta*, around 14:00, that she had been fired at by an enemy submarine near the western entry to the Oslofjord raised tension, as did a Danish Radio news broadcast from Kalundborg reporting heavy German naval units in the Great Belt, heading north. Towards evening, the ships were north of Hirsholmene, near the Skagen lightship, and the deep swell from the open Skagerrak could be felt. Darkness was not far away, but the sky remained clear. Suddenly, *Albatros* on the starboard side of the cruisers hoisted a signal and flashed a warning. Submarine contact! This time it was real. Torpedo tracks were sighted, apparently aiming for *Lützow*, but she was already in a starboard gear as part of a routine zigzag manoeuvre and they all passed harmlessly ahead. *Albatros* stayed with the contact, dropping depth charges while the group resumed a north-north-easterly course into the Skagerrak.

The British submarine *Triton* was on patrol off Skagen when at 16:50 Lieutenant Commander Edward Fowle-Pizey discovered that several heavy ships were overtaking him. He identified the first ship as *Gneisenau*-class (actually *Blücher*), the second as

Blücher in Kattegat on 8 April, seen from *Emden*. (Bundesarchiv Koblenz)

Nürnberg or *Leipzig* (actually *Lützow*) and the third correctly as *Emden*. The flotilla was travelling fast and he had little time to position his submarine. Rather than miss the chance, Fowle-Pizey aimed all his ten torpedoes at *Lützow*, the second ship in the line. Just as he was about to fire though, *Blücher* zigzagged, coming into a more favourable position. Fowle-Pizey decided she was the more important target and risked an 85-degree angle shot of ten torpedoes from seven thousand metres. *Blücher* was travelling faster than he had estimated and all torpedoes missed astern, coming close to *Lützow*. *Albatros* came down the tracks but never found *Triton* and eventually disappeared. Fowle-Pizey put his mast aerial up, sending a brief sighting signal at 18:25 before an aircraft appeared and made him go deep, the signal not being received in Britain. At 19:45 he was able to surface and sent: '1 German battleship *Gneisenau*-class with one heavy cruiser escorted by *Emden* and destroyers having passed Skaw westward 18:00. Speed 20 knots.'

At 20:31, *Sunfish* reported observing '1 *Blücher*-class, 2 cruisers, 1 destroyer', twenty miles north of Skagen at 18:12, steering north and zigzagging away before coming close enough to attack. Admiral Horton was delighted and ordered *Trident* and *Orzel* to proceed with utmost despatch to a position off Larvik, where he believed the flotilla was heading. In addition, *Seal*, *Clyde* and *Truant* were ordered to the western Skagerrak in case the German ships were heading for the North Sea.[150]

Leaving *Triton* behind, blackout was ordered from the flagship, and the battle ensigns were taken down as dusk approached. There was a light, south-westerly breeze and hardly any sea at all. It was a cold and at first a fairly clear night, with a misty haze developing later. Distance between the larger ships was reduced to some 600 metres. Nearing the mouth of the Oslofjord, rainsqualls and patches of fog reduced visibility further. *Blücher* remained in the lead with the others in line-astern, maintaining contact through screened lanterns aft. All soldiers were below deck.

At 23:00 GeT, Norwegian-speaking Sonderführer Willi Behrens listened in to the Norwegian Radio evening news. He heard about the discussions in the Parliament over the British mine-laying, the sightings of German ships heading north through the Belts and the sinking of *Rio de Janeiro*. Towards the end of the bulletin, he also heard the order from the Norwegian Admiral Staff to the naval districts, ordering all lighthouses and radio beacons south of Bergen to be doused. Behrens forwarded the information to his officers and was eventually called to the bridge to inform Konteradmiral Kummetz in person.[151] The same newscast was heard by *Lützow*'s radio operators and Kapitän Thiele took it as a sure sign that the Norwegians knew they were coming; all hope of surprise being lost. He sent a signal to the flagship, suggesting maximum speed to surprise the defenders at Drøbak before they were fully organised. Kummetz, annoyed at the uninvited suggestion contradicting his orders, answered that they would pass the Narrows as planned. The rear admiral was of the opinion that even if the Norwegians knew they were coming, they would not open fire in earnest. A signal was sent to all ships on the USW radio: 'Mission is peaceful occupation of Norway. Searchlights or warning-shots do not justify use of own weapons. Only fire back if fired upon.'[152] Group V continued as planned.

Shortly after, the lighthouses at Færder and Torbjørnskjær were sighted. They were still burning as normal, but within minutes were doused. Passing between Færder and Torbjørnskjær in total darkness, the German ships were in Norwegian territory and inside Oslo Krigshavn, which meant they were unquestionably trespassing. It was midnight German time and 23:00 Norwegian time; action stations was ordered onboard all ships.[153]

The Norwegian auxiliary *Pol III* was patrolling the outer reaches of the Oslofjord, between the lighthouses at Færder and Torbjørnskjær.[154] The 214-ton vessel had been built in 1926. With low freeboard, tall funnel, central wheelhouse and the nest for the lookout in the top of the foremast, *Pol III* looked like the whaleboat she was. Nothing much had been done to her after the commissioning eight months earlier, other than mounting a searchlight and a 76-mm gun on the foredeck. The fifteen men onboard were largely conscripts, many of them whalers. They had expected to spend the winter in the South Atlantic, but instead had been drafted for the Neutrality Watch together with their ship.[155] Kaptein Leif Welding-Olsen, a reserve officer from Horten, had received orders for increased readiness from SDS1 in Horten, but no explanation as to why they had been issued. At 22:00 the order for all lighthouses to be shut down was overheard. The night was dark with swirling fog and rain and Welding-Olsen ordered a sharp lookout. Around 23:00, two darkened ships were sighted briefly, 300–400 metres away, steering north. Welding-Olsen was called to the bridge and ordered full ahead on a following course while manning the 76-mm gun and the searchlight.

At 23:06 heavy engines were heard ahead and the searchlight turned on. To the amazement of captain and crew, several large warships emerged in the mist. One immediately veered towards *Pol III*, turning on a counter-light while the other ships

The 214-ton auxiliary *Pol III* was patrolling the outer reaches of the Oslofjord in the evening of 8 April. (Marinemuseet)

continued northwards. The approaching ship, the torpedo boat *Albatros*, eventually turned off her lights and signalled 'Stop engines. Do not use radio.' *Albatros*'s radio operator had been warned to watch the 600m band, and reported that the Norwegian was transmitting, but that he was effectively jamming the signal. Even so, the radio signal 'Alien ships incoming at high speed,' was received at Horten from *Pol III*.[156] Approaching the auxiliary somewhat apprehensively, Kapitänleutnant Siegfried Strelow ordered a prize crew to prepare for transfer. To his surprise, the defiant Norwegian fired a warning shot and in the ensuing melee slammed into the forward port side of the torpedo boat. A hole was opened in the side of *Albatros* but damage-control crews made sure there was no serious leakage. Two sailors jumped or were thrown onto the deck of *Albatros* and promptly detained. Onboard *Pol III* shouts were heard from the opponent in unmistakable German. Welding-Olsen ordered one white and two red flares fired to warn the other auxiliaries further up the fjord as well as the shore batteries. It was 23:10.

Strelow hailed the auxiliary, repeating the order to stop and cease all signalling. Captain Welding-Olsen answered back in German, refusing to accept any orders and instead instructed the torpedo boat to surrender or leave Norwegian territory immediately – otherwise he would open fire. Strelow pulled *Albatros* some 200–300 metres away to assess the situation, turning the searchlights onto *Pol III*. Shortly after, in spite of the clear order from Konteradmiral Kummetz, *Albatros* opened fire. It is unclear what actually

Kaptein Leif Welding-Olsen of *Pol III*. (Marinemuseet)

happened at this point but the gun on the foredeck was manned and may have been moved, while further aft one of the radio operators climbed the mast, trying to re-erect the radio antenna, which had come loose during the collision. Perhaps Strelow believed they were preparing to open fire. Regardless, at least two 10.5-cm shells slammed into the auxiliary and machine-gun fire raked the deck and wheelhouse. Kaptein Welding-Olsen was seriously wounded in both legs. Fire was not returned from *Pol III*.

The tackle for lowering the lifeboat was destroyed by the gunfire, but a small barge was still intact. Welding-Olsen, bleeding heavily from his legs, was carried from the bridge and laid in the barge before it was lowered. He had lost a lot of blood and was very weak. Too many men crowded the barge in the choppy sea and it capsized. Most men climbed back onto *Pol III*, but Welding-Olsen did not manage to hold on for long and drifted away. 'Don't worry about me. Save yourselves,' he is said to have told the others as he vanished.

The crew of *Pol III* was taken onboard *Albatros*, who set the auxiliary on fire with high-explosive shells and tracers before turning northwards up the fjord to rejoin the fleet. It was midnight Norwegian time on 8 April 1940.[157]

Norway was at war.

The Oslofjord

The Fjord

COMMANDER-IN-CHIEF OF 1ST SEA Defence District (SDD1), Kontreadmiral Johannes Smith-Johannsen at Karljohansvern in Horten, was responsible for the defence of the Norwegian coast from the Swedish border to Egersund. There was no doubt that the Oslofjord was his priority but, with the exception of three obsolete submarines, only minesweepers, minelayers and auxiliaries with very limited fighting value were usually deployed there and the defence of the capital rested with the coastal forts. These were organised in two lines of defence: the outer, with smaller guns and minefields, and the inner, centred on the heavy guns of Oscarsborg at the head of the Drøbak Narrows. None of the minefields was in place and few of the secondary batteries were manned.

C-in-C of 1st Sea Defence District (SDD1), Kontreadmiral Johannes Smith-Johannsen. (Marinemuseet)

Kommandørkaptein Andreas Anderssen (1879–1945). (Marinemuseet)

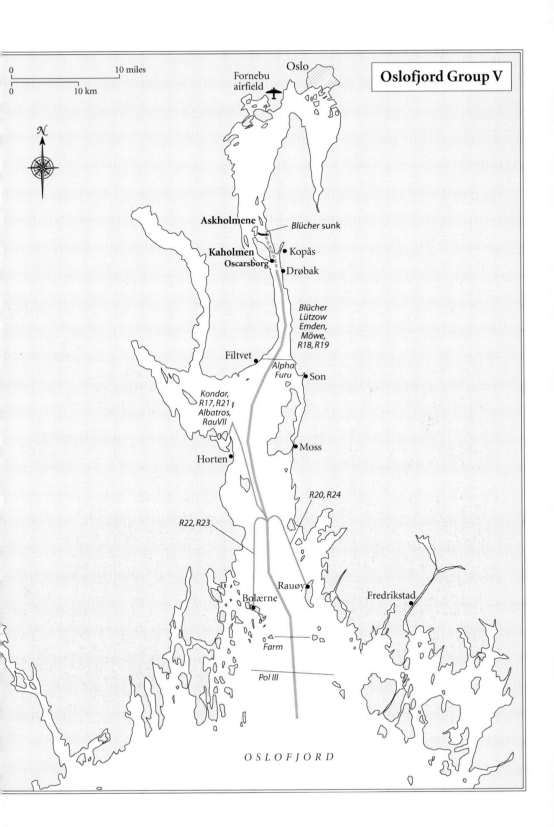

0 _____ 10 miles
0 _____ 10 km

𝒩

Oslofjord Group V

Oslo
Fornebu
airfield

Askholmene — *Blücher* sunk

Kaholmen ● Kopås
Oscarsborg ● Drøbak

Blücher
Lützow
Emden,
Möwe,
R18, R19

Filtvet ●
Alpha
Furu ● Son

Kondor,
R17, R21
Albatros,
RauVII

● Moss

Horten ●

R20, R24

R22, R23

Rauøy ●
Bolærne ●
Fredrikstad ●

Farm

Pol III

O S L O F J O R D

The key forts of the outer Oslofjord were at the islands of Bolærne (three 15-cm and four 12-cm guns and two searchlights) and Rauøy (four 15-cm and two 6.5-cm guns and three searchlights). Neither fort had complete manning, but there were small army units on each island as defence against landing attempts. On the night of 8/9 April, the naval auxiliaries *Pol III*, *Farm*, *Kjæk* and *Skudd II* were on station outside the Rauøy–Bolærne line.

Håøy Fort on the western side of the fjord had two 21-cm guns for the defence of Tønsberg city and Melsomvik naval base, but these could not fire into the Oslofjord. The 30.5-cm howitzer battery at Måkerøy Fort could in theory fire into the fjord, but had no rangefinders and limited ammunition. Neither Håøy nor Måkerøy were operationally manned in April 1940.[1]

During 8 April, a series of signals with news of German ships passing through Danish waters were received at SDD1. The sinking of *Rio de Janeiro* and *Stedingen* made it clear that British submarines were on the prowl outside the territorial limit, but aerial reconnaissance over outer Oslofjord and some thirty miles southward sighted nothing untoward.

At 13:30, SDD1 received the two compiled signals from the Naval Intelligence Staff in Oslo regarding German ships moving north. In response, Kontreadmiral Smith-Johannsen ordered the 1st Minelayer Division to start taking mines onboard from the depots and to prepare to lay the barrage between Bolærne and Rauøy.[2] At 15:40, a signal from the Admiral Staff informed that a British force was heading into the Kattegat to counter the German ships and at 18:20 orders came to draft additional personnel to man the 12-cm guns at Bolærne and the secondary searchlights there and at Rauøy. Engineers and personnel necessary to lay the minefields at Oscarsborg should also be called, but it was stressed that no mines should be laid anywhere until further orders arrived from the Ministry of Defence (i.e. the government).[3] A copy of the signal from Denmark confirming German ships moving northward was received just after 19:00 and all forts and vessels were instructed to raise preparedness to the highest level. Kaptein Wendelbo of the 1st Air Wing decided to move his reconnaissance aircraft away from Horten to safety behind Oscarsborg as they would be of no use during the night. The aircraft were not equipped for instrument flying and were to be taxied on the water. At 21:30, a request for permission to shut down the lighthouses within the district was sent to the commanding admiral and shortly after approved.[4]

The signal rockets from *Pol III* were observed by *Farm*, the second auxiliary of the outer patrol line, around 23:10, followed by gunfire and use of searchlights. Kaptein Amundsen, following instructions, stayed away, but sent a radio signal to the communication centre at Outer Oslofjord Sea Defence Sector. From here, it was forwarded to SDD1 in Horten, where at the same time a telephone call from Færder coastguard station reported rockets having been seen and shots heard in the fjord. Both reports were immediately forwarded to the Admiral Staff and Oscarsborg.

On sighting *Pol III*'s rockets, the alarm was sounded at Rauøy and guns reported ready at 23:28. The two 110-cm searchlights proved useless in the mist and only the 150-cm was eventually used. Minutes later, the contours of two ships were sighted coming up the fjord at about ten knots. The searchlight was turned in their direction, but counter-lights were shone back, preventing identification. Two warning shots were fired; one blank followed by a live round, aimed ahead of the lead ship. The vessels did not stop and another four rounds were fired for effect from Rauøy's southern 15-cm battery at a distance of some 4,500 metres. No return fire was observed and at 23:43 the ships vanished in the thickening fog. At Bolærne, three unidentified ships were outlined in the searchlight beam. The fort commander, Major Færden, gave orders to shoot, but wavering and inexperience at the battery resulted in only one blank round being fired before the fog set in, covering Bolærne until long after dawn.

Both forts reported to Horten, and at 23:50 SDD1 reported to the Admiral Staff: 'Rauøy and Bolærne in battle'. Within half an hour, a signal came back with orders to start laying the mine-barrage between the islands. At this time, though, the minelayers had not yet taken onboard a full complement of mines and those onboard were not armed, so nothing could be done.[5]

Leaving *Albatros* to deal with *Pol III*, the remaining vessels of Gruppe Oldenburg continued northwards through the darkened Oslofjord. At midnight German time, the first officer of *Blücher*, Fregattenkapitän Erich Heymann, climbed the ladder to the bridge to inform his captain that the ship was ready for battle. All men were at action stations and the Landsers were below deck. Doors and hatches were clamped shut and all communication systems had been tested and found in order. Kapitän zur See Heinrich Woldag acknowledged the report and ordered his first officer to remain on the bridge, contrary to standing orders, giving him a grandstand view of the events.[6]

Approaching the Rauøy–Bolærne line, Kummetz ordered *Blücher* and *Lützow* to train their guns on Rauøy to starboard while *Emden*, *Möwe* and *Kondor* covered Bolærne to port. The distance between the forts at Rauøy and Bolærne is some seven thousand metres and the misty gloom in the fjord largely concealed the ships and forts from each other. Around 23:25, searchlights from the forts illuminated *Blücher* and shortly after she was challenged by a signal lamp from the auxiliary *Kjæk*, patrolling just outside the forts. *Blücher* shone her own searchlights back, but otherwise continued up the fjord at eighteen knots, ignoring *Kjæk*. The sound of gunfire was heard from the direction of Rauøy, but no splashes were seen and Kummetz concluded the shots were only a warning.

From *Lützow*, the fire from Rauøy and the splash of several shots were clearly observed. Kapitän Thiele and his officers took this to mean that, as expected, the Norwegian defences were alarmed and had received orders to shoot, even if the feebleness of the fire puzzled them somewhat. No communication took place between the ships on the issue. At 23:50 the fog thickened rapidly and visibility was reduced to less than 800 metres. Gruppe Oldenburg continued up the fjord.

Meanwhile, Kapitänleutnant Forstmann and the eight boats of 1st R-boat flotilla joined Gruppe Oldenburg, having left Kiel the previous afternoon, and proceeded independently across the Kattegat. The R-boats were 120-ton fast vessels for inshore minesweeping and escort duties. In addition to the minesweeping equipment, they were armed with two 20-mm machine cannons and depth charges. The auxiliaries *Rau VII* and *Rau VIII* had accompanied the R-boats across the open sea, but were left behind at Færder.

Off Horten Konteradmiral Kummetz ordered the flotilla to halt. It was time to regroup. Six of the R-boats drew alongside *Emden* to embark troops for the capture of Rauøy,

Emden was a robust and functional vessel, but basically a WWI design. Her maximum speed was a mediocre 29.5 knots; armaments were eight 5.9-inch guns in shielded single mountings – the only guns available at the time of building. (Author's collection)

Bolærne and Horten while *R18* and *R19* approached *Blücher*. *Kondor* and *Möwe* screened for submarines. Fumbling somewhat in the darkness, the transfer took time, but there was no rush yet. Some time after 01:00, *R20*, *R24*, *R22* and *R23* were ready and detached with orders to land the troops at Rauøy and Bolærne at Weser-time, when the main force was scheduled to pass the Narrows. At 02:30, *Kondor*, *R17* and *R21* were also detached for Horten while the course of the remaining ships was set towards the Narrows at eight knots. *Blücher* was in the lead with *Lützow* some 600 metres astern and *Emden* following at the same distance again. *Möwe*, *R18* and *R19* made up the rear. Over the tannoy system, the crews and soldiers were informed that the Narrows were approaching. Only a few lights could be seen, but some of the lighthouses and sea-marks could be identified though they were darkened, giving the pilot officers reasonably certain position checks most of the time.[7]

At Horten, Kontreadmiral Smith-Johannsen had no information on the nationality of the intruders even if, based on the reports from earlier in the day, he believed they were German. As they had not returned fire at Rauøy, however, it could also be that they were part of the British fleet that had (falsely) been reported in the Kattegat. To find out, Smith-Johannsen decided to send the minesweeper *Otra* into the fjord. His Chief of Staff Kaptein Gunnar Hovdenak suggested he should join and this was accepted. *Otra* left Horten harbour around 02:30. About half an hour later, a darkened ship was sighted coming north, off Jeløya. When the searchlight was turned on, a strong counter-light was shone back and the ship vanished in the haze before it could be identified. Kaptein Hovdenak gave chase.

The ship was *Albatros*. After leaving *Pol III* behind, believing her sunk, Kapitänleutnant Strelow had navigated with some difficulty up the darkened Oslofjord before *Kondor* could be contacted on the USW radio to get a bearing. Picking up the German auxiliary *Rau VII* on the way, *Albatros* steered to join the force detached for Horten when intercepted by *Otra*. Approaching a second time, Hovdenak closed to within a couple of hundred metres before turning on the searchlight again. Counter-lights were shone back once more, but not as promptly as the first time and not as blinding. 'Two destroyers and two minesweepers' were identified from *Otra* and radioed to SDD1 at 04:03. A second signal at 04:10 confirmed that the ships were German; the first positive identification of the intruders for Kontreadmiral Smith-Johannsen. The news was immediately forwarded to the commanding admiral and Oscarsborg.[8]

Following at a distance, Kaptein Hovdenak realised the German ships were heading for Horten and that he was cut off from his base. Engaging the four ships was unrealistic as *Otra* had only one 76-mm gun and two machine guns. Hence, he reported, 'Enemy off Karljohansvern' at 04:25 and turned north, heading for Filtvet to find a telephone to talk to the admiral in person.[9]

The Drøbak Narrows

In spite of being the key defence line of the capital, Oscarsborg was in no better general shape than any of the other Norwegian coastal forts. The 65-year-old commander, Oberst Birger Kristian Eriksen, had repeatedly requested funds to modernise and improve the installations since the outbreak of the war, but little had been approved. The main artillery at Oscarsborg was three 28-cm Krupp guns in open, shielded mountings at Søndre Kaholmen. Supplementing these were three 15-cm guns at Kopås on the mainland as well as two 57-mm guns at Husvik near Drøbak and three at Nesset near Hurum. On Nordre Kaholmen, behind the main guns, a torpedo battery was built into the rock with underwater launch tubes.

With less than one-third of the full draft in place, manning of Oscarsborg was well below any minimum needed to operate the 28-cm guns, which needed at least eleven men to load and fire. Shells and cartouches needed cranes and carts to be handled and specialised personnel were necessary for maintenance and ammunition storage. There were only twenty-four trained men and four officers on duty that evening and Eriksen decided to concentrate these at two of the guns while ordering another seventy non-combat personnel to report for ammunition and communication duties. Sersjants Rækken and Strøm were ordered to take command at no. 1 (east) and no. 2 (centre) guns, respectively. Battery commander Kaptein Magnus Sødem and his senior officer, Løytnant August Bonsak, settled in the command bunker. The 75-cm searchlight at the fort was already manned and to replace the searchlight on the mainland, which was under maintenance, the auxiliary *Kranfartøy 2*, moored near Drøbak, was ordered to man its light instead.

The three 28-cm Krupp guns at Oscarsborg totally dominated the approaches to Oslo.
(E Skjold collection)

On the mainland batteries at Kopås and Husvik, the majority of the men had arrived
only a week earlier, replacing the first contingent of the Neutrality Watch. To reinforce the
inexperienced crews and to man as many of the guns as possible, Kaptein Vagn Jul Enger,
the landside commander, asked for and was permitted to call the cadets of the nearby
coastal artillery school.[10] The fifty or so cadets and their officers made a valuable addition.
Some were spread out where needed, while no. 1 15-cm gun at Kopås was manned entirely
by cadets.

None of the planned minefields in the Narrows were in place and there would be no
time to even consider laying them should the order come.[11] Torpedoes were available,
though, and the torpedo battery at Nordre Kaholmen was given orders to prepare. Its
regular commander had fallen sick in March, and Oberst Eriksen had requested the
retired 60-year-old Kommandørkaptein Andreas Anderssen to return to service. This
he had done without hesitation and in spite of new equipment and routines, the quiet,
unassuming officer had quickly settled into his old job.[12] Anderssen had left Oscarsborg
earlier in the evening, but when Oberst Eriksen called him at his home near Drøbak
around 23:00, he returned to the fort as soon as possible. Assisted by Løytnant Karlsen,
NCO Bexrud and eight ratings, Anderssen brought the 50-cm Whitehead torpedoes into
the battery and started preparing them. The first three were set to run at three metres
and loaded into the shafts. In spite of having been produced some fifty years earlier and
test-fired numerous times, the torpedoes were in immaculate order and their 100-kg
trinol warheads were lethal. Once the first torpedoes were in place, the sights and firing

mechanisms were tested and reloading procedures drilled. If the intruders that had passed Rauøy and Bolærne dared to try the Narrows, they would be in for a nasty surprise.[13]

Onboard *Blücher*, Konteradmiral Kummetz had decided to enter the Narrows just before first light, around 03:30. This would be earlier than intended, but he took it for granted the Norwegians knew they were coming anyway. After the event, several of the officers both on *Blücher* and the other ships held they had been sceptical about this decision. The pre-dawn light would give the Norwegian gunners an advantage as the ships presented silhouettes on the fjord while the batteries were still in darkness. Some reports say both Kapitän Woldag and Generalmajor Engelbrecht argued against sending the heavy cruiser first, but Konteradmiral Kummetz had made up his mind. They would go through before dawn and *Blücher* would lead.

The presence of the torpedo battery and the absence of the mine barrage had been reported by the Abwehr group at the embassy, but appear to have been lost somewhere along the chain of command. Kummetz's adjutant, Oberleutnant von Freyberg, later wrote that there were intelligence reports of a remote-controlled mine barrage across the Narrows. This makes the use of *Blücher* in the van even more questionable – to say nothing of having virtually all the administrative and command personnel for Oslo onboard the lead ship.

According to the orders for Group V, the auxiliaries *Rau VII* and *Rau VIII* were to proceed ahead of the warships to verify that the waters were clear. The two ships never turned up in time and Kummetz, for some reason, did not use *Möwe* or the R-boats instead. Oberst Eriksen believed he was facing a breach of Norwegian neutrality and would most likely have opened fire on any large ship in the van of the group. Kummetz was not aware of Eriksen's deliberations, of course, but perhaps he should have realised that *Möwe* was large enough to provoke a reaction while small enough to turn away behind a smokescreen if there was one. And, should *Möwe* be lost, it would in any case be of less consequence than the flagship. Cynically, it would even have been better to risk *Emden*, which was of lesser naval value and had already disembarked a large part of her troops.[14]

Passing Filtvet, two Norwegian auxiliaries – *Alpha* and *Furu* – patrolling the head of the Narrows approached *Blücher* and her consorts. Both vessels shone their searchlights briefly, identifying the intruders as large warships. *Alpha* was near enough to hear orders shouted in German onboard the lead ship, and Kaptein Bøhmer headed for the signal station at Filtvet to report to Oscarsborg. The copy of the signal, entered by hand in the signal book of Oscarsborg at 03:40, does not contain the word 'German'. Kaptein Bøhmer later asserted that Oberst Eriksen had been informed by him that the ships were German, but disregarded it as he did not accept he could know this. Other reports hold that the signal station at Filtvet saw the ships themselves and reported on their own initiative, not bothering to resend Bøhmer's almost identical signal a few minutes later.[15] For Thiele onboard *Lützow*, the appearance of the auxiliaries was further evidence of Norwegian vigilance. He wished for the admiral to give the order for maximum speed; but no such order came.[16]

Continuing up the fjord, tension grew on *Blücher*'s crowded bridge. In spite of the emerging dawn, it was not possible to identify any details ahead, neither on the mainland

Konteradmiral Oscar
Kummetz (left)
and Kapitän zur
See August Thiele.
(Bundesarchiv
Koblenz)

nor on the islands. A powerful searchlight on the east side of the fjord barred the Drøbak Narrows proper (this was the 90-cm searchlight of *Kranfartøy 2*). Around 04:15, it raked the cruiser from bow to stern and back; dazzling everybody onboard and then shone its beam up into the fog from where it was reflected onto the ship. Absurdly, at that moment, a tiny seaplane on its floats emerged just ahead of *Blücher's* bow. It looked as if it would be run over, but turned to port and vanished into the shadows, just in time.[17]

The first warning of intruders in outer Oslofjord was received at Oscarsborg from SDD1 at 23:30 and the alert was given. The guns at Kopås and Husvik were ready shortly after midnight while Nesset reported all set a few minutes later. Meanwhile, Kontreadmiral Smith-Johannsen made a personal call to Oberst Eriksen, informing him that Rauøy and Bolærne had opened fire. Several signals followed, in part contradictory and confusing. At 01:32, a signal from Outer Oslofjord SDS reported that 'four large cruisers and submarines' had passed Bolærne.

No further instructions or orders came from higher authorities during the night and Oberst Eriksen was left entirely to his own devices. He was usually a reserved man, but that night he discussed the situation several times with his intelligence officer Kaptein Unneberg. One thing was clear: if the foreign warships attempted to pass the Drøbak Narrows they would have to be stopped with all means available, whatever their nationality. They were inside the restricted krigshavn area and had received ample warnings. There was no need for further warning shots. The commander of the warships knew what risk he was taking.

For Oberst Eriksen, the intrusion was a breach of neutrality; he had no knowledge of any invasion. Thus, he could actually bring Norway into the war if he made a mistake, whether he fired or not. In the end, he decided the largest risk was that of his own career – a fairly low price for a man of his age. A signal from Filtvet at the mouth of the Narrows confirmed that the intruders were not turning away. At 03:58, Kommandørkaptein

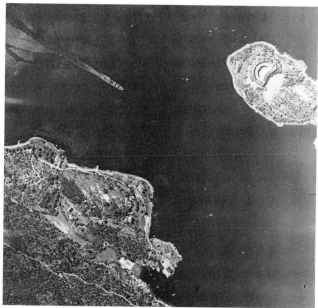

The Drøbak Narrows. Oscarsborg fort is the horseshoe shaped building on the island. The Kopås batteries are on the mainland in the lower left corner of the photo, with Drøbak town just out of view to the left. (Marinemuseet)

Anderssen in the torpedo battery asked for orders and received a clear answer: 'The torpedo battery *shall* open fire.' Oberst Eriksen had made up his mind.[18]

To have the best possible viewpoint, Eriksen climbed the grassy hill between the two manned guns. There was no cover whatsoever, but it was the best place from where to control the guns. The tall shadow of the first ship appeared in the glare of the searchlight. From Kopås two more ships could be seen and this was reported to Oscarsborg at 04:17. A minute later, *Kranfartøy 2* detailed: 'five ships, one large in front, four following'. Eriksen gave orders for the sights to be set at 1,400 metres. Actually, the distance to the point where the ship would be when he intended to open fire was only some 950 metres, but by increasing the distance, the point of impact would be above the waterline and the damage would be large, but not lethal. Oberst Eriksen was defending Norway's neutrality and gave the intruders a fair chance of pulling back before reaching the torpedo batteries.

Sersjant Rækken at no. 1 gun reported problems observing the target through his binoculars and Løytnant Bonsak instructed him over telephone to set the given range and aim the gun along the barrel. When everything was reported ready, Oberst Eriksen cast an eye at his watch and gave the order to shoot. It was 04:21.[19]

Death of a Cruiser

The first 28-cm high-explosive shell passed close over *Blücher*'s bridge, impacting with devastating effect in the lower part of the command tower, sending large parts of it overboard. The main flak fire-control platform was totally destroyed and most of the personnel there, including the second gunnery officer, Kapitänleutnant Pochhammer, were killed. Inside the foretop there were few casualties, but it filled with acrid smoke and had to be evacuated, including the main fire-control centre. On the crowded bridge, everybody was pounded by the pressure of the passing shell and the shock of the blast. Splinters rained, but nobody was seriously hurt.[20]

Seconds later, the second shell slammed into the port side just aft of the funnel, destroying the port III 10.5-cm mounting and killing a large number of army soldiers gathered on the 'tweendeck below. The aircraft hangar was wrecked, bursting into flames. Both aircraft ignited, including the one on the catapult, partly fuelled. Most of the personnel waiting in the hangar to help fly off the Arados were killed or severely wounded.[21]

Below deck, the violent crash of the first hit was taken to be the cruiser's own guns opening fire; the second hit made the reality clear. The lights went out in the boiler and engine rooms and asbestos-filled smoke made conditions almost unbearable. When the emergency lighting came on the fans could be seen to draw smoke from the fires above instead of fresh air and at times flames were coming out of the ducts.

Kapitän Woldag rang for full power, hoping to pass through the Narrows before a second salvo could be fired. In spite of advice from the chief engineer, Fregattenkapitän Thannemann, however, Woldag had decided not to run with all boilers lit. Emergency procedures were initiated, but these took time and the speed of the cruiser increased agonisingly slowly.[22]

The gunnery officer, Korvettenkapitän Engelmann, received permission to shoot but no targets could be identified even though Kaholmen was less than one thousand metres to port. The target indicator sights fell out from the hit in the foretop, and the glare from the searchlight effectively blinded the main rangefinders. The secondary directors were not of much use either and there was no co-ordinated use of the cruiser's own searchlights to try to find any targets. Third Gunnery Officer Kapitänleutnant Hagene, controlling the main guns, never obtained any targets, and the 20.3-cm guns did not open fire. The secondary guns fired individually on anything they could glimpse – trees, houses, sheds and telegraph poles. Tracers stretched onto the sides of the fjord in a spectacular play, but not one Norwegian soldier or gun was hit during this phase.[23]

Blücher was too far up the fjord for the guns at Nesset to bear, but as soon as Oscarsborg fired, the batteries at Kopås and Husvik opened up, raking the cruiser with 15-cm and 57-mm shells. Between twenty-two and twenty-four 15-cm shells were fired from Kopås and a further twenty-five to thirty 57-mm shells from Husvik, virtually all hitting the cruiser before she was through the fire zone. The 15-cm guns at Kopås in particular – positioned above the fjord and firing down onto *Blücher*'s deck and superstructure – had a devastating effect. Because of the short distance, most shells hitting the superstructure penetrated, exploding on the opposite side, turning seventy to seventy-five metres of the port centre section of *Blücher*, between the two 28-cm hits, into a mass of burning debris. A number of serious fires were started on the 'tweendeck, gun deck and upper deck, spreading rapidly and merging as petrol, ammunition and explosives from the army stores were ignited. Flak Control B and the adjacent 10.5-cm mounting were completely destroyed. Most of the electricity gave out and utter chaos reigned.

One of the early hits severed the rudder and engine telegraph cables from the superstructure. As the rudder at that moment was trained to port from a brief course-change when passing Småskjær, Woldag had to order 'full astern' via voice-pipe on the starboard outer screw to avoid *Blücher* running aground on Kaholmen. Emergency steering from the tiller-flat eventually restored some degree of control, but due to the time-lag between rudder orders being given and executed, *Blücher* started to reel and the speed dropped from the twelve knots briefly gained.[24]

The torpedo battery at Oscarsborg was literally built into the rock face of Nordre Kaholmen and could not be seen from the fjord. Kommandørkaptein Anderssen and NCO Bexrud were in the central cupola three storeys above where Lieutenant Karlsen and his men were waiting to reload once the first set of torpedoes had left the underwater launch shafts. There were nine torpedoes available, lowered individually into the shafts by steel cradles, a process that took about two minutes per torpedo. The shafts were fixed and could not fire a spread, but this made no difference in the confined waters. Anderssen had no information on the number or speed of the ships and set his sights at ten knots. A few small-calibre shells from *Blücher* accidentally hit near the bunker while they waited; frightening but not dangerous.

Just before 04:30, a large ship emerged in the sight, smoke pouring from multiple fires. It was moving slower than anticipated and Anderssen calmly adjusted the sights to seven knots; distance was about five hundred metres and it would be impossible to miss. Shaft no. 1 was reported ready, and in the darkness of the command bunker Kommandørkaptein Anderssen fumbled for the firing key. 'I had never thought I would fire my torpedoes in anger,' he later said. With the aim point underneath the main part of the superstructure, he pressed the firing key and to his immense relief heard the torpedo rumble away. The sights were readjusted to five knots and aligned on a new aim point a little further aft before the firing key was pressed again. The third torpedo was reported ready, but before it could be fired an explosion shook the ship, followed shortly after by a second, and with professional pride Kommandørkaptein Anderssen knew his torpedoes had worked as they should. Expecting further ships, he retained the third torpedo and ordered an immediate reload of the empty shafts.[25]

Everybody onboard *Blücher* could feel the heavy shocks as the torpedoes impacted close together on the port side in boiler room K1 and turbine room T2/3. Most personnel in these rooms were killed instantly and the turbines seized. Several bulkheads were opened to the sea. Water poured into the ship and as the pumps soon stopped, it continued into adjacent compartments through cracks and leaky cable gates. A slight list to port developed. Sonderführer Behrens wrote:

When *Blücher* approached the Drøbak Narrows, we were all ordered below the armoured deck. The ship was moving slowly and the engines could barely be noticed. Then a gun duel commenced, lasting about ten minutes. It was not possible from below to distinguish between hits and our own artillery. Speed was increased. Suddenly the cruiser was violently shaken and shifted sideways. The engines shut down and the light went out; emergency lighting turning on shortly after. Nobody could tell us what had happened.[26]

The fight for survival had started.

Kapitän zur See Heinrich Woldag (right) and his first officer, Fregattenkapitän Erich Heymann. (Author's collection)

* * *

Chief Engineer Fregattenkapitän Thannemann reported to the bridge that the centre turbine had fallen out, reducing the speed to slow ahead. Not long after, both outer turbines shut down as well, leaving *Blücher* unmanoeuvrable, but still with a forward momentum. An enquiry from the bridge was, according to Heymann, answered by an indication that at least one of the outer turbines could be restarted within an hour. Thannemann later categorically denied having authorised any such answer. Shortly after, all communication with the engine room was lost and Woldag, not realising the perilous condition of his ship, decided to drop anchor to stop *Blücher* from running ashore. Korvettenkapitän Czygan and Leutnant Bertelsmann were sent to the forecastle with an anchor party. Due to the list, the bow anchor would not drop, but eventually the starboard anchor rushed out, finding the bottom at sixty metres. The burning cruiser was halted in the middle of the fjord, turning slowly with the current.[27]

Onshore, there was no damage to any of the batteries and the guns at Kopås and Husvik turned their attention to *Lützow*, some 600 metres behind the flagship. Kapitän Thiele immediately ordered fire, but *Lützow's* gunnery officers could see little more than those on *Blücher* had, and they were at a further disadvantage being down the fjord with a limited sector of fire. The secondary guns opened up, but had no clear targets. Instead, the cruiser received three 15-cm hits in quick succession.

The first shell hit on top of the central gunbarrel of the forward Anton turret, near the crenel shutter, destroying the hydraulics and the cradle of the gun. The impact lifted the turret roof a few millimetres and splinters and fragments peppered the interior of the turret. Cabling, hydraulics and instruments were destroyed, fuses blew and the main turret motor was put out of action, rendering the turret unserviceable. Four men were wounded.

The second shell hit the hull between the portholes of compartment XIII, exploding on the 'tweendeck. The hospital isolation room and operating theatre were wrecked, starting a serious fire. Two soldiers were killed and six more severely wounded while one of the

Heavy cruiser *Lützow*, a sister ship of *Graf Spee*, was revolutionary in many aspects: electrical arc-welding eliminated rivets, saving over 15 per cent of weight in the hull alone. The 28-cm triple turrets were also new to the German Navy. Diesel-engine propulsion gave a high endurance, but the engines had teething problems. (Author's collection)

doctors and some ratings were wounded. Twelve to fifteen large holes were counted in the bulkhead, a traverse frame was damaged and the upper deck pierced in three places. The third 15-cm shell exploded ondeck behind the port crane. Splinters flew over a large area killing four gunners and wounding several others. One of the two aircraft was damaged and the optics of the aft A/A fire-control destroyed. For several minutes, machine-gun and light cannon fire from the Drøbak side raked the decks and starboard superstructure, causing minor damage and forcing everybody in the open into shelter.[28]

Thiele would not risk receiving the same treatment as *Blücher* and, assuming command of the remainder of the group, ordered retreat. Just before the flagship vanished blazing behind Oscarsborg, two huge explosions were seen. Thiele assumed these were from mines and that the passage to Oslo for all practical purposes was closed. He ordered 'full astern' and when *Emden* approached from behind he added 'hard a-port', stopping his ship towards the western shore of the fjord behind Storskjær. All light and medium guns on the port broadside fired up the fjord, even though targets remained elusive. Turning smartly, Thiele ordered 'full ahead' again and *Lützow* set off down the fjord while damage control and fire parties were ordered into action. Smoke from the fire in the hospital area shrouded *Lützow*, but it was extinguished within twenty minutes. A splinter from a near miss had slashed open a trim tank below the waterline, but the hole was not large and quickly sealed. 'A' turret was operational again after half an hour, even if the centre gun was beyond repair for the moment and hung limply down at its lowest elevation. Otherwise, there was no serious damage to the cruiser. While turning, *Lützow* received a few brief USW signals from *Blücher* that her engines were out and that she was anchoring. According to Thiele, Konteradmiral Kummetz added in the signal that he should take command of Gruppe Oldenburg. In September 1941, Kummetz's adjutant, Oberleutnant Freyberg, wrote that Thiele asked by USW if he should assume command and received a negative answer from Kummetz. He also alleged that Thiele turned back on his own initiative, unknown to Kummetz and Woldag.

Emden did not open fire, nor did she receive any hits. When *Lützow* turned, she made a similar manoeuvre towards the eastern shore and followed. *Möwe* and the two R-boats took the van.[29] The Kopås battery continued firing until the ships vanished in the haze around 2,500 metres down the fjord at 04:40.[30]

Early that morning, the 107-ton Norwegian freighter *Sørland* was heading towards Oslo with paper and food and ventured by misfortune into Gruppe Oldenburg coming back down the fjord. *Möwe* challenged *Sørland* with a signal lamp, but seeing they were warships Kaptein Martinsen curbed his lanterns and headed for the eastern shore. *R18* and *R19* opened fire, setting the wooden hull ablaze. Desperately, Martinsen headed for land and grounded near Skiphelle where the burned-out wreck sank later in the morning. Two of the six men onboard perished.[31]

Meanwhile, conditions onboard *Blücher* worsened. Saving the ship and the men took priority and Woldag ordered Heymann to leave the bridge and assess the situation. He found utter chaos. The centre parts of the main deck, 'tweendeck and superstructure were all a red-hot mass of flame. Explosive fires going through several decks raked the area of the aircraft hangar, hindering movement between fore and aft. Below the port forward 10.5-cm gun the ship's side was torn open with thick smoke and flames pouring out of the opening. At the site of the torpedo workshop, where much of the army ammunition had been stored, there was now nothing but a large hole in the deck. Small arms ammunition and hand grenades were detonating continuously and smoke canisters ignited by the many hits from the Kopås and Husvik batteries added to the inferno. Ill-trained fire-fighting parties struggled in vain to douse the fires, all the more so as splinters had riddled many of the hoses and made them of no use. Flooding and wreckage blocked companionways and hatches, and communication with more and more sections of the ship was breaking down, hampering co-ordination. The number of dead and wounded was increasing, and medical personnel worked desperately to cope. Some men managed to move into the blazing hangar, but most of these were killed when several aircraft bombs exploded. The fires spread out of control and as the pumps failed, even hand-held Minimax extinguishers were used – to no avail. Some of the ready-use ammunition from the ship's guns was hastily returned to the magazines below the armoured deck, some dumped in the fjord. Aft, the torpedoes in the starboard tubes were fired off as a precaution, two exploding against the eastern shore, the third grounding south of Drøbak. On the port side, it was only possible to remove the firing pistols as the tubes could not be swung out. Forward, the port-side tubes were gone, and the starboard ones could not be reached due to the flames and explosions.

Shaken, Heymann returned to the bridge reporting to his captain that in spite of the efforts of the men, the fires were getting out of hand. Hearing this, Woldag ordered all gun crews to be detailed to the fire-fighting parties as there appeared to be no immediate danger from further attacks. Priority was given to move as many of the wounded as possible to the less-threatened areas fore and aft. The only undamaged boat was the starboard cutter. Kapitänleutnant Mihatsch was detailed to take command of this once it was lowered, bringing the seriously wounded ashore, accompanied by two medical officers. The boat struck a rock on its second trip to shore and only a few casualties were rescued in this manner. The way to safety was a ten- to fifteen-minute swim through the icy water.

At dawn, a fresh wind fuelled the fire and the current turned the ship around on the anchor, pointing the bow south-eastwards. The smoke billowed forward across the bridge and forecastle, worsening the conditions there significantly. With water rising and thick smoke filling the rooms, Korvettenkapitän Grasser evacuated all boilers and turbines around 05:00, using everyone in the fire fighting as soon as they could find their way onto the 'tweendeck. Above, neither Woldag nor Heymann had any idea yet that *Blücher* would not be saved, but at 05:30 the 10.5-cm magazine in compartment VII exploded. There was a perceptible jolt through the ship and the list, which up to this point had been no more than five or six degrees, started to increase significantly. The explosion ruptured the bulkheads between the boiler room and the adjacent fuel tanks and the first flames of burning oil spread on the sea.

Blücher going down. The photograph was taken from Askholmene shortly after 06:00. (Marinemuseet)

Kapitän Woldag finally gave the order to start preparations for abandoning ship, including the destruction of code lists, orders and other secret material. Standard procedure was to throw this overboard in designated laden bags and boxes. Some of the documents did not fit into the boxes, though, and some areas seemed to be short of bags. Several officers later reported having thrown the papers they were responsible for into the fire amidships, but it is obvious from the number of documents retrieved from the fjord that numerous sets of documents were left behind or just thrown directly into the water.[32]

As communication was largely down, the order for 'all men on deck' went by mouth from man to man. Aft, Fregattenkapitän Thannemann on his own initiative had already ordered all men on deck when the list increased towards 20°. Confused and scared, the Landsers streamed up from below, struggling to open the hatches and doors. No fire or evacuation procedures had been reviewed and none of them had been instructed to close the hatches again once they had passed through. Most were left open and smoke, fire and eventually water quickly spread. Few of the soldiers could swim and many found to their despair that the fires had destroyed most of the kapok lifejackets strapped to the guardrails. Most German reports praise the disciplined behaviour of soldiers and sailors during the evacuation and there are abundant stories of sailors giving away their lifejackets or helping by throwing buoyant material to those already in the sea. Norwegian eyewitnesses however, speak of men running back and forth on the listing deck with much shouting and crying for help.

From the stern of *Blücher* to the island of Askholmene was about 300 metres. From the foredeck to the mainland was some 400–500 metres. Attempts to extend or slip the anchor chain so the ship could drift closer to shore failed due to the list. The fires amidships had effectively divided the ship in two with no communication except for those willing to climb across on the slippery side of the ship outside the starboard railing. Korvettenkapitän Czygan had moved to the quarterdeck after the anchor handling and managed to get two dinghies afloat. When the list of the cruiser reached 45°, he gave orders to start abandoning the ship. By then, however, many soldiers had already gone overboard of their own accord. Later Fregattenkapitän Thannemann appeared and took command aft. Undamaged Marks floats were thrown overboard as were hammocks, mattresses, crates, gas-mask canisters and other buoyant material. The floats took some ten minutes before being fully inflated, and several soldiers drowned sliding off when trying to enter too early.[33] Thannemann and a few soldiers were among the last to get into the water – after the ship had rolled past 90°.

Heymann took command on the foreship and ordered all men to assemble on the slanting foredeck. Around 06:00, Woldag gave a short address and called three cheers for the ship and the Fatherland, after which Heymann called cheers for the captain. What the army personnel thought of this display, which was followed by the order to abandon ship, has not been recorded.

Konteradmiral Kummetz, Kapitän Woldag, Fregattenkapitän Heymann, Navigation Officer Korvettenkapitän Förster and Senior Gunnery Officer Korvettenkapitän Engelmann went into the water without lifejackets. They swam together and were halfway to shore when the end came. *Blücher* capsized slowly to port with the battle ensign flying at the mainmast where Signalman Heidmann had set it on orders from Korvettenkapitän

Survivors watching the final moments of *Blücher* from Askholmene. (J Asmussen collection)

Czygan around 05:40. The burning superstructure reached the oil on the water and several intense fires were started. Fully capsized, the bow started sinking and the stern rose quickly, showing the three bronze propellers, before slipping under around 06:25. Many still clung to the rudder and shafts as she went. Norwegian eyewitnesses report having heard the singing of 'Deutschland, Deutschland über alles . . .', the German national anthem, as the ship went down. Some minutes after disappearing, there was a violent underwater explosion. A huge burning bubble followed, igniting the remaining oil on the surface and turning the fjord into a furnace, killing many of the last to get away. It was a little over two hours since Oberst Eriksen had decided to open fire on the unknown warship.[34]

The fire from the 28-cm guns at Oscarsborg damaged *Blücher* seriously, but would not have sunk her alone. The fires would in all likelihood have come under control, even with the additional damage from the Kopås and Husøy batteries, had it not been for the torpedoes. On the other hand, without the previous damage and fierce fires resulting from the hits in the region of the aircraft hangar and the subsequent explosion of the 10.5-cm magazine, it is quite possible that the damage from the torpedo hits might have been controlled too. Had the ship been grounded or taken into Lortbukta, north of Drøbak, the loss of life might have been significantly less and she could in all likelihood have been saved. Thus it was the combined effect of the shells and torpedoes hitting so close plus the inexperience of the crew and the delayed understanding of her officers as to the dangerous situation the ship was in, that eventually sank her.

The Survivors

At 04:54, the Kopås battery reported to Oscarsborg that the remaining ships had withdrawn to the south and that at least one of them was on fire, possibly sinking. The Narrows had been successfully defended and Oberst Eriksen allowed his men to stand down. They emerged from the batteries and shelters to discuss what had happened. Dawn was approaching and the stricken ship was seen to the north, near Kaholmen, burning fiercely. At first, there were several explosions, then disturbing cries for help. She was obviously in trouble.

Sailors and soldiers struggled for their lives in the icy fjord. Those that did not reach shore within fifteen to twenty minutes were at peril from the freezing water. Norwegian fishermen and other locals rescued at least fifty men in their boats; most others would have to struggle ashore alone.

The majority of the survivors, including many wounded, landed on the mainland at Digerud and Hallangen north of Drøbak. After a while, a headcount gave some 750 *Blücher*-men and about 170 soldiers, nearly all from the foreship, including Kummetz, Engelbrecht, Generalmajor Süssmann of the Luftwaffe and Oberst Blomeyer, commander of IR 307. They were all exhausted and very miserable. Air temperature was below zero. Many were smeared in oil and several had burns on their face and hands from swimming through burning fuel. Others had frozen limbs from the icy water or walking barefoot in the snow. Some had no strength to drag themselves out of the water and died on the shore. Fregattenkapitän Heymann walked tirelessly among the shaken survivors, making sure they stood up and moved around while others organised fires from wood gathered on the beach to get warm and dry the uniforms. The wounded were given priority and only a few men died once ashore.

Around 10:00, Engelbrecht set off in the repaired cutter to reconnoitre towards the south.[35] The cutter returned after some time ordering a move-out along the shore towards some summerhouses where the general had established quarters for the wounded. This turned out to be no easy task, as most survivors were without shoes and improvised footwear was made from cut-up lifejackets. Only around midday did the move-out start.

While installing the wounded in the huts, the Germans were surrounded by a group of Norwegian soldiers and ordered to continue to a farm about a mile inland. The soldiers came from 4th Guards Company, whose commander, Kaptein Aksel Petersson, had received orders to take his seventy men south from Oslo to take care of the survivors. There was little the Germans could do but oblige. Leaving the most seriously wounded behind in the huts with the medical personnel, what was by now a fairly miserable crowd set out on a sluggish hour-long march through the snow towards a farm at Søndre Hallangen, where as many as possible were installed in the farm buildings. The attitude of the Norwegian soldiers is described in all reports as 'correct and polite, even friendly'.[36] By 18:30 Kaptein Petersson approached the German officers, telling them that he had received orders to withdraw, which he did with his men, leaving the Germans to themselves.[37] Around 22:00 a requisitioned bus left for Oslo with the German senior officers. Generalmajor Engelbrecht and Konteradmiral Kummetz thus arrived in the capital around midnight. Korvettenkapitän Förster was given the task of organising food and transport for the 900 remaining men at Hallangen as soon as possible; no easy task in an occupied country. Next morning, buses arrived and started bringing the wounded to Oslo. Woldag joined this group. The rest of the senior officers and the Wehrmacht soldiers followed during the day in trucks and buses in a steady but slow shuttle while food, cigarettes and hot drinks were brought to those remaining at the farm. The most seriously wounded from Hallangen were taken onboard *Lützow* and *Emden* while the last 250 men embarked the R-boats and were taken to Oslo during 10 April.[38]

Most of the survivors from the stern, including Fregattenkapitän Thannemann and Rittmeister Goerz, one of the Group XXI staff officers, struggled ashore on Askholmene and some nearby rocks. Goerz was senior officer of those not wounded and took command, using the Marks float he had arrived in, to try to rescue others:

> The island was some 200 metres long and fifty metres wide and consisted of snow-covered rock with a few bushes. A small wooden hut contained a few pieces of old clothes taken in use by those arriving first . . . Using a steel helmet and a spade to row, I took the float back towards *Blücher*, helped by a naval petty officer named Scheer, to assist at least some of those still struggling in the water, crying for help instead of using their strength to swim. [Soon] we had eight to ten people clinging onto the float and with the current against us were hardly making any progress at all with our primitive rowing gear. The situation was getting desperate. The float sank below the surface and those clinging on were too cold to help us move towards land. Only after vigorous shouting were we able to make them assist us somewhat . . . Most of them had to be dragged ashore as they were not capable of hauling themselves onto the steep banks.[39]

When Obermaat Peter Schüller swam ashore at Askholmene, he found a flag somebody had brought along. He kept the flag and eventually had it brought back to Germany, where it is now to be found in the garrison church in Willhelmshaven. (J Asmussen collection)

Some died from only metres from the beach or even after being hauled ashore. A fire was lit from pieces of driftwood and planking from the hut and while gathering around the fire the shocked men watched the cruiser capsize and slip under.

Norwegian Løytnant Erling Carelius was guarding a nearby oil depot with thirteen soldiers when he was informed that survivors were struggling ashore on the islands. He requisitioned two fishing vessels and brought as many as he could find on the shores of Askholmene to the depot, where they were given dry clothes and food. Thannemann and Goerz accepted the internment as with only four pistols among them, resistance would be pointless. They were convinced the situation would not last long and would be infinitely preferable to a freezing day in the open waiting for rescue. In the afternoon, the steamer *Norden* arrived, sent by Kapitän Thiele, to try to find out what had happened to the flagship. The survivors were taken care of while the Norwegian soldiers were disarmed and sent away. Løytnant Carelius was brought to Oslo with the survivors.

Later, *Kondor* and three R-boats managed to go through the Narrows and take part in the search for survivors. Many hundreds were rescued from the islands and rocks in the fjord during 9 April, having spent a miserable day or even the following night in the open. Kapitänleutnant Forstmann's R-boats searched the area for several days, but found mostly bodies.[40]

For propaganda reasons, German authorities preferred to keep the casualty figures from *Blücher* unknown at the time and it has since been difficult to ascertain how many actually died. From some sources the figure is as high as 1,500, but the real number is most likely

Many of the dead from *Blücher* were buried at Vestre Gravlund near Oslo in the morning of 16 April. (Author's collection)

between 350 and 400. Some 320 Germans were buried in Oslo during the following weeks, most of them probably casualties from *Blücher*. In mid-May, documents from the German naval command in Oslo listed thirty-six confirmed dead, 114 missing and twelve 'uncertain', in addition to 195 army casualties. The highest ranking officer lost was Kapitänleutnant Pochhammer, killed inside the foretop by the first shell from Oscarsborg. The official burial ceremony for the dead from *Blücher* was held at Vestre Gravlund near Oslo in the morning of 16 April. Sailors from *Emden* and soldiers from the army made up the Guard of Honour and von Falkenhorst, Boehm, Engelbrecht, Heymann and most officers and men in Oslo that could be spared were there. To their anger, no *Blücher*-men were allowed to attend as Boehm decided they 'were not properly dressed'.[41]

Horten

The naval base at Karljohansvern had been the undisputed nerve centre of the Norwegian Navy when Sweden was the main adversary at the turn of the century. When focus shifted towards the North Sea and the north during WWI, its importance diminished and in 1940 Karljohansvern, besides SDD1, hosted the main naval yard and training centre of the RNN as well as the naval aircraft factory and flying school. On the evening of 8 April, the minesweepers *Otra* and *Rauma* were preparing to leave early next morning for western Norway to sweep the alleged British minefields off Bud and Stadt. The minelayer *Olav*

Three MF11 floatplanes over Karljohansvern naval base at Horten. The MF11 was the mainstay of the Naval Air Arm; twenty-eight of them were in service in the evening of 8 April. (Marinemuseet)

Tryggvason was also about to leave the yard, following a month-long overhaul, and return to SDD2 in Bergen. Only a few tests remained and she was for all practical purposes fully operational. The two decommissioned panserships *Tordenskjold* and *Harald Haarfagre* were moored side-by-side at the quay as accommodation ships for recruits but, apart from a few A/A guns, they were of no value to the defences of the naval base.

The first warning of the intruders came from outer Oslofjord to SDD1 at 23:10. Shortly after, Kontreadmiral Smith-Johannsen called Kommandørkaptein Briseid of *Olav Tryggvason* to his office. Briseid, who arrived at 00:10, was one of the most senior captains of the RNN and a highly respected officer. Since his ship was to leave the next day, provided the tests went well, he had given half of the crew leave until midnight and those of his officers with families in Horten, until 07:00. Briseid was updated on the reports of intruders in outer Oslofjord and the admiral's thoughts on the disposition of his meagre forces. Armed with four 12-cm, one 76-mm and two 20-mm guns, *Olav Tryggvason* was one of the most powerful vessels in the Norwegian Navy and she would have to be deployed in the defence of Horten regardless of regular chains of command. The two officers agreed *Olav Tryggvason* should cast off from the wharf and move to a buoy from where she could cover both Horten harbour and the Karljohansvern docks. Smith-Johannsen later wrote that he had given Briseid orders to 'open fire on unknown intruders'. Briseid, however, denied this.[42]

What was agreed was that *Olav Tryggvason*'s whaler should be sent to the merchant ships in Horten harbour, ordering them to darken their ships and turn off all lanterns. In addition, *Otra* and *Rauma* were to cast off as soon as they had sufficient crew onboard and take positions outside the harbour, sending up red signal rockets if anything irregular was observed.[43] As related above, however, Smith-Johannsen later decided to send *Otra* into the Oslofjord, forgetting to inform Briseid of this change of plans.[44]

Just after midnight, the very limited A/A defences of Horten and Karljohansvern were ordered in position, as was the company of army soldiers intended to secure the perimeter of the naval base. Recruits and personnel onboard the accommodation ships were ordered onshore to safer quarters. They had no military training and Smith-Johannsen would not deploy them for combat. Electricity in the harbour and city was cut to enforce complete blackout and the naval hospital was evacuated. Civilians inside Karljohansvern were evacuated, but the population of the city was not, as the chief of police found this too complicated before daylight.

By 02:15 *Olav Tryggvason* was moored to a buoy in the inner harbour with all but a handful of the crew in place. Guns were manned and ready-use ammunition brought to the lockers. Most of the men had been onboard for over six months and knew their ship well. Watches were set and Kommandørkaptein Briseid ordered coffee to be made. It would be a long night.

Otra departed on her reconnaissance mission at 02:30, followed by the submarine *B4*, ordered out of harm's way because she had faulty engines. Onboard *Olav Tryggvason* the departure of two ships was heard but not seen due to the misty darkness. Briseid assumed the ships were *Otra* and *Rauma* taking up station in the fjord as agreed. He was not informed that *Otra* had been sent on a reconnaissance mission and that *Rauma* was still heating her boilers. *Rauma* would not be all set until after 04:15 and thus not in the intended position outside the harbour when the German ships arrived.

At 03:00, the minelayers of 1st Division reported that a full load of mines was onboard, ready and primed. Now, though, Smith-Johannsen felt the situation was unclear, so he ordered them to await further orders. The intruders were already well past the Rauøy–Bolærne line and in the heavy fog positioning of the field would be very difficult.[45]

The original German plan for the capture of Horten was to send the torpedo boats into Karljohansvern at dawn. As it was now obvious that the Norwegians knew they were coming, Kapitänleutnant Hans Wilcke, captain of *Kondor* and senior officer, decided to transfer the vanguard of the soldiers to the smaller R-boats. The rest of the soldiers he wanted onboard *Rau VII* to free up his ship for maximum preparedness. Falling behind schedule, Wilcke agreed with Kapitänleutnant (Ing.) Erich Grundmann, chief engineer of the 1st R-boat Flotilla and senior officer of the two R-boats that they would have to risk a direct approach into the harbour. If they met with opposition the torpedo boats would lend gun support from the fjord.[46]

The entry beacons could be sighted even if the lights were off and at 04:35, *R17* ran smartly through Vealøsgapet, the entrance to Horten harbour, at high speed with *R21* right behind. Some 140 soldiers were onboard the two R-boats, mostly from IR 307 under the command of Oberleutnant Kurt Budäus. Sighting the jetties at Apenes ahead to port, Grundmann ordered *R17* to steer for them and the landing force to prepare for disembarkation while *R21* turned to starboard for the headland Reverumpa. *Kondor*

When commissioned in 1934 the 1924-ton minelayer *Olav Tryggvason* was the largest and most powerful vessel of the RNN, equipped with four 120-mm guns in single-shielded mountings, one 76-mm and two 40-mm multipurpose guns. She was a successful ship with good seagoing characteristics, but out of context and not what the navy needed – or indeed wanted. (Author's collection)

R17 burning fiercely after being hit by shells from *Olav Tryggvason*. (Marinemuseet)

remained outside, transferring the remaining soldiers to *Rau VII*, while *Albatros* approached the entrance slowly, well behind the R-boats.

Rauma finally cast off just before 04:30. Two dark shadows had been observed coming through Vealøsgapet and Løytnant Ingolf Winsnes decided to check it out. Why he had not left and taken station outside as ordered, in spite of his ship being ready for some time, is unclear. Most likely he decided to wait for further men to show up as less than twenty were yet onboard. On the bridge of *Olav Tryggvason*, *Rauma*'s presence in the harbour was registered when she cast off, but before anything could be clarified, unknown vessels were reported coming through Vealøsgapet.

Kommandørkaptein Briseid ran towards the foredeck where his first officer, Kaptein Dingsør, and gunnery officer Kaptein Lowzow were trying to identify the incoming ships. They still believed *Otra* was patrolling outside as they had been told, and no signal rockets had been seen. The intruders were fast, but did not have an obvious military appearance in the misty backdrop of the islands, and their decks were seen to be crowded. Briseid became indecisive and called for a loose warning shot. When this had no effect, he ordered a live warning shot; only when the two vessels continued undaunted into the harbour, the second turning starboard away from the minesweeper, did he open fire in earnest. At this point, *R17* passed in front of *Olav Tryggvason* and was recognised as German. Lowzow took control of the guns while Briseid headed for the bridge. It was 04:45.[47]

With the bow of *R17* scraping along the pier at Apenes, Grundmann, Budäus and some soldiers jumped ashore, surprising the guards of the two A/A machine guns positioned there. Unceremoniously, the guns were kicked into the water while the men were allowed to escape. The rest of the soldiers disembarked just as the first shell from *Olav Tryggvason* slammed into the stern of the boat. Stabsobersteuermann Arthur Godenau called for help from the torpedo boats and backed away from the pier as soon as the last soldier was off. Before he had come far, two more shells hit – one forward and one in the engine room. Fires from the latter spread rapidly and the doomed R-boat drifted helplessly in the harbour. At 05:20, the flames reached the depth charges on the afterdeck and *R17* blew up with a mighty explosion. By then, Godenau had abandoned his ship and, though several were wounded, there were only two dead from the crew of *R17*. Onshore, however, there were several casualties among the soldiers and numerous buildings were on fire.[48]

With *R17* duly ablaze, Briseid and Lowzow turned their attention to *R21*. *Olav Tryggvason's* fire-control system had fallen out after a few shots, and the guns had to be operated manually. *R21* fired back with her two 20-mm machine cannons, injuring two men at no. 1 gun who had to be taken below and replaced, while the R-boat vanished behind Reverumpa without being hit. When *R21* escaped from *Olav Tryggvason's* line of fire, *Rauma* gave chase, opening up with her 76-mm gun and machine guns. The R-boat was hit several times, but Leutnant von Pommer-Esche's capable gunners turned their cannons onto the new adversary – intense fire raked the forepart of *Rauma*. One man was killed and the rest of the 76-mm crew wounded. On the bridge, Løytnant Winsnes was mortally wounded and the first officer knocked unconscious. Below deck, steam pipes were severed, reducing the pressure on the boilers. Damage was limited, but the minesweeper was temporarily out of control. The helmsman, Peder Aalvik, who was also wounded, steered back towards the pier as best he could to try to save the captain's life, but it was too late; Winsnes died after having been brought ashore. Behind Reverumpa, *R21* headed for shore, where she was grounded on the sandy beach, listing heavily. The soldiers jumped into the water and waded ashore, while the sailors took care of the wounded and tried to get their ship afloat again.[49]

Meanwhile, Kommandørkaptein Briseid backed *Olav Tryggvason* off her moorings and moved towards Vealøsgapet to see if further adversaries lurked outside. *Albatros*, coming slowly through the sound, was sighted and *Olav Tryggvason* opened fire. The torpedo boat was straddled repeatedly, but not hit. *Albatros* fired back from her forward gun, which was the only one that could bear, but the shots went wide. Kapitänleutnant Strelow ordered full astern and withdrew behind Østøya. *Olav Tryggvason* remained inside Vealøsgapet. Kapitänleutnant Wilcke of *Kondor* decided to run and get help from the cruisers, which were outside USW range, and after having re-embarked the soldiers from *Rau VII*, took off to try to locate them. Meanwhile, *Albatros* commenced an indiscriminate fire into the harbour; partly firing blind over the island and partly through the sounds. Shells fell randomly over Karljohansvern and the yards. Venturing too close during one of her firing runs around 06:30, *Albatros* took hits from a well-placed salvo from *Olav Tryggvason*. One of the shells hit near the waterline, killing one soldier and wounding another three, one of whom later died. *Olav Tryggvason* was not hit, but shrapnel sprayed her hull on a couple of occasions.[50]

Once *R21* had completed the embarkation of the troops, Leutnant von Pommer-Esche decided to try to escape, dashing through the shallow Løvøy Sound. As he had reckoned, *Olav Tryggvason* could not follow, but the R-boat was hit twice before she was safe. The damage was serious, but largely above deck and she did not take water. Now Strelow had also had enough and pulled *Albatros* away towards the safety of the cruisers, followed by *R21*.[51] Around 07:00 *Emden* was sighted off Horten, but she did not open fire and things remained quiet.

Once the attention of *Olav Tryggvason* was drawn away from the soldiers landed at Apenes, they regrouped and attended to their dead and wounded. The survivors from *R17* joined the landing party, arming themselves with weapons from the casualties. Most of the equipment, including several machine guns, ammunition and radios had been lost. Eventually, some sixty men moved out from Apenes in the direction of Horten and Karljohansvern under the command of Grundmann and Budäus. Nine dead and five severely wounded were left behind with some medical personnel. Every civilian in Horten had been woken by the gunfire and the explosion of *R17* and the streets were filled with confused and scared people, including unarmed soldiers and sailors. Reaching the first group of houses, the Germans headed for Tårngården, a rather large building offering good defensive positions and a view towards the harbour and Karljohansvern. From there, they attempted to reach the office of Kontreadmiral Smith-Johannsen by telephone without success. Meanwhile, the chief of police had been alerted to the presence of the Germans in Tårngården and drove there to find out what was going on. He was brusquely pushed back into the car and, joined by Grundmann and Oberleutnant Körner, ordered to drive to Karljohansvern while a white handkerchief was held out of the window. The car arrived at the gate shortly before 07:00. In the meantime, telephone communication with the rear admiral's office had been established from Tårngården and he was informed that German representatives were on their way to meet him.

Kapitänleutnant Gustav Forstmann (right), commander of 1st R-boat Flotilla, and Kapitänleutnant (Ing.) Erich Grundmann, his chief engineer. (Bundesarchiv Koblenz)

Unknown to the Germans, the Norwegian soldiers defending Karljohansvern had been notified of their presence in Tårngården and had moved in to attack. Just as they were getting ready, the police car was seen leaving the house with a parliamentary flag and Kaptein Fuglerud called off the assault, assuming it was the Germans surrendering to the SDD.

At Karljohansvern, Grundmann and Körner were met at the gate by Kontreadmiral Smith-Johannsen. Brazenly, Grundmann stated he represented the commander of the German forces in Oslofjord and that they had come to 'help protect Norwegian neutrality from British attack'. He demanded resistance to cease immediately, lest Karljohansvern and Horten would be destroyed through naval and aerial bombardment. The bombardment would start at 09:00, unless a radio signal verifying Norwegian surrender called it off. He added that a strong German force was in position on the other side of the harbour and any resistance would be futile; this last assertion was pure deception.[52]

Smith-Johannsen replied that he had no knowledge of a Norwegian request for help. Anyway, he was not authorised to make such decisions on his own and needed to consult his superiors in Oslo. Grundmann gave him fifteen minutes and continued his bluff by calling Budäus at Tårngården from the gate and, while making sure he was duly overheard, 'begging him to hold back the bombardment as negotiations were ongoing'. Telephoning the Admiral Staff turned out to be difficult, as by this time it had left its offices in Oslo. Eventually, after about half an hour, the commanding admiral was found and connected with Smith-Johannsen. Diesen was less than helpful however, merely authorising the admiral to decide whatever he considered appropriate. Smith-Johannsen had no reason to doubt Grundmann's insistence that Horten would be bombed unless he surrendered. Only a small part of the population had been evacuated and casualties would inevitably be high. There were no A/A defences to speak of and *Olav Tryggvason* alone could do little against several German cruisers. Smith-Johannsen found he had little choice and, calling Grundmann to his office, stated he was willing to surrender Karljohansvern and its forces. Any other ship or fort in the Oslofjord region would have to decide independently what to do. This was accepted and a written statement (in poor Norwegian) was signed at 07:35.[53] Five minutes later a white flag was hoisted over Karljohansvern and Kontreadmiral Smith-Johannsen gave the order to cease fire. The most critical command level of the RNN in eastern Norway had been neutralised through a German bluff. Kapitänleutnant Grundmann underlined that in his opinion there was no state of war between Germany and Norway and the measures taken were largely to avoid any complications or outbreak of hostilities. Thus, the ships in the harbour could keep their Norwegian flags as long as they were made temporarily inoperable and key parts removed from guns and radios. Most officers and men were free to move as they wished within Horten and Karljohansvern.[54]

Kontreadmiral Smith-Johannsen immediately called Oberst Eriksen at Oscarsborg in person to make him aware of the situation and let him know that contact with SDD1 would be severed. At the same time Kommandørkaptein Tandberg-Hanssen of Outer Oslofjord SDS called Horten. As the rear admiral was busy, he was connected to acting Chief of Staff Kaptein Blich. The two officers discussed the situation and concluded that the surrender included the forts and ships in outer Oslofjord as well. After the two telephone conversations, Blich repeated this to the rear admiral, who angrily said he had misunderstood and asked to be reconnected with Tandberg-Hanssen to correct the mistake. This was done, but took some minutes and it was 08:00 before Outer Oslofjord SDS was given the correct information. In the meantime Tandberg-Hanssen had issued orders for the ships and forts of his sector to terminate the resistance; before these could be recalled, most of the auxiliaries were heading back to base and Rauøy Fort had surrendered.[55]

At 07:50 *Olav Tryggvason* moored, flying a white tablecloth on the main mast after having been ordered to do so by a courier from Kontreadmiral Smith-Johannsen.[56] Thirty-five 20-mm hits from *R21* were counted in the superstructure, but there was no serious damage to the ship and, except for the two gunners wounded early in the fight, there were no casualties onboard. Fifty-five 12-cm shells had been spent. Except for the wasting of time in the first phase through the firing of warning shots, *Olav Tryggvason* and her crew had defended Horten well. *R17* had been destroyed, *R21* damaged and *Albatros* and *Kondor* fended off through accurate fire.[57]

Further German soldiers were landed at Karljohansvern from *R22* and *R23* during the late morning of 9 April and those from *R21* eventually reached the town. During the 10th, the Norwegian lower ranks were allowed to depart, apart from those needed for the running of the base and yard while the officers were encouraged to remain where they were and to go about their business as usual. The friendly atmosphere lasted a few days until it was clear that Norwegian opposition was being organised.

German casualties at Horten are not fully known, but probably reached some twenty dead and an equal number of wounded. Because of a misunderstanding, German aircraft dropped a dozen bombs over Karljohansvern at 09:00 before the correct signals could be given. Four Norwegian soldiers and two Germans were killed. Otherwise, Norwegian casualties were restricted to the two dead onboard *Rauma* and about a dozen wounded.[58]

Oscarsborg

At Oscarsborg, Oberst Eriksen had long since realised that the events of the early morning were more than a neutrality breach and that the intruders would return with a vengeance. Around 07:45 Kontreadmiral Smith-Johannsen called from Horten with information that he was surrendering and that the Admiral Staff had moved to Smestad. After this, it was not possible for Eriksen to communicate with any higher naval or political authorities. Eventually, telephone contact was established with Akershus, where Generalmajor Jacob Hvinden Haug, the C-in-C of 2nd Division, came to the telephone. Eriksen learned that Fornebu was lost, Oslo threatened and that several of the cities in the west had fallen. Asking the general for assistance, Eriksen was told there was very little available, but it was agreed that a company of the King's Guard should come south by bus to handle the expected survivors from *Blücher* and try to prevent an advance towards Oslo, should infantry be landed on the eastern side of the fjord. Otherwise, Eriksen was on his own.[59]

Kapitän Thiele took command of Gruppe Oldenburg when contact with *Blücher* was lost. Being more senior, however, Kapitän Werner Lange of *Emden* seems to have had some problems with that; repeated orders from Thiele to proceed towards Son and disembark troops were ignored. Instead, Lange took *Emden* towards Horten on his own initiative to 'clear the situation' there. In *Lützow*'s war diary, there are repeated entries of Lange's failure to comply with orders. In *Emden*'s diary there are a similar number of 'suggestions' submitted to the new commander, including one for a renewed attempt at passing through the Drøbak Narrows. The situation must have been rather complex. Still, Thiele held in his final report that 'the unease' in the group was of 'limited consequence'.

The fate of *Blücher* remained unknown to Thiele, who had had no contact with the flagship after the USW signal at 04:50, which allegedly gave him command of the group. A signal at 05:26, ordering *Möwe* to come to *Blücher*'s assistance was picked up by *Möwe* and *Emden*, but immediately countered by Thiele when forwarded, saving *Möwe* from running the gauntlet of the Drøbak batteries. Thiele was in a difficult situation: Horten was heavily defended and neither Rauøy nor Bolærne had been captured. He noted in his diary that unless the situation had been cleared by nightfall, he would have to take the larger ships out of the fjord. Further artillery duels with the guns at Oscarsborg were out of the question until the Luftwaffe had reduced their strength significantly. Air support was requested from X Fliegerkorps and while waiting for this, Thiele decided to land the troops at Son, from where they could reach Oslo overland.[60] His decisions, including pulling the group out of harm's way after *Blücher* was hit, were later endorsed by Konteradmiral Kummetz as correct, considering the situation.[61]

R18 and *R19* were detached to land their troops at Moss, which was done without incident. *R19* remained in Moss harbour, while Kapitänleutnant Forstmann returned to *Emden* with *R18* to receive further orders. Once there, he was told to pick up the soldiers at Moss again and move them to Son. This accomplished, both R-boats returned to the cruisers to refuel, after which they were ordered to assist at Rauøy and Bolærne. Meanwhile, *Lützow*'s own boats landed some 250 men at Son, assisted by the captured local steamer *Oscarsborg*. *Möwe* landed her troops at Son and later *Albatros* and *Kondor* were ordered to do the same before returning to Horten. By 08:10, the disembarkation was completed and Major von Poncet, CO of the Gebirgsjägers from *Lützow*, started the advance towards Oslo in whatever trucks and buses could be commandeered.[62]

Aircraft from KG 100 and III/KG 26 were already over Oslo and some of these were diverted to Oscarsborg where they arrived at 07:45. From then on, the island was subjected to an almost continuous bombardment until early evening. Maximising the amount of fuel that could be carried, the first aircraft had only a small load of 50-kg bombs, which made little damage at the fort beyond breaking windows and creating a huge cloud of dust.[63] To accommodate Thiele's request for support, X Fliegerkorps in Hamburg would have to activate its reserve squadrons, KG 4 and the dive-bombers of I/StG 1. At 10:43, nine He111s of II/KG 4 took off from Fassberg and set course for the Oslofjord loaded with 150-kg bombs. Some fifteen minutes later, 22 Ju87 R-2 Stuka dive-bombers from I/StG 1 took off from Kiel-Holtenau; sixteen of them heading for Oscarsborg. The rest of KG 4 followed in batches. There were up to forty aircraft in any one attack wave.[64]

Oberst Eriksen wrote:

It was obvious that the aircraft were aiming for the flagpole of the fortress, standing in isolation on an eight-metre high platform. Several bombs fell nearby . . . but the flagpole and the flag remained unharmed. During the worst phase of the bombardment,

The Drøbak Narrows seen from the aft cockpit of a He111 of KGr 100, heading up the fjord towards Oslo. Oscarsborg is the large island just left of the tailfin and Askholmene are the smaller islands above the tailplane. (Author's collection)

when the whole island was covered in smoke and dust, the flag could be seen above the smoke. Most bombs created a disturbing, eerie sound when falling, but there was ample time to take shelter before they hit . . .'[65]

Some bombs fell near the 28-cm guns and they were sprayed with rock fragments and dirt, but suffered no harm. Other bombs fell inside the fortress where damage to buildings was extensive, even if the stone walls stood firm. There were no casualties at Oscarsborg from the bombardment. Most of the personnel, including non-combatants and officers' family members, sought shelter in the deep tunnels and caverns below the fortress where they were physically safe. Around midday, a lull in the bombing occurred and Thiele decided to move *Lützow* in for an artillery bombardment, which he expected would be at least as effective as the bombing. Twenty-seven 28-cm shells were fired between 13:17 and 13:24 from both turrets at a distance of around eleven thousand metres and some of the 15-cm guns were allowed to join in. The men on *Lützow*'s bridge and foretop believed the bombardment a success and Eriksen later said this part of the bombardment was the most frightening. A huge column of smoke rose above the fort, but actual damage was limited and the smoke stemmed from shells bursting on the ramparts or in the courtyard. As soon as *Lützow* turned away, the aircraft returned. Their main target remained Oscarsborg, but Kopås also received attention at times, through strafing in particular.[66]

Under cover of the bombardment, the small German steamer *Norden*, which had been commandeered by an NCO and some sailors from *Lützow*, broke through the Narrows and at 13:45 reported that *Blücher* had sunk. By now, Son, Horten and Rauøy were secure, while reports from Oslo indicated the city was in German hands and Thiele had a more optimistic view of the situation. Still, a signal from Group East to attempt a breakthrough during the renewed aerial bombardment was ignored, as there was no clarity regarding the presence of mines or the status of the torpedo battery. Instead, Thiele took *Lützow* to Horten. The initial reports had included disturbing reports of 'coastal panserships' taking part in the defence and he needed to see for himself that the situation was under control. To his relief he found the town and naval base secure. The German soldiers still numbered only some two hundred and a landing party was disembarked to give support until reinforcements could be sent from Oslo. Thereafter, *Lützow* and *Emden* once again headed back towards the Drøbak Narrows. *Albatros* and *R21* were sent to the submarine base at Teie to render the torpedo batteries and guns there harmless and secure the radio station.

Kontreadmiral Smith-Johannsen was requested to come onboard *Lützow* for a 'conference'. He was picked up in Horten by *R18* around 17:20 and brought to Filtvet where the two cruisers waited. Taken to Thiele's cabin, the rear admiral was greeted politely and Thiele expressed his regrets that Germany had been compelled to invade the country. The Norwegian defences in the Oslofjord had fought bravely, he said, but as Narvik, Trondheim, Bergen, Stavanger and Kristiansand were all in German hands, it was time to give up and Smith-Johannsen was asked to order Oscarsborg to surrender to avoid further bloodshed. This Smith-Johannsen declined, holding that after his surrender at Horten, the fort was no longer under his command. Thiele then urged the admiral to use his influence with the government for a general capitulation of all Norwegian forces. Somewhat bemused, Smith-Johannsen answered that unfortunately he did not have that kind of influence with the government and as he had no knowledge of the situation in other parts of the country, he could not be expected to consider such a request. Asked whether there were further minefields in the Narrows, Smith-Johannsen refused to reply at all and Thiele gave up. The rear admiral was politely taken back to the R-boat, which returned him to Horten. In the meantime, the bombing of Oscarsborg continued.[67]

From Kopås, the main fort appeared to have been obliterated. Smoke and fire was everywhere and at each explosion earth, wood and pieces of rock were thrown about. At 09:00 the telephone line across the fjord was severed. Kaptein Enger and his men were convinced that casualties on the island must be severe. Around 16:30, the intensity of the bombing lessened noticeably and German ships were again seen coming up the fjord. Enger ordered his men to the guns. The ships halted and *Lützow* turned broadside on at about nine thousand metres but did not open fire. Enger considered the distance too great for effective fire and did not shoot either.

When the bombing lessened, Oberst Eriksen risked an inspection of his guns. He found them covered by sand and grit from the explosions, needing extensive cleaning, but otherwise apparently in order. He wanted to attempt manning at least one gun, but was advised by his officers that many of the men were severely shocked by the bombardment and as the aircraft would undoubtedly start strafing if the activity picked up, it would be virtually impossible to make the guns operational without losses. Reluctantly, Eriksen had to accept. A signal was flashed across to Kopås at 17:15: 'Do not open fire; await further orders.' This was originally intended to keep Kopås from opening fire while the officers at Oscarsborg considered what to do, but as no further signals came, it put Enger, who did not know what was happening at the main fort, in a difficult situation. Meanwhile, the bombing continued sporadically and the German ships remained at a distance.

Möwe and *Kondor* approached the Drøbak Narrows around 17:30. They followed the eastern shore, accompanied by some of the R-boats, while *Lützow* and *Emden* remained off Filtvet. Some distance up the fjord, the torpedo boats halted while *R21* approached Drøbak harbour. The ships were clearly seen from Kopås, but Enger had received no further orders from Oscarsborg and did not open fire. The landings at Drøbak thus went unopposed. Having secured the harbour, the German soldiers reorganised and, leaving a small unit behind, headed for Husvik. The guns there had already been abandoned and the Germans continued towards Kopås. Enger could see them coming, but instead of organising a defence he left his command bunker and walked unarmed towards the officer who appeared to be in charge.

Oberleutnant Wetjen saluted and demanded a surrender of the Kopås batteries within twenty minutes. Otherwise, the ships would open fire and the aircraft resume bombing. Kaptein Enger said he needed to confer with his commander at Oscarsborg and this might take some time as he had to use signalling due to severed telephone lines. Wetjen at first accepted this, but then changed his mind. Enger was kept under strict guard and not allowed back into his bunker. Instead, he was told that as the main ports of Norway were in German hands and the Norwegian government had surrendered, there was no reason for him to hesitate. At 18:25 a signal was flashed from Enger towards Oscarsborg: 'Kopås battery and Drøbak occupied by German forces.' Some three hundred Norwegians had surrendered to less than fifty Germans.[68]

From Oscarsborg, German soldiers were seen landing at Drøbak, and Oberst Eriksen invited his senior officers to air their opinions on what should be done next. There was no contact with any naval authority and the situation in the rest of the country was known only from the public radio. Oslo appeared to be under German control while King Haakon and the government had left the capital. Further opposition seemed futile, considering the state of the men and the guns. At this time, the signal from Enger arrived and the decision made itself. Shortly after, *Möwe* approached with a white flag at the masthead. Kaptein Sødem and Kommandørkaptein Anderssen were sent in a boat to meet her. Kapitänleutnant Neuss demanded the two officers should surrender the fortress immediately, or an aerial bombardment would be initiated over Oslo and Drøbak. He had to accept that they could not agree to anything without their commander's consent though. The young Leutnant Döhler accompanied Sødem and Anderssen back to Oscarsborg around 19:00 with an NCO and four soldiers. Meanwhile, *Kondor* and three R-boats slipped through the Narrows to assist *Norden* in looking for survivors.

Oberst Eriksen dragged his feet, arguing the formalities of the surrender for several hours. Eventually, Thiele lost his patience and sent Kapitänleutnant Karl-Egloff von Schnurbein to conclude the negotiations. Arriving at Oscarsborg, he arrogantly demanded information on all defences in the Oslofjord including forts, ships and minefields. Eriksen grumpily refused to tell him anything, except there were no mines in the Narrows proper and the rescue work could be stepped up. Von Schnurbein had to bend to the stubborn Oberst and accept that ratings and civilians should be released as soon as possible and sent home, while the officers should remain in freedom at the fortress until their status had been clarified. There was no written agreement, Eriksen did not sign a declaration of surrender and there was never a white flag on Oscarsborg. Thiele was so impressed by

The scarred walls of Oscarsborg after the surrender. (Author's collection)

Eriksen and his fortress that he accepted his demand for the Norwegian flag to remain
flying next to the German one next morning.[69]

Only at 08:45 in the morning of the 10th did *Lützow*, *Emden* and *Möwe* finally pass
the Narrows behind four R-boats with sweeping gear set, partly to avoid wreckage from
Blücher, partly in case there should be mines after all. They reached Oslo harbour at
10:45, almost thirty hours behind schedule.

Generalmajor Engelbrecht came onboard *Lützow* to co-ordinate the management of
the invasion forces and to learn what had happened at Drøbak and Horten. Based on
instructions from Group East, it was decided to leave some three hundred of *Blücher's*
survivors in Oslo at the disposal of Korvettenkapitän Förster, temporarily appointed
'Commanding Admiral Oslo', while specialists and officers not needed should accompany
Lützow and the torpedo boats back to Germany. Of the three hundred, two companies,
each of seventy-five men, were equipped and armed from the stores of *Emden* and *Lützow*
and shipped to Horten and Drøbak to bolster the meagre occupation forces there. The
rest were installed onboard *Emden* or in various schools and public buildings around
town and eventually employed onboard captured Norwegian naval vessels. At 14:40,
Lützow cast off and headed down the fjord again. The R-boats were ordered to find and
mark the wreck of *Blücher* and start recovering the dead. *Emden* remained in Oslo for
communication and support. Several of her officers were detailed in the coming days to
assist in the takeover of captured Norwegian ships and securing the approaches to the
capital. Within a week, some fifteen ex-RNN boats were operating under German flag,
largely manned by survivors from *Blücher*.[70]

In his war diary, Kapitän Thiele later described the co-operation with the torpedo boats (Senior CO Kapitänleutnant Neuss of *Möwe*) and the R-boats (Kapitänleutnant Forstmann) as 'quite outstanding'. Notably he does not mention *Emden* and Kapitän Lange at all.[71]

Kapitän Woldag was called to Berlin to report and joined Thiele onboard *Lützow*. When she was torpedoed in the Skagerrak, Woldag was flown to Kiel in *Lützow*'s Arado, arriving in the morning of 11 April. The next day he continued to Berlin to tell his story in person to Hitler, Raeder and the SKL. Woldag was supposed to return to Norway on 16 April after a few days with his family in Kiel, but never arrived in Oslo as expected. There are several uncertainties shrouding what actually happened. Woldag's then 11-year-old son Jochen later held he followed his father to the airfield and saw him off in the early morning of 16 April. The funeral of the victims from *Blücher* was on this day and Thiele wanted to be present. Heymann in his diary writes that he and some other officers went to Fornebu the following day, the 17th, to pick up the captain, who never turned up. Woldag's aircraft vanished, some say over the Baltic or the Kattegat, others over the Oslofjord. Fregattenkapitän Heymann's narrative is generally very detailed, but on the issue of the disappearance of 'der Kommandant' he is surprisingly brief. He does, however, state that on 20 April letters from his own wife, which Woldag was supposed to have brought from Germany, were found floating in the Oslofjord. Legend has it that Woldag somehow made the Ju52 crash near Oscarsborg, but this has never been ascertained and is very hard to believe.[72]

Commanding Admiral Norway, Admiral Boehm, asked Fregattenkapitän Nieden to lead an investigation committee into the events in the Narrows. Nieden worked methodically and the report was not ready until July 1941. By that time, myths and rumours about *Blücher* were rife, especially after the disappearance of Kapitän Woldag. Nieden's report showed that the army put the blame for the failure and loss of so many lives directly on Woldag, particularly as he had anchored the damaged cruiser and not beached her. After an argument between Woldag and Generalmajor Engelbrecht, the army believed, the general had himself organised the disembarkation and rescue of the troops. Konteradmiral Kummetz was rarely mentioned, possibly as most army officers did not distinguish between his role and that of the captain. Most interviewed officers believed a smaller and less valuable ship should have been used to test the defences of the Drøbak Narrows. The army's conclusion was that in any future combined operation, one of their officers must be assigned the overall command and the navy only responsible for the transport. In case a ship should be disabled, the senior army officer onboard must take command. General von Falkenhorst left no doubt as to his opinion: 'The presence of torpedo batteries and their location was known [and] the commander of *Blücher* must have been well aware of the risk associated with passing through the Drøbak Narrows.' Onboard a warship, he added, the navy was in command and therefore fully responsible for what happened.

On 30th July 1941, Admiral Boehm forwarded the report to the SKL with the comment that as far as the disagreement between the naval and army commanders was concerned, Generalmajor Engelbrecht had, just after the event, spoken of how the conduct of the ship's crew and their efforts to rescue the soldiers had greatly impressed him. Raeder found the report unbalanced and ordered further reports to be obtained from the surviving members of the ship's officers, now scattered throughout occupied Europe.[73]

Few of them had much to add to the reports already filed a year earlier. Konteradmiral Kummetz wrote a brief addendum, strongly denying any conflict between Woldag and Engelbrecht and repeating that most sailors had given their lifejackets to the soldiers. As for the anchoring, Kummetz held that in spite of the shut-down turbines, nobody on the bridge realised the seriousness of the situation. When the true state of the ship emerged, the list and the fires were impeding all efforts to do anything other than what was actually done; and he repeatedly praised the efforts of sailors and officers to assist the soldiers getting ashore. Fregattenkapitän Heymann also submitted a brief statement, similarly dismissing the army's allegations, referring to his earlier report. Everything had been done to save as many as possible. Raeder and the SKL appear to have been content that the honour of the Kriegsmarine had been upheld, and the case was closed.[74]

After the war, Oberst Eriksen was the subject of no less than two investigation committees. Unbelievably, the main conclusion from both was that he had acted without specific orders. Eriksen died a bitter man in 1958. He has since been fully exonerated and, as part of the fifty-year commemoration of the liberation from the German occupation, King Harald unveiled a statue of him at Oscarsborg in 1995.[75]

Rauøy

Having cast off from *Emden* around 01:00, *R20* and *R24* headed for Rauøy with some ninety men from 1./IR 307 onboard under the command of Hauptmann Meng. The boats got lost in the fog and at the time they were supposed to have landed, an officer was sent ashore to find out where they were – and where to find Rauøy. He came back with directions after talking to some locals and they proceeded, trusting their luck. By the time they finally approached Rauøy, the fog had started to lift. The guns of the fort turned in their direction and there was no doubt they had been sighted, even if fire was not opened. Leutnant Jaeger of *R20* reckoned it would be possible to land the troops behind a headland north of the fort and eased his boat into the cove until the bow touched the bottom. The soldiers scrambled ashore in dinghies while *R24* continued to try to find a second landing site.

R20. (Author's collection)

* * *

Major Hersleb Enger at Rauøy knew it was not over when the unknown ships vanished northwards in the fog just before midnight. More ships were likely to follow and sooner or later those that had just passed would come back. An attack on the fort itself was possible and he ordered his men to remain at their guns while further ammunition was brought forward. Double manning was arranged for all sentries and lookouts. Around 04:30, Enger received a phone call from the mainland with information that a German officer had been asking for directions to Rauøy, and so he knew they were coming. Further infantry support was requested from Fredrikstad, but events developed too fast for this to arrive. At 05:30, *R20* was seen heading into the bay behind the headland while *R24* continued north. The cove could be seen from the battery but the landing site proper was covered. Kaptein Sørlie at the northern 15-cm battery ordered the crew of gun no. 1 forward with their handguns to a position at the battery perimeter while gun no. 2 was ordered to open indirect fire with high-explosive shells. Sørlie positioned himself at the gun, adjusting the sights in person, while Løytnant Eriksen was sent forward to the edge to observe and give corrections. The improvisations worked well and the disembarking German soldiers had to spread out and take cover to avoid casualties. Leutnant Jaeger backed *R20* off behind a smokescreen as soon as the last soldier was in the dinghy. Sørlie let his gun follow the boat, but no hits were scored and she suffered only splinter damage. Return fire from the R-boat's 20-mm guns was ineffective. During the battle, the fort's 40-mm A/A guns opened up on an approaching German aircraft. No hits were observed, but it later crashed north of Rauøy, killing its crew.[76] Disappearing in the fog, *R20* set course northwards to join up with *R24*, which had landed her soldiers without any resistance on the northernmost part of the island. Sørlie turned the fire of his gun back to the beach. There, however, the soldiers had regrouped and slipped away while out of the line of fire. Joined by the soldiers from *R24*, they prepared to move towards the fort.

Being informed of the German landings north of the northern battery, Major Enger ordered every available man on the island, including most of the crew from the southern battery and the A/A guns, into a defensive line close to the landing site. About a hundred men were in place around 06:15, including two heavy Colt machine guns. The Norwegians were too few and too inexperienced for a counter-attack, but the German soldiers could not advance either and had a steady attrition of their limited forces, as shelter was in demand.

Just before 08:00, Major Enger considered he had a firm upper hand, controlling the situation. Just then, a signal came from Oberstløytnant Notland, the commander of Oslofjord Fortress: 'Orders from Outer Oslofjord SDD. Stop all hostilities, cease firing.' Angered, Enger asked for the order to be verified, which it was. He had no choice but to instruct his soldiers to cease firing. No white flag could be found, but one of the soldiers had a reasonably clean shirt, which was hoisted on a pole, after which the German fire died down.

Hauptmann Meng, somewhat perplexed at the development, straightened his uniform and walked across to the Norwegian lines. He acted very politely towards Major Enger and expressed distress at being met by so much opposition when the German soldiers 'had come to help defend Norwegian neutrality'. He demanded that the fort should be surrendered intact. All NCOs and soldiers should hand in their weapons and uniforms, after which they were free to go home. The officers should remain and await further orders. After another conference with Notland, this was accepted. Enger was given some time to sort out his 'personal matters', which he used to burn files and destroy maps and codebooks. In the afternoon, he and his officers were taken to Horten by *R20* and *R24* while German naval gunners occupied Rauøy.

Two Norwegian soldiers were killed during the battle. German casualties have not been ascertained, but appear to have been substantial. Major Enger later held that his soldiers could have maintained the opposition for a considerable time and even been capable of defeating the landing force altogether. An extensive bombing attack would have been disastrous, though, as there was only limited shelter on the island; the final outcome was inevitable as long as German air and sea superiority was total.[77]

Bolærne

Completing the embarkation of two reinforced platoons from 2./IR 307 onto *R22* and *R23* from *Emden*, Stabsobersteuermann Karl Rixecker set course towards Bolærne around 01:00. The dousing of the navigation lights in the fjord made the passage difficult in the dense fog. Shortly after 04:00, anchors were dropped off a strandline Rixecker hoped to be the right one. He was far from sure, however, and decided to send a small reconnaissance force ashore to try to ascertain that they could reach Bolærne Fort from the landing site. Unknown to the Germans, they were off Vallø, which was not connected to Bolærne. Some twenty soldiers were disembarked to reconnoitre as dawn approached and the fog started to lift. Just as the last man jumped into the dinghy, a lookout sighted a submarine through the haze. Both R-boats raised anchor and turned towards the submarine, which started to dive when a warning shot was fired. Orders were given to prepare the depth charges.

Stabsobersteuermann Karl Rixecker of *R23*.
(Bundesarchiv Koblenz)

Kaptein Fjeldstad, commander of the 1st Undervannsbåtdivisjon at Melsomvik and captain of the submarine *A2*, received orders from Naval Command in the small hours of 9 April to deploy the boats at their operational area in the Oslofjord at dawn and prepare for battle. Before departure at 04:00, additional signals confirmed that the intruders were most likely German and, as they were inside Oslofjord Krigshavn, should be attacked on sight. *A3* and *A4* headed south from Teie while *A2* headed north towards its designated position north of the Bolærne–Rauøy line. The three submarines were of pre-WWI vintage and considered at least as dangerous to their own crews as to anything that might venture in front of their torpedo tubes.

Entering the main fjord around 05:00, Fjeldstad sighted two unknown vessels close to Vallø. Considering them too small for a torpedo he decided to dive to avoid them rather than engage in a gunfight.[78] The last thing Fjeldstad saw in the periscope as he dived were both vessels approaching at high speed, obviously attacking. The R-boats were fast and *A2* was only at twenty-five metres when they passed overhead, dropping six or seven depth charges. The submarine was forced back to surface by the explosions and the conning tower broke surface. The R-boats opened fire and the hail of 20-mm projectiles damaged the periscope. *A2* submerged again, this time diving so fast that bottom was touched at thirty-five metres. Continued depth-charge attacks damaged the submarine further and water started to leak into the boat at an alarming rate. To avoid total loss, Fjeldstad decided to surface and surrender. *R23* immediately came alongside and the shaken crew were taken onboard at gunpoint and locked below deck. A German naval flag was hoisted on *A2*, but she was left drifting in the fjord. *A3* and *A4* remained submerged all day due to 'intense aircraft activity' and returned to Teie by nightfall having achieved nothing.[79]

Having finished with *A2*, Stabsobersteuermann Rixecker realised that Bolærne could not be reached from Vallø and headed south, leaving the landed soldiers to themselves for the time being. On the way, the R-boats ran into the two auxiliaries, *Oter I* and *Skudd I*, which had been sent from Tønsberg to look for them. After a few inconclusive shots, the auxiliaries turned away while *R22* and *R23* hid behind a smokescreen.

A2 and *R21* at Teie on 14 April. *A2*, commissioned in 1913, held the dubious honour of being the oldest submarine in combat during WWII. (E Skjold collection)

The R-boats were observed from Bolærne, approaching from the north. Major Færden held his fire until the boats were only two thousand metres away; when he opened up, the 15-cm shells fell close. Rixecker ordered a zigzag course, but the Norwegian gunners followed skilfully. There was no way the lightly armed R-boats could fight back with any hope of success and Rixecker decided to turn back, lest the boats should be lost. Kaptein Fjeldstad was asked to go ashore to negotiate a ceasefire, but refused and was locked up again. Heading back to Horten for help, the R-boats again passed the auxiliaries at Vallø, which had been reinforced by *Ramoen* and *Treff*. A few shots were exchanged again, but as before, the R-boats sped off behind smoke. The soldiers onboard *R22* and *R23* were eventually landed at Åsgårdstrand and transferred to Horten in support of the meagre forces there.[80]

Kapitän Thiele requested that Bolærne was attacked by the Luftwaffe. The bombing commenced in the afternoon and everybody not strictly needed outside gathered in a tunnel behind the batteries. Apart from chasing the gunners into shelter, the aircraft inflicted little damage.

Next morning at 07:25 fire was opened on a German transport coming from the south. *Kondor* and *Albatros* were also sighted coming from the north in the company of some auxiliaries and fire was also opened on them. All ships turned away and Bolærne effectively controlled the traffic at the mouth of the Oslofjord. The guns could not take the extended live firing, however, and broke down one by one. The air attacks continued, but still had limited effect, aside from burning down some of the wooden houses on the island. The status of the 15-cm guns was discussed with Outer Oslofjord SDD at Tønsberg and it was agreed around 10:00 that further resistance was meaningless. Because of the air attacks, dismembering of the remaining guns and machine guns took some time and it was only at 12:30 that the Norwegian flag was lowered and the white flag was hoisted. Some sixty to sixty-five shells had been fired from the three 15-cm guns before they broke down. Later in the day, Bolærne was taken over by a force of German sailors from *Kondor*.[81]

By nightfall on 10 April, most of the Oslofjord was in German hands.[82] Still, few if any German transports dared venture up the fjord until the 11th, fearing submarines and mines.

Fornebu

In the spring of 1940 Oslo-Fornebu airport was the base for Jagevingen, the fighter wing of the army air force, equipped with nine Gloster Gladiator bi-plane fighters.[83] The 41-year-old Kaptein Erling Munthe-Dahl was C-in-C, but normally not flying, and Løytnant Rolf Tradin was in operative command of the squadron. For defence, the ground crew had three heavy Colt machine guns in pits south-east of the runways and two light machine guns in open positions to the north. A searchlight platoon was deployed south-west of the runways. This also had two Colt machine guns, but a limited field of fire onto the airfield proper.

In the evening of 8 April, seven Gladiators were serviceable. One aircraft was kept at five minutes' readiness, two more at stand-by. The engines of the remaining aircraft were run every two hours to keep them ready on short notice. Most of the men not on duty turned in before midnight. At 00:45, Munthe-Dahl returned from Oslo with the news of the forts in outer Oslofjord having opened fire on unidentified naval vessels and that air-raid sirens had been sounded in the city. It was too dark to fly yet and the aircraft were dispersed, pending dawn and further information. Around 04:00, the alarm went off: multi-engine aircraft were reported above the fog in the fjord. It was just light enough for two of the Gladiators to be sent off. Both encountered twin-engine aircraft, at least one of which was identified as a Do17, establishing the intruders as German. The aircraft vanished in the clouds before they could be intercepted.[84] Just before 06:00, three more Gladiators were sent off on a second patrol, but encountered nothing and returned some fifty minutes later.

Three airfields, Aalborg in northern Denmark, Sola-Stavanger and Oslo-Fornebu, were considered to be of such importance for German air superiority during Weserübung that they needed to be captured as early as possible: first, to bring in troops and supplies, secondly to use as forward bases to meet the inevitable Allied counter-attack. Hence, it would be critical to capture the fields in operational condition, including runways, defence installations and fuel dumps. Kjeller airfield north of Oslo would be strafed and bombed in the morning of 9 April, and secured later.

According to plan, some 340 Fallschirmjägers from 1st and 2nd Company of the 1st Battalion of the 1st Parachute Regiment would jump over Fornebu, led by Hauptmann Erich Walther.[85] Once the airfield was in German hands, IR 324 of 163rd ID would be flown in by transport aircraft, some 900 men in all. Supplies and heavy equipment would come by sea. To achieve tactical air superiority and to suppress the A/A defences, a flight of eight Bf110 heavy fighters from 1./ZG 76 under Oberleutnant Werner Hansen was added to the first wave. These would fly independently to Oslo and meet with the transports over Fornebu.[86]

The twenty-nine Junkers Ju52 transports of 5th and 6th Staffel of KGzbV 1, carrying the paratroopers of I/FschJgRgt 1, plus a special communication aircraft took off from Schleswig before dawn.[87] Over the Skagerrak they ran into low cloud and fog. Oberstleutnant Karl Drewes, commander of the first wave, was worried. Few of the pilots had much experience in instrument flying and when one aircraft reported by radio that two of the Junkers in its section had vanished, Drewes assumed they had collided in the fog and crashed. He had no reports of the conditions ahead and decided that this could not go on; they would have to turn back. The pilot of his aircraft, Oberleutnant Wilhelm Metscher wrote:

> Our mission this morning was on the edge of what I felt we were capable of. I was quite tense, and I am sure many of the others were as well. After taking off, we received two radio signals. The first saying that Denmark had surrendered, the second, which came a little later, over the Skagerrak, said there was opposition in Norway. Flying north, the weather gradually worsened and we encountered fog. Eventually, it was just one grey soup . . . Hauptmann Walther protested strongly at Drewes's decision [to turn back]. The other paratroopers later said the two argued loudly, shouting at each other. Walther meant the conditions were far from impossible. Here and there, openings in the fog

could be seen. Drewes, however, had made up his mind and as senior commander, enforced his decision. Walther was deeply disappointed.[88]

While Oberleutnant Metscher banked his aircraft in a wide left-hand turn, Drewes ordered the radio operator to notify the other aircraft and then send a radio signal to Oberst von Gablenz, Transportchef Land in Hamburg, informing him that the formation was turning back due to poor weather conditions. Three of the aircraft, the two carrying the battalion staff and the communication aircraft, did not receive the order to turn, or ignored it, and continued.

Von Gablenz forwarded the signal to Generalleutnant Geisler, commander of X Fliegerkorps, who found himself in an agonising dilemma. The second wave of Ju52s from KGzbV 103, with soldiers from II/IR 324, was already airborne. These fifty-three aircraft carried infantry and would have to land at Fornebu to unload their troops. Geisler had no choice: landing the slow, fully laden Junkers on a non-secured airfield was too much of a risk. The second wave would also have to turn back. The airborne attack on Oslo was about to fall apart.

Hauptmann Richard Wagner, in charge of the second wave, was a Luftwaffe airborne infantry officer and subordinated to Transportchef Land. The order to turn back, however, came from X Fliegerkorps. It read: 'Wegen Wetterlage Ruckflug Schleswig' – 'Return to Schleswig due to weather conditions' – and was not specifically addressed to KGzbV 103. As conditions over the Skagerrak were improving rapidly, Wagner decided the signal did not apply to him and continued towards Oslo as planned. At about the same time, Oberleutnant Hansen's eight Bf110s came out of the fog into clear weather south of Oslo.

Ju52 aircraft coming up the Oslofjord in the morning of 9 April. (Forsvarsmuseet)

There were no sign of any Junkers, but a large number of He111 bombers were going up the fjord.

When further aircraft were reported over the Oslofjord shortly before 07:00, five Gladiators led by Løytnant Tradin were scrambled from Fornebu. The last two operational aircraft followed shortly after. Tradin took his group south towards Nesodden and soon sighted a column of smoke north of Oscarsborg. They reckoned it was from a sunken ship, but had no idea what had happened. After having been airborne for some forty minutes, eight 'twin-engine fighters' were sighted, followed by numerous bombers, around fifty altogether. With ten to one against them the Gladiators could not hope to stop the German attack, only inflict maximum damage and survive to fight another day. Tradin ordered every man for himself. The Bf110s were completely surprised by the nimble Gladiators, which could outmanoeuvre them with some ease. The Germans used tracer ammunition and the Norwegian pilots later agreed this made it easy for them to avoid the stream of bullets. Of the eight Bf110s, two were shot down and two more seriously damaged. At least two He111 bombers were also shot down. Only one Gladiator was lost, force-landing purposely to avoid further damage. The Gladiators eventually ran out of ammunition and landed wherever they could as Fornebu was under attack. Most of them were damaged and none flew into battle again.[89] At least one Ju52 from KGzbV 103 was shot down by the A/A batteries around Oslo and almost all aircraft of the first wave were damaged. Some fifty to sixty soldiers and crewmembers were dead or wounded inside the aircraft when they landed.[90]

With the Gladiators out of the way, the remaining Bf110s began strafing the A/A defences at Fornebu as planned. The machine-gun crews took the challenge; if the stream of tracers got too close, they had time to dive into cover and only a few were lightly wounded. On the other hand, the A/A fire seemed to have a limited effect on the aircraft, the bullets bouncing off the armour as long as they stayed high. The two light machine guns at the northern end of the field ran out of ammunition, and as the key to the depot bunker could not be found, so the guns had to be abandoned. The men in the concrete pits south-east of the runways had more ammunition stacked, and stubbornly stayed by their guns.

There was no sign of the Junkers with the paratroopers; the situation was becoming difficult for Hansen. It had been taken for granted that the Bf110s could land once the airfield had been secured and could then refuel from Norwegian supplies. Now, the fuel gauges of the Messerschmitts were sinking towards empty and they would have to land somewhere, or end up as wrecks around the countryside. Just as things were getting desperate, around 08:20, Hansen was relieved to see three Ju52s approaching. The lead aircraft lined up on the airfield, but did not drop parachutes as expected; instead, it continued descending towards the runway. This was the Junker commanded by Hauptmann Wagner. Unaware that the airfield was still in Norwegian hands, he ordered his pilot Oberfeldwebel Sievert to approach for a landing from the south. Just as the wheels touched down a hail of machine-gun bullets tore into the lumbering transport. Sievert instinctively pushed the throttles forward, climbing out of range, with Wagner and several of the troopers dead inside. Sersjant Tellefsen, who had fired a full band of tracer ammunition into the hull of the Junker from his Colt machine gun, looked at the aircraft taking off again with amazement.

The situation had gone from bad to worse and Hansen realised he would have to make some decisions – quickly. Lieutenant Helmut Lent was ordered to try to land while Hansen and the other Messerschmitts kept the Norwegian machine-gunners down. Lent had no problems accepting the order. He was almost out of fuel and had already shut down his starboard engine to conserve what was left. Landing a Bf110 with one engine was no easy task, and the heavy plane was well above normal landing speed as it bounced onto the airstrip at a crazy angle. Machine-gun bullets riddled the fuselage, but none hit the cockpit. Continuing beyond the runway and down a grassy bank, the undercarriage broke off and with bent propellers the Bf110 came to rest halfway through the picket fence of a nearby house. Shaken but unhurt, Lent and his navigator Gefreiter Walter Kubisch climbed from the wreckage, watching the other Bf110s come in one by one. Fire was still coming from the Norwegian machine-gun positions, but all aircraft landed safely and were parked to the north of the runway, as far away as possible. Lent and Kubisch scrambled to rejoin the group and some of the rear-gunners dismounted their machine guns, making a defensive position behind a nearby brink.[91]

Some of the Junkers of Wagner's KGzbV 103 followed their lead aircraft south after the unsuccessful landing attempt. Others, seeing the Bf110s landing, believed the airfield was captured and set down. The first was Hauptmann Peter Ingenhoven, Wagner's second-in-command. Safely on the ground, he took charge and started to organise the situation.[92] Most of the aircraft landing early were riddled by the Norwegian machine-gun fire and damaged, several with dead or wounded inside. At 08:33 the aircraft carrying the staff

A Ju52 transport coming in to land at Fornebu. Below is the crashed Bf110 of Lent and Kubisch. (Bundesarchiv Koblenz)

of 1st Battalion of the Parachute Regiment led by Oberleutnant Götte arrived. Seeing German aircraft on the ground, he decided there was no reason to jump and the flight landed swiftly. Thus, there would be no paratroopers jumping at Fornebu that day.

Air Attaché Spiller had spent the early hours of the morning at the house of Alfred Kleinman, very near to where Lent's aircraft crash-landed. Seeing the first Ju52s landing, he dodged the Norwegian guards and ran for the German perimeter. After duly welcoming the Messerschmitt pilots and their observers, Spiller urged for a signal to be sent to Hamburg that Fornebu was under German control. Hansen, never one to diminish his own role, had the following signal sent from the communication Junker, which had just landed: 'Fornebu in own hands. 1. Staffel, Zerstörergruppe 76.' The signal was received at Aalborg and forwarded to Hotel Esplanade in Hamburg where it was received with astonishment.

The order to turn back from Fornebu was immediately reversed and all aircraft ordered to head for Oslo. Some Junkers turned round in mid-air once more, expecting to be refuelled at Fornebu; others took off from airports, fields, roads or wherever they had landed in Denmark, pending new orders. They arrived randomly, heavily laden and low on fuel. Fornebu was small, the approach was difficult and with no air-traffic control it went wrong for many. At least fifteen German transport aircraft crashed fatally at or near Fornebu on invasion day. Others collided on the tarmac. Many soldiers died and many more were wounded. The Norwegian machine-gun fire gradually subsided as the guns ran out of ammunition or overheated and the gunners watched helplessly as more and more aircraft landed. The Junkers able to take off again were sent to Aalborg for repairs and to reload as soon as ready to clear the way for others; slowly some kind of order was established. During the morning, most of I and II/IR 324, a pioneer company, parts of III/IR 159 and some administrative personnel landed at Fornebu – as did Hauptmann Walther and his paratroopers, having temporarily landed at Aalborg. Oberst Nickelmann, C-in-C of IR 324, could start considering the move towards Oslo.[93]

At 12:15, Oberstleutnant Pohlman sent a telegram from the embassy: 'Just back from Fornebu. Five companies with Oberst Nickelmann have landed. Only twelve paratroopers arrived. Eight transport machines from 6th Group crashed due to ground fire. Few losses. A/A machine-gun fire suppressed by landed troops. Embassy secured by guards. Entry to Oslo by Group Nickelmann imminent. No news of the warships.'[94]

As the Germans were growing in number and seemed to be getting organised, Kaptein Munthe-Dahl saw no other solution than pulling back in order to avoid being overrun. The reinforcement requested was apparently not coming. Most of the personnel of Jagevingen left Fornebu on foot or in trucks around 10:00. There were still armed Norwegian soldiers scattered around at the airfield, some of them sniping the incoming aircraft throughout the day.[95]

At Fornebu, the three operational Bf110s were refuelled from captured fuel depots, which nobody had apparently considered destroying, and established a continuous patrol around the airfield securing the inbound flight routes. During the afternoon, this was reduced to a standing patrol on the ground to conserve fuel. Around 17:30, a British Sunderland flying-boat was reported over inner Oslofjord. The Sunderland, flown by Flight Lieutenant Peter Kite of 210 Squadron, was ill suited for low-level reconnaissance over land, but the mission was improvised, as were most other things on the Allied side that day. The intruder was hit by A/A fire over Oslo harbour, and shortly after intercepted by Hansen and Lent, who mercilessly shot it down. Of the ten-man crew, only the 21-year-old wireless operator Sergeant Ogwyn George survived, tumbling out of the aircraft when it broke up in mid-air and falling some one thousand metres without a parachute.[96]

Chaos

The first German bombers, twenty-five He111s of III/KG 26, arrived over Oslo at dawn. Later a further fourteen He111s of KGr 100 appeared. These aircraft were to 'demonstrate' over the capital, intimidating the Norwegians into accepting the occupation. Passing up the Oslofjord, they saw the burning *Blücher* behind the Narrows and realised there would be no peaceful occupation. Indeed, shortly after, orders were given to attack Fornebu, Kjeller and Oscarsborg while others bombed and strafed targets opportunistically. Around 12:15, six Ju87 Stuka dive-bombers from I/StG 1, led by Oberleutnant Bruno Dilley, arrived.[97]

At Oscarsborg the bombs of the rest of the squadron had made little impression. At Akershus, however, there were a large number of soldiers or civilians in the open courtyards. Hearing the scream of the diving Stukas, they scrambled into any archway or building believed to give protection. Luckily, Dilley's flight was not up to standard on this day, most probably because they were disturbed by dense A/A fire, and three of the bombs went into the sea, one hit a nearby island and only two hit the fortress, both of them outside the centre courtyards. Nobody was killed, but many were wounded and those not under order to remain evacuated rapidly. Thus, when the first Germans arrived at Akershus not long after, they could drive their trucks right into the fort. Oberst Nickelmann sought out the commander, Oberst HP Schnitler, who had been left behind at Akershus when the General Staff evacuated, and demanded an immediate surrender. Schnitler managed to contact Prime Minister Nygaardsvold at Hamar and received permission to surrender the city to avoid bloodshed. The capitulation was agreed at 14:00

German soldiers marching into Oslo. The brazen bluff succeeded and no shots were fired. (Forsvarsmuseet)

A photo taken at Akershus shortly after the capitulation at 14:00. Oberst Schnitler is seen talking to some German officers. The man on the left is wearing a Fallschirmjäger jump-suit. (T Eggan collection)

and half an hour later the first German troops marched brazenly into Oslo in columns of five. Some spectators booed, but most watched, dazed, trying to comprehend what was going on.

By nightfall on 9 April there were probably less than one thousand Germans in Oslo. They had all come by air and lacked heavy weapons. Next day, *Lützow* and *Emden* arrived, more soldiers were flown in and the situation improved somewhat. The transport ships, which should have arrived in the afternoon of the 9th, eventually did not arrive until the 12th and it would take a week before the German forces were established in Oslo and could consider securing the rest of eastern Norway.

General von Falkenhorst was supposed to arrive in Oslo in the afternoon of 9 April. This was cancelled as the events unfolded, and it was not until 16:00 on the 10th that he arrived at Fornebu with Admiral Hermann Boehm, the designated 'Commanding Admiral Norway'.[98] In accordance with previous decisions, Boehm did not report to von Falkenhorst, but the two senior officers had orders 'to collaborate'.[99] Boehm later told Raeder that upon arrival he found a chaos he was not prepared for. Nobody had any overview of what was under German control and what was not. Army, air force and navy personnel were deployed as they appeared and just about everything had to be improvised. Oberstleutnant Pohlman took charge of the efforts and Oberleutnant Kempf was ordered ashore from *Widar* to help Oberst Nickelmann secure control of key points of Oslo, including the by now mostly abandoned A/A positions. Erich Pruck, the Abwehr agent, was assigned a temporary staff for his newly established intelligence office, Abwehrstelle Norwegen, until a proper intelligence staff could be transferred from Germany.[100] On the 10th, Korvettenkapitän Förster, *Blücher*'s navigation officer,

General von Falkenhorst arriving at Fornebu around 16:00 on 10 April, one day later than planned. The man in civilian dress talking to von Falkenhorst is Curt Bräuer, the German ambassador, with Oberstleutnant Hartvig Pohlman next to him. To von Falkenhorst's left, in naval uniform, is Admiral Hermann Boehm, the designated 'Commanding Admiral Norway'. (Author's collection)

was appointed harbourmaster, replacing the missing Korvettenkapitän Karlowa. Naval Attaché Schreiber was sent to Horten to take care of matters there and ensure the yard remained operational. Communication with Germany and within Norway was difficult, and when *Emden* arrived, Kapitän Lange received instructions to make its radio room available to the commanders. Slowly things became normal, not least because no British or Norwegian counter-attacks developed, but only on 13 April had the 163rd ID reached its goals of securing the Oslo area as far as Hønefoss, Drammen and Kongsberg.[101]

— 6 —

Ultimatum

The War Has Already Started

LATE AT NIGHT ON 8 April, Halvdan Koht went for a stroll in the quiet streets of Oslo to relax and clear his mind. To his surprise, his thoughts were interrupted by air-raid sirens just after midnight and the streetlights were turned off. He found a public telephone and called the front desk of the Foreign Office where he learned that warships had entered the Oslofjord and that Prime Minister Nygaardsvold had called for a Cabinet meeting at 01:30. Taxis were not to be found and so the foreign minister hastened through the darkened city on foot.

At Oslo Militære Samfund, King Haakon had retired early, but many officers remained discussing the recent events. Shortly after midnight, the air-raid sirens aroused a frantic ringing of telephones in the reception. Few waited to take the calls, but hurried back to their offices at the Ministry of Defence or Akershus. None of them realised that Norway had just entered the war.

Towards midnight, while the General Staff dispersed for the night, the commanding admiral, most of the Admiral Staff and the naval intelligence office remained in the naval wing of the Ministry of Defence. When the signal from SDD1 in Horten of warships in outer Oslofjord came at 23:15 followed by the signal 'Rauøy and Bolærne in battle' at 23:50, tension rose sharply. Though not confirmed, it was believed that the intruders were German, but it was not clear whether they were escaping from a superior Allied naval force in the Skagerrak or some sort of attack was under way. Orders were issued to Kontreadmiral Smith-Johannsen in Horten that the mines between Rauøy and Bolærne should be laid. Around 01:00, the British naval attaché, Rear Admiral Boyes showed up again, forwarding information of German ships passing through the Belts and asking if there were mines in the Oslofjord. After conferring with the commanding admiral, Chief of Staff Corneliussen answered, no, there were no mines in the eastern seaways. According to Steen, there was no discussion at this point between Boyes and the Admiral Staff regarding British ships in the Skagerrak and the attaché left a few minutes later.[1]

The events escalated when SDD2 in Bergen reported at 02:06 that 'five large and two small German warships' had entered the Leads. This was more than an occasional breach of neutrality. Twenty minutes later, Bergen reported that Lerøy Fort had opened fire. Just before 03:00 SDD1 reported 'four large cruisers and submarines' heading up the Oslofjord and shortly after, Trøndelag SDS in Trondheim reported unidentified warships penetrating the Agdenes defences. At 04:14 SDD3 in Tromsø reported intruders in Ofotfjorden off Narvik. The first report from Oscarsborg came at 04:28 and when Kristiansand reported at close to 06:00 that Odderøya Fort in Kristiansand had beaten off warships attempting to enter that harbour too, there was no longer the slightest doubt that a German attack on Norway was underway. Hence, it was decided to implement the SOK.[2]

The neutrality instructions called for all available measures to be used against intruding warships in the krigshavn or restricted areas and the commanding admiral saw no need to issue any further orders to the units in Oslofjord, Kristiansand, Bergen or Trondheim. Narvik was not a krigshavn and the commanding admiral confirmed a request from Kommandørkaptein Askim that fire should be opened. When it was clear that the intruders were German, a supplementary order was issued at 04:20 after Diesen had been in contact with Koht: 'Do not fire on British vessels, fire on German.' Except for the order to SDD1 at 00:12 to start the laying of mines between Rauøy and Bolærne (which could not be implemented as the minelayers were not ready) and at 01:40 for the submarines at Teie to move to their patrol areas, no other direct orders were issued from the commanding admiral or the SOK to any of the SDDs during the night of 8/9 April.[3]

Receiving notification from the Admiral Staff at 23:23 of unknown warships in outer Oslofjord, the officer on duty at the General Staff, Kaptein Rolstad, telephoned Oberst Hatledal. The Chief of Staff had asked not to be disturbed unless something special happened, but Rolstad considered this to be well within requirements. Hatledal agreed and said he would come to Akershus immediately. Meanwhile, he told Rolstad to alert 1st Division at Halden and the commanding general. Laake lived on a farm some way outside Oslo and, having just arrived home, he at first declined to come back. Rolstad then held the telephone receiver out of the window for him to hear the air-raid sirens, which had just started, and he grudgingly agreed to come as soon as he could find a taxi.[4]

Prime Minister Nygaardsvold was wakened at 23:30 by a call from Ljungberg with information of warships in outer Oslofjord. Ljungberg called again just before midnight, this time with news that Bolærne and Rauøy had opened fire on the ships, without being able to ascertain their nationality. Shortly after, Minister of Justice Terje Wold called, suggesting the government should assemble and they agreed on the Foreign Office at Victoria Terrasse as the most convenient place. He dressed and hastened from his home. Most of the other ministers had gone to bed, or were about to, when they received the call to gather. Koht arrived at 01:15 as one of the last. The reports poured in fast, each more sinister than the last. As King Haakon was not present, there was no formal Statsråd and no minutes were taken during the night. Thus, it has been difficult to reconstruct accurately what happened and who said and did what.[5]

Shortly after 02:00, Diesen forwarded reports from SDD2 that warships identified as German were approaching Bergen. The British notes of the day before, stating that the Royal Navy would 'guard the minefields for forty-eight hours', made the ministers take it for granted there was an Allied fleet off the coast and that this would intercept the German warships in the west. Neither Ljungberg nor Koht found the time to summarise the incoming warnings of the day before, and the government remained unaware that a German fleet was reported to be heading for Narvik.

Nygaardsvold later wrote:

It was an ominous night. I understood we faced a war-game between the belligerents. It was not we, but the powers at war that would fight over Norway. We however, would pay the price. A call was made to the British minister to find out if he had any information from his government, but he was asleep and knew nothing. England slept . . .[6]

It was Koht who called the British minister in Oslo, Cecil Dormer, at 02:10 to tell him that 'four big German warships' were coming up the Oslofjord. The ships had been fired at and Koht believed that 'The defences of Oslo might succeed in repelling them.' Further warships were approaching Bergen and Stavanger, and Koht stated explicitly 'so now we are at war'. When Dormer asked if the government intended to remain in Oslo, Koht said they did, as he 'thought the defences strong enough' and that it would therefore be unnecessary to evacuate the capital. Not long after, Naval Attaché Boyes returned from the Admiral Staff with additional information and Dormer called the US ambassador, Mrs Harriman, asking her to take over the British Legation. He must have had a premonition that they would have to leave Oslo, even if Koht said he would stay. A telegram summarising the information was sent to London, where it arrived about an hour later and was forwarded to the duty officer at the War Cabinet, as well as the Admiralty, War Office and Air Ministry. Around 04:00 Koht telephoned again informing Dormer that German warships were now also approaching Trondheim. Koht knew that the British Legation was in possession of a wireless telegraphy set and expected that Dormer would be able to forward the information to London independent of the public networks.[7]

Neither commanding admiral nor commanding general was invited to Victoria Terrasse. Neither did the commanders take any initiatives to meet with the government themselves or have any liaison officers attached to the administration. All communication between the government and the military during the night would depend on Defence Minister Ljungberg. This was to be most unfortunate and would lead to irreparable misunderstandings. Apart from Ljungberg, few of the ministers were familiar with the procedures and terminology for the mobilisation of the armed forces and none of them

Cecil Dormer (right), British minister in Oslo, here with Trygve Lie, minister of supply, onboard *Glasgow* after they had left Tromsø for Britain in June. (Krigsarkivet/Scanpix)

realised that even if armed and in uniform, the poorly trained soldiers of the Norwegian Army were not necessarily fit for combat. Likewise, none except Ljungberg, and possibly Wold, knew that, fearing civil unrest in the 1920s, tens of thousands of rifles and hundreds of artillery guns had been stored in an unserviceable manner with firing pins, box staples and ammunition kept in bunkers or forts kilometres apart; until all parts were issued and assembled, the guns were useless. Steps had been taken by Laake and Hatledal to restore the depots, but little had happened.[8]

Around 02:30, Ljungberg accepted a telephone call from the commanding general, who had just arrived in his office. Laake suggested mobilisation of the field brigades in southern Norway, the smallest of the alternatives discussed the day before. How he could propose this – which by definition was 'partial and quiet' and would take several days, unless specifically decided otherwise – is beyond belief, considering there were warships coming up Oslofjord.[9] To the Investigating Committee, Laake held there were 'no reports of any landings' and he never even considered 'to mobilise the whole lot'. Laake did not appreciate the seriousness of the situation; 'It won't hurt to give these units a bit of practice,' he is alleged to have told his staff. Ljungberg asked Laake to wait by the telephone while he consulted the government. Not long after, he was back saying it was acceptable to mobilise 'the field brigades of southern Norway'. Laake referred the conversation to Oberst Hatledal, who had tried several times himself to get in touch with Ljungberg over the telephone, without success. Hatledal argued angrily that a quiet mobilisation was not possible and would be catastrophic in the current situation. Commanding General Laake fended off the protests, referring to the minister who was on his way from Victoria Terrasse. Meanwhile, perturbed commanders from all over the country called the General Staff. German warships were entering the fjords and they needed orders. No orders were given and they were left to act on their own initiative.

When Ljungberg arrived at the General Staff around 03:00, accompanied by Trygve Lie, Hatledal once more protested firmly. A partial mobilisation meant calling the men by mail or telegram, which would take a minimum of three days – as Ljungberg very well knew. The only process feasible at this stage, Hatledal held, would be a full and open mobilisation whereby the call could be made immediately over radio. Ljungberg was firm, however: a partial mobilisation was what had been decided by the government. Lie wanted to get back as soon as possible and urged Ljungberg to finish, which he did, and the two ministers left. The officers of the General Staff were shocked, Hatledal so much that he defiantly set the first mobilisation day as 11 April. The orders were drafted during the night and hand delivered to the telegraph office in Oslo by an officer around 05:30. As no warnings had been given, the telegraph office had closed as normal the evening before. Hence, the mobilisation orders were not sent until it reopened at 08:00 on the 9th – by which time it was meaningless.[10]

All ministers except Ljungberg later held that a decision for 'general mobilisation' had been taken during the morning, 'before the arrival of the German minister'. When asked by the Investigating Committee the exact nature of the decision, though, the answers became more diverse and the orders given by Ljungberg to Laake cannot be verified. Trygve Lie wrote that a decision to oppose was taken by the government, including a 'full and immediate mobilisation of all forces'. He even held he had this verified after coming back from the General Staff, but he did not ensure that Hatledal and Laake were aware of this. Ljungberg later maintained that a decision of general mobilisation was taken by the government between 04:30 and 05:00 – after the ultimatum from Bräuer had been rejected. He also asserted that he immediately telephoned the revised order to the General Staff. Nobody there could recall taking such a call from the minister, and Laake, Hatledal, Wrede-Holm and Rolstad later firmly denied having received any revised orders. Trygve Lie supported Ljungberg's account, but could not verify any details of the conversation he supposedly overheard.[11]

The mobilisation issue remains one of the most controversial issues of 9 April. Apparently most members of the government *believed* they had ordered a general and immediate mobilisation some time during the early hours of the 9th. The ministers did not have the competence to formulate their intention in military terms, however, and it was never properly ascertained that Ljungberg and the General Staff understood what the government wanted – a situation of misperception and poor communication, for which the responsibility rested with the government. The responsibility for having the government formulate clear instructions and forwarding them, through the Ministry of Defence, to the commanding general, commanding admiral and their respective staffs rested with Birger Ljungberg. Judging from the other minister's accounts, it is almost inconceivable that he did not understand what Nygaardsvold, Koht, Lie, Torp and the others believed they had decided. The responsibility for making sure the government had all the information it needed and that the consequences of its orders, or lack of them, were understood rested with Laake and Diesen, who also must take responsibility for not letting the government appreciate that their instructions were ambiguous and, as the situation developed, meaningless. The government, on their side, however incompetent in military matters, must take the responsibility for failing to call the commanding officers or their Chiefs of Staffs to Victoria Terrasse to share information, ascertain that intentions were understood and to verify that orders could be implemented – and if not, what alternatives existed. From the time it was known that German ships were entering more than just outer Oslofjord, nothing but a full and immediate mobilisation would do, irrespective of previous plans and concepts.

At 04:30, German Minister Bräuer was at Victoria Terrasse, insisting that he speak to Koht.[12] They met in the library next to where the government was assembled. Appropriately for the situation, there was only candlelight due to the blackout, giving the room an eerie atmosphere. Bräuer was polite and correct as always, but there was an 'uncommonly cold tone' to his voice, Koht later wrote.

Bräuer presented a nineteen-page memorandum, where it was held that Germany, against its wishes, had been drawn into a war with the Allies. As they did not dare to attack Germany on mainland Europe they had 'shifted the theatre of war to neutral territory' and Norway was neither able nor willing to oppose the Allied pressure. The German armed forces had therefore commenced 'certain military operations [to] take over the protection of the Kingdom of Norway'. The sole purpose of the operation, it was held, was to prevent 'the intended occupation of bases in Norway by Anglo-French forces'. All military installations would have to be surrendered, but there were no 'hostile intentions'. If opposition was met, however, all necessary means would be employed and the German forces entering Norway at this very moment were formidable. To avoid unnecessary bloodshed, an 'immediate military and administrative co-operation' was advised 'and information thereof sent to the armed forces, with orders to avoid friction or difficulty'.

Koht listened to Bräuer's monologue, emphasising key points from the memorandum, with a sinking heart. This he had feared, but not really expected. Should the ultimatum be accepted, it would mean the end of Norway's independence and most certainly war with Britain and France.

When Bräuer eventually finished, Koht, who knew that fire had been opened on the German ships and that the plan of a fait accomplis had failed, answered that this was such an important matter it would have to be decided by the government. Bräuer said, no, there was no time for that, events were unfolding too fast. Koht insisted, and as the government was only next-door, Bräuer would have to wait. 'As I left,' Koht later wrote, 'I quoted to him the words of his own Führer: "a people who submissively give in to a violator, does not deserve to live."'

Hearing a brief résumé of the German demands, Prime Minister Nygaardsvold and the other ministers unanimously dismissed the demands as totally unacceptable. Koht returned to Bräuer with the brief answer from the government, adding that Norway wished to maintain its independence and Germany 'had no right to do what they were now doing to the Norwegian people'. Dismayed, Bräuer answered: 'Then nothing can save you. This means war.' Koht concluded: 'The war has already started.'[13]

Bräuer hurried back to the embassy. Too upset to use any predetermined codes, he sent the following telegram in standard code:

> Have presented the Foreign Minister at 05:20 German time with our demands in firm, insisting manner and explained the reasons for them as well as handed the memorandum to him. The minister withdrew for consultations with the government . . . After a few minutes he returned with the answer: We do not willingly give in; the war has already started.[14]

The Norwegian government made several wrong or at best confused decisions during 9 April. The decision to defend Norway's independence, however, was clear and undisputed, even if this would bring the country into the war. Stortingspresident Hambro had been crystal clear in the Storting on 8 April: 'The thought of going to war against Great Britain is absurd.' Thus, even if Nygaardsvold and his government were unprepared and stumbled severely, they made a swift and resolute decision when needed, which placed them firmly on the Allied side. The weakest armed forces in Europe would stand up to the strongest – contrary to all expectations.

To Feed the Flames

After Bräuer had left the Foreign Office, Prime Minister Nygaardsvold called the president of the Parliament, Carl Joachim Hambro, asking him to come to Victoria Terrasse.[15] Hambro had to be awakened by his wife and only grudgingly gave up his first chance to rest properly for several days. Once awoken though, Hambro initiated a series of actions that eventually would frustrate the German plans to capture the king and government and change the course of the ensuing campaign. A few telephone calls to the prime minister and defence minister, as well as some news agencies, put him in the picture and towards 03:30 Hambro realised a German invasion of Norway had commenced. The capital was an obvious target and the German intruders had for several hours been reported coming up the Oslofjord. If they entered Oslo, detaining King Haakon, the government and the Parliament, everything would be over in a few hours. Hambro decided they would have to evacuate to a safer place. Hamar, some 130 kilometres to the north, was a natural choice; not too far away and with good communications back to the capital as well as onwards, should that become necessary. Not conferring with anybody else for the moment, he called key staff at the Parliament, instructing them to prepare an evacuation of protocols, files and other secret material. He also called the National Railway Company, leaving instructions for a priority train to be ready at Oslo main station around 07:00. Then he went to the Parliament to check the status of the packing and verify that the MPs were being given notice to leave within a couple of hours, before he continued to the Foreign Office.

At Victoria Terrasse, Hambro advised an immediate evacuation of the administration to Hamar. Koht was reluctant to leave the capital as he reckoned the Germans would not get past Oscarsborg and there were no reports of landings yet. Hambro had his way, though. Nygaardsvold called King Haakon to update him on the dismissal of the German ultimatum and the decision to depart. The king accepted immediately and agreed to be at the railway station with his family when the train was ready. The ministers left Victoria Terrasse between 05:30 and 06:30, most of them hurrying to their respective departments to ensure a proper evacuation of personnel, documents and other material. Some prioritised their families and went home or at least called to ensure they were aware of the situation and what to do. When the train eventually left at 07:23, King Haakon was onboard with most of his family and staff, as were five of the ministers (Koht, Ystegaard, Støstad, Frihagen and Hindal), several MPs, civil servants and senior staff from the ministries and administrative personnel of the Parliament. A number of ministers and members of the Diplomatic Corps who had been made aware of the evacuation also joined the train and civilians wishing to get out of the city were allowed onboard if they could find a place. Nobody asked for tickets.[16]

On the platform, just as he was entering the train, Koht was approached by some journalists, asking what was going on. He explained that the German minister had visited him that same morning informing him that German troops had landed at several places on the coast. The government considered this an unprecedented act of violence and had unanimously refused to succumb, he said, adding that he hoped the situation could be resolved shortly. Koht revealed that the government and king were relocating to Hamar and concluded by saying that a general order to mobilise the armed forces had been issued that same night. His words were transcribed into a statement, which was read over the radio several times that morning. His words on the mobilisation, which differed from what was actually going on, added to the confusion, but also made many hasten to the depots and barracks, not waiting for the mobilisation papers.[17]

*   *   *

Finance Minister Oscar Torp and the managing director of the Bank of Norway (Norges Bank) Nicolai Rygg had long since agreed that should a crisis emerge, money, bonds and gold reserves would have to be evacuated from the capital. Most of the gold reserves had been sent to the USA in 1938–39, but some 120 million NoK remained in the vaults. Packing of this was initiated during 8 April and transportation planned for the next morning. During the night, Rygg was awakened by a call from one of Torp's secretaries with instructions to commence the evacuation at once. Within a few hours, some fifty tons of gold and other valuables were loaded onto the trucks and just before dawn they started for Lillehammer, one by one.[18]

At the British Legation, Minister Dormer dressed hurriedly after Koht's first telephone call and gave instructions for the staff to start preparing for the destruction of files and documents. Margaret Reid, assistant to Frank Foley, passport control officer and head of MI6, put the events into her diary a few weeks later:

> I slept soundly while the Germans were sailing up Oslofjord until the . . . telephone brought me leaping from my bed . . . 'Come to the office at once, will you – and be ready to go!' . . . The taxi exchange refused to send me a car, but fortunately I hailed one in the main road and reached the office in time. [MI6 officers Foley and Newill,] were tearing files out of their drawers in the open safes . . . We drove in a taxi to the Legation by the back way to avoid being seen from the German Legation, which faced ours on Drammensveien. We saw a great bonfire before we reached the grounds . . . and were soon frantically rending code books and files to feed the flames.[19]

At 03:55, a brief telegram from Dormer arrived at the Foreign Office in London, leaving no doubt as to the seriousness of the situation: 'Am burning cyphers archives'. It was followed within half an hour by a request no less sinister: 'Can you give me any information helpful in deciding direction of eventual evacuation from here?'[20]

Rear Admiral Boyes was instructed to call French Minister de Dampierre and invite him and his attachés to come to the British Legation for information and coordination.[21] At 05:30, Undersecretary of State Jens Bull called from the Foreign Office, informing him that a train would be leaving Oslo at 07:00, taking 'the government, members of the Storting, and the Diplomatic Corps who wished to stay with the government' to Hamar. There was no new information on the German warships in the Oslofjord, but Dormer and de Dampierre decided it was time to leave. After having confirmed that the US Legation would take care of British interests in Oslo, the two ministers left by car around 06:45, accompanied by their spouses and staff. At that hour everything in Oslo appeared normal and there was little traffic. The rest of the staff and other British citizens alerted during the night followed as soon as cars could be provided, or they headed for the railway station.[22]

After issuing the orders for the partial mobilisation, the General Staff decided to evacuate from Akershus, which was vulnerable to air and sea attacks and headed for Slemdal Hotel, north of Oslo. Oberst Hatledal was among the last to leave, around 06:30. Commanding General Laake, who still did not see the gravity of the situation, decided to go via his home and told Hatledal he would arrive at Slemdal 'around 10:00'. At the same time it was

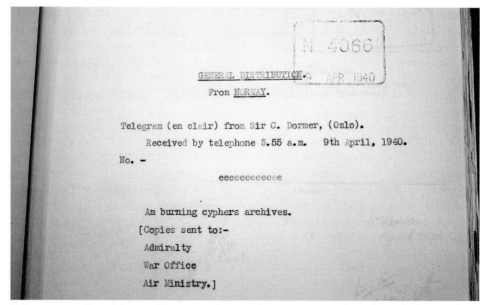

Telegram sent from Minister Dormer at the British Legation in Oslo in the early hours of 9 April (FO 371/24834)

decided to dissolve the General Staff and establish Hærens Overkommando (HOK) – the Army Supreme Command. A number of the officers usually assigned to the General Staff were meant to join field units during mobilisation and the HOK would in theory consist of the commanding general and some ten officers.

At Slemdal, nothing was prepared for the arrival of the HOK and the hotel was full of civilian guests, making the place completely unfit for purpose, in spite of their elaborate plans. After a while Hatledal decided they should continue towards Eidsvoll. Laake had not yet turned up and as nobody was left behind to wait for him, he found the hotel empty when he arrived. Laake eventually found a seat on one of the last trains leaving Oslo and was reunited with his officers at Eidsvoll in the early afternoon. Contact with most divisions and field units was sporadic during the day. Later, Defence Minister Ljungberg came by and after a brief update ordered Laake and Hatledal to join him near Hamar and the government, once again separating the commanding general from his staff. For all practical purposes, HOK did not function on 9 April.

Being informed of the German ultimatum and the likely consequences of its dismissal, the SOK also decided to withdraw to a safer location around 06:30. At that time, information had just been received from Tromsø that German warships were in Narvik and that one of the panserships had probably been sunk. At their chosen place, Smestad, the SOK immediately discovered they were cut off because of the overloaded telephone network and they moved on to Eidsvoll during the afternoon. Notably, many naval officers who found their way to Smestad during the day were told to 'go home and await further orders'.

During the coming days, the SOK would more or less follow the HOK towards Gudbrandsdal, where they eventually established headquarters during 12 April. Until then, the commanding admiral and the SOK had a limited influence on the events, and the captains of the ships still operational had to make their own assessments and decisions.[23]

No Ships at Oslo

Shortly after 04:00, Naval Attaché Schreiber and Willhelm Scheidt drove towards Oslo harbour to receive Group V as ordered. Scheidt spoke basic Norwegian and knew Oslo well, so he would be an important liaison man for Generalmajor Engelbrecht when he arrived. On Schreiber's invitation he had spent the night in the attaché's apartment and been informed of the invasion a few hours earlier.[24]

No ships came and the two men returned to the embassy, where nobody had anything to tell. Nervously, they returned to the waterfront to contact Oberleutnant Kempf onboard *Widar* to find out what was going on. All Kempf could tell them was that there appeared to be trouble at Drøbak. Schreiber then decided to take the car to Fornebu, where he knew Air Attaché Spiller would be, while Scheidt headed for Hotel Continental to find Hagelin and learn what he knew of the situation. Remaining onboard *Widar*, Kempf had an excellent observation platform, not least of Fornebu airfield. By 06:00, communication was established with Abwehrstelle Hamburg, and during the next vital hours a steady stream of some 250 signals with various observations would arrive from *Widar* and be forwarded to Group XXI at Hotel Esplanade and the OKW in Berlin.

At 06:18 Oberstleutnant Pohlman sent a coded signal to von Falkenhorst in Hamburg using the radio at the embassy: 'No ships at Oslo, no sounds of battle to be heard. Air-raid sirens, people gather in the streets.'[25]

By 06:00, less than five hundred German soldiers had landed in southern Norway, outside Bergen and Trondheim. There, and at Narvik, the operation had gone well, but the troops were for all practical purposes isolated and the invasion as a whole was on the verge of being repelled. Oslo and Kristiansand were in a shambles and the situation at Sola-Stavanger was unclear. Von Falkenhorst cancelled his transfer to Oslo, later admitting, 'The incoming reports from Oslo in particular did not give a clear picture of the situation for quite some time.' This is probably an understatement; the tension in Hotel Esplanade must have been palpable. At Hamburg-Fuhlsbüttel airfield, Major Albrecht Philler, the most senior staff officer of 163rd ID not onboard *Blücher*, was called to the telephone shortly before 09:00, just as he was about to enter the transport aircraft taking him to Oslo-Fornebu. At the telephone was a very upset Oberstleutnant von Tippelskirch from Hotel Esplanade, informing him that things had gone badly and he was ordered to halt his transfer to Oslo and that of all staff and support personnel. Only infantry companies should fly north at this stage.[26]

Tragically, neither the Norwegian government nor the military realised this and a few hours later the situation had changed dramatically again. Oslo was in German hands, as was Kristiansand, and troops were pouring into southern Norway. It was not the result of a major strategic turn, but of individual German resolve, Norwegian hesitation and pure serendipity. Not at any time during the day did the Norwegians realise that the Germans landed from the warships and aircraft were lightly armed, lacking supplies, ammunition and heavy weapons – far less that the majority of their supply ships had been intercepted or delayed.[27]

In London, the British leadership strove to keep up with events during the night. Major-General Hastings Ismay, secretary of the Military Coordination Committee, wrote:

> The Twilight War ended for me in a most unexpected and dramatic way. In the very early hours of 9 April, I was wakened out of a deep sleep by the telephone bell. It was the Duty Officer at the War Cabinet Office . . . His report was brutal in its simplicity. The Germans had seized Copenhagen, Oslo and all the main ports of Norway . . . The gathering that assembled in my office at 6.30 a.m. was not exactly inspiring. I had hoped that one or other of the Chiefs of Staff would have a plan of action, but so far as I can remember not a single constructive suggestion had been put forward by the time that we had to break up the meeting and join the War Cabinet at 10, Downing Street.[28]

During the morning the War Cabinet, which was set at 08:30, decided air reconnaissance over Norway should be initiated as soon as possible to 'clarify the situation'. No bombing should commence until this had been achieved. Meanwhile, C-in-C Home Fleet should take 'all possible steps to clear Bergen and Trondheim of German forces', while the Chiefs of Staff should start preparations for military expeditions to recapture both cities and take control of Narvik. These expeditions should, however, 'not move until the naval situation had been cleared up'. The French were to be informed of these steps and asked to consider whether the chasseurs originally destined for Narvik could be redirected to Bergen or Trondheim. It was not until 10:30 in the morning that information of German landings at Narvik was received in London – through the press. At 14:00, the Admiralty issued orders to British naval authorities throughout the world that Norwegian and Danish ships were to be 'taken under British protection and detained to harbour'. Orders were also given to all ships in home waters that 'Merchant ships seen approaching the Scandinavian coast were to be advised to proceed to Kirkwall.'[29]

In Copenhagen, the German ambassador Cecil von Renthe-Fink telephoned Danish Foreign Minister Peter Munch at 04:00, requesting an immediate meeting. When they met some twenty minutes later, Munch received an ultimatum similar to the one Koht had received in Oslo, while being told that German troops at that moment were moving into Denmark. Von Renthe-Fink advised no opposition to be offered, lest the capital was bombed.

The German landings had all gone according to plan. Paratroopers had taken control of the Storstrøm bridge and the fortress at Masnedø, without opposition. The greater part of the IR 326 had landed at Korsør and Nyborg, securing the Great Belt strait between Funen and Zealand, while at Gedser, III/IR 305 had landed with the ferry and was moving north across Falster. Meanwhile, some 8,800 men of ID 170 and the 11th Armoured Brigade had crossed the border, moving swiftly across Jylland supported by tanks and armoured scout cars. The Danish Air Force had been destroyed on the ground by strafing while paratroopers secured Aalborg airfield.

At 04:20, the passenger steamer *Hansestadt Danzig* docked at Copenhagen harbour and II/IR 308 disembarked. The Danish garrison was taken by surprise and the citadel was secured without a shot. The German troops moved on towards Amalienborg, where the king was. There the guard was alarmed, however, and fighting broke out. Casualties were light on both sides, but the German advance was halted. Inside the castle, the king, his government and the supreme commander, General William Prior, were discussing the situation. Apart from Prior, who wanted to continue the resistance, all agreed that any prolonged opposition was impossible and the only solution was to cease fighting. A messenger was sent to deliver the Danish answer to the German ambassador and King Christian ordered the fighting to stop. By 07:00 all units of the Danish Army had received the order to lay down their guns.[30]

Meanwhile in Norway, the train taking the king and his government out of Oslo arrived at Hamar at 11:10. Hambro and Nygaardsvold had gone ahead by car and while waiting at the platform Nygaardsvold, according to Hambro, was deeply depressed and shaken 'as if something basic in his perception of human integrity and decency had been broken'. Nygaardsvold was physically exhausted after the events of the last days and lack of sleep, and asked if Hambro would be prepared to take responsibility. Hambro argued that this was not the time to make hasty decisions and did his best to calm 'the Old Man' down. When the train arrived, a quick breakfast was served and then the king, most ministers and slightly more than 100 of the 150 members of the Storting gathered at 12:30 in Festiviteten, a local assembly building.

Hambro chaired the meeting, and Nygaardsvold and Koht recounted what had happened during the night and morning. Koht ended his account by stating that Norway was now at war with Germany. After a brief discussion, Hambro decided there was not much more to do at the moment and asked the MPs to take a rest and reconvene at 18:00 with, it was hoped, more and better information of the situation.[31]

The diplomats following the government settled at Høsbjør, a hotel some fifteen kilometres outside Hamar.[32] By 12:30, Foley's MI6 staff had rigged an aerial to a flagstaff, setting up communications with London through the portable wireless telegraph (W/T) set brought from the embassy. Meanwhile, Minister Dormer, Foley and Assistant Air Attaché Wing Commander Alan Dore went back to Hamar to find Koht or somebody from the government to learn what was going on, and to let them know a line of communication to London had been established. Eventually, at 16:00, they met with Oberst Thomas Gulliksen, inspector general of the army air force, who brought an urgent, formal request from the Norwegian government for 'immediate military and aerial assistance'.[33] The text of a telegram describing the situation at Hamar was set up, followed by an urgent request for help. Both telegrams were brought back to Høsbjør to be ciphered and transmitted over Foley's W/T set.

At 16:25, the telegram from Dormer arrived at the Foreign Office:

Oslo has capitulated. Government are at Hamar, fifteen kilometres north of which I and several members of staff are staying . . . United States Legation has taken charge of His Majesty's Legation. Reported one German ship sunk by fire from Droebak. Tonsberg,

Bergen, Trondhjem, Narvik occupied . . . Lillestrom bombed and in flames. French Minister and I would be grateful for any reassuring news as Government anxious and are subject to strong pressure to declare a war on His Majesty's Government.

Less than half an hour later, it was followed by: 'Norwegian Government stress need for *strong* and *quick* assistance before Germans establish firm footing on Norwegian soil. Please reply by 6 p.m. whether strong assistance can be (?immediately) forthcoming.' And at 18:10: 'German land and air forces have occupied Fornebu and Sola (Stavanger) aerodromes . . . forces at Trondhjem, Egersund, Bergen and Oslo Fiord. Size and number of ships at various ports unknown at present. Information will be sent later if possible.'

Actually, the British Cabinet had already decided to assist Norway. It appears that Dormer never received a telegram sent from London at 06:45, stating that 'The whole British fleet is operating in the North Sea and we are planning to re-capture the ports in German occupation.' A second telegram, originally timed 12:55, was received once Høsbjør was connected:

You should at once assure the Norwegian Government that in view of the German invasion of their country; His Majesty's Government has decided forthwith to extend their full aid to Norway and will fight the war in full association with them. You should at the same time inform the Norwegian Government that His Majesty's Government are taking immediate measures to deal with the German occupation of Bergen and Trondjem [and] will be glad to learn what the Norwegian Government's own plans are, so that subsequent British dispositions may be in conformity with them. His Majesty's Government would in the meantime suggest that the Norwegian Government should if possible destroy the Stavanger aerodrome should they be unable to hold it.

This telegram was forwarded to Koht via Oberst Gulliksen around 18:00, just before the second meeting of the Parliament.[34]

Minister Bräuer had not accomplished his mission and found the situation deeply worrying. Nygaardsvold and Koht had decided to resist and there were no German troops in Oslo to change their mind. Worst of all, the king and government had left the capital. Alone with the responsibility, the experienced diplomat had little else to do but start improvising. Bräuer returned to the Foreign Office, where he was met by Undersecretary Malthe-Johannesen, the only senior civil servant remaining. Through him, Bräuer delivered a note to the Norwegian government indicating that the terms of the ultimatum were still open and a 'peaceful' solution not yet out of reach. The note was well formulated; pointing to the situation in Denmark and arguing that resistance in the long run would cost Norway dearly. Malthe-Johannesen could give no answer, but called Bräuer later in the evening to confirm that the government had received the letter and an answer would follow in the morning.[35]

In the second meeting at Hamar, which commenced at 18:30, Nygaardsvold raised the issue of negotiations, as offered by Bräuer. Hambro argued against. The Germans would not negotiate at all in his opinion, only make demands and drag their feet. Lie, Wold, Torp and Støstad supported Hambro. Others, including Koht, held that no options should be left and it was worth talking to Bräuer to see if the German terms had been modified. Eventually, it was agreed that Koht and three MPs should hear what Bräuer had to say and bring it back to the Parliament – provided the German advance was halted in the meantime. The mood of the Parliament was at an all-time low; news of landings all over the country, bombing and strafing in Oslo, loss of Norwegian lives and the confused mobilisation made the men falter in their determination.[36] A wave of positive feeling swept over the assembly when Koht referred to the telegram from the British government, given to him just before the meeting, stating that London would send help forthwith.

At 19:40, the meeting was interrupted. Hambro informed them that he had received information that German spearheads were only some twenty kilometres away, heading for Hamar. The train was ready at the station and they would have to leave for Elverum at once.[37] A scramble to depart ensued.

The foreign diplomats at Høsbjør were also notified and left immediately to try to stay in touch with the government. By the time Foley, Reid and others were ready to depart, however, it was difficult to find a car and when they eventually did, the road to Elverum was closed. Thus, they headed north towards Lillehammer, eventually ending up in Åndalsnes the next day. The radio and its operator went with Dormer, but during the night they became separated and Dormer was prevented from communicating further with London.[38]

Meanwhile, a small episode, which has since become known as 'Spiller's Raid' unfolded further south. Finding the king and government gone from Oslo, some German officers met and discussed what to do, among them Air Attaché Spiller. Somebody, most likely Spiller, suggested it might be possible to intercept the king if, as had been reported publicly, he was at Hamar. Here was a chance of glory not to be missed. Some seventy-nine paratroopers and twenty army soldiers under the command of Hauptmann Erich Walther of the Parachute Regiment were loaded into two cars, a lorry and three buses and with Spiller in the lead headed out of Oslo around 17:00. Bräuer later categorically denied having given Spiller any orders and von Falkenhorst asserted to his interrogators in 1945 that the expedition was initiated by Spiller alone, without his approval, calling it 'Spiller's private war'.[39] There is a note in the OKW War Diary, however, saying: 'The Norwegian government at Hamar. Paratroopers under way,' so Spiller and/or Walther had reported their departure and intentions and, one must assume, achieved sanction from somewhere.[40]

There was considerable confusion along the roads north of Oslo and at times shots were exchanged with Norwegian soldiers.[41] Some Norwegian officers encountered along the road were forced at gunpoint to act as guides. Others, who managed to stay out of captivity, reported the column moving north. Acting upon orders from Oberst Hatledal, an improvised timber barricade was established at Midtskogen between Elverum and Hamar during the early evening. Ninety-three men, a company from the guards reinforced by NCOs and officers, some recruits and a group of volunteers were sent forward and spread out on either side of the road. The recruits were given forty shots each, brief instructions on how to load, aim and fire and placed between the sergeants and young officers. There were only two machine guns.

The Germans came just before 02:00. The fight was short, but intense. The Falls-chirmjägers dismounted, spread out and advanced towards the roadblock. One of the

Norwegian machine guns was frozen solid, but the other opened up with considerable effect. Compared to the Norwegians, the paratroopers were well trained and armed with machine pistols, hand grenades, machine guns and small mortars. Their resolve was limited on that night, though, in spite of an impressive display of Verey lights and tracer ammunition. The Norwegian officers realised that this was more spectacular than perilous, especially as the German fire was consistently too high. Some Norwegians, including officers, panicked and ran away; some kept their heads down and did not open fire, but most stood firm. Eventually, the flanks started to fall back, but the Jägers did not pursue. Instead, they retired to their buses, leaving the battleground to the astounded Norwegians, who had but a few light casualties.

On the German side there were four to six casualties, among them Air Attaché Spiller. Left to make his own decisions, 150 kilometres inside enemy lines without backup, Hauptmann Walther found the venture too risky to continue. Taking advantage of the confusion on the Norwegian side, and where necessary forcing Norwegian prisoners to walk in front of the buses, the paratroopers headed back towards Oslo. Eberhart Spiller died in hospital the next day. In his wallet the staff at the hospital found a note on which was written: 'King Haakon, Nygaardsvold, Sundby, Hambro'; the latter underlined in red. The attaché had his priorities clear. It is certain that Spiller intended to bring King Haakon back to Oslo. Whether the others were to be brought back or 'eliminated' is not known.

A laconic signal was sent from Walther to Group XXI in the afternoon of 10 April: 'Not possible to detain Norwegian government due to strong defences.' For the second time in twenty-four hours, German attempts at gaining control of King Haakon and his government had been halted. No more than a skirmish, the episode at Midtskogen was almost as important as Oscarsborg. Symbolically, Midtskogen was to become a showcase for Norwegian opposition.[42]

Coup by Radio

Quisling was not part of the German plans for Norway after the invasion and there is no reference whatsoever to him in the orders from Group XXI regarding the occupation of Oslo. Quite the opposite: there is a paragraph showing clearly the German intention of maintaining the status quo:

> Once in Oslo, contacts shall be made as soon as possible with the German Minister Dr Bräuer and the Naval Attaché Korvettenkapitän Schreiber. With their help, urgent negotiations shall be initiated with the heads of the Norwegian military and government in order to secure implementation of our demands. Impediment of these negotiations must under no circumstance delay the swift occupation of Oslo.[43]

The only reference to Quisling in von Falkenhorst's files was a paper written by Major Benecke of the Abwehr, in which he was described as 'German friendly, but has no role to play. A fanatic.'[44] If King Haakon, the government and most other constitutional bodies continued with a minimum of visible changes, it was believed the Norwegian people would come to terms with the occupation. No replacement of the government was considered necessary; the iron fist inside the silken glove would suffice. In Denmark, this

Vidkun Abraham Jønsson Quisling.
(Author's collection)

system worked – for a while. What would have happened in Norway we shall never know as the events took a very different route.

After Scheidt and Schreiber parted company in the early morning, Scheidt hastened to Hotel Continental. He knew Hagelin was at the Continental, but it is unlikely that Scheidt knew of Quisling's presence when he entered the lobby some time before 08.00. Still, no doubt guided by Hagelin, he was shortly knocking on Quisling's door. In spite of the uncertainties, Scheidt gave Quisling a very positive summary of the military situation. He added, as he had learned from Bräuer before he left the embassy, that Nygaardsvold and his government had decided to resist, and he asked if there was any way such a catastrophe could be avoided. Exactly which options were discussed is not known, but sometime during the morning Quisling decided to establish a 'national government', believing he had German support to do so. In his mind the situation must have been more or less as discussed in Berlin four months earlier – except that the Germans were already in the country. Scheidt, who undoubtedly encouraged Quisling towards his decision, hurried back to the embassy to telegraph Berlin for approval.

The timing of events is somewhat confused this afternoon, but sometime around 17:00 Scheidt appeared in Quisling's room once more. He was very upset, claiming Hitler was furious over the loss of *Blücher* and Koht's refusal to Bräuer. Unless there was an immediate surrender, orders would very likely be issued for the Luftwaffe to initiate a ruthless bombing of Norwegian cities. Should Quisling assume power, however – for which Scheidt held he had Hitler's approval – conditions would be different and a solution might be arrived at. Again, it is not known exactly what was discussed, nor is it possible to ascertain what kind of 'approval' Scheidt actually had from Berlin, though he later claimed it to be 'official' and 'from Hitler in person'. During the ensuing hour, the framework of a proclamation was set up, whereupon Scheidt and Hagelin left while Quisling fine-tuned the wording. He also set up a list of 'ministers' for his new 'government'. With the exception of Hagelin, none of the 'ministers' knew they were being considered for a position that would brand them as traitors for years to come.

Quisling then headed for the Radio House, accompanied by Scheidt. The last Norwegian news broadcast had been at 12:50, after which a German communication unit had occupied the house, closing it down. Scheidt, claiming he had special orders from Berlin, bluffed his way into the studios, followed by Quisling. At 19:25 the broadcast recommenced with music until Quisling at 19:32 came on the air, implementing a one-man coup d'état, unique in history.

His proclamation was largely based on the leaflet issued in Oslo the day before. Following the British mine-laying, to which the Nygaardsvold government had barely protested, Quisling claimed, the German government had offered 'its inoffensive assistance accompanied by a solemn assurance to respect national independence and Norwegian life and property'. After initiating a futile mobilisation, Quisling continued, the government had fled and left the population to its fate. NS was the only party that could save the country from this desperate situation and it was his 'duty and right' to take over the government with himself as prime minister and foreign minister. He then read a list of names for the other ministerial positions, of which most were totally unknown to the public. Concluding his five-minute speech, Quisling added that opposition would be 'meaningless and equal to criminal destruction of life and property'. It was the duty of every public servant and officer to take instructions only from the new government, and any aberration from this would result in 'the gravest personal responsibility'.

The statement was a bombshell and when it was repeated at 22:00 the number of listeners was considerable. It created severe confusion among senior officers; several ordered their men not to shoot, unless attacked, until the situation had been clarified. There was intense telephoning to reach higher authorities, which was virtually impossible. By the morning of 10 April, however, order had been restored. In most cases it was followed by bitterness over Quisling's actions, strengthening the willingness to fight.

The appearance of Quisling on the scene came as a total surprise to Bräuer – and to Engelbrecht and von Falkenhorst. Bräuer called Foreign Minister von Ribbentrop in Berlin late in the evening, asking for instructions. Von Ribbentrop had nothing to say before he had talked to the Führer and asked his minister to wait. Not long after, the baffled Bräuer had Hitler himself on the line with clear instructions: Germany would go for Quisling. Nygaardsvold had spoiled his chances when he ordered Norwegian soldiers to fire on their German comrades. Bräuer's task was now to have the king acknowledge Quisling. Hitler did most of the talking and was not interested in Bräuer's futile comments that Quisling was not suitable as head of a government and that King Haakon might not appreciate suggestions taking him outside his constitutional directive.

It is possible that Hitler had some long-term ideas for Quisling in Norway after the situation had settled down, but this was certainly not to be announced by radio on the invasion day and there is little doubt the plot was improvised as a result of the events during the morning. Unfortunately for Quisling, the country was not 'without a government' and there was no parliamentary, legal or other basis for the 'national government'. Quisling's treason was only made possible by the vacuum created by the sinking of *Blücher* and the absence of German military authority in Oslo.[45]

As Long as Possible

At Elverum, the Storting and government reconvened at 21:20 in a local school. It was confirmed, against the advice of Hambro, that Koht and three MPs should meet Bräuer and hear him out. No mandate was given and it was not clarified what the Parliament or the government might be willing to accept in terms of compromises. It was clear, though, that unless Bräuer had something substantially more positive than the conditions of the first ultimatum, the decision from the early hours of 9 April would stand. If, on the other hand, the German minister had something to offer, many of the MPs felt negotiations could be a positive way out of a dire situation. The news of Quisling's radio speech was known and any solution involving him would be unacceptable.[46]

Hambro realised that it would be difficult to assemble the Parliament in the days and weeks ahead and suggested a constitutional *prokura* should be given to the government empowering it to 'attend to the interests of the nation and make those decisions deemed necessary . . . until such times as it is possible to convene formally again'. There was no formal vote, but nobody voiced any serious comments and Hambro declared the *prokura* valid. The meeting ended at 22:25 and the Norwegian Parliament would not meet again for over five years. A statement was prepared to be issued by radio the next day, confirming the Nygaardsvold government as the only legal authority of the country, endorsed by the king.[47]

After the meeting, the government decided to ask Hambro to go to Stockholm to take care of Norwegian foreign affairs and other matters needing communication from neutral ground. He should also try to purchase weapons and supplies from Sweden, as direct military assistance was not expected. Hambro's political insight, administrative skills and cool head had, during the first critical hours of the crisis, made use of the breathing space created by Oscarsborg and Midtskogen to ensure the government and king remained in charge. He left for Stockholm in the morning of the 10th.[48]

Bräuer passed through the lines early in the morning of 10 April, arriving in a small rural school building near Elverum around 15:00. King Haakon arrived too, asking that Koht and the MPs attend the meeting.[49] Bräuer refused and insisted on seeing the king alone. King Haakon, who wanted a witness to overhear what he expected to come, told Bräuer that he, as a constitutional monarch, could not make any political decisions without his council and besides, he held, he did not speak German well and needed an interpreter. Outsmarted, Bräuer, who probably believed it would be possible to convince King Haakon to return, had to give in and accept Koht to join the meeting. At first he repeated tersely that the Germans had come as friends, forced to act through British provocations, and did not wish to change 'the prevailing dynastic situation'. He then complained bitterly that the Norwegian forces had not laid down their weapons 'as had been agreed'.[50] Nygaardsvold's government had shown itself to favour the Allied cause, he said, and as it had ordered a pointless resistance, the situation was totally changed from that of the morning of the previous day. Nygaardsvold and his government would have to go. Quisling had founded a new government, which King Haakon would have to recognise and return to the capital as soon as possible. By refusing to do so, he would personally be responsible for the inevitable loss of Norwegian lives. Rather than being mellowed, the German demands were now sharper than those presented at Victoria Terrasse. King Haakon, who said very little during the meeting at all, did not answer directly, but held that he could not appoint a government that did not have the confidence of the people. Bräuer answered that it might be possible to discuss some of the ministers, but Quisling remained an absolute demand. The meeting ended with a promise of a final answer within the day, and it was agreed that he should telephone Koht from Eidsvoll on his way back to Oslo.

When alone, King Haakon turned to Koht, noticeably distraught, saying that he felt terrible taking responsibility for the bloodshed that would follow from a war. He could not, however, accept 'this fellow Quisling' as prime minister and would have to abdicate if the German demands were accepted by the present administration. King Haakon continued to Nybergsund by car, where he met the government and recounted the meeting with Bräuer, repeating he could not approve Quisling, 'who had no public or parliamentary support'. If the government wished to accept the demands in order to avoid war, he would understand, but then he would have no choice but to abdicate. Minister Hjelmtveit later wrote:

> This made a great impression on us all. Clearer than ever before we could see the man behind the words; the king who had drawn a line for himself and his task, a line from which he could not deviate. We had through the five years [in government] learned to respect and appreciate our king and now, through his words, he came to us as a great man, just and forceful; a leader in these fatal times to our country.[51]

There was no discussion; the entire government, deeply moved, but also somewhat relieved, made common cause with the monarch. Koht, who had remained at Elverum, was informed, and when Bräuer telephoned from Eidsvoll around 20:00, the decision was referred to him. Bräuer asked if this meant that the Norwegian resistance would continue, and Koht answered in German: 'Ja, soweit wie möglich' – 'Yes, as long as possible'. Hitler's demand for the acceptance of Quisling as prime minister had effectively excluded all possible options for a ceasefire.[52]

At 11:40 on 10 April, Group XXI received orders from the OKW signed by both General Keitel and Generalmajor Jodl to 'detain the old Norwegian government'. If they would not come back to Oslo and start co-operating, they had to be 'disposed of'.[53] 'Peaceful occupation' was no longer an option.

The Commanding General

Having come to Hamar with Defence Minister Ljungberg for a meeting with the government, Commanding General Laake and Oberst Hatledal were left waiting outside the room where the politicians met.[54] After a while, a telephone call came through to Hatledal from Oberstløytnant Wrede-Holm back at the HOK: several buses with German soldiers were heading north. The message was forwarded to the meeting and resulted in the hurried departure. Nobody had time for Hatledal and Laake, other than asking them to halt the German advance, and not even Ljungberg invited one of them to join the entourage to secure proper communication. After a few hours administering the defence against Spiller and his paratroopers by telephone, the two officers headed for Elverum by car. Here, they snatched a few hours of rest before meeting up with the rest of the HOK and eventually continued to Rena, where they all arrived during the early hours of 10 April.[55]

The situation was confused; hearsay flourished and communication with the divisions was unsystematic and unreliable. Virtually nothing was written down and it became very difficult to have a consistent picture of what was happening. In the forenoon of the 10th, Generalmajor Laake assembled his senior officers to discuss the situation. Learning that Minister of Justice Terje Wold happened to be nearby on another undertaking, Laake invited him over in the afternoon for an impromptu update, which was to have wide-ranging consequences. Besides Wold, Laake and Hatledal, most senior officers of the HOK also participated. Generalmajor Laake presented a rather negative assessment of the situation. Depots and barracks had been seized by the Germans, and those units that had managed to mobilise were low in equipment and ammunition. Laake concluded by advising that negotiations with the Germans were 'held open for military reasons'. None of the other officers expressed any diverging views, but some voiced complaints about the belated orders for mobilisation and lack of communication and co-operation between the government and the military.

For Wold, the officers appeared resigned, almost defeatist, and he later maintained that Laake had stated that the only alternative to continued negotiations was surrender. Wold was also upset by the open criticism of the government. Unfortunately, he left in anger without seeking a solution or finding out what was needed to secure clarification and decisions. Wold had no knowledge of Hatledal's efforts to get things right and included him among the officers he characterised as 'weak and not the right men for the situation'.[56]

Returning to the government in the evening, Wold described the meeting at Rena in strong words. As by now the basis for negotiations with the Germans had already disappeared, Wold's account created a very negative impression. It was decided that Laake was not the man needed in the current situation and 'his resignation would be accepted'. The 58-year-old inspector general of the infantry, Otto Ruge, would be promoted to generalmajor and appointed in his place. Ljungberg, who for once voiced some opposition, was overruled and instructed to arrange the replacement as 'gently as possible'. Generalmajor Laake was asked to come to Nybergsund and arrived in the early morning of 11 April, accompanied by Oberstløytnant Roscher-Nielsen. Ljungberg took Laake into a private room and broke the news to him: he was no longer commanding general. Laake returned to Roscher-Nielsen 'unhappy, but also somewhat relieved'. Officially, the commanding general had been granted a voluntary resignation due to his age.[57] Characteristically, Ruge learned of the decision through a telephone conversation with Trygve Lie in the evening of the 10th, but dismissed it as a misunderstanding. Only the next morning was he informed by Ljungberg and asked to come to Rena.

The 58-year-old Otto Ruge was promoted to generalmajor and appointed as commanding general in the early morning of 11 April 1940. (NTB arkiv/Scanpix)

Commanding Admiral Diesen accepted willingly to be subordinated to Ruge and the Norwegian forces had a unified command for the first time.[58]

Otto Ruge immediately took command and initiated the establishment of a series of defensive lines to hold the Germans at bay while the mobilisation continued. During 13 April orders were issued to blow up all road and railway bridges and to sever telephone and telegraph lines as close to Oslo as possible. 'Fight we shall – and we must fight with what we have,' he said repeatedly. All over the country youngsters and some not so young wished to fight. Slowly, the mobilisation took effect and the first new elements of the army were reported ready. Ruge's determination was largely based on the certainty of imminent Allied help and his strategy was to fall back slowly while maintaining the fighting capacity of his units, pending Allied support.

Some of those wanting to fight were met at the camps and depots by NCOs and officers not understanding the seriousness of the situation and incapable of acting pragmatically. There are numerous verified stories of men being dismissed and sent home because they did not belong to the 'right' unit. The units that did come together were desperately short of artillery, machine guns, anti-tank weapons and, above all, anti-aircraft guns. These weapons to some extent existed in depots, but were not issued in time. When the Allies failed to deploy adequately trained and equipped men as well, the outcome of the campaign was inevitable, in spite of both Norwegian and Allied troops putting up stout resistance in many places, proving themselves on equal footing with the intruders when not overwhelmed by air superiority and heavy weapons.

The situation at Rena was difficult – partly because of lack of proper accommodation, partly because of the bombing of Elverum, and it was decided to move again, this time

Young men – and many not so young – flocked to the mobilisation centres. (Author's collection)

to Øyer near Lillehammer. Oberst Hatledal's health continued to deteriorate and to his despair Ruge had to insist that Hatledal took a spell of leave due to his indispositions. He was released on the evening of 14 April and Kaptein Leif Rolstad was appointed Ruge's adjutant in the meantime.[59]

At Nybergsund, there had been several air-raid alarms during the morning of 11 April, but no aircraft had appeared. Around 17:00, several He111 bombers suddenly appeared over the houses where King Haakon and the government were staying, dropping bombs and strafing. An improvised alarm was sounded by a car horn and people ran out of the houses, seeking shelter where they could. The king, Prince Olav and several of the ministers escaped by a hair's breadth into the woods nearby. Nygaardsvold and others only survived by taking refuge in a solid wooden shed where they were shaken by several near-misses. Koht hid behind a car and escaped a stick of incendiary bombs by a few metres. 'They were so close, I could see how they were working,' he said, 'it was like a furnace gushing from a bottleneck.' Miraculously, nobody was hurt, but the material damage to houses and equipment was significant. Nygaardsvold and others took off in a car during a lull and when the car got stuck, continued through the deep snow on foot.[60]

Nygaardsvold was visibly shaken by the ferocity of the German air attack. He was worn out by running around in the deep snow and felt intimidated by being shot at. Having a rest at Innbygda, Nygaardsvold suggested to the ministers with him that maybe they should consider crossing into Sweden. It is not known if he meant to go there for a short while to recuperate or to try to set up a permanent seat, though it is likely it was the latter he had in mind. The proposal created a heated argument and was dismissed. Instead, it was decided to continue towards Rena, where General Ruge was about to settle in, and from there up Gudbrandsdal, should it become necessary.

It was, however, discreetly enquired if it would be possible for King Haakon and Prince Olav to enter Sweden for a brief period of rest. The answer given by Foreign Minister Günther after consultation with King Gustav, was that if they crossed the border, the king would run the risk of becoming interned and not be able to return to Norway. Hearing this, King Haakon and Prince Olav refused any further talk of going to Sweden. During the subsequent trek to Gudbrandsdal, the government was split up for safety reasons. Some of the cars got lost and it would be almost a week before Nygaardsvold could assemble the majority of his ministers again at Otta.[61]

The British minister to Norway, Sir Cecil Dormer, who usually was considered a bit 'dull and phlegmatic', was to show an unperturbed resilience after he had been awakened by Koht in the early morning of 9 April. There were episodes during the retreat when he had differences with Koht and Nygaardsvold, partly because Dormer could not always understand their concerns for life and property or their wish to consider several options, but as a whole the efforts of Dormer and his staff for Norway during this period were highly valued.[62]

On the morning of 11 April, Dormer and Assistant Air Attaché Dore were introduced to Ruge. Dore later described him as having 'the reputation of being a soldier and a man of outstanding quality. The subsequent relation of the other attachés and myself with him at the GHQ fully confirmed this.' Ruge urged the vital importance of prompt and effective Allied action, which Dormer, in view of the signals they had received the day before from the War Cabinet, confirmed was forthcoming. Dormer then headed for Nybergsund where, to his relief, he was assured that both the king and government had dismissed any German attempts for continued negotiations, as well as Quisling's coup in Oslo. In the evening, Dormer was informed that the government would be travelling 'north', but no details were included. After the bombing at Nybergsund, the Norwegian government was reluctant to disclose its whereabouts and Dormer had to guess. He eventually found them at Drevsjø, near the Swedish border, and noted that:

> ... with the exception of the Crown Prince, who looked none the worse, they were all very exhausted, and I urged that, if possible, they should take it in turns to sleep a night or two in peace across the border. The king would not leave, but a few of them went to Särna for the night; amongst them M. Koht, who was going to discuss the question of financial credits with a representative of the Swedish Government and hoped also to set up the nucleus of an office as a liaison with Stockholm until it could function in Norway.[63]

Dormer later wrote to Lord Halifax of his experiences in Norway:

> His Majesty and his Government were called upon to decide [on many critical issues] at a moment's notice in a more or less complete unpreparedness and physical exhaustion. I was in touch with them most days, but there was no time for conversation. When they

asked me to come to them it was invariably to discuss on a particular question, in a crowded room, standing up; in the kind of conditions that might be described as chaos and confusion. And yet, although they had no administrative machine to work with – since everyone became scattered – they have succeeded in establishing some semblance of Government in districts free of Germans.[64]

In Oslo, Quisling moved into the Parliament building during the morning of 10 April, after having it cleared of German soldiers. Quisling chose to stay away from his NS Party, much to their confusion, and continued instead to work closely with Hagelin and Scheidt. There were relatively few German soldiers around, giving a comparatively peaceful impression of the occupation. In this, the original German intention was achieved, except that it stemmed from the absence of opponents on either side, not from co-operation. Apart from a brief episode of panic on 10 April when rumours of Allied air attacks made a large portion of the civilian population flee the town, things were surprisingly quiet in the capital. Some opportunistic youngsters reported at the NS offices, where they were heartily welcomed. Equipped with Norwegian army uniforms, guns and an armband with the yellow NS 'sun-cross', they were placed as 'guards' in strategic positions around Oslo. For a brief period, soldiers of the Royal Guard stood sentry outside Hotel Continental next to German soldiers, while the NS youngsters covered the lobby.

Few of the 'ministers' appointed by Quisling on 9 April actually showed up and at least five of the eight declined or never responded. This was a severe blow for Quisling and it was most likely registered in Berlin, where it added to the impression of a precarious situation in Oslo. Worse, many long-term supporters did not wish to become involved in an obvious coup and turned their back on 'Føreren' ('The Leader', as he was affectionately known by his supporters), some even defying his orders and joining the Norwegian forces. There were no plans for the work in the rebel 'government', no declared ambitions, no agenda, and everything had to be improvised – something Quisling was not good at. Some of the ministers who actually did show up were left alone with nothing to do and were not involved in anything of importance. Very few of the supporters he had told Hitler he had 'in central positions' materialised and most civil servants quietly ignored his instructions, undermining his authority and creating confusion. Quisling was a thinker and ideologist, not a man of action who might have achieved something in the prevailing situation.[65]

'Quisling is more critical than productive and is not up to the task,' Bräuer wrote in one of his reports to Berlin. Benecke, the Abwehr agent, also sent several critical reports on the new 'prime minister' through his channels to Berlin, asserting that his self-declared rise to head of state actually stiffened the resolve among the Norwegians to resist.

Quisling sensed that things were moving against him, and Hagelin was sent to Berlin. Not even he could restore confidence, however, and the support from Berlin was fading as fast as it had come. On 13 April, Quisling was banned from using the radio, the NS youngsters were ordered off the streets and at 17:00 on the 15th it was all over. Bräuer informed Quisling that Hitler had decided he would have to go. His 'government' was history; it had for all practical purposes never functioned and nothing had been achieved during its five days in existence.[66]

Norwegian soldiers preparing to make a stand at Norderhov Church in Haugsbygd.
(Forsvarsmuseet)

A hybrid 'government' or administrative council was established instead, masterminded by Bräuer. Led by the Lord Chief Justice Paal Berg, it was to have jurisdiction
over and administer the occupied areas. Having no foundation in the constitution and
no ambition to be anything but an emergency solution, this did not work either. On 19
April, Hitler cut through the mess and appointed Josef Terboven as his representative
and Reichskommissar in Norway.[67] Terboven, who was an old comrade of Hitler, would
be the supreme ruler of Norway in the five years to come. All attempts at a peaceful
occupation had failed and only with an iron fist – without the slightest attempt to cover
it in silk – did Germany gain some sort control over Norway. The country would have to
be 'Nazified' the hard way. On 24 April Admiral Boehm, the newly established supreme
naval commander, Norway, reported to Raeder that on the surface, things were quiet
in the occupied areas, but there was a 'marked stiffening of the negative attitudes of
the population and an increased passive opposition'.[68] Two days later, on the 26th, the
German-controlled radio announced, in case anybody was in doubt, that a state of war
existed between Germany and Norway.[69]

For Vidkun Quisling a course had been set that would inevitably lead to the firing
squad and make his name synonymous forever with treason and collaboration with the
enemy. His strange name, pronounceable in most languages, would travel through the
world press within a few days and create a whole new concept of treason.

— 7 —

Kristiansand–Arendal

Southern Pearl[1]

KAPITÄN ZUR SEE FRIEDRICH Rieve of the cruiser *Karlsruhe* was a very unhappy man in the morning of 9 April. It was almost 10:00, and Kampfgruppe IV, of which he was in command, should have started disembarkation of the landing troops almost six hours earlier. But things were not going well at all. Fog had delayed his flotilla and the coastal forts had put up a fierce defence, fending off the ships several times in spite of repeated bombing and shelling. In desperation, Rieve regrouped his ships and gave orders to enter the fjord once more.

In 1927, during the defence budget reductions, Kristiansand Fortress had been put in the reserve and for all practical purposes abandoned. Oberstløytnant Ole Fosby, the 64-year-old C-in-C, had maintained it as best he could in spite of minimum manning and meagre funds, and the old guns were in fair condition. Modernisation of the defences of Kristiansand had been accepted by the Parliament in 1937, but lack of qualified personnel meant that little had happened, except for upgrading part of the ammunition. During the neutrality, a minimum force was drafted to man the main batteries at Odderøya Fort. By the spring of 1940 the first draft had served their time and an almost complete change of crew took place during March. In the evening of 8 April, through sickness, leave or guard duties, only about twenty-five officers and 150 ratings manned the batteries at Odderøya. The average age of the men was around 30, while most of the officers and NCOs were either much older or much younger. Major Sandberg, the senior gunnery officer, was 56 years old and had not served since 1918. Sergeant Eichinger, one of the 21-cm gun commanders was 22 years old.[2]

The main fort at Odderøya was equipped with four 24-cm howitzers, two 21-cm guns and six 15-cm guns. Due to restricted elevation, the 21-cm batteries had a maximum range of only twelve thousand metres, covering the fjord, but unable to fire into the open sea; the other guns had even lower range. Two elderly 75-mm A/A guns were not manned and the only practical defence against aircraft was four obsolete 7.92-mm machine guns. There were no mines or torpedo batteries, nor any infantry to protect from landside attacks.

The secondary fort at Gleodden between the city and Marvika had three 15-cm guns for defence of the inner part of the fjord. This fort had not been manned during the neutrality, but Oberstløytnant Fosby had quietly made the guns ready during March and brought about a hundred rounds of ammunition to its magazine. On 1 April, a group of corporal trainees from Oscarsborg arrived in Kristiansand for exercises. When in the afternoon of the 8th, an order came from SDD1 for these men to move to Gleodden and put the battery in fighting condition, most of the job was already accomplished and all they had to do was to cut down some trees and shrubs to gain a fair field of vision

Aerial photo of
Kristiansand. Odderøya
Fort is on the island
protruding from the very
regular network of streets
in the city proper. The
main harbour is to the
right (west) of the city.
(Marinemuseet)

and fire. By nightfall, two of the guns were operational. The corporals knew the 15-cm guns well but there had been no time for the officers to familiarise themselves with the local conditions. The only communication between Gleodden and Odderøya was via the public telephone network.

Commander-in-Chief of Kristiansand Sea Defence Sector, Kommandør Severin Wigers, reported to Kontreadmiral Smith-Johannsen in Horten. His office and staff were at Marvika naval base. Two torpedo-boat divisions were allocated to Kristiansand SDS with a total of eight boats, deployed at various smaller harbours around the sector.[3] The submarines *B2* and *B5* had their base at Marvika and both were operational. In addition there were nine auxiliaries in or around Kristiansand and three MF11 reconnaissance aircraft at Marvika. Kristiansand Krigshavn was defined by the chain of lighthouses that marked the entrances to the fjord.

Generalmajor Einar Liljedahl was C-in-C of the limited army forces in Kristiansand. In April, these consisted of the inexperienced I/IR 3 stationed at the Gimlemoen barracks. Most of them came from Telemark further east and neither officers nor men were familiar with the Kristiansand region. In the evening of 8 April, one machine-gun and one infantry platoon were deployed at Kjevik airfield; one company had been sent to Lillesand to take care of the *Rio de Janeiro* survivors and two companies were on general guard duty in Kristiansand city. No army units were deployed for defence of the forts.

There were no military aircraft at Kjevik airfield on the 8th, the only concrete airstrip between Sola and Fornebu. During the afternoon the area outside the main runway was blocked and preparations were made to close the rest at short notice.[4]

In Kristiansand 8 April was a nice, wintry day. It was cold, a few degrees of frost, and a thin layer of ice had developed in the inner harbour; patches of fog started to drift in from the sea later in the day. During the morning, people flocked around the newsstands or listened to the radio for news of the British mine-laying. Kommandør Wigers ensured the coastguard stations were alert, and he confirmed with Oberstløytnant Fosby that the observation posts at Smørvarden, Oksøy and Høgfjell were adequately manned. The torpedoing of *Rio de Janeiro* would take the main attention of Kristiansand SDS on this day. In the afternoon, the destroyer *Odin* came in with eighteen dead Germans and seventeen wounded. Many people had come to watch and the sight of the casualties made a great impression. The war had never been closer. Wigers and Liljedahl met to discuss the event, and concluded that, due to 'lack of evidence of German warships or other transports heading for Norway', it was unlikely to be true that Bergen was the target. At 16:21, a signal arrived from the Admiral Staff informing that a British naval force was heading into the Kattegat; the Royal Navy was on its way and would handle the situation.[5]

At 19:35, an order for increased preparedness came from Horten and was forwarded to Marvika and the fortress. Because of the encroaching fog, auxiliaries had routinely been deployed at the entrances to the fjord – *Hval IV* and *Hval VI* in Oksøygapet, *Lyn* and *Kvik* in Vestergapet and at Randøysund, respectively – but these were not informed of the alert. Neither was the army.

From the west, the German freighter *Seattle* approached Kristiansand, escorted by the Norwegian destroyer *Gyller*. It was nearing the end of a long and dangerous journey for *Seattle* and Kapitän Lehmann was looking forward to entering German-controlled

Odderøya's 24-cm St Chamond howitzers. (Author's collection)

waters within a day or two. His ship, loaded with wheat, planks and timber, had entered the Norwegian Leads near Tromsø a week earlier after slipping away from internment in Curaçao and passing successfully through the British patrols north of Iceland.[6] *Gyller* had taken up the escort off Egersund but progress had been slowed by the fog, and it was decided both ships should spend the night in Kristiansand. Entering Oksøygapet, Lehmann dropped anchor on the western side of the inlet, near Oksøy Lighthouse. *Gyller* continued up the fjord towards Kristiansand harbour, where she refuelled and moored at the customs quay (Tollbodkaia) around 21:00. The men not needed for general duty were given leave for the evening while Kaptein Lorentz Holck made his way to Wigers in Marvika to get an update of the situation and to receive orders for the night. Wigers requested that the destroyer was kept at readiness and the men recalled. This was done and all were back onboard by 22:30. *Gyller*'s sister ship *Odin* was already at Marvika. The two destroyers were usually subordinated to the commanding admiral and used for escort duties along the southern coast. By being in Kristiansand they fell under the operational command of Kommandør Wigers, but neither Kaptein Holck nor Kaptein Gunvaldsen of *Odin* were given any tactical orders or specific instructions regarding what to do if anything happened during the night.

Around midnight, news that Rauøy and Bolærne had opened fire arrived by telephone from Horten. It was immediately forwarded to the fortress, the naval air base and the ships in Marvika and Kristiansand harbour – but again, the auxiliaries were forgotten. Oberstløytnant Fosby had earlier in the evening given orders for 'condition III' at the 21-cm battery – guns manned and ready. The other batteries had 'condition II', which meant that the men were at the guns but allowed to relax and sleep inside the shelters, and he saw no need to change this. Major Sandberg, the artillery commander, asked for and was given permission to bring live ammunition to the batteries.

At the naval air base, Kaptein Eliassen gave orders for his MF11s to be ready for take-off at dawn. Kapitänleutnant Stiebler and the first officer of *U21*, interned at Marvika since its grounding in March, were taken off their boat and handed over to the army for detention. The lighthouses had already been shut down on orders from the commanding admiral and when electricity was cut in the city and parts of Marvika, an eerie but tense atmosphere spread.

Shortly before 02:00 a signal that unknown ships were approaching Bergen arrived. Kommandør Wigers called Horten and spoke to Kontreadmiral Smith-Johannsen, but he could not add much. The fog, which had been thick throughout the night, lifted slowly over land and by 04:30 visibility started to improve. At 04:45 an officer onboard the torpedo boat *Skarv* called from Egersund saying his ship had been captured by German soldiers, who were now moving into the town. Nobody knew how to react to this.[7]

One MF11 took off some twenty minutes later, and around 05:00 a signal arrived from the aircraft that unknown naval ships were heading for Oksøygapet. Shortly after, Sotåsen coastguard station telephoned: 'Several warships can be seen, large and small, heading west. Moderate speed.' Within minutes, Smørvarden observation post also reported: 'Large warship sighted one mile off Torsøy. Slow speed. Course west.'

Oberstløytnant Fosby sounded the alarm. None of the signals indicated nationality or type of ships. It was only clear that they were not Norwegian and, if entering the krigshavn, were to be stopped by any available means. Fosby called Wigers, informing him that he intended to open fire should the ships continue towards Kristiansand; the C-in-C concurred. Shortly after, all batteries reported ready and were ordered to load their guns. When the warships could be seen through the fog, approaching Oksøygapet in line-astern, two loose warning shots were fired and a black warning flag hoisted. When the lead ship appeared to be off Dvergsøy, well inside the krigshavn, Fosby ordered Major Sandberg to fire a 21-cm warning shot. This he did, and as none of the ships changed course or reduced speed, Oberstløytnant Fosby ordered him to shoot in earnest. It was 05:32.[8]

First Run

Besides the light cruiser *Karlsruhe*, Group IV consisted of the torpedo boats *Luchs* and *Seeadler*, the depot ship *Tsingtau* and seven S-boats. The third torpedo boat, *Greif*, had been detached for Arendal and was on its own. Onboard the ships were some 970 soldiers, largely from I/IR 310 (163rd ID), and some naval artillerymen.[9] Oberstleutnant Wachsmuth, the C-in-C of IR 310 was onboard the cruiser, as was Konteradmiral Otto Schenk, the designated admiral of the Norwegian south coast. Both were passengers and had no influence on Kapitän Rieve's dispositions, other than giving advice.

Group IV reached the 200-metre contour off the Norwegian coast at 02:45 and turned east, following this by echo-sounder as it followed the coastline at a suitable distance. The fog was heavier than ever and persistently shrouded the land. None of the ships had radar and unless the fog lifted, delays would be inevitable; running aground would jeopardise the whole operation and could not be risked. Shortly after 04:15, the time by which Group IV should have commenced disembarkation, the fog lifted slightly and the darkened Torsøy Lighthouse east of Kristiansand could be identified. Transfer of the Landsers to

The 1320-GRT torpedo boat *Luchs*, under the command of Kapitänleutnant Karl Kassbaum, was of the *Raubtier* class. Its main armament was three 10.5-cm guns and two triple torpedo mountings. *Seeadler* and *Greif* were of the slightly smaller but otherwise similar *Raubvogel* class. (Author's collection)

S14. Kapitänleutnant Rudolf Petersen's 2nd S-boat Flotilla assigned to Group IV (*S9, S14, S16, S30, S31, S32* and *S33*) was a motley mix of boats of different designs, which caused operational challenges. The small, 86-ton *S9* was from a batch commissioned in 1935. The others were similar in basic design and armament but larger (*c.*100 tons). *S14* and *S16* from 1936/37 had old, unreliable MAN engines whereas the four '30 boats' were equipped with Daimler-Benz engines. These latter boats had been commissioned after the outbreak of hostilities, the last, *S33*, as late as 23 March. (Author's collection)

the S-boats as planned would result in further delays, so Kapitän Rieve decided to go straight into the harbour. All troops were sent below decks and the sailors closed up at action stations. Just then, a seaplane appeared to starboard. It made a sweep over the ships and turned away before fire could be opened. Fenrik Oscar had no bombs, and once it had been ascertained that these were not Norwegian ships, he turned his MF11 back into the fog, signalling the observation to Marvika. Rieve realised that the element of surprise had been lost. A very hard day for him and his men had just begun.

At 05:23, course was changed to north-north-west through Oksøygapet. On the starboard bow, Grønningen Lighthouse was visible, and to port the smaller Oksøy Lighthouse; neither was burning. *Karlsruhe* was in the lead with the two torpedo boats in line-astern; the S-boats and *Tsingtau* further behind. All guns were trained fore and aft, with the gunners out of sight inside their turrets or behind the shields to give a non-aggressive appearance. Speed was low. To begin with, all went well. What looked like a fishing boat fired off two red signal rockets when the ships approached Oksøy (this was the auxiliary *Hval VI*) but nothing further happened for a few minutes.[10] A brief moment of tension flashed over the bridge when one of the lookouts on the starboard side shouted 'submarine alarm' when he thought he glimpsed a periscope. Whatever he had seen in the murk, it was not a periscope and nothing happened.

The Norwegian pilot vessel *Oksøy I* was, as usual, waiting off Oksøy. There was no radio onboard and nobody had thought to inform the pilots of the situation during the night. Now it approached *Karlsruhe* to transfer the required pilot. Slightly bemused, Rieve decided to accept the offer, as it might be useful further in. *Oksøy I* matched the speed of the cruiser and headed for the rope ladder thrown over her side. Pilot Thomas Aanundsen climbed onboard, but by the time he was taken to the bridge, events had escalated and Kapitän Rieve had his attention elsewhere. To his amazement, Aanundsen was left standing in a corner of the bridge with an unprecedented view of the first run.[11]

Next, *Seattle* approached the German column through the fog. Kapitän Lehmann had decided to enter Kristiansand and request escort to continue eastwards. Rieve at first welcomed the disturbance as he thought he might shelter behind her, but abandoned the idea when he realised *Seattle* was a civilian German ship. Instead he ordered a signal to be sent to get her out of the way. Lehmann never observed any signal, but believing the warships to be British; he turned away to port to shelter behind the island Kinn. At that moment, the first shot from the Norwegian battery rang out across the fjord.

Major Sandberg concentrated all guns on the lead ship. After the first warning shot, well ahead of *Karlsruhe*, the following salvoes landed close. The spray from the exploding shells drenched the superstructure of the cruiser and there was significant surprise among the officers on the bridge at the determination of the Norwegian opposition. Rieve ordered fire but he was at a disadvantage as only the forward turret would bear.[12] *Luchs* and *Seeadler* also opened fire with their single 10.5-cm guns, but these were rather inaccurate at this range and after a few salvoes *Luchs* reported problems with her forward gun. The situation was unsustainable. Not only were the ships and their crews at risk, but there were almost a thousand soldiers onboard, including the entire designated command echelon of occupied southern Norway. A second submarine alarm worsened the situation. Kapitän Rieve was forced to accept that the fortress would have to be neutralised before he could proceed and ordered an about-turn to starboard.[13] For a while all guns could bear but after completing the turn the distance was quickly opened and only a few salvoes were fired from the aft turrets. The retreat was covered by smoke from

Karlsruhe turning back after the first run around 05:40. Smoke is emitted to cover her retreat. (Kapitän Rieve's photo collection via K Mæsel)

the cruiser, and the torpedo boats dropped smoke rafts. When the ships could no longer be observed from Odderøya, the fire ceased, shortly before 05:45. The run had lasted about twenty minutes – with about ten minutes of actual bombardment.[14]

The first shots from *Karlsruhe* went low and landed below the fort. The fire was lifted but even if there were several near misses, shaking the gun emplacements and bunkers, there were no serious hits. Firing upwards in a flat trajectory, some of the shells overshot the fort and landed in the city. Panic broke out among the population, which had just tumbled out of bed a few minutes earlier, awakened by the warning shots. Those who could do so loaded family and valuables into their cars and drove off. Others withdrew to basements and shelters, while some ran half-dressed in terror in any direction that would take them out of harm's way. A few, not realising what was going on, sought high ground to get a view of events.[15]

The first of the Luftwaffe bombers arrived as the ships turned into Oksøygapet. Vigilant A/A gunners onboard *Luchs* and *Seeadler*, annoyed at having missed the MF11 earlier, promptly opened fired, but a recognition signal soon cleared the situation. The six He111 from 7./KG 4 made a sweep north of the city while assessing the situation. Hauptmann Erich Bloedorn and Leutnant Hajo Herrmann of the lead aircraft saw the ships turn back under gunfire, and the bombs were made ready. The He111 had a variable-delay mechanism in its bomb-release system. By adjusting to the height and speed of the aircraft, the bombs would in theory be released at intervals to make them hit from ten to

Around 05:50. The western ammunition store of Odderøya explodes: pieces of shrapnel, shells and cartridges were flung across the batteries and into the trees, starting numerous fires. (Karl Eilert Grøndahl via K Mæsel)

a hundred metres apart. The German pilots had been warned not to drop any bombs over the city and, as Odderøya was a rather compact target, Bloedorn gave orders to adjust the release mechanism to ten metres. Herrmann dropped his bombs carefully over the fort. The next aircraft mistakenly set the release mechanism to maximum, however, and at least two bombs overshot, landing in the harbour area starting several fires.[16]

The remaining aircraft concentrated on the top of Odderøya. One aircraft had a lucky hit in the western ammunition store. The ensuing explosion shook the whole island and pieces of shrapnel, shells and cartridges were flung across the batteries and into the trees, starting numerous fires. Another stick of bombs hit near the signal station next to the main command bunker, killing two men and wounding several. This hit also severed most external communication to and from Odderøya. Chaos reigned for a while, but few of the gunners were hurt and none of the guns was damaged. The Norwegian Colt machine guns could not reach the aircraft, which stayed mostly above one thousand metres.[17]

Second Run

From the bridge of *Karlsruhe*, the bombing looked efficient. Smoke was everywhere and the mighty explosion of the ammunition storage appeared to be devastating. Expecting the fighting-power of the fort to have been reduced significantly, Rieve ordered his ships to enter Oksøygapet once more at 05:55.[18] The torpedo boats and *Tsingtau* were now en-échelon to the cruiser, with a better field of fire. The S-boats were left outside, securing the rear. Oberstløytnant Fosby, who believed the returning ships had been reinforced by 'one more large ship', opened fire as they passed Dvergsøy once more.[19] The eastern battery was now inoperable because of a faulty mechanism. The other guns, as before, concentrated their fire on *Karlsruhe*. The splashes crept closer and one shell ricocheted off the aircraft catapult on the starboard side.

This time *Karlsruhe*'s own fire was more accurate. Several high-explosive shells hit inside the fort and a number of men were wounded from blast and splinters. Two shells hit the concrete right in front of one of the 21-cm guns. The men were knocked over by the blast and several were wounded by shrapnel and rock fragments. Sergeant Eichinger, though wounded, had his gun firing again within minutes.[20] The He111s were still overhead. They had no more bombs but harassed the gunners through strafing. By now, however, the destroyers *Odin* and *Gyller* were using their A/A guns to some effect and the pilots dared not fly low enough for the strafing to become effective.

As before, several shells also went over the island, landing in the city, where they added to the panic among the civilians. Many small wooden houses were destroyed and it became very dangerous to move about among the ruins. Casualties were reported and it was soon evident that lives had been lost.[21]

The guns at Odderøya were, as were all Norwegian guns, of a significant vintage, and keeping up the rate of fire was difficult, even if the crews worked hard. The strain of the extended fire made the breaches lock or malfunction and the engineering officer, Gunsmith Bekken, rushed from one gun to the next as best he could. Thanks to him most guns remained operational throughout the morning even if the rate of fire inevitably dropped. Onboard the German ships, this was barely noticeable and a deeply concerned Kapitän Rieve was compelled to turn back once again at 06:23. Oberstløytnant Fosby later held that he had observed several hits on the ships, but there is nothing in the German reports to support this.

Rieve realised grimly that it would not be possible to subdue the fort in this manner, and a change of tactics was required. Landing the troops in Vestergapet, as suggested in the operation orders, was considered no better option under the foggy conditions. Rieve decided to withdraw to the south-west outside Oksøygapet, where there would be room to manoeuvre and engage the fort with a full broadside. The longer range meant an indirect, plunging fire, which he believed would be more effective on the open emplacements. Most importantly, the cruiser would be outside the range of the Norwegian guns. The long-range bombardment started around 06:50. Many of the German shells continued to overshoot, landing in the city. Those that hit the island landed mostly near the top, shaking the command bunker, but nobody was seriously hurt. The muzzle flashes could be seen in the haze, outside effective range, and fire was not returned.[22]

Luchs and *Seeadler* were ordered to try to force the narrows under cover of the fire from *Karlsruhe*, but before the torpedo boats could comply, the fog settled again and the attempt was called off. Frustrated, Rieve submitted a request to Kiel for renewed air attacks. The long-range naval bombardment lasted some forty minutes, after which *Karlsruhe* and her consorts vanished.

As the shelling died down, Kapitän Lehmann of *Seattle* decided to move out of harm's way and emerged from the shelter behind Kinn. The officers at Odderøya believed *Seattle* to be a troop transport and saw no reason not to engage her. A 15-cm shell from Vestre Batteri hit the freighter amidships, igniting some gasoline barrels stored there for scuttling purposes. A course was set for Flekkerøy, where *Seattle* was grounded after being hit at least once more. The crew took to the boats and set off, away from the burning wreck. One sailor was seriously injured and several others had light bruises and cuts. The auxiliary *Hval IV* eventually arrived and took the lifeboats in tow, heading for Marvika.[23]

Seattle burning. This photograph was taken from Gleodden, which did not open fire. (Karl Eilert Grøndahl via E Skjold)

* * *

Around 07:30, a twin-engine aircraft approached from the south-west. It flew across the fjord, south of Odderøya, and passed low over Marvika, strafing *U21* and the auxiliary *William Barents*. The A/A machine guns at the naval depot opened up, as did the destroyer *Odin*. The aircraft was identified as British, however, and orders to cease fire were given. After another sweep over Marvika, Flying Officer Charles Wright of 220 Sqn pulled his Hudson back into the clouds. The aircraft was hit; not seriously, but enough for him to set course back to base. En route he sent a signal that he had been fired at by a Norwegian destroyer and had observed a burning transport ship at Flekkerøy (*Seattle*) but otherwise Kristiansand had been quiet. In the fog he had not observed any of the German ships lurking offshore.[24]

Around 07:30. Flying Officer Charles Wright of 220 Sqn took his Hudson twice over Kristiansand in spite of being fired at by the Norwegian A/A defences before being recognised as British. The aircraft was hit, but not seriously, and returned safely to base. (Karl Eilert Grøndahl via K Mæsel)

* * *

A period of calm ensued in Kristiansand. Dead and wounded were attended to, food was distributed and broken telephone lines were repaired. Gunsmith Bekken did the best he could to maintain the guns. The howitzer battery reported that it had only enough unwounded men to man one gun, and the other batteries were also critically low. Oberstløytnant Fosby ordered the guard platoon at the main gate to come to the batteries and the men who had been detached to Marvika for guard duty were also recalled. Further telephoning resulted in forty army cadets being sent to help fight the fires at the ammunition depot.

At Odderøya a perception spread that the battle was over or at least that there would be a lengthy pause. Major Sandberg later wrote: '. . . a hope grew that the ships had received such thrashing that they had abandoned the attack.' Around 07:35 Kristiansand SDS was informed from SDD1 that there had been fighting in Horten harbour and, as Karljohansvern was about to surrender, all further communication with the district would be severed. Kommandør Wigers tried to contact both Horten and the Admiral Staff in Oslo to receive instructions regarding measures against further British aircraft. Neither could be reached, but he was eventually connected to an unidentified officer at the HOK at Slemdal Hotel. From him, Wigers received orders to 'let British forces pass'. Wigers accepted this and forwarded the order to Odderøya at 08:05, adding that further

British aircraft were not to be fired at. Similar orders were subsequently forwarded to the destroyers *Odin* and *Gyller*.[25]

Around 09:00, the fog lifted briefly and the visibility improved sufficiently for Kapitän Rieve to attempt another solo entry through Oksøygapet. The conditions were deceptive, however, and the cruiser missed the entrance, very nearly running aground on the western side of Oksøy. Rieve decided it was not worth risking his ship and settled for another period of idle waiting.[26]

At 09:30, Kommandør Wigers ordered his adjutant Kaptein Boehlke to follow and he left Marvika for Odderøya Fort. There, he walked about, inspecting the batteries and congratulating the crews and officers on a fine job. Oberstløytnant Fosby accompanied him for a while but soon returned to his bunker. Both men believed the German attack had been repelled. Some time later, between 10:00 and 10:30, information was forwarded by telephone from the A/A centre that 'British forces are not to be fired at.' Again, the information was forwarded to the fortress. Added to the earlier false signal regarding the British Navy in Kattegat, these new signals created a strong expectation among the Norwegian officers that an Allied naval force was underway to help them.[27]

Bitter Moments

Meanwhile, the mood on the bridge of *Karlsruhe* was becoming very tense. Rieve realised he was facing a career-damaging failure. The longer he stayed at sea the more exposed his fleet would be to British aircraft and submarines, and they still had troops onboard. By 09:25, a light breeze sprang up and the fog started to clear; Rieve decided there was no time to waste. *Tsingtau* was ordered to take the four most modern S-boats alongside and disembark soldiers for the final attack. These boats were the fastest and sturdiest. As many men as possible were crammed onboard; among them fifty naval artillerymen and their commander, Kapitänleutnant Michaelsen. The troops were to be landed irrespective of opposition under cover from *Karlsruhe* and the others. Once ashore, they should secure the harbour and Odderøya as soon as possible. This would have to succeed! At 10:10 the transfer of the Landsers was complete and *Luchs* and *Seeadler* were ordered towards Oksøygapet at high speed, followed by *S30*, *S31*, *S32* and *S33* in zigzags just behind. *Karlsruhe* and the remaining S-boats followed, with *Tsingtau* bringing up the rear.[28]

At 10:25 the signal station at Smørvarden reported 'two cruisers towards south-south-west', followed a few minutes later by the station at Høyfjell reporting ships approaching Oksøygapet from the south. The wording of the reports and the direction from which they came made most of the officers in the command bunker at Odderøya believe that these ships belonged to a different force. The signalmen at Sotåsen coastguard station, however, recognised the German vessels, and realised these were the same ships again. All four men there later held that the report, 'the same ships are approaching,' was given by telephone to the communication room in Marvika, in accordance with procedure. Here though, no such report was entered into the signal book and was consequently not forwarded to Odderøya. There are indications that the communication personnel at

Around 10:00, Kapitänleutnant Michaelsen's men have embarked onto one of the S-boats from *Tsingtau* and are ready to head for the harbour. (Kapitänleutnant Michaelsen's photo collection via K Mæsel)

Marvika did not trust the 'civilians' on duty at Sotåsen and therefore disregarded their messages.[29]

The fog had not lifted quite as quickly in the fjord as it had further out and the German ships were not observed from the command bunker at Odderøya until they were inside Dvergsøy. At 10:30 they emerged from the fog, heading straight for the entrance to the western harbour and Oberstløytnant Fosby gave the order to shoot again. The senior gunnery officer, Major Sandberg, believed this to be an order for a warning shot against another group of ships and telephoned accordingly to Vestre Batteri. Before they were ready to fire, though, hurried reports arrived from several observers, including the rangefinder in the command bunker. The incoming ships were flying the French tricolour! Fosby immediately countered his last command and ordered 'cease fire'. No shots were therefore fired from any of the guns at Odderøya this time.

Two of the S-boats heading inshore, fully loaded with soldiers. (Kapitänleutnant Michaelsen's photo collection via K Mæsel)

After a few minutes, some believed they could see a swastika inside a roundel on the foredeck of the ship in the van. Others saw a red flag aft. Not until the ships were so far inside the fjord that only the guns of Vestre Batteri could reach them was the German naval flag positively identified on one of the torpedo boats. Oberstløytnant Fosby is said to have shouted 'Fire, God damn it!' At Vestre Batteri, however, only one gun was manned, prepared for a warning shot and trained in the wrong direction.[30]

It is clear that the German ships did *not* fly any French flag. All ships had British flags onboard, but the order to use these during the approach had been countered during the afternoon of 8 April. Konteradmiral Schenk and his Chief of Staff later gave written statements that no foreign flag had been hoisted during any of the entry attempts to Kristiansand and there is no report of any change of flag on any of the German ships before the last run or after they had arrived in the harbour, where all were seen to fly the regular German naval ensign. In any case, Kapitän Rieve had no reason to expect that his ships would not be recognised as the ones that had already been fended off twice: masquerading as another group of ships would not have made sense to him. Neither could he have known that Allied help was anticipated. Still, several officers and men observing through binoculars and rangefinders from the fort were absolutely certain they had seen the tricolor fly and held that they were correct in reporting this to the command bunker.

The Investigation Committee concluded in 1946 that Group IV had not been flying the French flag and the question of what had happened was among the most controversial issues in Norwegian naval history for many years after the war. Many of the men present at Odderøya that day felt mistrusted and accused of making poor excuses for failing at a critical moment and the stamp of an 'easy excuse' smeared the history of an otherwise respectable defence of Kristiansand.

After corresponding with several of the surviving German officers, the naval historian Steen concluded in 1953 that there had been 'some signalling by flag between the ships during the last entry' with, among others, the German naval signal flag 'H'. This is similar in colours to the French tricolour but with the red bar nearest to the mast. In the German Navy of 1940, flag signalling was very much in use. Radio was new and vulnerable, and communication was still left to flags during the day and Aldis lamp at night. Once the signals were issued, two signalmen made the appropriate combinations and hoisted the message in the assigned place on the signal mast. There could be several signals on the mast at any one time in different positions and they would normally be up until countered or replaced. The codebook was a massive volume of single, double and three-letter combinations; it was old fashioned, but very efficient to those used to it. Only the S-boats had for practical purposes changed fully to radio or Aldis lamp, but they could still read the signals from the flagship.

In *Karlsruhe*'s war diary, there is a note at 09:29 (10:29 GeT), of an order to hoist the signal '*heranschliessen*' or 'close up and follow me' and it is quite possible that this remained on the signal mast during the entry. According to the German book of signals, this order would be shown by the flags 'H-Ch' or in other words the inverted 'tricolour' and one other flag. Local historian William Berge asserts that *Luchs* in the van almost certainly was flying the same 'H-Ch', while Knut Mæsel produced a photograph of *Karlsruhe* (in black and white), showing that she might have been flying the signal 'D-H-O' at some

Around 11:00. *Karlsruhe* has just dropped anchor inside Kristiansand harbour. (Author's collection)

stage, meaning '*durch*' or 'steer through'. Hence, several of the German ships were flying red–white–blue flags on their signal masts during the last run.[31]

The combination of orders received that British forces were not to be fired at and incorrect reports of British naval units in the Skagerrak created an expectation that Allied help was imminent in the late morning of 9 April. At the critical moment, a glimpse of what somebody believed to be a French flag gave hope that the returning German ships was the Allied help arriving. With hindsight it is easy to argue that they should have understood more quickly that it was not. These men, however, had a few hours earlier been in battle for the first time and seen their friends and colleagues dead or mutilated. Their hopes lay with the arrival of outside help and it was easy to believe that these ships were friends arriving rather than the enemy once more. It might be said that, according to the Neutrality Instructions, Oberstløytnant Fosby should have opened fire on the ships regardless, as they were entering Kristiansand Krigshavn without permission. He later argued that the order not to fire on British aircraft undoubtedly also meant that Allied ships could enter. Fosby was under huge stress that morning and had only minutes to make decisions of great military and political consequence.

Onboard the German ships, the officers and men could hardly believe what was happening. Not a single shot was fired. At twenty-seven knots the torpedo boats raced through the narrow sound between Odderøya and the small island Dybingen, closely followed by the S-boats. *Luchs* and *Seeadler*, who almost collided in the rush towards the inner harbour, moored at Kommunebrygga, near *Gyller*. The S-boats headed for the 'grain-silo' quay at Odderøya. *Karlsruhe* and *Tsingtau* followed; the latter mooring near the torpedo boats while the cruiser dropped anchor at 10:50.[32]

Kommandør Wigers was at one of the batteries talking to the crews when he was warned of warships approaching once more. He could see the ships coming but also the auxiliary *Hval IV*, which appeared to be heading undaunted for Marvika with two whalers (from

Seattle) in tow. Wigers walked towards the command bunker, followed by his adjutant Kaptein Boehlke, to find out what was going on. The latter went into the bunker and returned with the information that the approaching ships were French. Wigers was very much encouraged by the news of Allied help arriving and decided to drive back to the harbour for a conference with the French C-in-C. It never occurred to him that the identification of the intruders could be false and to his immense surprise, he only realised that the ships were German when he was half-way up the gangway of *Luchs* some twenty minutes later. Seeing who had arrived onboard his ship, Kapitänleutnant Kassbaum demanded that Wigers should immediately give orders for a full surrender. If not, he threatened, Kristiansand would be bombarded ruthlessly. German soldiers were already pouring off the ships and running up the streets towards the centre of the city. The baffled Wigers felt he had no choice but to give in.[33]

As soon as the S-boats had moored, Kapitänleutnant Michaelsen and his men, armed with machine pistols and hand grenades, jumped ashore and advanced up the hill towards the fort. They soon encountered two trucks and forced one of them to take them up the steep road towards the batteries. There was no opposition. Virtually all the guards had been withdrawn to replace casualties at the batteries. Meanwhile, an army unit from 3./IR 310, led by Leutnant Westphal, also disembarked from the S-boats and started to climb the rear of the island.

Kapitänleutnant Michaelsen reached the command bunker at Odderøya around 10:45. Only a handful of his men had followed on the truck, but Michaelsen walked up to Oberstløytnant Fosby, saluted and stated that the Germans 'had come in the name of the Führer to help Norway defend itself against British occupation'. He said that the

Oberstløytnant Fosby experienced the bitterest moment of his life. (Kapitän Rieve's photo collection via K Mæsel)

Kapitänleutnant Michaelsen, holding a hand grenade, forces Major Sandberg to accept the surrender. (Kapitänleutnant Michaelsen's photo collection via K Mæsel)

fort should be surrendered to avoid unnecessary bloodshed. Fosby was very perturbed and replied that the Germans 'had come under false flag'. Michaelsen did not argue, but gave him one minute to accept the situation, after which, he said, his men would start using their guns. Fosby felt helpless; his unarmed men would stand no chance against the German machine pistols. 'One experienced the bitterest moment of one's life,' he later wrote.[34] Michaelsen told Major Sandberg that the officers could keep their sidearms and the men their personal belongings, but the batteries had to be surrendered intact and the officers should facilitate the handover. Michaelsen and Sandberg signed the capitulation; Odderøya Fort was under German control. The radio station in the command bunker was also taken over and contact established with *Karlsruhe* as well as Konteradmiral Schenk and Oberstleutnant Wachsmuth, who were about to establish themselves in the town. At 11:08, Kapitänleutnant Michaelsen could proudly report to Kapitän Rieve, who was stunned by the swiftness of the events: 'All batteries of Odderö are under control.' Half an hour later, *Greif* arrived from Arendal, having completed her mission there.

Leutnant Westphal and his men arrived in hot pursuit of Michaelsen's gunners, heading for the flagpole at the highest point of the island while Michaelsen negotiated with Fosby. The Norwegian flag was lowered and the German swastika raised. Westphal was apparently annoyed at having been beaten to the fort by Michaelsen and acted very brusquely towards the Norwegian prisoners, demanding that the officers should surrender their handguns, contrary to the agreement. Most of the men and NCOs from Odderøya were allowed to leave in the afternoon, while Oberstløytnant Fosby and twenty-nine of his officers were detained.

The three 15-cm guns at Gleodden did not open fire at all during the morning. The battery commander Løytnant Sannes had orders from Oberstløytnant Fosby to fire at any intruders within seven thousand metres range − equivalent to six thousand metres from Odderøya. Sannes later held that during the first two runs he judged that the intruders had always been at least ten thousand metres away, and as the rangefinders at Gleodden could not be used beyond six thousand metres, he could not shoot. When the German ships came back for the third time, Odderøya did not open fire and neither did Løytnant Sannes. Oberstløytnant Fosby was later very critical of the handling of the battery at Gleodden and claimed that the officers there had failed in their duty. Gleodden was surrendered together with Odderøya and taken over by German gunners late in the afternoon.[35]

In all some sixty rounds were fired from the 21-cm guns at Odderøya. The 15-cm guns also fired about sixty rounds and the howitzers twelve to fourteen rounds. One officer, two sergeants and five soldiers were killed, while more than forty were wounded, some seriously. Thirteen civilians were killed and about twenty wounded. There were no German losses. Had the fortress opened fire during the last run, it is likely that this attack might have been repelled as well. At this stage, however, additional aircraft were on their way with heavy bomb loads. If there had been extensive bombing, casualties would likely have been severe and the ultimate outcome the same, even though it would probably have taken longer and incurred German losses.

Eight He111s from I/KG 26 sent in response to Rieve's request for additional air support arrived over Kristiansand, shortly after the German ships had reached the inner harbour. Flying low over the city, Major Gerhard Schäper's aircraft took hits in the port engine, probably from fire from *Odin*. The pilot, Oberleutnant Hippel, struggled to keep the machine airborne, but the engine seized and he had to land at sea, some thirty kilometres offshore. Three of the five-man crew were wounded, one seriously, but they managed to get into the rubber dinghy before the aircraft sank. Several of the other aircraft were damaged too, but all the others returned to base.

Shortly after 15:00, a British Wellington of 9 Sqn flying from Lossiemouth appeared over the city. Squadron Leader Jarman had been tasked with reconnoitring the coastline from Kristiansand to Bergen. Coming in very low, he totally surprised the German gunners and was out of sight before they could open fire. Heading north, he sent a signal reporting 'one *Emden*-class cruiser and four smaller warships' in Kristiansand harbour. Two hours later, Pilot Officer Heathcote, also from 9 Sqn, swept his Wellington over the city, taking several photographs and registering that a 'K-class cruiser' was still in the harbour while the minesweepers were just leaving. The German A/A guns opened up but Heathcote and his crew escaped, though thoroughly shaken. At 20:42 the last British reconnaissance aircraft of the day arrived: this time a Hudson from 220 Sqn piloted by Pilot Officer Carey. This also got a warm welcome, even if by now *Karlsruhe* and the torpedo boats had left, and it was too dark to observe much except the burning wreck of *Seattle* outside the harbour.[36]

The landing of the troops and equipment was largely concluded by 14:00, and by 16:00 a relieved Kapitän Rieve received confirmation from Major Schröder, the commander of I/IR 310, that Kristiansand was now firmly in German hands. It was considerably later than expected, but was a success – and not a single German life had been lost. Mission accomplished, Rieve had no wish to remain in Kristiansand overnight. As had been demonstrated several times, the city was well within reach of British bombers and the longer he stayed, the more likely an attack would be. Hence, *Karlsruhe* weighed anchor and passed Oksøygapet outward bound in the company of *Greif*, *Luchs* and *Seeadler* at 18:00.

Meanwhile, Konteradmiral Schenk was acknowledged as admiral of the Norwegian South Coast and established a temporary headquarters onboard *Tsingtau*, which was to remain there for the time being. A request from Kommandør Wigers to meet with Konteradmiral Schenk was dismissed. There was much to consider and the Norwegian commander was irrelevant, having surrendered.

The transports *Westsee*, *August Leonhardt* and *Wiegand* arrived during the afternoon and unloading immediately commenced. These brought supplies, heavy weapons, fuel, vehicles and the remaining one third of the men of I/IR 310. The fourth transport, *Kreta*, with heavy A/A guns, was chased into Norwegian territorial waters by *Trident* and did not arrive for another couple of days. In the morning of 11 April, the torpedo boats *Falke* and *Jaguar* arrived from Kiel. They had a small number of troops onboard; their presence was mainly to augment the defences. During the following days, they remained in harbour or patrolled offshore.[37]

Arendal

The task of maintaining the neutrality of the Norwegian coast east of Kristiansand towards the Oslofjord was in the hands of the young Løytnant Thore Holthe, captain of the torpedo boat *Jo* and commander of 3rd Torpedo Boat Division. In the evening of 8 April, *Jo* was in Arendal, *Grib* in Risør and *Ravn* in Langesund, while *Ørn* and *Lom* were at the naval yard in Horten for repairs. *Jo*'s normal mooring was at Hisøy, a little off Arendal harbour, where she was tied up with her stern pointing towards the town and a telephone landline connected to the radio room. Because of the alerts, ammunition had been brought to the two 37-mm midship machine cannons and the Colt machine gun. Both torpedoes had recently been inspected and everything was in perfect order. During the evening, Holthe was copied in on some of the signals reporting German ships moving through Danish waters as well as intruders in the Oslofjord. After midnight, he did not receive any further information or orders. Thus, the first and only knowledge Holthe and his eighteen-man crew had that something was happening was the radio news-broadcast at 07:00.

Being detached off Hanstholm after midnight, Kapitänleutnant Wilhelm Freiherr von Lyncker set the torpedoboat *Greif* on an independent course towards Arendal. Onboard were ninety men from Bicycle Squadron 234 of 163rd ID under the command of Rittmeister Schmidt-Wesendahl. As at Egersund, the place was only important because of the presence of a telegraph cable to England, which had to be severed to prevent the Norwegian government communicating with the Allies. To do this and to secure control of the telegraph station, which was important for communication between Oslo and most of southern Norway, ten signal experts were also onboard *Greif*. Once landed the Landsers would establish contact with IR 310 in Kristiansand and 163rd ID in Oslo and wait for reinforcements. No significant opposition was expected and the soldiers were lightly armed. *Greif* had orders to depart once the town was under control and to rejoin Group IV in Kristiansand. Korvettenkapitän Wolf Henne, leader of 5th Torpedo Boat Flotilla, was onboard *Greif* and in overall charge of the operation.

As in Kristiansand, the dense fog forced Henne and von Lyncker to wait for hours beyond Weserzeit before they dared enter the narrow inlet to Arendal. Only at 08:20 did the grey torpedo boat move slowly through Galtesund, heading for the customs quay. The boat moored and the soldiers jumped ashore with their bicycles, spreading into the town. There was no opposition and the signal experts also disembarked. Within twenty minutes, all men and equipment had been landed and Henne ordered von Lyncker to cast off. *Greif* left Arendal shortly after 09:00, heading for Kristiansand at 23 knots.

Rittmeister Schmidt-Wesendahl posted sentries at the railway station, police station and other buildings, while he himself marched off to secure the main prize: the telegraph station. Another platoon was sent off on their bicycles to find where the cable ran into the sea and severed it. Once communication had been established with superior units, they all settled down to wait. Not a single shot had been fired. It is not known when the Germans learned that the Arendal cable had not been operational since Christmas due to a malfunction.

Løytnant Holthe contacted the captains of *Grib* and *Ravn* by telephone during the morning, agreeing that the three boats should meet in Lyngør in the afternoon. Preparations were made to depart Arendal as soon as the fog had lifted. Around 08:30 a grey, sleek warship emerged through the fog. 'It is *Sleipner*,' somebody remarked but Holthe, recognising the German naval flag, corrected him: 'It's a bloody German destroyer.'

Holthe's instinctive reaction was to fire his torpedoes. Arendal was no krigshavn, though, and therefore not an area where force should be applied without further orders. Holthe had no such orders. Nor had he information of what was going on in the country other than what he had heard on the public radio, and he did not know if Norway was at war. Moreover, *Jo* would have to cast off and turn around to be able to fire her torpedoes at all. Holthe reckoned the German, vastly better armed than his own tiny boat, would open fire before *Jo* could get into position, which was likely to be devastating in the confined waters.[38] While pondering what to do, the quay behind *Greif* had filled up with curious civilians: an explosion onboard the German boat would certainly result in collateral damage. Before the young lieutenant could make up his mind, *Greif* solved the issue by

The torpedo boat *Jo* at her mooring outside Arendal. (Marinemuseet)

casting off, leaving the way she had come, apparently never registering the presence of *Jo*, which had her slim stern pointing towards the harbour. Holthe also cast off and took his boat east through Tromøysund at maximum speed in order to be in a favourable position for attack, should *Greif* head that way after entering open sea. She did not, and was never seen again from *Jo*.

After waiting for some time, Holthe ordered speed and set course for Lyngør to meet up with the rest of his division. Neither of the two other boats had seen any German ships or aircraft at all during the morning. Holthe tried to contact a superior to receive orders. Eventually, he learned that a German attack on Norway was developing and that SDD1 had surrendered. The three boats stayed in the area trying to establish a seaward defence for the Norwegian forces mobilising in Telemark. Contact with superiors was sporadic and largely confusing. Holthe considered the possibility of going to Britain, but deficiency of intelligence and a shortage of coal for his boats eventually precluded this. German aircraft were constantly chasing them and all boats sustained damage fighting back. By 17 April ammunition was running low and the situation was unsustainable. A last stand seemed pointless and after having brought ashore weapons and equipment, *Jo*, *Grib* and *Ravn* were sunk south of Lyngør. The crews were dismissed to go home, the three captains headed for the remains of the RNN in the west.[39]

Shambles

The account of the Norwegian Navy ships at Kristiansand is a sad story. Though smaller than the German torpedo boats, the armament of *Odin* and *Gyller* were of similar magnitude and their nimbleness should have been to their advantage inside the confined waters of Kristiansand Krigshavn.[40] In addition, the two submarines, however obsolete, had four torpedo tubes each and if utilised with resolve could have made a significant difference – even if acting as no more than floating torpedo batteries lurking in the fog behind the islands. Had the forewarnings been taken seriously, additional positions of defence, augmenting the shore batteries, would have made Kristiansand virtually impenetrable for Group IV. Oberstløytnant Fosby later stated that he had been assured by Kommandør Wigers in the evening of 8 April that one destroyer would be deployed in Vestergapet, one behind Dvergsøy and one submarine at Oksøygapet. This was not to be.[41]

At nightfall on 8 April, Kommandør Wigers gave orders to Kaptein Bro of *B2*, the senior of the two submarines stationed at Kristiansand, to deploy outside Oksøy, so as to be ready at first light in case an attack should materialise. Unbelievably, Bro questioned the order, claiming the crews would be too tired if they were to be on station during the night. Instead, he suggested the boats should move out at first light. Even more incredibly, Wigers accepted this and left Bro to decide for himself when to depart.[42]

At 04:45 Marvika received a call with information that the two submarines would cast off in fifteen minutes and asking if there was any news during the night. Bro later held he was told there was none and he concluded that the reported incident in outer Oslofjord had been between British and German units and of no consequence to them in

Kristiansand. Shortly after 05:00, both submarines slipped their moorings – some time after 'first light'.[43] As the boats sailed, the first warning shots from Odderøya could be heard. According to standing orders for the Neutrality Watch, alien ships entering the krigshavn should be engaged with all means and the fact that Odderøya had opened fire should have left no doubt as to what was happening.

While B2 was diving, her gyrocompass became unserviceable and Kaptein Bro decided he could not operate without it. Thus he resurfaced and set course for Fiskå Verk, where he could shelter his boat under a huge crane while trying to repair it and inform Marvika what had happened. It is difficult to accept the loss of the gyrocompass as sufficient reason not to risk a surface attack from a sheltered position in the confined and familiar ranges of the fjord.

As B5 trimmed for diving, aircraft were sighted overhead. These were identified as non-Norwegian; as B5 dived, one swooped down on the submarine, strafing the tower. Kaptein Brekke decided it was inadvisable to proceed down the shallow waters of the fjord at periscope depth with aircraft about. He therefore took his boat down to the bottom of the harbour at forty metres where he stayed for several hours. Surfacing around 10:00 and mooring, Brekke went ashore looking for a telephone just as Group IV entered Kristiansand. Later he moved to Fiskå Verk where both B2 and B5 were immobilised by German officers.[44]

Kommandør Wigers believed that the two destroyers Odin and Gyller were best suited to augment the air defence of Kristiansand and 'found it was best they remained where they were'. Thus, neither Kaptein Gunvaldsen nor Kaptein Holck received any tactical orders during the night and, through a grave oversight, neither was informed that warships were approaching. Once the firing started from the fort, Odin left Marvika heading for Topdalsfjord, where Kaptein Gunvaldsen felt his ship would be better protected from air attacks. The destroyer opened fire on aircraft identified as German with its 20-mm Oerlikon and two 12.7-mm Colt cannons on several occasions, but in spite of definite hits effects appeared limited. Some of the aircraft returned the fire and some dropped bombs but there was no damage to the destroyer. Around 10:00, a signal was received from Marvika that 'British ships shall pass', which was interpreted to mean that a force was actually on its way. During a subsequent air attack, warships were sighted heading for the harbour at high speed, and it was assumed these were British; especially as the fortress did not open fire. Later, an officer was sent to Marvika for information and he returned with the news that the SDS had surrendered and ordered the ships to cease fire. Kaptein Gunvaldsen called Kommandør Wigers and suggested Odin should try to escape eastward. Instead he was ordered to return to Marvika, where an S-boat approached, sending an officer onboard. He verified that all ammunition was stored but otherwise left the destroyer alone, leaving the Norwegian flag flying.

Gyller remained at the customs quay, firing at aircraft within reach until 08:00, when Kaptein Holck cast off, taking his destroyer to a position between Dybingen and Odderøya, where he could cover the entry to the inner harbour. Around 10:00, Gyller received the signal 'British ships shall pass', and, like Gunvaldsen, Holck took this to indicate that a British force was actually approaching. During the morning, Holck decided his position at the harbour entrance was too exposed and decided to join Odin at Topdalsfjord. First, however, he returned to the harbour to discuss matters with the SDS over the telephone. While he was mooring, two ships entered the harbour at high speed (*Luchs* and *Seeadler*) followed by half a dozen small torpedo boats. Holck at first assumed they were British and only later did he see the German flag. He ran ashore to find a telephone to inform Marvika of the nationality of the ships; as he returned he could see Kommandør Wigers walk up the gangway of one of them. Shortly after, Kapitän Klinger of *Tsingtau* came onboard *Gyller* with some of his officers. He assured them that they had come as friends and asked for Holck's co-operation. A guard was posted on the quay and parts of the radio were removed – but the Norwegian flag was allowed to remain at the mast.[45]

Wigers later wrote that he felt he could not order the two destroyers to attack the intruders as he had been informed they consisted of 'two large ships and several cruisers'. No attempt was made to verify the strength of the intruders from the fort, or to discuss with the two captains what might have been done. For the auxiliaries in the fjords around Kristiansand, the morning was generally confused and uncertain. As their standing order was to observe, report and stay out of harm's way, there is little to criticise them for.

At Kjevik, little happened during the early morning and none of the German aircraft ventured in the direction of the airfield. At 09:30, half a dozen Fokkers and a Caproni that had escaped from Sola landed briefly, but took off again after a quick refuel, heading east. By afternoon, the commander of the guard force, Kaptein Kristian Sundby, believed he was about to become isolated from the retreating Norwegian forces; between 15:00 and 16:00 he ordered his men to block the runway and started pulling out. At the same time one of the Ju52s of KGzbV 106, returning from Sola, was getting desperately low on fuel over the Skagerrak. Hauptman Bøhner ordered his pilot, Oberleutnant Roll, to head for Kjevik. They landed safely among the rubble on the runway just as the last soldiers drove off. Kjevik was in German hands. During the night, the runway was cleared and secured and next day reinforcements started to arrive.

During 9 and 10 April some twenty thousand people, about 85 per cent of the population, evacuated from Kristiansand. Most left by train northwards, up Setesdal. British attacks and bombing of the city was expected and after the casualties and destruction of the morning, few wished to remain. The Germans let the evacuation take place. It facilitated their taking over of the city and made the establishment of Norwegian defence lines difficult.

By the morning of 10 April, Kristiansand Fortress was fully in German hands and, bar heavy A/A guns, which would not be available until the transport *Kreta* arrived some days later, ready to defend the entry to the Skagerrak. Reinforcements started arriving in the form of 2nd and 3rd Battalion of IR 310. They first came through Oslo, but once Kjevik airfield had been cleared, the airlift was shifted there, to speed up the process and relieve Fornebu from further chaos. By evening on the 11th, some three thousand men and their equipment had been flown in.[46]

After departing Egersund in the early morning of 9 April, *M1*, *M9*, *M2* and *M13* were already on their way back to Kiel when orders were received from Konteradmiral Schenk around 09:00 to head for Kristiansand to assist Group IV. Luckily for Major Schäper and his miserable crew drifting in the Skagerrak, the minesweepers passed right by their little dinghy. *M1* hove to and picked up the airmen before rejoining the others. Korvettenkapitän Thoma and his minesweepers arrived in Kristiansand in the afternoon, by which time their assistance was no longer required. Hence, they left within a few hours after landing the rescued airmen, apart from *M1*, which developed a temporary engine problem and stayed behind.[47]

Konteradmiral Schenk decided to order most of the Norwegian ships to Marvika, where *Odin* already was, to keep them out of the way in case of British air attacks. Wigers was finally invited onboard *Tsingtau* in the afternoon of 11 April. Konteradmiral Schenk informed him that there was a condition of war between the two countries and that it had become necessary to take command of the Norwegian ships. The men should leave immediately, taking nothing but their personal belongings; the officers would be released as soon as they had signed a declaration of non-resistance.[48] At the end of the meeting, Wigers was informed by Schenk that Oberstløytnant Fosby and twenty-nine of his officers had been taken hostage and would be shot, unless Kapitänleutnant Wolf-Harro Stiebler of *U21* and those of his men still in Norwegian custody were released. The Germans were released on 14 April, but Oberstløytnant Fosby and his officers were held until the middle of May. Kommandør Wigers, having signed the required declaration, was allowed to travel to Horten to report to Kontreadmiral Smith-Johannsen.[49]

When the Germans landed in Kristiansand, Generalmajor Liljedahl pulled his widespread forces north to try to establish a defence line in Setesdal. After a while, however, the Norwegian lines were swamped by refugees and when German reconnaissance units broke through, confusion was almost total. All kinds of rumours flourished and stories of strong German forces moving north, supported by tanks and aircraft, were taken at face value. The Germans had no more than one battalion and no armoured vehicles at all. They did, however, have support from aircraft and these were flown as much as possible over the Norwegian lines to intimidate soldiers and refugees alike, bombing and strafing at will. The tactics worked, and on 15 April the Norwegian forces in Setesdal, some two thousand men, surrendered unconditionally without a single shot having been fired. It was one of the most shameful episodes during the invasion and severely damaged the strategic position and morale of the Norwegian Army in southern Norway.[50]

— 8 —

Stavanger–Egersund

North Sea Corner

IN EARLY APRIL, HAUPTMANN Günter Capito, commander of the Ju52-equipped transport squadron 7./KGzbV 1 was invited to meet Oberleutnant Otto von Brandis, commanding officer of the 3rd company of the Parachute Regiment (3./FschJgRgt 1). He was taken into a locked room, empty apart from a huge sandbox, presenting a detailed miniature landscape with beaches, hills and woods – and in the middle of it all, an airfield. Von Brandis admitted he did not know where the airfield was, but he did know that it would be the target of an operation within the next few days and that Capito and his pilots would fly the paratroopers into battle. The two officers spent the evening discussing how to approach the airfield, where to make the drop and how to get away. Not until the evening of 8 April, after he and his pilots had been quarantined at Stade airport, did Capito learn that the model he had seen was of Sola airfield outside Stavanger in south-western Norway.[1]

In the late 1930s, the newly opened Sola-Stavanger airfield was nearer to Britain than any German-controlled airfield and only 500 kilometres from Scapa Flow.[2] A blockade of

Sola-Stavanger airfield, opened in 1937, was Norway's first regular civilian airfield with concrete runways and a seaplane harbour. (T Ødemotland collection)

the northern entrances to the North Sea would be virtually impossible should Germany secure possession of Sola. Likewise, British control of the airfield would be catastrophic for Operation Weserübung. The German planners had Sola as a high-priority target that would have to be secured at all costs at the start of the invasion. It was agreed that this could best be accomplished as a Luftwaffe affair with paratroopers spearheading airborne troops flown in by transport aircraft. Heavy equipment would be brought to Stavanger harbour by ship. No naval forces were assigned to this part of the operation as there were no fortifications or artillery positions protecting the harbour.[3]

The Hunter Hunted

The 6,780-BRT freighter *Roda* was one of the seven transport ships of the Ausfuhrstaffel. She left Brunsbüttel on 7 April, disguised as regular traffic to the Russian Arctic, but her cargo consisted of four 10.5-cm guns to protect the entrance to Stavanger harbour, A/A guns, vehicles, ammunition and other provisions for the troops of IR 193 that were to be flown in to Sola airport. *Roda* arrived at Stavanger late in the evening of the 8th and anchored at Hundvåg. She was flying a German merchant flag and signalled for customs clearance to enter the port. The three other freighters destined for Stavanger, *Mendoza*, *Tijuca* and *Tübingen*, chose to wait offshore.

The RNN had a significant numerical presence in the south-west in April 1940, but most of the ships were old and small. The most modern vessel, the destroyer *Æger*, was on patrol offshore in the morning of 8 April when Kaptein Niels Bruun heard of the British mine-laying on the radio. Bruun later wrote that he became 'convinced that Norway was

Kaptein Niels Bruun of *Æger*.
(Marinemuseet)

about to be dragged into the war' and, obtaining approval from his superior in Bergen, Kontreadmiral Tank-Nielsen, returned to Stavanger to prepare his ship accordingly. By early evening *Æger* was moored in Østre Havn, fully fuelled, with torpedoes and depth charges armed, all guns ready and a telephone cable to land. At 22:00, Bruun received instructions from SDD2 to 'prepare for war' and could confidently report that his ship was as ready as could be. The signal gave no indication of what was to be expected, or who the potential adversary might be.

Around 01:00, two police officers came onboard, reporting that *Roda* had been inspected upon anchoring. Papers had been insufficient and as the hatches were covered by a deck-load of coal, it had not been possible to ascertain her cargo. Hence, she had not been given permission to enter Stavanger harbour and the captain had requested the German consul be allowed to come onboard. Kaptein Bruun decided that anybody wanting to board the ship should be brought to him first. Half an hour later, the assistant consul, Kapitän Mathy, arrived. He could give no explanation as to why it was necessary for him to go onboard *Roda* and Bruun denied him access.[4] Instead, the two police officers were sent across with an officer to find out what cargo she carried and where she was heading. Kapitän Wiersbitzki was less than co-operative, though, and the Norwegians returned none the wiser.

Around 02:30, a brief signal notified Bruun that *Bolærne* was 'in battle' but not with whom or why. He radioed back for further information but received no answer. At 04:15, another signal arrived, informing him that 'warships were entering the Bergen Leads'. Still there was no information as to the identity of the attackers. 'Many thoughts went through my head during these hours,' Bruun later wrote. 'Above all, I thought it inappropriate of me to start a war all on my own, especially as I didn't know for sure who the intruders were.'

The destroyer *Æger* escorting the American freighter *City of Flint*. *Æger* was delivered from the naval yard in Horten in August 1936. She displaced 735 tons and the two De Laval turbines gave her a maximum speed of thirty-two knots. Armament was three 10-cm L/40 guns, one 40-mm Bofors and two 0.5-inch Colt machine guns, as well as two torpedo tubes and a fair number of depth charges on the quarterdeck. (Marinemuset)

Roda sinking off Stavanger harbour around 08:00 on 9 April. The lifeboats have been swung out but several are still in place even though at an angle, showing the urgency with which she was abandoned. (Marinemuset)

He decided the best thing to do would be to get the German freighter out of the way and free up *Æger* for other tasks. The pilot recommended a secluded fjord east of Stavanger and Bruun cast off. Gunnery Lieutenant Reinhardtsen and eight armed sailors were sent across to *Roda* with orders to make the radio unserviceable, replace the German flag with a Norwegian one and prepare the ship to move. Wiersbitzki remained unenthusiastic, and everything was delayed as much as possible in spite of repeated orders. The radio room was sealed off and put under guard, but, contrary to Bruun's specific instructions, the radio was left intact.

When daylight broke and *Roda* was still not under steam, Bruun lost his patience. He hailed across for the prize crew to return and for *Roda*'s crew to take to the boats. Once he had picked up his own men, *Æger* was moved into position and Bruun ordered a 10-cm cold grenade to be fired into the bow of the freighter, 'to get rid of her – even if that could mean war with Germany', Bruun wrote, adding, 'This was something my crew was not fully up to and I had to give the order three times before they would shoot.'[5]

At last the Germans took to the boats and at 07:00 Bruun started a systematic pounding with cold grenades into *Roda*'s starboard waterline. After about twenty-five shots he moved *Æger* to the other side. To his surprise, he found two men paddling away on a float. This turned out to be Kapitän Wiersbitzki and a sailor. A nearby civilian vessel was ordered to pick them up and bring them to shore while *Æger* continued the pounding. What Bruun did not know was that Wiersbitzki had broken into the sealed radio room and sent a signal that had been picked up by *Tübingen* at anchor off Sola and forwarded to the Weserübung command in Hamburg. With *Roda* listing heavily, Bruun ceased fire and pulled away to assess the situation.[6]

*   *   *

Around 08:00, a couple of aircraft were sighted to the west, black under-wing crosses clearly visible. The events at Sola were unknown to Bruun, but, certain that the intruders reported elsewhere in the country were German, he ordered fire to be opened from Æger's 40-mm Bofors and two 12.7-mm Colt machine guns. No aircraft were hit and they vanished northwards. Not long after, a further eight to ten aircraft appeared, circling the destroyer. These were Ju88s of 8./KG 4. Several sources claim they had been called by the distress signal from *Roda*, forwarded from *Tübingen*, but this cannot be verified and may give German inter-service communication too much credit. The radio signal from the aircraft after the engagement rather indicates that they attacked in response to being fired at, which is much more likely.

At first the aircraft stayed high and attacked in singles from a respectful distance. Bruun ordered maximum speed and the nimble destroyer zigzagged away from the bombs with relative ease. The Bofors gun was handled particularly well and proved hazardous for the attacking aircraft; several were seriously hit. Two were later held to have crashed, but this does not match confirmed German losses. At 08:30 disaster struck for *Æger*. Three aircraft attacked simultaneously at a very low level, and a 250-kg bomb hit *Æger* just aft of the funnel, exploding below deck in the confines between the two engine rooms. The blast wrecked the entire midship of the destroyer and the Bofors as well as the two Colts were put out of action. Several of the engine crew and anti-aircraft gunners were killed or seriously wounded. From twisting and turning at twenty-five knots, *Æger* had become a limp wreck with decks awash and smoke streaming from a mess of twisted plates.

The aircraft kept coming. One bomb grazed the mast and another hit the side of the forecastle without exploding. Seeing the Bofors gone, the aircraft moved in to strafe the men who were moving about on deck, trying to help the wounded. Incredibly, no one was

Æger aground in Kråkenesbukta north-west on Hundvåg with her back broken.
(Marinemuset)

hit. Bruun had no further means of defence and, to limit the perils of his men, decided to strike the flag, which had been flying since first light. The German pilots acknowledged and held back, shortly before heading home, as fuel was getting low. A signal was sent: 'Attacked Norwegian destroyer due to resistance. Sunk after two hits.'

Kaptein Bruun ordered his men to abandon ship. It was not far to the island of Hundvåg where the shocked people in the nearest houses did what they could to help. Seven men had been killed. Another eleven were seriously wounded and taken to hospital, where one later died. Bruun dismissed the rest of his men, advising them to rejoin the navy where they could.[7] The wreck of *Æger* drifted ashore at Hundvåg. Finding the two 10-cm guns and the Bofors undamaged, the Germans removed these to use in the defence of Stavanger port, replacing the guns lost when *Roda* sank.[8]

First Blood

On 29 March, eight hundred men of Jegerbataljonen (the Ranger Battalion) of IR 2 from Oslo arrived to take up the defence of Sola and the Stavanger peninsula. These men, quartered at Madlamoen between the airfield and the city, had been given sixty to eighty days' training before being sent west and were supposedly among the better-trained units of the Neutrality Watch. Oberst Gunnar Spørck, the C-in-C of the Norwegian Army in the Stavanger area, deployed one rifle platoon and one machine-gun platoon to Sola on a weekly rotational basis and kept a similar force in reserve. Nine machine guns were available, three of which had A/A mountings. One bunker had just been completed, another was under construction.[9] The rest of the guns were in open positions. Significant private funds had been collected to purchase A/A guns for the airfield, but it had been difficult to find suitable guns to buy and none was in place.

The bomber wing of the Army Air Arm had four Fokker CV bi-planes and four Caproni Ca310 bombers at Sola under the command of Løytnant Halfdan Hansen.[10] In mid-March, it had been decided by the General Staff that the bomber wing and the scout wing at Kjeller should change places and the first men of the scout wing had arrived to prepare the exchange.[11] At Sola seaplane base, west of the airfield proper, the Navy Air Arm operated two MF11 reconnaissance aircraft and one He115 under the command of Lieutenant August Stansberg.[12] These regularly patrolled the coast and territorial waters from Egersund to north of Haugesund.

Løytnant Hansen was certain that the British mine-laying was only the start of serious events. A request to division in Kristiansand for permission to prepare for demolition of the runways at Sola was to his surprise and irritation denied.[13] Nevertheless, he ordered all aircrews to remain at the base overnight and be ready to fly at short notice. The news of battles in the Oslofjord made him order the machine-gun positions manned and all aircraft made ready immediately. Around 02:00, Hansen called SDD2 in Bergen to let them know that the Fokkers and Capronis were standing by with bombs loaded, in case any maritime targets should be considered. To his frustration he was told that there was no use for them at the moment and no orders. The army forces at Stavanger, including the army aircraft at Sola, reported to 3rd Division in Kristiansand. The naval forces, including the naval aircraft, reported to SDD2 in Bergen. Inter-service liaison and communication were not facilitated by such an arrangement. Hansen discussed the situation with Løytnant Stansberg at the seaplane base, but he had already received orders to conduct a reconnaissance patrol at dawn and had little to add. Hansen discussed matters with the civilian airport manager Ullestad-Olsen. They agreed to close off as much as possible of the airfield and rolls of heavy wire were placed across the runways a hundred metres apart, keeping only a small section open should the bombers need to take off at short notice.

At 05:00, Stansberg took off from the seaplane base in his MF11.[14] Off Feistein Island south of the airport, he came across the freighter *Tübingen* and returned to Sola, dropping a message bag with its position before resuming the flight. More than a dozen other freighters were sighted offshore, as was a U-boat (*U4*) and several German aircraft. When returning to Sola around 08:00, Stansberg found the airfield under attack. He decided there was little he could do other than to get out of danger and headed north towards Haugesund, low on fuel. Acting on Stansberg's report in the drop bag, Løytnant Hansen ordered Løytnant Christian Jean-Hansen to investigate. He took off at 06:00 in a Fokker loaded with four 50-kg bombs. After he had left, an order came by telephone from SDD2: 'Do not bomb.' Hansen found the order meaningless but was obliged to forward it to Jean-Hansen, who had no option but to obey and head back to the airfield.[15]

Meanwhile, some two hundred kilometres from Sola, the aircraft of the first German attack wave were in trouble, enshrouded in heavy fog.[16] Oberleutnant Gordon Gollob in charge of the Bf110s from 3./ZG 76 decided it was not going to work and turned around, intending to land at Aalborg airfield in Denmark – which he expected to be in German hands – and to wait for the fog to lift. Gollob was under strict radio silence and could only hope that the other aircraft of his Staffel would see what he was doing and follow. Three did. One more probably started to turn but collided with one that did not, as two aircraft vanished without a trace. The last two, flown by Oberfeldwebel Fleishmann and Feldwebel Gröning, continued unknowingly through the murk towards Stavanger.

Hauptmann Capito was in a similar situation. His twelve Ju52s had taken off from Stade airfield west of Hamburg loaded with paratroopers, twelve to each plane. With almost 650 kilometres to Sola the lumbering Junkers would need over three hours to get there and it was critical that the paratroopers arrived at exactly the right time: after the bombers and fighters had subdued the defences, but in time to capture the airfield before the transports arrived. Half-way across the Skagerrak, the fog was so thick that Capito could barely see his own wingtips and he had no knowledge of what lay ahead. 'It was difficult,' he later wrote:

> . . . the whole squadron was swallowed up and despite the closest formation, the nearest plane was like a phantom. Even if the soldiers had parachutes, they would land in the sea if they managed to get out and none had a lifebelt. And what if the fog extended over land? It would be certain suicide. On the other hand it was our first war effort and the paratroopers were as eager as I to succeed and if we turned, those coming behind would have nowhere to land. The mission would have to be completed! I was only 27 at the time and the decision was based as much on youthful light-headedness as bravery.[17]

The Junkers continued. Another tense half-hour passed. All of a sudden there was a glimmer of light and as if by magic, Capito was in the clear. He was about a hundred kilometres from his target and could just see the rugged Norwegian coastline ahead. Banking slowly, so as not to disturb the paratroopers, he looked back at the wall of fog and saw all but one of his aircraft emerge. There was no time to wait for the last. Fuel was precious and they were behind schedule.[18] With the other Junkers gathering on him, the young hauptmann continued towards Sola at wave-top height. His courageous gamble had succeeded. Not far behind, a hundred Ju52s followed with I and II/IR 193, including Oberst von Beeren and his regimental staff.[19]

Shortly before 08:00, orders came from Oslo that the aircraft of the bomber wing at Sola were to move east as soon as possible. Løytnant Hansen had to fly with them in his own aircraft and leave Sola at the time when he would be needed most. Command of the airfield was handed over to the intelligence officer, Løytnant Thor Tangvald. Just as the Capronis and Fokkers were taking off, eight Ju88s of 8./KG 4 roared over the airfield a few hundred metres above the ground, guns blazing. There was no advance warning and everybody was taken by surprise. One Caproni was hit repeatedly and had to make an emergency landing between the wire rolls. The other aircraft headed off. Neither of them would be of much use in aerial combat.[20]

The Ju88s came down to twenty to thirty metres, dropping bombs and firing their guns at anything that moved. Many of the rangers, caught off guard, were almost paralysed with fear. The three A/A machine guns led by Løytnant John Kristensen opened fire but the guns had little effect on the aircraft other than attracting their attention. The inexperienced gunners fired indiscriminately at the Junkers and the water-cooled machine guns soon overheated and Løytnant Kristensen ordered his men into cover. When the machine guns fell silent, many of the rangers pulled back and some deserted. The Ju88s headed off after a while but were immediately replaced by two Bf110s: Oberfeldwebel Fleishmann and Feldwebel Gröning had arrived according to schedule. Had the two Bf110s turned as the others did, the defenders might have had time to regroup and deploy properly and the situation for the paratroopers could have been far worse than it eventually turned out to be. However, the defenders remained pinned down and fear and uncertainty prevailed.

At 08:20 the Bf110s pulled up, making room for eleven three-engine aircraft coming in from the south-east. Hauptmann Capito had taken his Junkers over land south of the airfield and, hugging the ground, approached the target behind some hills. While climbing to 120 metres, the doors were opened and the paratroopers made themselves ready. Capito had a brief glance at the airfield and registered that it looked just like the model: 'As we had discussed over the sandbox, I aimed for the hangar and saw the other aircraft following. Back with the throttle, lights on green. The troopers were gone in seconds and we dived back down to pick up speed and avoid any A/A-fire and headed away. Our mission was completed.'[21]

To the amazement of the Norwegian soldiers, parachutes started to open up behind the aircraft as they passed over the airfield. Oberleutnant von Brandis and his 134 men jumped into battle. They were a good hour behind their comrades in 4th Company that had landed to secure the Storstrøm Bridge in Denmark, but unlike the situation there, this would be real combat.

Fallschirmjägers landing on Sola in the morning of 9 April. At least sixty parachutes are on the ground, some of them from equipment containers. The group in the air have just jumped from the aircraft in the upper right corner and are among the last to land. The bunker with Johansen's machine gun was hidden inside the shed with the black roof just in front of the wing of the aircraft from which the photo was taken – probably the communication aircraft in which Oberst von Beeren was waiting to land as soon as the airfield was secure. (Fotosamlingen, Flyhistorisk Museum Sola)

The German Fallschirmjäger had two particular tactical disadvantages on their way into battle. First, the trooper was connected to his parachute by a single strap in the harness at the centre of his back. After leaving the plane in a tumbling dive, a static line opened the parachute and he would be dangling below with little control over his descent. The result was a hard landing, requiring a forward roll that often resulted in injuries. Secondly, due to the difficult landing, the Jägers jumped with no equipment, except for a pistol and a knife. Weapons and equipment were dropped in containers, between the troopers. After landing, they had to locate the right container and retrieve their guns before they were ready for combat. No easy task under fire.

The Norwegian defenders had no knowledge whatsoever of this, and wasted their limited ammunition on the aircraft. One of the few men to keep his head was the 25-year-old machine gunner Ragnar Johansen in the only completed bunker, at Svihus, east of the runway.[22] Most of the Fallschirmjägers landed in Johansen's fire sector and were pinned down, virtually helpless. Eventually, some Jägers landed further away and after a while managed to reach their containers, retrieving guns and hand grenades. Approaching the bunker from behind, they blew the door open and a wounded Johansen was confined.

Once Johansen's machine gun was silenced, the Fallschirmjägers spread out, mopping up what was left of the opposition. Løytnant Tangvald tried to gather his soldiers for a

The three dead Fallschirmjägers awaiting transport back to Germany. Some records have this photograph as being from 'the Narvik area', but it is undoubtedly taken at Sola in the morning of 9 April. (Author's collection)

counter-attack but by now the Germans had the upper hand and attacked ferociously, keeping the defenders down.[23] Tangvald decided further resistance would result in the pointless killing of his inexperienced men. He managed to get in contact with von Brandis, asking for a ceasefire. Shortly after 09:00 Sola-Stavanger airport was in German hands. It had been accomplished through the aggressive use of paratroopers for the first time in history – a form of attack the defenders were not prepared for. Johansen later estimated that some forty of the Fallschirmjägers were hit during the gunfight, but German sources list three troopers dead and ten wounded, four seriously.[24] Two or three Norwegian soldiers were wounded, but none was killed. Some eighty Norwegians, including seven officers, were taken prisoners; another forty or so escaped, some during the battle.

As soon as control had been established at the airfield, some of the Jägers started clearing the wire blockade on the runways and soon several dozen Ju52s landed in rapid succession, turning onto the grass to make room for more. Oberst von Beeren's was the first aircraft to touch down, loaded with communications equipment. Unlike the chaos at Fornebu, no Junkers were lost at Sola on 9 April. As soon as the aircraft were emptied and refuelled, they were rushed off again to avoid congestion. This worked beyond all expectations and by early afternoon, more than two thousand men had been airlifted in, plus ground crew, administration officers, ammunition, A/A guns and communication equipment as well as some nine thousand litres of fuel. Having concluded their task, most of the paratroopers left Sola during the day on the returning transport aircraft.[25]

At about the time the paratroopers started to gain control at Sola, twelve He59 seaplanes of KGzbV 108 landed at Hafrsfjord and taxied towards the seaplane base. There were no machine guns there and the handful of soldiers and naval aircrew were taken by surprise by the forty soldiers jumping ashore from the floatplanes.[26] At 11:00, ten He115 floatplanes from 1./KüFlGr 106 also arrived after having performed reconnaissance over the North Sea.

Once a perimeter had been established at Sola, the first companies moved towards Madlamoen and Stavanger city. Løytnant Tangvald was forced at gunpoint to walk in front of the German vanguard that followed, carrying a white flag. Many civilians lined the road close to Stavanger; few of them were friendly, but nothing happened. The radio station, telephone exchange, police station and other public buildings were occupied and within a few hours, Stavanger was secured without a single shot having been fired. Oberleutnant Taraba of 7./IR 193 found events almost bizarre:

> Equipment and ammunition were hurriedly unloaded from the aircraft and stacked on the grass next to the runway . . . 5th Company headed for the Madla Camp, between Sola and Stavanger. They encountered no opposition as all units there had withdrawn towards Sandnes; hence the way to Stavanger was free . . . Oberleutnant Christ captured a bus and the driver was ordered to take us to town. We secured the port and there Oberleutnant Weissenberg appeared with several maps that he had bought in a nearby bookshop – a strange war![27]

A signal from X Fliegerkorps reaching von Falkenhorst's staff at 14:00 reported the town quiet and the airfield fully secured, adding that the scene was 'one of tranquillity'. By early evening, the transports *Tübingen*, *Tijuca* and *Mendoza* docked and started to unload ammunition, fuel, equipment, A/A guns, heavy weapons, horses, vehicles and another nine hundred soldiers, mostly administrative support personnel. A disappointingly high number of dockhands accepted the German invitation to assist unloading the ships: money, cigarettes and alcohol being the lures. During 10 April, 3rd Battalion of IR 193 was flown in and von Beeren set about his task of securing the area. On the 12th, the aircraft tender *Karl Meyer* arrived with aviation fuel, buoys and other equipment for the Sola seaplane base. *Meyer* had originally been heading for Kristiansand but was diverted to Sola. The Luftwaffe had not registered that there was a swing bridge at the mouth of the Hafrsfjord, whose columns were too narrow to let the broad-beamed *Meyer* through and the equipment had to be brought from Stavanger harbour to Sola-Sjø by lorry.[28]

* * *

The freighter *Tijuca* unloading in Stavanger harbour. (Author's collection)

The British Consulate in Stavanger had been significantly 'reinforced' during March and April. In addition to the consul, Mr Spence, there was Commander Frank Platt and Captain John Olsson of the Royal Navy, Howard Coxon and W/T operator Albert Ware of the army and the Military Intelligence Research (MIR) officer Captain Malcolm Munthe.[29] The latter arrived on 5 April via the embassy in Oslo as a vanguard for Plan R4 to establish himself as liaison officer to the Norwegian Army in Rogaland. By the first week of April, Platt, Munthe and the others were quartered at Hotel Victoria with a wireless set and windows overlooking the harbour.

As news of the German attack spread during the morning, Consul Spence left, taking his Norwegian wife and family to their country cottage. At Hotel Victoria the British agents were taken by surprise when the Germans, who had no idea they were there, arrived, commandeering the hotel for their harbourmaster. They literally escaped out of the back door as the Germans entered at the front. The wireless equipment was destroyed and the officers eventually joined the consul and his family. The entourage, with Norwegian help, managed to evade capture while Munthe, who was convinced the British would initiate the landings he had been sent to prepare for, left the others in search of the Allied forces. To his frustration, they were nowhere to be found.[30]

Too Old for Comfort

The four-stack destroyer *Draug* had its base in Haugesund during the Neutrality Watch, but was constantly moving up and down the coast on various escort missions. In the afternoon of 8 April, she was heading home after leaving the German *Seattle* with *Gyller* outside Egersund. Mooring at 16:00, several signals from SDD2 awaited Kaptein Thore Horve, telling him of German ships in the Kattegat and the sinking of *Rio de Janeiro*. There seemed to be plenty of work ahead, and coaling started immediately while Horve called Kontreadmiral Tank-Nielsen in Bergen to discuss the news and receive orders.[31] Since Horve was alone in Haugesund and communication might become difficult, Tank-Nielsen advised him to judge how the situation developed and if necessary act on his own. Horve interpreted this to mean that a German attack on Norway was to be expected and, after a discussion with his first officer, ordered the coaling to be hastened and ammunition brought to the guns. Some time after midnight, a signal from Bergen informed him that the fortresses in Oslofjord were in battle. The nationality of the intruders was not given, but Horve took it for granted they were German. During the night, several German ships came through the Leads from the south. One that carried the German state flag was allowed to proceed at its own risk. The others were ordered to wait. Horve tried to contact Bergen but could not get through.

Around 03:00 a darkened merchantman hurried through the sound, carrying no flag: an open breach of the Neutrality Act. A signal to stop had no effect, neither had a warning shot, and *Draug* cast off in pursuit, in spite of a 12-degree list to port from the incomplete coaling. The ship, which turned out to be the 7,600-ton German freighter *Main*, was overtaken in open waters just north of Haugesund. After two more warning shots the captain finally turned back to sheltered waters. First Officer Løytnant Sjur Østervold went onboard with two customs officers and demanded to see the ship's papers. These showed

The ancient destroyer *Draug*, here photographed after being rebuilt in the UK, where she was given several A/A guns and the forward stack was removed. She was used for protection of coastal convoys until November 1943. (Marinemuseet)

a mixed cargo of seven thousand tons for Bergen, but all hatches were covered by coal and the arrogant German captain would do nothing to help the customs officers inspect what was below. Østervold decided to arrest the ship. He sealed off the radio room and ordered the German captain to follow him across to *Draug* for further interrogation.

Like *Roda*, *Main* was one of the ships of the Ausfuhrstaffel. She had orders to arrive in Trondheim on Wesertag, but had been forced to wait at Kopervik because of an unforeseen lack of pilots. Only at around 23:30 on 8 April did a qualified pilot arrive. By then, *Main* had been redirected by the Weserübung command to Bergen, replacing the unfortunate *Rio de Janeiro*. While Løytnant Østervold was onboard *Main*, Kaptein

Kaptein Thore Horve of *Draug*. (Marinemuseet)

Horve took *Draug* back to the depot to complete the coaling and went ashore to find a telephone. He called Marineholmen in Bergen and talked to Orlogskaptein Sigurd Årstad. To Horve's bewilderment, Årstad told him that he was actually a prisoner of war, with a German officer standing next to him, so he really couldn't say much. The connection was severed and a disturbed Horve hastened back to his ship. Shortly after, Løytnant Stansberg landed his MF11 nearby and taxied across to *Draug*. Stansberg told Horve of the German bombers over Sola, what he had seen during his reconnaissance and what little he knew of the attack on *Æger*, concluding that a German occupation of Stavanger was in progress. Having refuelled, Stansberg took off again, continuing northwards.

Kaptein Horve was deeply alarmed. German forces appeared to have occupied both Bergen and Stavanger and the Kriegsmarine was inside Norwegian territory in the Oslofjord. *Draug* was old, poorly armed and no match for a modern warship and Horve felt it would be meaningless to sacrifice his crew in a suicidal stance against superior German forces. There was in his mind no question at all that Norway would enter the war on the Allied side and he found it much more sensible to preserve his men for another day and a better chance to fight back 'onboard British ships rather than old *Draug*'. After some consideration, he decided the best thing he could do was to cross the North Sea to Britain and bring *Main* along as a prize.[32] Horve sent the captain of *Main* back to his ship with instructions to prepare to continue towards Bergen, seeing no reason to upset the man prematurely. *Draug* and *Main* left Haugesund around 09:00.

Offshore, Horve turned *Draug* westward and signalled for *Main* to follow. Predictably, the instructions were not obeyed and the German maintained his northerly course. *Draug* turned back and only with guns and torpedoes pointing at him did the freighter captain reluctantly change course. Later in the morning, some forty miles off shore, six aircraft appeared. One of them broke out of the formation, diving on *Main*. At least two bombs were dropped before it rejoined the others heading for the Norwegian coast. The aircraft were never properly identified. Onboard *Draug* it was assumed they were German, while the crew of *Main* held the attackers were British. Like the other ships of the Ausfuhrstaffel,

Main reluctantly following *Draug* westwards. (Marinemuseet)

The sulking crew of *Main* closely guarded on the afterdeck of *Draug*. (Marinemuseet)

Main was under orders not to be captured or surrender under any circumstance. Only minutes after the aircraft had turned away, the surprised men of *Draug* saw *Main*'s crew take to the boats. The sea was rough and it took some time to pick them up – sixty-seven in all, including the Norwegian pilot Eriksen – making sure they carried no guns.[33] Meanwhile, it became obvious that the seacocks of *Main* had been opened and she was sinking. To accelerate the process Horve fired half a dozen shots at her waterline before ordering speed again, continuing west. There was no room for the Germans below and they were kept under guard on deck. To Horve's delight, most of them became seasick and caused no trouble.

Next morning, three British destroyers appeared and one of them, *Sikh*, escorted *Draug* to Sullom Voe on Shetland. British vessels in the port manned the rails, cheering as they arrived, and Horve ordered his crew to respond. After unloading the sulking German prisoners, *Draug* continued to Scapa Flow, where she arrived next morning. In a meeting with Rear Admiral Hallifax on 12 April, Horve was asked to join a British destroyer as liaison officer. This he willingly accepted, suggesting that other men from *Draug* could be useful too, and some fifteen officers and NCOs were sent onboard the destroyers of the Fourth and Sixth Flotillas about to leave for Norway.[34]

In 1942, Kaptein Horve was, with five other officers, awarded the War Cross with Sword by the Norwegian government in London, endorsed by King Haakon, for 'outstanding merits during the invasion and afterwards'. After the war, the Military Investigation Committee concluded that, 'under the circumstances and with the information available', Horve's decision was 'acceptable'.[35]

Walkover

The port of Egersund is about eighty kilometres south of Stavanger and is one of the few places on this part of the Norwegian coast where a sizeable ship can find shelter and provisions. In 1940, it was also the starting point for a telegraph cable to Peterhead in Scotland, which the Weserübung planners decided would have to be under German control. Furthermore, they believed it necessary to secure the port to prevent it from being used by Norwegian or Allied troops to establish a bridgehead from where Sola-Stavanger might be threatened.

The narrow sound leading to Egersund stretches from the south, past Eigerøy, before one arm bends north-east into the harbour proper. In 1940, the port facilities and piers were largely on the southern side of the inlet. RNN presence in Egersund on the evening of 8 April was limited to the 24-year-old Fenrik Hjalmar Svae and his seventeen-man crew onboard the torpedo boat *Skarv*. The destroyer *Gyller* had its usual station in Egersund, but was in Kristiansand that evening.

There had been no army presence in the town so far during the Neutrality Watch. On the 8th, Oberst Spørck ordered a small unit from Madlamoen to move south, just in case. Arriving late in the evening, Kaptein Dæhli contacted Fenrik Svae onboard *Skarv* to discuss the situation while his men established quarters. Svae informed Dæhli that he had received orders from Kristiansand for increased preparedness and his ship was armed, fuelled and ready to leave at short notice. His suggestion to patrol outside the entrance to the Egersund Leads had been denied, and he had been told to stay in the harbour and keep an eye on things from there. Neither of the officers believed Egersund was under any immediately threat and decided to catch some sleep while it was still possible. Fenrik Svae usually slept at a hotel in town, but this night he decided to stay onboard.

Unknown to anybody in Egersund, the two minesweepers *M1* and *M9* were at this very moment closing in on the Norwegian coast. Contact had not been regained with the ships lost in the fog during the night, but Korvettenkapitän Kurt Thoma took it for granted they were not far away. The knowledge Thoma and Rittmeister Friedrich Eickhorn, the C-in-C of the troops onboard, had of their target was limited.[36] They had been told there were no fortifications or troops in the town, but Thoma knew there might be one or two torpedo boats or destroyers. The soldiers below deck were mostly overcome by seasickness and wished they were in Egersund already, resistance or not. Eickhorn later said he was so tense from the uncertainty and the loss of half his force that he had no time to be seasick. To his great relief, the fog lifted and the contours of the coastline could be seen some time after 02:30. With the fog gone it was a cold night and the snow on the mountains gave a profile to the landscape, even if it was overcast and no moon.

Shortly before 04:00, a light could be observed ahead to starboard. Through the binoculars it was recognised as the easternmost beacon at the entrance to the Egersund Leads, and within a few minutes the western light was also identified; they were spot on! That the lights were burning probably meant that no one knew they were coming and surprise was still possible.[37] The two missing minesweepers were nowhere to be seen. Eickhorn was less than comfortable landing with only the seventy-five men onboard *M1* and *M9*, but it would have to do. Time was running out and waiting was not an option. The minesweepers were fairly well armed and two of them would be a match for even a

M1. In spite of some stability problems, the 874-ton minesweepers were one of the more successful designs of the German Navy; well-armed and highly manoeuvrable, they were dreaded adversaries. They were complicated and expensive, though, and engine maintenance needed tools and skilled personnel. Commissioned in 1938, *M1* had two 10.5-cm guns, the forward one in a shielded mounting, one 37-mm cannon, two 20-mm cannons and about thirty mines. Cruising speed was around eighteen knots. (Author's collection)

destroyer in the narrow waters. *M1* had Voigth-Schneider propulsion instead of regular rudder and propellers; this increased her manoeuvrability and she was expected to be the faster of the vessels to moor. Thus, Eickhorn was onboard Kapitänleutnant Hans Bartels's *M1* rather than with Thoma on *M9*. After a brief conference inside the shelter of the sound, Thoma, Bartels and Eickhorn decided to proceed as planned. Bartels and Eickhorn talked quietly together, controlling tension as best they could. The two officers were very different personalities and, reading between the lines of Bartels's narration of the events, there was substantial mistrust between them from the start. The tension seems to have eased off during the night and now they had a common task requiring their full attention. Below deck, the soldiers started to prepare for the landing, any remaining effects of the seasickness disappearing fast.[38]

At precisely 04:15, *M1* turned starboard around the Vardberg headland into Egersund harbour. *M9* remained outside in the sound. This early in the morning all was quiet and calm. A few lights were burning and dawn was approaching, making it possible to see the outline of the piers. Eickhorn and Bartels started to look for a place to land. The lookout reported a submarine moored in the harbour, the slim, unfamiliar profile of *Skarv* fooling him. Bartels realised that this was one of the Norwegian torpedo boats and decided to get the soldiers off *M1* as soon as possible. By chance, the place he chose to make fast was near *Gyller's* usual mooring, less than a hundred metres from *Skarv*. The watchman onboard *Skarv* heard an approaching ship but it was too dark for him to see more than a vague outline and he did not raise the alarm. Eickhorn was one of the first to jump ashore and while he secured the landing, a dozen soldiers ran quietly along the quay.[39] Onboard *Skarv*, the watchman suddenly had a submachine gun pointed at him and his rifle was snatched away. Later he claimed he had heard *Gyller* was to return that night and, believing it was her coming back, did not pay much attention to the whole thing until it was too late.

Below deck in his cabin Fenrik Svae had just been woken by the unfamiliar noises when three armed soldiers burst in. Taken totally by surprise, Svae was angry that *Skarv* had not been given a chance to defend herself. Her main weapons, the torpedoes, could not be used inside the narrow harbour and her two 47-mm guns were no match for the minesweepers' two 10.5-cm guns, and heavy machine cannons. It might have been a different story had Svae been allowed to take *Skarv* outside the sound as he had requested.

Fenrik Svae was permitted to dress and was taken to a German officer, who told him that the Germans had come to assist in the defence of Norwegian neutrality and that the two governments had agreed to co-operate. The young sub-lieutenant did not believe this and his scepticism and anger must have shown as he was not allowed back onto his ship. He somehow managed to get a message to those still onboard *Skarv* to destroy maps and files and to notify Kristiansand SDS, which was done before the Germans realised there was a telephone onboard.

As soon as the soldiers and their equipment had been landed, *M1* cast off again and headed out of the harbour. It was less than fifteen minutes since she had arrived and Bartels was very pleased. Not a shot had been fired and everything appeared to run smoothly. *M9* moved in and more soldiers were disembarked. Bicycles, motorcycles, heavy machine guns, mortars and ammunition followed. On Eickhorn's orders, a dozen men were left to guard *Skarv* and the quays while the rest spread into town. Machine-gun posts were established at the telephone and post office, railway station and police station.

The torpedo boat *Skarv* after being captured. (Dalane Folkemuseum)

M2 and *M13* casting off
shortly before 06:00.
(Dalane Folkemuseum)

One troop mounted bicycles and headed south along the coastal road to establish a warning post at the narrowest part of the sound. The only direct contact between Norway and Britain was in German hands.

It appears that Kaptein Dæhli got his first and only warning of the landing by telephone from a civilian in the harbour at more or less the same time as the Norwegian and German soldiers became aware of each other. The man on the telephone spoke of Egersund being 'full of Germans' and the shocked Dæhli tried to call Oberst Spørck in Stavanger to inform him, rather than alarming his men. Eickhorn was no less startled to learn of the Norwegian soldiers, but acted decisively and, with only a handful of his men, stormed into the Norwegian quarters. Surprise was total and no opposition encountered. Dæhli believed, according to what he had just been told, that a large force waited outside and so he surrendered immediately. Just before being detained he got through to Spørck in Stavanger, telling him that 'a large invasion force' was present in Egersund.

M2 and *M13* arrived an hour later, by which time it was all over. They unloaded their troops and equipment as fast as possible and by 05:57 all four boats were heading down the sound. Korvettenkapitän Thoma's initial orders were to return to Kiel but a few hours after leaving, orders were received to head for Kristiansand to assist Group IV.

Rittmeister Eickhorn must have felt isolated, left behind with a small force in an alien country, in spite of having completed his mission so easily.[40] He decided not to sever the telegraph cable to Scotland, but posted a guard where it entered the sea with orders to blow it up if anything should happen. Later, orders came to cut it permanently and this was done.[41]

Guerrilla

As soon as the German landings at Sola were confirmed, Oberst Spørck decided to abandon the defence of the Stavanger peninsula. He was of the opinion that it would not be possible to create an effective defence of the beaches and coastal areas with only one battalion and wanted to move his forces to a more suitable terrain. He was concerned that soldiers would be landed on the coast from the German transport ships reported offshore, and the telephone call from Kaptein Dæhli in Egersund mentioning (wrongly) large German forces there confirmed his fears. That through this, Sola airfield as well as Stavanger town and harbour were laid open for the invader, was a price Spørck was willing to pay.[42] For the Germans, it was quite convenient that the Norwegian forces moved out of the way. Even if it gave Spørck time to mobilise additional local forces and prepare a defensive position, it also gave the Germans time to bring in troops, heavy weapons and above all establish an air-support base at Sola.

The first skirmishes between the German and Norwegian forces occurred on 15 April. A series of minor actions developed as the Norwegians first advanced out of their positions and, as German pressure mounted, gradually pulled back into the mountains, making a stand in Dirdal, where the steep mountainsides and narrow canyons gave good defensive positions. Heavy casualties eventually made the German Army leave it to the Luftwaffe at Sola to wear the Norwegians down. By the end of April, the Norwegian ammunition supplies were exhausted and, having received no reinforcements or Allied help, Spørck saw no other solution than surrender.[43]

Controlling Sola-Stavanger in additions to the airfields at Kristiansand and Aalborg gave the Luftwaffe effective air superiority over the Skagerrak and the eastern North Sea. During 9 April the remaining Bf110s of 3./ZG 76 returned to Sola from Aalborg.[44] Later, the Stukas of I/StG 1 arrived, as did the Ju88s of Z/KG 30 and on 16 April most of KG 26 transferred to Sola to support the ensuing campaign in Norway. Many units also used the airfield as a forward base. British air attacks were inevitable and Allied landings on the beaches south of Stavanger were feared, as were Norwegian counter-attacks. The air attacks came sure enough, but no invasion, and within weeks a significant expansion of the airfield was initiated. Runways were extended, hangars were built and equipment, provisions, fuel and ammunition stored in dispersed dumps around the area. Buildings were camouflaged and bunkers and A/A positions set up around the airfield – work in which a number of local Norwegians participated.[45]

Coastal Command initiated the attacks on Sola in the afternoon of 10 April when Sergeant CF Rose of 254 Sqn strafed the airfield from his Blenheim. One Ju52 was damaged and one destroyed, as was one He59 at the seaplane base.[46]

On the 11 April, two directives arrived at RAF Bomber Command:

Aircraft have general permission to attack without warning any ships, merchant or otherwise, under way within ten miles of the Norwegian coast south of latitude 61° 00'N and anywhere east of longitude 06° 00'East, as far south as latitude 54° 00'N. Ships at anchor may be attacked if definitely observed to be enemy.

Confirming conversation between A.O.C-in-C and D.H.O. today, guerrilla bombing operations against Stavanger aerodrome and seaplane anchorage should be carried out as soon as possible and continued until further orders with the object of destroying aircraft installations and runways. Effort should not exceed one Wellington Squadron a day. Attacks should be carried out by small formations or single aircraft spaced out in time best to avoid fighter defences.[47]

In addition, Commander-in-Chief Bomber Command, Air Vice Marshal Charles Portal, was instructed to initiate operations against German sea communication in the Skagerrak, Kattegat and Kiel Bay. Portal was reluctant to commit to what he considered a sideshow and wanted to conserve his squadrons for the Western Front. He considered that, in Norway, his men were asked to perform 'in a role for which they were neither trained nor suitably equipped', and were being wasted for little gain. The Blenheim-equipped 107 Sqn and 110 Sqn and the Wellington-equipped 9 Sqn and 115 Sqn had already moved to Lossiemouth and Kinloss in Scotland to be closer to the North Sea and Portal decided this would suffice also for Norway. Other squadrons would fly from further south if necessary, with subsequent loss of efficiency and range.[48]

In the first RAF bombing raid of the war on a mainland target, Stavanger airfield was targeted in the evening of 11 April by six Wellingtons of 115 Sqn with a nominal escort of two Blenheim Mk IV-Fs of 254 Sqn, Coastal Command.[49] The Wellingtons were late and running low on fuel, one of the Blenheims strafed the airfield before turning home, alerting the A/A defences and scrambling the fighters. Hence, several Bf110s bounced the Wellingtons when they arrived. The aircraft of Pilot Officer Barber ventured over Stavanger town during evasive actions and was shot down by fire from the recently installed A/A guns there. It crashed into the centre of town, killing three civilians in addition to the crew, and damaging several houses.[50]

On the following day, twelve Wellingtons from 38 Sqn and 149 Sqn, engaged in the search for returning German battleships, were attacked by Ju88s and Bf110s off Stavanger and three were lost. Combined with catastrophic losses at Kristiansand, Portal saw his concerns justified and on 14 April the two Wellingtons squadrons were ordered south and replaced by further Blenheims and the Whitley-equipped 77 Sqn, earmarked for

A 35-mm A/A gun just outside Stavanger. These required a fairly large crew to operate efficiently, but were very effective against low-flying aircraft. (Author's collection)

attacks in the Trondheim region because of their long range.[51] After 12 April, most raids, except those by Blenheims or Coastal Command Hudsons, were carried out in darkness, largely to avoid fighters, but also because it was believed that there were more aircraft on the ground to be destroyed at night. Besides Sola, the airfields at Værnes, Kjevik, Fornebu and Kjeller as well as Aalborg in Denmark and Westerland on Sylt were targeted, as were naval ships or transports encountered inshore. On occasions, even the precious Wellingtons and Hampdens were targeted to fly over southern Norway from bases in England.

The brunt of the 'guerrilla' bombing of Sola was handed to the Blenheim squadrons. The nearly 1,800-km round trip was near their maximum endurance, straining men and matériel to the limit. Difficult navigation, unpredictable weather and a hostile reception at the target added to the perils of flying over long stretches of dangerous waters. Between 15 April and 10 May, when the German offensive on the Western Front opened and changed the situation totally, some thirty-five attacks were carried out on Sola airfield, disturbing its expansion, but achieving little else. There were few large installations at the airfield to target and the aircraft were well dispersed. Holes in the runway were filled in overnight and the airfield was kept operational most of the time, as was the seaplane base. By 15 April one heavy and one light A/A battery had been set up in the vicinity of the airport. In addition to the fighters, this made it a risky target and during April, Bomber Command lost twenty-seven and Coastal Command five aircraft at or near Sola. These were losses that could be ill sustained and the number of attacks lessened as pressure mounted in France.

The ordnance used by the RAF at Sola and other airfields was rather limited: 40-lb, 250-lb and 500-lb general-purpose bombs and 4-lb incendiaries. The damage to runways

The graves of British airmen at Sola churchyard in late April. Notice the Norwegian flag and flowers put there by local Norwegians. (Author's collection)

Stereographic photographs taken during the attack on Sola on 17 April by Blenheim Mk IVs of 107 Sqn. On the right-hand photo, four 250-lb bombs can be seen falling; there were several hits on runways and dispersed aircraft. (Author's collection)

from anything but the 500-lb bombs was negligible and easily repaired.[52] Trials were performed with delayed fuses from three to thirty-six hours to try to close the airfield, but unless the bombs landed on the tarmac the effect was limited. Diving attacks from about 2,500 to 1,000 metres were considered to give the best immunity from the A/A fire, gaining speed to get clear without getting too low. Experiments with smaller bombs, incendiaries and strafing to destroy oil tanks and depots were carried out but found to achieve little beyond normal use of incendiaries. Decoy aircraft to attract the attention of the searchlights and co-ordinated simultaneous attacks from different heights and directions were more effective while, as expected, strafing from low altitude was found to give the best and most reliable direct results. This, however, required large amounts of ammunition, skilled pilots and gunners with steady nerves.

One particularly negative factor for the attacks on Sola was the lack of precise weather forecasts for southern Norway. Insufficient meteorological data were available for accurate predictions, resulting in a significant waste of resources. Routines were established to forward weather reports from ships in the area and Coastal Command patrols, but these were scarce and irregular and only helped to a certain extent. On 16 April, Flying Officer Edwards from 110 Sqn was awarded Distinguished Flying Colours for pressing on to the target, while five other aircraft turned back because of severe icing. Three days later, seven of nine aircraft from 107 Sqn abandoned the sortie due to clear skies as they had been ordered not to attack unless cloud cover was sufficient.[53] Of the remaining two, one bombed 'an airfield' and one was lost. On 20, 21 and 24 April most of the aircraft sent towards Sola also abandoned their sorties because of unfavourable weather.

During the withdrawal from central Norway, attacks on Sola were intensified to lessen the pressure on the operations at Åndalsnes and Namsos. By now the Germans had managed to install makeshift seaward-looking radars on the coast near Stavanger, however, and the fighters stationed at Sola became an even more dangerous threat. On 3 May, after carrying out 113 bombing sorties against Stavanger airfield alone, 107 Sqn and 110 Sqn were ordered back to Wattisham. The last Bomber Command attack on Sola occurred on the night of 7/8 May. Eight of the nine aircraft failed to locate the target as it was covered by low cloud. Sporadic attacks on Sola still occasionally took place, largely by single aircraft, and with no system to them.[54]

Operation Duck

To augment the bombing of Sola-Stavanger and to ease the pressure on the naval forces supporting the Allied landings in the Trondheim area, the Admiralty wished to 'inflict the greatest possible damage to the aerodrome so as to restrict the operation of aircraft therefrom'. The heavy cruiser *Suffolk* with four escorting destroyers, *Kipling*, *Juno*, *Janus* and *Hereward*, were chosen for the operation, codenamed Duck. *Suffolk* carried 8-inch guns in four twin turrets and secondary batteries of 4-inch guns. The anti-aircraft protection had been increased to sixteen pom-poms and a fair number of 20-mm and 40-mm Bofors and Oerlikon guns during a refit in 1938, but her armour was limited, in particular in decks and superstructure.

In support, it was intended that Bomber Command should undertake a heavy night attack just prior to the arrival of the cruiser, causing as much destruction and distraction as possible and to illuminate the target through fires amongst the buildings and parked aircraft. A subsequent attack by twelve Blenheims at midday would suppress any retaliatory attacks while the cruiser withdrew. For reconnaissance and artillery spotting, *Suffolk* carried two Walrus seaplanes and Coastal Command would provide additional air cover and supplementary artillery observation.

Churchill endorsed Operation Duck, which was to be under the direct order of the Admiralty. It would be the first time since WWI that large-scale shore bombardment from a heavy naval vessel was initiated. It had been forgotten or overlooked that, since then, aircraft and their capacity to deliver heavy bombs with precision had improved by several orders of magnitude. That *Suffolk* and her crew had no previous experience in shore bombardment was likewise disregarded, as was the fact that there was only a limited amount of high-explosive shells in *Suffolk*'s magazines. A lesson of naval operations under total enemy air superiority was to be learned the hard way.

Captain JW Durnford took *Suffolk* and the destroyers to sea from Scapa Flow at 16:25 on 16 April. The escort was late coming in and their refuelling took some time, so the North Sea was crossed at twenty-six knots so they could be in place as ordered. The submarine *Seal*, which had been in the area for a couple of days, positioned herself off Skudeneshavn and, using her hydrophones to pick up the flotilla, guided them towards land by flashing light signals with a box lamp. This worked well and the ships passed *Seal* at 04:35 on 17 April off Kvitsøy, north of Stavanger.[55]

From then on, few things went as planned. The twelve Wellingtons that were to perform the night attack met poor weather over the North Sea and only two actually found the airfield. For some reason, these believed that the airport already destroyed and did not bomb. One of the two Coastal Command Hudsons also encountered problems and turned back. The second Hudson from 233 Sqn, piloted by Flying Officer Gron Edwards, arrived as planned at 03:55. After circling to assess the conditions, he dived in from one thousand metres, dropping 25-lb incendiaries and flares over the airfield as illumination for *Suffolk*'s gunnery officers. Edwards had Lieutenant Commander Fleming onboard as an observer and he transmitted on the agreed frequency to establish contact with *Suffolk*. Communication was erratic, though, and failed altogether after a few minutes.[56] At 04:55, a Ju88C from Z/KG 30 stationed at Sola attacked Edwards. Neither of the two aircraft was much damaged in the ensuing dogfight and Edwards eventually managed to lose his adversary. Meanwhile, *Suffolk*'s first Walrus seaplane was catapulted off to commence spotting. It climbed to four thousand metres, from where Sola airfield was easily seen, but the observer was unable to reach *Suffolk* on the radio. He kept sending, in case there was reception.

At 04:45 *Suffolk* reduced speed to fifteen knots, and two minutes later the force turned to a course parallel to and some eighteen kilometres off the coast. To Captain Durnford's intense annoyance it was not possible for *Suffolk* to obtain radio contact with any of the aircraft. The situation was becoming critical as full daylight was approaching and time was getting short. Eventually fire was opened without spotting at 05:13, waking people up all over the Stavanger area. Land could be clearly observed from the cruiser, but with no detail. In addition, fresh snow on the mountains in the background meant that the fires and flares dropped by Edwards could hardly be distinguished. *Suffolk*'s first two salvoes landed to the north of the airfield. The next four salvoes fell in the sea, before the fire was lifted and eventually hit the seaplane base. Black smoke rose from several fires. At 05:22, fuel was running low and the Walrus headed for Scotland.

The second Walrus had been standing by over the cruiser with orders to take over when the first aircraft left. This it did, but obviously from a lower altitude or different position as the observer had a hard time seeing anything at all except the smoke from the seaplane base. The subsequent salvoes from *Suffolk* appeared mostly to be falling between this and the hangar at the northern edge of the field. At 05:48 the second Walrus had to leave for home. The spotters onboard both aircraft later noted that the high-explosive shells landing on the ground were very difficult to observe because of the snow and lack of visible flash when exploding.

Suffolk fired 202 8-inch rounds during three sweeps along the coast, until at 06:04 Durnford decided enough damage was done and turned westward at thirty knots. The rising sun behind the mountains in the east meant that observations became even more difficult and the gunnery officer was almost firing blind in the end. Most of the shells from *Suffolk* landed north of the airfield proper, near the seaplane base at Sola-Sjø. Flight Officer Edwards saw that the hits were not in the intended place when he returned after getting away from the Bf110, but the continued lack of radio communication prevented him from giving corrections. Damage at Sola-Sjø was limited, except for the very last salvo, which destroyed the administration building and four He59 transport seaplanes and four He115s from 1./KüFlGr 106. Sola airfield itself was virtually untouched, except for minor damage caused by the incendiaries dropped by Edwards, who returned to base without further incident.[57]

After the bombardment, *Suffolk* was originally to head west under cover of a fighter escort from Coastal Command. The day before the operation, however, a group of German destroyers had (falsely) been reported off the Norwegian coast near Stadtlandet and cruisers of the Home Fleet had been sent to catch them. During the evening it was decided that *Suffolk* and her escort should head north after the bombardment to take part in the chase and a signal was sent from the Admiralty at 23:00 on 16 April, ordering *Suffolk* upon completion of Operation Duck to 'sweep to the northward to intercept enemy destroyers'. It was a decision that disrupted the whole operation and severely delayed the force's withdrawal from danger.[58] The signal ended with the information that '. . . air reconnaissance is being arranged.' Something went wrong in the communication between the Admiralty and Coastal Command, however, and when the Blenheims of 254 Sqn came to take up the escort, *Suffolk* and the destroyers were not to be found where the pilots expected. Following the new orders, Durnford stood westward until 07:04 and then altered course to the north, reducing *Suffolk*'s speed to twenty-five knots to conserve fuel. The Admiralty was informed of the cruiser's position at 07:20, but this information was not forwarded to Coastal Command until five hours later.

Do18 flying-boats from KüFlGr 106 and 406 shadowed the retreating ships as they withdrew and at 08:25, ten He111s from I/KG 26 recently stationed at Sola-Stavanger arrived. Most of them concentrated on *Suffolk* while some attacked the destroyers. As the aircraft stayed high and bombed from level flight, the ships turned safely away from all but two 250-kg bombs, which exploded close to *Kipling*, resulting in cracks in her machinery mounts. Two He115s from 3./506 armed with torpedoes also tried to attack but had to give up due to the high seas. The attacks made Durnford realise he was at risk without fighter cover and he decided to abort the search for the German destroyers and head for home.

Believing there was a major British naval force off Stavanger, all available aircraft of II/KG 4, KG 26 and KG 30 were alerted and sent westwards from Sola, Oslo-Fornebu, Aalborg and Westerland. During the morning, a clear sky emerged, giving excellent visibility and only a few patches of clouds. The Heinkels of II/KG 4 had limited experience in operating over the sea and few of the aircraft from this group found the British ships at all, in spite of the favourable conditions. Those that did bombed without results. KG 26 also had limited success in their search for the cruiser. Since the capture of Sola-Stavanger, the anti-shipping experts of KG 30 had used the airport as a forward base for their sweeps into the North Sea, and from 11 April parts of the wing had been stationed there. In the morning of 17 April, twenty-eight Ju88 bombers, largely from II Group, were ready, including some that came in from Westerland; they took off in small groups between 10:00 and 13:00. Of the twenty-eight, twelve found and attacked *Suffolk* a hundred kilometres off the coast. The pilots of KG 30 had by now perfected their tactics against enemy warships and came in from several directions and heights in steep dives. Having experienced the less aggressive level attacks of KG 4 and KG 26 earlier in the morning, Captain Durnford presumed the same was to happen now and turned the beam of the cruiser on the nearest aircraft to make his guns bear, making *Suffolk* an easier target for the experienced pilots of KG 30.[59]

He111s of 7./KG 26 searching for prey. (Author's collection)

At 10:37, a 500-kg bomb struck the heavy cruiser just forward of the X-turret. It passed through the wardroom, the warrant officers' flat and several store rooms before detonating on the port side of the platform deck between the after engine room bulkhead and X shell room and cordite-handling room The blast created havoc in the engine room and set off a charge in the cordite-handling room that vented up the hoist into the X turret, where further explosions lifted the turret roof; the Y-turret was disabled too. Flames shot through several hatches as well as the engine room exhaust trunks, causing the flames to reach the gaff of the mainmast, destroying the ensign. Severe structural damage was incurred and splinter damage was extensive. The fire raged uncontrollably until the magazines were flooded. Fifteen hundred tons of water entered the cruiser in less than twenty minutes and her speed was reduced to eighteen knots, later to fifteen. The radio was disabled and signals had to be forwarded by visual means to *Kipling* for transmission. Ruptured oil tanks left a distinctive trail for the aircraft to follow.

Continued search by Blenheims and Hudsons during the morning failed to locate the force. The twelve Blenheims coming in for the midday attack on Sola, however, came right into the attack by pure chance. Wing Commander Embry of 107 Sqn was not entirely sure what was going on, but recognised British warships being attacked by German bombers and decided to engage, in spite of a heavy bomb load. Hoping the Germans might mistake them for Blenheim IV-F fighters, he ordered five of the aircraft to follow him in an attack, while the rest continued towards Sola. Embry's ruse succeeded and the approaching bombers diving through the attack with blazing guns scattered the German aircraft, which largely headed for home. It also scattered the Blenheims, however, and by the time Embry arrived over Sola the defences were fully alerted by the first group. Two Blenheims were shot down by the Bf110s while a third was badly damaged and crashed on landing at Lossiemouth.[60]

During the peak of the attacks on *Suffolk*, a signal came in from C-in-C Home Fleet that *Repulse* and *Renown* with escort were under way from Scapa Flow. Captain Durnford responded back that he advised the fleet to stay away, and asked for urgent air support instead. The Ju88s of KG 30 kept coming during the afternoon as *Suffolk* continued westwards at reduced speed. For a while, the steering motors broke down and the cruiser was unable to take avoiding action. During this, at 13:25, two 500-kg bombs exploded five or six metres off the starboard side, just aft of the already damaged X turret. In addition to extensive splinter damage, the whole after compartment of the cruiser became completely flooded and the situation was desperate.

Eventually, at 13:15, three Hudsons from 233 Sqn found *Suffolk* and her consorts. The gunners of the tormented ships were not taking any chances and a spirited barrage met the British aircraft in spite of repeated recognition signals. Nine Skuas of 801 and 803 Sqn arriving half an hour later were also fired at, but eventually recognised for what they were and a patrol established. During the afternoon, KG 4 dispatched another two dozen He111s on one last attack. Eleven of them found *Suffolk*, but by now the Skuas and Hudsons had created an effective screen and few bombs fell near the cruiser. By 15:15, her plight was over and the last Heinkel headed off.

While recording a total of thirty-three attacks (twenty-one horizontal high-altitude and twelve dive), *Suffolk* received one direct hit and three near misses. Eighty-eight bomb

The damage to *Suffolk*. When she reached Scapa Flow on 18 April, she had a pronounced list to port, her quarterdeck was awash and her forefoot level with the waterline. (Imperial War Museum)

To prevent *Suffolk* from sinking, Captain Durnford beached her at Long Hope for temporary repairs and eventually sailed for the Clyde on 5 May. *Suffolk* would be out of action for almost a year. (Imperial War Museum)

splashes were counted in total during almost seven hours. The Luftwaffe deployed at least sixty bombers, of which around twenty-three located and attacked the ships. The German pilots were, however, never able to concentrate their efforts or engage in multi-directional attacks as they largely came in groups that were too small. None of the attacking aircraft were lost in spite of British gunners reporting at least one shot down.[61]

When *Suffolk* eventually reached Scapa Flow late on 18 April she had a pronounced list to port, her quarterdeck was awash and her forefoot level with the waterline. The rudder was wrecked and Durnford had been steering by the propellers for at least 160 miles. Her survival was a major achievement for the damage-control crews. Thirty-two men had been killed and thirty-eight wounded – many of them from severe burns and scalds. To prevent his ship from sinking, Durnford beached at Long Hope for temporary repairs and eventually sailed for the Clyde on 5 May. *Suffolk* would be out of action for almost a year.[62]

— 9 —

Bergen

Await Further Orders

In 1940, Bergen had a population of well over a hundred thousand. Not many of the people were overly anxious in the evening of Monday, 8 April. Through radio and newspaper updates they knew of the British mine-laying, the sinking of *Rio de Janeiro* and of German ships at sea, but few believed it would have much consequence for themselves. There had been violations of the neutrality before and this would probably, as with the others, end up as little more then a protest. It was a dark, cold evening with a bitter wind and when flakes of wet snow started to fall, most people remained indoors. By midnight the city was asleep.

From his headquarters at Marineholmen naval base Kontreadmiral Carsten Tank-Nielsen, C-in-C of SDD2, had links to the intelligence and communication centre of the Admiral Staff, other SDDs, subordinated commanders in Trondheim, Måløy, Haugesund and Stavanger and Bergen Fortress. Communication had also been established with the army, the coastguard and the air-raid centres. Few of the ships deployed in the district had a radio onboard, though, and most captains needed to find an onshore telephone to report and receive orders.

The most modern ship of SDD2, the minelayer *Olav Tryggvason*, was at Horten for upgrading. The torpedo boats *Storm*, *Brand*, *Sæl*, the submarine *B6* and the destroyer *Garm* were old, slow and poorly armed and would be outclassed against any modern

Kontreadmiral Carsten Tank-Nielsen, C-in-C of SDD2. (Marinemuseet)

naval vessel. Still, their torpedoes could be lethal. Four minelayers and two minesweepers were at Tank-Nielsen's disposal but these had no combat value outside their designated tasks. At Flatøy naval air base, Kaptein E Manshaus had two He115 and three MF11 floatplanes.[1]

There are several entry routes to Bergen harbour. To secure these, Bergen Fortress had been built with an outer perimeter of smaller forts covering minefields (Herdla and Håøy Forts in the north, Færøy in the west and Lerøy in the south), and the two main forts Kvarven and Hellen protecting the harbour proper, supported by a torpedo battery. The fortress was designed in the 1890s, when the ships of the potential invaders had many guns but moved slowly. By 1940, the main forts were too close to the city for an efficient defence. Several committees had suggested a reinforcement of the outer forts with larger guns to increase the defensive range, but these had all come to nothing within the available defence budgets.[2] Instead, a network of observation and signal posts had been established on islands and mountains to try to give the batteries time to prepare and, in theory, control indirect fire.

Oberst Gunnar Isaachsen Willoch, the commander of Bergen Fortress, was subordinated to Kontreadmiral Tank-Nielsen and acted as his deputy. His forts were manned with the third contingent of the Neutrality Watch, drafted during March, and there had been little time for exercise or familiarisation. The ratings, mostly in their late thirties or early forties, had at best been given a rudimentary military training. None of the men and few of the officers had ever fired live rounds. There was no infantry for landward defence of the forts.

Kvarven Fort, under the command of Kaptein Peder Waage, had three 21-cm St Chamond guns and three 24-cm howitzers. In all, some sixty officers and four hundred

View from the Kvarven 21-cm battery looking northwards across Vestre Byfjord. (Knudsen/ Sedal collection)

ratings were at the fort, including staff, A/A defences, searchlights, signal stations, communication and intelligence. Three signal stations were manned, one high up on the Kvarven mountain itself, one on Lyderhorn and one on Store Kongshaug, all overlooking the southern approaches to Bergen.

Hellen Fort, under Kaptein Kristen Valde, had three 21-cm St Chamond guns. As a result of men being off sick and on leave, only nine officers and eighty-three men were at the fort in the afternoon of 8 April. The howitzers and 6.5-cm guns at Sandviksfjellet battery were not manned at all.

Willoch was very clear in his reports after the invasion that the guns and their sighting mechanisms were obsolete and that the cumbersome ammunition handling in particular prevented an efficient rate of fire. The guns were well maintained, though, and during the morning of 9 April they worked reasonably well for a while. Problems were eventually experienced with the breach-seal mechanisms and the rate of fire slowed as there was nowhere near enough technical personnel available to keep the guns firing. The rangefinders were generally in good condition but the optics required daylight or searchlights for the operators to see the targets. The most serious defect was the poor ammunition, with some of the fuses being up to twenty years old.

The outer forts were equipped with 65- or 57-mm guns and searchlights in addition to a signal station. Each fort had one minelayer and a number of auxiliaries attached. No mines were laid and until this was done, Oberst Willoch considered the outer forts to be 'without any significance'. The decision to lay the mines rested with the minister of defence and thus the government.[3]

Three heavy A/A batteries were deployed around Bergen, each with two 7.5-cm guns and a few Colt machine guns. One battery was near Kvarven, one near Hellen and the third south of the city.

The medieval Bergenhus Castle on the north-east side of the inner harbour housed the headquarters of Generalmajor William Steffens, C-in-C of 4th Army District Command. If troops were mobilised, it was intended that 4th Brigade should muster four battalions (two each from IR 9 and IR 10). Only one battalion was called at any one time, on a rotational basis, and on 8 April the 775 men of I/IR 9 under Major Carl Stenersen were deployed at the Ulven barracks south of Bergen. A good number of the officers had already served one or more periods and were quite experienced, even if most of the men, few of whom were younger than 25, had been drafted during March. Communication between the army and navy had been limited during the winter and little else had been agreed except that the army should be ready to deploy an emergency force to the forts, if requested.

For Kontreadmiral Tank-Nielsen, the British mine-laying on 8 April added to a disturbing picture that had developed over the previous days. He feared the mine-laying would result in German countermeasures, which might escalate out of control and bring Norway into the war. Kaptein Manshaus was instructed to reconnoitre along the coast during the day, but the aircraft came back reporting nothing out of the ordinary. During the morning, Tank-Nielsen called the commanding admiral, asking for instructions. The conversation developed into a regular quarrel when he was told to do nothing other than 'observe the neutrality instructions'. Tank-Nielsen was furious and ordered all ships within the district not already preoccupied with the alleged minefields to complete bunkers, stores and ammunition and proceed to their war stations. Bergen Fortress and the air wing also received orders to prepare for war. Satisfied that measures were in progress, Tank-Nielsen called 4th Army District Command. Generalmajor Steffens agreed the situation was serious, but, as before, the two officers did not decide on any co-ordinated measures.

Around 14:00, several signals arrived at Marineholmen from the Admiral Staff regarding German ships moving through Danish waters. Tank-Nielsen called Oslo again, this time talking to Kommandørkaptein Danielsen, who assured him that the Admiral Staff was well aware of the German activity. They were, however, of the opinion that they were not heading for Norway, but 'had a different address'.[4] Shortly after, the first news of the sinking of *Rio de Janeiro* off Lillesand came in; later followed by signals that surviving crewmembers were wearing uniform and saying they had been heading for Bergen 'to assist the Norwegians in their defence against British aggression'. At 15:39, a signal came from Kopervik reporting that many of the German ships there had received instructions from the German Embassy to await further orders before proceeding.[5] This information was forwarded to the Admiral Staff at 16:00.

Convinced that a German attack on Norway was developing and that Bergen was a likely target, Tank-Nielsen called a conference at Marineholmen. His staff and senior officers were all present, including the captains of the ships at the base. Willoch was not invited: a telephone conversation with him afterwards was considered sufficient. This cannot be seen as anything but a blunder. Willoch was Tank-Nielsen's deputy and, besides being responsible for preparing the fortress, he needed to know what was going on in general and which orders had been given to others to co-operate fully and to take over command if necessary. It is possible, and if true very unfortunate, that Tank-Nielsen preferred to deal with 'the artillery' as a separate chain of command. It was only a few years since the coastal artillery had been subordinated to the navy and there were still issues of competence, seniority and tactics between the two branches. It is clear from Willoch's reports that he was uncomfortable taking orders from 'the navy' and saw himself as 'singularly in command of the fortress'.[6]

At the conference, Tank-Nielsen went through the information available and concluded that in his opinion the threat of aggression from Germany was real. He underlined that no orders had come, neither from the Admiral Staff nor the Ministry of Defence, and the Neutrality Act applied. During the ensuing discussion, it was believed to be likely that a German attack would come before Allied help. It would be critical that the auxiliaries patrolling the outer lines could identify intruders correctly and report swiftly to command. Firing on British ships was to be avoided if possible.[7] The most likely entry to Bergen was the southern one, through Korsfjorden; Løytnant Thorleif Pettersen, captain of the torpedo boat *Storm*, suggested placing his boat there, just inside the krigshavn with *Brand* and *Sæl* further in. This was accepted. The ban on foreign warships in the restricted krigshavn zones was well known by all parties and a forced entry past the auxiliaries would be an act of aggression, justifying the use of force according to the Neutrality Act.

After the conference, Tank-Nielsen issued a general instruction to Bergen Fortress, Flatøy air base and the naval ships under his command to be aware that something might

Løytnant Thorleif Pettersen, captain of the torpedo boat *Storm*. (Marinemuseet)

happen during the night and that all levels were to maintain 'increased preparedness' and 'make ready for war'. It was largely left to each captain or commander how to interpret this. Oberst Willoch received a telephone call with a summary of the situation and confirmation of the instructions to prepare for combat. Some of the captains of the vessels stationed outside Bergen, such as Bruun of *Æger* and Horve of *Draug*, were also called and told that if the situation became critical they would have to act independently, based on their own judgement. At Flatøy, Kaptein Manshaus started to prepare his aircraft for takeoff at dawn.

At 18:40, a signal arrived from the commanding admiral to Willoch and Tank-Nielsen, ordering the deployment of heavy machine guns with ammunition at the outer forts. Around 19:00, a further two signals arrived from Oslo. The first stated that reports from Copenhagen confirmed that a German fleet of warships carrying troops was heading north through the Belts. The second asked for a report by telephone on whether it was possible to mobilise a guard company for protection of Bergen Fortress. Tank-Nielsen called Generalmajor Steffens to discuss the issue, but once again the two otherwise decisive officers failed to agree any concrete measures.[8] Tank-Nielsen called the commanding admiral's office at 22:00. He confirmed that army troops could be arranged if required and at the same time requested permission to lay mines in the approaches to Bergen. The answer, which came via Kommandørkaptein Danielsen, was brief and disappointing: 'Await further orders.' Such orders would never come and Kontreadmiral Tank-Nielsen's freedom of action remained limited.

At 22:18 an order was issued from the commanding admiral through the public radio for all lighthouses north to Marsteinen, off the southern entrance to Bergen, to be extinguished. Tank-Nielsen called Oslo to discuss the situation with the commanding admiral, but neither he nor Chief of Staff Corneliussen was in the office, and the kontreadmiral again talked to Danielsen. Tank-Nielsen asked if, as a minimum precaution, the lighthouses north to Utvær and the lights of the inner leads around Bergen could be extinguished. This was accepted and implemented as soon as the order could be forwarded to the keepers.[9] Lights at Marineholmen were also doused, and a call was made to the chief of police, proposing the streetlights be turned off. Tank-Nielsen and his staff remained at Marineholmen during the night but several of the NCOs and officers that had been on duty during the day were released to go home shortly before midnight.

Oberst Willoch ordered 'condition I' at the forts after talking to Tank-Nielsen. This meant additional guards and manning at the batteries and command posts. Live ammunition was hoisted into the batteries and the A/A machine guns were brought into position. By 22:00, all batteries had confirmed 'preparations complete'. How much these measures added to the battle-readiness of the forts and fulfilled the admiral's intentions is arguable. No drills or practical preparations were initiated and most NCOs and officers believed it was just another exercise. The one order not given was for the torpedo battery below Kvarven to prepare – an omission that has not been satisfactorily accounted for. Willoch later reasoned that he had received direct orders from the commanding admiral *not* to prepare the torpedo battery for the Neutrality Watch and hence, as there was no mobilisation, had no authorisation. He never asked for this to be changed, though, and everybody else seems to have forgotten it existed, or assumed that it was being made operational. Willoch drove across to Hellen Fort to inspect the preparations around 22:00. Returning to Kvarven an hour and a half later, he stopped to talk to Tank-Nielsen at Marineholmen. The first signals of intruders in the Oslofjord arrived while he was there and Willoch had his adjutant Løytnant Kvammen alert the forts by telephone. As he left, Tank-Nielsen gave Willoch orders to open fire with all batteries on warships trying to enter Bergen Krigshavn.[10]

Konteradmiral Hubert Schmundt, acting Flag Officer Scouting Forces in charge of Group III approaching Bergen, had orders to land the troops embarked onboard his ships at Weserzeit – 04:15 Norwegian time. An operational order dated 24 March instructed that if challenged by patrol boats or coastal forts during the entry, answers should be given in English in the form of 'Calling at Bergen for short visit, no hostile intent.' *Köln* should identify herself as 'HMS *Cairo*', and *Königsberg* as 'HMS *Calcutta*'. It was hoped that the invasion should be unopposed but if necessary the ships should give fire support during the landing and defend the bridgehead against subsequent British air and sea attacks. As soon as a safe perimeter had been established and the forts secured, the cruisers and torpedo boats would depart, to avoid being trapped.

Half an hour after midnight, Schmundt's ships passed north of the doused Marsteinen Lighthouse at ten knots, entering Korsfjorden, the southern entrance to the Bergen Leads, shortly after. Some of the inner navigation lights were burning and the profiles of the mountains and the larger islands could be discerned sufficiently to keep a bearing. Within minutes, the ships were challenged by a Norwegian patrol boat.[11]

The Attack

Just inside the mouth of Korsfjorden, the auxiliary *Manger* was on patrol. Further in, *Lindaas* was covering the entry to Lerøyosen, the first of the narrows. Close to 01:00 Kaptein Birger Brynhildsen on the bridge of *Manger* sighted the shadow of a darkened warship coming up the fjord and the lookouts reported further ships following behind. While challenging them in the prescribed manner by Aldis lamp, Brynhildsen fired two red Verey lights notifying Lerøy Fort and the signal stations further in. One of the stations telephoned Marineholmen, where the message was received at 01:10.

As the rockets climbed, partly illuminating the flotilla, a signal lamp started flashing from the superstructure of the larger of the two ships in the van, which unknown to Kaptein Brynhildsen was *Köln*. The signal sent was 'HMS *Cairo*', but onboard *Manger* it was read as the German words 'Sei ruhig' ('remain calm'), establishing that the intruders were German![12] Two more rockets were fired from *Manger* and the message 'Five large and two small German warships have passed' was sent by lamp to the nearest signal station from where it was forwarded to Marineholmen at 01:35. When the flotilla was observed from the next auxiliary – *Lindaas* at Børnestangen – more Verey lights went up. *Köln* flashed 'HMS *Cairo*' again and the ships continued.[13] Meanwhile, two converted trawlers, *Schiff9* and *Schiff18* fell in, taking station at the rear of the German formation. These were intended for assistance during landing, harbour communication, mining operations and so on.[14]

Receiving the signals at 01:10 and 01:35, identifying the intruders as German, Kontreadmiral Tank-Nielsen called Commanding Admiral Diesen in Oslo. Apparently, he still received no instructions other than a reference to the Neutrality Act. This stated that warships entering the krigshavn should be challenged and, if refusing to turn back, should be considered hostile and fired at. A vigorous discussion ensued in the Intelligence and Communication Centre at Marineholmen where Tank-Nielsen had gathered most of his staff and senior officers.[15]

Kaptein Johan Ulstrup of the minelayer *Tyr* at Sotra was senior commander in the southern approaches. Being informed from Marineholmen at 00:30 of intruders in Oslofjord, he ordered the mines onboard *Tyr* to be armed and made ready. When a copy of the signal from *Manger* arrived an hour later, Ulstrup requested permission to lay the mines in the narrows at Lerøyosen. At Marineholmen Tank-Nielsen decided he could no longer wait for Oslo and gave permission on his own account. The torpedo boats *Sæl* and *Brand*, still at Marineholmen, were ordered to leave immediately and, heading for Lerøy and Alvøy respectively, to attack the intruders. The minelayer *Uller* was ordered to lay mines in the northern narrows, while the destroyer *Garm* was ordered south through Hjeltefjorden to be ready for a torpedo attack should the intruders reach Vestre Byfjord. Kaptein Eriksen of the submarine *B6* was ordered to make his boat as ready as could be and move to Flatøy, from where he could attack ships that might have entered Bergen harbour after dawn.[16]

Tank-Nielsen called Generalmajor Steffens at Bergenhus at 02:30, updating him on the situation. It was by now clear that German ships were heading for Bergen harbour instead of, as most exercises had anticipated, landing sites outside the city.[17] It was agreed that now was the time to act and Major Stenersen was shortly after ordered to head for Bergen with his battalion (I/IR 9), leaving only a small rearguard at Ulven. At 03:35, a signal arrived from the General Staff: '4th Brigade to mobilise all units. Quiet mobilisation. First mobilisation day is Friday.' Steffens found this ridiculous and instructed his Chief of Staff, Kaptein Pran, to inform Oslo that 4th Brigade would mobilise on 10 April unless they heard otherwise, and would shut down the telephone exchange. At 04:30, Steffens and his staff left Bergenhus to establish a safer headquarters at Nestun, along the railway line to Voss.[18]

When Oberst Willoch arrived back at Kvarven, he made a brief inspection of the batteries, finding things to his satisfaction. At 01:20 a telephone call from Tank-Nielsen came with the information that warships had entered the krigshavn and that he should open indirect fire if they reached the area north of Lerøy. Willoch answered that this was not possible as the rangefinders of the observation posts could not be used during darkness. Tank-Nielsen had to accept that fire could only be opened once the intruders entered Vestre Byfjord and emphasised that this was to be done.[19]

Willoch sounded the alarm and moved with his staff to the command bunker inside the fort. By 01:30 all batteries had reported ready. No attempts were made to man the secondary guns or any of the mobile artillery units. Løytnant Kalsås, commander of gun no. 1 at the howitzer battery, later wrote that his crew questioned the orders to load the guns with live ammunition. This had never been done before and nobody in the emplacement had any idea of what was going on.[20] The torpedo battery below Kvarven also received the alarm signal but reported back that it would require at least twelve hours to become ready, partly because equipment had been placed off-site for security reasons.[21]

In the midst of the preparations, a request came from the Civil Air Defences asking whether the fortress had any objections to darkening the city. Both Kvarven and Hellen forts were connected to the public network and would lose their power supply if the

Oberst Gunnar Isaachsen Willoch, the commander of Bergen Fortress. (Ellen M Willoch)

electricity was severed, affecting the guns, command posts, ammunition hoists and searchlights. Among other things, the 140-kg shells would have to be manhandled by rope and shackle. Willoch hesitated but eventually accepted the shutdown. Later, he held he had prioritised the safety of the city above convenience at the fort, but it is possible that he did not fully realise the consequence of his approval for the fighting ability of the fortress. The senior searchlight officer, who almost certainly would have objected to the disabling of his hardware, was on leave and nobody with authority had been appointed in his place. The electricity works were shut down at 01:45 and most of Bergen was darkened.[22]

Løytnant Pettersen had left Bergen with the torpedo boat *Storm* as agreed after the conference and had taken up position near Lerøy Fort around 22:00. Unknown to Pettersen, who had no radio onboard, the two other torpedo boats *Brand* and *Sæl* did not leave Marineholmen in time because they lacked a large number of their crews, who had been given leave in spite of the order for 'increased preparedness'. The defensive barrier that had seemed such a good idea at the conference looked very fragile from the tiny bridge of the lone vessel:

> I must admit, as time passed and the two other torpedo boats never appeared, I felt very lonely. This, in addition to having to prepare for war and most likely having to attack a superior enemy, created a frustrating feeling of impotence; but also of anger that somebody could consider invading our country with force. I was filled with fear for the immediate future. On the other hand the Germans were coming as intruders and I felt a desire to fight back . . . Waiting felt long, and this is the worst period of all operations. The answer was to keep the crew active; and we had lots to do. The torpedo sights were meant for another kind of war forty years earlier, and not very useful in the darkness. I calculated the sighting angle for a target at sixteen knots and we trained the tube accordingly. Thus I could aim directly for the target and fire at the pre-set range. This would in addition give *Storm* a small silhouette not very visible during the critical phase of the attack.[23]

The torpedo boat *Storm*. (Marinemuseet)

Shortly after 01:00 the first signal rockets arched into the sky to the southwest. Intruders! *Storm* was turned towards Korsfjorden and everybody on deck ordered to look out for the enemy. After about an hour, warships were identified in the narrows in the glare of the searchlight at Lerøy Fort. The large ships in the van were too far past already, and Pettersen aimed for one of the ships further behind. At 02:20 a torpedo was fired from some twelve hundred metres, most likely towards *Carl Peters*. The attack was never registered onboard the cruisers, but the launch was seen onboard *S21* and *S24*, which gave chase.[24] The S-boats could do forty knots versus *Storm*'s sixteen and they closed fast. Pettersen called the engine room for maximum power and headed for a narrow passage between some small islands east of Lerøy. The chief engineer closed the safety valve by sitting on it and the old boat had never moved faster. She reached the narrows just ahead of the S-boats, vanishing into the shadows. The Germans dared not follow and returned to the flotilla. No shots were fired from either side. *Storm* still had one torpedo left and Pettersen headed for a second attack north of Lerøy. Before he could get there, however, the Germans had already passed and he returned to Lerøyosen to wait for the troopships that he expected would follow.[25]

Navigation was difficult in the narrows and as Group III approached Lerøyosen speed was reduced further. *Tyr* had started laying her mines, but only seven were in the water before the German ships were so close that Kaptein Ulstrup had to break off to get out of the way. On the bridge of *Köln*, it was not realised what *Tyr* was doing and the group continued unperturbed, lit up by Verey lights and searchlights from the minelayer. *Leopard* signalled 'British destroyer' towards *Tyr* and *Köln* her usual 'HMS *Cairo*', neither being understood. None of the mines laid by *Tyr* were activated early enough to be dangerous to Group III as it would take some time for the seawater to dissolve the safety mechanisms and arm the fuses.

For a while, the German ships were also illuminated by the searchlight at Lerøy Fort. *Køln* signalled 'Entering Bergen for short visit', in English, but the message was not understood. The ships were inside the krigshavn, and after a warning shot, Kaptein Tangen gave his two 6.5-cm guns the order to shoot in earnest. Fifteen rounds were fired at the ships in the back of the column. *Schiff9* had a near-miss but suffered only minor damage even if both trawlers fell back for a while. The warships continued through Lerøyosen without returning the fire; Schmundt considered the fire from Lerøy Fort as warning shots. Shortly after, two merchantmen appeared ahead. Seeing the warships, they turned back and to Schmundt's annoyance he had to slow down even further to avoid overtaking them in Vatlestraumen.[26]

The torpedo boat *Sæl* had left Marineholmen at 02:30. About an hour later, she rounded a headland in Vatlestraumen, running into the ships of Group III at close range. The men of *Sæl* scrambled for the guns and torpedo tubes while *Köln* started signalling in English. On his tiny bridge Fenrik Gulbrandsen was preoccupied with avoiding a collision and never observed any signalling. Shaken by the encounter, he took his ship into Dolvik, where also *Tyr* had retired from her mine-laying sortie. Kaptein Ulstrup ordered *Sæl* to pursue the Germans, but it took some time before the torpedo boat got underway and eventually Gulbrandsen found it was 'too light' to risk any attack. Meanwhile Ulstrup took *Tyr* into the southern approaches to Vatlestraumen and laid a further sixteen mines there.[27]

* * *

Reaching Stangen Light at the last headland before Vestre Byfjord around 03:40, Group III paused and *Königsberg* pulled out of the formation, followed by *S21*, *S24* and the trawlers.[28] According to the plan, troops from the cruiser were to embark on the smaller vessels and, depending on how the situation developed, be landed close to the forts to ensure a swift capture. The embarkation would take at least half an hour and as time was running short, Konteradmiral Schmundt decided to carry on, leaving *Königsberg* behind. *Wolf* and *S22* rejoined the flotilla at this time and, while ordering *S22* to *Königsberg*, Schmundt signalled for *Bremse*, *Carl Peters*, *Wolf* and *Leopard* to follow and proceeded towards the headland a few minutes before 04:00.[29] The torpedo boats were ordered into the lead. The order formulated by Schmundt was confusing and *Schiff9* and *Schiff18* followed *Köln* rather than staying with *Königsberg* as intended. Kapitän Ruhfus also believed he was ordered to follow and *Königsberg* picked up speed, forcing the S-boats to cast off. Clarifying orders came to continue the embarkation, however, and the cruiser backed into shelter again.

Schmundt knew all chance of surprise had been lost but speed was kept moderate with troops below deck and guns trained fore and aft, trying to maintain an impression of friendly vessels as long as possible. All ships were closed up at action stations, and the guns were loaded and fully manned.

Located on a steep cliff some hundred to a hundred and fifty metres above the sea, the batteries at Kvarven had an excellent field of fire. Their effective fire zone was only some three and a half thousand metres deep, though, and at ten knots a ship could cover this distance in eleven to twelve minutes. Opening fire as soon as targets came in sight was therefore vital for the battery commanders at Kvarven. The signal station at Store Kongshaug reported it could see three warships at 03:34, and some fifteen minutes later another four. Hence, the defenders expected warships to round the headland into Vestre Byfjord. Instead, two freighters came into view. 'This was a surprise,' Willoch wrote. 'If the ships belonged to the intruders, it would be highly irregular for them to be in the lead. It looked more as if they were civilian ships commandeered in front. I found it inappropriate to open fire before they had proceeded far enough for us to fire above them without risk. Thus, valuable time was lost.' Willoch was right. The freighters were no targets and the warships followed some four to five hundred metres behind. Very little time was lost, however. According to Willoch, 'another few minutes' passed while attempting to measure the speed and distance of the warships, but in all likelihood this period did not last as long as he later recalled. According to German sources, fire was opened almost instantly as *Köln* turned into Vestre Byfjord, close to 04:00. By this time, *Leopard* was in the lead, followed by *Wolf*, who had just overtaken the cruiser, and according to Korvettenkapitän Marks, *Leopard* was no more than 150 metres into the fjord when the first shot fell. Hence, fire must have been opened less than a minute after *Leopard* could be sighted.[30] After the war, Willoch was blamed for the 'loss of time', which ironically seems to be due to his own narration of the events rather than reality.

Kaptein Waage ordered: '21-cm battery fire on the first vessel, 24-cm battery fire on the second.' At first, the shots fell short of the torpedo boats. Eventually they came closer, one exploding near enough for splinters to fall on the deck of *Wolf*. Both boats increased speed and zigzagged towards the cliffs of Kvarven to get underneath the guns. The searchlight at Håbsøy was turned on, but its effect was weak through the haze and the rangefinders and gun layers could not see the targets properly. The battery commanders used their binoculars but lost the nimble boats in the murk, resulting in confusion and delay.[31] The fire was shifted to *Köln*, which kept a straight course and presented an easier target. There were no hits, but several near misses and one 21-cm shell passed between the funnels. As the fire was somewhat erratic and appeared to come in singles rather than salvoes, Schmundt still considered them warning shots and ordered all ships to hold fire. Instead, the cruiser's signal platform started to send repeatedly, 'Stop firing, English ship, good friends.'[32] Kapitän Kratzenberg noted in the war diary of *Köln* that, 'Had the Norwegians been fully determined and prepared, there is no doubt they could have prevented the entry of the German ships.' Korvettenkapitän Marks onboard *Leopard* noted in his war diary that he found the Norwegian fire 'rather aimless' and probably 'meant to save honour' rather than hit the ships. In his opinion the defenders had all the advantages and 'Every shot ought to have been a hit.'[33]

When fire had been opened, Kvarven reported the fact to Marineholmen adding that no return fire was experienced and asking for confirmation that the shooting should be continued. According to Løytnant Marstrander, the intelligence officer, Tank-Nielsen hesitated for a short while, considering the consequences for the city should a serious gunfight ensue, but on advice from his staff confirmed that the fire should be maintained.

Tense moments occurred when the German ships approached the torpedo battery below the cliffs of Kvarven and speed was briefly increased to above twenty knots. No torpedoes came and relief was great. *Wolf* and *Leopard* turned smartly into the harbour at 04:13, unharmed and without having fired a single shot, followed by *Köln* a few minutes later.

A fourth ship appeared behind the cruiser and the howitzer battery was ordered to turn its fire to this, which was *Bremse*. Kaptein Haugstad, the battery commander, fired

The torpedo battery at the foot of Kvarven dominated the entry to Bergen harbour, but the fire sector was short. (Knudsen/Sedal collection)

his guns individually to get the bearing and distance right and reckoned the third shot was a hit. With *Köln* out of sight, Kaptein Olsen also turned the fire of his 21-cm guns to *Bremse*, which was close enough to be clearly observed through the gun sights. Olsen later claimed that he scored two hits; one near the waterline forward and one on the afterdeck. There is no record of any hits on the afterdeck of *Bremse*. There were numerous near-misses though and most likely both battery commanders observed and claimed these for hits. One shell ricocheted off the water before going straight through the thin hull of *Bremse*'s forecastle, without exploding – most probably a 21-cm shell.[34] Two howitzer rounds were fired indirectly after she passed into the harbour, but both missed.

The fire was shifted to the next ship, *Carl Peters*, but seeing *Bremse* hit, Kapitänleutnant Hinzke turned back towards Stangen. While on opposite course, a shell passed through the foremast from astern, without exploding, destroying the rangefinder. [35]

The distance from Hellen Fort to Stangen is some nine kilometres, but Kaptein Valde's guns had few dead zones and could engage the ships throughout Vestre Byfjord, right into Bergen harbour. During the first phase of the engagement, Willoch held back the fire from Hellen. The mist made observation impossible anyway and both rangefinders and gun layers reported 'no targets'. As the ships got closer they could vaguely be discerned through the optics. Valde estimated the range to the nearest ship at 7,800 metres and shouted this to his gun commanders when the order from Kvarven to shoot eventually came. Seven or eight shots were fired from Hellen during this phase. Kaptein Valde later claimed two hits, but this is not correct. At least one shell exploded on land. Gun no. 1 malfunctioned and had to stand down according to procedure to reload. After a short while, it reported 'ready' again but the recoil break was destroyed when firing and the gun could no longer be used at all. The sealing mechanism of gun no. 2 over-expanded during each shot, making it difficult to open, slowing down the rate of fire. Gun no. 3 functioned well but was short on crew. The gun commander Fenrik Dalene manned the gun layer's seat himself, while some cooks volunteered to handle the ammunition. At 04:15 Valde ordered 'cease fire'. 'I had just received a signal from central that own torpedo boat was in position near Kvarven for a torpedo attack,' he later wrote, 'and another signal informed me that one of our auxiliaries was expected to come up Vestre Byfjord so I decided to hold my fire as I could not recognise friend from foe in the poor light.' A pause in the bombardment ensued.[36]

The torpedo boat that Kaptein Valde had been informed of was *Brand*. Fenrik Midtland received orders from Kontreadmiral Tank-Nielsen some time before 02:00 to take his boat to a position south of Stangen and attack the intruders. *Brand* was not ready to depart before 03:30, though, and before she left, orders had been revised for *Brand* to act as a substitute for the Kvarven torpedo battery, which the admiral had just learned was not operational. Shortly after leaving Marineholmen, gunfire was heard from Kvarven, and Fenrik Midtland took his torpedo boat into the embayment at Gravdal. The torpedoes were ready and all men were at action stations. After fifteen to twenty minutes the first warships passed the mouth of the inlet. The light was improving fast and Underminør Jensen at the torpedo sights could see several targets clearly at six hundred to one thousand metres. He considered the chances of a hit to be great but to his annoyance no order to fire came. Fenrik Midtland was very young and had not been in command for long. He felt it was too light and 'the chances of a successful attack very small and very hazardous as the enemy was already operating in the fjord'. Instead, Midtland moored *Brand* at a nearby pier, left his ship and returned to Marineholmen, where he arrived around 10:00 – only to be interned by the German soldiers now in charge there.[37]

Inside the harbour, *Köln* tried to anchor off Nordnes, but ended up keeping a dynamic position as the anchor would not hold the ship. The soldiers of 3./IR 159 disembarked in cutters and motorboats, landing on the eastern side of the harbour and securing the part of the city known as Sandviken. From there, they spread out to make safe that side of the port before advancing on Bergenhus, the telegraph office and the railway station. By 05:15, white star-shells fired from Bergenhus, followed by a fluttering Nazi flag, signified German control of the eastern harbour.

The damaged *Bremse* moved from a brief anchorage off Laksevåg to Skoltegrunnskaien, unloading the rest of her troops and equipment there; *Leopard* and *Wolf* tied up at Dokkeskjærskaien where 1st Company secured the quays and gas works before approaching Marineholmen.

Running the Gauntlet

Completing the transfer of the troops from *Königsberg* to the three S-boats and the cutter, the order was for Kapitän Ruhfus to follow the other ships into Bergen harbour. He had heard the gunfire from Kvarven, but as there was no return fire from the flagship, believed it was only warning shots. At 04:40, Ruhfus ordered 'full ahead', leaving the shelter of the cliffs at Stangen.

Meanwhile, at Flatøy, an MF11 was ordered airborne at 03:52 and a He115 at 04:10. Both aircraft had orders to find and attack ships off Bergen harbour. Løytnant Svenning returned with the MF11 after an hour, reporting that he had sighted the intruders but decided it was not viable to attack as they were already being engaged by Kvarven. Løytnant Bugge in the He115 sighted a ship north of Kvarven and dropped two of his 250-kg bombs from 3,000 metres with no result. He then continued westward where around 04:30 he sighted another ship 'south of Stangen'. He took the Heinkel down to 1,500 metres, dropping his last bomb, which also missed. With no more bombs left, Bugge took his aircraft back to Flatøy.[38]

There is a significant amount of confusion around Bugge's report and which ships he actually attacked. At about the same time, the four-stacker *Garm*, which Kontreadmiral Tank-Nielsen had ordered to attack the intruders, was approaching Vestre Byfjord from the north. It was heard that Kvarven had opened fire and Kaptein Skjolden decided to take up a position off Hjelteneset across the fjord from Stangen. From there, he sighted *Königsberg*, which had just left shelter behind the headland. According to Skjolden, the cruiser opened fire on his destroyer and he turned back behind a smokescreen. At the same time, what was identified as a 'German aircraft' appeared and Skjolden decided to take his destroyer into a nearby fjord, where he remained for the rest of the day, trying to contact Marineholmen. There are no records of *Garm* being sighted from *Königsberg*, far less being fire at. Kapitän Ruhfus is firm that the guns were trained fore and aft when he left Stangen and that he did not shoot until fired at from Kvarven. Furthermore, there were no German aircraft over Bergen at this time. Hence, it is likely that Bugge lost his bearing and mistook *Garm* for a German ship in the poor light, while Kaptein Skjolden was confused by the He115 and her bomb and mistook some of the subsequent gunfire to be aimed at him.[39]

By the time *Königsberg* entered the fire zone of the guns at Kvarven, visibility had improved somewhat and the crews were alert. The first salvo from the 21-cm battery fell at 04:43 and the shells landed very close to the cruiser; one in front of the bow and a second twenty metres starboard of the C turret, drenching the afterdecks and alarming the engine crews. Ruhfus still hoped it was only a warning shot and ordered 'Stop firing – good friends' to be flashed in English from the foretop while holding his own guns back. The engine telegraphs remained at 'full ahead'. The next salvo made things clear. A 21-cm shell hit the starboard side amidships, opening a hole at the waterline. The shell appears to have broken up against the bulkhead of no. 3 generator room, rather than detonating properly. Fragments and splinters continued into no. 3 boiler room, damaging it severely. Several pipes and cables were severed and steam pressure in at least two circuits started to fall, reducing speed. The leaking oil ignited, forcing an evacuation and partial flooding of both rooms, as well as the above 'tweendeck, before regaining control. The second shell hit the starboard forecastle, abreast the forward starboard 37-mm gun. This shell also apparently broke up on impact: one part continued through the lower superstructure and forward funnel, destroying one of the port 37-mm guns, the rest tore through the deck, starting several fires below while bulkheads were wrecked, pipes and cables severed and power fell out. Casualties were numerous.[40]

Kapitän Ruhfus returned fire. He later credited *Königsberg*'s guns with silencing the fort, but the effect was actually limited: only one 15-cm shell exploded near gun no. 2 of the 21-cm battery, throwing fragments into its barrel and putting it out of action. The other two guns kept firing. By now, however, the sealing mechanisms started to over-expand from the extended shooting with live ammunition and at 04:52 gun no. 1 was reported out of action. Four minutes later gun no. 3 also jammed. The howitzer battery did not shoot on *Königsberg* in spite of orders to do so and the artillery commander Kaptein Waage was about to call and enquire why when he was overtaken by an order from Oberst Willoch to halt the fire.[41]

Carl Peters left Stangen in the wake of *Königsberg*. Seeing the cruiser hit, Kapitänleutnant Hinzke ordered starboard rudder and headed for Olsvik, a small embayment on the south side of the fjord, out of reach from the guns. Here, *Carl Peters* remained until some time after 07:00.

Onboard *Königsberg*, steam pressure continued to fall. Acrid smoke from the fires and fumes from punctured exhaust pipes made conditions very difficult for the damage-control teams. The electrically driven rudder engine failed, but was quickly restored. Water pipes had been punctured and for a while the boilers were endangered by lack of water and had to be shut down until emergency couplings could be prepared. Ruhfus gave the order to anchor when safely inside the harbour. Both anchors failed to drop, though, and for a few minutes the cruiser drifted out of control. Eventually, one anchor came loose and the cruiser halted on the western side of the fjord, off Laksevåg.[42]

* * *

When the fire from Kvarven ceased, Kaptein Valde at Hellen became confused. He called to find out what was going on and learned that most of the gunners had left the batteries and were now preparing to defend the fort against ground attack. Valde then called Marineholmen, where he was informed that they were also under attack and that the admiral had left. He talked to Kaptein Årstad, one of the senior officers remaining, and received orders to maintain fire as long as he could.[43] Valde assessed the situation for a while and opened fire a few minutes after 06:00. Both he and the commander of gun no. 3, Fenrik Dalene, are firm in their reports that they aimed for the cruiser at anchor off Laksevåg some 4,600 metres distant. This would indicate that they aimed for *Königsberg*, but the shells landed near *Köln*, at the time hovering nearby, offloading troops to the *Schiffs* and S-boats. Three salvoes were fired and the nearest shell landed no more than five to ten metres away from *Köln*, but she sustained no damage. Both cruisers returned fire, *Königsberg* with full broadsides while *Köln* could only make her A turret bear. The shells all went low, however, hitting the cliffs below the fort.[44]

The first German aircraft, six He111s of 9./KG 4, arrived over Bergen shortly after 05:00 and after exchanging recognition signals with *Köln* fanned out over the city, where they started dropping leaflets. Fire was opened from the Norwegian A/A batteries and one aircraft was eventually shot down.

When fire was opened from Hellen, the Heinkels dived on the fort, dropping sticks of 250-kg bombs. Kaptein Valde ordered all men into an ammunition tunnel, behind the guns. Soon after, he learned that no. 3 gun had been hit, killing or wounding most of the crew. Some of the men at the gun had already been injured by strafing and were receiving first aid behind the shield when a bomb struck among the medical personnel. Five men were killed outright and another six wounded. Valde left the safety of the tunnel with a volunteer to see if anything could be done. The dead were covered, to be taken care of later, while the wounded were helped into shelter. Two of the aircraft remained overhead, strafing everybody in sight. The A/A machine guns fired back for a while, with little effect, and in a duel with one of the Heinkels, Sersjant Hans Tjelflaat was mortally wounded. After this, the guns at Hellen did not open fire again.[45]

Good Fortune

When Kontreadmiral Tank-Nielsen realised the German intruders were about to succeed in entering Bergen harbour, he decided at around 04:30 to leave Marineholmen for a more secure place. The Chief of Staff, Kommandørkaptein Kjelstrup, was left behind, as was the commander of the base, Kommandørkaptein Jacobsen, with most of his officers and men. A signal was sent to Kvarven that the admiral had left, but this apparently never reached Willoch. From a viewpoint in the mountainside, Tank-Nielsen could see the German ships in the harbour unloading troops before continuing towards Nestun, where he had been informed that Generalmajor Steffens had set up temporary headquarters. There, however, German aircraft were already overhead and Tank-Nielsen and Steffens decided they needed more time to set up a proper defence. Hence, at 05:30 they left by train for Voss where they arrived some three hours later. By moving to Voss, Tank-

Nielsen for all practical purposes excluded himself from further influencing the events in and around Bergen.[46]

Meanwhile, the soldiers of I/IR 9 arrived at Krohnsminde, a kilometre south of Marineholmen. One of the companies was ordered forward to take up positions near the Nygårds bridge, supported by several machine guns, while the other was ordered to hasten towards Kvarven to assist in the defences there.[47]

Kommandørkaptein Kjelstrup had about twenty sailors available for the defence of the naval base, but when he discovered that they had no more than fifty shots between them, he decided it would be futile to initiate any opposition. Instead, he held up the Germans landed from *Leopard* and *Wolf* through talk and parleying, giving the soldiers at the Nygårds bridge a chance to come to assist. They saw the Germans approaching Marineholmen but, as the bridge and streets around were full of civilians woken by the gunfire and trying to find out what was going on, decided that opening fire was out of the question. Their officers found the position unsustainable and decided to pull back to find a better defensive position. Marineholmen was quietly surrendered.[48]

When *Königsberg* left Stangen, the S-boats followed, landing the soldiers and naval gunners at designated places below Kvarven, from where they started the ascent towards the fort. At least one of the S-boats hit an underwater rock, damaging propellers and rudder. *Königsberg*'s cutter headed for Håbsøy, where the Germans believed there was another battery. Finding only a searchlight, a few soldiers were left to guard this, while the rest crossed the fjord to Kvarven.

Shortly after the bombardment of *Königsberg* had ceased, reports of several German landings started coming in. The most dangerous appeared to be in Hestviken below Kvarven, close to the main road to the fort and the torpedo battery. At 05:05 Oberst Willoch ordered his men out of their batteries and into defensive positions at the perimeter of the fort, which thus effectively became inoperable.

About 160 German soldiers landed at Hestviken. The few Norwegian soldiers there were taken prisoner and forced at gunpoint to lead the way towards the fort. As soon as they started up the hill, Norwegian machine guns opened up. Several Germans were killed as well as two of the Norwegian prisoners and many were wounded. The advance halted but the inexperienced Norwegian gunners kept firing their machine guns and after a while started to run out of ammunition.[49] As the machine-gun fire subsided, the Germans fanned out into the terrain, advancing in a well-practised manner.[50] The S-boats came close to land and used their 20-mm cannons with precision; some of the larger ships used their secondary guns in support. A couple of aircraft also came in to bomb and strafe. The Norwegian gunners were compelled to retreat towards the fort. A second German platoon landed at Kvarvepynten and advanced up the other side of the mountain, joining those advancing from Hestviken near the top. A third group landed at Olsvik and after capturing the A/A battery there also commenced the advance towards Kvarven.

After inspecting the perimeter, Willoch was talking on the telephone to Oberst Østbye of IR 9 about the non-appearance of the infantry, when their connection was interrupted by another incoming call. This was Kommandørkaptein Kjelstrup from Marineholmen, who said he had a German officer next to him insisting on talking to 'Der Kommandant'.

The German, Hauptmann Müller, urged Willoch to lay down the guns to avoid further bloodshed. When Willoch referred to Kontreadmiral Tank-Nielsen and Generalmajor Steffens, Müller said they had both left Bergen and the responsibility now rested with him. Willoch did not want to give any answer and managed to sever the connection for a while. A renewed call to Østbye established that the infantry sent to defend the fort should have arrived a long time ago and something had obviously gone wrong. Müller was reconnected and after stating that the harbour and Marineholmen were under German control, threatened that the city would be bombed unless he received a constructive answer. Willoch found himself in a difficult situation and as he by now could hear gunfire and see German soldiers outside his office, decided there was little else to do but surrender. At 06:20 he gave the order to cease firing and by 07:00, Kvarven Fort was in German hands. Two of the three 21-cm guns were inoperable at the time, but no further attempts were made to put the fort out of action.

After *Königsberg* had anchored, one of the trawlers came alongside, embarking troops allocated for the capture of Hellen Fort. They landed unopposed at Eidsvåg north of Hellen and from there advanced on Øyjord A/A battery and Hellen Fort. Troops from *Carl Peters*, still at Olsvik, were taken onboard one of the S-boats and, landing at Sandviken, also moved towards Hellen. Kaptein Valde found his fort surrounded and, after a short parley, surrendered at 07:35. By 08:00, Bergen city and its defences were in German hands.[51]

Generalmajor Tittel established his headquarters at Bergenhus while von Schrader, the new commanding admiral of the Norwegian West Coast, established his onboard *Carl*

The S-boats of Kapitänleutnant Birnbacher's 1st S-boat Flotilla had a top speed of forty knots under favourable conditions but were vulnerable to damage when operating inshore. (Author's collection)

One of the S-boats taking onboard soldiers from *Köln*. (Author's collection)

Getting organised on the quay. The ship on the left is the *Flying Fish*, the only American freighter in Bergen harbour at the time. (Author's collection)

Soldiers waiting to be taken ashore from *Köln* by *Schiff 18 – Alteland*. (Author's collection)

Peters, which was tied up alongside Skoltegrunnskaien. The depot ship had a powerful radio station, convenient for communication with Group West. Eight radio technicians were transferred from *Königsberg* to ensure constant operation.[52] During the morning, the aircraft tenders *Hans Rolshoven* and *Bernhard von Tschirschky* arrived with aviation fuel, buoys and other equipment, setting up a seaplane base at Kristiansholm island in Sandviken.[53] During the afternoon, Major Lessing and his float-equipped Ju52s from KGzbV 108 landed, as did a group of He59 floatplanes with 5./IR 159, having been delayed by fog.

There were some sixty civilian ships in Bergen that morning. Most of the non-Norwegian were Danish, Swedish or Finnish – regular traffic. At least one was US registered and one German.[54] The ships were inspected during the day, sealing their radio rooms and placing armed guards onboard each. Most were loaded with timber, cellulose and other wood products. Two Finnish ships carried assorted British equipment for the Finnish Army, including trucks, weapons and ammunition. This was confiscated and taken into use as soon as it could be unloaded.[55]

The British Consulate was a prioritised target for the Germans. The British consul CA Edmond was detained with three of his vice-consuls, some of whom later escaped. Another of the vice-consuls, Lieutenant James Chaworth-Musters RNVR (Royal Naval Volunteer Reserve), who undoubtedly had connections to British intelligence, managed to avoid German detention through active help from Norwegian friends. Eventually things got too hot, and he left for Britain on a Norwegian fishing vessel in early May. The MIR officer Captain AC Croft had just arrived a few days earlier via the embassy in Oslo to establish himself as liaison officer with the Norwegian Army in Bergen for the Plan R4 forces. At first Croft intended to stay behind, anticipating that an Allied force would arrive in due course. He maintained contact with Chaworth-Musters and McKennedy, assistant shipping adviser from the consulate, but eventually decided they would have a better chance of escape if they split up. After an adventurous journey through occupied Norway, Croft finally met up with British forces at Ålesund and was taken to Britain onboard the destroyer *Ashanti*.

Lieutenant Commander George Villiers was Naval Control of Shipping (NCS) officer in Bergen. In the morning of 9 April he was woken by gunfire and ran to his office, where he met with the night duty officers, Captain St John and Lieutenant Miller. Neither had any idea of what was going on, but soon German soldiers were seen outside. Captain St John advised that they dispersed while he remained to tear up cipher books and codes. Villiers and some of the others escaped from Bergen with their families and, reaching the Norwegian forces in Hardanger, were eventually taken home by flyingboat in early July. Captain St John also escaped but at least four of the shipping office staff were detained.[56]

After the capitulation of Kvarven, Oberst Willoch was taken to Vizeadmiral von Schrader onboard *Carl Peters*. The vice admiral gave him the usual 'we came as friends', and then Willoch was taken to Marineholmen where his men had already been interned. In addition to the two Norwegians killed by their own fire at Hestviken and the six killed at Hellen, there were about twenty casualties. Four Germans were killed at Kvarven in addition to a large number of light casualties.[57]

The detained officers felt powerless and the mood was sombre. Bergen had fallen to a daring German operation. In spite of ample warnings (almost three hours had passed from the first signal from *Manger* until *Köln* rounded Stangen Light) the relatively light German force had been able to penetrate the defences with small losses. In his report Willoch largely put the blame on old and deficient weapon systems, inadequate manning and unsatisfactory preparations. His points are well warranted, but he himself must take part of the responsibility for the battle-readiness of the forts, or lack of it, as well as the way the weapons were utilised. Willoch, unlike many other commanders around the country that morning, was in communication with his superior officer most of the time and did not have to take decisions alone. Perhaps he saw himself more as alone than he in reality was due to the lack of rapport between him and Tank-Nielsen. The admiral must also take his share of the failure to stop the German invaders. The guns and ships available to SDD2 were old, but numerous enough to be dangerous when used with resolve. There is no doubt that Tank-Nielsen tried to act decisively, but his intentions were hampered by lack of authorisation from above and even more by indecisiveness below. Had approval to lay mines been given by Oslo in time, had the torpedo battery been made operational, had the three torpedo boats been deployed in Lerøyosen as agreed, had it been feasible to open indirect fire on the German ships, had the emergency generators – and thus the main searchlights – been operational, had the soldiers at Ulven been deployed in the evening of 8 April, and so on, the quality of the equipment might not have been such an issue. The one torpedo fired by *Storm* missed, but *Storm*, *Brand*, *Sæl*, *Garm* and *B6* had thirteen torpedoes between them; had even half of these been launched, they were very likely to have had results.

A relieved Generalmajor Tittel, realising how close it had been, commented to some of his officers that the capture of Bergen was '95 per cent luck and 5 per cent reason'.[58]

As soon as things were settling down, Konteradmiral Schmundt sent his fleet engineer onboard *Königsberg* to assess her damage and invited Kapitän Ruhfus to report to the flagship. While waiting for Ruhfus, Schmundt went through the signals that had arrived during the morning. Heavy British warships were at sea and at least one battle group was observed off western Norway. At the same time, several cruisers and destroyers appeared to be heading for the approaches to Bergen. An attack on the city could well be under development and the risk of facing superior enemy forces when leaving the fjords seemed to increase by the hour. On the other hand, sailing in the company of a damaged ship with reduced speed and battle-worthiness could become a liability.

The fleet engineer reported that in his opinion *Königsberg* could be made ready for sea in a relatively short time, but was uncertain whether her inexperienced crew was capable. After conferring with his own engineering officer, Ruhfus said they would need at least one, possibly two days to regain operational status. If *Königsberg* were to sail that evening, she could only do a little over twenty knots and the makeshift repair of the hole in her starboard side would undoubtedly affect her seaworthiness in the poor weather prevailing. Ruhfus proposed to plan for a joint departure in the afternoon of 10 April. Vizeadmiral von Schrader added eagerly that he believed all ships should remain in Bergen for the time being. Schmundt disagreed with both; the longer he waited, the more exposed he would be. A signal of his intentions was submitted to Group West at 11:45: '*Königsberg* damaged. Length of repair not yet known. Intend break out 22:00–23:00 hours with *Köln*, *Leopard* and *Wolf*. Exit-route depends on enemy position.' Meanwhile, *Königsberg* was to complete repairs and plan for an independent return to Germany whenever possible. Sending the damaged cruiser into the fjords to reduce the danger of air attacks was considered, but eventually Schmundt decided that it was better to keep her in Bergen where her guns could augment the shore batteries in case of a British attack. Ruhfus was instructed to have *Königsberg*'s Arado aircraft reconnoitre off the coast during the afternoon and evening.[59]

Several British aircraft appeared over Bergen during the day. The first was a Hudson of 224 Sqn shortly before 09:00, followed by a London flyingboat of 240 Sqn at 10:45 and a Blenheim of 254 Sqn around 13:00.[60] Bombing attacks were at first restrained but at 15:10, twelve Wellingtons of 9 and 115 Sqn were authorised to attack the German ships. The aircraft of 9 Sqn arrived over the city just before 18:30 and, identifying two cruisers, attacked *Köln* in a 'losing-height attack from 6,500 feet to 2,000 feet'. Eighteen 500-lb bombs were dropped. Some landed near the cruiser, but did not explode and she suffered no damage. Squadron Leader GE Peacock's bombs hung up. He boldly made a second attack, after which he took his Wellington low over *Köln*, in spite of heavy fire, while his rear-gunner strafed the A/A positions to suppress fire on the other aircraft. Through this, three sailors were killed and five wounded. 115 Sqn arrived a few minutes later and concentrated their attack on *Königsberg*. One bomb-hit was reported at the stern, but this is not correct. All aircraft retuned to base after more than five hours in the air.[61]

Shortly after the attack, *Köln*, *Leopard* and *Wolf* left Bergen harbour. Cautious as ever, Schmundt let the torpedo boats in the van set their mine-sweeping gear when going down the fjord. This was well justified as – passing the minefields laid by *Tyr* the night before – at least two mines were cut loose, floating to the surface. Around 20:00, twelve Hampdens of 50 Sqn arrived, some attacking the harbour and some the departing ships. By now the sun was down and in the growing darkness no hits were obtained. One or two of the Hampdens stayed near the ships for a while, in spite of heavy A/A fire, and Schmundt supposed they were shadowing him.[62] Receiving further reports from Germany of British destroyers and cruisers off Norway, he took it for granted their departure would be intercepted and ordered the ships into the network of fjords south of Bergen to wait for the following night, which the weathermen predicted would be better suited for a breakout. *Köln* dropped anchor in Maurangerfjord around 02:00 and her consorts took up screening stations nearby.[63]

At dawn, Løytnant Stansberg, flying his MF11 on a reconnaissance sweep out of a temporary air base near Voss, sighted the two torpedo boats patrolling in Maurangerfjord. In the hazy twilight he identified them as Norwegian of the *Trygg*-class and decided to check if they had any information worth sharing. Stansberg landed some thousand metres away from *Leopard*, onboard which the surprise was notable. Taxiing towards her, signals started flashing and, realising his mistake, Løytnant Stansberg slammed the throttle forward and turned away while Fenrik Abildsø in the backseat opened fire. The fire was returned, and a hail of 20-mm bullets chased the wake of the speeding aircraft. Just as the MF11 lifted off to safety, a bullet hit Abildsø's gun, knocking him onto the floor of the cockpit, stunned but unhurt. Stansberg landed in Eidfjord at 08:00, shaken but with a priceless story and a valuable lesson in ship recognition.

Leopard in Maurangerfjord. (Author's collection)

Köln hiding in Maurangerfjord. The turret tops, painted bright yellow for aircraft recognition purposes, were covered by tarpaulin. Notice the low clouds. (Author's collection)

Later in the morning, Løytnant Hansen of the torpedo boat *Stegg* was notified by some fishermen that there were several 'enemy destroyers' moving about in Maurangerfjord. He had the report confirmed and after a brief telephone call to Kontreadmiral Tank-Nielsen at Voss decided to attempt an ambush. Towards dusk, *Wolf* and *Leopard* were approaching the trap and everything looked set when they suddenly turned away, hastening after *Köln*, which had raised anchor and was heading south as darkness settled. Schmundt had decided it was time to sail for home.

The German ships followed the Leads south towards Haugesund and slipped into the North Sea at midnight. No British ships or aircraft intervened and the flotilla anchored in Wilhelmshaven just after 19:00 on 11 April. In his final comments on the operation, Schmundt noted that while he and his staff had done all they could to ensure success, luck had played a major role during the operation. It was luck that fog had disguised the ships' outward passage, luck that *Köln* was not hit in the engagement with the Kvarven batteries, and luck that the bombs dropped by the British aircraft in Bergen harbour did not explode. Finally, in his opinion, it was extremely fortuitous that the low clouds over Maurangerfjord had concealed the ships during 10 April.[64]

The Sinking of Königsberg

Upon the departure of Konteradmiral Schmundt from Bergen, von Schrader was left with *Schiff9*, *Schiff18*, *Bremse*, *Carl Peters*, *Rolshoven*, *Tschirschky* and the four S-boats in addition to *Königsberg*.[65] *Schiff111* also arrived during the day with a load of mines underneath a cover of wood, but like the two other *Schiffs* she had no combat value beyond her mines.[66] It was clear that the Norwegians would oppose the invasion, but their intentions in Bergen were unknown. There was limited intelligence and neither von Schrader nor Generalmajor Tittel felt the situation secure. Neither of them was confident that a combined Norwegian–British counter-attack could be repelled. The batteries of Kvarven and Hellen would not be operational for some time.[67]

During the early evening of 9 April, *Königsberg* moored with her starboard side to Skoltegrunnskaien, assisted by a tug. The stern was left free of the quay so that her guns could engage potential intruders in the Byfjord. The two aft 15-cm turrets could engage ships coming from the south, while all three turrets and the port torpedo tubes covered the northern entrance. Artillery spotters with radios were sent up to some of the signal stations overlooking the western fjords in order to guide indirect fire, should that become necessary.

Bremse moored at Dokkeskjærskaien from where her guns could cover Puddefjorden, while *Carl Peters* tied up north of Marineholmen. The merchant ships in the harbour were moved so that they blocked any blind spots while not disrupting the warships' field of fire. The damaged S-boats were ordered alongside *Königsberg*, for lack of torpedo nets, while those operational patrolled the approaches to the harbour. About a hundred sailors not needed for repair works or manning of the guns were ordered ashore to reinforce the meagre land forces.

Kapitänleutnant Birnbacher, the C-in-C of the 1st S-boat Flotilla approached Vizeadmiral von Schrader's Chief of Staff, Kapitän Schomburg, pointing out that his crews were totally exhausted after more than forty-eight hours on constant duty and needed to rest. The direness of the situation was reflected in Schomburg's response: 'Stay alert, the British will come tonight – or never.' During the early night, *Schiff9* and *Schiff111* laid four minefields in the approaches to Bergen but no enemy came and the night passed calmly. Apart from the medical teams and engineering crews of *Königsberg* and *Bremse*, who worked throughout the night, most men were actually able to snatch a nap, sleeping in shifts at their posts.[68]

British reconnaissance over Bergen in the evening of 9 April confirmed that there were German warships in the harbour and that the Wellington and Hampden attacks had achieved little. For a number of reasons, Bomber Command would concentrate its operations in the following days to the Helgoland Bight; Bergen was left with the Fleet Air Arm, which eagerly accepted. *Furious* had not yet joined the Home Fleet, and the choice fell on the Blackburn Skuas of 800 and 803 Squadrons, currently shore-based at Hatston in the Orkney Islands, providing fighter protection for Scapa Flow.[69] The round trip from Hatston to Bergen would exceed 560 miles, leaving little room for navigational errors or bad weather. Still, the departure of *Köln* had not been registered and two German cruisers within range were worth some risk. All the more so as no fighter opposition was anticipated, even if there might be heavier aircraft around.[70]

Sixteen Skuas took off from Hatston at 05:15, each armed with a single 500-lb semi-armour-piercing (SAP) bomb. Seven aircraft were led by Captain Richard 'Birdie' Partridge, the C-in-C of 800 Sqn; the other nine by Lieutenant William Lucy; C-in-C of 803 Sqn.[71] Lieutenant Edward Taylour lost touch with the rest of the aircraft in a rain shower shortly after take-off, but, confident in the skills of his navigator, Pilot Officer(A) Cunningham, he continued undaunted on his own. The aircraft made landfall just south of Korsfjorden after almost two hours' flight. The squadrons had become separated during the last leg and approached Bergen independently. Partridge wrote:

> Ahead of us was Bergen, looking quiet and peaceful in the sparkling, early morning sunlight. To port were three large fuel storage tanks and ahead and to starboard ships, but merchant ships only – no cruiser. There was no sign of activity of any sort, no enemy fighters and no A/A fire. We were almost down to 8,000 feet when we spotted her, a long thin, grey shape lying alongside a jetty. I pulled away to port in order to make a great sweep up to the mountains and over the town of Bergen itself and so attack out of the rising sun. Now I was heading back towards the German cruiser and concentrating hard to get my Skua and those following me into the correct position for starting our dive . . . Having reached a suitable position, I did a 90° turn to port, eased back on the stick, flaps down, further back on the stick, a half stall turn to starboard and then I was in a well-controlled dive with the cruiser steady in my sights.[72]

It was 07:20. To his pleasure, Partridge found 803 Sqn diving right in front of him. All the Skuas had found their target and delivered a concentrated punch. Below a thin layer of cloud at 2,500 metres, visibility was good and the stationary ship presented an excellent target.[73]

The Blackburn Skua fighter/dive-bomber used by the FAA in the early years of the war. The Bristol Perseus XII engine gave a maximum speed of 225mph at 6,700ft and 204mph at sea level. One 500-lb semi-armour-piercing bomb was held in a bomb crutch under the centre fuselage and swung it clear of the propeller when released in dive-bombing attacks. (Author's collection)

*   *   *

Some thirty minutes earlier, the air-raid alarms had sounded over Bergen but the intruder was identified as an He111 and the A/A crews relaxed. The aircraft, actually a Hudson of 233 Sqn, flew in large circles over the city.[74] When the flock of smaller aircraft was sighted at great height, they were assumed to be German fighters. The mistake appears to have been realised onboard the seaplane tender *Rolshoven* first, where the Luftwaffe personnel presumably had a better grip on aircraft recognition. The air-raid sirens were sounded and fire opened, but it was too late.

Of *Königsberg*'s nominally proficient A/A armoury, only the two forward 20-mm guns could fire effectively on the Skuas approaching in a 60-degree dive. The ship's superstructure and the many cranes and tall buildings on the pier hampered the 8.8-cm guns aft. The surviving 3.7-cm guns forward fired intermittently, but were also to a large extent obstructed. One of the first hits shut down the power system of the cruiser, making the 8.8-cm guns virtually useless in their electrically operated mountings and the 3.7-cm

Bergen harbour around 06:50 on 10 April. This photo is taken from the Hudson of 233 Sqn setting off the air-raid alarms at that time. *Königsberg* can be clearly seen tied up at Skoltegrunnskaien, just left of centre of the photo. (National Archives, AIR 28/470)

guns sluggish on manual power. Thus the British aircraft had a relatively safe escape. The most dangerous A/A fire came from a handful of 20-mm guns on Kristiansholm island. The fire from *Rolshoven* was also intense, causing some of the Skua pilots to describe her as a 'flak ship' in their combat reports. Partridge wrote:

> I was attacking the ship from bow to stern and the only resistance being offered was coming from a light Bofors type A/A gun on the fo'c'sle which kept firing throughout the engagement, tracer bullets gliding past on either side. My dive was still firm and controlled with the ship held steady in my sights and I could see water and oil gushing out of her below the waterline and guessed that she had been already damaged. Down to 3,500 feet now and beginning to watch my height . . . At 1,800 I pressed the release button on the stick and let my bomb go, turning violently away to starboard and then down to water level when clear.[75]

The Skuas released their bombs from six to eight hundred metres. After the attack, each aircraft headed west across Askøy while gaining height. Lieutenant Church from 803 Sqn did not release on the first dive as he was not satisfied with his position and brazenly made a second attack over the stern. It was all over in minutes, the final attack being made by Taylour and Cunningham, who arrived late. All aircraft were seen to leave the harbour but shortly after, while climbing back through the thin cloud layer, the aircraft of Lieutenant Brian Smeeton and Midshipman(A) Watkinson went into a spin and crashed in the sea, forty miles west of Bergen.[76] The other aircraft made it back to the Orkneys, two of them with flak damage, having been airborne for four and a half hours.

One of the first bombs to hit *Königsberg* bounced off the pier, penetrating the starboard side-armour, leaving a large hole into no. 1 boiler room amidships. Even if the crane and the oil-drums appear largely undamaged, part of the plating around the upper part of the hole seems to be bent outward, probably from the bomb spinning after hitting the quay. (Author's collection)

On debriefing, the Fleet Air Arm pilots were thrilled at their apparent success, but acknowledged that it had to be attributed largely to an almost total lack of opposition. Three certain hits were claimed and several near-misses. There was no doubt that the cruiser had taken major damage, but information from Bergen was scarce and it was to be some time before it became clear which cruiser had been attacked and what had happened to her.[77]

Königsberg had indeed been very badly hit. Within minutes, at least six bombs hit the cruiser or exploded so near as to make no difference. One of the first bombs bounced off the pier, impacting the starboard side-armour, and leaving a large hole into no. l boiler room amidships. Bunker tanks were cracked and steam pipes severed by splinters, filling the room with steam and burning oil. A second bomb passed through the port-side signal deck to explode in no. 4 generator room. The bomb ripped a hole in the ship's side below the waterline and the generator room, as well as the adjacent no. 4 boiler room, filled with water, spreading into the command centre, radio room and gunnery control room. A list to port began to develop. The third bomb impacted some forty metres further aft, exploding in the 'tweendeck auxiliary boiler room. Numerous fires broke out, hampering the damage-control teams and evacuation of the casualties.

Two more bombs exploded on the 'tweendeck, one in the auxiliary machinery room in compartment VI and one damaging no. 2 boiler room. A sixth bomb exploded in the water on the port side, causing leakages aft. The list to port increased through water pouring into the hull. All four boiler rooms were taking water and the electrical plants

Immediately after the aircraft had left, the situation did not appear too dramatic. (Sperbund/ Sedal collection)

had to be shut down. The diesel generators that had been damaged the day before gave out completely and could not be restarted. Hence, there were no pumps functioning, neither to extinguish the fires, nor to pump out the water. The fire mains on the quayside were of no use as the bombs also destroyed these.

A tall, black column of acrid smoke rose from *Königsberg*, increasing as the fires got out of hand. Aircraft fuel, bunker oil and ready-use ammunition added to the inferno. As it became clear to Kapitän Ruhfus that his ship could not be saved, he ordered her to be abandoned, saving most of the men but little equipment except two 20-mm A/A cannons that were hurriedly dismounted and carried off. The list to port, away from the pier, increased and *Königsberg* capsized off the mole just before 10:00, leaving her screws and part of the bottom protruding for a while. Eighteen men were killed and around twenty wounded – half of them seriously. Arguably, it was not the bombs alone that sank *Königsberg*, but the inability of her crew to control the fires and flooding, added to the damage caused by the hits from Kvarven the day before.[78]

A number of the survivors from *Königsberg* were deployed to the forts at Kvarven and Hellen, where they were sorely needed, both as guards and to man the guns.[79] Ruhfus was made harbourmaster and kept the remaining parts of his crew for guard and defence duties in port, releasing two companies of the army to be set up as a mobile reserve in case of counter-attacks. Most sailors were not repatriated to Germany until late May.[80]

The Admiralty was 'much satisfied', but for somewhat obscure reasons did not seek to publicise the achievement of the Skuas, far less build on their unique experience. For the men of the Fleet Air Arm, it must have been ironic that the first sinking of a major

The ship could not be saved, however. The list to port, away from the pier, increased and just before 10:00, *Königsberg* slid off the mole and capsized. (Author's collection)

warship by aerial bombing could be achieved for the loss of a single aircrew on the first occasion when the Skuas were used for the purpose for which they had been designed – only to be met by indifference.

In the Hands of the Enemy

During 10 April the remaining Norwegian forces were pulled back to Voss and the Bergen peninsula was for all practical purpose in German hands. It was Generalmajor Steffens's intention to counter-attack once the mobilisation had become effective and he had sufficient units under arms.[81] Critics later held that Steffens pulled away from Bergen too early and it is possible that he believed that the German forces landed in Bergen were stronger than they actually were. It may also be that the reports of *Köln* and the two torpedo boats in Maurangerfjord led him to believe that Voss was threatened, and all men needed there.

In the late morning of 10 April the German trawler *Cremon* came into Bergen with survivors from the transport *Sao Paulo* picked up during the night in Vatlestraumen. She had struck what in all likelihood was one of the mines laid there by *Tyr* and sunk with a great loss of life the night before.[82] Vizeadmiral von Schrader ordered an investigation, and when Kommandørkaptein Kjelstrup, interned at Marineholmen, during interrogation asked the Germans to ensure civilian vessels did not venture into the minefields, it was clear that a problem was at hand. To the vice admiral's annoyance a delayed signal from Group West arrived at noon on 11 April, informing him that the torpedo boats during their departure two days earlier had cut the cables of at least two Norwegian mines. Several supply vessels were expected over the next days and the mines had to be swept – only there were no minesweepers. Makeshift gear with cables and paravanes were rigged on *Schiff9* and *Cremon*, which in the early evening of the 11th left for Vatlestraumen.[83] Two motor launches from *Carl Peters* and a dory from *Bremse* joined them. Closing the narrows, *Schiff9* ran onto one of the mines laid by *Schiff111* the night before. The powerful explosion ripped her bow off and she sank in minutes. *Schiff18*, moored on picket duty near Stangen, could see the accident and cast off to try to rescue the crew of her unlucky companion. Before she could reach the scene, however, *Cremon* blew up in an explosion that also destroyed the dory from *Bremse*. *Schiff18* approached very carefully and managed to rescue a large number of men – even if some chose to swim towards shore rather than be rescued by a ship they reckoned could blow up at any time. Having brought the survivors to Bergen, the captain of *Schiff18* obviously had had enough for one day and reported 'boiler problems', forcing von Schrader to ask Group West to suspend all traffic towards Bergen for the moment. A sharp signal to *Schiff18* ordered her to fix the problems as soon as possible and leave with the two remaining motor launches for the narrows to continue the minesweeping. This was done and by the morning of 13 April a passage through Vatlestraumen was reported clear, though not guaranteed due to lack of proper sweeping gear.[84]

Schiff111, with its remaining load of mines, was sent to Sørfjorden in Hardanger to block potential British landing sites to the south. There, she went aground in the early morning of 12 April in a snow squall. The barrage across Sørfjorden was completed, though, and *Schiff111* managed to limp back to Bergen, but was for all practical purposes out of service.[85]

Things improved somewhat when *Bremse* reported ready for service on the 13th. The S-boats had already on the first day proved to be ideal for operations in the fjords and leads around Bergen and their repairs and return to service were given maximum priority. *S19* eventually arrived from Selbjørnsfjorden and on 14 April *S23* and *S25* arrived from Germany. It would take time for all six S-boats to become fully operational.[86]

Before the Leads were temporarily closed, the two freighters *Marie Leonhardt* and *Bärenfels* came through and docked on 10 April. *Marie Leonhardt* was the only transport scheduled for Bergen that actually arrived; *Curityba* ran aground on the Swedish coast and was diverted to Oslo, while *Rio de Janeiro* was sunk off Lillesand. *Bärenfels* was originally destined for Narvik with supplies for Dietl's Gebirgsjägers. She was held up in Kopervik, however, due to lack of pilots and redirected to Bergen. *Marie Leonhardt* was emptied during the 12th and departed.[87] The 7,569-ton *Bärenfels* took longer to unload. It was found to be dangerous to have such a large ship moored at the quays during daylight hours as she would inevitably attract attention should further British air attacks occur.

The first attack came in the afternoon of 12 April when twenty Skuas of 800, 801 and 803 Sqn from Hatston again crossed the North Sea. *Bärenfels* was in the fjord, fully steamed-up, and moved out of harm's way as the Skuas concentrated on ships alongside or moored in the harbour. No bomb hits were scored, but strafing of the docks damaged *S24*, killing nine German sailors and wounding at least eight. *Bremse* and *Carl Peters* also had casualties and some warehouses were destroyed. Pilot Officer(A) Gardner had to ditch his aircraft because of damage from A/A fire, but he and his observer Alan Todd were helped by Norwegians to Molde from where they returned to the UK.[88]

By nightfall *Bärenfels* moored at Skoltegrunnskaien mole, on the other side from where *Königsberg* had sunk. There were no dockhands to unload her; the regular workers refused, partly as they were not keen to unload a German ship, but also because the work was obviously dangerous. Next day, groups of men were rounded up and sent onboard with promises of good money and alcohol if they worked well. German soldiers were sent to supervise them. During the day and following night some eighty-seven thousand litres of aviation fuel were taken on barges to Kristiansholm. Sixty thousand litres remained onboard with other stores, and *Bärenfels* was still alongside at dawn on 14 April.

By 07:15, the Skuas of 800 Sqn were back. The workers fled, as did most of the German soldiers. None of the bombs hit the ship, but one struck a stack of oil drums on the mole. These detonated, blowing a hole in the freighter's side and starting a fire, which quickly got out of hand. An hour later 803 Sqn arrived. The weather had deteriorated but Lieutenant Lucy and two others of the nine aircraft got through, sealing the fate of the freighter. At least one bomb hit, opening the hull aft. The German Flak Regiment claimed two Skuas shot down during the attack, but only one was actually lost: that flown by Captain ED McIver.[89] The fires onboard the freighter intensified and with 150 tons of ammunition in the hold explosions were inevitable. Buildings nearby were evacuated and at 09:00 *Bärenfels* started to blow up. Luckily for the city, she did not go all at once but kept exploding at intervals throughout the day with significant damage to the mole,

Bergen, showing *Bärenfels* burning on the other side of Skoltegrunnskaien from where *Königsberg* had sunk. (National Archives, AIR 28/942)

including cranes and warehouses. Windows burst all over the city but few people were hurt. Eventually, *Bärenfels* keeled over to starboard and sank by the stern, submerged as far back as the bridge. The bow remained afloat hanging by the moorings and when the fires subsided it was found that the forward holds remained practically undamaged. As much as possible was emptied from these, including three 15-cm field guns, a 10.5-cm A/A battery, parts of the ammunition and some trucks.[90]

On 16 April the Skuas were back again, this time damaging *U58* and the captured torpedo boat *Brand*. The next day, *Bremse* was attacked as well but suffered no damage. After that, the Skuas of 800, 801 and 803 Sqn transferred to *Ark Royal* and *Glorious* for operations further north and Bergen was left in relative peace for a few weeks until 806 Sqn was worked up and could continue the attacks from Hatston, destroying several oil tanks at Askøy in a series of attacks between 9 and 16 May.[91]

Between 11 April and 17 May, not a single German supply ship arrived in Bergen. Oslo, Trondheim and Narvik were prioritised. Von Schrader and Tittel were left waiting, in spite of protests, partly as the strategic importance of Bergen was limited in the current

The wreck of *Bärenfels*. Damage to the buildings and cranes of Skoltegrunnskaien are severe. (P Sedal collection)

situation, partly because the Allies appeared to be focusing their efforts further north. An Allied attack on Bergen co-ordinated with a Norwegian counter-attack from Voss would put their limited forces at a great disadvantage, but neither materialised. In the evening of 15 April the minesweeper *M1* came from Stavanger with 220 men of IR 193 from Stavanger and a steady trickle of men from 1st and 3rd Battalions moved north by air or sea. A seaplane shuttle for men and supplies was set up from Stavanger to Bergen on the 18th and the situation became less critical. After a while, some of the stores could even be forwarded to Trondheim. As they became operational, the S-boats were used in the traffic between Stavanger, Haugesund and Bergen. Eventually, Generalmajor Tittel could turn his attention to the expansion eastwards while Vizeadmiral von Schrader settled in as the supreme commander of Western Norway. By 20 April Generalmajor Tittel felt strong enough to consider the breakout from the bridgehead. Von Schrader concurred and it was agreed to commence the push on 25 April. The history of the battle for western Norway is beyond this narration. Suffice to say it would be bloody for both sides – and it would be 16 June before the railway line to Voss was open for traffic.

The Germans tried hard from the start to normalise things in Bergen and get on a friendly footing with the population. One issue they saw as important was the funeral of the fallen soldiers and sailors from the invasion days. They wanted a common grave in the city centre with a large memorial. Norwegian authorities opposed this and insisted on individual graves in one of the regular cemeteries. This was eventually accepted, and in the afternoon of 13 April, seven Norwegians and nineteen Germans were buried. Both Vizeadmiral von Schrader and Oberst Willoch gave speeches, as did Mayor Stensaker.[92] In spite of German efforts to create an atmosphere of camaraderie and friendship, there was no denying that the Norwegian soldiers had been killed during an invasion that nobody had asked for; if anything the event actually turned out to be the start of what was to become five difficult years for the Germans in Bergen. The population was negative and hostile towards the invaders from the start, and for several reasons the city would become more of a front line than other cities in Norway.

Seven Norwegians and nineteen Germans killed on 9 and 10 April were buried in the afternoon of 13 April. (Author's collection)

— 10 —

In Harm's Way

Anti-Shipping

AT 04:46 ON 9 April, Admiral Forbes was informed by the Admiralty that 'four German warships reported entering Oslo Fjord . . . engaged by defences, five ships approaching Bergen, at least one at Stavanger [and] two . . . at Trondheim.' Norway was being invaded. Forbes, steering south during the night with *Rodney* and the Home Fleet, decided the best course of action at the moment would be to continue southwards for a rendezvous with the cruiser squadrons, while preparing an attack on Bergen. He advised the Admiralty to consider sending submarines 'to sink enemy at Stavanger' and asked for intelligence 'on nature of enemy forces in Bergen'. The answer came at 08:25 and was of limited value: 'No intelligence, but air reconnaissance being carried out. Bergen reported to be in the hands of the enemy and minefield there. Submarines ordered to attack enemy forces in Stavanger.'[1]

Vice Admiral Geoffrey Layton with 18th Cruiser Squadron joined the Home Fleet at 06.30, followed by Vice Admirals Edward-Collins, Cunningham and Derrien with their seven cruisers and thirteen destroyers some three hours later.[2] A second signal from the Admiralty confirmed that they also considered Bergen the primary target. Orders were added to prepare attacks against German warships and transports in Bergen and, if possible, in Trondheim, 'on the supposition that defences are still in the hands of the Norwegians'. Narvik should be watched 'to prevent German landings'.

Forbes replied that the *Tribal*-class destroyers *Afridi, Mohawk, Somali, Gurkha, Sikh, Mashona* and *Matabele*, under the command of Captain D(4) Vian and covered by the 18th Cruiser Squadron under Vice Admiral Layton with *Manchester, Sheffield, Glasgow* and *Southampton*, were being prepared to attack the *Köln*-class cruiser believed to be in Bergen. One destroyer force was to enter the Leads from the south through Korsfjorden and another from the north through Fejeosen with the cruisers remaining outside for support. The destroyers would be ready to enter the fjords on three hours' notice from the receipt of a definitive order to do so. If the Norwegian batteries were in German hands, Forbes suggested it might be better to mount an attack by *Furious*'s torpedo aircraft at dusk the next day.[3] The Admiralty endorsed the operation against Bergen at 10:15, while the attack on Trondheim was cancelled to avoid an undue dispersal of forces while the German battleships were unaccounted for. *Tartar* and the three Polish destroyers *Blyskawica, Grom* and *Burza* were detached to take the thirty-nine ships of convoy HN25 to Britain from Hovden in western Norway while the remainder of the Home Fleet continued southwards.[4]

Vian and Layton were detached at 11:25. At this time they were considerably south of Bergen and found the passage slow going in the face of strong north-westerly winds and rising seas, the destroyers doing sixteen knots at best. Vice Admiral Layton, never one to conceal his opinions, did not hide the fact that he regarded an attack on Bergen by destroyers hazardous. 'Owing to the movement southward of the fleet during the forenoon it was unfortunately necessary to retrace a lot of ground to windward,' he later wrote, adding – after he learned there were two cruisers in Bergen – 'With only seven destroyers available, the prospect of a successful attack appeared distinctly less, though there was some hope that the enemy could not yet have got the shore guns effectively manned.' Vian was also sceptical, believing it to be 'a considerable proposition'. The attack would be made during darkness, and there was no knowledge of the German defences – shore batteries, mines or booms – or the number of adversaries and their locations.[5]

Around 14:00, the RAF reported two K-class cruisers at Bergen. With only seven destroyers available and growing uncertainty about the control of the shore defences, the Admiralty cancelled the operation just as the destroyers were approaching the Leads, changing orders to maintain a patrol offshore to prevent reinforcements entering and warships leaving Bergen. 'Looking back on this affair, I consider that the Admiralty kept too close control upon the Commander-in-Chief, and after learning his original intention to force the passage into Bergen, we should have confined ourselves to sending him information,' Churchill later wrote. Vice Admiral Layton's force turned back to rejoin the Fleet.[6]

The pilots of the bomber wing KG 30 were amongst the most experienced of the Luftwaffe. They had already had several brushes with the Royal Navy in the Nasse Dreieck (wet triangle) between Britain, Norway and Germany and perfected the tactics for dive-bombing heavily defended warships. British naval reactions to Weserübung were inevitable and as the acknowledged 'anti-shipping experts' of X Fliegerkorps, Oberstleutnant Loebel's Ju88-equipped KG 30 had been retained as a strategic air reserve at Westerland on Sylt in the morning of 9 April.

German aircraft had been shadowing the Home Fleet as well as Vice Admiral Layton's detachment most of the day. In mid-afternoon, forty-seven Ju88s of KG 30 were ordered

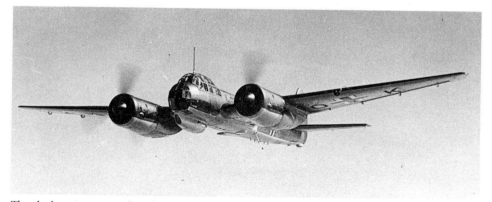

The sleek, twin-engined Junker Ju88s of KG 30, pressed into service in the early days of the war, took on the warships of the Royal Navy. They were equipped with dive-breaks and could deliver bombs from a low level after a steep dive, a tactic far more suited against warships than traditional level bombing. (Author's collection)

up from Westerland and later forty-one He111s of KG 26 followed from Sola-Stavanger. After a good hour flying, the first of the Ju88s sighted the British ships south-west of Bergen. The attacks on the cruisers commenced at 14:25, some thirty miles to the west of Korsfjorden. In spite of considerable A/A fire, both *Southampton* and *Glasgow* were near-missed by bombs and suffered damage, the latter having five casualties, of which two died.[7]

Heavy seas were breaking over the destroyers' forecastles, spraying forward guns and gun directors, rendering their A/A fire largely ineffective. Commander Anthony Buzzard of *Gurkha* was increasingly frustrated and eventually turned his ship away from the wind and sea to facilitate conditions for his gunners and fire-control officers. For some reason Vian let him proceed, even if the manoeuvre took *Gurkha* towards the rear of the screen, and it was apparently never realised that she was about to detach herself rather than taking independent evasive action. The single destroyer attracted the immediate attention of the Ju88s, all the more so as she could put up nowhere near as much A/A fire as the cruisers. Buzzard later wrote:

> At 15:07 when about five miles on the quarter of the cruiser squadron, steering 290°, one of the several enemy aircraft then in sight, a four engined bomber, was seen to be approaching on a steady course from the starboard quarter, at about 10,000 feet. Course was altered to bring the aircraft on the beam so that all guns could bear, but after a few rounds were fired the angle of sight became too great for the limited elevation of the 4.7" guns. The target was, however, kept abeam so that the pom-poms were able to bear in the event of the aircraft starting a dive-bomb attack. It was soon clear, however, that a high level bombing attack was being made, and the rudder was then put to 'hard-a-starboard' in an attempt to take avoiding action . . . A stick of six bombs fell on the starboard side abreast the gear room from about 150 yards to right alongside. The gear room quickly filled followed shortly by the engine room and by the majority of the after compartments.[8]

Intensive damage control prevented immediate disaster, but soon the stern was awash and the destroyer drifted helplessly with a 45-degree list to starboard. Lower decks were evacuated and all wounded brought onto the forecastle. Many were blinded by fuel oil and everyone had to cling to the guardrails or anchor chains to keep from falling overboard in the heavy seas. All radio equipment failed, and it was not possible to attract the attention of the other ships by any visual means. The forward guns remained operational and further aircraft attacks were repelled during the day. Towards evening it became clear the destroyer would not remain afloat.

Emergency aerials were rigged, and after an hour *Gurkha*'s telegraphist Petty Officer Rainer began transmitting for help. No answer was obtained from the squadron, but after attempting several frequencies and adjusting the length of the emergency aerials, Rainer could report to Buzzard that the cruiser *Aurora* answered, 'Am coming to your assistance.' *Aurora* was alone, having sailed from the Clyde looking for the fleet, but Captain Louis Hamilton set course for *Gurkha* without hesitation. Buzzard ordered the firing of high-explosive shells at maximum elevation as a guide for *Aurora* and at 18:55 she was sighted at the horizon. Conditions made transfer of *Gurkha*'s company slow and only about half had been taken off when she could hold no more. At 20:45, Buzzard ordered 'abandon

Tribal-class destroyer HMS *Gurkha* was commissioned in October 1938. On 21 February 1940 she sank *U53* south of the Faroe Islands. (Author's collection)

ship' and she sank shortly after. The rest of the men were picked up from the water or from Carley floats through excellent seamanship from *Aurora* and her crew. Just as *Gurkha* went down, some of the other destroyers sent looking for her appeared and assisted in the rescue work. Of the 215 officers and men onboard, 199 were picked up alive.[9]

While *Gurkha* fought her lone battle, the rest of the squadron fell in with the Home Fleet and the German bombers, Ju88s of KG 30 and He111s of KG 26, turned their attention to the capital ships. At the time, the Home Fleet consisted of battleships *Rodney* and *Valiant*, cruisers *Galatea*, *Devonshire*, *Berwick* and *York*, and destroyers *Codrington*, *Griffin*, *Jupiter*, *Electra* and *Escapade*. In addition, the French cruiser *Emile Bertin* with destroyers *Tartu* and *Maillé-Brézé* were attached. Under a clear sky, the Home Fleet was about to receive more attention from the Luftwaffe than anything experienced previously.

Intense A/A fire from the British ships kept most of the German aircraft at a distance, but in the process, some of the ships used up to 40 per cent of their stock of ammunition. A few of the aircraft pressed home attacks through steep, high-risk dives. At 15:30, a Ju88 dived on *Rodney* and hit her with one 500-kg bomb. Fortunately, the bomb broke up on the six-inch armoured deck and failed to explode properly. Structural damage was slight and casualties low, but the impact looked serious at the time.[10] In subsequent attacks, several more bombs fell near the *Rodney*. *Valiant*, *Berwick*, *Devonshire* and several destroyers also suffered near-misses. Four Ju88s were shot down, including that of Hauptmann Siegfried Mahrenholtz, the Gruppenkommandeur of III/KG 30. The attacks continued until shortly before 18:00, when darkness started to approach.

Forbes steered north for some hours after the attack, then west at sixteen knots during the night, turning to the east again at 05:00 on 10 April, making for a suitable position from which to launch *Furious*'s aircraft for the attack on ships in Trondheim. This course also provided cover for convoy HN25, which, after its successful escape from the Norwegian coast, was making its way to Britain, escorted by the four destroyers allocated the day before. At 07:30 *Warspite* and *Furious* joined the fleet with several new destroyers, upon which the original destroyer screen went home for oil. The fleet then consisted of *Rodney, Valiant, Warspite, Devonshire, Berwick, York, Furious* and eighteen destroyers.[11]

Considering the ferocious air attacks, Admiral Forbes concluded that, with a carrier present, the Home Fleet should not operate within the zone controlled by German land-based air power. He preferred to 'leave Bergen to Skuas from Hatston' and to concentrate the forces of the Home Fleet in the north, starting with Narvik, which had also been captured by the Germans, it was now realised. On the way north, the warships in Trondheim could be attacked by aircraft from *Furious*. In consequence, the C-in-C steered north with the fleet. During the evening of 10 April, the Admiralty agreed that 'Recapture of Narvik takes priority over operations against Bergen and Trondheim [while] interference with communications in southern area to be left mainly to submarines, air and mining, with intermittent sweeps when forces allow.' Churchill added in a signal to Forbes from his private office that he considered the Germans had 'made a strategic error in incurring commitments on the Norwegian coast, which we can probably wipe out in short time.'[12]

Meanwhile, the 2nd and 18th Cruiser Squadrons were sent back to the coast, following the orders of the Admiralty, to watch German forces in Bergen and prevent them being resupplied. *Glasgow, Sheffield* and 6th Destroyer Flotilla patrolled off the entrance to Korsfjorden during the night of 9/10 April while *Manchester, Southampton* and 4th Destroyer Flotilla covered Fejeosen. *Aurora* joined *Glasgow*'s force after having rescued most of the crew from *Gurkha*. She was positioned off Bømmelfjorden further south during the night, before proceeding to Scapa Flow with the survivors the next day. During the early morning Vice Admiral Layton left the coast to rendezvous with the fleet again while Pegram took *Glasgow* and consorts southward before turning north-west and to seaward around 05:00 off Utsira. It was not realised that *Köln* and her torpedo boats still hovered in the fjords.[13] No contact occurred during the night, except for *Manchester*, who vainly attempted to ram a U-boat sighted on the surface. The boat dived just in time but suffered 'a glancing blow'. It appears that no depth charges were used and no search instigated.

At the rendezvous site, around 09:00, the cruiser squadrons found Captain D(1) GE Creasy in *Codrington* and some of his destroyers sent by the C-in-C with orders for them all to proceed to harbour for fuel; the destroyers to Sullom Voe, the cruisers to Scapa Flow. By evening, the cruisers arrived at Scapa Flow, commencing ammunitioning and refuelling immediately.

Nineteen Ju88s of I and II/KG 30 took off from Westerland in the afternoon and set course for Scapa Flow. They arrived at dusk, attacking in four waves, each of four to six aircraft, diving from 20,000 feet. Ample warning had been received by radar, and shore and ship guns were ready, as was a group of fighters. None of the aircraft managed to get near the cruisers and no bombs actually landed in Scapa Flow at all. Two Junkers were lost to British anti-aircraft fire.[14]

*　＊　＊　＊*

Having recovered the aircraft after the raid on Trondheim in the morning of 10 April, the Home Fleet stood to the north again. Later in the day, German aircraft attacked again for about an hour, but with nothing like the ferocity of 9 April. *Eclipse* was hit by one bomb on the starboard side of the engine room while three other bombs bracketed the ship and exploded within twenty metres of the hull on both sides. The engine room was flooding rapidly and had to be abandoned, as did some of the magazines, while the boiler room had to be shut down. The pumps held while the hole in the side was covered to above the waterline and *Eclipse* was taken in tow by *York* towards Lerwick.[15]

At 15:00 on 11 April, Vice Admiral Cunningham with *Devonshire*, *Berwick*, *Isis*, *Ilex*, *Inglefield* and *Imogen* were detached from the Home Fleet to search along the inner Leads north of Trondheim for German warships or freighters. It was during this sweep that *Ilex* and *Isis* ventured into Trondheimsfjorden, drawing fire from Brettingen fort. No German ships were encountered, but *Isis* met with the Norwegian auxiliary *Nordkapf* off Sandessjøen, who informed her that she had sunk the German tanker *Kattegat* in Glåmfjord. At 15:30 on 12 April, the destroyers rejoined the cruisers just south of the Arctic Circle and they all fell in with the Home Fleet the next morning off Lofoten; Admiral Cunningham reporting the Leads 'clear of the enemy'. The destroyers continued to Skjelfjord to fuel while the cruisers remained with the flag.[16]

Trondheim

Ancient Capital

TRONDHEIM HOLDS A SPECIAL place in Norwegian history and culture. It was the first capital of Norway and is still the city where new kings receive their ceremonial blessing. Strategically, Trondheim is in the very centre of Norway; from the south, several roads and railways converge on the city, along the coast, through the mountains from Oslo and from Sweden. The road northwards starts here – a road that in 1940 was primitive at best. Being a centre for agricultural and timber industries, the city had an extensive harbour with good accommodation for deep-draught vessels.

The entry to Trondheim from the sea was protected by three forts collectively known as Agdenes Festning, in April 1940 under the command of Oberstløytnant Frithjof Jacobsen. Coming up the fjord, intruders would have the Brettingen and Hysnes Forts to port and Hambåra to starboard. Brettingen Fort on the northern shore was built into the side of a rocky promontory, dominating the entrance to Trondheimsfjorden. It had one battery of two 21-cm guns and one with three 15-cm guns in addition to two 110-cm searchlights and light A/A defences. Rosters were arranged so that one 15-cm gun was always manned, as well as the command and communication centre, and at night, one of the searchlights would be shone across the entrance of the fjord towards Agdenes Lighthouse. The commander of the fort was Major Henrik Schlytter. Three 6.5-cm guns were not manned.

Hysnes Fort, about two and a half miles further in, on the same side of the fjord, had one battery of two 21-cm guns and one with two 15-cm guns in addition to one 110-cm searchlight and light A/A defences. The commander of the fort was Kaptein Øyvin Lange. As at Brettingen, the 6.5-cm guns were not manned. Hambåra Fort on the southern side of the fjord, with two 15-cm guns, was not manned at all.

In all, there were less than 350 men at the forts on 8 April 1940, including non-combat and auxiliary personnel. This was one-third of the officers and less than a quarter of the men required for a full combat set-up of Agdenes. No land defence forces were mobilised and nor were any reserve or support units. The guns and equipment of the fortresses were old and worn and the crews had only received limited training since their arrival four to six weeks earlier.

It was generally acknowledged that if an enemy naval force penetrated the fortress, it would not be possible to defend the city nor the army barracks and magazines of the region that were deliberately located close to the fjord for ease of supply and transport. The C-in-C of 5th Division, Generalmajor Jacob Laurantzon, had several times during the neutrality period urged the High Command to set up Agdenes fully, including the land defences, as had Oberstløytnant Jacobsen. Nothing had happened though and on 8 April the Agdenes defence line protecting one of Norway's most strategic cities was at best an illusion.[1]

The guns at Hysnes Fort. The main guns of the coastal forts were 21-cm St Chamonds, purchased between 1895 and 1900; they had a nominal range of up to 16,000 metres. Semi-armour-piercing, high-explosive and star-shell projectiles existed but were not always available. (Marinemuseet)

The C-in-C of Trøndelag SDS was Kommandørkaptein Olav Bergersen in Trondheim. The relationship between Jacobsen at Agdenes and Bergersen was strained and it appears that the two officers kept their communication to a minimum.[2] In the afternoon of the 8th, the ships of the SDS were deployed as follows: the destroyer *Sleipner* was guarding the assumed British minefield at Hustadvika; the torpedo boat *Sild* was heading for Kristiansund to detain *Hipper*'s Arado (see below) and the torpedo boat *Skrei* was at anchor off Hitra. The two auxiliaries *Fosen* and *Steinkjær* were patrolling the approach to Agdenes, while *Heilhorn* was at anchor below the fortress as back-up. With hindsight, the auxiliaries outside Agdenes were far too close to the fortress. It was only fifteen kilometres from the patrol line to the forts and any intruder passing would be within firing range within minutes, even at moderate speed.

In the morning of 8 April, Kommandørkaptein Bergersen and Oberstløytnant Jacobsen were informed of the British mine-laying. For obscure reasons, though, very little of the information regarding German ships moving through Danish waters, the sinking of *Rio de Janeiro* and the warning from the Admiralty regarding a likely attack on Narvik was forwarded to Trøndelag SDS from SDD2 in Bergen. Neither were any assessments of the situation received, nor the instruction for increased alert issued to other parts of the district. This lack of communication has never been explained, but can most likely be ascribed to human error rather than deliberate neglect. Bergersen received some information from Vevang coastguard station, which seems to have been well informed, and, listening to the radio during the day, he realised something was going on in the Skagerrak, but had no sense of threat to his own region. When he heard through the public radio that the lighthouses and sailing lights were to be doused south of Bergen, he took that as confirmation that no special measures were necessary in Trondheim for the coming night.

At Agdenes, Jacobsen heard even less. After the report of the British mine-laying, orders came from the coastal artillery command to prepare the manning of the Hambåra Fort on the southern side of the fjord. There was no urgency to the order, however, and the mobilisation cards were made ready and delivered to the post office in the evening for distribution during the days to come.[3] The commanding admiral requested Trøndelag SDS to report by telephone whether it was possible to reinforce the land defences of the forts by local army units. Bergersen contacted 5th Division and learned that II/IR 13 had gathered at the Steinkjærsannan barracks north of Trondheim a few days earlier and was getting ready to transfer to Narvik, where it would replace 1st Battalion, which had served its time. It was decided that the transfer should be deferred and Generalmajor Laurantzon gave orders for one company to prepare to deploy at Agdenes. In spite of repeated calls to the General Staff on the issue, though, Laurantzon was unable to obtain permission for them to move to the forts, and they remained at Steinkjærsannan.[4]

The fact that he heard virtually nothing from any higher command during the day made Jacobsen draw the same conclusion as Bergersen: there was no threat to Trondheim and no need for any special measures. Confident that it would be a quiet evening, Oberstløytnant Jacobsen went to his home outside the fortress. The two senior naval officers did not consider it necessary to discuss the situation between themselves – or with the army.[5]

Following the ceasefire in Finland, the 870-ton minelayer *Frøya* had been ordered to return to Horten from her temporary deployment to Finmark. In the morning of 8 April, Kaptein Schrøder-Nielsen heard over the radio about the (false) minefields at Hustadvika and Stad and decided to wait in Trondheimsfjorden for 'the situation to become clearer'.

The 595-ton minelayer *Frøya*, originally commissioned in 1916. She was armed with four 10-cm guns and one 76-mm, in addition to two torpedoes and some 180 mines. (Author's collection)

Frøya dropped anchor at 19:15 in Ørlandsbukta west of Agdenes. Kontreadmiral Tank-Nielsen endorsed the decision to wait but advised Schrøder-Nielsen to contact Trondheim and Agdenes with information of his presence. This was done. Tank-Nielsen also asked if it would be possible to use the mines to block the fjord in front of the forts, but *Frøya* had only 200-metre-type mines onboard, with wires too short for the depth in question, and the idea was abandoned.[6]

The night started off quietly. It was cold and a northerly gale was blowing with occasional snow, limiting visibility. The first indication of something came at 00:54 when a brief signal arrived at the communication centre, saying Rauøy and Bolærne had opened fire and that there was an air-raid warning at Oslo. The signal was forwarded to Agdenes, SDD3 in Tromsø and the army. After this, nothing more was heard until 02:15, when Bergen reported: 'Air-raid warning called off in Oslo. Fighting at Færder. Unknown vessels penetrating Korsfjorden,' followed half an hour later by 'German warships forcing entry to Bergen.' Kommandørkaptein Bergersen received the signals and ensured they were forwarded to Agdenes and Tromsø but saw no reason to do anything else.

The first of the above signals was received at Agdenes at 00:56. Kaptein Lange at Hysnes immediately sounded the alarm and manned the guns. Major Schlytter at Brettingen did nothing. Oberstløytnant Jacobsen was called at his home and had the signal read to him. He agreed with Schlytter, and Lange was ordered to stand his men down again. There were no replacements for the gun crews, and Jacobsen later held he feared they might become tired if they were to be on alert the whole night. Instead, the men were ordered to take part in hauling ammunition to the guns; a fairly arduous task as the magazines were some distance away from the batteries.[7]

No Unfriendly Intentions

After the encounter with Flight Lieutenant Hyde's Sunderland, Kapitän Heye expected British and Norwegian forces to be aware of his presence. Hence, at 16:50 one of *Hipper*'s Arado reconnaissance aircraft was launched to search Halten, Frohavet and the approaches west of Trondheim. Oberleutnant Werner Techam and Leutnant Hans Polzin were instructed to stay at the coast and under no circumstance to approach Trondheim or Agdenes for fear of alerting the Norwegian defences further. The Arado did not have sufficient fuel to return to *Hipper* and after having reported their sightings the airmen planned to land at a suitably remote place and wait for recovery. Techam and Polzin saw two merchant ships at the entrance to Trondheimsfjorden but no warships and reported as much before landing at Lyngstad near Kristiansund around 19:00.[8] Group II turned towards Trondheim, passing Halten Lighthouse at nightfall.

The darkened ships entered Frohavet at 23:30, closed up at action stations. *Riedel* and *Jacobi* were in the van with mine-sweeping gear set. *Hipper* followed with *Eckholdt* and *Heinemann* in line-abreast as anti-submarine defence. When sighting Tarva Lighthouse at 00:40, Heye turned south for the narrows at Flesa. All lighthouses were burning, as well as the sailing lights and there was no indication that the ships were expected. At 01:55 they turned into the Leads, approaching the Agdenes patrol line. *Hipper* took the van,

Kapitän Heye and Oberst Weiss, the C-in-C of Gebirgsjäger Regiment 138 on the deck of *Admiral Hipper*. (Bundesarchiv Koblenz)

with the destroyers pulling in the paravanes and falling into line-astern, close behind the cruiser. The waters off Trondheim are unclear and studded with islands, rocks and shallows, requiring expert navigation. Still, speed was increased to twenty-five knots. Ahead, the Agdenes massif could be sighted when the snow was not falling too heavily.[9]

After a turn to port around the Smellingsflua shallows, Agdenes point and the entrance to Trondheimsfjorden proper could be sighted ahead. The mood on the bridge of the cruiser was sombre: a signal had just come in from Group West that the lighthouses in southern Norway had been doused and that the forts in the Oslofjord had opened fire on Group V. At 02:53, a shadow appeared to port and a signal lamp lit up, demanding the identity of the intruders. It was the auxiliary *Fosen*, patrolling the outer line of the Agdenes defences. *Hipper* answered back in English identifying herself as HMS *Revenge*, adding 'Am ordered by government to proceed towards Trondheim. No unfriendly intentions.' Kaptein Nic Bryhn of *Fosen* did not understand the signal and turned a searchlight on the warship to try to identify her. Before he could see much, he was blinded by an intense counter-light that engulfed the whole of his tiny vessel. Heye had turned one of *Hipper's* huge searchlights on her, blinding the crew completely. If fire was opened from the Norwegian batteries, he intended to enter the fjord at maximum speed, all guns blazing, in order to saturate the defences. Prior to being fired at, though, it was searchlights only. Bryhn recovered quickly and even if he did not know how many ships there were and far less what nationality they had, he fired two red signal rockets, signifying enemy ships intruding, repeating the information by lamp to the nearest signal station.[10]

Two miles further up the fjord, the crew of the second auxiliary *Steinkjær* could see the lights and read part of the signalling from *Hipper*. Fenrik Olsen also fired off two rockets and flashed a signal to Beiarn coastguard station: 'Alien warships passing B1' (ie *Fosen*).[11] At this stage, the German ships started making smoke and by the time they passed *Steinkjær*, Olsen could only identify one cruiser and one destroyer, which he signalled to Beiarn.

The rockets from the two auxiliaries were observed at both Brettingen and Hysnes and the alarm was sounded at 02:55. Within minutes, calls rushed in from several of the coastguard and signal stations confirming the intrusion. Oberstløytnant Jacobsen had been on an inspection tour to Hysnes and just returned to his house when alerted by a messenger with a car that came to take him to the fort. Before leaving, he called Major Schlytter and gave him orders to open fire on the intruders without warning shots; Hysnes received the same order. Nearing Brettingen, Jacobsen could see the fort was under fire and that there were ships passing in the fjord. He ordered the car to turn back towards Hysnes. By the time he reached there, however, the German ships had also passed this fort and the C-in-C had missed the whole battle.

At Brettingen, Major Schlytter ordered the batteries to shoot as soon as targets could be identified. This took some time: many of the men had to hasten from hauling ammunition, and then the electrical firing mechanisms did not work when everything was eventually ready and had to be switched to manual. Only at 03:12 did the guns at Brettingen open fire, almost fifteen minutes after the alarm had been sounded. By this time, *Hipper* was past the fort and the guns were turned on the destroyers. The first salvo landed close by *Riedel*, but Heye turned *Hipper*'s searchlight onto the fort, blinding the crews, and the rest of the shots went wild. *Hipper* also fired two salvoes from her aft turrets. There were no direct hits, but one of the shells severed the fort's main electrical network that powered the searchlights and most other lights, so the gunners had to operate in total darkness.[12] The exploding shells also threw up large clouds of sand and smoke, reducing visibility further. Two salvoes were fired from Brettingen's 21-cm guns and seven from the 15-cm guns.[13]

At Hysnes, the alarm was to be sounded by a bugler – who happened to be asleep. Only after Brettingen had opened fire did the men at Hysnes arrive at their guns. By this time, *Hipper* was already opposite the battery with the destroyers right behind. Just as fire was about to be opened, the lights went out (with the severing of the main cable at Brettingen). Bewildered by this and blinded by the searchlights, no targets were identified by the battery commanders. One of the 15-cm guns was outside the glare from the searchlights and could see the ships but the gun commander would not shoot without orders and none came due to a fault at the telephone exchange. No shots were fired from Hysnes – and none from the ships. At 03:20, Jacobsen sent a signal to Trondheim reporting that at least two warships of unknown nationality had passed the forts. It was less than twenty minutes since rockets had been fired from *Fosen*.

Safely through the danger zone, *Jacobi*, *Riedel* and *Heinemann* were detached while *Hipper* and *Eckholdt* continued up the fjord, dropping anchor in Trondheim harbour at 04:25 and immediately commencing the disembarkation of the troops. 13th and 14th Company of IR 138 were taken ashore in cutters from the cruiser, the first men stepping ashore just before 05:00 at the piers in Brattøra and Ravnkloa. A perimeter was secured and the landing continued with the help of three requisitioned steamers. *Hipper*'s two remaining Arado aircraft were sent on reconnaissance, one over the forts and the fjords, the other over land towards the east. Apart from sighting *Frøya* in Stjørnfjorden, everything was reported quiet.

At 05:10, Trøndelag SDS sent a signal to the commanding admiral and the Admiral Staff: 'One German battleship and one destroyer at anchor in Trondheim harbour.' Trondheim, Norway's third-largest city, lay open to the invaders and over a thousand men were being landed. Outdated equipment, technical shortcomings and failings at higher command must take the blame, but so must the weakness of the men in charge at the scene. Had all guns been manned as soon as *Fosen* gave the signal, had each battery commander been given the freedom to open fire at will, had the vessels available been used as forward pickets instead of lying in reserve, things might have been different. For a number of reasons, nothing was done and Agdenes remained unprepared until it was too late. Kapitän Heye must have been relieved beyond all expectations. He later wrote: 'The Norwegian batteries were ready a few seconds too late. They fired just as we had passed the danger zone.'[14]

We Can Stand Firm

To capture and secure the forts, *Jacobi*, *Riedel* and *Heinemann* each had one Gebirgsjäger company onboard, reinforced by flamethrower, mortar and heavy machine-gun units. *Jacobi*, followed by *Heinemann*, headed for Kalurdalsbukta on the western side of the fjord. Here the water is quite deep almost to the shore and the destroyers were presumed to be sheltered under land while the soldiers used the motor launches to land troops further north, from where they could scale the hill up to Hambåra (which, unbeknown to the Germans, was unmanned even if the guns were fully operational). The company onboard *Heinemann* would be held in reserve and only landed if needed.

Riedel headed for the eastern side of the fjord to unload her soldiers to capture Hysnes and thereafter Brettingen. The shots fired from Brettingen told Korvettenkapitän Böhmig that it was unhealthy to be too close to the batteries and he decided to land the troops further down the fjord than intended. This would mean a longer overland hike for the Jägers but be safer for the destroyers. During the disembarkation, *Riedel* touched an underwater rock, damaging her bottom, and the Jägers were hurriedly sent ashore.

As dawn grew, *Jacobi* and *Heinemann* were sighted from Hysnes and Brettingen. Troops were seen to disembark from one of the destroyers and the batteries at both forts reported 'good targets'. Oberstløytnant Jacobsen held back the order to shoot, though, and not long after, *Heinemann* disappeared up the fjord. The gun commanders continued to report 'good targets', repeatedly asking for permission to open fire on the remaining destroyer. Jacobsen held back until 07:00, when he finally allowed the 21-cm battery at Hysnes to shoot. Four salvoes were fired. The first was about eight hundred metres short; the rest straddled the Zerstörer. Løytnant Strande, the battery commander, later held he saw at least one of the shells hit below the waterline, but there is no German record of this. *Jacobi* fired back while heading for shelter, but all her shots fell short and there was no damage to the fort.

* * *

Kaptein Lange, the commander of Hysnes, anticipated that the intruders would try to capture his fort from the landside. At 03:30 he therefore ordered the A/A unit of the fort, reinforced by men not deployed at the batteries, some twenty-five men in all, to join him in the hills south of the fort to establish a makeshift defence line.[15] In addition to handguns, the unit carried six heavy tripod-mounted machine guns. Only a handful of the men had any experience in using them.

Meanwhile, it could be seen from Hysnes that soldiers were moving along the road on the western side of the fjord. It was anticipated that they were heading for the unmanned Hambåra Fort, but Jacobsen refused to open fire, claiming there were too many civilian houses on the western side. Instead, two men were sent across in a boat to make the guns unserviceable – which they did, just in time.

Lange and his twenty-five men established themselves in the hills south of Hysnes. At 06:45 one of *Hipper*'s Arado aircraft bombed the fort, but did not damage any of the guns. After the attack, the aircraft flew low over the machine guns, which opened fire, hitting the aircraft repeatedly.[16] Not long after, the first of the German soldiers were sighted. Fire was opened and the Jägers went into cover. To Lange's great annoyance, Jacobsen ordered him to return to the fort when he reported having opened fire. Lange was in a good defensive position and answered back angrily 'Disagree. We can stand firm.' Oberstløytnant Jacobsen believed from civilian telephone reports that as many as five hundred Germans were advancing on the fort. He upheld his order and Lange was compelled to start pulling back. The Germans followed, slowly at first, but attacked vigorously as they closed on the fort. The Norwegians dug in, but their position had become difficult in spite of some reinforcements. Still, the small group of largely untrained Norwegian soldiers held the Jägers at bay for over five hours until they eventually started running low on ammunition.[17]

The telephone network remained operational at Agdenes during the day; reports from Trondheim made it clear that the Germans were in control of the entire city around midday. Radio reports brought similar news from other towns, including Bergen and Narvik. Contact with SDD2 in Bergen or the commanding admiral was not possible and it would be up to Jacobsen alone to decide what to do. He called a war council; the senior officers concluded that as the forts were neither manned nor equipped for a defence from the land side and as no help seemed imminent, it would be a futile loss of life to try to resist. Hence, at 15:15, the white flag was hoisted at Hysnes and Kaptein Lange was sent forward to negotiate surrender. Twenty-two Germans had been killed during the attack, and two Norwegian were wounded.

The forts and batteries were surrendered intact. Løytnant Hauglie, on his own initiative, managed to remove parts of the firing mechanisms of the 15- and 21-cm guns at Hysnes and it would not be until the evening of 11 April that the new German commander of Agdenes could report to Oberst Weiss, the C-in-C of the German land forces, that the batteries were operational. The Norwegian gunners and NCOs were released on the 10th and the next day most of the officers were dismissed as well.[18]

Generalmajor Laurantzon had long since concluded he could not put up a defence of Trondheim once the warships had passed Agdenes as he had no troops in or near the city. Instead he decided to move with his staff towards Levanger, where a defence line could be

Soldiers of Gebirgsjäger Regiment 138 preparing to disembark. (Author's collection)

established with the available troops from IR 13 while the mobilisation became effective. The commander of IR 12, Oberst Erland Frisvold was ordered to remain and surrender the city 'without bloodshed'.[19]

After Laurantzon had left, Frisvold contacted Chief of Police Løchstøer and the two men decided it was preferable not to alert the general public in order to avoid panic or situations that might result in a confrontation between soldiers and civilians. Thus it was that the German soldiers entered a quiet, sleeping city; when the inhabitants of Trondheim eventually woke up they found armed foreign troops in the streets and machine-gun posts at the bridges across the river. Not a shot had been fired, and in some places there were still Norwegian soldiers standing guard next to the Germans, both looking somewhat uncertain.[20]

At 06:35 Oberst Weiss arrived with his staff at the headquarters of the 5th Division, asking for Generalmajor Laurantzon. He was informed by Frisvold that the general had left but authorised him to surrender the city. Later, Kommandørkaptein Bergersen and several members of the civilian administration were informed by Weiss, in a hastily arranged meeting, that the Germans had come 'to assist the Norwegian defences' and as a sign of good faith, both flags would fly from key positions.[21] The Norwegians had little say; the Germans were already in control of the city.

In the late morning of 9 April two Staffels of He115s from KüFlGr 506 under Major Heinrich Minner landed in Trondheim harbour. They had flown from the island of Sylt in the morning and spread out for a reconnaissance sweep across the North Sea on the way. Some of the aircraft had been damaged through encounters with Coastal Command Hudsons. Suitable fuel was scarce as the tankers had not arrived and only two or three of the Heinkels could be used for reconnaissance in the coming days. *Hipper*'s two Arados, on the other hand, were used extensively as long as the cruiser remained.

He115 from KüFlGr 506 of Major Minner landing in Trondheim harbour in the morning of 9 April. (Author's collection)

Of the three transports and two tankers intended for Trondheim, only the transport *Levante* eventually arrived, three days late.[22] Fuel soon became a critical issue for the Germans. Contrary to expectations, only limited dumps were encountered and those that were contained limited amounts suitable for the destroyers. The ten Norwegian merchant ships in the harbour were taken over by German prize crews, as well as one Swedish and two Finnish, but few of these contained anything useful for the occupiers.[23] An emergency operation using six U-boats was eventually set up, bringing in some 270 tons of supplies, but the situation would remain critical until an airlift from the Oslo region could be established.[24]

At Værnes airfield east of Trondheim, a signal was received at 03:00 ordering the eight aircraft of the Scout Wing to retreat inland. These aircraft were only equipped for reconnaissance and had no combat value. Some fifty men were left behind to defend the airfield. During the forenoon *Hipper*'s two Arado 196s arrived, strafing the field. The young Norwegians put up a spirited defence, using their three A/A machine guns effectively, and the Arados departed. Not long after, a Ju52 appeared, reconnoitring a landing ground. This was also driven away and had to make an emergency landing nearby. Twice more during the afternoon, groups of Ju52s attempting to land were forced to look elsewhere. During the morning of 10 April, some four hundred heavily armed Gebirgsjägers arrived and the Norwegians, now low on ammunition, retreated. No attempts were made to destroy the airfield or the runways. The surface of Værnes airfield was in a very poor condition and work was immediately initiated to improve the field. A large number of local men came to assist, tempted by ample money and liberal amounts of alcohol. Meanwhile, a temporary field was established at the nearby lake Jonsvatnet.

Stalemate

With the troops disembarked and Trondheim safely in German hands, the task of *Hipper* and the 2nd Destroyer Flotilla was concluded. The army had requested that some of the ships remained as defence against potential Allied attempts to retake the city. This had been accepted by Raeder in a conversation with Hitler. It is not entirely clear from the available documents how it was to be organised, but the solution more or less presented itself.

During the early evening of 9 April, Kapitän Heye and Fregattenkapitän von Pufendorf went ashore for a conference with Oberst Weiss and Major Minner. The situation was not encouraging; besides *Hipper's* own damage, the destroyers had various degrees of storm and battle damage and all were very low on fuel.[25] The expected supply tankers had not arrived and if *Hipper* was to meet up with the battleships as anticipated, several of the destroyers would have to stay behind. The cruiser had barely enough fuel to reach home and nothing to spare for the destroyers. Group West definitely wanted *Hipper* home, in spite of the prospect of her sailing without anti-submarine protection. Agdenes had surrendered, but the batteries were not operational and even with three to four U-boats ordered to enter the fjord, an Allied intervention was likely to be devastating.[26] Heye wished to head for open sea that same night but realistically settled for departure in the evening of the 10th, accompanied by the destroyer *Eckholdt*. Fuel would have to be transferred from *Jacobi* and *Heinemann* to *Eckholdt* for the return trip and this would take some time.[27]

During 10 April, Heye had a second conference with von Pufendorf and the destroyer captains. It was hard leaving the Gebirgsjägers and the destroyers behind, but there was no way he would risk the safety of *Hipper* by leaving her, though: the risk of being

Hipper disembarking soldiers in Trondheim harbour. The tug alongside is attending to the damage from *Glowworm*. (Bundesarchiv Koblenz)

intercepted during the return trip was the lesser of two evils. The conference supported this. As a supplement to the Agdenes guns, which started to become operational, the conference agreed to position the damaged *Riedel* on a sandy shallow in Strømsbukta as a stationary torpedo and gun battery. Fregattenkapitän von Pufendorf would remain in charge of the Zerstörers and their ultimate return to Germany.

In the afternoon, an Arado 196 flown by Oberleutnant Schreck with observer Oberleutnant Schrewe landed in Trondheim harbour. It came from *Scharnhorst* and had flown some one thousand kilometres, from south of Jan Mayen, having been sent off in the morning by Vizeadmiral Lütjens, who did not wish to break radio silence. The men carried a report to be sent to Group West from Trondheim (and copied to Heye) of the events off Lofoten, the position of the battleships and Lütjens's intentions. Based on this, Heye reported to Group West that his own intentions were now to head independently for German waters. Steering to meet up with a tanker or the battleships seemed to him an unnecessary risk. If intercepted by British forces, Heye intended to head for 'still unoccupied places on the coast' such as Åndalsnes or Tromsø.[28]

Landing of the troops was unopposed and almost an anti-climax. Note forward damage from *Glowworm*. (Bundesarchiv Koblenz)

Eventually everything was ready and *Hipper* and *Eckholdt* heaved anchor at 20:30 on the 10th. Reports of British submarines at the mouth of the fjord had been received during the day and both ships were at action stations. At 22:20, not long after passing the beached *Riedel*, a surfaced submarine was sighted and fire was opened from all guns that could bear. Total chaos erupted in the narrow fjord. The boat, which was *U30* (Kapitänleutnant Fritz-Julius Lemp), crash dived and narrowly escaped. Heye had been assured by Kapitän Rollmann of *U34*, who had arrived in Trondheim, that German U-boats would stay away during their departure and took no chance when they encountered one on the surface. *Hipper* and *Eckholdt* turned back, heading up the fjord while continuing to fire at the place where the boat had dived. *Riedel* also opened fire. *Jacobi* and *Heinemann* were alerted over the radio and in spite of almost empty bunkers, headed down the fjord to assist. Apparently *Heinemann* took some minor hits in the melee, but the misunderstanding was cleared and no further damage was sustained.

At 22:44, a signal was sent from Group West to Heye, instructing him to depart Trondheim during the coming night, even if no destroyers were ready to follow. By the time this reached the bridge of *Hipper*, however, the cruiser was on its way again. To avoid the submarines reported at the entrance to Trondheimsfjorden, Heye decided to go south and enter open sea via Ramsøyfjorden. This is a difficult channel to navigate for a ship of *Hipper*'s size even in daylight and it is a tribute to Heye and Pilot Officer Hintze that they got through unscathed, helped by the navigation lights. Once in open waters at 01:30, speed was increased to the maximum, heading westwards. To Heye's disappointment, *Eckholdt* signalled that she could not maintain twenty-nine knots under the prevailing conditions and he had no option but to let her turn back. *Hipper* continued alone.

Heye held a north-westerly course until dawn on 11 April when, some three hundred miles from the coast, he turned south on a zigzag course. The Home Fleet was near, but luckily for Heye they headed for the coast further north while *Furious* prepared to fly off her aircraft for a dawn air strike on Trondheim. Tension remained high onboard *Hipper* during the day – not lessened after radio reports were received from *Eckholdt* that she had been attacked by torpedo aircraft on her return to Trondheim. At least one carrier was about! Nothing happened, though, except for a few submarine alerts, which Heye believed were false or U-boats heading north.

The meteorologists predicted the weather to close in along the Norwegian coast and Heye steered *Hipper* east before continuing south. After nightfall, in a Force 9 gale, some ships, probably British destroyers, were tracked by *Hipper*'s vigilant radar crew and the cruiser turned smartly away. Twenty-nine knots was maintained throughout the night, in spite of the upper decks forward of the bridge having to be vacated because of the mountainous seas. At 08:24 on the 12th, *Hipper* fell in with *Scharnhorst* and *Gneisenau* south-west of Egersund and the three ships made Wilhelmshaven without further incident at 11:00. Close to one hundred British aircraft failed to find the German warships due to low clouds, rain and sleet. When docking, *Hipper* had only 120 m³ left in her bunkers, less than 5 per cent of what she had left with, barely enough for a couple of hours more at high speed.[29]

Hipper was taken into the floating dock for inspection. There was a thirty-metre tear in the plating below the waterline and the collision had left dents and bruises along the cruiser's side armour. Damage was worse than anticipated, but the belt armour had prevented anything really serious. After a fortnight of intensive repairs, *Hipper* was released from the yard, fully operational and transferred to the Baltic for exercises.[30]

On 12 April, a limited amount of suitable fuel oil was discovered and *Heinemann* and *Eckholdt* left Trondheim two days later. They arrived in Germany the next day without incident. *Jacobi's* engines were ready in early May, when also she sailed back through the Leads after having supported the German troops fighting the British and Norwegian forces in inner Trondheimsfjord. *Riedel* was refloated on 20 April and docked in Trondheim. She would not be ready to sail home until June. While in the yard, *Jacobi's* aft torpedo tubes were dismantled and remounted in pairs on two small confiscated boats. Likewise, a set of *Riedel's* torpedo tubes was removed and mounted on land near Agdenes.[31]

The minelayer *Frøya* remained at anchor in Ørlandsbukta during the night of 8/9 April. Shortly after 03:00, Kaptein Schrøder-Nielsen was wakened by his duty officer with information that warships had been observed entering Trondheimsfjorden and gunshots heard from the direction of Agdenes. Schrøder-Nielsen tried to reach Bergen, Trondheim and even the Admiral Staff, without success. Eventually Beiarn signal station informed him that warships were approaching Bergen and Oslo. During the morning one of *Frøya's* officers succeeded in making telephone contact with Trondheim from onshore and learned that German forces occupied the city and that several German warships were in the fjord. *Frøya* had ninety-six mines onboard. These would make her vulnerable during an engagement and Schrøder-Nielsen decided to dump the mines for the time being, after which he moved further into Stjørnfjorden.[32] He believed his ship would stand little

While *Jacobi* was in the yard at Trondheim, her aft torpedo tubes were dismantled and remounted in pairs on two small confiscated boats. (T Eggan collection)

chance against German destroyers, but considered the odds better inside the fjord than in open waters and decided to remain inshore. British ships were likely to come sooner or later and if the Germans came first, he was determined to prevent *Frøya* falling into enemy hands. Reconnaissance aircraft were overhead during the day but otherwise things remained quiet.[33]

On 10 April very little happened. On the 11th several aircraft appeared, both British and German. Just after midday two Swordfish aircraft from *Furious* attacked *Frøya*, but she was not hit. The British pilots identified her as a German and apparently did not find it strange that she did not fire back at them. At 13:30, gunfire was heard from the direction of Agdenes but unfortunately Schrøder-Nielsen did not realise that this was the British ships he had been waiting for. Also 12 April remained quiet until just before darkness, when *Frøya* was raked by machine-gun fire from shore. Nobody was hit and there was no damage to the ship, which pulled away into a neighbouring fjord. Here, guards were posted and guns manned through the night. Early next morning reports were received of soldiers approaching over land, and Schrøder-Nielsen decided to head out in order not to be trapped. At 11:45, as she moved down the fjord, the ship was again raked by heavy machine-gun fire. This time there was damage to the ship, but none of the crew was hit. Fire was returned and *Frøya's* guns seemed to get the upper hand until the Germans were able to bring a 10-cm gun to bear. One or two shells hit the port side of the bridge and Schrøder-Nielsen steered *Frøya* through a shallow passage behind some islands. Ground was touched several times but she got through and out of danger again. Damage from the cannon shells was largely superficial but there were several leaks from the grounding.

Kaptein Schrøder-Nielsen decided the best thing to do was to abandon the ship and sink her, lest she fell into German hands. Supplies were getting low and with Agdenes held by Germans, the chance of getting out was 'realistically zero'. Maps and codebooks were destroyed and the guns made inoperable while machine guns and rifles were loaded into the lifeboats. When all was ready, the crew was sent ashore and *Frøya* ran aground, after which the engine room was filled with water. At 12:30, the minelayer was sinking in shallow water some twenty metres from shore. Most of the deck and superstructure remained above water. Late in the afternoon, *U30* and *U34* arrived en route to Trondheim. The latter fired a torpedo that impacted aft, breaking *Frøya* in two. Meanwhile, Schrøder-Nielsen and his crew had requisitioned some trucks and headed for Namsos, where they arrived at midday on 14 April. *Frøya* was armed with four 10-cm guns, one 76-mm and two torpedo tubes. She would be no match for *Hipper*, but with proper reconnaissance she might have been used aggressively against the damaged German destroyers with a fair hope of success.[34]

The torbedo boat *Laks* was in Trondheim naval yard on the morning of 9 April. Her young captain, Løytnant Rangvald Tamber, was disgusted with the German attack on Norway and above all with the ease with which Trondheim had been captured. After gaining approval from Kommandørkaptein Bergersen, torpedoes, ammunition and coal were discretely brought onboard and the torpedo boat made ready for a night attack on *Hipper*, which was still at anchor in the harbour. Just as Tamber was about to sail, he received word that the cruiser had left with the destroyers. Not realising that the destroyers would come back, the attack was aborted and the boat abandoned.[35]

*   *   *

Trondheim and Værnes were at the extreme range of RAF aircraft operating out of Britain. From Coastal Command it was only the Sunderlands that could venture that far, and from Bomber Command only the Whitleys of 77 Sqn based at Kinloss. Several attempts were made by the latter to raid the airfield and the temporary base at Jonsvatnet, but they were few in number and the sorties were largely frustrated by weather. Results were negligible.[36]

Around 08:30 in the morning of 9 April, Admiral Forbes received instructions to prepare a plan for attacking German warships and transports anticipated to be in Bergen and Trondheim and to take control of the approaches to the two cities – assuming sufficient forces were available and the defences were still in Norwegian hands. During the day, the Home Fleet experienced severe bomb attacks off Bergen and as the carrier *Furious* was about to join the fleet, Forbes decided to 'leave Bergen to the Skuas and use *Furious*'s aircraft for attacking enemy ships at Trondheim'.[37] The carrier joined the flag in the morning of 10 April. Her two TSR Swordfish units, 816 Sqn and 818 Sqn, had been landed on her but no fighters.[38]

German ships were confirmed in Trondheim during the afternoon of the 10th by a Sunderland of 228 Sqn and at 04:00 on 11 April *Furious* started to fly off her complement of eighteen Swordfish aircraft from a position some ninety miles off the coast, in what would be the first aerial torpedo attack of the war. Unknown to Forbes, *Hipper* had already left Trondheim and was at this moment actually west of the Home Fleet.

Arriving over Trondheim at 05:14, 816 Sqn found the harbour obscured by cloud. Undaunted, Lieutenant Commander Gardner took his squadron through the clouds in a diving attack but found the roads empty. Continuing towards Skjorenfjord, a destroyer was sighted at anchor, an ideal target. All nine aircraft dropped their ordnance but to their astonishment the torpedo tracks ended abruptly some five hundred metres from the ship. The target was *Riedel*, grounded on her shallow. Four of the nine torpedoes exploded harmlessly, the others expended their energy on the sandy rocks.[39]

Meanwhile, 818 Sqn sighted *Eckholdt* returning from her sortie with *Hipper*. Considering her a valid target, Lieutenant Commander Syndey-Turner attacked. Of the eight torpedoes released, two exploded prematurely while the other six were skilfully avoided.[40] It was a very disheartened band of airmen that returned to the ship at 06:30. Irritated by the meagre results, Admiral Forbes ordered a 'proper reconnaissance' of Trondheim. Two aircraft of 816 Sqn made a lengthy investigation of the fjord and harbour. In Trondheim, only a handful of seaplanes were observed moored in the roadstead. No ships were sighted except *Frøya*, which was identified as 'a small enemy warship, probably a destroyer of the Wolf-class', and attacked with bombs. Luckily, the Norwegian minelayer was not hit by the British bombs and she did not fire back so the Swordfish planes suffered no harm. Both aircraft returned safely at 13:45. An unidentified seaplane shadowed the two Swordfish when they headed back to the carrier and, predictably, an attack by the Luftwaffe followed in the afternoon, off Vikna. The attack was not pressed home with much enthusiasm though, just a series of high-level bombing runs.

During the morning of 11 April the Admiralty instructed Admiral Forbes to investigate reports of a German merchantman off Trondheimsfjorden, and the destroyers *Ilex* and

Isis were sent into Frohavet. Finding nothing, Commander JC Clouston of *Isis* decided to continue towards Trondheim and while *Ilex* found her way northward into Stjørnfjorden, *Isis* boldly turned starboard into Trondheimsfjorden. At 13:20, she was approaching Hysnes when fire was opened from Brettingen Fort, by now abaft the port beam, at a range of some three thousand metres. The fire was returned; even if the German gunners did not appear to handle their new guns well, Commander Clouston found the environment unhealthy and ordered both destroyers out of the fjord at high speed under a smokescreen. Shots were exchanged with the fort as long as the guns could bear, *Ilex* also joining in. No damage was sustained by either side. After reporting the incident to the commander, the two destroyers were ordered to join 1st Cruiser Squadron in a continued search for German transports in the fjords north of Trondheim.

It was only the batteries at Brettingen that opened fire, as the guns at Hysnes and Hambåra were still not operational. The fire from the guns at Brettingen was reported ineffective and not very accurate, but the mere fact that they were operational and obviously manned by German gunners brought about some significant changes in the dispositions of the Home Fleet, with profound effects on the subsequent campaign. Having received signals from the Admiralty in the evening of 10 April that recapture of Narvik was to take priority over Bergen and Trondheim, Admiral Forbes decided there was little to gain off mid-Norway and he set course for Lofoten.[41]

Encounter in the Storm

Am Engaging Enemy

AFTER DETACHING THE NARVIK destroyers at the mouth of Vestfjorden in the afternoon of 8 April, *Gneisenau* and *Scharnhorst* headed north-west, into the Norwegian Sea. There was a west-north-westerly full storm raging, which towards midnight reached hurricane strength. Kapitän zur See Kurt Cäsar Hoffmann of *Scharnhorst* was not a happy man. Mountainous seas were breaking over his ship, distorting bulkheads and developing cracks. Evidence of metal fatigue was even reported from the bows and the upper works. Just after midnight, one malicious wave broke a ventshaft, which let seawater flood through the intake, polluting seven oil tanks and making some 470 m³ of fuel oil unusable. The port engine had to be temporarily shut down. The flagship instructed nine knots with one boiler on line per shaft. Hoffmann thought this imprudent under the prevailing conditions and ordered his engineer officer, Fregattenkapitän Leibhard, to keep two boilers on line per shaft. By 02:00 they were about thirty miles south-west of Lofoten on a north-westerly course. A slight decrease in the sea was experienced and

The nine 28-cm guns of *Scharnhorst* and *Gneisenau* fired a broadside of just under 3,000 kg at a rate of 3.5 rounds per minute. Twelve 15-cm guns, in two twin turrets and two single mountings on each side, and fourteen 10.5-cm multipurpose guns in twin mountings made up the secondary armament. Fire control for the main and secondary guns was handled by several stereoscopic rangefinders. The foretop and aft fire-control centre as well as each turret had 10.5-m instruments. The forward control centre had a 6.5-m rangefinder in a rotating cupola. (Author's collection)

speed was increased to twelve knots. To the west, the visibility was poor, with frequent snow and hail showers. To the north and east it was an almost cloudless horizon. It was cold, with temperatures falling well below freezing during the night.[1]

The destroyers following Vice Admiral Whitworth in *Renown* – *Esk*, *Greyhound*, *Hardy*, *Hotspur*, *Havock*, *Hunter*, *Ivanhoe*, *Icarus* and *Impulsive* – were, somewhat to their own surprise, afloat and in reasonable condition in the morning of 9 April. It had been a terrible night, and even old hands could barely remember anything similar.[2] With the first hint of daylight, conditions were still appalling, but improving just enough for Whitworth to turn back towards Vestfjorden, where he should have been, according to the orders from the Admiralty.[3] Unbeknown to the vice admiral, the German destroyers he was supposed to intercept were nearing Narvik at twenty-seven knots.

'From midnight onwards, the weather improved,' Whitworth later wrote, 'but knowing that the destroyers would be widely strung out on account of the weather, I decided to wait until the first sign of dawn and sufficient light to make the turn to the south-eastward without losing touch with them.' The destroyers managed to turn without damage in the heavy seas and by 02:40 the British ships were on course 130° at twelve knots. The sea was still heavy, and the destroyers kept station astern of the flagship.

At 03:37, *Renown* sighted a darkened ship emerging from a snow squall some ten miles to the east, followed within minutes by the shadow of another. The two ships were on a north-westerly course approximately opposite to that of the British, some fifty miles west of Skomvær Lighthouse. The ships were identified as German – one *Scharnhorst*-class battlecruiser and one *Hipper*-class cruiser. Vice Admiral Whitworth kept *Renown* on course for ten minutes, picking up speed and preparing for battle. At 03:37, he altered

HMS *Renown*, one of two 26,500-ton battlecruisers completed in September 1916. She was extensively rebuilt and refitted to increase protection against gunfire and torpedoes several times between the wars. The last refit was completed in September 1939. (Wright and Logan)

to 080° and ten minutes later to 305°, roughly parallel to the German ships. The bulky battlecruiser was just in the position Whitworth wanted: about seventeen kilometres away, with the German ships silhouetted against the eastern morning horizon. At 04:05, *Renown* opened fire on *Gneisenau*, which was straddled with the sixth salvo. It was twenty-five years since a British battlecruiser had fired on a German one.[4]

Engaging the two German ships was an audacious undertaking, possibly made easier by believing that one of them was a cruiser. *Renown* had six 15-inch (38-cm) and twenty 4.5-inch (11.5-cm) guns but she was WWI vintage and slow. Various rebuilds and modernisations had added almost five thousand tons to her displacement, reducing speed to less than thirty knots and lowering the freeboard by a foot, making her very wet forward in heavy seas. *Scharnhorst* and *Gneisenau* were under-gunned, but still carried nine 28-cm guns and twelve 15-cm each.

Whitworth ordered 'full ahead' but to his annoyance, the seas breaking over the forecastle made this impossible, and he had to settle for the maximum *Renown* could sustain: twenty-four knots. The British destroyers fanned out astern of the flagship and brazenly opened fire too. At that range the 4.7-inch fire from the rolling destroyers had no effect whatsoever and when *Hardy* and *Hunter* narrowly escaped being hit, Vice Admiral Whitworth ordered them out of harm's way. There was no hope of them catching up in the heavy seas to obtain a position from where torpedoes could be fired. At first the order for Captain D(2) Warburton-Lee was to turn back to a position east of Lofoten, later amended to head for Vestfjorden.[5]

At 04:07 a signal was sent from *Renown* to the C-in-C and the Admiralty: 'Am engaging enemy.' It must have been a most welcome report, even if it also created considerable anxiety. At last some German ships had been found.[6]

In an Unfavourable Position

At 03:50, a contact aft on the port quarter was reported from the DeTe-Gerät radar to the bridge of *Gneisenau*.[7] The radar had not performed well during the previous days due to the poor weather and Kapitän zur See Netzbandt wanted visual confirmation before alerting the admiral. Hence, he joined his senior gunnery officer, Fregattenkapitän von Buchka, at the rangefinder to try to verify the sighting. In the shifting visibility towards the south-west, it was not until 03:59 that the foretop could report a shadow in the direction of the contact. Von Buchka was sent to alert Vizeadmiral Lütjens while Netzbandt returned to his bridge, from where the alarm was sounded at 04:00. The sighted ship was less than twenty kilometres away, but in the murk it was first identified as a tanker and then as a '*Nelson*-class battleship – very long bow section and bridge structure well astern'. From *Scharnhorst*, east of the flagship, nothing had been sighted prior to the 'Alarm' signal and it would be another few minutes before her lookouts reported a shadow on the dark, western horizon.[8]

At 04:05, the shadow identified itself as an enemy by opening fire. Muzzle flashes were seen through the snow and shortly after, incoming shells landed some three to five hundred metres abreast the bridge of *Gneisenau*. From the size of the waterspouts, it was clear that these were shells from heavy-calibre guns. The first indication of range reported to the admiral was 14.8 kilometres. *Scharnhorst* returned fire at 04:10 and *Gneisenau* a minute later. It is notable that it took eleven minutes from the 'Alarm' until the main guns of *Gneisenau* opened fire, and another five minutes before a logbook entry at 04:16 stated that the ship was 'battle ready'. The delay made Whitworth comment in his report that he did not believe the Germans had sighted *Renown* before she opened fire. He also found the fire from both ships 'ragged both for line and range and the spread was very variable'.

Vizeadmiral Lütjens had orders to avoid battle with superior opponents if possible and, believing this was the case, he steered away. At first, the adversary could not be seen properly from the vice admiral's bridge, but only recognised from the muzzle flashes. Hence, Lütjens and his staff were not sure what they were up against. When visibility improved for a while, a 'Renown-class' battlecruiser was correctly identified, but as some of the destroyers also opened fire, their muzzle flashes made Lütjens believe there was more than one heavy ship to the south-west. From the first identification of a *Nelson*-class battleship and later a *Renown*-class battlecruiser, Kapitän zur See Netzbandt and his officers also believed there might be two enemies. From *Scharnhorst*, only one battleship was sighted, while at the start of the encounter it was believed there might be 'one or two further targets' behind.

Lütjens ordered a 40° change of course to starboard, steering 350°, even if this meant that only the after turrets could bear. He also asked for maximum speed and the German ships eventually reached twenty-seven knots. Huge seas fell on the forecastle, making observation very difficult from the bridge and gunnery-control stations as the optics misted up and the electric motors for the clear-screens kept short-circuiting. Kapitän Netzbandt suggested a course somewhat more to port and Lütjens agreed to steer 330°, which also allowed the use of all turrets. The wind was rising again, and during the engagement it shifted from north-north-west to north-north-east.[9]

In spite of the 'ragged' German fire, at least one of the battleships found the range and some time around 04:15, *Renown* was hit by two 28-cm shells. One shell hit the foremast, severing most of the W/T aerials, destroying cables for the radio direction finder and tearing adrift some lanterns. The second shell impacted aft, wrecking storage rooms and creating minor flooding but otherwise doing little damage. British reports suggest that both shells failed to explode properly, but as flames and smoke were observed from the bridge of *Gneisenau* it is more likely that the hits were high-explosive shells rather than armour piercing.[10] There were one or two more near-misses, but no further hits. An emergency W/T aerial was soon rigged.

Kapitän Netzbandt instructed one of the signalmen on the bridge to telephone von Buchka, 'Your fire lies well, let him have it.' At that very moment, 04:17, *Gneisenau*'s foretop was hit on the port side aft by a 15-inch projectile from *Renown*'s sixteenth salvo. Six men were killed, including Fregattenkapitän von Buchka, and at least nine wounded. The rangefinder, radar and main fire control fell out and *Gneisenau*'s guns fell silent for a few minutes until command could be transferred, first to the forward port director then to the aft director under the command of no. 3 gunnery officer, Korvettenkapitän Bredenbreuker. By the time *Gneisenau*'s guns were under command again, only the after turret could bear, together with the port 15-cm guns. Two 4.5-inch shells from *Renown* hit *Gneisenau* some minutes later. One exploded on the port side of the aft flak-gun platform, doing little damage; the other tore off parts of the A turret's rangefinder cupola, opening the turret to flooding and it eventually fell out altogether.[11] Seeing the flagship hit, *Scharnhorst*, which had so far been engaged by *Renown*'s secondary guns, drew across behind *Gneisenau*, making smoke in an attempt to draw fire. This worked and *Renown* changed target for her main armament at 04:20.

Gneisenau turned away to the north-north-east, and *Scharnhorst* followed, forcing Whitworth to also alter north, directly to windward and into a heavy sea. *Renown* was, on paper, only a few knots slower than her adversaries, but in the heavy seas she took enormous amounts of water over the forecastle and forward turrets, making conditions extremely difficult. In addition to the hazards of handling ammunition in the moving ship, the gun houses and working chambers of the forward turrets were filled with steam from seawater boiling off the hot guns, with water flowing down the barrels when the breeches were opened to reload. Heavy spray also hampered the director optics and turret rangefinders, which were all washed out during most of the action. Fire control was hence largely based on observing the splashes of the 15-inch shells from the director control tower – not easy in the poor visibility as the targets were continually covered by sheets of spray from driving into the sea. As the distance between them and their pursuer increased, there was time for the Germans to alter course when the muzzle flashes from *Renown* were seen; to the frustration of the British gunnery officers they slipped out of line of their shells each time. Attempts were made to increase speed a few knots when the German ships were out of sight in the squalls and fire suspended, but, not knowing exactly which course to steer, this was at times counterproductive. *Renown*'s gunnery became increasingly intermittent.

Fire was maintained from the after turrets of the German battleships when *Renown* was visible through the murk, *Scharnhorst* yawing occasionally to fire a broadside. At 04:28 Lütjens wrote in his war diary:

Speed 27kt. Course 30°. It became clear that after the last change of course that the enemy had come in an unfavourable position for the efficient use of his guns. As he followed the turn, he could only apply his two forward turrets and the firing from these became very erratic and inaccurate. The smoke we were making due to the emergency engagement of the idle boilers also hampered his observations. The battle range was increasing rapidly [and] rain showers made it impossible for both parties to maintain covering fire. On the other hand, our own observation improved, although with only one turret bearing [per ship] and a narrow target, the chance of a hit was small.[12]

At 04:40, *Renown* was forced to reduce speed further to twenty knots to keep the forward guns in action at all. Steering an easterly course from 04:59 to 05.15 to try to take more speed while the Germans turned north-north-east in a prolonged sleet shower meant that the distance between the ships was increasing. Sighting the adversaries again at 05:15, Whitworth also turned north-north-east, but by now the distance was over twenty-five kilometres and firing at the diminishing targets from only the forward turrets was largely ineffective – all the more so as one of the guns of the A turret ceased firing for a while because of mechanical failure.

Another photograph of *Renown*, taken in heavy seas. Note how the forward turrets are turned away from the sea. (Author's collection)

At 05:57 the German ships vanished in yet another squall and the chase was for all practical purposes over. In one last effort to keep up, Vice Admiral Whitworth ordered the turrets turned away from the sea and speed increased to twenty-seven knots and later to twenty-nine knots. This strained the old battlecruiser to the maximum, but had little effect. At 06:15, when the snow lifted briefly and the German ships were sighted for the last time, they were out of range and soon vanished for good. Whitworth stood on to the northward until a few minutes after 08:00 when he turned westward, hoping to cut off the enemy, 'should they have broken back to southward', but no further contact occurred.

Renown's main armament had fired 230 shells, mostly from the A and B turrets. In addition, the starboard 4.5-inch guns fired 1,065 rounds. Considerable damage was done to *Renown* by the blast from her own 15-inch turrets, including a hatch abaft the breakwater, which was blown in, allowing large amounts of water to enter the foreship. The forward turrets also took much water through the blast bags, which were burst early in the action. The only casualty onboard the battlecruiser was the navigating officer, Lieutenant Commander Martin Evans, who was wounded in his left leg by a splinter from a near-miss.[13]

After losing contact with the German battleships, Whitworth signalled for *Repulse* and her group to steer for Vestfjorden, where his destroyers were heading, before he turned westward.[14] The Admiralty intervened, and at 09:18 Whitworth received orders to end the chase and turn back, concentrating his forces off Vestfjorden to prevent German landings in Narvik. This he did, signalling for *Repulse* and her consorts as well as the destroyers to join him south-west of the tip of Lofoten. By the time *Renown* met up with *Repulse* at 14:05, however, the Admiralty had been informed that German ships were at Narvik and Captain (D)2 had been ordered to investigate.

Admiral Forbes later commented somewhat arrogantly that the action 'confirmed the experience of that off the River Plate, namely that the enemy has little liking for close action and his morale deteriorates rapidly if the ship is hit'. He may not have been entirely wrong, but it is nevertheless dangerous for any Commander-in-Chief to underestimate his adversary. It also does not appear that Forbes recognised that Whitworth had been compelled to fight alone with an elderly battlecruiser against two modern battleships because of his and the Admiralty's failure to read German strategic intentions correctly.[15]

Having finally lost contact with the British battlecruiser, *Scharnhorst* was back in her usual position, line-abeam to starboard of the flagship, at 06:22. The loss of *Gneisenau's* foretop gunnery control station was serious. It hampered her capability for long-range engagement and could not be repaired at sea. *Scharnhorst* had not taken hits, but both electrical motors of her A turret had short-circuited, partly because water poured in through the shell-case ejection ports when the rear of the turrets faced into the oncoming seas, firing at maximum rearward traverse. An emergency hand-steering was rigged but worked poorly and the turret became inoperable from around 05:25. The B turrets and some of the forward secondary guns also experienced flooding. In addition, a steam valve tripped at 06:18 and the centre turbine stopped for almost an hour, reducing her maximum speed to twenty-five knots.

Lütjens decided to continue away from potential danger and repair as much as possible of the damage to his ships beyond the range of British air reconnaissance. He therefore stood north at twenty-four knots until midday before turning west around latitude 70°N. The weather cleared and the rest of the day remained uneventful. The only casualties were those in the foretop of *Gneisenau*; action stations were stood down at 09:00.

Forty-four high-explosive and ten armour-piercing shells had been fired from *Gneisenau's* main guns. It is difficult to justify the use of high-explosive shells against a well-armoured target such as *Renown* and that may well be why she only sustained light damage in spite of two hits. *Scharnhorst* had fired 182 rounds of 28-cm AP shells and was running so low in the C magazine that shells had to be transported aft from A magazine.

All told, the German battleships did not stand out as reliable gun platforms. A great wetness combined with complicated and sensitive engines was not the best starting point for a naval battle in the Arctic. Both ships had been modified since commissioning and given an 'Atlantic bow', as had the heavy cruisers. The low-stem clipper-bow was intended to minimise plunging of the foreships in heavy seas, but under certain conditions turned out to do the opposite. Recovery was slower than anticipated and, added to the low freeboard, made them very wet. In addition, the high-pressure superheated steam-power plants proved vulnerable, keeping the engine-room personnel on their toes. There is little doubt that had Lütjens not been willing to risk sea damage and had a more modern capital ship been chasing them, *Scharnhorst* and *Gneisenau* would have been in deep trouble.[16]

Once things became less urgent, Lütjens started to have some doubts about his decision to withdraw. Already at 05:07 a signal was sent to *Scharnhorst* questioning the number

Damage inflicted to the port side of *Gneisenau's* foretop by a 15-inch projectile from *Renown*. Parts of the unserviceable radar set are seen to the left of the officer. (J Asmussen collection)

of enemy ships observed. *Scharnhorst* reported back half an hour later that 'so far, only one' had been recognised. Later, an interesting sequence of signals is recorded in Lütjens's war diary:

> 08:05 hrs: USW to *Scharnhorst*: Are you sure there was only one enemy ship? From here two were seen.
> 08:17 hrs: USW from *Scharnhorst*: Have looked into matter, appears there were two enemies at the beginning of the engagement.
> 08:29 hrs: USW from *Scharnhorst*: All shipboard aircraft unserviceable. Judging from shell fragment found on quarterdeck, enemy was firing 38-cm guns.
> 08:34 hrs: USW from *Scharnhorst*: A third enemy was seen aft of *Scharnhorst* at start of the battle.[17]

It was apparently important for Lütjens to have this recorded, and the last signal has an addition in brackets '(. . . not seen from *Gneisenau*)', as if underlining that the other adversaries were not invented on the flag bridge.

Proceed to Sea

Incoming signals from Group II said *Hipper* and her destroyers had entered Trondheim with only light resistance. From Group V in the Oslofjord, however, disturbing signals from *Lützow* reported *Blücher* to be in trouble and the Drøbak Narrows to be closed. Operation Weserübung had commenced, but was not going quite according to plan: '. . . the operations in the south seem to have run into unexpected Norwegian resistance,' a worried Lütjens noted in his war diary.[18] Based on further incoming signals from Group West during the afternoon, Lütjens concluded in his diary at 21:00 that there were two groups of heavy British ships at sea, one off Vestfjorden, consisting of '*Repulse* and apparently another battleship (one *Nelson* or one *Barham*?)', and one north of the

Bergen–Shetland Narrows consisting of 'three heavy ships with three heavy and five light cruisers'. In addition, a French force consisting of three ships, 'one of which is probably a *Dunkerque*', was reported to be in 'Scottish waters'. The general situation in Norway is described as 'unclear' – particularly as regards the ships of Groups I and II and their preparedness for the return home.[19]

During 10 April, reports of the dramatic events in Narvik were received between reports of *Blücher* sunk at Oslo, *Königsberg* capsized in Bergen, *Karlsruhe* sunk off Kristiansand and *Lützow* struggling for her life in the Kattegat. For Lütjens and his staff, Operation Weserübung must have seemed anything but a success. In the absence of an accurate overview and with no knowledge of British intentions, Lütjens described the situation to be 'completely changed', so much so that he felt there was a lack of orders as to what to do next; both on his own account as well as for Bonte in Narvik and Heye in Trondheim. An attack on the British forces reported off Vestfjorden to relieve the pressure on the Zerstörer in Narvik was considered, but abandoned on the grounds that they would be difficult to locate and bring to action under favourable conditions. Taking the battleships into Vestfjorden proper was out of the question. In the end, Lütjens concluded that the destroyers, as well as *Hipper*, should be able to sneak home through the Leads alone. His own fuel situation was favourable and the battleships would remain at sea, repairing damage. The weather forecast predicted a worsening of the weather and Lütjens settled for a breakthrough into the North Sea on the night of 11/12 April.

Group West had limited knowledge of the battleships' position and asked for information in the morning of 10 April. Lütjens did not wish to break radio silence, suspecting (correctly) that several of the brief position signals to Wilhelmshaven were not coming through. Thus, towards midday, one of *Scharnhorst*'s Arado aircraft was patched up sufficiently from the damage obtained during the battle and flown off, south of Jan Mayen Island. The pilots, Oberleutnants Schreck and Schrewe, had orders to set course for Trondheim, some one thousand kilometres away and close to the maximum distance for the little floatplane, sending a detailed report from there, including the position of the battleships and the admiral's intentions.[20]

At 15:00, a signal arrived from Group West: 'All available cruisers, destroyers and torpedo boats are to proceed to sea tonight. Narvik destroyers are to concentrate with the Commander-in-Chief. It is left to your discretion whether *Hipper* with three destroyers join you or break through and proceed direct to home port.'[21] Lütjens assumed the order was based on a lack of information as to the position of the battleships and anticipated the order would be cancelled when the signal from *Scharnhorst*'s Arado had been received.

At 22:38, the cancellation came, adding that the Home Fleet, including *Furious*, was somewhere north of the Bergen–Shetland Narrows. The battleships were ordered to keep on towards the west as planned and the destroyers were ordered to stay inside the Leads.[22] *Hipper* was to decide her own measures, but to leave Trondheim as soon as possible; even without any destroyers. Lütjens was not unhappy with this and steered south-westward for an entry to the North Sea near the Shetlands. The news of the carrier-borne aircraft attacks on Trondheim meant that the Home Fleet was most likely in a position north of Trondheim, favouring his original plan of slipping southwards in the coming night. Lütjens anticipated (correctly) that besides *Warspite* and the French *Dunkerque*, all heavy Allied units were by now north of him. Provided *Hipper* managed to leave the Norwegian coast safely, she should also have a fair chance of getting through. Towards midday on 11 April, when the battleships were some seventy-five miles to the north of the Faeroes, *Scharnhorst* reported being capable of twenty-eight knots, and some hours later 28.5 knots. Course was set for home. Sheltered by rain and fog, the two battleships slipped unseen into the North Sea at maximum speed and were joined by *Hipper* in the morning of 12 April.

The first British aircraft were sighted at 06:45 in the morning of the 12th. The ships were shadowed throughout the morning until an escort arrived in the form of He111s and long-range Bf110 fighters. By late morning, the destroyers *Beitzen* and *Schoemann* fell in and by 20:00 the fleet entered the mouth of the Jade. By 22:30, the two battleships had anchored in Wilhelmshaven Roads. Lütjens left *Gneisenau* for his command vessel, the *Gazelle*, at 09:00 on 13 April. As far as the Kriegsmarine was concerned, Operation Weserübung had come to an end.

Hipper was in dire need of repairs and taken straight into the dock where she remained for three weeks. Of the battleships, *Scharnhorst* in particular needed an extended overhaul of her machinery, at least ten to twelve days in dock in Hoffmann's estimates. The OKM ordered that all repairs should be accelerated as much as possible and work should not be initiated that might prevent the ships from taking to sea. Daily reports on their status were requested. Eventually, the OKM had to accept that both ships would, for all practical purposes, be out of service for at least the remainder of the month.[23]

Vizeadmiral Lütjens was awarded the Knight's Cross) on 14 June. His reputation stood very high in the Kriegsmarine and in July 1940 he was appointed C-in-C of the fleet. In early 1941, Lütjens, by now a full admiral, went to sea with *Gneisenau* and *Scharnhorst*, sinking or capturing twenty-two merchant ships during Operation Berlin. In May 1941, Lütjens took to sea again, onboard the brand new *Bismarck*, on a mission from which he would not return.

Vice Admiral Whitworth returned his flag to *Hood* when she was recommissioned later in 1940. His recall to the Admiralty in early May of 1941 came just weeks before *Hood* was to sail for the last time in pursuit of *Bismarck*, and the two admirals never crossed swords again. Whitworth was assigned the position of Lord Commissioner of the Admiralty and Second Sea Lord, which he would hold until 1944 when appointed Commander-in-Chief, Rosyth. William 'Jock' Whitworth was promoted to a full Admiral in December 1943. He retired in 1946 and died on 25 October 1973 at the age of 89.[24]

— 13 —

Narvik

The Ore Town

'WE HAD NEVER EXPECTED the war should come this close. The smoke from our neighbour's burning houses and the smell of dead soldiers drift into our country and we know little of our own future,' wrote Theodor Brock, the mayor of Narvik, in January 1940 in the newspaper *Fremover*. Within four months, the war would come to his own town and many would die, both soldiers and civilians.

Wedged between the deep fjord and the steep mountains some two hundred kilometres north of the Arctic Circle, Narvik has always been a special place. In 1940 it had a population of close to ten thousand, grown from some three hundred in 1898 when the first plans for building a railway from the Kiruna–Gällivare iron-ore district to the ice-free Norwegian port were discussed. By the time the railway and ore-loading pier were completed in 1906, the strategic significance of Narvik had grown out of all proportion.

The seaward entry to Narvik is through the funnel-shaped Vestfjorden where the Lofoten Islands create a protective barrier against the rages of the Norwegian Sea. Off the head of Vestfjorden, Tjelsundet makes a safe passage north to Harstad and Tromsø. Eastwards, Ofotfjorden opens up after the Barøy Narrows towards Narvik town. The tidal difference in the fjord exceeds three metres, creating swift currents in the

Narvik harbour in the late 1930s. (Author's collection)

Narrows. Vestfjorden is one hundred and twenty kilometres long and there is another sixty kilometres through Ofotfjorden before reaching Narvik. Ofotfjorden is three to four kilometres wide at its narrowest, west of Narvik, widening to fifteen to eighteen kilometres between Ballangen and Evenes. Beyond Narvik, Rombaksfjorden – from the head of which there is no more than ten kilometres to the Swedish border, continues east while Herjangsfjorden opens to the north.

There had long been plans for the building of a fortress at the entrance to Ofotfjorden, protecting Narvik and the naval depot at Ramsund. Parliament had approved the plans for the Ofoten Fortress and work had started just before WWI. Two batteries were intended: three 15-cm guns on Ramneset south of the fjord and two 10.5-cm guns north of the fjord.[1] After the end of WWI, construction was halted and the guns stored. Plans had been revived in 1927, but the cost was too high and the plans were shelved again.[2]

Unlike most other large ports in Norway, Narvik had not been declared a krigshavn, in order to avoid complications with the international traffic. This meant there were no restrictions for ships in and out of the harbour as long as the neutrality regulations in general were respected. On 29 March 1940, the commanding admiral drafted a memorandum to Foreign Minister Koht, at his request, regarding the issue of establishing a krigshavn in Narvik. The handwritten draft is strongly in favour of establishing such a zone, as it would significantly improve the navy's capacity to control the traffic in the area.[3] The official memorandum was never submitted.

The winter of 1939/40 was the hardest for many years. The cold was crippling and there was so much snow around Narvik that the roads could not be kept open. Snowdrifts packed solid by the howling winds closed even the railway at times. The fjord remained ice free, though, and in the evening of 8 April, no fewer than twenty-six civilian ships, ten of which were German, were moored in or around Narvik harbour. The vice-consuls in Narvik – Mr Gibbs of Great Britain and Herr Wussow of Germany – were well-known men in town and everybody knew they both reported diligently back to their respective Foreign Offices any ship movements in and out of the harbour. Fritz Wussow was particularly known for his frequent evening strolls into the hillsides, carrying a nice pair of binoculars. In the last few days, in addition to the ore ships, they had also been able to report the presence of Norwegian warships in Narvik.[4]

After Finland had capitulated, and it seemed certain the Russians would stop short of Norwegian territory, most navy ships sent north during the winter were redeployed to the south. The panserships *Norge* and *Eidsvold* were ordered to take station in Narvik, however, where they arrived on 1 April. Together with the submarines *B1* and *B3*, their tender *Lyngen* and the auxiliaries *Michael Sars* and *Kelt*, they constituted the Ofoten Division under the command of the 59-year-old Kommandørkaptein Per Askim, who reported to SDD3 in Tromsø. When German Naval Attaché Schreiber asked the Admiral Staff the purpose of the increased force at Narvik, he received the answer 'exercises'. The real reason was Foreign Minister Koht's concern that the Allies might use the German ore traffic as an excuse for intervention, now that the pretext of Finland was gone. On 5 April the C-in-C of SDD3, Kontreadmiral Hagerup, went on leave, approved by the commanding admiral, and Askim took over as acting commander of the district. He remained onboard *Norge*, except for a brief visit to Tromsø, but the additional responsibility meant that Askim could not fully concentrate on the defence of Narvik and the two panserships had only one reconnaissance tour into Ofotfjorden to assess suitable positions during the first week of April.[5]

The army forces in northern Norway were under the command of the C-in-C of 6th Division, Generalmajor Carl Gustav Fleischer. Following a request from Finland, the army's increased neutrality forces in the north had not been demobilised at the end of the Winter War and on 8 April Fleischer and his Chief of Staff were on an inspection tour, reviewing the situation.[6]

Shall Be Met with Force

In the morning of 8 April, *Eidsvold* and *Norge* were at anchor in Narvik, stern to shore, with telephone lines onboard. The depot ship *Lyngen* with *B1* and *B3* was also in the harbour, as well as the harbour patrol vessel *Senja*. *Kelt* and *Michael Sars* were patrolling the narrows.

Receiving the news of British destroyers laying mines in Vestfjorden around 06:00, Kommandørkaptein Askim ordered steam to be raised on the panserships and preparations to be made for battle. Everyone onboard realised something serious was going on when each quarter was ordered to put on clean underwear before coming on duty.[7] Askim was well aware of the strategic importance assigned to the ore traffic by the Admiralty and feared the German ships in the harbour might be tempting enough to risk a raid into the fjord. *Syrian* reported the departure of the British destroyers from the minefield at 10:45 but Askim took it for granted they were not far away. To augment the defences, Askim ordered the two submarines to move to Liland, some twenty kilometres down the fjord on the northern side, followed by *Lyngen*. Things remained quiet, though, and at midday reduced steam was ordered, but both ships were to remain ready at short

The panserships *Norge* and *Eidsvold* in Narvik harbour in the afternoon of 8 April 1940. (Forsvarsmuseet)

notice. 'I and the rest of the officers of the division realised that important events were imminent on the Norwegian coast,' Askim wrote in London in June 1940.[8] The statement was probably not meant as a criticism at the time, but it casts doubt on the higher military and civilian command, who from their position in Oslo did not manage to see the same threat.

Around 17:30, the 12,000-ton German tanker *Jan Wellem* made its way into the harbour. Løytnant Lundquist of *Senja* went onboard, together with a customs officer to inspect the papers and cargo, according to routine. The captain of the tanker informed them that he carried 8,500 tons of fuel oil and 8,089 crates of various provisions. His ship had been to Arctic Russia, he said, and was now heading back to Germany. Lundquist found everything in order and left after a short inspection, though he did wonder why the ship had come up the fjord to Narvik, which was a dead end. What he had been told was true enough. What he had not been told was that *Jan Wellem* intended to stay at Narvik for a while and that the fuel was meant for the Zerstörers of Group I, at that very moment closing the mouth of Vestfjorden.[9]

Receiving information at 19:30 of the telegram from the embassy in London that the Admiralty considered a German attack on Narvik to be under development, Askim invited Kommandørkaptein Odd Willoch of *Eidsvold* to *Norge* for a conference. Meanwhile, steam was raised on both ships again and all men ashore were called back.[10] The two captains agreed that the line of defence should be outside the crowded harbour and *Eidsvold* should move out as soon as she was ready. *Norge* would remain for the time being and maintain telephone contact with Naval Command, SDD3 and the rest of the Ofoten Division. Calling the Admiral Staff and asking for comments regarding the signal, Askim learned from the officer on duty that 'Nobody here believes this is true.' At 22:00, *Eidsvold* left Narvik harbour, anchoring six or seven hundred metres off the lighthouse at Framnesodden. Both panserships were at war stations (half the crew at stations, half at rest). The weather was very poor with a howling wind and dense snow showers.

At 23:45 Askim, who still feared the German ships in the harbour might be tempting for the British destroyers, sent the following signal to Commanding Admiral Diesen: 'Fourteen German freighters in Narvik, partly loaded, and a large tanker with fuel oil and provisions. In case British warships enter Narvik, please advise if force (gunfire) shall be applied to prevent attack on German ships.'[11] Just before midnight a clear answer came back from the commanding admiral: 'Attack on Narvik shall be met with force (gunfire).'[12] This signal was forwarded to all ships of the Ofoten Division. Kaptein Brekke, the commander of the submarines at Liland, suggested that the boats moved into the fjord but was ordered to remain where he was for the time being.

Later, in the early hours of 9 April, three signals arrived from Trondheim.[13] The first, at 01:25, said: 'Rauøy and Bolærne have opened fire. Oslo out of communication due to air-raid warning.' The second, at 02:35, said: 'Air-raid warning called off in Oslo. Combat at Færder. Unknown vessels penetrating Korsfjorden at southern entry to Bergen.' The third, at 03:00, said: 'German warships forcing entry to Bergen, five large, three small, three transports. Fortress in combat. Unknown vessels penetrating Trondheimsfjorden. Agdenes prepared for combat.' Askim requested updated instructions from the commanding admiral. Diesen, who at this stage had confirmation that the intruders were German, responded at 04:20, after conferring with the foreign minister: 'Do not fire on

British vessels, fire on German.' This signal arrived via SDD3 just before the hostilities commenced and was not forwarded to *Eidsvold*.[14]

At 20:00, Generalmajor Fleischer received a copy of the warning that German naval forces might be heading for Narvik. The information was forwarded to Oberst Konrad Sundlo, the army commander at Narvik, with orders to deploy the rifle company and machine-gun units at his disposal.[15] In addition, Major Spjeldnes at the Elvegårdsmoen barracks was ordered to move towards Narvik at once with the rest of I/IR 13. II/IR 15 was ordered from Bardufoss to Elvegårdsmoen, as a replacement, together with a mountain artillery battalion that was to continue towards Narvik as soon as possible. A few hours later there was a signal from Oslo that further mobilisation would not be considered until the next morning. Fleischer ignored this and at 04:45, after receiving signals of intruders at Oslo and Bergen, ordered IR 16 to start mobilising. Major Spjeldnes arrived in Narvik around 01:00 with his battalion. The men were tired and cold after a long march and ferry transport across Rombaksfjorden. Sundlo ordered one company and some further machine guns posted at strategic positions and the rest of the men billeted.[16] Oberst Sundlo was a well-known member of Quisling's NS Party from long before the war and made no secret of this, or the fact that he was a keen admirer of Hitler.

The auxiliaries *Michael Sars* and *Kelt* were stationed at the mouth of the Ofotfjord some fifty kilometres west of Narvik. Normally, one vessel would patrol the narrows between Barøy and Tjeldodden while the other was moored, resting the crew and maintaining telephone contact with Narvik. Both vessels had radio, but it was not as reliable as a landline. Kaptein Jackwitz of *Michael Sars* talked to Askim in the evening of 8 April and was ordered to patrol the narrows with *Kelt*, lest anything should slip past them in the snow. By 23:00 both vessels were in the narrows, *Kelt* in the southern part, *Michael Sars* in the north. The radio connection from both ships to *Norge* worked satisfactorily; there were frequent snow squalls limiting visibility, but the fjord is only about three kilometres wide here and they could see each other and the shoreline most of the time. If any foreign warships were observed, German or British, the instruction was to report to Narvik and stay out of trouble. *Michael Sars* was armed with two 47-mm guns and *Kelt* with one 76-mm, but orders were that fire should only be opened in self-defence.[17]

At 03:10, the Zerstörers of Group I steamed past Barøy into Ofotfjorden at twenty-seven knots. It was still dark but dawn was approaching.[18] All ships were closed up at action stations. The crews were exhausted after two nights and a day without sleep, but at least the seas had calmed and the decks became stable again. The Jägers, still shaken and miserable from seasickness, slowly started to clean up and prepare for landing.

Heidkamp was in the lead. Kommodore Bonte was on the bridge, as was Generalmajor Dietl, commander of the landing troops, and Korvettenkapitän Erdmenger, captain of the flagship. The atmosphere was tense. What would meet them in Narvik? Would the Norwegians oppose them? The fuel tanks of the destroyers were almost empty and until they refuelled their tactical manoeuvrability was limited. According to plan, one tanker should be in Narvik waiting for them and a second would arrive during the day. *Giese* had not been able to catch up, and USW reports indicated she was about three hours behind. The destroyers were observed from both *Michael Sars* and *Kelt* as they passed and several signals were received in *Norge*'s radio room. The last, at 03:20, summed up: 'Nine German

(Left) The 44-year-old Kommodore Friedrich Bonte. (Author's collection)

(Right) Korvettenkapitän Hans Erdmenger, captain of the flagship *Wilhelm Heidkamp* had, before he joined the Navy in 1925, a short spell at the officer school in Ohrdruf where Hauptman Dietl taught tactics. They had, as the story goes, not had a smooth relationship. (Author's collection)

'You must gain the hearts of your soldiers,' Generalmajor Eduard Wolrath Christian Dietl used to say, 'then, and only then, can you take them to Hell and back, asking them to bring the Devil out.' In this photo from June 1940, he is seen with the senior officers of 139th Mountain Regiment. From left, Oberst Alois Windisch, C-in-C of 139th; Dietl; Major Wolf Hagemann, C-in-C III/139; Major Ludwig Statutner, C-in-C I/139; and Major Arthur Haussels, C-in-C II/139. (Author's collection)

destroyers have entered Ofotfjorden.' It was immediately copied to SDD3, from where it was forwarded to the commanding admiral at 03:37 and thereafter to the army units in the area. The signal was sent in clear text and intercepted onboard *Heidkamp*, so Bonte knew they were expected. After the destroyers had passed, the two auxiliaries continued to patrol the fjord as instructed.

At 03:40, the destroyers passed the Ramnes–Hamnes line and Fregattenkapitän Hans-Joachim Gadow, commander of the 3rd Flotilla, was detached with *Lüdemann*, *Schmitt* and *Roeder* to capture the forts, which they wrongly believed guarded the fjord. Not long after, Fregattenkapitän Erich Bey, commander of the 4th Flotilla, was detached with *Zenker*, *Koellner* and *Künne*, whose troops would secure the army camp and depots at Elvegårdsmoen at the head of Herjangsfjorden, north of Narvik. Kommodore Bonte continued towards Narvik with *Heidkamp*, *Thiele* and *Arnim*. Operation Weserübung was about to reach Narvik.[19]

Senja had left Narvik at 01:35 with orders to proceed to the minefield in Vestfjorden and escort merchant ships past, waiting for it to be swept. Løytnant Lundquist had been informed that German warships were heading for Norway, but if he ran into any of these he had strict orders not to engage, only to observe and report. *Senja* headed down Ofotfjorden in dense snowfall and did not see the inbound German destroyers. As she passed Ramnes, however, the snow lifted and a destroyer was sighted near land. Believing this to be British, Lundquist sent the signal, 'British destroyer at Ramnes', to Narvik. It was coded and reception was poor onboard *Norge*, where it was read as 'British cruiser at Ramnes'. 'Thank God there are British ships in the fjord,' was Askim's comment when he was handed the signal. In fact, no British warships would be in Ofotfjorden for twenty-two hours. Lundquist headed for the destroyer to find out what it was doing in the fjord and quickly realised his mistake. The destroyer was *Schmitt* and *Roeder* was also sighted shortly after. A revised signal was sent immediately: 'Two German destroyers approaching'. This was never received onboard *Norge*, and it is quite possible that the first flawed signal caused Askim to become careful, so as not to make any mistakes.[20]

In Narvik harbour, Captain Nicholas of the British ore ship *Blythmoor* awoke around 02:00 and saw the wind rising with heavy snow falling. Just to be safe, he called his first officer and told him to let go the second anchor. While turning in again, he heard two or three of the other vessels doing the same.[21]

We Shall Fight

Contact between *Eidsvold* and *Norge* was maintained by USW radio, which usually worked well over short distances inside the fjords. Both ships were still at war stations and live ammunition had been brought to the ready-use lockers. Due to the limited visibility, at times down to a few hundred metres, the gunsights had been preset to 1,400 metres.[22]

Receiving the signals from *Kelt* and *Michael Sars* of the intruding German destroyers at 03:20, Kommandørkaptein Askim immediately ordered the aft mooring of *Norge* with the telephone line to be cast off and the anchor hoisted. Action stations were sounded and the guns loaded.[23] Askim informed Willoch by USW what he was doing and ordered

Kommodørkaptein Odd Willoch of
Eidsvold.
(Ingrid Willoch)

him to prepare his ship for war too. A radio signal was sent to SDD3 summarising the situation and concluding that from now on, all communication would have to be by radio. While the anchor lifted, *Norge* steered towards the harbour entrance. At 04:30 she was in position, about three hundred metres off Malmkaia with port broadside towards the entrance and starboard lifeboats lowered to the waterline. 'It was the strangest weather I have seen,' wrote First Officer Langeland of the Norwegian freighter *Cate B* in the harbour. 'Gale force winds with snow and sleet. The air was thick and almost yellow. Perfect for the Germans!'[24]

Onboard *Eidsvold*, steam was raised, guns were loaded, watertight doors closed and all crew on deck ordered to put on lifebelts. The lifeboats were swung out and those on the starboard side lowered to the waterline. A whaler manned with two sailors was made fast aft as an extra precaution. Daylight was approaching but the snowfall was as heavy as ever and visibility remained poor. At 04:15 everything was reported ready and Willoch ordered the anchor to be weighed. Almost immediately, while the anchor was still lifting, two warships emerged from the snow three or four hundred metres away. Willoch ordered the leader to be challenged with an Aldis lamp while both the 21-cm guns and those of the 15-cms that could bear were trained on the ship.[25] When no answer came back, he ordered a 76-mm warning shot to be fired and hoisted the signal 'Bring your vessel to a halt.' The shell landed in *Heidkamp*'s wake and had the desired effect. She started to slow down and signalled back: 'Sending boat with officer.' *Arnim* and *Thiele* continued into the harbour. It speaks highly of Bonte's capacity as a destroyer commander that his ships were almost dead on time after more than a thousand nautical miles through vicious seas.

Lowering the whaler took some time, as the heavy seas of the day before had damaged the boat, but eventually it got underway. In the boat was Korvettenkapitän Gerlach, one of Bonte's staff officers and a signalman. The guns of *Heidkamp* remained pointing fore and aft, but the torpedo batteries were quietly swung towards the pansership. Gerlach and the signalman entered the starboard quarterdeck of *Eidsvold*. They were received by the pansership's first officer, Kaptein Jansen and taken to the bridge. There, Gerlach saluted Kaptein Willoch and stated the standard phrases of the Germans coming as friends to help Norway defend its neutrality against British aggression. He advised Willoch to submit to the new situation and surrender his ship by removing breeches and shutting down engines. Opposition was pointless as most Norwegian cities were already under German control.[26] Willoch answered that he was under orders from his C-in-C to oppose the German intruders and could not comply with such instructions without conferring with the flagship. Gerlach refused to wait and headed back for the whaler. Willoch called Askim on the USW from the radio room underneath the aft bridge, recounting the conversation with Gerlach and asking for orders. The answer was not to be misunderstood: 'Open fire.' Willoch replied: 'I will attack!'[27]

Korvettenkapitän Gerlach had just cast off when he was hailed back and met by Willoch on the quarterdeck. He informed the German officer that *Eidsvold*'s order to resist had just been confirmed and the German request for surrender rejected. Gerlach saluted and returned to the whaler, which cast off once more. Shortly after, a red signal rocket was sent up, arching towards *Heidkamp*, signifying that the Norwegians would not surrender. Whether Willoch saw the rocket is uncertain, as he ran towards the bridge across the gun deck on the opposite side from where Gerlach's boat was. On his way, passing one of the guns, Willoch shouted to the crew: 'Man the gun, boys, now we shall fight.'[28] Once Willoch reached the bridge, the engine telegraph rang out and *Eidsvold* started to move forward.

During the parleying onboard *Eidsvold*, *Heidkamp* had circled the pansership and was now some thirty degrees on her port bow, about seven hundred metres away. Kommodore Bonte was in an awkward situation. His orders were clear, only to open fire if the Norwegians fired first, as a gunfight would jeopardise any hope of a tacit occupation. Now the guns of the pansership were trained on his flagship and the red signal rocket indicated fire might be opened at any time. Still, firing the first shot as an aggressor was not Bonte's preferred manner. Generalmajor Dietl, on the other hand, had the safety of his troops foremost in his mind. He was a passenger onboard the destroyer and in principle had no say in what was happening while at sea. One did not become the commander of a mountain division of the Third Reich without a large portion of tenacity, though, and Dietl insisted the torpedoes should be fired to eliminate the threat of the pansership. Bonte was undecided, but Korvettenkapitän Erdmenger was also becoming uncomfortable. Not only were two 21-cm and three 15-cm guns pointing at his destroyer from point-blank range, but the range was rapidly being reduced! *Eidsvold* had picked up speed and was nearing fast. It looked as if the pansership might ram the destroyer. Erdmenger ordered full ahead and turned to increase the distance. With some urgency he requested repeatedly for permission to fire the torpedoes. Waiting for the first shot from *Eidsvold* could become a very costly gesture of honour, he argued. All hopes for a peaceful solution vanishing, Bonte finally conceded and nodded his approval. Erdmenger gave the order and four torpedoes left the tubes of the aft torpedo battery of *Heidkamp*.[29]

No shots were fired from any of *Eidsvold*'s guns after the initial warning shot. There are few accounts of what happened onboard the pansership in the last minutes of its history, and, as there were no survivors from the bridge, we shall never know what orders Willoch gave. Around two minutes passed between Gerlach firing his rocket and the first torpedo hit.[30] There was no need to close the distance before commencing fire. All guns had confirmed target and, if anything, getting too close would be a disadvantage, as the 21-cm guns would have to fire downwards to hit the low hull of the destroyer. Did Willoch hesitate to draw first blood? Did he wish to test how serious the Germans were before he fired? Neither is very likely. His orders were clear and he had discussed this with Askim on several occasions. Willoch knew very well the limitations and vulnerability of his ship and must have been acutely aware of the dangers of a torpedo attack on the old, thinly armoured hull. If Willoch did not see Gerlach's red signal rocket it is possible that he may have given the negotiator grace to get out of the way, expecting similar German chivalry. That he considered ramming, as Erdmenger feared, and many of the German reports later held, is highly unlikely considering his ancient ship.[31]

Kvartermester Henry Backe, one of the eight survivors, later said he heard the order 'Port battery. Shoot!' being given by the gunnery officer, Kaptein Thorkelsen, in the fighting top and repeated by the portside gun commander. Two other survivors, Nielsen and Opstad, confirmed this. Before the order was executed, however, the first torpedo hit. Underoffiser Ludolf Holstad, the commander of the aft 21-cm gun, also received the order to fire but held that at that very moment *Heidkamp* moved from starboard to port across the bow of *Eidsvold* and his gun did not carry. Before he could turn the turret on the new bearing and reconfirm target, the torpedoes struck. Why the other guns did not fire, he could not say. The sea was rough and guns and sights corkscrewed. Perhaps the gunners had problems keeping the target in their sights even if the gun commanders confirmed target. Perhaps there was a missing order to load the guns in advance, or the crew hesitated. There are several examples of Norwegian sailors and soldiers hesitating to fire the first shots in the early hours of 9 April. Their mindset was for neutrality, not war. Carl Carlson, a gunner onboard *Norge*, recounted that his first reaction when ordered to fire in earnest on *Arnim* was: 'Are you mad, we might hit them!'[32] What really happened onboard *Eidsvold* we shall never know. It seems clear that Kaptein Willoch did give the order to open fire – while for some reason the guns remained silent.

Four torpedoes were fired from *Heidkamp*. Norwegian sources mostly agree on three hits, but German sources claim only two. The first impacted on the port side, just below the aft turret and very likely ignited the 21-cm magazine. One or two torpedoes hit forward of amidships seconds later. A mountainous explosion followed, probably from another magazine or boiler exploding, and within seconds the ship was gone in a nightmare of flames, smoke and steam.[33] The last that was seen of the pansership was the stern going vertically into the deep at 04:37, some twenty minutes after *Heidkamp* had been sighted for the first time.

One hundred and seventy-seven men from *Eidsvold* perished, including Kaptein Willoch and all but one of his officers. Only eight men survived. Four were pulled out of the water by a whaler from *Martha Heinrich Fisser* and two men drifted ashore on a float.

The two men in the rescue boat aft managed to cast off, fearing being dragged under, but, shocked beyond belief, they did not find anybody to rescue.[34]

Norge's position at the mouth of the harbour was ideal in theory, but the extremely poor visibility because of the heavy snow and the large number of ships at anchor reduced the advantage. Based on Senja's misleading signal an hour earlier, Kommandørkaptein Askim believed that there were both British and German warships in Ofotfjorden and when Arnim and Thiele were observed coming into the harbour, he ordered them to be challenged, signalling 'Stop. What ship?' No answer was given and neither of the ships appeared to reduce speed. Askim ordered a warning shot to be fired, but before this could be done, the snow closed in again and the destroyers vanished. Meanwhile, Willoch called on the USW, recounting the discussions with Gerlach. It was now clear the intruders were German and according to orders from the commanding officer should be actively opposed. Shortly after, a muffled explosion was heard from outside the harbour, but nothing was seen, even though the distance between the two panserships was no more than a nautical mile.

Korvettenkapitän Curt Rechel of Arnim could see little as he entered Narvik harbour. Keeping his nerve, he at first steered towards the northern part of the bay, where he eventually got a glimpse of the tall ore quay through the snow and then turned east, where he knew Dampskipskaia would be. Eventually seeing this in the murk, he stopped the engines and let his destroyer drift onto the wooden pier where he made fast, starboard side-to. Shortly after, Thiele moored on the other side. The Jägers started to disembark at once.

At 04:45, just minutes after Eidsvold had sunk, Arnim and Thiele were again observed from Norge, apparently berthing at Dampskipskaia. Askim ordered 'Fire for effect!' No warning shots this time. The snow had lifted somewhat but it was virtually impossible to see the destroyers or anything else through the rangefinders; the first salvo was short, most of the shells went over and exploded on land. Five 21-cm shells and seven or eight 15-cm shells from the port secondary guns were fired at a distance of six to eight hundred metres.

Once fired at by Norge, Korvettenkapitän Rechel fired back with the 12.7-cm and secondary guns that could bear. None of the shells hit but a couple of the machine-gun salvoes struck the bridge and superstructure of the pansership, causing minor damage.[35] Seven torpedoes were fired from Arnim, individually aimed due to the limited space between the freighters. The first five missed in spite of Norge being virtually stationary in the water.[36] The sixth and seventh torpedoes impacted simultaneously on the pansership, one amidships and one aft. As on Eidsvold, the explosions were devastating, probably as one or more of the magazines exploded. With propellers still turning, the once-mighty ship rolled starboard over. As the lights went out, shouts were heard in all compartments: 'Abandon ship! Save yourself!' Men on the port side climbed the gunwale, edging across the hull towards the keel as she rolled, smokestacks crashing into the water – an unforgettable sight. Once upside down Norge hesitated for a while, but within a minute she had vanished from the surface.[37] When the sea calmed, many men were alive among the flotsam in the icy water. Boats sent from Arnim and several of the merchant ships picked up ninety-six men, among them the unconscious Askim; 105 men perished.

Meanwhile, Erdmenger had taken *Heidkamp* into Narvik harbour, mooring at Fagerneskaia and commencing the disembarkation. It was 05:00 and the snow was still heavy, obscuring the tragedy from all but those very close.

The captains of the British freighters in the harbour were in a difficult situation. They could not escape and their ships would undoubtedly be captured. Anxiously they started burning secret papers, maps and codes. The crews of the German ships, on the other hand, were very excited and started singing 'Deutschland, Deutschland über alles.' Apart from Kapitän Esser of *Bockenheim*, that is. He had heard rumours of a possible British attack from Consul Wussow the night before and when the shooting started did not recognise his own navy. To avoid capture, he deliberately ran his ship aground at Ankenes and, ordering the men off, ignited the demolition charges.

Kommandørkaptein Askim remained in hospital until 15 April, and acting first officer Kaptein Sandved took charge of registering and caring for the survivors of both ships and burying the dead that could be recovered.[38] The sinking of *Eidsvold* and *Norge* horrified the Norwegians more than anything else that happened that day. Losing 282 sailors in what was seen as a needless act of violence added greatly to the determination of the Norwegian population to oppose the invasion. Amongst the armed forces especially, the memory of *Eidsvold* and *Norge* created a grim determination to join the Allies in the struggle against Nazism. Kommodore Bonte was proved right: the sinking of the two panserships jeopardised all hopes of a peaceful occupation.

The disposition of the panserships in the morning of 9 April has been questioned. The short range of the guns, poor fire-control systems and limited armour made the ships vulnerable, restricting tactical options. Their advantage was the power of their guns. A broadside from either ship could wreak havoc with any destroyer or light cruiser and as floating batteries the panserships in theory went a long way towards compensating for the lack of coastal defences in Ofotfjorden. The audacity of the German attack, however – greatly assisted by the atrocious weather – neutralised this to a large extent as the sights and rangefinders were almost useless in the driving snow.

During the court martial of Oberst Sundlo after the war, Kommandørkaptein Askim said: 'Had I known how matters would develop, I would have run one ship aground on each side of the harbour entrance. Willoch and I had discussed this option but it could not be done without consent from the commanding admiral.' Questioned whether he should have sought to meet the German invaders further out in the fjord he answered: 'Under the prevailing weather conditions with extremely poor visibility, this would have been pointless. We were blind in the heavy snow. The only place to meet the intruders was at the entrance to the harbour. I realised, however, that this meant any encounter would quickly become conclusive – one way or another.'[39]

No Guns

The troops disembarking from *Arnim*, *Thiele* and *Heidkamp* spread into Narvik, setting up machine-gun positions at strategic places. The Norwegian soldiers had no clear orders and were confused. The Austrian Jägers had been told they came as friends and hoped for a non-violent outcome. Most of them, some five hundred men from II/IR 139 under

Around 07:30 in Narvik. Soldiers coming ashore from *Wilhelm Heidkamp* at Postkaia. (Author's collection)

Major Haussels, were still miserable from seasickness and saw no reason for assertive aggressiveness. No shots were fired.

From his headquarters, Oberst Sundlo heard explosions from the harbour and was shortly after informed of Germans soldiers 'swarming into the city'. He sent Kaptein Gundersen to find out what was going on and he himself walked to the school where Major Spjeldnes was mustering his troops in spite of only a few hours' sleep. Before they could move out, however, they were surrounded by a force of Gebirgjägers. A German officer approached, handing Sundlo a note in Norwegian, where it said that Denmark and several Norwegian cities had been taken over and that the Norwegian government had decided no resistance should be offered. 'We will not open fire unless you do,' he added. Sundlo asked for a half-hour 'ceasefire' to consider. This was agreed, but the Germans continued into town, and soon hoisted the Nazi flag from the town hall. Sundlo found a telephone and called the district in Harstad, who in the general's absence had no answer other than that Sundlo had to decide for himself what to do, based on the orders he had received.

When Generalmajor Dietl came ashore, Fritz Wussow, the German vice-consul, waited for him at the pier. Kaptein Gundersen came across Wussow and Dietl and was promptly detained. Dietl confiscated the consul's car and set off with Korvettenkapitän Fritz-Otto Busch and Kaptein Gundersen to find the Norwegian C-in-C. They found him at the school, surrounded by the Jägers. Dietl greeted Sundlo amenably, obviously anticipating a similar reaction back. Sundlo was not as friendly as expected, though, and with no time to lose, Dietl switched to threats. Unless the Norwegians surrendered immediately, he said, the destroyers would reduce Narvik to ruins. Sundlo gave in and said he would issue orders to surrender the town. It was 06:15.[40]

Major Spjeldnes in the meantime managed to get in touch with Generalmajor Fleischer, who gave clear orders to resist and 'throw the enemy back into the sea'.[41] When Sundlo came on the telephone, telling him what had just happened, Fleischer became enraged. He considered that Sundlo had failed his duty and relieved him of his command on the spot, appointing his second-in-command Major Omdal in his place.

Major Haussels's men had continued to establish a foothold in the city during the parleying; resistance inside the town would now result in severe damage and loss of civilian life. The best plan would be to pull the troops out and regroup to the east, preparing for a counter-attack. Brazenly, Major Omdal ignored the agreed surrender and, with Spjeldnes in the lead, marched more than two hundred soldiers in single file straight through the German lines, saluting the German officer in charge of the guard. Before he or anybody else realised what was happening, the Norwegians had vanished in the snow. Those who did not escape were rounded up during the morning and disarmed. Omdal continued east along the railway line and after a minor skirmish near Djupvik, eventually established a defence at the bridge crossing the Nordal valley on 10 April. The many refugees along the railway and at every station prevented Omdal's men from destroying the line, but the bridge was prepared for demolition should the Germans advance.[42]

The British MIR officer Captain Torrance, who had reached Narvik on 4 April via Stockholm, was awakened by the sound of gunfire in the morning of the 9th. He at first assumed it was the British arriving ahead of the time he had been told, but when he saw the streets full of German soldiers he realised that this was not the case. Torrance made his way into the mountains and settled out of harm's way in a small hut, effectively isolating himself from forthcoming events.[43]

Once Fregattenkapitän Gadow had been detached with *Lüdemann*, *Schmitt* and *Roeder* at the Ramnes narrows, he proceeded to land soldiers on either side of the narrows to capture the forts supposedly there. *Schmitt* steered for Ramnes on the southern side of the fjord, where 1st Company of I/IR 139 under Major Hans von Schlebrügge was landed, while *Lüdemann* approached Hamnes on the northern side, landing 6th Company under Leutnant Obersteiner. *Roeder* was positioned in the narrows as picket and could be called upon to give support if needed. The naval gunners were held back for the moment but would be landed as soon as the Jägers had secured the forts.

The soldiers immediately started inland, searching for the forts. The snow was deep, the men were heavily loaded and there were no roads. In fact, there was nothing at all on either side. After slogging through the snow for hours it dawned on the officers that perhaps they were chasing ghosts. At Ramnes the shape of some foundations could be outlined in the snow, but that was all. The only garrison found was the twenty men at the Ramsund naval depot, who were taken completely by surprise and surrendered their stock of mines without a fight. Around 07:00, Gadow radioed Bonte: 'Search for batteries so far without luck.' The troops were ordered back to the boats and only a small unit left on either side. Around 11:00 all Jägers were back onboard and Gadow set course for Narvik.[44]

S/S *Riverton*, one of the British freighters in Narvik harbour. Unlike the German ore ships, many of the British were openly armed even if this was against Norwegian neutrality regulation. German protests were ignored and the Norwegians largely looked the other way. (E Skjold Collection)

It is worth noting that Kapitän Lindemann of the merchant navy, who had sailed for years in the Narvik ore trade and was recruited to assist Bonte onboard the flagship as a pilot, held firmly from the day he arrived onboard *Heidkamp* that there were no guns at Ramnes. He had never seen or heard any evidence of this and was certain the information was faulty in spite of what the German Admiral Staff handbook said.[45] Quisling had been asked by Oberst Piekenbrock in Copenhagen to confirm that there were guns at Narvik and had done so, but there is no evidence that Consul Wussow had been asked what he knew. Even if he could not go there and see for himself, it should have been easy for him to verify whether the guns were actually there.[46]

Michael Sars and *Kelt* continued to patrol the narrows during the morning. At 04:15 a report was sent to *Norge* that a destroyer (*Roeder*) could be seen from time to time. An hour or so later two destroyers were sighted (*Giese* had arrived). This time, no contact could be made with *Norge* and the signal was sent to SDD3 in Tromsø. *Giese* continued for Narvik at slow speed on nearly empty bunker tanks, while *Roeder* approached the two auxiliaries, ordering them to proceed to Narvik. Both captains protested but after a series of warning shots decided there was nothing to do but comply and head east. Later in the morning, *Roeder* ran into the Swedish ore ship *Stråssa*, which had left Narvik fully loaded for the USA, and sent her back.[47]

Reaching Narvik around 09:00, *Michael Sars* dropped anchor off Gammelkaia while *Kelt* moored at Dampskipskaia. The panserships were nowhere to be seen but on many of the merchant vessels in the harbour the flags were flying at half-mast and at one place there was an inexplicable bubbling on the surface. A German officer came onboard *Michael Sars* with regrets that the German destroyers had been forced to sink the panserships and that loss of life had been due to foolhardy resistance. A shaken Jackwitz informed his crew and that of *Kelt* and ordered the flags of both vessels to be lowered to half-mast. Jackwitz expected a British counter-attack on Narvik and asked for and was granted permission to move his crews onshore to a safe location away from the harbour.

Meanwhile *Senja* had been ordered back to Narvik by *Schmitt*, which Løytnant Lundquist at first had mistaken for a British destroyer. Under the threat of the destroyer's guns the young officer could do little but deliver his protest and head east. Lundquist found the town full of German troops, but managed to locate a telephone and succeeded in getting a call through to Tromsø to report the events.[48]

Fregattenkapitän Bey had been detached from the main force with *Zenker*, *Koellner* and *Künne* to land Kampfgruppe Elvegård, led by Oberst Windisch, the C-in-C of IR 139, at the head of Herjangsfjorden to capture the army barracks and depots there. They arrived pretty much on time, 04:15, and immediately started disembarkation. Major Spjeldnes had left Elvegårdsmoen with I/IR 13 the evening before to reinforce the garrison in Narvik, while heavy snow bogged down the troops from Setermoen that should have taken over the defence of the barracks and depots. Hence, Windisch's soldiers had an easy task, meeting no resistance from the few men left behind. By early morning he could report to Dietl that Elvegårdsmoen and its valuable depots and the main road northwards were firmly secured. The unloading of the destroyers took some time, as there was only a small wooden pier and most of the equipment had to be taken ashore via whalers and a single hand-winch. Meanwhile, *Giese* arrived to unload her troops too. It would be late afternoon before the destroyers could head back towards Narvik.[49]

* * *

Erich Koellner ran aground manoeuvring in Herjangsfjorden, but damage was moderate. (T Eggan collection)

Kaptein Brekke, senior officer of the submarines at Liland, was uncomfortable being moored inside the fjord, where he would be trapped if there was an attack. At 03:30 he attempted to call Askim again, asking for permission to cast off and move out. He was unable to gain contact with his superior, but a sentry answering the telephone told Brekke that the pansership had just slipped moorings, including the telephone line, and was about to weigh anchor. Brekke decide to act independently and take both submarines into the pre-arranged positions in the fjord. It was pitch dark and the driving snow prevented all use of periscopes. Brekke trimmed *B3* down but kept the conning tower above surface to observe from there. The German destroyers had already passed and nothing was seen. When dawn approached and the snowfall eased somewhat Brekke dived, continuing to patrol the area submerged. *B1* was also met by heavy snow when entering Ofotfjorden and Løytnant Melsom decided to stay submerged.

Some time after 06:00, Brekke observed *Michael Sars* and *Kelt* coming up the fjord. He raised his radio antenna above surface and called them to find out what was going on. The reply from *Michael Sars* was a brief signal that they had been ordered back to Narvik, but there was no information of where this order came from. Brekke found this strange and decided to head back to *Lyngen* and use the telephone to find out what was going on. There he learned of the sinking of *Norge* and *Eidsvold* and the occupation of Narvik and received orders from SDD3 to proceed westwards and take up new positions in Vestfjorden.

B3 headed off again at 08:00 and, after unsuccessfully attempting to contact *B1* through underwater signalling, steered west at periscope depth. Near Ramsund, two destroyers were sighted lying still. Identifying them as German, Brekke decided to attack. Before he could get in position, both took off at high speed, turning towards the submarine in line-abreast. Brekke took his boat as deep as he could (about fifty metres) and managed to lose the adversaries. At this depth several leaks occurred in the forward torpedo room and Brekke decided to continue towards Vestfjorden and fight another day. Arriving in the evening, the boat was camouflaged with tarpaulin and, after informing SDD3 of his whereabouts, repairs were initiated.[50]

B1 did hear the underwater signalling, but by the time it surfaced, *B3* had dived and so Løytnant Melsom steered back to *Lyngen*. Here, he received orders from SDD3 to stay where he was. In the afternoon Melsom decided, with support from his officers, to leave the boat and take the crew ashore until he had 'a better picture of the situation'. In the morning of 13 April, after conferring with SDD3, *B1* was submerged completely some twenty metres deep. *Lyngen* managed to sneak out of Bogen and arrived in Tromsø some days later.[51]

By 06:30, the Gebirgsjägers were in control of Narvik and Elvegårdsmoen, but their position was very exposed. All the guns of 112th Mountain Artillery Regiment had been washed overboard in the storm and there were no A/A guns or other heavy weapons because the Norwegians had destroyed the few guns they left behind in the city. The supply ships *Bärenfels*, *Rauenfels* and *Alster* were supposed to arrive during the day, but none of them did, and Dietl never received the equipment and provisions he had expected.[52] Ironically, the only guns to be found were those onboard the British ships in the harbour.[53] As many as possible of these and their ammunition were taken ashore and used to supplement the harbour defences. The nearest German troops were nine hundred kilometres away in Trondheim, having their own challenges. Communication with the rest of XXI Corps was difficult but eventually established through the radio of *Heidkamp*. What would happen when the destroyers left, nobody knew.

Before they could leave, however, they needed to refuel. The tankers *Kattegat* and *Jan Wellem* should, according to plan, have arrived in Narvik ahead of the destroyers, ready to commence refuelling as soon as the troops had been disembarked. *Jan Wellem* arrived, but *Kattegat* did not. Her captain had received information of the British mines in Vestfjorden and decided to wait south of the minefield until the situation was clear. In the morning of 10 April the auxiliary *Nordkapp* found her and she was scuttled by her own crew to avoid capture.[54]

The missing tanker and the non-existent batteries at Ramnes made the situation precarious for Kommodore Bonte. His ships were trapped in the fjord without proper defence. The refuelling would be severely delayed with only one tanker and it was very likely that they would not be able to leave in time to meet up with the battleships for the return home. Every hour they had to remain in the fjord increased the chances of British intervention and with no guns at Ramnes there were only the U-boats left for protection during the refuelling. At 13:57, Bonte sent a report to Group West, copied to Vizeadmiral Lütjens, that he would not be able to depart Narvik before nightfall on 10 April. He did not wish to split up his ships and decided to wait for as many as possible to be refuelled before departure.[55]

Jan Wellem's cargo of oil was a mixture of 4,000 m³ of fuel oil for the destroyers and 5,000 m³ of diesel for the U-boats. This was insufficient for the all the Zerstörers but the oils could be mixed to some extent without a dramatic loss of efficiency. A solution for the U-boats would be found later. A larger problem was the low pumping capacity of *Jan Wellem*. She was a former whale-factory and had never been upgraded fully to the task of supply tanker. It would take up to eight hours to complete the transfer of sufficient fuel to each destroyer and only two could come alongside at the same time.[56] *Arnim* was the first destroyer to complete her disembarkation and she started taking on fuel from *Jan Wellem* some time during the morning, followed by *Thiele* and later by *Heidkamp*.

Information from Group West that all U-boats were in position according to plan comforted Bonte to some extent as he expected them to report British warships entering the fjord and most likely damage them or even prevent them from entering altogether should they try. This overestimation of the capacity of a few U-boats under very unfamiliar conditions was to become costly, all the more so as it would emerge that their torpedoes were faulty. At first, there were three U-boats in Vestfjorden; *U25*, *U46* and *U51*. *U25* came straight from Germany, but others had been on patrol since the second week of March and were low on fuel, and the crews were starting to show signs of fatigue. When it became clear that there were no guns at the narrows and that the Zerstörers could not depart as planned, Dönitz was instructed to increase the number of submarines in Bonte's support. *U47*, *U48*, *U49*, *U64*, *U65* and *U38* received orders to converge on Narvik at maximum speed. The latter three were large Type-IX boats, totally unsuited for operations in the confined Vestfjorden. *U64* and *U65* were, in addition, brand new, no more than a few days into their first operation.

Bonte did not live long enough to commit his thoughts and impressions to paper, but there is no doubt that he was greatly upset in the evening of 9 April. He had been under tremendous pressure since the flotilla left Wesermünde two and a half days earlier and had probably not slept much. Those who lived to recount the events from Narvik and had been near Bonte often related a picture of a very unhappy man. In addition to the dangerous situation for his destroyers, he was deeply discomforted by the fact that he had been persuaded to torpedo *Eidsvold* before she had opened fire and spoke of this to several of his officers. Korvettenkapitän Rechel of *Arnim* wrote that when he reported to Bonte, after the landing, the Kommodore said he 'owed him thanks' as he had let *Norge* fire first, while he had 'been forced to sink the other, without it having defended itself'.

By midnight *Heidkamp*, *Arnim* and *Thiele* were fuelled and the latter two ordered to Ballangen. Bonte wished for *Heidkamp* to patrol in the fjord during the night, but Generalmajor Dietl asked for the flagship to remain in harbour to ease co-ordination and maintain radio contact with the Weserübung staff. *Zenker* was given a moderate amount of fuel and ordered to Herjangsfjorden with *Koellner* and *Giese*. *Künne* and *Lüdemann* then moved alongside *Jan Wellem*. As a precaution against air attacks, some of the freighters were moved into the centre of the harbour to shelter the tanker and the Zerstörers. Moving *Jan Wellem* out of Narvik was considered, but disregarded as it would interrupt the refuelling and expose the tanker to air attack, which Bonte apparently feared more than a naval intervention.

Bonte's almost careless dismissal of the risk of a British surface attack is difficult to comprehend. He knew from the efficient sigint department of Group West – which, unknown to the Admiralty, could intercept and interpret British naval communication – that two battlecruisers and a large destroyer force was off Lofoten and that a group of destroyers had been ordered to attack an unknown target.[57] Bonte's belief in the submarines as a safeguard against intruders is also questionable, considering his own arrival during the snowstorm that same morning. *U25* was stationed off Barøy and *U46* off Ramnes, where the fjord was narrow enough for them to see and attack everything that tried to pass – in theory. The fact that the pickets depended on conning towers or periscopes at sea level in heavy snowfall, or sonar operators in unfamiliar conditions, does not seem to have worried him much. Still, it is hard to accept that Bonte thought that the Royal Navy would not risk an attack under conditions similar to those prevailing during his own attack. Unless, that is, he was so tired from lack of sleep and disturbed by the responsibility he felt for the sinking of *Eidsvold* and *Norge* that he lost his otherwise firm grip of command.

Concluding that things were under control and that his ships were safe, Bonte ordered only one extra safeguard: one destroyer should patrol in Vestfjorden outside the harbour during the night. No precautionary orders were given in case of an attack and no attempt made to plan a co-ordinated use of the ships in Herjangsfjorden and Ballangen with those remaining in Narvik, should it be needed. Bonte left it to Fregattenkapitän Gadow to organise the refuelling and the protection of the harbour and retired to his cabin on the afterdeck of *Heidkamp*. *Künne* was the first ship to go on picket duty and she was relieved by *Schmitt* at midnight.[58]

'You alone . . .'

After losing contact with *Gneisenau* and *Scharnhorst* in the early morning of 9 April, Vice Admiral Whitworth steered *Renown* west until ordered by the Admiralty to concentrate on the approaches to Narvik, 'as we shall probably want to land a force there'.[59] Whitworth complied and turned south-east for a rendezvous with *Repulse*, *Penelope* and their destroyers off Lofoten. At the same time, he instructed Captain (D)2 Bernard Warburton-Lee, who had been patrolling the entrance to Vestfjorden since 09:30, to rejoin the flag at 18:00 south-west of Skomvær. Again, however, he was overruled. First, at 09:52 when Admiral Forbes sent a signal directly to Warburton-Lee, instructing him to 'send some destroyers up to Narvik to make certain that no enemy troops land there', adding that Norway was at war with Germany. Then at noon when the Admiralty also addressed Captain (D)2:

> Press reports one German ship arrived Narvik and landed small force. Proceed to Narvik and sink or capture enemy ship. It is at your discretion to land forces if you think you can recapture Narvik from number of enemy present. Try to get possession of battery, if not already in enemy hands. Details of battery to follow.[60]

The signal was repeated to Forbes and Whitworth but, by addressing a junior commander directly and overriding their authority, it effectively inhibited either of them from applying any initiatives in the operation. The direct order to Warburton-Lee isolated him in an unnecessary manner and more than likely precluded Whitworth from deploying a balanced force, which was available. The 'details of battery' followed shortly

Captain D(2) Bernard Warburton-Lee. (John Warburton-Lee via Alister Williams)

after 13:00 and described 'three 12 or 18 pounders mounted on Framnes and facing northwest. Guns 4-inch or less may be in position on both sides Ofotfjord near Ramnes.' All this was faulty information as none of the batteries existed.

The casual manner in which Churchill and the Admiralty handled the issue of Narvik on 9 April is intriguing. The information available should have left no doubt that a German invasion of Norway was unfolding and that a substantial German force was heading for the town – if not already there. Vice Admiral Phillips had informed the Norwegian Embassy the previous afternoon that 'German operations against Narvik are intended.' Accepting 'press reports' as a basis for tactical dispositions of ships and men seems in this case to be rather arrogant, all the more so as Narvik had been foremost in the Scandinavian deliberations for the last seven months. A more qualified assessment of the situation could have saved many Norwegian and Allied lives in the days and weeks to come.

Warburton-Lee decided the best manner to comply with his orders would be to take only the ships of his 2nd Destroyer Flotilla, *Hardy*, *Hotspur*, *Hunter* and *Havock* to Narvik.[61] The mine-laying destroyers had neither torpedoes nor guns aft. Captain (D)20 Bickford was therefore instructed to remain in Vestfjorden with *Esk*, *Ivanhoe* and *Icarus*, supported by *Greyhound*.[62] *Penelope* was on station south of Skomvær Lighthouse, while *Renown* and *Repulse* stood further west screened by *Bedouin*, *Punjabi*, *Kimberley* and *Eskimo*.

At 16:00, 2nd Flotilla hove to off the pilot station at Tranøy in the inner Vestfjorden and Captain Warburton-Lee sent his secretary, Paymaster Lieutenant Geoffrey Stanning, ashore with Lieutenant George Heppel, the torpedo officer, to seek information on the German forces in Narvik. At this time, *Hostile* joined the flotilla. On 9 April she had joined up with *Repulse* and her destroyers but been advised to continue towards 2nd Flotilla in Vestfjorden.

At Tranøy, the pilots welcomed the British officers and in spite of some language problems, informed them that they had seen six German destroyers 'larger than the *Hardy*' and a submarine heading up the fjord. The one pilot who spoke some English asked how many ships the British had and when told, advised Stanning and Heppel 'not to attack until [they] had twice as many, as the place was very strongly held'. Heppel was not convinced that anybody at Tranøy had actually seen the German ships and wondered if the superior force might be 'hearsay'.

With Stanning and Heppel back onboard, Captain Warburton-Lee gathered his senior staff officers for counsel. The new information put him in a very tricky situation. The order from the Admiralty to attack Narvik was unambiguous and it would be a major issue to argue against it. The information from Tranøy might be incorrect and it was quite conceivable that the Admiralty had other information, unknown to Warburton-Lee and his staff, justifying the risk of sending the destroyers up the fjord. Captain (D)2 was known throughout the fleet as a brilliant destroyer man but also to be reserved, even remote. He rarely addressed his own crew and was not well known to the men of the other ships. On this afternoon, Warburton-Lee must have felt the mask of command to be an even heavier burden than usual. He left for half an hour to think matters through alone and returned to his staff with a decision to proceed. The Admiralty had chosen to give him a direct order that only they could recall, and that was the way it was going to be. Asking for reinforcements or even advice was no option. At 17:51, he sent the following 'Most Immediate' signal to the Admiralty, repeated to Forbes and Whitworth: 'Norwegians report Germans holding Narvik in force, also six repetition six destroyers and one submarine are there and channel is possibly mined. Intend attacking at dawn, high water.'[63]

Vice Admiral Whitworth was not happy with the situation and considered sending reinforcements to Warburton-Lee when he received the decoded signal just after 18:30. He even considered making a signal to *Penelope* to take *Punjabi*, *Bedouin*, *Eskimo* and *Kimberley* at speed up Vestfjorden to join the attack but eventually decided against. Had he made that move, the history of Narvik might well have been very different. Whitworth later wrote: 'I have always regretted that I did not intervene and order Warburton-Lee to postpone his attack until *Renown* could join him. Now that I know that the Admiralty had no special intelligence not available to myself, this regret is all the more poignant.'

Meanwhile, Warburton-Lee had made up his mind. A signal from the Admiralty to patrol east of Tjeldøy in case the Germans tried to escape northwards through Ramsund was either not received or ignored, probably in order not to be observed by the batteries that the Admiralty had said were located on either side of the narrows. The destroyers were observed by *U51*, though, which surfaced at 20:00, reporting five British destroyers at moderate speed on a south-westerly course. When the signal arrived at Narvik, Bonte drew the conclusion that it was a routine patrol heading away from Ofotfjorden, posing no danger. Half an hour later when Warburton-Lee ordered his ships back on a reciprocal course up the fjord, *U51* had dived and moved away.

Conditions were poor when the British destroyers passed Barøy an hour after midnight in 'continuous snowstorms with visibility seldom greater than 1½–2 cables.'[64] The uncertainty of what would meet them was great, and they were at action stations travelling in a narrow quarterline to starboard so that all forward guns would bear immediately if needed. It was pitch black in addition to the snow, and the skills of the fleet navigator, Lieutenant Commander 'Rusty' Gordon-Smith, were put to the ultimate test. Stanning later wrote that navigation was by 'dead reckoning asdic and echo sounding, as we never saw either side of the fjord – except early when we nearly hit it . . .' The captains were hard pressed to maintain contact while avoiding running into the ship in front. Through the narrows where there are only about three kilometres from shore to shore, speed was reduced to twelve knots. None of the ships had radar, no lights could be seen nor had anybody considered bringing pilots along from Tranøy. At one stage a shadow loomed ahead but an instant 'hard-a-starboard' took the destroyers away from whatever it was, if anything at all. The line was thrown into a shambles but contact eventually regained with the help of USW and asdic. Just before entering the narrows, a ferry with all lights burning loomed out of the murk and *Hostile* had to veer off, losing touch with the others. Commander 'Willy' Wright ordered his navigating officer, in whom he had full confidence, to find his own way towards Narvik.

A signal received from the Admiralty just after 01:00 suggested that the Germans might have arrived in disguised ore ships, which might still have cargoes and equipment onboard and should be eliminated.[65] At 01:36 a final signal came from the Admiralty, also copied to Forbes and Whitworth: 'Norwegian coast-defence ships *Eidsvold* and *Norge* may be in German hands. You alone can judge whether, in these circumstances, attack should be made. We shall support whatever decision you take.'[66] The signal did not affect Warburton-Lee, who had made his decision several hours earlier, but it must have distressed Vice Admiral Whitworth to be totally sidelined yet again.

Shortly after 02:30, the destroyers were through the narrows and speed was increased again. *Hostile* was a few minutes behind but also came through unharmed. Unbelievably, neither *U25* nor *U46*, at either end of the narrows, noted any of the destroyers. Both boats were most likely on the surface to charge batteries and get fresh air. That nothing was seen through the blizzard is understandable but the fact that neither U-boat picked up the destroyers on their hydrophones can only be explained by the combination of unfamiliar conditions and intermixed civilian traffic. That both captains, Schütze and Sohler, should have relaxed their vigilance to a degree where the destroyers just slipped through is inconceivable.[67]

Roeder relieved *Schmitt* as picket off Narvik at 03:00. Korvettenkapitän Böhme took *Schmitt* in between the merchant ships and dropped anchor. Conditions on the picket station had been difficult, with visibility usually less than four hundred metres in the driving snow, and the night was bitterly cold, creating misery for the lookouts. Böhme looked forward to the warmth of his cabin but remained fully clothed when lying down, folding the lifebelt under his head. *Künne* and *Lüdemann* were alongside *Jan Wellem*, refuelling.

It has since been difficult to ascertain which orders Bonte actually gave to Fregattenkapitän Gadow regarding the picket duty. Gerlach and Erdmenger held that Bonte had intended for a Zerstörer to patrol in the harbour entrance. Bey, after his conference with Bonte before departing for Herjangsfjorden, believed there would be a patrol line inside the narrows. Gadow, on the other hand, appears to have believed he was to organise a patrol off the harbour mouth but in its vicinity, as the U-boats would cover further out. When *Roeder* relieved *Schmitt*, there were no orders for any other ship to take over after that. On his way out, Korvettenkapitän Holtorf of *Roeder* claimed he received instructions over USW from Gadow to 'patrol against submarines outside harbour entrance until daylight'. It was not specified where in the fjord the picket should be positioned, and Holtorf took *Roeder* into the fjord rather than staying near the entrance. Around 04:20, a few minutes before sunrise, Holtorf considered his task ended and took *Roeder* into the harbour, dropping anchor off Postskaia without being relieved, leaving the entrance unprotected. Gadow later claimed that it had been his intention that *Roeder* stayed on picket until relieved by *Lüdemann* after she had completed refuelling about half an hour later.[68]

Lieutenant Commander Gordon-Smith took the British ships, all now in contact, close to Ankenes. Around 04:05, land appeared to starboard when visibility temporarily improved in the growing light and Warburton-Lee halted the flotilla to get a firm bearing. *Roeder* must have been very close, perhaps less than a mile away, but the ships remained unaware of each other. *Hotspur* and *Hostile* received orders to take care of the (non-existent) batteries on Framnes should they engage, while securing the escape route from Germans hiding in the north. The two were thus detached at 04:20 as the others continued around Ankenes in the growing light. The snow had lessened and visibility was a little over half a mile. At 04:30 *Hardy* entered the harbour, while *Hunter* and

Havock waited their turn. Unlike the Zerstörers, the British destroyers could not direct their torpedoes to run on a course other than that in which the tube was pointing at the time of firing. Warburton-Lee had therefore agreed with torpedo officer Heppel to enter the harbour along the south-western shore, off Ankenes, and to take a port turn inside, being prepared to fire as targets emerged.

Blythmoor was the first ship sighted from the bridge of *Hardy* as she crept into the harbour and shortly afterwards the grounded *Bockenheim*. Both were ignored for the moment as it was more important to locate the warships. One was eventually sighted between the shadows of the freighters and as Warburton-Lee commenced a slow turn to port, Heppel fired three torpedoes to starboard from the forward tubes. With the torpedoes away, *Hardy* increased speed and continued the turn. Two more destroyers came into sight and four torpedoes were fired at them from the aft tubes before fire was opened from the main guns. The last four torpedoes from *Hardy* appear to have missed altogether, detonating against the ore quays in the north-east, causing great damage.[69]

Alarms were sounded onboard the Zerstörers, but it was too late for *Heidkamp*. The first of the torpedoes missed and hit the stern of a freighter further behind. Seconds later, the second torpedo impacted on *Heidkamp*'s port stern, igniting the aft magazine in a tremendous explosion. More than eighty men were killed outright, among them Kommodore Bonte and most of his staff. Kapitän Erdmenger had been in his cabin at the bridge and survived, in spite of a shell hitting the port side of the superstructure shortly after. The three aft turrets were thrown into the air and the stern sank until water was lapping against the afterstack. With some effort, Erdmenger managed to secure the wreck of his ship to a nearby ore vessel.[70]

Hunter was the 'junior destroyer' of the flotilla and, as usual, followed closely in *Hardy*'s wake. Lieutenant Commander de Villiers entered with guns blazing, firing one salvo of four torpedoes at what appeared to be a destroyer at anchor and a second

Heidkamp hanging onto the Swedish freighter *Oxelösund*. Most of her after ship had been blown away and she sank the next day. (T Eggan collection)

indiscriminately into the mass of ships in the harbour. Several merchantmen were hit and a 12-cm shell slammed into *Schmitt*, immediately after which she was hit by a torpedo in the forward engine room. Korvettenkapitän Böhme, who was wakened abruptly after no more than an hour of sleep, found to his horror that he was trapped in his cabin by a jammed door.

Havock followed *Hunter*, in spite of increasingly accurate fire from the defenders. The poor visibility had been further reduced by the gunfire as well as a smokescreen laid by *Hardy*, and a brief exchange of gunshots with *Künne* still moored to *Jan Wellem* was inconclusive. *Schmitt* came into *Havock*'s sights and a second torpedo rammed the heavily listing Zerstörer aft.[71] Böhme had meanwhile managed to wrench open the door to his cabin and climb onto the listing quarterdeck, from where the explosion threw him into the icy water. Fortunately, he had put on his lifebelt and as he floated in the harbour he saw his ship break in two and sink rapidly with a large loss of life. A shaken Böhme climbed ashore near Jernbanekaia with a handful of his men, frozen to the bone. No targets could be identified for the aft guns of *Havock*, which did not open fire.[72]

Korvettenkapitän Holtorf in *Roeder* must have been devastated when he realised that British destroyers had more or less followed in his wake into the harbour. He had just ordered anchors to be dropped and the crews were standing down when all hell broke loose. Fire was ordered, aiming for the gun flashes, which could be seen through the blizzard, but the snow closed in and the shots went wide. Instead, all eight torpedo tubes were fired blind towards the harbour entrance. They came out of the murk, totally surprising the British destroyers. Disaster seemed inevitable but, incredibly, all torpedoes passed harmlessly, some underneath, scaring the wits out of the men on deck.

The German torpedoes were usually set to run at three to four metres and seem to have done so with a slight margin, as the regular draft of the H-class destroyers was 12.4 feet or 3.8 metres.[73] The German destroyers had a draft of some five metres and the German torpedo officers, who disliked setting their torpedoes running too shallow in case they ended up on the surface, in all likelihood had no time to consider the shallower draft of their British adversaries. The British ships were also low on fuel and probably higher than usual in the water. It is also possible that the German torpedo officers, who most likely did not know they were heading for Norway when inspecting their torpedoes at Wesermünde, later did not realise that they would run slightly deeper than usual in the less salty waters of the fjords. Whether the storm and/or ice had some additional effect on the depth keeping is less certain.[74]

Confusion reigned among the Germans; resistance was erratic at best, with few attempts at co-ordination. Some small-arms fire came from land, but did little damage to the destroyers. *Künne* and *Lüdemann* were moored to *Jan Wellem* with engines down when *Hardy* opened fire. By the time *Havock* came out of the smoke, *Künne* was under way and backed off the tanker, ripping off moorings and hoses as she went. By the time *Schmitt* was hit for the second time, *Künne* was only some forty metres away and shockwaves from the underwater explosions seized *Künne*'s engines, immobilising her. She drifted out of control into the sunken wreck of *Schmitt*, where she lay entangled during the remainder of the melee. Some of her crew panicked and jumped overboard; only a few of them were rescued from the icy water.

After having left the harbour, *Havock* was fired at by *Roeder* and *Lüdemann* – the latter now free from *Jan Wellem*. *Havock* was not hit and fired back from her aft guns, scoring twice on *Lüdemann*. One of her forward guns was knocked out while a fire was started aft, severing the rudder control and forcing a flooding of the magazine. Listing heavily and not answering the helm, Korvettenkapitän Friedrichs had no choice but to pull his ship out of the battle.

For the second morning in a row, Narvik harbour had turned into carnage. The torpedoes that miraculously passed through the almost compact wall of ships, detonated against land with tremendous explosions echoing between the steep mountainsides, spreading panic through sailors, soldiers and civilians alike. Some A/A guns opened up as well, increasing the noise level, and many fled into the mountains or along the shoreline away from the harbour.

Meanwhile, *Hotspur* and *Hostile* had encountered neither enemy destroyers nor shore batteries to the north. Hearing the gunfire from the harbour, they returned, as their orders could justifiably be said to be fulfilled. Off Framnes, they saw the three other destroyers coming out and laid a smokescreen behind which they could hide. *Hotspur* was ordered to fire a salvo of four torpedoes into the harbour and did so, sinking at least two more merchant ships. Commander Wright steered *Hostile* into the harbour shortly after *Havock* came out, engaging *Roeder* in a gunfight. *Roeder* was hit in quick succession by at least five 12-cm shells. The rudder control was severed, gun control broke down and forward aft turret was destroyed. Nos 2 and 3 boiler rooms were both hit, and a ruptured fuel tank ignited, filling the ship with dense, black smoke. *Roeder*'s anchor was stuck because of lack of power, but Korvettenkapitän Holtorf turned his ship by the engines and pulled back towards the piers, dragging anchor and chain. Eventually, *Roeder*'s stern was secured to Postkaia by a hawser while the anchor held her bow off at an angle.[75] The fires were extinguished, but damage to the destroyer was severe and most of the crew was ordered ashore. *Roeder* was no longer battleworthy.

At 05:30, Warburton-Lee gathered his ships outside Skjomnes and called his staff to the bridge for a consultation. It was full daylight, but still misty with occasional periods of snow. None of the destroyers had received any significant hits. The information from the Norwegian pilots at Tranøy indicated six German destroyers at Narvik. It appeared that most of these were inside the harbour and none had been encountered outside – yet. Some quick signalling between the ships concluded that four or five German destroyers had been identified and two, at most, might be somewhere outside (actually five were inside and five outside). These could be dealt with if encountered and, encouraged by his positive staff, Warburton-Lee turned his ships back for another swoop on the harbour. Twenty-four torpedoes had already been fired. *Hunter* had expended hers, while *Hostile* had a full outfit, *Hotspur* four, *Havock* three and *Hardy* one left. It was taken for granted that all non-German merchant ships had been commandeered and were thus legitimate targets.[76]

Meanwhile, some of the German officers had regained their composure and did what should have been done a long time ago: alert the five destroyers outside the harbour. Around 05:15, a signal was sent from *Lüdemann*: 'Alarm, attack on Narvik.' It would be just in time.

Jan Wellem was one of the few ships undamaged inside the harbour. Several torpedoes had been close and her shaken captain prepared to move his ship behind Malmkaia for shelter, should there be further attacks.[77] Captain Charles Evans of the British freighter *North Cornwall*, detained onboard *Jan Wellem*, argued that they should be given a fair chance to get away and asked to be allowed to take a whaler and row ashore. To his surprise, they were granted permission, and immediately set course for Ankenes, where there were no Germans at this stage.[78]

The British did come back, passing close to the entrance in a loose line-astern at fifteen knots. Little could be seen through the smoke and snow, though, and there were few targets left. *Lüdemann* had regained some control and fired four single torpedoes towards the gun flashes. One of these intercepted the course line of the destroyers but again passed harmlessly underneath. *Hostile*, going further into the harbour to seek targets for her torpedoes, was hit by a 12.7-cm shell high up on the forecastle, but damage was slight.

Completing the run, apparently without causing much damage, time had come for the decision on whether landing parties should be set ashore or not. Before Warburton-Lee could give it much consideration, the decision was made for him. Three obviously enemy ships were sighted coming down Herjangsfjorden at full speed. *Hardy* engaged at 6,400 metres with a full broadside and fire was immediately returned. Warburton-Lee called for thirty knots and sent a signal to Captain (D)20, picked up onboard *Renown*: 'One cruiser, three destroyers off Narvik. Am withdrawing to westward.'[79]

Fregattenkapitän Bey, C-in-C of the 4th Zerstörer Flotilla, had been at anchor in Herjangsfjorden with *Zenker*, *Giese* and *Koellner* when the radio signal from *Lüdemann* alerted him to the presence of the British destroyers. He reacted at once and, as soon as engines were ready, weighed anchors and headed south. Bey was acutely aware that his ships were low on fuel and at a severe disadvantage versus the intruders. *Giese* in particular was running desperately low, and *Koellner* was so depleted that she was limited to four boilers. Their fifteen 12.7-cm guns would be a mouthful for the British destroyer, though, and all Zerstörers had a full complement of torpedoes. In Herjangsfjorden the weather was clear and the sight good, but mist encroached as they approached Narvik.

Warburton-Lee steered his ships westwards north of Ankenes, making smoke, while shooting from the guns that would bear. A running fight ensued down the fjord, where Bey had the tactical initiative. The first British salvoes were short and they never got the distance right during this part of the battle. British sources state the distance to have been some six and a half to eight thousand metres whereas German reports say eight to ten thousand metres.[80]

At this time, a second signal came from *Lüdemann*: '*Heidkamp* sunk, Bonte killed. Three destroyers ready in harbour as protective batteries.' The effect must have been shocking onboard the Zerstörers, but there was little time to reflect and it appears that Bey jumped to the conclusion that such damage must have been inflicted by a substantial enemy force. Added to the precarious fuel situation of his ships, this made him very careful, especially as the British smoke was effective and he could not really see what he was chasing. Just as the German destroyers started to gain on their adversaries, they had to turn away to port to avoid the three torpedoes fired by *Lüdemann* coming out of Narvik harbour, losing any advantage gained.

Fregattenkapitän Erich Bey, commander of the 4th Zerstörer Flotilla. (Author's collection)

Fregattenkapitän Friedrich Berger, in command at Ballangen with *Thiele* and *Arnim*, had also picked up both USW signals from *Lüdemann* and was about to get underway. Visibility was momentarily less than two hundred metres due to a dense snow squall and Berger held back for a while, but by 05:40 the snow lifted and he ordered ships away. Both Zerstörers were flying large *wimpels* (pennants) to ensure recognition. Approaching Ofotfjorden, visibility improved further and at 05:50 five warships were sighted ahead and, in spite of emitting heavy smoke, recognised as British H-class destroyers. An almost perfect trap was about to develop. 'Crossing the T' of the British flotilla, the two German destroyers opened fire, *Thiele* only four thousand metres away from *Hardy*. The Germans were broadside-on with all guns bearing, and in spite of their numerical inferiority they matched the British in number of usable guns, reduced further as only *Hardy* and *Havock* could see properly through the smoke.[81]

For Warburton-Lee, the appearance of two ships coming out of Ballangen created a brief glimmer of hope. The newcomers were bow-on, slightly to port, and believed at first to be friendly cruisers come to their rescue. The mistake was quickly corrected, however, when the first of the two ships turned to port and opened fire. Warburton-Lee also swung to port, opposite the course of the Germans, to open for his own aft guns. The last signal from Captain (D)2 at 05:55 leaves little doubt that he believed the situation to be grave: 'Keep on engaging enemy.' The pursuing Zerstörers could not be seen and nobody realised that they were not actually in hot pursuit behind the smokescreen. Thus, Warburton-Lee did not recognise that he had a potential tactical superiority.

The third salvo from *Thiele* straddled *Hardy* and shortly after she was hit several times in quick succession. Both forward guns were put out of action by direct hits and shortly after *Hardy*'s bridge, wheelhouse and forward superstructure were soon smashed to a blazing mess. Captain Warburton-Lee was mortally wounded. Both legs were crushed and he had a serious head wound. Most others on or below the bridge were killed instantly. The only officer alive was Lieutenant Stanning, who had been at the rear of the bridge, recording events. The explosion threw him into the air and he landed on the gyrocompass binnacle. Recovering his senses, Stanning found himself the only man standing in the carnage. In spite of a lifeless left leg and shrapnel wounds to his back he took command of the burning ship careering down the fjord at some considerable speed with the rocky shore close to port. Struggling down from the bridge to the empty wheelhouse, Stanning took the wheel himself for a short while before he was relieved by Able Seaman Smale and could return to the shattered bridge. Several more shells from *Thiele* and *Arnim* hit *Hardy* from point-blank range and it appears she took more than a dozen strikes in all. When a shell exploded in the boilers, all steam was lost and she started losing way. Stanning decided it was best to save as many of the crew as possible and shouted 'Port 10' to Smale to beach the ship. At this time Torpedo Officer Heppel, who had only been lightly wounded came to the bridge; he first cancelled the order, but then concurred when he realised the severity of the situation. With what speed she still had left *Hardy* ran neatly aground on the south side of the fjord at Vidrek, some five kilometres east of Ballangen.[82]

Lieutenant Commander Mansell, the first lieutenant, who had not been on the bridge during the disaster, now took charge and ordered 'abandon ship' as the fiercely burning wreck was still under heavy fire. Lieutenant Heppel fired his remaining torpedo at one of the Zerstörers that appeared in the mist, without result. No. 4 gun also boldly continued firing after the grounding but soon ran out of ammunition. Meanwhile, the men were struggling ashore in the icy water using planks, rafts, lifebelts and whatever else was at hand. Stanning completed his sterling service of that morning by dropping confidential documents and codebooks over the stern in a loaded bag before leaving the ship; his watch stopped at 07:12 as he slipped into the water.[83] Warburton-Lee was briefly conscious as he was brought onto a raft, but died from his wounds shortly after. Lieutenant Heppel, Leading Seaman Mason, Stoker Bowden and Able Seaman Slater made their way back onboard *Hardy* to rescue the badly wounded Navigating Officer Gordon-Smith, who was brought safely to shore as the last man off the destroyer, in spite of having a fractured skull.

Of *Hardy*'s complement of 175, 140 managed to get ashore, twenty-seven of them seriously wounded. In the house nearest the grounding site, Mrs Christiansen and her daughter had been woken by the gunfire. Seeing the destroyer in front of their house with men scrambling ashore, they rushed outside and started to tend the wounded. Any dry clothes that could be found were distributed, while tea, coffee and hot soup were produced in large quantities.[84] There were not enough facilities to stay at Vidrek, however, and as soon as transport could be arranged, the survivors were transferred to Ballangen, where the local hospital took care of the wounded. Lieutenant Heppel and a number of the less wounded had to walk. Most of the survivors were repatriated to Britain a few days later when they were picked up after the events of 13 April.[85] A few weeks later,

The wreck of *Hardy* floated off during high tide and drifted across the bay, grounding again at Skjomnes, where she keeled over. (Author's collection)

Warburton-Lee was awarded a posthumous Victoria Cross – the first to the Royal Navy during this war.[86]

With *Hardy* gone, *Havock* took the lead of the British line and received the attention of *Thiele* and *Arnim*, the other British ships largely being hidden in the smoke. The distance between the adversaries was now down to 2.5–3 kilometres and *Havock* was straddled repeatedly but took no serious hits. One shell landed near an ammunition locker, but did not explode and was thrown overboard. Both sides fired torpedoes; all of them missed in the melee. *Hotspur* fired two at *Thiele* and claimed a hit, but this is not correct.[87] Many of the surviving British officers later commented that the short range of the encounter with multiple, swiftly moving targets was very different from anything they had practised for in peacetime.

The Zerstörers turned west, running parallel to and north of the British ships, and slightly ahead of them. Fregattenkapitän Berger believed that Bey and the 4th Flotilla was pursuing the British destroyers from behind the smoke and wanted to keep them under double fire. Bey, however, appearing to have been concerned about the fuel situation and nothing as aggressive as Berger, stayed well behind.

The smoke from the foremost British destroyers kept hampering those coming behind and few of the captains had a good understanding of what was happening. Lieutenant Commander Courage of *Havock* may not have been fully aware of Berger's presence ahead of him and turned back, running down his own line to relieve the pressure he believed came from behind and to find out what had become of *Hardy*. At the critical moment, the forward guns failed and he had to turn again, skirting *Hostile*, which was last in line, to let his aft guns engage. This fire appears to have discouraged Bey further, and 4th Flotilla remained at distance.

Up front, *Hunter* – now forward in the line – started to take hits. So did the Zerstörers, which so far had escaped unmolested. On *Thiele* a shell impacted on the port side, starting a fire in no. 1 boiler room, shutting it down. Shortly after, a second hit aft started a fire that endangered the aft magazine, which had to be flooded. As she turned east again for the final assault on *Hunter*, a 12-cm shell exploded behind the shield of the forward gun, killing nine men and setting the ammunition host on fire. Two more shells impacted in rapid succession, causing significant damage above and below decks and starting several fires. Many were killed or wounded. The fire-control systems fell out, and the remaining four guns had to operate on local control.

Hunter was hit several times in succession and turned into an inferno within a few minutes, especially because the German destroyers also used their 3.7- and 2-cm guns. Several fires, ignited by a series of secondary explosions, destroyed the engines and boilers. In all likelihood she was also hit by one of three torpedoes fired by *Thiele* at this stage. *Hunter*'s speed dropped rapidly and *Hotspur*, herself under heavy fire and temporarily out of control from two hits, rammed her from behind. While locked together, the two ships received the full attention of both *Arnim* and *Thiele*. It was not possible to steer *Hotspur* from the bridge and Commander Layman had to make his way aft to the X gun deck and shout orders from there to the engine room and tiller flat. When *Hotspur* eventually managed to extricate herself, *Hunter* keeled starboard-over and sank with a heavy loss of life. *Hotspur* was alone with five German destroyers for a while, Bey having reappeared with the 4th Flotilla, but Sub-Lieutenant Tillie kept the two aft guns firing and, when the forward guns eventually joined in, the adversaries stayed at a distance.[88]

Havock and *Hostile* drew clear at first, but boldly turned back, *Havock* for the second time, fighting the Zerstörers off *Hotspur*. She regained some speed and, under a smokescreen from *Hostile*, escaped the claws of *Arnim* and *Thiele*, which were compelled to pull back, licking their wounds. *Thiele* was particularly severely hit with multiple fires and flooded magazines. Grudgingly, Fregattenkapitän Berger had to leave the rest of the business to Bey.[89] Bey, however, lobbed a few shots at the retiring destroyers before turning back, pounding the wreck of *Hardy* instead. Fregattenkapitän Schulze-Hinrichs let *Koellner* follow as far as Djupvik before he also turned back.[90] *Hostile*, *Hotspur* and

Some of the fifty survivors from *Hunter* picked up by the Germans being brought into Narvik. (T Eggan collection)

Havock were thus saved from total destruction and continued down the fjord as fast as *Hotspur* could make it, scarcely believing their luck.[91]

At 06:45, Commander Wright of *Hostile*, who was now in command, sent a signal to *Penelope* and *Renown*: 'Returning with *Hotspur* and *Havock*. *Hunter* sunk in Vestfjord. *Hardy* ashore. 5 or 6 large German destroyers in Narvik.'[92]

The Zerstörers picked up some fifty survivors from *Hunter*, five of whom later died.[93] The following morning, *Künne* returned to search the wreck of *Hardy*, which floated off during high tide in the afternoon, drifting across the bay and grounding again in the evening at Skjomnes, where she keeled over.[94]

Kapitänleutnant Sohler of *U46* had no idea that British destroyers had passed up the fjord some hours earlier and his boat was still surfaced at the narrows, charging its batteries.[95] When three destroyers emerged out of a snow squall he dived and was not sighted. The ships were out of reach before he could stabilise his boat and move it into a potential attacking position.

Through the narrows at the mouth of Ofotfjorden the British destroyers ran into the German supply ship *Rauenfels* heading for Narvik where she should have arrived the previous day. In her holds were A/A guns, 15-cm artillery pieces and other heavy

Rauenfels burning, shortly before she blew up. The photo is taken from *Havock*. (Lt Burfield via David Goodey)

Havock was hit by several fragments from the exploding *Rauenfels*. Here the crew of *Havock*'s X gun are grinning over a nasty hole made by 'German mice'. From left: John Dodds, SA Brown, Jim 'Buster' Brown, Gun Captain 'Shits' Gilbert and Seaman Grimes. (Lt Burfield via David Goodey)

weapons as well as 12.7-cm shells for the Zerstörers. *Hostile* opened fire and *Rauenfels* was run aground on the south side of the fjord by her crew, who scrambled ashore in panic. *Havock* remained at the site while the other two continued. An inspection to verify her identity found the transport on fire and Lieutenant Commander Courage ordered the search party off. With the men safely back, two 12-cm rounds were fired to hasten *Rauenfels*'s destruction. These probably hit some of the ammunition as she blew up with a spectacular explosion and a column of smoke that could be seen from the Zerstörers returning to Narvik. They did not realise this meant that none of the supply ships or tankers intended for Narvik would arrive, except *Jan Wellem*. One German sailor from *Rauenfels* was killed; the rest were taken into custody by Norwegian forces.

Fregattenkapitän Bey took his Zerstörers back to Narvik at 10:00. It was a sorry sight that met them. *Schmitt* had sunk with over fifty casualties. On *Heidkamp* eighty-one men were dead, among them Kommodore Bonte. Five shells had hit *Roeder*, damaging her oil tanks as well as the rudder and she was not battleworthy; thirteen of her crew were dead. *Arnim* had suffered an equal number of hits and was also out of action. *Thiele* had taken seven hits, seriously damaging a boiler room, the fire-control room and one of her guns, killing thirteen men.[96] *Lüdemann* had been hit by two shells and had two dead but her guns were all working. *Künne* had nine dead from splinter damage and needed work on her engines before becoming fully operational. *Zenker* and *Giese* had suffered no hits and went straight to *Jan Wellem* to commence fuelling. Neither had *Koellner* but she suffered engine problems and needed to shut down her boilers. Large amounts of ammunition had been expended and few magazines were more than half full.

Eight merchant ships were sunk (plus *Rauenfels*) and many others damaged. Narvik hospital and the makeshift emergency station at the 'Seamen's House' were filled with

Narvik harbour, 10 April 1940. The wrecks of *Hein Hoyer* and *Cate B*. Behind the latter can be seen the bow of *Bockenheim*. (E Skjold Collection)

Narvik harbour shortly after the first British attack. *Roeder* is seen at an angle to Postkaia, while *Lüdemann* is moored on the other side and *Zenker* is moving alongside. The freighter aground close to shore in the upper part of the photo is *Bockenheim*, with the bow of *Hein Hoyer* further out and the light hull of *Cate B* further still. The half-sunken ship inside the smoke is *Saphir*, while *Riverton* appears to be on fire amidships. The apparently undamaged ship beyond *Roeder* is *Aachen*. (Author's collection)

wounded. Norwegian doctors and nurses worked side by side with German medical personnel as naval, merchant and civilian casualties were brought in. Smoke hung heavily over the town in the growing daylight and there was a strong smell of fire, cordite and oil all over the area.

Tactically, the brutal encounter between the destroyers on 10 April looked like a fairly even affair with two ships lost on each side. Strategically, however, it sealed the fate of the Kriegsmarine's destroyer force for the rest of the war. To the British, for whom the element of surprise had been decisive, the casualties had no practical consequences, neither at Narvik nor in general, beyond the grief for the loss of some two hundred men.

How necessary Warburton-Lee's sacrifice was is arguable. Had he waited for reinforcements the damage to the enemy might have been even greater and he might have lived to fight another day. What would have happened had Vice Admiral Whitworth sent *Penelope* and the Tribals in support in the evening of 9 April remains speculation. They would most likely have arrived too late for the first attacks on Narvik harbour, where they were not needed anyway, but they might have tipped the balance in the ensuing battle and reduced British losses.[97]

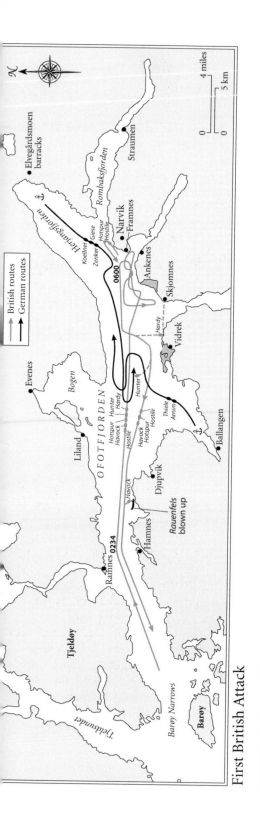

First British Attack

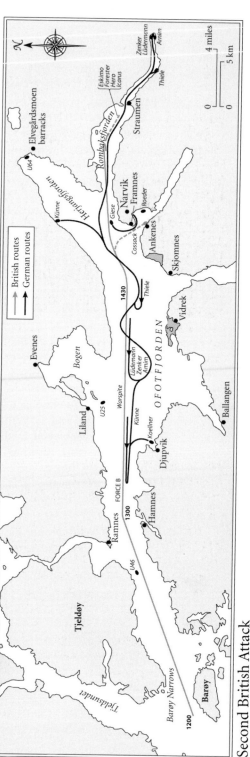

Second British Attack

Trapped

Hostile, *Havock* and *Hotspur* met up with *Greyhound* off Tranøy at 09:30. Having received Warburton-Lee's signal just before 06:00 that a cruiser was chasing his flotilla, Vice Admiral Whitworth had finally put all discretion aside and ordered *Penelope* and the destroyers of his own screen into Vestfjorden with orders to support the retiring 2nd Flotilla. *Greyhound* was nearest and met the survivors first; *Penelope*, *Kimberley* and the Tribals being encountered at 11:00. The badly damaged *Hotspur*, which had around twenty casualties, was sent towards Skjelfjord with *Hostile* as escort. While underway, Commander Wright sent a more comprehensive report to his superiors. He repeated that there had been five or six large destroyers in Narvik, of which one had been sunk and at least three damaged. He made no mention of any cruiser, but believed there had been fire from a number of shore guns of up to 6-inch calibre.[98]

Eskimo and *Bedouin* patrolled the head of the fjord when, around 19:00, closing the Barøy Lighthouse, two large explosions occurred in short succession some two hundred metres in front of the ships. Believing they were approaching a remote-controlled minefield the two captains agreed to turn away and withdraw towards Tranøy. Actually, they were torpedoes from *U25*, that had exploded prematurely again, saving the destroyers from severe damage. Surprisingly, the British did not at this stage realise that there were several U-boats in the confined fjord and the episode further strengthened the misconception that there were strong German shore defences and minefields.[99]

Havock and *Greyhound* took up a patrol line across outer Vestfjorden, between Skjelfjord and the British minefield. At 15:25 they obtained a sonar contact and shortly after sighted the conning tower of a submarine breaking surface. The boat, which was *U64* on its way to Narvik, had sighted the destroyers and was positioning itself for an attack when something happened to the depth-control system and she broke surface. Kapitänleutnant Schulz crash dived as the destroyers attacked and, as soon as he was safely below, turned away from his original course. Depth charges were dropped liberally and an oil slick appeared on the surface but *U64* suffered only minor damage. Schulz and his crew were thoroughly shaken and had to take their boat below 125 metres before being able to sneak away.[100]

Captain Yates took *Penelope* and the rest of the destroyers down the fjord as backup. Their objective was to prevent German reinforcements from reaching Narvik and to ensure that no German ships, including the submarines, could escape from Ofotfjorden. Whitworth, who at this stage operated *Renown* and *Repulse* south-west of Lofoten without escort, elaborated the instructions in a signal to Captain Yates and the destroyers, timed at 11:16 on 10 April:

> Enemy forces reported in Narvik consist of one cruiser, five destroyers and one submarine. Troop transports may be expected to arrive through Vest Fjord or through Inner Leads disregarding minefield. Your object is to prevent reinforcements reaching Narvik. Establish a destroyer patrol between positions 67° 47' N., 14° 20' E., and 68° 2' N., 13° 40' E., one destroyer also to patrol northeast of minefield during daylight. Enemy submarines may operate in West Fjord . . . Establish warning and A/S [anti-submarine] patrol 30 miles north-eastward of your patrol line.[101]

Commander Wright and Lieutenant Commander Courage wanted to go back to Narvik to finish the job and search for survivors before the Germans could recover, but Yates considered this to be beyond his orders and decided to stay in Vestfjorden. Later in the evening Yates received a signal directly from the Admiralty that asked him to consider 'taking available destroyers in Narvik area and attack enemy tonight or tomorrow'. Whitworth, once again bypassed, pointed out that this would weaken the patrol line in Vestfjorden and might lessen his abilities to prevent reinforcements or German break-out attempts. Yates, who lacked Warburton-Lee's panache, wanted more time to gather superior forces and advised the Admiralty to accept waiting until the morning of 12 April before attacking. Their Lordships concurred.

In the evening of 10 April the Admiralty informed the C-in-C at 19:04 of their considerations regarding Narvik, copied to Whitworth.

> As enemy is now established at Narvik recapture of that place takes priority over operations against Bergen and Trondhjem. Expedition is being prepared as quickly as possible . . . It is of primary importance to prevent Narvik being reinforced by sea. [The possibility to seize] and hold a temporary base near Narvik with small military force is under urgent examination. In the meantime, you will presumably arrange for a temporary refuelling anchorage in North. As Narvik must also be of primary importance to the Germans, it seems possible that battlecruisers may turn up there.[102]

The 'temporary refuelling anchorage' had already been found at Skjelfjord on the south side of Flakstadøy in Lofoten. *Hotspur* was already there and a repair depot was being organised. The German transport *Alster*, captured by *Icarus* in the morning of 11 April, was taken to Skjelfjord and her cranes used as makeshift repair facilities.[103] When the oiler *British Lady* arrived on the 12th, escorted by *Grenade* and *Encounter*, a routine was set up for the destroyers to be refuelled as needed. In the weeks to come, Skjelfjord would become a very efficient repair workshop, affectionately known as 'Cripples Creek'. The efficiency was in large part due to the arrival of the Norwegian salvage vessel *Stærkoder* (under Andreas Emblem) and the many Norwegian fishermen, used to fixing their own vessels with welding apparatus and whatever else was around, coming to help. The Norwegian Hartvig Sverdrup, who spoke good English, became a 'civil liaison officer' almost by default and organised an effective service at Skjelfjord together with Mr Krogstad, a civil engineer from Kabelvåg. British officers and naval engineers were at first highly sceptical of the Norwegians, whom they considered backward and simple natives. In particular they were horrified when the Norwegians wanted to use wooden plugs greased with sheep tallow to plug bullet holes. The greasy plugs kept the water out, though, and with solid craftsmanship the Norwegians got the ships ready to sail home and won the respect and gratitude of the Royal Navy. Many British sailors found their final resting places outside the mouth of the fjord, while the hospitals at Gravdal and Reine became unexpected havens for the wounded.

In the afternoon of 11 April *Penelope* ran aground off Fleinvær Light north of Bodø while searching for (wrongly) reported German merchant ships. The cruiser was badly damaged with a fractured bottom, propeller damage and distorted rudder frame. The forward engine and boiler rooms were flooded and once off the ground at high tide she had to be towed to Skjelfjord by *Eskimo*. The attack planned for the 12th was postponed.[104]

* * *

After the death of Bonte, command of the remaining German destroyers at Narvik was given to Fregattenkapitän Bey as oldest commander on site. Reporting status to Generaladmiral Saalwächter and Group West, he received orders at 13:06 to refuel the remaining battleworthy Zerstörers as soon as possible.[105] *Lüdemann* and *Roeder* were too damaged to leave without extensive repairs. Men not needed onboard for this were sent ashore and put at the disposal of Generalmajor Dietl with the survivors from *Heidkamp* and *Schmitt* in a 'naval battalion' under Korvettenkapitän Erdmenger. The sailors were deployed to secure the harbour and town of Narvik, releasing soldiers for more important duties. The radio equipment from *Roeder* was taken ashore and set up as a communication centre, significantly improving Dietl's communication with Group XXI and other German commands.

At 14:00 a signal arrived from Group West with orders to depart with the seaworthy ships that same evening and join up with *Scharnhorst* and *Gneisenau* for the return trip to Germany. Bey reported back that only *Zenker* and *Giese* would be ready. *Thiele*, *Künne*, *Arnim* and *Koellner* required more time for refuelling and repairs. At 18:30 a signal came from Wilhelmshaven: '*Zenker* and *Giese* to depart with C-in-C at nightfall.' Consequently, Bey left Narvik with the two destroyers at 19:40 on 10 April. The feeling of the sailors remaining in Narvik was rather gloomy; nobody knew if or when they would be able to depart. Those onboard *Zenker* and *Giese* were probably not too excited either; the prospect of two destroyers penetrating the British forces waiting in Vestfjorden was rather slim, especially as the snow had stopped and the clouds lifted.

Damage to *Z17 Diether von Roeder*. Her stern is secured to Postkaia by a hawser while the anchor holds her bow off at an angle. At least three holes from British 12-cm shells can be seen. (Author's collection)

Off Tranøy the shadows of *Penelope* and two destroyers came into sight and Bey promptly turned back.[106] Breakout would have to be another day with poor weather conditions, even if this meant that the Zerstörers would have to return to Germany without the protection of the battleships. Bey signalled to Group West that he had run into superior British forces at Tranøy and that it was not possible to depart under the prevailing weather conditions, adding an urgent request for increased U-boat support in the fjord.

An hour later, Group West answered that any ruse of war may be applied during subsequent breakout attempts, including the use of the British flag (which all the German ships had in their lockers). The tanker *Skagerrak* had been redirected from Trondheim and would remain offshore as long as possible; if she could not be reached, fuel could be found in Bergen or Kristiansand. Trondheim was to be avoided, as there were already Zerstörers there, needing whatever fuel and repair facilities were available. It was later added that additional U-boats could not arrive for at least forty-eight hours. During the morning, *U46* arrived to refuel from *Jan Wellem* and discuss communication and co-ordination of operations with the Zerstörers. Prior to this, there had been no direct radio connection between the U-boats and the destroyers. Signals from the U-boats were received at headquarters in Germany, decoded, forwarded to Group West, recoded and sent to Narvik. There was therefore a time delay and potential vulnerability to mistakes and atmospheric disturbances to the radio connections. Means of direct communication were now agreed, and Fregattenkapitän Bey and Kapitänleutnant Sohler apparently departed in a relatively agreeable manner, Sohler having spent a considerable part of the meeting conveying to the destroyer captain the difficulties the U-boats had encountered operating in the fjord.

During 11 April, *Koellner* and *Künne* completed repairs and refuelling. *Lüdemann* also reported ready, earlier than expected, and the men sent ashore were called back. Still, Bey did not attempt another breakout in spite of fog and poor visibility during the ensuing night. Instead, he sent a signal to Group West stating that he considered '. . . breakout of Zerstörers as impossible tonight as last night', and that a return through the Leads was 'unfavourable' because of the threat from British and Norwegian naval forces.

At 22:00, *Koellner* was sent to Ballangen on picket duty for the night. Shortly before midnight, she ran hard aground, suffering substantial damage to her bottom. There was no immediate danger of her sinking, but she was taking water in several compartments and limped back to Narvik in the morning. *Zenker* also touched bottom and damaged her port propeller while at anchor during the night, limiting her maximum speed to twenty knots.[107]

On the 11th, *U48* ran into parts of the Home Fleet off Vestfjorden. Kapitänleutnant Schultze audaciously fired two salvos of three torpedoes, both times aiming at cruisers venturing close. Four of the torpedoes exploded prematurely and the other two missed. Frustrated, Schultze surfaced to report the encounter and the failure of his torpedoes.[108] This caused grave concern in Kiel. Of twelve torpedoes fired in Norwegian waters in the last two days, over half had exploded prematurely and the rest missed easy targets. Something was very wrong! Dönitz called his experts but they could offer few explanations and even less help. It was decided to apply a mix of contact and magnetic pistols adapted to the assumed draft of the target and hope for the best. Recalling the boats was not an option and little could be done in the field until the nature of the problem was fully understood.[109]

At 18:45 on 12 April eight Swordfish aircraft from 818 Sqn of *Furious* attacked Narvik, the carrier having arrived off Lofoten with the Home Fleet at 05:00 in the morning. After the failure of the torpedo attack in Trondheim harbour the day before, Forbes and his staff decided bombs would be more effective than torpedoes, and the 'Stringbags' were accordingly armed with four 250-lb and four 20-lb bombs. The weather was appalling, with strong winds and snow from low clouds, and the inexperienced navy pilots were hampered by poor reconnaissance. For once, the German early-warning systems worked and all A/A guns on the ships were manned and ready, putting up a deterrent fire against the slow, ungainly bi-planes. In addition, the clouds opened just as the attack commenced, exposing the aircraft. No bombs hit any of the German ships, but eight sailors were killed and some twenty wounded from splinters on land. The auxiliary *Senja* was damaged during the attack and sank off Fagerneskaien. She had just been manned by a crew from *Roeder*. The unmanned *Michael Sars* moored in the harbour was also damaged and sank the following day.[110]

Two aircraft were shot down and crashed in Ofotfjorden, where the crews were rescued by *Punjabi* and *Penelope* respectively. The six other aircraft returned to *Furious*. 816 Sqn, following some fifty minutes behind 818 Sqn, encountered even worse conditions and turned back at the mouth of the fjord. The carrier was pitching heavily in the coarse seas and Lieutenant MD Donati touched his lower port wing onto the deck when landing and, in spite of being hooked on the arresting wire, swung round and went over the side. Luckily, the stand-by destroyer was alert and Donati and his air-gunner Leading Airman Smith were picked up from the icy sea; they were wet but ready to fly another day. Lieutenant S Keane of 818 Sqn, having had his undercarriage damaged by A/A fire over Narvik, waited until all other aircraft had landed on before nursing his damaged aircraft onto the carrier with one wheel missing and nearly empty tanks.[111]

Fregattenkapitän Bey had at this stage given up all hope of a breakout in spite of continued pressure from Germany. A signal from Group West at 00:44 on 13 April, informing him that aircraft had sighted one large naval vessel with seven or eight destroyers in Vestfjorden, made Bey expect an attack similar to that of the 10th. *Koellner* was for all practical purposes unmanoeuvrable and ordered to move to Tårstad, inside the Ramnes Narrows, and to take position on the northern side of the fjord as an early-warning picket and a floating barrage battery. The water is shallow at Tårstad and not suitable for torpedoes, so her remaining stock was taken off and divided between *Thiele* and *Arnim*, as was excess fuel. Some ninety men not needed onboard were ordered ashore and most of the engine-room crew would be taken off after arriving at Tårstad. Few doubted this was a suicide mission or 'Himmelfahrtskommando' that would mean the end of *Z13 Erich Koellner*. When she left harbour, escorted by *Künne*, the other destroyer's crews manned the rails and cheered.[112]

At 10:10, a signal sent an hour and a half earlier from Wilhelmshaven was received, saying: 'Expect enemy attack this afternoon. *Repulse*, *Warspite*, five Tribals, four destroyers and probably carrier.' Bey ordered the remaining Zerstörers to be ready at

13:00, irrespective of their condition and the crews started working in earnest, in spite of being desperately short of sleep. Only *Künne* was fully operational with all guns working and full torpedo batteries. *Arnim* was also in fair shape, capable of thirty-three knots, all guns working and with six torpedoes left. *Lüdemann* had four operational guns and four torpedoes left and was in relatively good condition. Ammunition from the flooded aft magazine had been retrieved and found to be in order when dried. *Giese* and *Zenker* had full torpedo loads, having been replenished from *Heidkamp* and *Koellner*, but were still under intense repair. *Giese* reported she would be capable of twenty-eight knots, while *Zenker's* maximum speed was estimated at twenty knots. *Thiele* had four operational guns and six torpedoes; it was estimated she could do some twenty-seven knots in an emergency but for the moment she was tied up at Malmkaia with engines shut down for repair, and she would not be combat ready for several days. *Roeder* was not a complete wreck as first feared, but it would be a week or more before she might become mobile. Most of the crew had already been sent ashore, and now she was stripped of light guns and other equipment needed elsewhere. Her stern was moored to Postkaia in the inner harbour, her bow held by the anchors at an angle from the pier. Only the two forward guns had a free field of fire.[113]

Ram if Necessary

With *Penelope* having become unavailable, the Admiralty decided to attack Narvik 'on a far heavier scale'. Admiral Forbes and the Home Fleet had come north from the Trondheim area during the night of 11/12 April and met up with Vice Admiral Whitworth at 07:30 on the 12th at about 67°N, 6°E. In the afternoon of 12 April Admiral Forbes received orders from the Admiralty to 'clean up enemy naval forces and batteries in Narvik by using a battleship heavily escorted by destroyers with synchronised dive-bombing attacks from *Furious*'. The number of ships at Forbes's disposal was at this stage becoming limited. The first of the troop convoys – NP1 – had left Britain but required attention, so *Valiant*, *Repulse*, and three destroyers had just been detached to meet the convoy and augment her escort. *Valiant* was to stay with NP1 all the way to Harstad, while *Repulse* and the destroyers would have to proceed to Scapa Flow for fuel. Admiral Cunningham's cruisers were still searching the fjords, *York* and two destroyers having taken the damaged *Eclipse* home, and a number of destroyers had left for Britain to refuel. Thus, the C-in-C had *Rodney*, *Warspite*, *Renown*, *Furious* and six destroyers directly at his disposal.[114] Twelve more destroyers were operating in or around Vestfjorden.

Forbes tasked Whitworth with the attack (Operation DW) and ordered him to strike in the afternoon of 13 April with 'Force B', made up of *Warspite*, *Bedouin*, *Punjabi*, *Eskimo*, *Cossack*, *Kimberley*, *Forester*, *Icarus*, *Hero* and *Foxhound*.[115] His objective was clear: 'destruction of German warships, merchant ships and defences in Narvik area'. The senior officer of the destroyers was Commander James 'Bes' McCoy, onboard *Bedouin*.

Whitworth transferred his flag to *Warspite* and sailed for Vestfjorden in the evening of the 12th, accompanied by *Cossack*, *Foxhound*, *Forester* and *Hero*. *Bedouin*, *Punjabi*, *Kimberley* and *Icarus* fell in during the night and following morning. The C-in-C remained some thirty miles off Lofoten with *Rodney*, *Renown*, *Furious* and five destroyers, with four

HMS *Warspite* had a long and distinguished career from her commissioning in 1915. She was extensively modernised in the late 1930s, with changes to armament and propulsion systems and her superstructure was radically altered. This photograph shows her as she appeared after recommissioning in 1937. (Medway Studio)

more standing by off Skjelfjord. Captain Crutchley addressed *Warspite's* company over the loudspeakers in the evening. He informed them of his intention to proceed to Narvik and did nothing to hide the potential dangers from minefields, U-boats and torpedoes. A grim determination spread onboard the battleship and a special communion at 08:00 the next morning was attended by more than three hundred men.[116]

The greatest threat to Force B was perceived to come from mines and shore batteries, none of which actually existed. Attacks from enemy aircraft would be serious in the confined waters but not really considered a high risk as the area was far from the nearest German-controlled airport. Covering patrols from the *Furious* would be mounted as soon as the fleet entered Ofotfjorden. The one risk that was real, U-boats, was seriously underestimated at all levels of the British command, in spite of ample evidence of their presence. Unknown to Whitworth and McCoy, there were no fewer than five U-boats in the area. *U48* was off Tranøy, *U46* was in the narrows west of Ramnes, *U25* had moved further up the fjord and was now off Liland, *U51* was in Narvik, refuelling from *Jan Wellem*, and *U64* – having completed refuelling – was at anchor in Herjangsfjorden resting the crew.[117]

In the morning of 13 April, action stations were closed up onboard the ships as they passed Tranøy Lighthouse at twenty-two knots. The sky was heavily overcast, with cloud base at 350 metres, and rain and sleet showers reduced visibility at times. *Hero* and *Foxhound* were one mile ahead of the battleship, with their two-speed destroyer sweep (TSDS) gear set.[118] *Icarus*, fitted with bow protection gear, was ahead of them. *Kimberley*,

Forester and the Tribals formed an anti-submarine (A/S) screen around *Warspite*. At 11:30 action stations lunch was served, consisting of hard-boiled eggs and thick corned-beef sandwiches.

Eskimo, the last destroyer assigned to Force B, had been patrolling off Tranøy during the night to secure the entrance to Ofotfjorden. At 10:40 just as Force B hove into view, a submarine was sighted, surfacing some four miles away, in the path of the approaching fleet. 'It was a small boat and it flashed the letter "U" to me as a form of recognition,' Commander St John Micklethwait later wrote. 'I acknowledged this signal by light. He then made "A.A.A." but receiving no answer and seeing *Eskimo* turn towards, the submarine hurriedly dived.' The culprit was *U48* and Kapitänleutnant Schultze crash dived once he realised it was no Zerstörer he was approaching. Micklethwait let go a pattern of depth charges over the area where the boat was expected to be, but no result was observed and no asdic contacts obtained, so *Eskimo* joined the fleet once it had passed the danger area. Whitworth suggested the submarine 'may have been a Norwegian'. *U48* had just arrived in Vestfjorden and had not been warned of British presence this far up the fjord. The sound of the explosions from *Eskimo*'s depth charges was magnified greatly in the narrow firth and Schultze and his crew had their biggest scare of the war. Still, they succeeded in sneaking away and, after recovering, brazenly fired a full salvo after *Warspite*, with no result.[119]

Vice Admiral Whitworth ordered the A/S screen to fall into two lines abreast *Warspite* behind the sweepers when closing Barøy, to be protected by the guns of the battleship should there be fire from the supposed shore batteries. No guns were observed and no mines encountered by the sweepers. Tension ran high and fire was almost opened on some Norwegians watching from a hilltop. Eventually Ofotfjorden opened ahead and with relief the A/S destroyers pulled away from the battleship and drew level with the minesweepers: *Punjabi*, *Bedouin* and *Eskimo* to starboard, *Cossack*, *Kimberley* and *Forester* to port. Following tradition, all ships were flying battle ensigns at the foremasts.

While passing Ramnes, *Warspite* had, unknown to all onboard, once again been at an acute risk. Staying submerged, Kapitänleutnant Sohler had managed to bring *U46* inside the screening destroyers. The battleship was only some six hundred metres away and it would be impossible to miss. Just as he was ready to fire, though, *U46* ran onto a shallow, exposing the bow and conning tower. Incredibly, none of the British ships saw the mishap, possibly as they were too busy keeping position and avoiding each other in the narrows. *U46* managed to back off the shallow with engines full astern, but by then Force B was out of reach. If Sohler had fired, and hit the battleship, it would have been a very different encounter for both parties.

Warspite's Swordfish aircraft was catapulted off at 11:52 off Barøy to scout ahead of the fleet and in particular to look for German vessels in the side fjords. During the ensuing operations this aircraft and its crew, Petty Officer Frederick 'Ben' Rice, Lieutenant Commander W 'Bruno' Brown (observer) and Leading Airman Maurice Pacey (gunner), were to give exceptional service in spite of difficult flying conditions, and show results way beyond normal expectations. 'I doubt', wrote Vice Admiral Whitworth later, 'if ever a ship-borne aircraft has been used to such good purpose.'[120] Ten minutes after its launch, the Swordfish reported sighting an enemy destroyer in the vicinity of Kjelde and a few minutes later, yet another further up the fjord.[121]

Warspite moving into Ofotfjorden, screened by destroyers. (HMS Cossack Association)

* * *

Koellner had been moving westwards in Ofotfjorden since early morning at less than ten knots, escorted by *Künne* some two hundred metres ahead. At 12:00, about three miles off Tårstad, a British aircraft was seen. Fire was opened, but the seaplane stayed at a distance. Shortly after, several destroyers were sighted from *Künne* off Barøy. Korvettenkapitän Kothe at first picked up speed and approached to investigate, but when he realised that they were undoubtedly British and there were nine of them, he turned *Künne* around and headed back while sending an alarm signal to Narvik.

For some reason, the sighting report from Rice and Brown was not forwarded from *Warspite*, and as only *Hero* was listening in on the aircraft frequency the British destroyers were at first not aware that an adversary was approaching. Only at 12:28 was *Künne* sighted and *Bedouin* opened fire some minutes later, followed by *Punjabi* and *Cossack*. *Icarus* also fired a few salvoes from her forward position leading the sweep. The shells all fell short as *Künne* had already turned, zigzagging up the fjord. The wind had freshened and an attempted smokescreen from *Künne* was swept away but Kothe made optimal use of remaining fog patches and rain showers, occasionally firing a few shots back. *Warspite* held her fire for the moment.

Receiving *Künne's* alarm signal at 12:20, Fregattenkapitän Bey was caught unprepared. He was expecting the attack to come in the afternoon and none of the Zerstörers had yet deployed in the side fjords as intended. The order to depart was given at once, but the U-boats were not properly alerted, in spite of the mutual agreement of two days earlier. *U64* received a signal to depart, but with no urgency; needing to repair a minor deficiency on the periscope, Kapitänleutnant Schulz remained at anchor in Herjangsfjorden. *U25* received no warning but, seeing the Swordfish, Korvettenkapitän Schütze gave the order to dive out of harm's way. Kapitänleutnant Knorr of *U51* believed that the alarm was for an air attack like the day before and, casting off from *Jan Wellem*, dived to the bottom of the harbour basin, where he remained.[122]

Meanwhile Rice and Brown continued their reconnaissance. After checking the side fjords, they passed Narvik at a distance before continuing into Herjangsfjorden where *U64* was discovered. The U-boat was at anchor, fifty metres from the jetty at Bjerkvik; without hesitation, Rice put his lumbering double-decker into a daunting dive-bombing attack. Two 50-kg A/S bombs were dropped from about one hundred metres on the unprepared boat. One bomb hit the bows, the second exploded close to the side of the boat between the bow and the conning tower. The combined effect of the bombs cracked the hull open and water poured in; *U64* started to sink. The majority of the crew managed to escape and swam through the icy water to be rescued by the Jägers at Bjerkvik, but eight men perished.[123] Pacey opened up with the rear gun as the Swordfish pulled away, striking the conning tower. One of the lookouts replied with his own gun, hitting the tailplane of the Swordfish, making her controls sluggish. The extent of the damage could not be seen, but Rice considered it safe to continue, provided he 'flew slowly and manoeuvred gently'. Brown agreed and they stayed in the air.[124] Returning towards Narvik at 12:30, they found that none of the Zerstörers had left the harbour and reported 'all fjords empty with the exception of Narvik itself', before setting course westward to regain visual contact with Force B.[125]

Koellner could not reach her designated position at Tårstad and Fregattenkapitän Schulze-Hinrichs decided to turn back towards Djupvik on the south side of the fjord instead. Here, he anchored his crippled destroyer about a kilometre from land, using the engines to keep the ship's broadside onto the fjord. Schulze-Hinrichs, now regretting the decision to take his torpedoes off, hoped he had not been sighted and that the British destroyers would emerge unsuspectingly behind the headland. Returning from Narvik, however, Rice and Brown could see *Koellner* from the air and signalled *Warspite*. *Koellner*'s masthead was also visible above the bank, so when *Bedouin*, *Punjabi* and *Eskimo* rounded the foreland at 13:05, it became a brief but violent encounter. The ships were so close (2,500–3,500 metres) that the pom-poms were used with devastating effect. None of the Tribals were hit, but the immobile *Koellner* was systematically pounded, silencing her guns one by one. She was soon ablaze and when *Warspite* rounded the naze and turned her 15-inch guns on the hapless Zerstörer, her fate was sealed. The large semi-armour-piercing (SAP) shells impacted like 'express train coaches', tearing through the lightly

Other destroyers were pulling ahead of the battleship. (National Archives, ADM 199/473)

armoured destroyer without exploding, but tilting her visibly over each time. At least one British torpedo hit the burning wreck, breaking the forecastle off and she sank rapidly. Thirty-one men perished. Norwegian forces detained most of the survivors, including Schulze-Hinrichs. Brave though the stance had been, it was completely in vain. *Koellner* was disposed of in passing and none of the British ships even slowed down.[126]

Meanwhile, Fregattenkapitän Bey hoisted the red standard 'Z' on *Zenker* and led *Arnim* out of Narvik at 12:45.[127] *Lüdemann* was already a mile ahead. *Thiele* followed a while later, but *Giese* had not worked up sufficient steam and stayed behind. Korvettenkapitän Kothe saw the other Zerstörers leaving the harbour and, turning *Künne* back on a westerly course, intensified the efforts to lay a smokescreen to hide them as long as possible. Coming out of the narrows, Force B spread out on a solid front ahead and abeam of *Warspite*, but had limited room to manoeuvre. The German destroyers, on the other hand, were in the wider part of the fjord and, zigzagging in broad sweeps, managed to use their broadsides to maximum effect in spite of being seriously outgunned. The Tribals each had eight 12-cm guns, as had *Kimberley*, but only the forward ones could bear. The smaller destroyers had single mountings and *Hero*, *Icarus* and *Foxhound* were in addition tied down by their sweeping gear and took little more than a symbolic part in the encounter at this stage.

Initial fire was exchanged at a distance of 15,000–17,000 metres and later varied from 10,000 to 21,500 metres, the destroyers generally firing at the shorter distances. The weather continued to clear, but smoke from the ships and their guns made observation and fire control difficult throughout. None of the Zerstörers were hit during the running battle but the British ships were straddled several times by a fire they felt to be 'uncomfortably good' and 'with considerable accuracy'. Between 13:20 and 13:47, *Cossack* counted sixteen near-misses. Her W/T aerial was shot away and splinters perforated the mess deck and no. 2 provision room, causing considerable flooding. The lack of direct hits by either side during the hour-long encounter is remarkable. Fog and smoke must take part of the blame, as must pure chance, but it is nevertheless an example of the quality of gunnery control at the time; hits by a destroyer on a moving target at anything over five thousand metres could largely be ascribed to chance.[128] Target holding was made difficult for the British destroyers by the German ships criss-crossing, but there is little doubt that the German gunnery control was superior that day. The Germans noted with awe that the shells from the four barrels of the Tribals' forward guns made a compact and deadly salvo. They were far less impressed by the gunnery control and tactical use of the British weapons, though, as few shells landed close. Commander McCoy, on the other hand, found the German fire 'accurate, especially for line' and, although no direct hits were suffered, splinters were continuously striking his ship.[129]

Fregattenkapitän Pönitz manoeuvred *Zenker* into position for a torpedo attack on *Warspite* but was driven off by the combined fire from the battleship and the screening destroyers of the northern group and the torpedoes missed.[130] Shortly after, Korvettenkapitän Rechel managed to take *Arnim* close enough to fire two triple salvoes of torpedoes. *Cossack*, *Kimberley* and *Forester* dodged these, although one running deep was spotted late and passed under the bridge of *Cossack* before any defensive action could be taken.[131]

Closing Narvik. (HMS *Cossack* Association)

After diving away from Rice's Swordfish, Schütze took *U25* back to periscope depth and soon saw the British destroyers approaching. Being nearest the northern group, he fired two torpedoes at *Cossack* and her consorts but, as was becoming the norm, with no results.[132] In the melee the torpedoes were not recognised as coming from a U-boat and no search was instigated. Returning to periscope depth, Schütze could now also see *Warspite*, but she was too far to the south. He decided the best he could do would be to proceed westward and wait for the return of the British ships at the Ramnes Narrows.[133]

Entering Ofotfjorden proper, *Hero* and *Foxhound* slowed down to recover their sweeping gear and dropped out of the battle for some time while *Warspite* and the others continued pushing the Zerstörers back. No tactical orders were given from McCoy or Whitworth at this stage and the destroyers acted more or less individually as their captains interpreted the situation.

The confined waters and the need to keep inside the destroyer screen meant that *Warspite*'s two forward 15-inch turrets would bear. On average she fired two rounds every minute but the smoke from the destroyer engagements disrupted fire control at intervals, as did her own smoke from firing straight ahead. No hits were scored in this part of the engagement, but the metre-long muzzle flames from the big guns and the howling of the heavy shells in almost flat trajectories low over the fjord made for a terrifying spectacle. The noise echoing between the cliffs and shells exploding on land caused avalanches of rocks and snow to tumble down the mountainsides.[134]

At 13:29 nine Swordfish aircraft from *Furious*, led by Captain AR Burch, were sighted from *Warspite*. The unwieldy double-deckers dived audaciously down on the German destroyers from just below the cloud base, dropping their bombs from 250–300 metres, but with little effect. Two hits were claimed but were in fact only near-misses on *Künne* and *Arnim*. The only ship sunk was the auxiliary *Kelt*. Two aircraft were shot down.[135]

The German ammunition reserves started to dwindle. In particular the Zerstörers that had taken part in the chase on 10 April were virtually empty. At 13:50 Bey broke off the engagement behind a series of smoke floats, ordering his ships into Rombaksfjorden;

at least the battleship could not follow them there. *Künne* missed the signal and Korvettenkapitän Kothe steered north into Herjangsfjorden where he set his ship aground near Bjerkvik as the magazines had been completely emptied. Even practice shells and star shells had been fired. Depth charges were prepared and, after the crew had been evacuated, exploded. *Künne* had received no damage during the preceding actions and she had no casualties. *Eskimo* and *Forester* followed *Künne* into Herjangsfjorden and Commander Micklethwait put a torpedo into the beached wreck for good measure, breaking off her stern.[136]

Meanwhile, *Giese* was at last ready and got under way. Korvettenkapitän Smidt knew from the radio signals that the other Zerstörers were heading for Rombaksfjorden and that he would be on his own against an overwhelming enemy. Still, he considered it 'the proper duty of an officer and soldier . . . to inflict as much damage on the enemy as possible. We had about ten minutes' worth of ammunition and all torpedoes, so we could fight. But I had no hope that we would ever reach port again.'

At the harbour mouth, *Giese*'s port engine seized, leaving her almost dead in the water. *Bedouin* and *Punjabi* approached, firing five torpedoes among them, which all missed in spite of the German being virtually motionless. *Giese*'s torpedoes were no more successful. Smidt focused his artillery on *Punjabi*, hitting her with six or seven 12.7-cm shells in short succession. Several exploded inside the ship, resulting in extensive damage. Two holes were opened in the starboard side just above the waterline, while subsequent hits wrecked the fire-control system, put most of the W/T out of action, severed steam pipes and started several fires. Seven men were killed and fourteen wounded. Commander Lean was forced to withdraw and at 14:00 sent the following signal to the flagship: 'Am damned sorry I have got to come out of it, main steam pipe and guns out of action.'[137]

After some ten minutes' frantic work in the engine rooms, *Giese*'s chief engineer could report to the bridge that engines were ready again and the Zerstörer left the harbour at her maximum speed, twelve knots. She ran straight into the guns of at least five of the British destroyers and had no chance at all. Commander McCoy took *Bedouin* to point-blank range and *Giese* was hit hard. Korvettenkapitän Smidt and his crew fought back defiantly, firing guns and torpedoes as long as they could. *Bedouin* received at least one shell, putting the A turret out of action. By 14:15, having taken more than twenty shell hits and possibly a torpedo, *Giese* was a blazing inferno adrift and out of control. Orders to abandon ship were given, but for eighty-three men it was too late. Two officers and nine ratings were picked up by *Foxhound*; two of the latter subsequently died. The rest of the survivors scrambled ashore as best they could through the freezing water.[138] The wreck of *Giese* drifted listing and burning in the fjord until it sank just after midnight.[139]

Roeder remained moored to Postkaia inside the harbour. At least one of the torpedoes intended for *Giese* passed into the harbour, exploding at the pier and barely missing *Roeder*. Her two forward guns brazenly opened fire when targets could be sighted through the harbour entrance, first *Punjabi* and *Bedouin* when they went after *Giese*, then even *Warspite* as she came into sight. Several shells fell close to the battleship, one hitting the bridge but doing only minor damage. The British at first believed the fire came from shore batteries and *Warspite* fired several round towards land without hitting much. A signal from Rice's Swordfish indicated there was a destroyer alongside the southern jetty inside the harbour and, once *Giese* was eliminated, *Cossack* and *Kimberley* moved in to

The burning wreck of *Giese*. (Author's collection)

investigate. Manoeuvring *Cossack* carefully between the wrecks of the sunken freighters, Commander Sherbrooke found *Roeder* at her moorings and opened fire from 2,500 metres. For the third time in less than a week, the harbour of Narvik became an inferno of noise, smoke, shells and metal fragments. *Cossack* scored with her second salvo but soon after took seven hits herself. Three holes were opened forward on the portside waterline, in addition to extensive splinter damage. Splinters holed the main steam pipe to no. 1 boiler room and there was much damage in no. 2 boiler room. A fire in the lower mess deck led to precautionary flooding of the forward magazine. The steering gear was thrown out of action and, unable to control her course, *Cossack* went hard aground on the beach at Ankenes between the wreck of *Bockenheim* and a small lighthouse.[140]

Roeder had taken hits too and she was on fire aft. Still, her two forward guns upheld their fire as long as there was ammunition left. The X and Y turrets of *Cossack* continued firing at the Zerstörer, even after grounding, and *Kimberley* came to her support from the harbour entrance, where she had held back. *Warspite* also opened fire on *Roeder* and she was hit by at least one of the huge shells. By this time, however, the twenty-five gunners that had remained onboard had abandoned ship and there were no casualties. When the fire from *Roeder* died down, *Foxhound* approached to investigate. A party of three had remained onboard and, seeing the destroyer nearing, they lit the fuses of the demolition charges and ran ashore. The charges exploded while *Foxhound* was less than fifty metres away, boarding party ready, and *Roeder* sank in the shallow water.

Onboard *Cossack*, nine men were dead and twenty-one wounded, two of whom later died. Damage-control parties were swiftly organised and went to work, repairing the damage to her engines and cleaning up the mess decks that had been badly damaged. Hawsers were brought onboard from *Kimberley* but *Cossack* was firmly stuck and would have to wait for the next high tide. That meant spending the night fifty metres off an enemy-occupied coastline, and Sherbrooke gave orders to start destroying codebooks and

Kimberley moving into Narvik harbour to assist *Cossack*, which has grounded between the freighters in the background off Ankenes. (National Archives, ADM 199/473)

Damage to *Cossack*. (HMS *Cossack* Association)

secret papers, just in case.[141] In addition, anything not considered necessary was thrown overboard to lighten the ship. During the afternoon, occasional rifle shots became a hazard for sailors moving about on deck and at one stage a field howitzer or heavy mortar was brought up and started firing at the destroyer from behind the town. A few well-aimed 12-cm shells silenced the latter while the pom-poms took care of the snipers and by nightfall things quietened down.[142]

Lüdemann, Zenker, Arnim and *Thiele* had a brief respite after entering Rombaksfjorden. None of the four had been hit so far but their position was rather hopeless and preparations were made to sink the ships should the situation worsen further. East of Narvik, Rombaksfjorden passes into the shallow Rombaksbotn through the narrow sound of Straumen, only 460 metres wide. From here there was no way out. *Zenker* and *Arnim* had both depleted their ammunition supply and could fight no more. They steered for the head of the fjord and were run onto the sandbanks there.

Thiele and *Lüdemann* still had ammunition left, including torpedoes, and prepared an ambush inside Straumen. As expected, *Warspite* did not follow into Rombaksfjorden. *Forester*, *Hero*, *Icarus* and *Eskimo* did, however, followed by *Bedouin*. Rice's ubiquitous Swordfish reported two and later three German destroyers at Rombaksbotn. The British could not see them, partly due to the foreland at Straumen and the sheer walls of the fjord, partly due to smoke from floats dropped into the fjord from the fleeing Zerstörers. Commander Micklethwait took *Eskimo* through the entrance at 14:45, followed by *Forester*. *Hero* halted in the sound, while *Bedouin* and *Icarus* remained outside.

Lüdemann opened fired from about three miles as the British came into sight. All remaining ammunition had been sent to the three aft guns. The remaining four torpedoes were fired blindly towards Straumen. One of these ran underneath *Forester*'s forecastle. Shortly after, one or two shells from *Eskimo* hit *Lüdemann* aft, destroying the D and E guns, killing most of their crews, and damaging the C gun. Korvettenkapitän Friedrichs decided he could do no more and headed for Rombaksbotn and grounded *Lüdemann* next to *Zenker* and *Arnim*. *Thiele* remained in position behind the smokescreen, starboard broadside towards Straumen. Her four operational guns were under local control as the fire-control room was inoperable. Korvettenkapitän Wolff had a few torpedoes left and was determined to delay the British as much as possible, giving his fellow captains time to demolish their ships and save their crews.[143]

When *Lüdemann* left, the British fire was shifted to *Thiele*. She was hit repeatedly, killing many and starting several fires, but remained stubbornly in position, fighting back. Micklethwait wished to finish this one off quickly in order to pursue the others

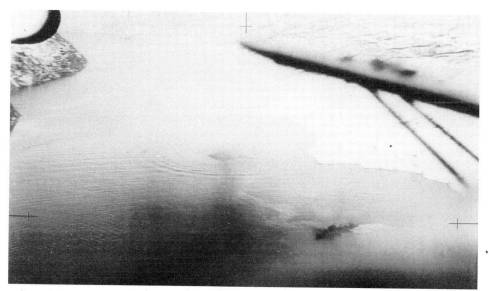

Eskimo (inside the circular wake) has just been hit by the torpedo from *Thiele*. *Forester* is temporarily pulling out of harm's way. The tailplane is from Rice's Swordfish, from which the photograph was taken. (National Archives, ADM 199/473)

up the fjord and he started to put *Eskimo* in position for a broadside torpedo attack. The fjord is narrow, and with slow speed ahead, he ordered astern on one of the screws to turn on the spot. Just then, three of the torpedoes fired from *Lüdemann* were observed and Micklethwait was obliged to order 'full ahead all' to avoid them. The starboard torpedo track was skirted by a matter of metres, but land was approaching fast and 'full astern' followed. *Eskimo* pulled up just a few metres from shore with every plate in the ship vibrating, but her luck was about to run out.[144] Oberleutnant Sommer, *Thiele's* torpedo officer, had received a free hand from Wolff and fired when he sighted the British destroyers coming through the narrows.[145] The torpedo ran on the surface and while it could probably have been avoided under normal circumstances, *Eskimo* could not respond to further rudder or engine orders. The very last German torpedo fired slammed into the destroyer just below no. 1 turret at 14:50 while everybody on the bridge watched helplessly. The impact took away everything below the forecastle deck and, when the spray settled, the remains of the bow, with the turret still attached was hanging vertically into the water. Fifteen men in the magazine, shell room and turret died immediately, while ten were wounded (two fatally).

Incredibly, no. 2 turret continued firing, almost uninterruptedly, even though its crew must have been badly shaken by the explosion. The aft turrets kept firing too, and *Eskimo's* last remaining torpedo was fired as Micklethwait gave orders to move back towards Straumen, stern first. The torpedo just missed *Thiele's* bow. Cables and anchors hanging down from the damaged section got stuck at Aspeneset while backing through the narrows, but the forecastle eventually broke off and the journey back towards Narvik could continue – stern first and very slowly. Superb damage control saved *Eskimo*: bulkheads were shored up, accessible leaks stopped and everything heavy jettisoned to save weight. Slowly the crippled destroyer came under control.[146] *Forester* was low on ammunition and assisted *Eskimo* out while *Hero* and *Icarus* headed through the narrows to finish the job.

Thiele was in a sorry state. Fires were blazing and on the bridge all but Korvettenkapitän Wolff had been killed or severely wounded. Some of the guns still fired intermittently, but there was hardly any ammunition left. To save the remainder of his crew, Wolff, himself wounded, slammed the engine telegraphs to 'full ahead' and set his ship aground at Sildvik. In all fourteen men were dead and twenty-eight wounded onboard *Thiele*.[147] Her last stand gave the crews from the three other Zerstörers in Rombaksbotn time to evacuate their ships in an orderly manner and in addition to the wounded, guns, food and other equipment were brought ashore. Seacocks were opened and depth charges set off. While their ships listed and sank into the sand of the delta, Fregattenkapitän Bey and his men scrambled up towards the railway some three hundred metres above the fjord, where they were later picked up and transported back to Narvik.

Hero and *Icarus* eventually entered Rombaksbotn, very carefully and very alert in case of another ambush. They found the three German Zerstörers abandoned by their crews. *Arnim* was already keeling over heavily, almost capsized, while *Zenker* turned over as the British approached. *Lüdemann* was still upright, her demolition charges not having detonated properly. Whalers with boarding parties were dispatched from both *Hero* and *Icarus* and, after a race, which the boat from *Hero* proudly won, she was boarded without problems.

The search parties found *Lüdemann* 'extremely smart and very well fitted out . . . more like a yacht than a destroyer on war service'. She had been hit several times, some of the SAP shells apparently passing right through without exploding. The engine room was flooded and there was a fire in the tiller flat. Fearing the ship might blow up at any time, a rapid search was made. Little of interest was found except for a pile of charred papers on the bridge, but numerous souvenirs were brought back in the form of binoculars, pendants, ensigns and other Nazi symbols. The boarding parties were recalled when McCoy arrived in *Bedouin* with orders from Whitworth to destroy the Zerstörers without delay – 'ram or board if necessary'. A badly wounded petty officer found on deck was brought along, but he later died. A torpedo from *Hero* finished *Lüdemann* off at 16:55 and shells were put into the other wrecks to ensure nothing more could be salvaged. The back of the Kriegsmarine's destroyer force had been broken.[148]

Close to 16:00, *Warspite* halted off Narvik harbour. Rice's Swordfish made a last sweep up Rombaksfjord, dropped her remaining bombs on the wreck of *Thiele* and landed on the fjord to be recovered after a day of sterling work.[149] There were no air attacks and, though a U-boat alarm temporarily raised some anxiety, an almost relaxed atmosphere soon spread through the ship. The weather had steadily improved and now for the first time in more than a week the sun broke through the clouds. Men were allowed on deck to enjoy the sunshine and admire the view of the snow-covered mountains and the crews enjoyed their post-action helpings of tea, eggs and corned beef 'in a state of high elation'.[150] A launch with doctors and medical personnel was sent to *Eskimo*.

At 17:42 Vice Admiral Whitworth reported to Admiral Forbes that all German destroyers and a U-boat had been sunk. He later wrote that at this stage he considered 'the landing of a party to occupy the town as the opposition had apparently been silenced'. But, he continued: 'With the force available only a small party could be landed, and to guard against the inevitable counter-attack, it would be necessary to keep the force

Final resting place of *Zenker* and *Arnim* in Rombaksbotn. (Author's collection)

concentrated, close to the water front, and to provide strong covering gunfire. In fact, I considered it would be necessary to keep *Warspite* off Narvik.' Eventually, in spite of persistent arguments from Commander Sherbrooke of *Cossack*, Whitworth arrived at the conclusion that he did not have sufficient forces available for a landing in Narvik 'in the midst of a force of not less than 2,000 professional German soldiers'. In fact, there were probably no more than a few hundred Gebirgjägers in Narvik proper on 13 April. The eight hundred or so Jägers available to Dietl at this part of his bridgehead had been spread around the whole perimeter, along the fjord and in the mountains and were desperately thin on the ground in most places. Many of the soldiers as well as the stranded sailors (of which most were poorly armed) had fled in fear of the shells hitting the town. At one stage there was almost a panic situation as soldiers and sailors scrambled along the railway line or into the mountains to escape the expected British landing.[151] Whitworth's considerations were probably affected by a report received from *Foxhound* that an officer rescued from *Giese* had informed his rescuers that 'the disposition of *Warspite* was not safe due to submarine', and when a dozen German aircraft appeared at around 18:00, the thought of lingering in the fjord became unattractive.[152]

Once he had made up his mind not to recapture the town, Whitworth saw no reason to 'keep *Warspite* stopped in the fjord, subject to submarine and air attack' and at 18:30 he ordered *Foxhound, Icarus, Forester, Punjabi* and *Hero* to gather on him and headed down the fjord.[153] On the way, the flotilla was attacked near Hamnes by *U25* but again no torpedoes exploded. *Foxhound* gained contact and counter-attacked. The throwers misfired, but the attack nevertheless forced the U-boat deep while the fleet passed.[154] Whitworth, who had no idea how many torpedoes he had narrowly escaped, believed the U-boat was trying to escape and wrote arrogantly: 'I have since come to the conclusion that a submarine navigating in the narrow waters of a fjord would find himself in a not very enviable position with anti-submarine destroyers overhead, and his desire to get out is therefore understandable.'[155]

Eskimo tied up to *Alster* at Skjelfjord. (Author's collection)

Ivanhoe and *Hostile*, which had joined Force B during the afternoon, were left behind with orders to look after *Eskimo* and *Cossack*, together with *Kimberley* and *Bedouin*. *Eskimo* transferred wounded and unessential men and, keeping seventy-six men onboard, started a slow, wobbly descent down Ofotfjorden, stern first, assisted by *Bedouin*.[156]

Towards midnight, *Warspite* and her screen was back at Narvik to collect wounded from the destroyers. These were transferred as the destroyers came alongside two at a time. Just before dawn on 14 April *Warspite* and the destroyers left Narvik for good. In total, twenty-eight British sailors died and fifty-five were wounded, but the number of dead would rise in the days to come. *Cossack* managed to get off the ground under her own power at 03:15. She could only move stern first due to the damage to her engines but joined the others at Skjelfjord in the afternoon of the next day, escorted by *Forester*, which had also taken hits but without being seriously damaged. *Ivanhoe* stopped at Ballangen to pick up the survivors from *Hardy* and the merchant seamen that had made it there.[157]

The Germans were greatly surprised that the British did not take the opportunity to recapture Narvik and took it to be a sign of indecisiveness and lack of resolve even when in overwhelming superiority. They were not impressed.[158] Neither was Churchill. At 21:15, an Admiralty signal urged Forbes to consider 'the occupation of Narvik to ensure unopposed landing later'. That this signal actually reached Whitworth is not clear from his report. Nevertheless, he knew that a regular expedition was on its way to Vågsfjord and, being of the opinion that this expedition should be diverted directly to Narvik, he signalled to the C-in-C and the Admiralty at 22:10:

> My impression is that enemy forces in Narvik were thoroughly frightened as a result of today's action, and that the presence of *Warspite* was the chief cause of this. I recommend that the town be occupied without delay by the main landing force. I intend to visit Narvik again tomorrow Sunday in order to maintain the moral effect of the presence of *Warspite*, and to accept the air and submarine menace involved by this course of action.[159]

There is little doubt that had Whitworth's proposal been adhered to, the situation in Norway would have been very different in the weeks to come; many lives would have been spared. Next morning, the Admiralty asked for an account of the German strength at Narvik, to which Whitworth answered at 10:27 on 14 April:

> Information from Norwegian sources estimates 1,500 to 2,000 troops in Narvik. German Naval Officer prisoner states that there are many more than this, but I think this statement was made with intent to deceive. He also states that guns on shore are being positioned with the main object of opposing a landing, but *Cossack*, aground in Narvik bay for 12 hours yesterday, was not seriously molested. I am convinced that Narvik can be taken by direct assault without fear of meeting serious opposition on landing. I consider that the main landing force need only be small, but it must have the support of Force B or one of similar composition. A special requirement being ships and destroyers with the best available AA armaments.[160]

The dead from *Norge* and *Eidsvold* that could be recovered were buried on 15 April. Kommandørkaptein Askim was still in hospital, so the acting first officer, Kaptein Sandved, was in charge. (Author's collection)

Among the Norwegians, disappointment and frustration spread when nothing happened and eventually the British ships left. Few could understand why the British did not land to secure the victory they had won.

Warspite remained in Vestfjorden in case a landing decision was made. In the morning of the 14th the battleship passed in front of *U48* but zigzagged just as Kapitänleutnant Schultze was about to fire, escaping damage once again. On 15 April it became clear that a landing in Narvik was not imminent and Whitworth met briefly with the C-in-C, changing over destroyers, before taking up a supportive position south-west of Skomvær Light, screened by *Hostile*, *Havock* and *Foxhound*.

Admiral Forbes, who had been operating off Lofoten during 14 April, shaped course for Scapa Flow in the evening of the 15th with *Rodney* and *Renown*, escorted by *Esk*, *Ivanhoe*, *Forester*, *Icarus* and *Kimberley*. *Valiant*, which had taken the troop convoy NP1 to Vågsfjord, sailed independently for Scapa Flow on the same day, screened by *Fearless*, *Griffin* and *Brazen*. *Furious* headed north to Tromsø to fuel, carrying out air reconnaissance of the northern approaches to Narvik on the way.

The loss of all ten destroyers of Kampfgruppe 1 was a terrible blow to the Kriegsmarine and revealed the extreme risks that had been taken during Operation Weserübung. The German Navy could ill afford to lose any ships at all and it is difficult to approve of Fregattenkapitän Bey's timid handling of matters after Kommodore Bonte's death, both in the morning of the 10th and in the days following. Two, three or even five of the destroyers might have escaped had he acted more decisively and been willing to accept some risk, if not on the night of 10/11 April, than at least the night of 11/12 April, when the weather closed in again. It is unbelievable that he did not even reconnoitre the possibility of escaping through Tjeldsundet. There were no British ships there at all, at least not on the first night. In open sea, the speed and firepower of the German destroyers would have given them significant advantages against most ships that the Royal Navy could muster at this time. What they would encounter further south would be anybody's guess, but could hardly have been worse than being trapped inside a narrow fjord with no way out, waiting for certain annihilation. Even a move to Trondheim, Bergen or Stavanger would have been preferable.

Individually, each Zerstörer fought courageously and with as much determination as the tactical situation allowed; their captains can only to a small extent be blamed for what happened. With the odd exception of Korvettenkapitän Friedrichs of *Lüdemann*, the surviving commanding officers eventually commanded destroyers or even flotillas again. It is more perplexing that Bey seems to have continued his career almost unconstrained. Hitler wanted to hear first hand what had happened in Narvik and sent a special courier to interview Dietl and other key officers in Narvik. He arrived in a Dornier Do24 flyingboat on 22 April. When he left on the 24th, Erich Bey and Leutnant zur See Gerd Alberts, Bey's adjutant, were onboard the Dornier.[161] Upon returning to Germany, Bey was confirmed as Kommodore Destroyers and C-in-C of the 6th Destroyer Flotilla (created from the surviving first-generation destroyers). Later, after being promoted to admiral, he also commanded the North Norway Naval Squadron. He perished onboard *Scharnhorst* at Nordkapp on Boxing Day 1943, an affair for which he must take most of the blame.

Narvik harbour was an unforgettable sight, littered with debris floating in the oily water. In Kleiva on the Fagernes side of the harbour and on the Ankenes side a large number of houses were damaged and several burned to the ground. The church was also hit by a 12-cm shell but did not catch fire. From the sunken vessels, bows, masts and smokestacks protruded above the water as grim memorials. Of the German ships only the indestructible *Jan Wellem* remained afloat. She had actually been grounded and the seacocks opened when Force B was reported approaching but when they left, she was still undamaged, so the cocks were closed and the tanker refloated more or less in the same condition as she had been when she arrived in the afternoon of the 8th. Large supplies of food, invaluable for the remaining German forces, were still onboard.

In Germany the affair at Narvik was pictured as a heroic defeat against impossible odds. Medals and badges were awarded to commemorate the events and the new Type-36A destroyers, coming into service shortly after, was unofficially termed the Narvik-class. It is perhaps difficult to see how the Nazi propaganda machine could have done otherwise, as defeats in general were not allowed, but it appears to be a general belief at the time both in the Kriegsmarine and among the public that the navy fought bravely at Narvik and lost only to a very superior enemy. Had Bey been reprimanded or not given the same positive attention as the others, this would have questioned the inevitability of the losses and pointed an accusing finger at incompetence in the leadership. This was not acceptable in the Third Reich.

The approximately 2,600 sailors that suddenly found themselves on land with nowhere to go were a welcome addition for Generalmajor Dietl. His forces were more than doubled and without them it would most likely not have been possible for him to hold his position in Narvik as he did. Most of the crews from the destroyers sunk in

The wreck of *Thiele*. Parts of it are still there. (Author's collection)

Rombaksbotn were set up in a regiment under the command of Fregattenkapitän Berger and used to secure the railway to Sweden. Naval engineering personnel were tasked with maintaining the railway line and its rolling stock. Korvettenkapitän Kothe and the men from *Künne* were placed under the command of Oberst Windisch and 139th Regiment, together with Erdmenger and the survivors from *Heidkamp*. The rest of the sailors were gathered in Marinestammabteilung Narvik for guard and security tasks in the city proper. Some of them adapted so well to life on land that they also took part in the fighting. The 'naval' soldiers were equipped with whatever guns and uniforms were available, including Norwegian equipment from Elvegårdsmoen.[162]

Generalmajor Dietl and his troops faced an extended battle for Narvik and its surroundings, but that is a story for another day.

No Room For Mistakes[1]

Submarine Alert

Vice Admiral (Submarines), VA(S), Max Horton focused the majority of his boats in the North Sea, Skagerrak and Kattegat during the first months of 1940. This created great concern in the German Navy and diverted significant resources from other tasks to anti-submarine patrols. As one of a few in the British naval command, Horton was convinced Allied intervention in Norway would bring immediate German countermeasures and during March he started concentrating his boats along the Norwegian coast. Having been informed of Operation Wilfred, he summoned his flotilla commanders to a meeting in London on 1 April. Orders were given for all available submarines to be at sea by dawn on the 5th, covering the exits from the Bight, Kattegat and Skagerrak as well as likely German landing points in southern Norway.

At the time of the conference, *Triton* and *Swordfish* were off Skagen and *Trident* off Arendal. During the next few days, *Sealion*, *Sunfish*, *Unity* and the Polish *Orzel* took to sea to join them. *Narwhal* also sailed on 2 April to lay some fifty mines north-west of Helgoland, where there was believed to be an opening in the German minefield. In the evening of the 4th, after Operation Wilfred had been postponed to 8 April, Horton moved some of the boats deeper into the sea lanes; *Orzel* east of Lindesnes, *Trident* off Larvik, *Sunfish*, *Triton* and *Sealion* into the Kattegat. The boats received orders not to compromise their position by intercepting merchant vessels, but to focus on warships.

By midday on 7 April, on receiving information that a German fleet was at sea, Horton had no doubts that a German intervention was developing. He ordered all remaining boats to sea with utmost despatch, bringing the number of submarines at sea up to twenty, including two French boats. The next day, he discussed his dispositions with the Admiralty and to his surprise received instructions to withdraw the boats off Norway and redeploy them to a line in the North Sea, south of Stavanger, intercepting German naval forces heading home to bases in the Helgoland Bight. Before these instructions could be put into force, however, reports were received from Oslo that the German freighter *Rio de Janeiro* had been sunk east of Kristiansand and that German soldiers were being rescued. Horton took this to mean he had been right all along and made only minor adjustments to his dispositions, instead of the major realignment directed by the Admiralty.

Horton's measures were so effective that some fifteen German transports and supply ships were sunk or severely damaged between 8 and 29 April, in addition to half a dozen warships. This caused a crisis in the OKW and the plans for moving troops and supplies to south and west Norway had to be completely revised.[2]

Vice Admiral Horton knew from his own experiences in the Baltic in 1914/15 the navigational hazards of the eastern Skagerrak and Kattegat. The shallow waters and narrow straits greatly favour the A/S patrols and at times, the water is so still that the shadow of the submerged submarine can be seen from the air. The slightest oil slick or feather of a periscope or antenna may give the boat away over long distances. Tides are challenging and an irregular flow of fresh water from the Baltic causes rapid changes in the density of the water. Boats in perfect trim may suddenly find themselves breaking surface when entering an area of increased salinity or alternatively dip periscope and head for the bottom if entering a pocket of fresh water. Lieutenant Commander Bryant of *Sealion* wrote in his diary on 9 April:

> A most unpleasant day. Glassy calm, surrounded by fishing boats, and enemy aircraft being sighted continually flying low and close. It was not possible to go deep (owing to density) and continual action to avoid being trawled up was required. Boat was driven slow, shafts in series, at 34 feet . . . The boat could not be driven below 37 feet without flooding or speeding up.[3]

At 04:24 on 9 April, the British Admiralty issued a signal indicating that ports in south and west Norway were being invaded by German naval forces. On receiving this information, Horton ordered *Thistle* to patrol off Stavanger, while *Truant* was sent to the entrance of Oslofjord. Until this time, the submarine captains had only been allowed to attack 'enemy warships and transports'. Identifying which of the large numbers of merchant ships in the Kattegat and Skagerrak were German or indeed transports was no easy task, especially as escorts and air patrols precluded any attempt at surface interception. In the late morning of 9 April the War Cabinet, after heavy pressure from VA(S), approved that all German merchant vessels in the Skagerrak east of 8°E, or east of the German declared area, could be treated as warships and sunk without warning. This order was forwarded to all boats at 13:24.

While the signal was decoded onboard *Sunfish*, Lieutenant Commander Jack Slaughter was turning his periscope onto the 7,129-ton *Amasis*, outside Swedish territorial waters off Lysekil. 'Just as the sights came on', he later wrote in his report, 'the last part of VA(S)'s 1324/9 was read out to me, so I fired.' One torpedo hit, and the ship sank, opening a series of successful actions by the Allied submarines.[4]

Looking for submarines. The A/A measures were significantly heightened onboard the German transports (T Eggan collection)

All in Good Time

Kapitän zur See Rieve's orders after the seizure of Kristiansand were rather loose, except that he should return to Kiel as soon as possible. As had been clearly demonstrated, Kristiansand was well within reach of British bombers and the longer he stayed the more likely an attack would be. Having completed the disembarkation of the remaining troops and equipment in the afternoon, Rieve decided his task was concluded and there was no reason to linger any longer. He weighed anchor and *Karlsruhe* left with the three torpedo boats at 18:00. Offshore, *Greif, Luchs* and *Seeadler* took up screening positions around the cruiser, which was zigzagging at twenty-one knots.[5]

The 1,500-ton T-class submarine *Truant*, under the command of 34-year-old Lieutenant Commander Christopher Hutchinson, was loitering off southern Norway in the morning of the 9th. She had left Rosyth three days earlier but the fog in the Skagerrak had made things difficult and though several ships had been heard, none had been identified with sufficient certainty to justify an attack. During the morning of 9 April, the fog lifted and Hutchinson settled his boat at periscope depth. Explosions were heard at times and 'Dornier' aircrafts sighted above on several occasions during the day. Something seemed to be going on. At 17:23 three torpedo boats were sighted coming from the north-west, steering south at an estimated twenty-two knots. An attack was commenced, but discontinued when the ships were identified as 'Norwegian *Sleipner*-class destroyers'. This was definitely wrong; the only two such ships in the area, *Gyller* and *Odin*, at this time were in Kristiansand harbour, under German control. The vessels were most certainly Korvettenkapitän Thoma's three minesweepers *M2, M9* and *M13* heading for home and Hutchinson lost a good target.

HMS *Truant*. A T-class submarine launched in May 1939, the boat displaced 1,090 tons on the surface and 1,575 tons submerged. Six internal torpedo tubes faced forward, four external tubes faced aft; there were six reload torpedoes. She was capable of fifteen knots with her two diesel engines on the surface and nine knots below on electric motors. The normal crew was fifty-nine men. (Imperial War Museum FL 22602)

On the other hand, the misidentification kept *Truant* concealed for larger prey. At 18:33, a cruiser was sighted low on the northern horizon, steering south-south-east and screened by '3 *Maas* destroyers'.[6] Range was 4,500 metres and decreasing; *Truant* was in an excellent attack position. A sudden easterly course alteration increased the relative speed of the cruiser, but all four ships were within range and in an almost unbroken line. At 18:56 Hutchinson fired a full bow salvo of ten torpedoes at six-second intervals, at what was now estimated to be 3,500 metres. The two first torpedoes were set to run at ten feet, the next six at twelve feet and the last two at eight feet. The shallower setting was intended to try to catch the 'destroyers' forward and aft of the cruiser, respectively. In order to avoid breaking surface from the loss of the weight of such a large salvo, *Truant* was taken down as soon as firing commenced. About three minutes later, a loud explosion was followed by another and then a third, accompanied by the sound of 'rending metal'. Hutchinson took *Truant* to periscope depth and sighted *Luchs* approaching at high speed. She had narrowly escaped the torpedoes through emergency manoeuvring and was now combing down the tracks for retribution. Two depth charges exploded 'dead close' while the boat was going deep. The hunt was on.

For the next four and a half hours, *Truant* was chased by the torpedo boats, taking turns between assisting the cruiser. Thirty-one depth charges were counted, 'nearly all of them unpleasantly close', though not as close as the first two; possibly because *Truant* went deeper than anticipated, below 100 metres. All unnecessary machinery, including the Sperry gyrocompass, were shut down and lights and cooling switched off to save the batteries. A constant speed of 3.5 knots was maintained to keep trim and steering while courses were changed to keep the stern towards the adversary considered being the most dangerous. German anti-submarine tactics were not well known at the time, and Hutchinson devotes a paragraph in the logbook to his observations:

> After each attack, destroyers stopped to listen, used echo-sounding, but appeared not to transmit on any super-sonic set. They appeared to drop some form of device which made a sound like gravel dropping on the hull of the submarine. A/S conditions were very good and enemy appeared to be uncomfortably efficient at hunting and most persistent. I hoped forlornly that they would retire after dark on more important business.[7]

The torpedo boats were not easily shaken off. During the first attack, the explosions had caused the forward hatch to open, admitting water into the boat despite being fully closed. The trim of the submarine was affected, but the mechanism was fortunately not damaged and it was possible to close the hatch again before any serious danger developed. Adding to the problems, both hydroplanes jammed and, though later freed, had to be operated on local control. The magnetic compasses also became unserviceable and Hutchison was moving around blindly for a while. Later explosions made the aft trim tank burst, increasing the leaks. Numerous short-circuits affected the electrical system and sparks flew from the main motor switch gear. The high-pressure air system developed leaks too, increasing the pressure inside the hull and making breathing in the foul air very uncomfortable. One set of exploding depth charges jarred open the main engine cooling-water inlet valves, resulting in flooding aft and sent the bows up fifteen degrees. *Truant* was still under control, though, and level trim was not attempted, as using the pump would be noisy and there was a risk that oily water might reach the surface, revealing her location.

At 21:45 things had been quiet for some time and Hutchinson decided to risk going up for a look. On the way up, more explosions were heard, although not as close as before and *Truant* was taken down to 100 metres again. In all likelihood, these explosions were those of *Greif*'s torpedoes sinking the crippled cruiser. Things remained quiet after this and about an hour later when the batteries were running low and the air too foul to stand, Hutchison ordered his submarine to rise again; very slowly and quietly. *Truant* finally surfaced at 23:25, having been submerged for nineteen hours. Everything was quiet and nothing was seen of the enemy. All hatches were opened and the engines started to charge the batteries. None of the compasses worked, and the sky was overcast so it was difficult to know which way to go to clear the area. Assuming the direction of the wind had not changed much since last night, Hutchinson steered downwind, hoping this to be towards open waters. Eventually, the sky cleared sufficiently for his pilot to identify enough stars for a south-westerly course to be set for home. The crew was exhausted, and the boat damaged so Hutchinson informed Submarine Command of the attack and that he was returning to Rosyth in a signal at 01:12 on 10 April. Most of the damage was made good during the day and in an updated signal, Hutchinson asked if he should remain on patrol. The answer from Vice Admiral Horton was swift and clear: 'All in good time. I want to see you first.'[8]

Onboard *Karlsruhe*, four torpedo tracks were observed to starboard at 18:58. Kapitän Rieve immediately ordered 'both engines full ahead' and 'hard-a-port', but to no avail. In spite of three explosions being recorded by *Truant*, it appears that only one torpedo impacted on the starboard side near the bulkhead between the auxiliary machine room and the cruising turbine room, compartments V/VI. Both engines and steering fell out and the cruiser stopped, listing twelve degrees. The situation was serious and more so when the first officer, Korvettenkapitän Duwel, reported all pumps out of action. The compartments filled fast and water and oil was soon up to the floor plates of the main rudder engine room and no. 1 generator room, coming through cracks in the bulkheads. *Karlsruhe* was apparently sinking, and the survivors from below deck were evacuated. *Luchs* and *Seeadler* were ordered alongside to take the crew off, after which they set course for Kiel. Kapitän Rieve left his ship as the last man at 20:10, embarking *Greif*, which was ordered to remain. After a while, it was decided to sink the cruiser and a torpedo was fired from *Greif*. *Karlsruhe*'s forecastle was blown off but she remained afloat and it took another torpedo before she finally slid below, bow first, at 21:42.

The loss of the valuable cruiser to a single torpedo close to land was disconcerting to the SKL and Rieve was criticised for not attempting to take her in tow by the torpedo boats or call the minesweepers of Korvettenkapitän Thoma back to assist. Konteradmiral Schmundt pointed to the fact that in spite of being in submarine-infested waters, the ship had neither been fully closed up nor at action stations. He recognised that the condition of the ship had been serious but it should not have been hopeless under the existing weather conditions. Rieve maintained that based on the reports from Korvettenkapitän Duwel, the ship had been sinking and everything possible had been done, considering the low state of training of the ship's young company. Still, she took two more torpedoes before going down and perhaps a more energetic damage control might have saved her. Rieve was made Commander of the Sea Defences of the Oslofjord and took office in Horten around 25 April. In August he was promoted to Konteradmiral and appointed Chief of Staff at the North Sea Naval Command in Wilhelmshaven. His replacement in Horten was Kapitän Ruhfus of *Königsberg*.[9]

Holding Water

After finally reaching Oslo at 08:45 in the morning of 10 April, Kapitän Thiele was in a hurry to leave again and return to Germany as soon as possible. The risk of interference by the Royal Navy in the Oslofjord or the Skagerrak was considered low but British aircraft could appear at any time. The main reason for the rush, however, was the need to reach a yard where the auxiliary engine, which had led *Lützow* to Oslo in the first place, could be repaired, as well as the newly inflicted damage from the guns at Kopås. Merchant warfare in the Atlantic remained the raison d'être for the 'pocket battleship' and Thiele knew that every week passing would shorten the length of the nights in the northern waters, and thus his chances for a lucky breakout.

Emden and the R-boats were left behind while *Lützow* and *Möwe* headed back down the fjord around 15:00. *Albatros* and *Kondor* were already operating in the outer reaches of the fjord and would join later. Kapitänleutnant von Schnurbein and his men were picked up at Drøbak and replaced with survivors from *Blücher*. Further men from *Blücher* were landed at Horten. In the meantime, news came in of *Albatros* being in trouble, having run aground off Hvaler.[10]

The German sources are somewhat vague as to what actually happened when *Albatros* went aground. It appears she was screening the transport *Curityba*, trying to get through to Oslo, while at the same time landing additional men at Rauøy. *Kondor* was meanwhile closing Bolærne, still in Norwegian hands, and received fire from the guns there. To avoid similar attention, Kapitänleutnant Strelow took *Albatros* east of Rauøy. Unknown to him and the other men on the bridge of the torpedo boat, they were heading for the shoal Gyren where a sea mark had been broken off by the ice a few weeks earlier. Around 13:50, while at some twenty knots, breakers were observed ahead. Strelow ordered five knots, but before this took effect, *Albatros* hit the rock hard.

Almost running right over the shoal, she settled with her stern well above water, heeling sharply. At least one bunker tank was opened to the sea while oil and water poured into the turbine and boiler rooms. The boilers were hastily shut down and the rooms evacuated. Parts of the electrical systems fell out immediately and the rest was short-circuited within minutes. Several fires were ignited and as both steam and power had been lost, they could not be put out. Heavy smoke forced the crew on deck and the flames spread, augmented by multiple explosions. The auxiliary *V707* came alongside and tried to help extinguish the flames but it was in vain and eventually the crew were evacuated along with valuable equipment and secret papers.[11]

On receiving the news of *Albatros*'s grounding, Kapitän zur See Thiele detached *Möwe* to stay with *Kondor* in the Oslofjord while *Lützow* continued alone, in spite of several submarine alerts in the Kattegat. Thiele reckoned twenty-four knots – the

Albatros aground on the shoal Gyren, east of Rauøy. (E Skjold collection)

maximum that *Lützow* could make – would be sufficient for a safe trip home and he was not overly worried at losing his escort. Leaving Oslofjord behind, the night was clear and starry with good visibility, moderate seas and a Force 4 north-easterly wind. Signals filed during the previous days put most of the submarine contacts near the Swedish coast, and Thiele steered a westerly track in large zigzags. The general course was 138°, heading towards the gap between Skagen and the Paternoster Skerries. An hour after midnight German time, the ship's DeTe-Gerät radar picked up a contact ahead, fine on the starboard bow, at a range of 15,000 metres. The echo was small and taken to be a fishing vessel, but Thiele gave port rudder to give it a wide berth. The distance increased, and when the radar reported the echo lost, starboard rudder was ordered to get back onto the main course.[12]

Spearfish of the 6th Submarine Flotilla had reached her designated patrol area in the Kattegat in the morning of 7 April. There was extensive activity in the area, both in the air and at sea, and 8 and 9 April were largely spent hiding below surface. On the 10th *Spearfish* was chased by a group of escorts and A/S trawlers for most of the afternoon. Sixty-six depth charges were counted, causing high-pressure leaks and damage to hydrophones and periscope. The leaks increased the pressure inside the submarine and together with the foul air made the crew exhausted and dizzy. At 23:30 the hunters had finally been shaken off and Lieutenant Commander John Forbes could bring his boat to the surface after having been submerged for more than twenty hours.

About an hour later, the first lieutenant sighted the bow wave of a large ship on the starboard quarter at about three thousand metres. Forbes believed it might be one of the escorts again and altered course to port to put the boat stern-on to avoid detection. Some minutes later, the vessel was seen to be very large and, later still, identified as the heavy cruiser *Admiral Scheer*.[13] The torpedoes were set to run at four to six metres and, with both engines stopped, Forbes fired six torpedoes from the conning tower by eye while still on the surface. In spite of a very dark night, conditions were otherwise good and he risked a long-distance shot. Immediately after firing, *Spearfish* was turned on a westerly course, still on the surface, and a sighting report was sent to Submarine Command. After some five minutes, a large explosion was heard from the direction of the target.[14]

When Thiele gave the order to bring *Lützow* back on her main course, Forbes's torpedoes were underway, and she almost escaped. *Lützow* was still turning on starboard rudder when at 01:29 GeT, a tremendous impact shook the cruiser aft. Nothing was seen prior to the hit. Just after, two or three torpedo tracks were reported at an acute angle off the port side. The rudder was jammed at twenty degrees to starboard and the cruiser kept turning while speed was reduced. Nobody in compartment II answered the telephone or the rudder indicator and it was obvious that there was significant damage. Several of the compartments aft started to flood and *Lützow* settled by the stern with a list to port. Thiele gave orders for emergency steering to be rigged, but the rudder room could not be accessed and attempts to steer by the propellers had no effect; both propellers were lost.[15]

At 01:55 an urgent signal was dispatched to Group East giving the estimated position, adding: 'Need immediate tug assistance,' followed some ten minutes later by: 'Probable torpedo hit aft. Engines are OK. Rudder not operational. Submarine protection is required.' And later still: 'My position is ten miles off Skagen. Ship is unmanoeuvrable. Holding water. Both propellers lost.'

Eventually, the flooding was stemmed in compartment IV, but it was clear that the three after compartments were gone, including the aft magazines. With no propulsion or steering, *Lützow* drifted at about two knots south-westward towards Skagen, broadside to the sea. Further submarine attacks were to be expected and in the good visibility the immobilised ship would be a sitting duck. A sharp anti-submarine watch was set and all secondary guns manned. Thiele also ordered all crewmembers to don lifebelts and the lower decks to be evacuated, except by those assigned to the damage-control parties. Boats were swung out and made ready for launching. The aft turret was ordered to jettison all ammunition to help lighten the stern. By 03:00 the ship's trim had been improved by pumping oil, and the main part of the hull was almost upright, even if the after deck was at an angle, partly under water.

At 03:08 Oberleutnant Vogler was sent off in a motor cutter towards Skagen to summon assistance from tugs and escort vessels. At about the same time, 17th A/S Flotilla, 19th Minesweeping Flotilla and 2nd S-Boat Flotilla were ordered by Group East to gather on the cruiser while the torpedo boats *Jaguar* and *Falke* were under way from Kristiansand, *Greif*, *Luchs* and *Seeadler* from Kiel and *Möwe* and *Kondor* from the Oslofjord.[16] Meanwhile, *Lützow*'s launch was set on the water with a crate of demolition charges and orders to circle the cruiser, throwing one or two in the water every now and then, passing off as depth charges, to scare further submarines away.

Between 04:30 and 05:00 the trawlers and minesweepers arrived and as many as possible of the ship's company were transferred to these, which thereafter took up screening positions. A temporary tow was rigged from three of the minesweepers (*M1903*, *M1907* and *M1908*) to have a minimum of steering and keep the bow to the wind. *Möwe*, which arrived around 08:20, took charge ahead of the tow. Not long after Oberleutnant Vogler returned from Skagen. He had not found any tugs but brought numerous fishing vessels and the Skagen lifeboat should an evacuation become necessary. At dawn, a standing

Damage to *Lützow* was severe. (Bundesarchiv Koblenz)

patrol of He115 aircraft was established, reducing the danger of further submarine attacks significantly. The RAF mercifully stayed away.

The minesweepers found handling of the cruiser difficult as the wind and sea were building, but at in the afternoon the heavy tugs *Wotan* and *Seeteufel* arrived from Kiel to take over the job. When the rest of the torpedo boats arrived, taking up a proper anti-submarine station, it seemed as if it might be possible to save *Lützow* after all. Still, Thiele ordered all unnecessary men off, including most of the gun crews now that a proper escort was in place. Some five hundred men were landed at Fredrikshavn in Denmark, from where they were ingloriously sent home by train. Several of the men had sailed with *Lützow* for years and pleaded to be allowed to stay onboard during her time of plight, but Thiele had no time for sentiments. He was trying to save his ship, so off they went.

It was feared for a while that the increasing sea might break off the stern altogether, as it only appeared to be attached to the rest of the ship by the two drive shafts, but the sea calmed somewhat and the structure held. *Lützow* had eventually some 1,300 tonnes of seawater below decks when the flooding was checked. This and the angled stern gave her a twelve-metres draught astern, which became a huge problem because the Danish inland waterways are in some places rather shallow. On the other hand, Thiele preferred to risk grounding on a sandbank rather than having his ship sink in deeper water. Progress down Kattegat was slow. *Lützow* grounded on several occasions, but careful manoeuvring by the tugs and flooding of the bow to lift the stern freed her each time. Eventually at 20:22 on 14 April, *Lützow* made safe at the Deutsche Werke yard at Kiel.

Fifteen men died when the torpedo struck and their remains were buried in Kiel with full military honours. The repairs of the cruiser would last well into 1941. Kapitän 'Curry' Thiele left his ship and was within a few weeks posted to Norway as Naval Commander, Trondheim. [17]

Lützow safe at the Deutsche Werke yard at Kiel. She would remain there well into 1941.
(Bundesarchiv Koblenz)

Damned Un-English Vessels[18]

During the morning of 9 April, a signal was made for Lieutenant Commander Haselfoot of *Thistle* to enter Stavanger harbour at his discretion and attack German ships there.[19] Haselfoot reported back just after midday that he was steering for the fjord, expecting to enter the harbour the following evening, air activity permitting. It was added that *Thistle* had only two torpedoes left, as that same afternoon a salvo of six had been fired at a U-boat on the surface off Skudeneshavn, with unconfirmed result. This was the last ever heard from *Thistle* and her fate remained a mystery until after the war. Oberleutnant Hinsch of *U4* had not appreciated being attacked at all. Escaping *Thistle's* torpedoes, the nearest only ten metres away, he had stalked her until, in a favourable position off Karmøy, he was able to return the attention in the early hours of the 10th. The first torpedo missed from six hundred metres, but Hinsch repositioned his boat and at 02:13 fired a second torpedo that hit the target amidships. The British crew were apparently caught off guard and earned the dubious distinction of becoming the first Allied submarine to be sunk by a U-boat.[20]

The bulk of the troops and supplies to secure the immediate sustainability of Operation Weserübung were to come through Oslo in a series of transport convoys following the initial landing. There had already been a significant attrition of the first transport group, heading for the invasion ports outside Oslo. The following groups, bringing in more than a hundred thousand troops and their equipment, would go to Oslo only, partly because

HMS *Thistle* was torpedoed by *U4*, earning the dubious distinction of becoming the first Allied submarine to be sunk by a U-boat. (P A Vicary)

15th Vorpost Flottille. Auxiliaries like these were well suited for A/A work and did sterling service in the Kattegat and Skagerrak. (E Skjold collection)

the sea lanes further west were under total British dominance, partly because the main breakout towards the other bridgeheads was planned to come from the Oslo region.

This operation turned out to be not quite as easy as expected, mainly due to the one factor the Kriegsmarine had not fully prepared for: British submarines. Though not crippling, the attrition would be high enough for the set-up to be modified so that as many as possible were transported by air, while supplies and the rest of the troops were shuttled between northern Denmark and southern Oslofjord.

On 10 April the Admiralty informed C-in-C and VA(S) that they had decided '. . . interference with communications in southern areas must be left mainly to submarines, air and mining, aided by intermittent sweeps when forces allow.'[21] This was a formidable upgrade of the strategic significance of the Submarine Arm – probably not fully recognised at the time – creating an undreamt-of opportunity for VA(S) and his submarines.

At 16:35 on the 10th, *Triton* was patrolling in Kattegat, when a large convoy of some fifteen ships steering north was sighted off Gothenburg, just outside Swedish territory. This was the second transport group, 2.Seetransportstaffel, heading for Oslo.[22] The sea was 'glassy calm' and the periscope had to be used sparingly to avoid detection. At 17:26 the boat was in position and Lieutenant Commander Fowle-Pizey fired a right-angle shot of six torpedoes from about two thousand metres. Three ships were hit: the 5,200-ton *Friedenau*, the 3,600-ton *Wigbert* and the escort *V1507* (*Rau VI*). Total chaos broke out in the convoy. There had been no precautionary instructions and for a while it was every ship for itself. Some stopped to pick up survivors whereas others continued. Eventually, the transports were ushered along, while a few of the escorts stayed behind to pick up the remaining survivors. *Wigbert* sank on an even keel within fifteen to twenty minutes, while *Friedenau* remained for a while longer, floating on her forecastle. From *Fridenau* 384 officers and men from IR 340 perished and a similar number of men of IR 345 were lost from *Wigbert*. Nineteen men went down with *V1507*; 800 men were rescued; many by a Swedish destroyer that came to assist. The counter-attack on *Triton* was severe (seventy-eight charges) but inaccurate, and Lieutenant Commander Fowle-Pizey was able to get his submarine safely away within an hour.[23]

Survivors from *Friedenau*, *Wigbert* and *V1507* being rescued in the afternoon of 10 April. Whaler left is *V1501*, steamer background right is *Espana*.(Author's collection).

Friedenau sinking.
(Author's collection)

A third ship of this convoy, the 2,500-ton *Antares* was stalked by *Sunfish* later in the evening and sunk off Lysekil. This caused 'considerable activity overhead', but no counter-attacks developed and *Sunfish* slipped away to charge her batteries. Later still, *Trident* and *Orzel* both missed in further attempts at the remaining ships of the convoy. The surviving transports reached Oslo on 12 April, followed by the ships of the third transport group, 3.Seetransportstaffel, a few days later. After this, most of the larger ships were sent to Norway in small, heavily escorted groups. Troops that could not be accommodated by aircraft were taken by train to Denmark and shipped across from Frederikshavn or Aalborg to Larvik or Oslo, about three thousand men per day.

Also on the 10th, *Tarpon* attacked what turned to be the Q-ship *Schürbeck* (*Schiff 40*) west of Jutland. The torpedoes missed and in return *Schürbeck*, assisted by the minesweeper *M6*, chased the submarine, dropping depth charges for about four hours. *Tarpon* was never heard from again and was presumably lost with all hands in the counter-attack.[24]

Meanwhile, the War Cabinet agreed to extend the freedom of action for the submarines further, and at 19:56 on 11 April, VA(S) submitted a signal to his captains that any ships, merchant or otherwise, under way within ten miles of the Norwegian coast, south of 61°N, and anywhere east of 6°E, could to be attacked on sight, adding, 'You are all doing magnificent work.' By now, however, air and surface activity in the Kattegat and Skagerrak had increased considerably and it was becoming difficult to find safe areas in which to charge batteries during the shortening periods of darkness. Still, *Triad* sank the German transport *Ionia* at the mouth of the Oslofjord while *Sealion* sank *August Leonhardt* off Anholt on the 11th.[25]

The next day, following reports of German capital ships west of Lindesnes, Horton positioned *Severn*, *Clyde*, *Trident*, *Spearfish*, *Sunfish* and *Snapper* to cover the entrance to the Kattegat, between Lindesnes and Skagen, while *Shark* and *Seawolf* covered the German Bight. Only the tanker *Moonsund* was intercepted. Lieutenant Commander King of *Snapper* wrote in his report:

At 03:40, as dawn was breaking, a small steamer was sighted to the north-eastwards, making for the northward. As it was getting light and aircraft were expected, it was desired to sink her quickly and two torpedoes were fired on a broad track. These missed astern. It was then seen that the steamer was smaller and nearer than at first estimated and that torpedoes were wasted on such a target as she could be chased and brought to. *Snapper* proceeded to chase and overhaul the steamer, which zigzagged and took no notice of the signal to heave to . . . After a chase of seven miles, she was brought to with a shot across the bows. She then broke the German Merchant Flag. The order was shouted to abandon ship and the reply was heard, 'as you wish'. No efforts appeared to be made to get the boats out. The Lewis Gun was then fired over the masts but produced no results. One round of HE was then fired into the forepeak and the cargo of aviation spirit burst into flames and the crew jumped over the side. Six out of the seven were picked up; the seventh could not be seen. Two of these subsequently died of shock and exposure. The remaining four, including the Captain, kept in good heart for the rest of the patrol.[26]

Gneisenau, *Scharnhorst* and *Hipper* were not encountered. They slipped behind the declared area and vanished into German ports in spite of more than a dozen boats looking for them. Intense tracking by the B-dienst probably located some of the submarines so they could be chased deep while serendipity and the poor weather did the rest. On 12 April *Triton* and *Trident* started back for Rosyth while *Orzel* moved east and *Shark* and *Seawolf* moved north and into the Skagerrak.

At first, the British submarine captains frequently used a tactic of sneaking in behind the German screen to attack the convoy on a broad track pushed in from abaft the screen. The German escorts learned rapidly, though, and by having some ships staying astern of the convoys made undetected British attacks more and more difficult, especially as the number of A/S trawlers and escorts increased as fast as the SKL could move them into the Kattegat. To the British submariners, the German A/S tactics appeared 'curious'. 'They frequently pass one another, circle around and occasionally get stern-on to each other,' wrote Lieutenant Commander Slaughter of *Sunfish*, continuing that the Germans 'appear reluctant to trust their instruments to drop charges'. Lieutenant Commander Bryant of *Sealion* found the trawlers 'disciplined', operating in pairs, but still fairly easy to avoid.

The Kriegsmarine had two kinds of tracking equipment: active sonar similar to the British asdic, and passive hydrophones. The boats with active sonar usually drifted or moved slowly, directing other vessels. The passive hydrophones were usually towed behind and made distinct noises that made them easy to avoid as they had limited directional capacity. The pumps of the British boats were noisy and when they were used to maintain trim the A/S hydrophone operators could easily pick up the racket. When the pumps were stopped, it was usually possible for the boats to sneak away from the passive German sonar. It was known that German U-boats dived deep when depth charged and many of the British captains 'adopted shallow tactics', staying above twenty metres at slow speed, bursting away when believing to be out of contact.[27]

On the 14th, *Sunfish*, who had unknowingly revenged *Tarpon* by torpedoing the Q-ship *Schürbeck* (*Schiff 40*), forcing her into Swedish waters just north of Marstrand the day before, rounded off a most successful patrol by sinking the *Oldenburg* (*Schiff 35*) north of Skagen. Korvettenkapitän Selchow's A/S trawlers of the 11th Submarine Hunter Flotilla (U-Jagd Flottille) chased her for hours afterwards, but without gaining firm contact and no serious attack developed.[28]

Brummer in Oslo harbour, shortly before casting off on her last voyage at 16:30. (Author's collection)

On the same day, the gunnery training ship *Brummer* sailed from Kiel to Fredrikshavn, where she embarked 409 soldiers for Oslo. The embarkation was swift and *Brummer* headed to sea in the evening accompanied by *Jaguar*, *Falke* and *F5*.[29] Reaching Oslo the next morning, the soldiers and their equipment were disembarked and the ships cast off again at 16:30, heading back to Fredrikshavn for more troops. At 23:07 on 15 April, off the Jomfruland island, three torpedo tracks were seen from *Brummer*, who was in the van. The convoy had just passed through an area of fog and snow, and Korvettenkapitän Max Gebauer had ordered the other boats into line-astern in order for them not to lose contact and there was no A/S screen. Two torpedoes passed in front of *Brummer*, the third impacted below gun no. 1, detonating the forward magazine. The forecastle was cut clean off, leaving gun no. 2 pointing towards the water at a crazy angle.

At first it was unclear to the other ships from which side the attack had come and *Falke* and *F5* circled the scene, throwing depth charges and looking for a contact. Nothing was found, and *F5* was ordered to approach the wreck to take off the wounded while *Jaguar* joined *Falke* in the search. When complete, *F5* set course for Fredrikshavn and Korvettenkapitän Gebauer, himself wounded from being thrown off the bridge by the explosion, ordered *Jaguar* alongside to take off the remaining crew. The wreck appeared stable but the damage was significant and she could sink at any moment in the choppy sea. A submarine contact was briefly obtained and the two torpedo boats gave chase, but nothing was achieved and the contact was lost. A towing attempt was planned for dawn, but before it could be initiated, *Brummer* sank at 06:50 a mile off Tvesteinen Lighthouse.

HMS *Sterlet*, sister-ship of *Spearfish*. After having sunk *Brummer*, she was herself in all likelihood sunk two days later. (Wright and Logan)

There were fifty-one casualties of which twenty-five were fatal. Virtually all of the dead and wounded had been in the forecastle.[30]

The assailant was *Sterlet*. After attacking *Brummer*, however, her fate remains uncertain. No signals were ever received and she was eventually reported overdue and lost. From the reports of the German ships it seems likely that she escaped from *Jaguar*, *Falke* and *F5*, unless hit by chance by one of the two dozen depth charges dropped in singles or pairs, and sank to her destruction unnoticed. Two days later, north-east of Skagen, a submarine fired two torpedoes unsuccessfully on a convoy just after darkness. During the attack, the boat broke surface and was heavily attacked by the escort. This was most likely also *Sterlet* and she was possibly sunk on this occasion, or so damaged that she perished on the way home.

On 15 April, *Shark* fired five torpedoes at the depot ship *Saar* (mistakenly identified as *Brummer*) and two transports, but the torpedo tracks were sighted and the targets turned safely away. *Snapper* sank the two minesweepers *M1701* and *M1702* north-east of Skagen on that day, after which she was chased for hours, but got safely away. On the 16th, *Porpoise* fired six torpedoes at *U3* off Egersund; all missed. On the 18th, *Seawolf*, operating north of Skagen, sank the transport *Hamm* during a night attack.

The intense efforts of the German A/S flotillas and other escorts eventually paid off. On 20 April *Swordfish* was bombed by an aircraft when at periscope depth. A few minutes later, engines were heard and Lieutenant Cowell surfaced to investigate. Coming up, he found his boat surrounded by no fewer than five F-class escorts and one larger vessel. *Swordfish* crash dived and was chased for two hours. The depth charges, some of which came uncomfortably close, caused leaks in the outer tanks and the boat took water aft. To get away, all engines were stopped, including the gyrocompass. Undaunted, Lieutenant Cowell went on another search and within half an hour found a convoy of three merchant ships and four escorts. Six torpedoes were fired, but as the compass was still turned off, course keeping was disturbed and there were no hits. *Swordfish* crept away on one engine but was chased by the escort as well as the original hunting group for another six hours before she could surface. By then, pressure inside the boat had built up and when opening the hatch, it flew open, knocking Lieutenant Cowell and a signalman unconscious. The following week was spent off southern Norway, constantly harassed by A/S patrols and aircraft until course was set for home on the 27th.[31] The convoy they had attacked consisted of the freighters *Belgrano*, *Dessau* and *Curityba* and was escorted by Korvettenkapitän Selchow's 11.U-Jagd Flottille. They had left Oslo the day before, heading for Kiel for another load of equipment and troops. A few hours after having chased *Swordfish* away, a new submarine contact was reported. During this chase, a periscope was observed at least twice and some twenty-five depth charges dropped – probably against *Triad* this time. Contact was lost, however, and the convoy resumed course southwards, unharmed.[32]

By the second half of April, several of the submarines had been on patrol for nearly two weeks, some almost three, and they started running low on torpedoes. One by one, the boats headed home.

Throughout April, the submarines found the conditions increasingly difficult in the Skagerrak. The numbers of A/S patrols increased markedly and low-flying patrol aircraft were everywhere, continually forcing them to go deep. Several of the boats were bombed without warning, even when submerged. By the end of April, the rapidly shortening hours of darkness and the need for redeployment pending the expected attack in the west, forced VA(S) to suspend patrols in the Kattegat and the eastern Skagerrak. In early May, after the attack on France, the submarines were forced to give Norway and Skagerrak 'a bit of a rest' altogether. Operations east of the Lindesnes–Skagen line were terminated, effectively leaving the supply convoys alone.

The British success in the Kattegat and Skagerrak in April was not gained without loss. Four submarines came to grief: *Thistle* and *Sterlet* in the Norwegian area and *Tarpon* west of Jutland, while *Unity* was rammed and sunk by the Norwegian freighter *Atle Jarl* off Blyth on 29 April as she headed out for her second patrol.[33]

The boats truly earned the signal sent to them by the First Lord: 'Please convey to all ranks and ratings engaged in these brilliant and fruitful submarine operations, the admiration and regard with which their fellow countrymen follow their exploits.'[34]

A Tide in the Affairs of Men

AT 19:30 GeT ON 9 April, Group XXI issued a situation report to the OKW in Berlin: 'The occupation of Norway and Denmark has been accomplished according to orders.'[1] It was a gross oversimplification, contradicted by the fact that General von Falkenhorst, the C-in-C of the invasion forces, was still in Germany. True, the German forces were in control of Oslo, Horten, Arendal, Kristiansand, Egersund, Stavanger, Bergen, Trondheim and Narvik, but in little else of the country, and the situation for the troops was far from secure. The Norwegian government had dismissed the German demands and decided to resist. Britain and France had declared they were on their way to help and Norwegian mobilisation had started. Politically, the operation was a failure. King Haakon, the government and the Parliament had escaped and Quisling's improvised 'coup' already showed signs of being counterproductive. Negotiations would soon become impossible and the determination to resist would harden.

It would take a full two months before the occupation of Norway was fully accomplished; the sideshow in the north would actually take longer to conclude than the campaigns in both France and Poland.

Why did the Germans come in the first place?

No easy, unchallenged answer can be given to this question. Behind the events is a confusing blend of ideology, high-level strategy, personal ambitions, military deliberations and illogical reasoning. Hitler's irrational rage over *Altmark* and Churchill's obsession with Narvik must be taken into accounted, as must French internal politics and Quisling's political aspirations. Koht's failure to have the Allies understand his intentions is also important, as is Raeder's naval aspirations and Churchill's opportunism. Lesser factors also matter, such as Krancke's and von Falkenhorst's audacious planning of the operation actually making it look feasible.

The motives of Grossadmiral Erich Raeder, the C-in-C of the German Navy, in advocating a Norwegian venture were many, but the responsibility for the actual concept of Operation Weserübung must be placed with him. On one hand, he saw the need for Germany to protect the iron ore and other imports from Scandinavia as part of a greater strategic setting. On the other hand, he also wished for the Kriegsmarine to be seen as an important part of the armed forces, dominant in the North Sea and actively threatening British supply lines in the Atlantic. He believed both submarines and surface vessels could be helped in these tasks by bases in Norway and conversely that Germany's northern coast would be severely threatened by British bases. The army and the Luftwaffe would be in the lead as long as the focus of the war was in the west or on a long-term expansion in the east. It was imperative for Raeder to create alternative schemes where the navy could excel and not be left behind the other services in the allocation of resources. He

Grossadmiral Erich Raeder, here arriving at Fornebu, must take the main responsibility for the concept and execution of Operation Weserübung. (Author's collection)

was aware, however, that the strategic value of German bases in Norway should not be overrated and did probably not initially foresee a full-scale invasion.

On 15 April, just one week after Operation Weserübung, Hitler and Göring told the Swedish Admiral Tamm at a meeting in Berlin that it had been Germany's preference to keep Scandinavia neutral. Due to prolonged Allied aggression and threats to the German ore import, however, they had been forced to act in Norway.[2] At Nuremberg and in his later memoirs, Raeder also defended himself against accusations of initiating a war of aggression, claiming that the German intelligence had such detailed knowledge of the Allied plans for invading Norway that Operation Weserübung was purely preventive. This was true to some extent, but inadequate as an isolated argument. There was widespread concern among senior German naval officers during the first phase of the war over a potential British blockade of Germany and the ability of the navy to protect its merchant lines – above all, the iron-ore trade.[3] During the winter of 1939/40, Raeder, in a series of reports to Hitler and the OKW pointed repeatedly to the importance of the trade war in breaking British ability to oppose German expansion on the Continent. Above all, he highlighted the importance of securing the German import of iron, pyrite, nickel and other minerals from Scandinavia while denying the same to Britain. Hence, it is evident, in spite of a significant British pressure on these supplies, that the concept of aggressive actions to secure German interests was deeply rooted in Raeder and parts of his staff.

* * *

The crippling cost of WWI and the subsequent financial depression had caused Britain to enter the new war substantially unprepared. Time was needed to make up for the deficiencies. The Western Front could explode at any time and the War Cabinet had a vested interest in opening as many fronts as possible to divert German forces. The more nations that could be cajoled or goaded into the war against Germany, the more Germany's capabilities would be diluted. Winston Churchill saw this more clearly than most others in the War Cabinet and he was the unchallenged 'hawk' of the British government. He argued for mining of the Norwegian Leads throughout the autumn and winter, and finally had it his way on 8 April.

The Russian assault on Finland in November and widespread empathy with the brave Suomi defenders created an opportunity to send an expeditionary corps – taking control of the Swedish ore fields on its way. From Paris, sending an expedition to Finland via Norway and Sweden looked very promising and was strongly encouraged. It would take pressure off the Maginot Line and if it severed the flow of iron ore to German industry, so much the better. The British would carry the major burden, while a couple of thousand troops, mostly Foreign Legionnaires, could be used to hurt Germany away from the French borders. Hence, significant French pressure was mounted in the Allied War Council to commence the operation, which was hoped to engage German soldiers in a distant theatre of war. Parts of the British military also saw the advantages of taking the war to Scandinavia, wresting the initiative from Germany. General Ironside, supported by the CoS, developed an ambitious operation securing control of the Lapland ore deposits as well as the Norwegian west coast. What would have happened if this scheme had not been halted by the Finnish capitulation, we shall never know, but the Allied plans and intentions became well known in Berlin, underlining the necessity for countermeasures.

Churchill considered the mine-laying in the Leads in the morning of 8 April a 'technical infringement' and claimed brazenly in a press statement on the 10th that 'Norwegian Neutrality and our respect for it have made it impossible to prevent this ruthless coup,' referring to the German invasion. The infringement was now played down. The Germans had come to Norway by themselves, no provocation had been needed and while it could not be undone, it was best forgotten. Britain had deliberately decided to violate the neutrality of a country whose neutrality it had pledged to defend six months earlier. There is not the slightest doubt that the mine-laying – from every legal and moral standpoint – was a flagrant violation of Norwegian neutrality. That Hitler wrongly used the incident as a justification for his own aggression is irrelevant in this context.

On 6 October Hitler said in a speech to the Reichstag:

> Germany has never had any conflicts of interest or even points of controversy with the northern states. Neither has she any today. Sweden and Norway have both been offered non-aggression pacts by Germany and have both refused them solely because they do not feel themselves threatened in any way.[4]

The statement was nice to say, but dangerous to believe. The Norwegian Declaration of Neutrality was convenient for Germany only as long as it was respected by the

Allies. Hitler had no respect for international law and it is inconceivable that he held any moral obligation to respect Norway's desire to be outside the European conflict any longer than it served his own purposes. Norwegian neutrality was convenient, as it allowed blockade-runners, ore ships, trawlers and other civilian vessels to move safely inside the Leads between the Skagerrak and the Norwegian Sea. Germany benefited substantially from Norwegian neutrality, but only as long as Norway was clearly not swaying towards a preference for the Allies. Vidkun Quisling's statements during his visit to the Reichskanzlei in December sowed doubt about this, and the *Altmark* episode appeared to substantiate his allegations. Used by internal German forces looking after their own interests, Quisling authenticated warnings of Allied intentions in Scandinavia and brought the topic of Norway nearer the front of Hitler's mind. The British naval intervention against *Altmark* in Jössingfjord made the issue concrete and took Weserübung from a planning to an execution stage. When German intelligence reported that an Allied expedition to Finland via Norway and Sweden was under development, averted only by the Finnish capitulation, it was largely a question of *when* Operation Weserübung should be implemented. Hitler had long-term goals for dominance in Europe, but his short-term strategies versus each neighbouring country were very dynamic; probably because they were rather vague in the first place.

British occupation of bases in Norway would have interrupted the supply of Swedish ore to Germany, and would have allowed Britain to intensify her air war on Germany. It would also have brought Sweden under Allied influence, and seriously endangered German sea communications in the Baltic. In an extreme case, the loss of Norway to Britain could mean losing the war. Operation Weserübung originated through a series of more or less arbitrary decisions and an unpredictable combination of events. The German belief that Allied severing of the ore traffic and seizure of bases in southern Norway was imminent was a pretext for the invasion. Whether this threat was real or not is largely irrelevant, as long as Berlin believed it was genuine.

Why did Operation Weserübung succeed?

This is an equally complicated issue. Each stage of the operation had its own dynamics and each landing port its own independent development of events. In spite of the tight security, there were ample and timely warnings in London, Copenhagen and Oslo to allow for actions that should have turned Weserübung into a resounding fiasco. Still, Norway was occupied and where organisation and planning failed, brazen initiative and pure cheek won the day, ably assisted by the ruthlessly effective Luftwaffe.

The Norwegian men and women were not at war in April 1940. For the better part of the century, neutrality and pacifism prevailed and the defences had been reduced to the point where it was almost disgraceful to be an officer or NCO. Countless warnings from aggressive nations had created fear, but also an even stronger resolve not to become entangled. In spite of Spain, Austria, Czechoslovakia, Poland, Finland and seven months of war, with sinking of Norwegian shipping and loss of life, most people trusted that the government would steer the country through – as it had in the first war. For most Norwegians there was a ravine that needed time to be crossed between defending neutrality and fighting a war, and in the morning of 9 April the majority of the Norwegian officers and men believed they were still on the side of the Neutrality Watch. No declarations had come from the government or from any military authorities. There was no mobilisation and no warning beyond 'increased preparedness'. Neither was there firm information as to who the enemy was. Most believed they were facing a serious breach of the neutrality, but not war. Their reactions were therefore scaled accordingly.

Many soldiers found it opportune to remind their officers that their guns were loaded with live ammunition when ordered to open fire. Somebody might be hit. In all my discussions with Norwegian veterans, there is one thing they almost inevitably have in common: they admit they did not shoot to kill for several days into the campaign. Not until they had experienced the ruthlessness of the German attackers and some of their comrades had actually been killed or wounded, did they lower their sights onto the field-grey uniforms. Add this to the technical shortcomings, poor communication, malfunctioning guns, non-exploding shells, lack of electricity for the searchlights, missing crews and so on, and the disparity between the attackers and defenders becomes pronounced.

The Germans were not necessarily better equipped, but they knew they were at war, they had been trained well and, above all, they had officers with goals and timetables and resolve to meet them. Still, the success of Weserübung was not the result of meticulous planning and long-term preparations. The planning of the operation did not start in earnest until mid-February, less than two months before its implementation. Quite the contrary: it was improvisation and pragmatic application of available forces that won the day. To a large extent the whole concept was far beyond the comprehension of British and Norwegian military and civilian authorities.

The Norwegian armed forces had been decimated in the 1920s and 1930s, and the country's ability to defend itself atrophied. To gain consent, the military leaders had been chosen by their political masters and treasurers so as not to rock the boat and they were unwilling or incapable of presenting viable alternatives for a defence of the country against the growing threat from Nazism and Communism – with a few very remarkable exceptions.

Prime Minister Nygaardsvold left most of the international issues to Foreign Minister Koht, who made it his personal responsibility – almost to the exclusion of all others who should have been involved – to steer the country away from the threat of war. Both failed to seek the right advice and when they appointed Ljungberg as defence minister the road to catastrophe lay open. The ultimate responsibility for the state of the Norwegian armed forces and their lack of readiness rests with Nygaardsvold, Koht and Ljungberg. More than any other men they had the ability to do something about it. By making the choices they did – whether from personal, ideological or political reasons – the history of Norway was changed forever. Other men in their positions might have acted similarly or differently, but these three were there and the responsibility remains with them. Clear warnings were available and the fact that they were not disseminated, analysed, understood and acted upon was the responsibility of Halvdan Koht. The accountability for lack of communication and direction between the military and the politicians in the days leading up to the invasion as well as earlier cannot be put anywhere but on Birger Ljungberg. Responsibility for the fact that the system allowed such defects to take place remains with Johan Nygaardsvold.

One may sympathise with the initial assessment of the government in September 1939 that there was no immediate danger of an attack on Norway at the time, and that the Neutrality Watch would suffice. It is more difficult to understand why so little was done later, in particular after the *Altmark* affair and the obvious escalation of the threat to Norway from both sides. None of the regular ministers had sufficient insight in military matters to formulate their intentions in suitable terms, and it was never properly ascertained that Ljungberg, Diesen and Laake understood what the government wanted. Neither did Laake and Diesen take the burden of making sure that the reluctant government had all the information it needed on the military situation and that the consequences of its orders, or lack of such, were understood. Neither man made sure that the time and the resources needed to increase the strength of the Norwegian defences were appreciated by the government. They believed the 'prescient Foreign Office' would initiate necessary precautions in due course, should it become necessary. Nobody realised that this amounted to the judgement of one man, Foreign Minister Koht, as no others were involved. The government as a whole, however incompetent in military matters, must take the responsibility for failing to call the commanding officers to their meetings to share intelligence, ascertain intentions were understood and verify orders could be implemented – and if not, what alternatives existed.

The Royal Navy ruled supreme in the North Sea but failed substantially to cut off any part of the Weserübung forces or throw them back once they had landed. Not having adapted to the new era of warfare, where intelligence, or rather comprehension of intelligence, submarines and airpower would dominate, the Admiralty still remained in the battle fleet tradition where ships fought at sea and decisions were taken at high levels. Apart from the actions at Narvik and the outstanding contribution of the British submarines, much opportunity was missed and numerous lessons were not learned.

Still, the German Navy came out worse. Three cruisers, ten destroyers and about a dozen other ships were sunk. Virtually all the rest of the surface fleet involved was damaged and by the end of the campaign, for all practical purposes, only the U-boats would carry the war to the Atlantic while smaller forces operated in the Channel and in Norway. The new battleships were nowhere near operational and there was no question of the Kriegsmarine being a factor in a potential invasion of Britain.

From today's standards, it is virtually impossible to understand the acceptance of Operation Weserübung as a military plan. Disregarding the conventional limitations of contemporary naval strategy, Hitler, on the advice of Raeder and the SKL, relied on the effect of surprise. The SKL commented in its war diary that the operation 'broke all the rules in the book of sea warfare' but also called it 'one of the more creative operations of the modern history of war'. Operation Weserübung was considered likely to succeed because of its unorthodoxy, not in spite of it.

It was the first combined operation ever where air force, army and navy operated intimately together with interlinked tasks and objectives. Troops were transported directly into battle simultaneously by air and sea, and success required strict adherence to schedule and seamless co-operation between normally fiercely rivalling services. It was also the first time paratroopers were used actively, jumping into battle. The following days would see the first dive-bomber attack to sink a major warship, the first carrier task-force operations, the first naval shore bombardments of this war and the first instances where the positioning of naval fleets at sea was influenced by the presence of land-based aircraft.

The subsequent campaign would also see the first encounter between German and British land forces, and the first German defeat of WWII (the recapture of Narvik). Indirectly, Operation Weserübung would also topple the Chamberlain Cabinet and make way for Winston Churchill in Downing Street. What would have happened after Dunkirk with Chamberlain and Halifax in the seat is anybody's guess.

More than most other campaigns of WWII, Operation Weserübung has been shrouded in mystery, legend and forged impressions. What happened and why it happened has been told in many different manners by different people for different reasons. Strategic, political, legal and moral issues were at best unclear. Military issues were dominated by risk and untested concepts. For Europe, it was a sideshow overshadowed by events on the mainland. For the people of Norway, it changed their history forever.

Let those who fought and above all those who made the ultimate sacrifice be remembered in a manner worthy of the price they paid.

Appendices

— Appendix A —
The European Iron Ore Trade

Swedish Export of Iron Ore in thousands of tons

	1933	1934	1935	1936	1937	1938	1939	1940
Total	3,044	6,376	6,906	10,289	13,110	11,976	12,562	9,271
to Germany	2,153	4,804	5,006	7,479	8,818	8,441	9,981	8,170
to Britain	423	801	987	1,362	2,136	1,603	1,421	584

Swedish Export of Iron Ore via Narvik in thousands of tons

	1935	1936	1937	1938	1939	1940
Total	3,821	5,530	7,580	6,844	5,866	1,266
to Germany	2,592	3,843	4,919	4,771	4,027	504
to Britain	786	998	1,611	1,222	1,117	524
to Other	207	319	438	349	537	189

Source: Karlbom, *Sweden's Iron Ore Exports to Germany 1933–1944*; and Bröyn, *Den svenske malmeksport fram til besetingen av Narvik i April 1940.*

— Appendix B —
The Royal Norwegian Navy, April 1940

Supreme Sea Defence Command – Sjøforsvarets Overkommando

Commanding Admiral – Kommanderende Admiral – Kontreadmiral Henry Edward Diesen
Adjutants:
    Kommandør Birger Lund Gottwaldt
    Kaptein Oskar Alf Gunvaldsen
    Løytnant Tore Holthe
Chief of the Admiral Staff – Kommandør Elias Corneliussen
    Kommandørkaptein Edvard Kristian Danielsen
Liaison and Intelligence Office – Kaptein Erik Anker Steen
C-in-C Naval Air Force – Kommandørkaptein Finn Lützow-Holm
C-in-C Coastal Artillery – Oberst Hans Oscar Hammerstad

1. Sjøforsvarsdistrikt – 1st Sea Defence District (SDD1) at Karljohansvern, Horten

Kontreadmiral Johannes Smith-Johannsen
Chief of Staff – Kommandørkaptein Gunnar Hovdenak
Karljohansvern Naval Base – Kommandørkaptein Paul Münster
Intelligence and Communication Officer – Kaptein Knut Nergaard Blich
1st Minelayer Division (*Glommen, Laugen, Nor, Vidar*) – Kaptein Ernst Wilhelm Schramm
1st Air Wing – Kaptein Gøsta HA Wendelbo
Horten Air Defence – Kaptein OJ Johannessen
Naval Shipyard

Oscarsborg Sea Defence Sector at Oscarsborg

Oberst Birger Kristian Eriksen
Intelligence and Communication Officer – Kaptein Thorleif Unneberg
Oscarsborg Patrol and Auxiliary Division (*Kranfartøy II, Alpha, Furu*) – Kommandørkaptein Andreas Anderssen

Kaholmen Fort – Kaptein Magnus Sødem
    28-cm battery (3 guns – only 2 manned 9 April)
    57-mm battery (4 guns, not manned)
Kopås Fort – Kaptein Vagn Jul Enger (acting on order from Oberst Eriksen)
    15-cm battery (3 guns)
Husvik Fort – Løytnant Rolf Thorleif Bertelsen
    57-mm battery (2 guns)
    15-cm battery (3 guns, not adequately manned)
Nesset Fort – Løytnant H Strand
    57-mm battery (3 guns)
Nordre Kaholmen Torpedo Battery – Kommandørkaptein Andreas Anderssen
    3 x 45-mm torpedo tubes
Seiersten A/A Battery – Løytnant Hans Sollie
    2 x 40-mm A/A guns
    3 x 7.92-mm machine guns

Outer Oslofjord Sea Defence Sector at Tønsberg

Kommandør Einar Tandberg-Hanssen
Chief of Staff – Kaptein Trond Stamsø
Oslofjord Patrol and Auxiliary Division – Kommandørkaptein HH Finborud
1st Submarine Division (*A2, A3, A4, Sarpen*) – Kaptein Thorvald Frithjof Fjeldstad
1st Minesweeper Division (*Hauk, Hvas, Falk, Kjæk*) – Løytnant Olav Arnljot Apold
3rd Minesweeper Division (*Otra, Rauma*) – Kaptein A Dæhli

Oslofjord Fortress – Oberstløytnant Kristian Kristoffersen Notland, at Håøy Fort
Rauøy Fort – Major Hersleb Adler Enger
    4 x 15-cm guns
    4 x 12-cm guns (not manned)
Northern Battery – Kaptein B Sørlie
Southern Battery – Kaptein K Gullichsen

2 x 40-mm A/A guns and 2 machine guns – Løytnant Rønning
1 x 150-mm and 2 x 110-cm searchlight – Sersjant T Hansen
Bolærne Fort – Major Fredrik Wilhelm Færden
    3 x 15-cm guns – Kaptein Telle
    4 x 12-cm guns (not manned)
    1 x 150-mm and 1 x 90-mm searchlight – Sersjant Harrisland
Måkerøy Fort – Kaptein Ragnar Edgar Wølner
    2 x 30.5-cm howitzer guns (not adequately manned)
Håøy Fort – Kaptein Knut Aas
    2 x 21-cm guns (not adequately manned)

Kristiansand Sea Defence Sector in Kristiansand

Kommandør Severin Edward Wigers
Chief of Staff – Kaptein Martin August Tønnessen
Intelligence and Communication Officer – Kaptein Alexander Vercoe
Marvika Naval Base and Depot – Kaptein Martin August Tønnessen
2nd Torpedo Boat Division (*Kjell, Skarv, Teist*) – Løytnant F Halvorsen
2nd Submarine Division (*B2, B4, B5*[1]) – Kaptein Bjarne Bro
10th Auxiliary Division (*Kvik, Blink, Lyn*) – Kaptein Ludolf Eide Buvik
11th Auxiliary Division (*William Barents, Fireren, Lyngdal, Hval IV, Hval VI, Hval VII*) – Kaptein T Johansen
3rd Torpedo Boat Division (*Jo, Grib, Ravn, Ørn, Lom*[2]) – Løytnant Thore Holthe
Kristiansand Naval Air Base – Kaptein Erling W. Eliassen

Kristiansand Fortress – Oberstløytnant Ole Arnt Fosby
Senior Gunnery Officer – Major Johannes Sandberg
Intelligence and Communication Officer – Kaptein Reidar K Brynhildsen
Sjøbevoktnigssjef – Kaptein Karl J Schmidt

Odderøya Fort
    21-cm battery – Kaptein Sverre Geirulv
    24-cm howitzer battery – Kaptein BA Flisnes
    Western 15-cm battery – Løytnant Hilmar Hestmann
    Central 15-cm battery – Løytnant Jacob A Rynning
    Eastern 15-cm battery – Løytnant Thorbjørn Nielsen
    A/A defences – Løytnant AT Abusland

Gleodden Fort
    15-cm battery – Løytnant Harald Nikolai Sannes

1. Flyavdeling – 1st Wing

Kaptein Gøsta Wendelbo
Naval Air Base, Karljohansvern, Horten – Kaptein Gøsta Wendelbo
Naval Air Base, Kristiansand – Kaptein Erling Eliassen
Naval Air Base, Grasholmen, Oslo (provisional)
Naval Flying School, Horten

2. Sjøforsvarsdistrikt – 2nd Sea Defence District (SDD2) at Marineholmen, Bergen

Kontreadmiral Carsten Tank-Nielsen
Chief of Staff – Kommandørkaptein Hagbart Fredrik Kjelstrup
Marineholmen Naval Base – Kommandørkaptein HG Jacobsen
Intelligence and Communication Officer – Løytnant Ernst Bryne Marstrander
2nd Air Wing – Kaptein D Manshaus
Coast Guard units

Stavanger – Haugesund Sea Defence Area
Destroyer *Æger* – Kaptein Nils Larsen Bruun
Destroyer *Draug* – Kaptein Tore Horve
Torpedo boat *Stegg* – Løytnant Herman Magne Hansen
Auxiliary vessels *Sperm, Motorbåt nr.7*
Provisional seaplane base at Hafrsfjord, Sola
Haugesund Coast Guard and Communication Centre – Kaptein E Krogh

Florø – Måløy Sea Defence Area
Destroyer *Troll* – Kaptein Johan Dahl
Torpedo boat *Snøgg* – Kaptein N Simensen

Måløy – Ålesund Sea Defence Area
Auxiliary vessels *Hval V, Commonwealth*
Måløy Coast Guard and Communication Centre – Kaptein Bjarne Sjong

Bergen Sea Defence Sector at Marineholmen

Kontreadmiral Carsten Tank-Nielsen
Deputy – Oberst Gunnar Isaachsen Willoch.
Senior Staff officers – Kaptein Årstad, Kaptein Røssberg, Kaptein Cappelen-Smith
Bergen Naval Command – Kommandørkaptein I Evensen (Sjøbevokningssjef)
4th Torpedo boat Division (*Storm, Brand, Sæl*) – Løytnant Thorleif Pettersen
2nd Minelayer Division (*Gor, Tyr, Uller, Vale*) – Kaptein Johan Fredrik Andreas Ulstrup
2nd Minesweeper Division (*Derv, Dristig*) – Løytnant W Knutsen
Submarine *B6* – Kaptein HT Eriksen
Minelayer *Olav Tryggvason* – Kommandørkaptein Trygve Sigurd Briseid[3]
Destroyer *Garm* – Kaptein Sigurd Skjolden
13th Patrol and Auxiliary Division (*Oster, Smart, Bjerk, Veslefrikk, Veslegutt*)
12th Patrol and Auxiliary Division (*Alværsund, Manger, Lindaas, Haus Øygard*)
Lerøy Region – Kaptein F Ulstrup
Færøy Region – Kaptein KA Hagestad
Håøy Region – Løytnant K Backen
Herdla Region – Kaptein A Lea

Bergen Fortress – Oberst Gunnar Isaachsen Willoch
Kvarven Fort – Kaptein Peder Herman Waage
    21-cm battery (3 guns) – Kaptein O Olsen
    24-cm howitzer battery (3 guns) – Kaptein K Haugstad
    Torpedo battery (not operational)

Hellen Fort – Kaptein Kristen Martinus Valde
    21-cm battery (3 guns) – Kaptein Kristen Martinus Valde
    24-cm howitzer battery (2 guns at Sandviksfjellet – not manned)

Lerøy Fort (2 x 65-mm guns) – Kaptein OM Tangen   The outer forts were
Færøy Fort (2 x 65-mm guns) – Løytnant B Johannesen   tactically
Herdla Fort (2 x 65-mm guns) – Kaptein H Risnes   subordinated to
Håøy Fort (2 x 57-mm guns) – Kaptein S Vangen   Bergen Naval Command

Bergen Air Defences – Kaptein P Alvær
    Kvarven A/A battery – Fenrik S Torp
    Øyjord A/A battery – Fenrik J Strøm
    Slettebakken A/A battery – Fenrik EA Welle-Strand

Trøndelag Sea Defence Sector – Trondheim

Kommandørkaptein Olav Bergersen
Chief of Staff – Kaptein Brynjulf Bjarnar
Agdenes Naval Command – Kaptein H Pedersen (Sjøbevokningssjef)
14th Patrol and Auxiliary Division (*Fosen, Nauma, Steinkjær, Heilhorn*)
Destroyer *Sleipner* – Kaptein E Ullring
Torpedo boat *Trygg* – Løytnant FW Münster
5th Torpedo Boat Division (*Sild, Skrei, Laks*) – Løytnant Rangvald Tamber
Seaplane base at Aunøy, Hitra – Løytnant Kaare Strand Kjos
Coast Guard and Signal Stations

Agdenes Fortress – Oberstløytnant Frithjof Jacobsen
Intelligence and Communication Officer – Kaptein S Løvstad
Brettingen Fort – Major Johan Henrik van Kervel Schlytter
    21-cm battery (2 guns) – Kaptein H Isaachsen
    15-cm battery (3 guns) – Løytnant Patrich Hans Volckmar
    A/A defences – Fenrik S Elnan
Hysnes Fort – Kaptein Øyvin Lange
    21-cm battery (2 guns) – Løytnant Paul Magnussen Strande
    15-cm battery (2 guns) – Løytnant Haakon Myrholt
    A/A defences – Fenrik J Hageløkken

2. Flyavdeling – 2nd Wing

Kaptein Edvin Manshaus
Naval Air Base, Flatøy, Bergen – Kaptein Edvin Manshaus
Naval Air Base, Hafrsfjord, Sola Stavanger (provisional) – Løytnant Carl Johan Stansberg
Naval Air Base, Aunøya, Hitra (provisional) – Løytnant Kaare Strand Kjos

3. Sjøforsvarsdistrikt – 3rd Sea Defence District (SDD3) at Tromsø

Kommandør Leif Sarinius Thoralf Hagerup (on leave 8 April)
Acting Kommandørkaptein Per Askim
Chief of Staff – Kaptein Erling Kjær
Intelligence and Communication Officer – Kaptein Carl Fritjof Hassel Rode

3rd Air Wing

Coast Guard and patrol vessels (*Heimdal, Nordkapp, Thorodd, Kvitøy, Svalbard II, Syrian, Torfinn I, Aud I*)

Ramsund Naval Depot

Ofoten Detachment at Narvik – Kommandørkaptein Per Askim

1st Pansership Division (*Norge, Eidsvold*)

3rd Submarine Division (*B1, B3, Lyngen*)

Auxiliary patrol vessels (*Michael Sars, Senja, Kelt*)

Finmark Detachment at Kirkenes and Vadsø – Kaptein Peter Morten Bredsdorff

Fisheries Protection/patrol vessels (*Fridtjof Nansen, Børtind, Nordhav II, Rossfjord, Spanstind*)

Vardöyhus Fortress – Kaptein Johan Basilier

3. Flyavdeling – 3rd Wing

Kaptein T Sundt

Naval Air Base, Skattøra, Tromsø

Naval Air Base, Vadsø (provisional)

— Appendix C —
British Ships Involved in Norway, April 1940[4]

The Home Fleet

Flag, Admiral Sir Charles Forbes, GCB, DSO, Commander-in-Chief, Home Fleet, *Rodney*

2nd Battle Squadron[5]

Rodney	Captain FHG Dalrymple-Hamilton
Valiant	Captain HB Rawlings, OBE
Warspite	Captain VAC Crutchley, VC, DSC

Battlecruiser Squadron[6]
Flag, Vice Admiral WJ Whitworth, *Renown*

Renown	Captain CEB Simeon
Repulse	Captain EJ Spooner, DSO

Aircraft Carriers

Furious	Captain TH Troubridge

1st Cruiser Squadron[7]
Flag, Vice Admiral JHD Cunningham, CB, MVO, *Devonshire*

Devonshire	Captain JM Mansfield, DSC
Berwick	Captain IM Palmer, DSC
York	Captain RH Portal, DSC
Suffolk	Captain JW Durnford

2nd Cruiser Squadron
Flag, Vice Admiral Sir GF Edward-Collins, KCVO, CB, *Galatea*

Galatea	Captain BB Schofield
Arethusa	Captain GD Graham
Penelope	Captain GD Yates
Aurora	Captain LHK Hamilton, DSO

18th Cruiser Squadron[8]
Flag, Vice Admiral Geoffry Layton, CB, DSO, *Manchester*

Manchester	Captain HA Packer
Sheffield	Captain CAA Larcom
Southampton	Captain FWH Jeans, CVO
Glasgow	Captain FH Pegram
Birmingham	Captain ACG Madden

2nd Destroyer Flotilla[9]

Hardy (H87)	Captain (D)2 BAW Warburton-Lee
Hotspur (H01)	Commander HFH Layman
Havock (H43)	Lieutenant Commander RE Courage
Hero (H99)	Commander HW Biggs
Hyperion (H97)	Commander H St L Nicholson
Hunter (H35)	Lieutenant Commander L de Villiers
Hostile (H55)	Commander JP Wright

3rd Destroyer Flotilla[10]

Inglefield (D02)	Captain (D)3 Percy Todd
Isis (D87)	Commander JC Clouston
Ilex (D61)	Lieutenant Commander PL Saumarez, DSC
Imogen (D44)	Commander CL Firth, MVO
Delight (H38)	Commander M Fogg-Elliott
Diana (H49)	Lieutenant Commander EG Le Geyt

4th Destroyer Flotilla[11]

Afridi (F07)	Captain (D)4 PL Vian, DSO
Gurkha (F20)	Commander AW Buzzard
Sikh (F82)	Commander JA Gifford
Mohawk (F31)	Commander JWM Eaton
Zulu (F18)	Commander JS Crawford
Cossack (F03)	Commander Robert St V Sherbrooke
Maori (F24)	Commander GN Brewer
Nubian (F36)	Commander RW Ravenhill

5th Destroyer Flotilla[12]

Kelly (F01)	Captain (D)5 Lord Louis Mountbatten, GCVO
Kashmir (F12)	Commander HA King
Kelvin (F37)	Lieutenant Commander JL Machin
Kipling (F91)	Commander A St Clair Ford
Kimberley (F50)	Lieutenant Commander RGK Knowling

6th Destroyer Flotilla

Somali (F33)	Captain (D)6 RSG Nicholson, DSO, DSC
Ashanti (F51)	Commander WG Davis
Matabele (F26)	Commander GK Whiting-Smith
Mashona (F59)	Commander WH Selby
Bedouin (F67)	Commander JA McCoy
Punjabi (F21)	Commander JT Lean
Eskimo (F75)	Commander St JA Micklethwait, DSO
Tartar (F43)	Commander LP Skipwith.

7th Destroyer Flotilla[13]

	Captain (D)7 PJ Mack
Janus (F53)	Com JAW Tothill
Javelin (F61)	Com AF Pugsley
Juno (F46)	Lieutenant-Com AM McKillop
Jupiter (F85)	Com DR Wyburd

8th Destroyer Flotilla[14]

Faulknor (H62)	Captain (D)8 AF de Salis
Fearless (H67)	Commander KL Harkness
Foxhound (H69)	Lieutenant Commander GH Peters
Fury (H76)	Commander GF Burghard
Forester (H74)	Lieutenant Commander ER Tancock, DSC
Fortune (H70)	Commander EA Gibbs, DSO
Fame (H78)	Lieutenant Commander WS Clouston

1st Destroyer Flotilla[15]

Codrington (H65)	Captain (D)1 GE Creasy, MVO
Grenade (H86)	Commander RC Boyle
Greyhound (H05)	Commander WR Marshall-A'Deane
Glowworm (H92)	Lieutenant Commander GB Roope
Griffin (H31)	Lieutenant Commander J Lee-Barber
ORP *Blyskawica* (H34)	Lieutenant Commander J Umecki
ORP *Grom* (H71)	Commander Alexander Hulewicz
ORP *Burza* (H73)	Lieutenant Commander Stanisław Nahorski

12th Destroyer Flotilla[16]

Electra (H27)	Lieutenant Commander SA Buss
Escapade (H17)	Commander HR Graham
Encounter (H10)	Lieutenant Commander EV St J Morgan
Eclipse (H08)	Lieutenant Commander IT Clark

MINELAYERS

Teviot Bank	Commander RD King-Harman

20th Destroyer Flotilla[17]

Esk (H15)	Captain (D)20 JG Bickford, DSC
Impulsive (D11)	Lieutenant Commander RJH Couch
Ivanhoe (D16)	Lieutenant Commander WS Thomas
Icarus (D03)	Commander PH Hadow

SUBMARINES

2nd Submarine Flotilla at Rosyth (HMS *Forth*)[18]

Thistle	Lieutenant Commander WF Haselfoot	Sailed for patrol 7 April. Towards Utsira. Lost 10 April
Triad	Lieutenant Commander ERJ Oddie	Sailed for patrol 8 April. Towards position east of Skagen
Trident	Lieutenant Commander AGL Seale	Sailed for patrol 25 March. Off Larvik
Triton	Lieutenant Commander EF Fowle-Pizey	Sailed for patrol 29 March. In Kattegat
Truant	Lieutenant Commander C Hutchinson	Sailed for patrol 6 April. Off Egersund
Tarpon	Lieutenant Commander HJ Caldwell	On passage towards Skagerrak. Lost 10 April
Orzel	Lieutenant Commander J Grudzinski	Sailed for patrol 3 April. Off Kristiansand
Seal	Lieutenant Commander RP Lonsdale	Sailed for patrol 6 April. North of declared area
Taku	Lieutenant Commander V Van den Byl	Sailed for patrol 12 April
Porpoise	Commander PQ Roberts	Sailed for patrol 13 April
Tetrarch	Lt Commander RG Mills	Sailed for patrol 13 April

3rd Submarine Flotilla at Harwich (HMS *Cyclops*)[19]

Sealion	Lieutenant Commander B Bryant	Sailed for patrol 2 April. In Kattegat
Seawolf	Lieutenant Commander J Studholme	Sailed for patrol 7 April. German Bight
Shark	Lieutenant Commander PN Buckley	Sailed for patrol 7 April. German Bight
Snapper	Lieutenant WDA King	Sailed for patrol 4 April. North of declared area
Sterlet	Lieutenant Commander GH Haward	On passage towards Skagerrak. Lost *c.*18 April
Sunfish	Lieutenant Commander JE Slaughter	Sailed for patrol 2 April. In Kattegat

6th Submarine Flotilla at Blyth[20]

Unity	Lieutenant JFB Brown	Sailed for patrol 2 April. Horns Reef area[21]
Spearfish	Lieutenant Commander JH Forbes	Sailed for patrol 5 April. North of declared area
Swordfish	Lieutenant PJ Cowell	Sailed for patrol 22 March. Returned Blyth 8 April. Sailed again 16 April
Clyde	Lieutenant Commander DC Ingram	Sailed for patrol 7 April. Off Egersund from 03:00 9 April
Ursula	Lieutenant Commander WK Cavaye	Sailed for patrol 8 April. On passage
Severn	Lieutenant Commander BW Taylor	Sailed for patrol 5 April. On passage towards North Sea
Narwhal	Lieutenant Commander RJ Burch	Sailed for patrol from Immingham 10 April

— Appendix D —
Ships in Narvik Harbour, 8 April 1940

Name	Nationality	BRT	Built	Fate
S/S *Cate B*	Norwegian	4,285	1920	Severely damaged 10 April. Sunk 18 April. Raised and scrapped in 1954
S/S *Eldrid*	Norwegian	1,712	1915	Damaged and ran aground 10 April. Later sunk by German aircraft. Wreckage blown up in 1945
S/S *Haaleg*	Norwegian	1,758	1922	Sunk in shallow water 13 April. Salvaged 1940 but laid up. Repaired after the war
M/T *Rødskjael*	Norwegian	133	1914	Sunk by German aircraft 4 May. Salvaged 1940 and repaired
S/S *Saphir*	Norwegian	4,306	1905	Sunk by British destroyers 10 April. Raised and scrapped in 1957
S/S *Bernisse*	Dutch	951	1915	Abandoned after FAA attack 12 April. Further damaged on 13th, partly sunk. Scuttled 15 April. Raised and scrapped in 1949
S/S *Boden*	Swedish	4,264	1914	Damaged by British destroyers 10 April. Partly sunk on 13th and abandoned by crew on 15th. Later sunk. Raised and scrapped in early 1950s
M/S *Oxeløsund*	Swedish	5,613	1923	Damaged during attack on 10 April. Ran aground and abandoned. Sunk 8 May after having been further damaged during air attack. Salvaged in 1947 and rebuiLieutenant Scrapped in 1962
M/S *Stråssa*	Swedish	5,603	1922	Had left Narvik 6 April but anchored with engine problems. Intercepted by German destroyers and sent back. Damaged during attack on 10 April. Later sunk, probably through German demolition
S/S *Torne*	Swedish	3,792	1913	Ready to leave morning of 9 April. Shelled by British destroyers 10 April. Scuttled 12 April. Raised and scrapped in 1955
S/S *Blythmoor*	British	6,582	1922	Captured by Germans 9 April. Sunk by British destroyers 10 April (6 dead). Captain DJ Nicholas. Raised and scrapped in 1954
S/S *Mersington Court*	British	5,141	1920	Captured by Germans 9 April. Damaged on 13 April and sunk by Germans on 15th. Raised and scrapped in 1952

S/S *North Cornwall*	British	4,304	1924	Captured by Germans 9 April. Damaged on 13 April and sunk by Germans on 15th. Captain Charles Evans. Raised and scrapped in 1952
S/S *Riverton*	British	5,378	1928	Captured 9 April. Most likely sunk on 13 April. Raised and scrapped after the war
S/S *Romanby*	British	4,887	1927	Left Narvik during evening of 8 April but intercepted by German destroyers and sent back. Torpedoed and sunk on 10 April
S/S *Aachen*	German	6,388	1923	Lightly damaged 10 April. Scuttled on 16 as blockade. Kapitän Lieberum. Salvaged in 1951, but lost during tow
S/S *Altona*	German	5,398	1922	Hit by British torpedo, shelled and sunk 10 April. Three dead. Raised and scrapped 1954
S/S *Bockenheim*	German	4,902	1924	Run aground and set on fire by own crew 9 April. Broken up on site. Remains still visible
S/S *Hein Hoyer*	German	5,836	1937	Sunk by British destroyers 10 April. Raised and repaired in the early 1950s
S/S *Martha Hendrik Fisser*	German	4,879	1911	Sunk by British destroyers 10 April
M/S *Neuenfels*	German	8,096	1925	Scuttled by own crew during 10 April. Also hit by torpedo. Two dead. Had loaded 11,700 tons ore
Jan Wellem	German	11,776	1921	Arrived Narvik 8 April. Set on fire by own crew in late April. Repaired and use as depot ship. Scrapped 1947
S/S *Lippe*	German	7,849	1917	Damaged on both 10 and 13 April. Scuttled on 14th in shallow water. Later salvaged. Torpedoed 1944
S/S *Frielinghaus*	German	4,339	1922	Sunk by British destroyers 10 April. Salvaged and repaired. Mined 1942
S/S *Planet*	German	5,881	1922	En route from Murmansk to Germany, but not part of Weserübung forces. Sunk by British destroyers 10 April. Salvaged and repaired. Mined 1945
S/S *Diana*	Swedish	213	1922	Harbour tug. Sunk on 13 April or later. Salvaged and repaired 1940
S/S *Styrbjørn*	Swedish	167	1910	Harbour tug. Sunk after FAA attack on 12 April. Later salvaged and used by Germans in Narvik. Restored and can today be seen in Oslo harbour

— Appendix E —
The German Naval Invasion Forces

C-in-C Kriegsmarine Grossadmiral Erich Raeder
SKL Chief of Staff: Konteradmiral Schniewind
OKM Chief of Staff: Fregattenkapitän Schulte Mönting

C-in-C Marinegruppenkommando West, Wilhelmshaven Generaladmiral Alfred Saalwächter
Groups 1, 2, 3, 4, 6, 10, 11

C-in-C Marinegruppenkommando Ost, Kiel Admiral Rolf Carls
Groups 5, 7, 8, 9

Surface Ships

Cover force
Acting Flottenchef, Vizeadmiral Günther Lütjens[22]
Battleship *Gneisenau*   Kapitän zur See Harald Netzbandt, (flag)
Battleship *Scharnhorst*   Kapitän zur See Kurt Caesar Hoffmann

Group I: Narvik – Kampfgruppe Nienburg
C-in-C Destroyers (Führer der Zerstörer) Kapitän zur See, Kommodore Friedrich Bonte
Departure from Wesermünde 23:00, 6 April
Führerschiff (flagship for the C-in-C)
Z21 Wilhelm Heidkamp   Korvettenkapitän Hans Erdmenger

1. Zerstörer Flottille – Fregattenkapitän Fritz Berger (onboard *Z2*)[23]
Z2 Georg Thiele   Korvettenkapitän Max-Eckart Wolff

3. Zerstörer Flottille – Fregattenkapitän Hans-Joachim Gadow (onboard *Z18*)
Z17 Diether von Roeder   Korvettenkapitän Erich Holtorf
Z18 Hans Lüdemann   Korvettenkapitän Herbert Friedrichs
Z19 Hermann Künne   Korvettenkapitän Friedrich Kothe
Z22 Anton Schmitt   Korvettenkapitän Friedrich Böhme

4. Zerstörer Flottille – Fregattenkapitän Erich Bey (onboard *Z9*)
Z9 Wolfgang Zenker   Fregattenkapitän Gottfried Pönitz
Z11 Bernd von Arnim   Korvettenkapitän Kurt Rechel
Z12 Erich Giese   Korvettenkapitän Karl Smidt
Z13 Erich Koellner   Fregattenkapitän Alfred Schulze-Hinrichs

Support
Tankers: *Jan Wellem, Kattegatt*
Transports: *Rauenfels, Alster, Bärenfels*

Group II: Trondheim – Kampfgruppe Detmold
Kapitän zur See Hellmuth Heye

Departure from Cuxhaven 22:00, 6 April 1940
Heavy cruiser *Admiral Hipper* – Kapitän zur See Hellmut Heye

2. Zerstörer Flottille – Fregattenkapitän Rudolf von Pufendorf (on board *Z5*)
Z5 Paul Jacobi	Korvettenkapitän Hans-Georg Zimmer
Z6 Theodor Riedel	Korvettenkapitän Gerhardt Böhmig
Z8 Bruno Heinemann	Korvettenkapitän Georg Langheld
Z16 Friedrich Eckholdt	Korvettenkapitän Alfred Schemmel

Support
Tankers: *Skagerrak, Moonsund*
Transports: *Sao Paulo, Levante, Main*

Group III: Bergen – Kampfgruppe Bremen
Acting C-in-C Scout Forces, Konteradmiral Hubert Schmundt onboard *Köln*
Departure from Willhelmshaven and Cuxhaven 00:40, 8 April. The S-boats departed from Helgoland
Light cruiser *Köln*	Kapitän zur See Ernst Kratzenberg
Light cruiser *Königsberg*	Kapitän zur See Heinrich Ruhfus
Gunnery training ship *Bremse*	Korvettenkapitän Jakob Förschner
Depot ship *Carl Peters*	Kapitänleutnant Otto Hinzke
6th Torpedo Boat Flotilla	Korvettenkapitän Hans Marks (on board *Leopard*)
Leopard	Kapitänleutnant Hans Trummer
Wolf	Oberleutnant zur See Broder Peters,

1. S-Boot Flottille – Kapitänleutnant Heinz Birnbacher
S18, S19, S20, S21, S22, S24 (*S18* and *S20* collided at Helgoland and did not go to Bergen until later)

Auxiliary *Schiff 9 – Koblenz*
Auxiliary *Schiff 18 – Alteland*   Oberleutnant zur See Klaus Feldt

Schiff 111	Kapitänleutnant Borcherdt	arrived later, not
Hans Rolshoven	Kapitän Teich	part of invasion
Bernhard von Tschirschky		force proper

Support
Tankers: *Belt*
Transports: *Marie Leonhardt, Curityba, Rio de Janeiro*

Group IV: Kristiansand and Arendal – Kampfgruppe Karlshafen
Kapitän zur See Friedrich Rieve, commanding officer of *Karlsruhe*
Depart from Wesermünde 05:30, 8 April

Light cruiser *Karlsruhe*	Kapitän zur See Friedrich Rieve
Depot ship *Tsingtau*	Kapitän zur See Karl Klingner
C-in-C Torpedo Boats	Kapitän zur See Hans Bütow (on board *Luchs*)
Seeadler	Kapitänleutnant Franz Kohlauf
Luchs	Kapitänleutnant Karl Kassbaum
6th Torpedo Boat Flotilla	Korvettenkapitän Wolf Henne (to Arendal)
Greif	Kapitänleutnant Wilhelm-Nikolaus Freiherr von Lyncker

2. S-Boot Flottille – Korvettenkapitän Rudolf Petersen
S9, S14, S16, S30, S31, S32, S33

Support
Tanker: *Stedingen*
Transports: *Wiegand, Westsee, Kreta, August Leonhardt*

Group V: Oslo – Kampfgruppe Oldenburg
Konteradmiral Oskar Kummetz onboard *Blücher*
Departure from Kiel 03:00, 8 April

Heavy cruiser *Blücher*	Kapitän zur See Heinrich Woldag
Heavy cruiser *Lützow*	Kapitän zur See August Thiele
Light cruiser *Emden*	Kapitän zur See Werner Lange
Torpedo boat *Möwe*	Kapitänleutnant Helmut Neuss
Torpedo boat *Albatross*	Kapitänleutnant Siegfried Strelow
Torpedo boat *Kondor*	Kapitänleutnant Hans Wilcke

1. Raumboot Flottille – Kapitänleutnant Gustav Forstmann
R17 – Stabsobersteuermann Godenau
R18 – Kapitänleutnant Gustav Forstmann
R19 – Obersteuermann Wels
R20 – Leutnant zur See Jaeger
R21 – Leutnant zur See von Pommer-Esche
R22 – Stabsobersteuermann Scheurer
R23 – Stabsobersteuermann Rixecker
R24

Rau VII, Rau VIII

Support:
Tankers: *Euroland, Senator*
Transports: *Antares, Ionia, Muansa, Itauri, Neidenfels*

Group VI: Egersund – Kampfgruppe Elsflet
Korvettenkapitän Kurt Thoma of *M9*
Departure from Cuxhaven evening of 7 April

M1, M2, M9, M13 of 2nd Minesweeping Flotilla

Support
Transports: *Roda, Tübingen, Tijuca* and *Mendoza* to Stavanger. No transports to Egersund

Group VII: Korsör/Nyborg
Kapitän zur See Gustav Kleikamp
Schleswig-Holstein, Claus von Bevern, Nautilus, Pelikan, 7 auxiliaries, 2 transports (*Campinas* and *Cordoba*) and 2 tugs

Group VIII: Copenhagen
Korvettenkapitän Wilhelm Schröder
Hansestadt Danzig, Stettin. Escorted through the Belts by 13. Vp-Flottille

Group IX: Middelfart
Kapitän zur See Helmuth Leisner
Rugard, Otto Braun, Arkona, Monsum, Passat, M157, V102, V103, U.Jäg 107, R6, R7

Group X: Esbjerg
Kapitän zur See Friedrich Ruge
Königin Luise, M4, M20, M84, M102, M1201, M1202, M1203, M1204, M1205, M1206, M1207, M1208, R25, R26, R27, R28, R29, R30, R31, R32

Group XI: Limfjord, Thyborön
Kapitän zur See Walter Berger
Von der Gröben, M61, M89, M110, M111, M134, M136, R33, R34, R35, R36, R37, R38, R39, R40

Schlesien (Kapitän zur See Horstmann) was in southern entrance of the Danish Belts, covering the takeover of the Danish minefields and supporting groups 7, 8 and 9. When *Schleswig-Holstein* ran aground she helped pull her off

In the west, Kapitän zur See Böhmer led the minelayers *Roland, Cobra* and *Preussen* supported by *M10, M6, M12, M11* which laid a protective mine barrier off north-west Denmark on the night of the 8/9 April

Support Vessels

Ausfuhr Staffel

Ship	BRT	Destination	Depart	Fate
Bärenfels	7,569	Narvik	Brunsbüttel, 02:00, 3 April	Severely damaged and partly sunk by British aircraft in Bergen 14.04 after being delayed and diverted
Rauenfels	8,460	Narvik	Brunsbüttel, 02:00, 3 April	Delayed. Reached Ofotfjorden 10 April. Sunk by *Havock* coming out from first British attack on Narvik
Alster	8,570	Narvik	Brunsbüttel, 02:00, 3 April	Delayed. Captured by *Icarus* 10 April outside Bodø
Sao Paulo	4,977	Trondheim	Brunsbüttel, 21:00, 4 April	Delayed and redirected to Bergen where she struck mines laid by *Tyr* and sank early 10 April
Levante	4,768	Trondheim	Brunsbüttel, 02:00, 5 April	Arrived on 12 April
Main	7,624	Trondheim	Brunsbüttel, 02:00, 5 April	Captured by *Draug* at Haugesund and scuttled by own crew 9 April when taken to Britain
Roda	6,780	Stavanger	Brunsbüttel, 02:00, 7 April	Arrived according to plan. Shelled and sunk in Stavanger 9 April by *Æger.*

Tankerstaffel

Ship	BRT	Destination	Depart	Fate
Kattegat	6,031	Narvik	Wilhelmshaven, 3 April	Scuttled by own crew off Ørnes 10 April when intercepted by Nordkapp
Skagerrak	6,031	Trondheim	Wilhelmshaven, 4 April	Redirected to position offshore. Scuttled by own crew when intercepted by Sheffield 14 April
Jan Wellem	11,776	Narvik	Basis Nord, 08:00, 6 April	Arrived Narvik 8 April as planned. Set afire by own crew in late April
Euroland	869	Oslo	Hamburg, 13 April	Army tanker. Arrived Oslo as planed. Sailed with 3. Seetransportstaffel
Moonsund	322	Trondheim	Brunsbüttel, 08:00, 9 April	Luftwaffe tanker. Sunk by gunfire from British submarine Snapper outside Larvik 12 April
Senator	845	Oslo	Hamburg, 12:00, 6 April	Luftwaffe tanker. Arrived Oslo as planed. Sailed with 1. Seetransportstaffel
Belt	322	Bergen	Brunsbüttel, 08:00, 9 April	Luftwaffe tanker. Arrived Bergen as planned
Dollart	280	Stavanger	Brunsbüttel, 08:00, 9 April	Luftwaffe tanker. Possibly redirected to Kristiansand. Arrived Stavanger 28 April

Seetransportstaffeln[24]

Ship	BRT	Destination	Depart	Fate
1.Staffel				
Antares	2,592	Oslo	Stettin, 02:00, 7 April	Torpedoed and sunk by Sunfish 10 April. 6 miles off Lysekil
Ionia	3,102	Oslo	Stettin, 02:00, 7 April	Torpedoed by Triad 11 April in Oslofjord. Capsized and sank 12 April
Muansa	5,472	Oslo	Stettin, 02:00, 7 April	Arrived in Oslo early morning of 11 April
Itauri	6,837	Oslo	Stettin, 02:00, 7 April	Arrived in Oslo early morning of 11 April
Neidenfels	7,838	Oslo	Stettin, 02:00, 7 April	Arrived in Oslo early morning of 11 April
Wiegand	5,869	Kristiansand	Stettin, 17:00, 6 April	Arrived as planned 9 April
Westsee	5,911	Kristiansand	Stettin, 17:00, 6 April	Arrived as planned 9 April
Kreta	2,359	Kristiansand	Stettin, 17:00, 6 April	Escaped unharmed from Trident 9 April. Arrived 13 April
August Leonhardt	2,593	Kristiansand	Stettin, 17:00, 6 April	Arrived as planned 9 April. Torpedoed and sunk by Sealion 11 April south of Anholt on return

Tübingen	5,453	Stavanger	Stettin, 07:00, 6 April	Arrived as planned 9 April
Tijuca	5,918	Stavanger	Stettin, 07:00, 6 April	Arrived as planned 9 April
Mendoza	5,193	Stavanger	Stettin, 07:00, 6 April	Arrived as planned 9 April
Marie Leonhardt	2,594	Bergen	Stettin, 04:00, 6 April	Arrived 10 April
Curityba	4,968	Bergen	Stettin, 04:00, 6 April	Ran aground north of Helsingborg 7 April. Pulled off and arrived Oslo 11 April
Rio de Janeiro	5,261	Bergen	Stettin, 04:00, 6 April	Sunk by Orzel off Lillesand 8 April
2. Staffel				
Friedenau	5,219	Oslo	Gotenhafen, 16:00, 8 April	Torpedoed and sunk in Kattegat by Triton 10 April
Kellerwald	5,032	Oslo	Gotenhafen, 16:00, 8 April	Arrived Oslo 11 April
Hamm	5,874	Oslo	Gotenhafen, 16:00, 8 April	Arrived Oslo 11 April, two days late. Sunk by Seawolf 18 April on return
Wigbert	3,647	Oslo	Gotenhafen, 16:00, 8 April	Torpedoed and sunk in Kattegat by Triton 10 April
Espana	7,465	Oslo	Gotenhafen, 16:00, 8 April	Arrived Oslo 11 April
Rosario	6,079	Oslo	Gotenhafen, 16:00, 8 April	Arrived Oslo 11 April
Tucuman	4,621	Oslo	Gotenhafen, 16:00, 8 April	Arrived Oslo 11 April
Hanau	5,892	Oslo	Gotenhafen, 16:00, 8 April	Arrived Oslo 11 April
Wolfram	3,648	Oslo	Gotenhafen, 16:00, 8 April	Arrived Oslo 11 April
Wandsbek	2,388	Oslo	Gotenhafen, 16:00, 8 April	Arrived Oslo 11 April
Scharhörn	2,643	Oslo	Königsberg, 16:00, 8 April	Diverted to Fredrikshavn

3. Staffel consisted of several groups. First *Moltkefels, Köln, Dessau, Philipp Heineken* and *Thetis*. Later joined by *Leuna, Cordoba, Campinas, Entrerios, Buenos Aires* (which first went from Kiel to Korsør in Denmark). *Utlandshörn* and *Urundi* also sailed to Oslo. In addition, *Friedrich Breme* (10,397 GRT) carried fuel for the Luftwaffe.

Luftwaffe Support Vessels

Ship	BRT	Destination	Depart	Fate
Karl Meyer	1,351	Kristiansand		Diverted to Stavanger
Hans Rolshoven	985	Bergen		Arrived as planned in the morning of 9 April
Bernhard von Tschirschky	960	Bergen		Arrived as planned in the morning of 9 April
Stedingen	8,036	Stavanger	Hamburg, 7 April	Sunk off Stavern by British submarine Trident 8 April

— Appendix F —
Losses

In comparison to the expenditures of men and matériel, which became commonplace later in the war, the cost of the Norwegian campaign was modest. Still, it was as painful as all other losses to those involved.

German Losses

On 10 June, Group XXI summarised the losses of the army during the Norway campaign.[25] It is assumed that the Landsers lost onboard *Blücher* are included in 'losses during transport'. If so, the majority of the 'battle losses' occurred after 15 April. The Kriegsmarine reported the naval losses in Norway on the 21 June.[26] Most of these occurred between 8 and 15 April. The Luftwaffe losses are estimated at between 100 and 150, based on the number of aircraft lost during April.

	Dead officers / NCOs and men	Missing/PoW	Wounded
Army losses during transport	18/1093	–	–/64
Army battle losses	39/683	7/362	52/1323
Navy losses	26/178	28/327	12/211
Civilians	5	5	

British Losses

In the first phase of the invasion, before the campaign proper commenced, British losses amounted to some 500 men from *Ghurka*, *Eclipse*, *Glowworm*, *Hardy*, *Hunter*, *Hotspur*, *Eskimo*, *Cossack*, *Punjabi*, *Tarpoon*, *Thistle* and *Sterlet*. In addition some 110 airmen of the RAF and FAA were lost at sea or over Norway or Denmark between 7 and 13 April.

Norwegian Losses

During the invasion and ensuing campaign 853 Norwegian soldiers lost their lives. Of these, 283 were from the navy and most of these fell during April. Around 200 civilians also died. The number of military and civilan wounded reached almost 1,000, some of them were seriously wounded and remained cripped for life.[27]

Abbreviations and Glossaries

Abbreviations

A/A	Anti-aircraft
AP	Armour-piercing (shell or grenade)
A/S	Anti-submarine
BC	Bomber Command
B-Dienst	Beobachtungsdienst 'observation service'; German shipboard cryptanalyst service
BrT	British Time
CAP	Combat Air Patrol
CoS	Chiefs of Staffs
GC & CS	Government Code and Cypher School at Bletchley Park responsible for providing signals intelligence and information assurance to the UK government and armed forces
DCT	Director Control Tower
FAA	Fleet Air Arm
FO	Foreign Office
GeT	German Time
HOK	Hærens Overkommando (Norwegian Army Supreme Command)
ID	Infantry Division
JIC	Joint Intelligence Committee
KTB	Kriegstagebuch (German war diary)
MI6	Early name used for SIS foreign intelligence
MIR	Military Intelligence Research (intelligence section of the British War Office, formed in 1939)
NCO	Non-commissioned officer
NCS	Naval Control of Shipping
NS	Nasjonal Samling (Quisling's National Unification Party)
OIC	Operational Intelligence Centre
OKH	Oberkommando des Heeres (German Army High Command)
OKW	Oberkommando der Wehrmacht (German High Command of the Armed Forces)
SAP	Semi-armour piercing (shell or grenade)
SDD	Sjøforsvars Distrikt (Norwegian Sea Defence District)
SDS	Sjøforsvars Sektor (Norwegian Sea Defence Sector)
SIS	Secret Intelligence Service
SKL	Seekriegsleitung (German Naval High Command)
SOE	Special Operations Executive
SOK	Sjøforsvarets Overkommando (Norwegian Supreme Command of the Sea Defence Forces)
Sigint	Signals intelligence (assessment of intercepted radio traffic)
USW	Ultra-short wavelength (short-range radio for communication between ships)
VC	Victoria Cross
VHF	Very high frequency
W/T	Wireless telegraphy (basic radio for coded signals)

Norwegian Words and Terms

Avsnitt	Sector
Bevoktningsavdeling	Auxiliary unit
Etterretning	Intelligence
Festning	Fortress
Flystasjon	Air base
Føreren	'The Leader' – affectionate name for Quisling used by his followers
Gubben	'The Old Man' – affectionate name for Prime Minister Nygaardsvold
Indreleia	The Leads
Jager	Destroyer; also fighter aircraft
Kommanderende admiral	Commanding Admiral
Kommanderende general	Commanding General
Krigshavn	Restricted area
Kystartilleriet	Coastal artillery
Kystvakten	Coast guard
Marinen	Navy
Marinens Flyvevåben	Naval Air Arm
Minelegger	Minelayer
Minesveiper	Minesweeper
Norges Bank	Bank of Norway
Nøytraltetsvakt	Neutrality Guard
Panserskip	Armoured coastal cruiser; pansership
Sambandssentral	Communication central
Sjef	Commanding officer; C-in-C
Sjøforsvaret	Sea Defence Forces
Stab	Staff
Statsråd	Council of State (official meeting between king and government)
Storting	Norwegian Parliament
Stortingspresident	Parliamentary president
Torpedobåt	Torpedo boat
Undervannsbåt (U-båt)	Submarine

The three Norwegian letters Æ, Ø and Å (æ, ø and å) are used as in the original language.
Æ (æ) or ae is pronounced as in a drawn-out pronunciation of carry or marry.
Ø (ø) or oe is pronounced very much as in the English sir or the French *fleur*.
Å (å) or aa is pronounced much like the o in more or before.

German Words and Terms

Abwehr	German military untelligence
Aufklärungs Abteilung	Reconnaissance unit
Auswärtiges Amt	Foreign Office
DeTe-Gerät	Shipborn radar (Dezimeter-Telegraphie-Gerät)
Fallschirmjäger	Paratrooper
Fliegerkorps	Air force corps

FdT (Führer der Torpedoboote)	C-in-C torpedo boats
FdZ (Führer der Zerstörer)	C-in-C destroyers
Gebirgsjäger	Mountain ranger
General der Flieger	Air force general
General der Infanterie	Infantry general
Grossadmiral	Grand Admiral
Hauptmann	Army captain
Jäger	Ranger
Kapitän zur See	Naval captain
Kriegsmarine	German Navy
Landser	Affectionate name for German soldiers, referring to medieval mercenaries carrying a lance
Luftwaffe	German Air Force
Radfahrschwadron	Bicycle unit
R-Boot, Raumboot	Fast minesweeper (R-boat)
Reichskanzlei	Reich Chancellery, buildings of the German government, including Hitler's offices
Reichsleiter	National leader; the highest paramilitary rank of the Nazi Party
Rittmeister	Cavalry captain
S-Boot, Schnellboot	Motor torpedo boat, S-boat (known as E-boat later in the war)
Sonderstab Weserübung	Special Staff Weserübung
Studie Nord	Initial draft of plans for the invasion of Norway
Wehrmacht	German armed forces
Wesertag	Weser day. Codname for 'D-Day Weserübung'
Weserübung Nord	The invasion of Norway
Weserübung Süd	The invasion of Denmark
Weserzeit	Weser time. Codname for the timing of the landings on Weser day. 05:15 German time, 04:15 Norwegian and British time
Zerstörer	Destroyer. Also used for heavy fighters such as Bf110

Naval Ranks

Royal Norwegian Navy	Royal Navy	Kriegsmarine
Matros	Seaman	Matrose
	Able Seaman	Matrosen-Gefreiter
	Leading Seaman	Matrosen-Obergefreiter
	Leading Seaman (4.5 years)	Matrosen-Hauptgefreiter
	Senior Leading Seaman	Matrosen-Stabsgefreiter
		Matrosen-Stabsobergefreiter
Kvartermester	Petty Officer	—maat*
	Chief Petty Officer	Ober—maat
	Boatswain	Bootsmann
	Senior Boatswain	Stabsbootsmann

	Chief Boatswain	Oberbootsmann
	Senior Chief Boatswain	Stabsoberbootmann
Kadett	Midshipman/Cadet	Fähnrich zur See
Fenrik	Sub-Lieutenant	Oberfähnrich zur See
Løytnant	Lieutenant (Junior)	Leutnant zur See
	Lieutenant (Senior)	Oberleutnant zur See
Kaptein	Lieutenant Commander	Kapitänleutnant
	Commander	Korvettenkapitän
	Captain (Junior)	Fregattenkapitän
Kommandørkaptein	Captain	Kapitän zur See
Kommandør	Commodore	Kommodore
Kontreadmiral	Rear Admiral	Konteradmiral
Viseadmiral	Vice Admiral	Vizeadmiral
Admiral	Admiral	Admiral
		Generaladmiral
	Admiral of the Fleet	Grossadmiral

* A man's trade would prefix the word -*maat* such as Funkermaat for a radio petty officer or a Bootsmannsmaat for a deck petty officer.

Notes

Introduction

1 *Weserübung* means 'Weser Exercise', named after a river in north Germany.

Chapter 2

1 Albert Viljam Hagelin was born in Bergen in 1882; studied in Germany and settled in Dresden. He met with Quisling in 1936 and from 1938 was his representative and liaison in Germany.

2 Außenpolitische Amt der NSDAP; not to be confused with the traditional Foreign Office. Rosenberg was preoccupied with 'Germanic' theories and racial concepts, far from political reality and any relevant understanding of Scandinavia. The professional diplomats in the Foreign Office were not happy with this and considered it at best a distraction.

3 Raeder's motives for advocating a Norwegian venture are many and complex. Most importantly, he wished for the Kriegsmarine to be seen as an important part of the armed forces, dominant in the North Sea and actively threatening British supply lines in the Atlantic. Raeder realised the burden that would be put on the navy to defend a sustainable German presence in Norway and probably did not initially foresee a full-scale invasion.

4 The date of this meeting varies in different accounts between 13 and 16 December. Jodl's diary gives the 13th.

5 Scheidt was supposedly a 'specialist' on Norway and had visited Oslo frequently. He was hastily called to Berlin when the meeting emerged, evidencing its improvised nature. Neither Raeder nor Rosenberg was present.

6 Hagelin frequently had to translate or clarify what Quisling tried to say in his poor German.

7 Parliamentary President Hambro is referred to in Raeder's minutes of the meeting as 'Juden Hambrow'. Hambro's great-grandfather had converted to Christianity in 1810, before moving to Norway from Denmark.

8 Quisling's party Nasjonal Samling, the National Unification Party, was founded in 1933. The party programme was largely based on 'return to law, order, justice and tradition'. The elections in 1933 and 1936 were disastrous and the NS was never even close to entering Parliament. The party virtually collapsed and following a series of withdrawals and exclusions was reduced to a small core of followers faithful to Quisling in person.

9 Some 200,000 Reichsmarks were sent to the NS from Berlin and used to renew the party offices and re-establish the party newspaper. Quisling's request for military training for some of his men was deferred.

10 RM 7/180; RM 7/177; N 172/14; N 172/16 (*Nachlass Boehm*); *Innstilling fra Undersøkelseskommisjonen av 1945*, Appendix, vol. 1; *Straffesak mot Vidkun Abraham Quisling*; Raeder, *Mein Leben*, vol. 2; Halder, *Kriegstagebuch*; Krancke, *Norwegen Unternehmen*; and Gemzell, *Raeder, Hitler und Skandinavien*. Rosenberg noted in his diary that Raeder afterwards talked of Quisling as a 'handshake from fate' (. . . *ein Wink der Schicksals*) and already on 16 December, Schulte-Mönting, Raeder's Chief of Staff, referred to the 'Anglo-Norwegian conspiracy' as a fact to Kommendörkapten Forshell, the Swedish naval attaché in Berlin.

11 The Oberkommando der Wehrmacht (High Command of the Armed Forces) was in effect Hitler's personal staff, combining strategic, operational and ministerial functions. The army, navy and air force were subordinated to the OKW. General Wilhelm Keitel was head of the OKW, while Generalmajor Alfred Jodl led the operations staff (Führungsstab), which acted as a General Staff.

12 N 172/14, *Nachlass Boehm*. Scheidt uses the word '*integer*', which translates to 'untouched', indicating Quisling might become useful after a potential invasion. Whether these were Scheidt's or Hitler's thoughts is not obvious.

13 Quisling never acknowledged the consequences of his visit to Berlin; claiming he had only had 'political discussions'.

14 Halder, *Kriegstagebuch*. Jodl tasked Hauptmann von Stenburg, a Luftwaffe officer in the OKW, with compiling the initial report 'Studie Nord'.

15   Kapitän zur See Theodor Krancke was captain of the pocket battleship *Admiral Scheer*, which was about to dock in Wilhelmshaven for a lengthy overhaul. He was ordered to Berlin on the 30th and arrived a few days later.

16   KTB SKL A Jan40; RM 7/92; and RA II-C-11-2150/52. During WWI, Fregattenkapitän Wolfgang Wegener issued a series of memoranda to some of his colleagues. Bases in Norway, he argued, would hinder a British blockade of Germany by securing Scandinavian supplies to Germany and giving access to the Atlantic. Secondly, it would push the Royal Navy back to the Shetland–Faeroes–Iceland line and open possibilities for further German expansion towards these islands to really open 'the door to the Atlantic'. In 1929, Wegener, by now a retired Vizeadmiral, repeated his matured viewpoints in a book entitled *Die Seestrategie des Weltkrieges*, which became widely distributed in the German Navy. Wegener saw bases in Norway – and in Denmark and France – as means for an offensive sea war; not goals; and he never suggested occupying the country. Raeder opposed Wegener's concepts for political reasons, but also because it would be difficult to envisage a priority of resources necessary to produce the naval capacity required by Wegener's vision. That Wegener's book was 'Hitler's sea gospel' is a gross exaggeration – even if he was aware of its concepts.

17   RM 7/180; RM 7/177; and Raeder, *Mein Leben*, vol. 2; Jodl's diary, in Hubatsch, *Weserübung*; and Rosenberg's diary, in *Straffesak mot Vidkun Abraham Quisling*.

18   N 300/5, *Bericht und Vernehmung des Generalobersten von Falkenhorst, Gruppe XXI, Ia, Kriegestagenbuch* and Halder, *Kriegstagebuch*. General Keitel and Generalmajor Jodl were also present.

19   N 300/5, *Bericht und Vernehmung des Generalobersten von Falkenhorst*. According to von Falkenhorst, Hitler said he should be subordinated to the OKW to secure co-operation with the other arms and 'avoid problems with the Luftwaffe'.

20   All officers who became involved had to take a personal oath of secrecy. Von Falkenhorst brought most of his staff with him to Bendlerstrasse, including his Chief of Staff, Oberst Erich Buschenhagen, Oberstleutnant Hartwig Pohlman (Ia), Hauptman Egelhaaf (Ic), Major Treuhaupt, Major von Tippelskirch, Oberleutnant Bieler, Oberst Bäntsch, Hauptmann Michelly and Rittmeister Goerz. Oberstleutnants Schmidt, Boetzel and Bader and Hauptman Heil were specialists in transportation, signalling and intelligence while Major Hammersen and Lieutenant Johnsen spoke Norwegian. From the OKW, Oberstleutnant von Lossberg and Major Deyhle were involved. In the SKL the number of officers with knowledge of what was being planned grew quickly as the plans progressed.

21   RM 7/92. Scheidt came to Oslo during December and Hagelin in January. Both soon started to produce a series of intelligence reports painting a grim picture of the situation, seen from the German side. Neither man had real political or military contacts and the reports were largely analytical and very one-sided.

22   RA II-C-11-1200-1210; N 300/5, *Bericht und Vernehmung des Generalobersten von Falkenhorst*; Steen, *Norges Sjøkrig 1940–1945*, vol. 1; and Hubatsch, *Weserübung*.

23   RM 35 I /32; RH 24-21/23; Halder, *Kriegstagebuch*; and Hartmann, *Nytt lys over kritiske faser i Norges historie*.

24   A document describing Norwegians and giving advice on behaviour towards them was issued. In this it stated that: 'The Norwegian is extremely freedom loving and self-conscious, defying every attempt at forceful submission . . . He is introvert and reluctant and suspicious of strangers. Hence, no orders or harsh words. Use time.'

25   RM 35 I/32; KTB SKL A Feb40; N 300/5, *Bericht und Vernehmung des Generalobersten von Falkenhorst*; MSg 2/1882. Åndalsnes Namsos, Molde and Bodø were on the list of target ports but abandoned for lack of available ships.

26   Tankerstaffel (tanker echelon) and Ausfuhrstaffel (transport echelon). They were not to act as Trojan horses, though.

27   RM 7/11; RM7/92; and KTB SKL A March40. It was considered unlikely that the transport ships would arrive at all, if they had not done so by Wesertag. Many were indeed intercepted while others arrived late, with dire consequences.

28   RM 35 I/32; and RM 35 I/35. They did use Morse signals in English, though, and each ship received orders as to which British ship they should pretend to be.

29   N 300/5, *Bericht und Vernehmung des Generalobersten von Falkenhorst*.

30   RH 24-21/17; RM 35 I/32; RM 7/92; RM 7/11; RM 7/177; and KTB SKL A March40.

31   This was hardly the case. Oberst Knauss had been the Luftwaffe representative already in Sonderstab Weserübung.

32   A Geschwader is a large wing consisting of three Gruppen or squadrons and a Stab or staff unit: altogether some 100 aircraft. A KG or Kampfgeschwader is a bomber wing, so II/KG 30 is number II Squadron of the 30th Wing. 2./KG 30 is 2nd Staffel or flight in no. I Squadron of the 30th Wing (1st, 2nd and 3rd Staffels making up no. I Squadron).

33 RM 35 II/35.

34 The Foreign Office was probably aware that an operation was being deliberated through von Ribbentrop's connections with the Reichskanzlei, but was officially notified through a memorandum from Keitel on 2 April with instructions for the German ministers in Oslo and Copenhagen. Thus they had little time to prepare, far less influence the issue.

35 MSg 2/1882. General Pellengahr of 196 ID, for example, was briefed in person by von Falkenhorst in early March and had to swear silence by handshake. He was only allowed to include his First Staff Officer (Ia) Major Schäfer in his confidence. To everybody else in the division, the activities and preparations were related to exercises.

36 RH 24-21/17; RM 7/180; N 172/1, *Nachlass Boehm*; KTB SKL A March40; RM 7/9; N 300/5, *Bericht und Vernehmung des Generalobersten von Falkenhorst*; Raeder, *Mein Leben*, vol. 2; and Jodl's diary in Hubatsch, *Weserübung*.

37 The krigshavn or restricted areas were defined near fortifications and harbours such as inner Oslofjord, Kristiansand, Bergen and Trondheim. Narvik was not declared krigshavn due to the large international traffic. A krigshavn could only be passed by merchant ships in daylight and warships were forbidden altogether. The navy had instructions to apply force 'as appropriate' against ships not conforming to regulations.

38 FO 371/23658; Koht, *For Fred og Fridom i Krigstid 1939–1940*; Skodvin, *Norwegian Neutrality*; and Nøkleby, *Da krigen kom*. Like many Norwegian words, Nøytralitetsvakten (the Neutrality Watch) has a subtle double meaning, referring both to the forces guarding the neutrality and the concept that the neutrality is protected by military force.

39 The C-in-C of the Navy had since the nineteenth century been called commanding admiral – Kommanderende Admiral – with headquarters and Admiral Staff in Oslo. Henry Edward Diesen was appointed commanding admiral in 1938.

40 The auxiliaries were usually requisitioned fishing vessels, whale-boats and small freighters, mostly with a 76-mm gun or a couple of machine guns, intended for patrol and guard duties and not expected to engage in combat.

41 FO 371/21087.

42 In the Oslofjord, for instance, during WWI it was decided to fortify the Rauøy–Bolærne line in the outer part of the fjord by torpedo batteries, medium-calibre guns and mine barrages. Thirteen 15-cm guns were ordered from Bofors but not delivered until 1920/22. The guns were never mounted and remained safely in storage in 1940.

43 RA-II-C-11-51; and *Innstilling fra Undersøkelseskommisjonen av 1945*. The Investigating Committee was established in 1945 to 'investigate the dispositions of the Parliament, the government, the Supreme Court and other civilian and military authorities before and after 9 April'. It presented its conclusions in December 1946.

44 FO 371/21088.

45 During the autumn, negotiations took place between Britain and Norway regarding the use of Norway's merchant fleet in addition to the general war trade agreement. By mid-November 1939, an agreement was signed for the use of some 150 of the largest and most modern Norwegian tankers in addition to 700,000 BRT of tramp tonnage. By 8 April 1940, 2.45 million BRT of Norwegian vessels were sailing under British charter – flying the Norwegian flag – of which 1.65 million BRT were tankers. The War Trade Agreement was signed in March.

46 Hobson and Kristiansen, *Norsk Forsvarshistorie*, vol. 3; and Skard, *Mennesket Halvdan Koht.*

47 Koht, *For Fred og Fridom i Krigstid 1939–1940*. Koht wrote several memoirs during and after the war. These are invaluable as sources, but must, as all memoirs, be approached with caution.

48 In 1936, naval plans existed that would have created a small, but efficient RNN with modernised or new-built cruisers, destroyers, submarines, torpedo boats, aircraft and support vessels. This would have required a significant revision of the financial priorities of the government and Parliament and was never near reality, in spite of the number of jobs this might have created in yards and ports along the coast.

49 Hjelmtveit, *Vekstår og Vargtid.*

50 RA-II-C-11-51; Hjelmtveit, *Vekstår og Vargtid*; Skodvin, *Norwegian Neutrality*.

51 Hafsten et. al., *Flyalarm*; and Hobson and Kristiansen, *Norsk Forsvarshistorie*, vol. 3. Almost one hundred Douglas 8A-5 light bombers, Curtis H75A-8 fighters and Northrop N-3PB naval reconnaissance aircraft under contract in April 1940 were later delivered to the RNAF in Canada.

52 Eventually, two MTBs were commissioned by the RNN in Britain and served with distinction on the Channel coast.

53 In the meantime, the CoS had pointed out to the Cabinet and FO that it would not be possible to give direct help to Norway against German air attacks, but the FO decided it was not desirable to forward this information to Oslo.

54 It appears that Koht took Dormer's request for confidentiality so seriously he informed very few people apart from Nygaardsvold.

55 *Innstilling fra Undersøkelseskommisjonen av 1945*, Bilag, Bind II.

56 RA II-C-11-51; FO 371/23658; CAB 66/3; Koht, *Norsk Utanrikspolitikk fram til 9. April 1940*; Koht, *For Fred og Fridom i Krigstid 1939–1940*; and Kristiansen, *Krigsplaner og Politikk i mellomkrigstiden*.

57 Ljungberg was at the time of his appointment C-in-C of IR 1 *Østfold*. Within the army, Ljungberg was recognised as a competent officer and considered a respectable choice. CJ Hambro of *Høyre*, chairman of the Parliamentary Foreign Affairs Committee, considered Ljungberg too weak and 'cultured' for the task.

58 With the appointment of Ljungberg, the Norwegian government had the following ministers, also in office on 9 April 1940: Prime Minister Johan Nygaardsvold, Minister of Foreign Affairs Halvdan Koht, Minister of Justice Terje Wold, Defence Minister Birger Ljungberg, Minister of Finance Oscar F. Torp, Minister of Trade and Commerce Anders R. Frihagen, Minister of Labour Olav Hindal, Minister of Agriculture Hans Ystgaard, Minister of Church and Education Nils Hjelmtveit, Minister of Social Welfare Sverre K. Støstad, Minister of Supply Trygve Lie.

59 Hjelmtveit, *Vekstår og vargtid*; Lie, *Leve eller dø*; and Skard, *Mennesket Halvdan Koht*. Koht never blamed Ljungberg officially, but according to his son-in-law Sigmund Skard – with access to his diaries – he held him responsible for much of what went wrong on 9 April. After the war, Ljungberg fell sick and never answered the accusations.

60 Generalmajor Laake had been ill for some time. He turned 65 in April and it was expected he would retire to his farm outside Oslo soon after. British intelligence notes of January 1940 described Laake as 'a shrewd hard working officer with sound judgement and a certain faculty for handling political questions . . . appointed C-in-C for political reasons and in face of considerable opposition, . . . more successful than expected', WO 106/1840.

61 Kristiansen, *Krigsplaner og politikk i mellomkrigstiden* – lecture in Oslo Militære Samfunn, 15 December 2004.

62 RA II-C-11-51; Ruge, *Felttoget*; Kristiansen, *Krigsplaner og Politikk i mellomkrigstiden*; Steen, *Norges sjøkrig 1940–1945*, vol. 1; Skard, *Mennesket Halvdan Koht*; Koht, *For Fred og Fridom i Krigstid 1939–1940*; Koht, *Norsk Utanrikspolitikk fram til 9. april 1940*; and *Innstilling fra Undersøkelseskommisjonen av 1945*.

63 Signal issued from Whitehall, 3 September 1939 to all units on learning that Churchill had been appointed First Lord.

64 In the late 1930s, about 10 per cent of Britain's imports came from Scandinavia, mostly food (bacon, butter, egg and fish) or raw materials (iron ore, ferroalloys, timber, wood pulp and paper). Should these supplies be cut off, the 'fighting services would suffer', in particular from the loss of iron ore, timber and butter. The export to Scandinavia made up about 10 per cent of the total (coal, cotton, wool, machinery and chemicals). It was considered unproblematic if this came to a stop.

65 ADM 205/2; ADM 199/892; ADM 116/4471; ADM 1/10680; CAB 66/1; CAB 65/1; CAB 65/2; FO 371/22276; FO 371/23658; Butler, *Grand Strategy*, vol. 2; and Macleod, *Time Unguarded*.

66 Net figures were even higher due to the richness of the Swedish ore (62–66 per cent on average).

67 CAB 66/6; ADM 116/4471; FO 371/24821; RM 7/194; KTB SKL A Oct39; KTB SKL A Jan40; KTB SKL A March40; Karlbom, *Sweden's Iron Ore Exports to Germany*; Bröyn, *Den svenske malmeksport fram til besetingen av Narvik i April 1940*; and Munthe-Kaas, *Krigen i Narvik-avsnittet 1940*. British off-take through Narvik would be at an all-time high in March 1939. In February 1940, the Cabinet was made aware through a report from the Ministry of Shipping that the dependence in Britain on the Narvik ore was 'more serious' than previously realised.

68 RM 98/89. Kapitänleutnant Liebe held that *Garoufalia* carried no Greek markings and her flag was not lit.

69 CAB 65/4.

70 CAB 65/4; CAB 66/4; FO 371/24820; ADM 116/447; Butler, *Grand Strategy*, vol. 2; Dilks, *Great Britain and Scandinavia in the Phoney War*; and Macleod, *Time Unguarded*.

71 FO 419/34. The word *technicists* is used in the original.

72 FO 371/24820; ADM 199/892; CAB 66/4; CAB 65/11; CAB 65/4 and Dilks, *The Diaries of Sir Alexander Cadogan*. The French government would be informed and their concurrence obtained before the memorandum was sent.

73 CAB 65/11; ADM 116/4471; Koht, *For Fred og Fridom i Krigstid 1939–1940*; and Skodvin, *Norwegian Neutrality*.

74 Colban, *Femti år*. Laurence Collier was one of the few in the FO with indepth knowledge of Norway. He was appointed British minister to Norway in late February and meant to take over from Dormer in May, but events would not have it so. From 1941, Collier was made responsible for the political liaison with the Norwegian government-in-exile in London and in 1945 followed its return to Oslo, remaining as a British ambassador in Oslo until 1952.

75 ADM 116/4471.

76 CAB 65/11; CAB 66/5.

77 CAB 65/11; Macleod, *Time Unguarded*; Churchill, *The Second World War*, vol. 1; and Butler, *Grand Strategy*, vol. 2.

78 Macleod, *Time Unguarded*.

79 There were some initial objections from the Polish government-in-exile in Angers to the use of Polish troops in Norway, but eventually General Sikorski agreed that some 4,500 Poles, adequately equipped and trained, could be made available.

80 CAB 65/11; CAB 65/12; CAB 66/6; CAB 66/5; FO 371/24818; Macleod, *Time Unguarded*; and Butler, *Grand Strategy*, vol. 2.

81 Mannerheim, *Minnen*.

82 Reynaud, *La France a sauvé l'Europe*; and Kersaudy, *Norway 1940*.

83 CAB 65/12; Koht, *For Fred og Fridom i Krigstid 1939–1940*; and Lie, *Leve eller dø*.

84 CAB 65/12; FO 419/34; and Macleod, *Time Unguarded*.

85 Macleod, *Time Unguarded*; and Butler, *Grand Strategy*, vol. 2.

86 CAB 65/12.

87 Dilks, *The Diaries of Sir Alexander Cadogan*; and Kersaudy, *Norway 1940*.

88 CAB 66/6; CAB 65/12; PREM 1/419; Dilks, *The Diaries of Sir Alexander Cadogan*; and Butler, *Grand Strategy*, vol. 2. British violations of Norwegian territory by aircraft and destroyers became so frequent from mid-March that Koht on 23 May called First Secretary Lascelles of the British Legation to his office, making an official complaint and making him aware of the instructions issued to the A/A batteries throughout the country to fire on intruders.

89 CAB 66/6; CAB 66/7; CAB 80/105; WO 193/773; WO 106/1969; FO 371/24819; FO 371/22283; and FO 371/23674.

90 Hinsley, *British Intelligence in the Second World War*.

91 *Innstilling fra Undersøkelseskommisjonen av 1945*, Bilag, Bind II.

92 Prem 1/419. Dilks, *The Diaries of Sir Alexander Cadogan*; and Reynaud, *La France a sauvé l'Europe*.

93 The Ministerial Committee on Military Coordination or MCC had been formed in November 1939 to act as the main link between the War Cabinet and the CoS and their advisers.

94 CAB 65/12; and Churchill, *The Second World War*, vol. 1.

95 CAB 66/7.

96 FO 371/24819; CAB 66/6; CAB 66/7; ADM 199/388; and ADM 199/379.

97 Personal communication from John Warburton-Lee (grandson of the captain). This was to be Captain Warburton-Lee's second but last letter. On the next day, 5 April, just before departure, he finished yet another letter to his wife in which he wrote: 'I've been telling you repeatedly that you won't hear from me for a bit – I think now that it is really so.'

98 These reports, which had very little authenticity in them, came to Berlin through different channels. Virtually all originated in the same faction in Oslo, however, and were filtered through Scheidt's small group at the embassy, painting a one-sided picture of Allied threats and Norwegian compliance. Minister Bräuer, who saw things differently (and far more correctly) advised Berlin to strengthen Norwegian neutrality rather than sever it, but was ignored.

99 RM 7/92; MSg 2/1882; KTB SKL A March40; Halder, *Kriegstagebuch*; Jodl's diary, in Hubatsch, *Weserübung*; and *Lagevorträge des Oberbefehlshabers der Kriegsmarine vor Hitler 1939–1945*.

100 RM 35/I 35; RM 24-21/30; and Halder, *Kriegstagebuch*. Not until mid-March could the transport ships assigned to Weserübung start moving in the Baltic. It would be 22 March before Swinemünde was ice free.

101 RM 35 II/35; RNSM A1995/312; RM 7/180; and KTB SKL A March40.

102 KTB SKL A March40.

103 This is not in agreement with internal SKL notes. It is notable that every time Raeder pushed for an intervention in Norway he also watchfully covered his back one way or another. Hitler, probably as Raeder expected, listened more to his aggressive ideas than his cautions, but at least a warning had been recorded.

104 RM 7/180; RM 7/124; RM 7/92 and KTB SKL A March40; RM 35 I/32; Halder, *Kriegstagebuch*; and *Lagevorträge des Oberbefehlshabers der Kriegsmarine vor Hitler 1939–1945*.

105 RM 12/II/167; and RA-II-C-11-51. Dönitz ordered all Hartmut material (the orders for Weserübung) destroyed, and this was done. *U21* was taken to Kristiansand from where she was released on 9 April.
106 *Förspelet till det Tyska angreppet på Danmark och Norge den 9 April 1940*; RM 7/124; RM 35 I/31; RM 7/180; and KTB SKL March40. The German High Command paid close attention to what the international newspapers wrote. In the war diary of the SKL, for example, there was a daily morning summary of the main news regarding the 'Norwegian question'.
107 N 300/5, *Bericht und Vernehmung des Generalobersten von Falkenhorst*; RM 7/92; RM 35 II/35; and RM 7/11.
108 Letter from Buschenhagen 31 July 1957, in Hartmann, *Varslene til de Nordiske Legasjoner før den 9.April 1940*.
109 Weser-day is 9 April. RM 35 I/39; RM 7/11. German summertime was Middle European time + one hour. Dawn would be almost an hour earlier in Narvik than in Kristiansand, so Weser-time was a compromise.
110 RM 7/11.
111 RM 35 II/35.
112 Chamberlain complained bitterly that 'the trouble with the French is that they cannot keep a government for six months or a secret for half an hour', and General Ironside said, 'I don't know whether the politicians or the press are the worst; everybody knows what we are preparing.' Dilks, *Great Britain and Scandinavia in the Phoney War*; and Macleod, *Time Unguarded*.
113 KTB SKL A March40; and RM 7/11 '. . . einem "Wettlauf" zwischen England und Deutschland auf Skandinavien.'

Chapter 3

1   Harriman, *Mission to the North*.
2   The 'Foreign Office' increased from two or three officers in 1936 to seven in 1940. In addition to registration, dissemination and analysis of incoming data, it was also responsible for the internment of personnel from the belligerents and the making of 'handbooks' on the armed forces of neighbouring countries. There was no active intelligence anywhere at all.
3   A limited official military co-operation emerged between Sweden and Norway in 1938, including exchange of maps, air warning and intelligence. Other contact (as with Denmark) was on a personal level between individual officers. They met occasionally, but mostly communication was by telephone, telegram or letter.
4   Koht did discuss most of the incoming material with his senior staff, but they offered little in terms of differing views.
5   RA-II-C-11-51; *Innstilling fra Undersøkelseskommisjonen av 1945*; Koht, *For Fred og Fridom i Krigstid 1939–1940*; Kristiansen, *Krigsplaner og Politikk*; and Heradstveit, *Kongen som sa nei*.
6   FO 371/23667; Steen, *Norges Sjøkrig 1940–1945*, vol. 1; Hinsley, *British Intelligence in the Second World War*; Churchill, *The Second World War*, vol. 1; and Macleod, *Time Unguarded*.
7   ADM 223/82; Hinsley, *British Intelligence in the Second World War*; and Beesly, *Very Special Intelligence*.
8   Handwritten on the front page of the report is: 'I wish I could believe this story. German intervention in Scandinavia is what we want!' – signed by Laurence Collier.
9   FO 419/34; ADM 116/4471; and FO 371/24815.
10 ADM 116/4471; and CAB 65/12.
11 CAB 66/7.
12 FO 371/24815.
13 Two months later almost the same happened again when the aircraft carrier *Glorious* was lost.
14 AIR 22/8; AIR 41/73; ADM 116/4471; and ADM 223/82. In fact, the presence of *Leipzig*, *Nürberg* and *Prinz Eugen* at Kiel, all out of commission, added to the confusion of the number of German ships at sea.
15 Denham, *Inside the Nazi Ring*.
16 ADM 223/126; and Denham, *Inside the Nazi Ring*.
17 Hinsley, *British Intelligence in the Second World War*. See also Beesly, *Very Special Intelligence*.
18 Ismay, *The Memoirs of General the Lord Ismay*.
19 *Förspelet till det Tyska angreppet på Danmark och Norge den 9 April 1940*; N 300/5, *Bericht und Vernehmung des Generalobersten von Falkenhorst*; Hartmann, *Varslene til de Nordiske Legasjoner før den 9. april 1940*; and Koht, *Norsk Utanrikspolitikk fram til 9. april 1940*; and *Innstilling fra undersøkelseskommisjonen av 1945*. The letter from Berlin arrived at the Foreign Office in Oslo on 3 April. It was copied to the prime minister's office and to the MoD.

20 FO 371/24815.
21 The letter had a wide distribution and was copied to the king, the Ministry of Defence and the commanders. In another draft letter to the Parliamentary Committee, Scheel criticised Koht directly. Before submitting the letter, Scheel discussed its content with Hambro, who persuaded him not to send it. It is possible that Koht knew the draft existed.
22 Jervell, *Scener fra en ambassades liv*.
23 Steen, *Norges Sjøkrig 1940–45*, vol. 1; and *Förspelet till det Tyska angreppet på Danmark och Norge den 9 April*.
24 Koht, *Norsk Utanrikspolitikk fram til 9.April 1940*; and Koht, *For Fred og Fridom i Krigstid 1939–1940*.
25 The Dutch Investigation Committee interviewed Sas in March 1948; he was killed in an accident six months later.
26 Kjølsen, *Mit livs logbog*; and Hartmann, *Varslene til de Nordiske Legasjoner før den 9.April 1940*. The two accounts were in all likelihood 'near identical' as regards Denmark. Regarding Norway, there is more ambiguity.
27 *Innstilling fra undersøkelseskommisjonen av 1945*, appendix, vol. 2. See also Hartmann, *Varslene til de Nordiske Legasjoner før den 9. april 1940*.
28 RM 7/11. The exclamation mark is in the original text. Somehow this lead must have gone cold, as Hans Oster survived until April 1945 when he was executed with Canaris and others allegedly having been involved in the attempt on Hitler's life in July 1944.
29 *Betænkning til Folketinget*; and Kjølsen, *Mit livs logbog*. Stang did not disclose to Kjølsen that he had not only talked to Major Sas but also Undersecretary Boetzelaer at the Dutch Embassy. The latter later insisted they had discussed Norway being part of the German plans, which Stang denied.
30 *Betænkning til Folketinget*.
31 RA II-C-11-52.2/52.6. It appears that Scheel signed the telegram late on the 4th, but as the cipher personnel had left for the day, it was not coded and sent until next morning.
32 RA-II-C-11-51 and *Innstilling fra undersøkelseskommisjonen av 1945*, appendix, vol. 2. To limit the amount of paper, signals like this were circulated to the officers but not copied.
33 There were several rumours of mountain troops in northern Germany – and that these had been issued with seasickness pills. This was very unusual and indicated Norway or northern Sweden rather than Holland or Denmark.
34 *Betænkning til Folketinget*, Bilag, stenografiske referater 17.07.45; and Kjølsen, *Mit livs logbog*.
35 *Förspelet till det Tyska angreppet på Danmark och Norge*. Most likely, the warning was unrelated to Oster's initiatives and intended to reassure Stockholm they would not be threatened during the events to come.
36 Document in Lie, *Leve eller dø* and *Innstilling fra Undersøkelseskommisjonen av 1945*. Jens Bull had previously been attached to the embassy in Berlin and apparently shared Koht's scepticism towards the quality of its assessments.
37 *Betænkning til Folketinget*, appendix 4. This is not exactly what other documents indicate the Swedish government believed. Esmarch later wrote that Hamilton told him the Swedish Foreign Office 'did not put much faith in the rumours'.
38 During 8 April, a letter from Copenhagen arrived, explaining the background for the telephone call on the 5th, but this seems hardly to have been registered by anybody outside the staff at the Foreign Office.
39 Holm and Adlercreutz had communicated unofficially for years and knew each other well.
40 RA-II-C-11-51 and *Innstilling fra Undersøkelseskommisjonen av 1945*.
41 RA II-C-11-52.2/52.6; Jervell, *Scener fra en ambassades liv*; and *Aftenposten*, 20 June 2005. The radio and the news agencies were told to hold these 'rumours' back so as not to disturb the public.
42 The information came from the Danish Embassy, where Stang had been told a fleet had left Stettin with mountain troops onboard. Kjølsen, who had received the information from the US naval attaché, Schrader, was convinced the ships were heading for Norway. Stang later denied having received any information other than what was in the telegram. *Innstilling fra Undersøkelses-kommisjonen av 1945*, appendix, vol.2; and Kjølsen, *Mit livs logbog*.
43 RA II-C-11-52.2/52.6; Willoch Papers; Steen, *Norges Sjøkrig 1940–1945*, vol. 1; and Ræder, *De uunnværlig flinke*. Gudrun Martius figures in many documents as Gudrun Ræder, but she did not marry Johan Ræder until late 1940, in London. Miss Martius's version of the events of 7 April were written down in November 1941 at the request of Trygve Lie, who had replaced Koht as foreign minister in the Norwegian government-in-exile in London in November 1940. Koht played down the whole episode. The diary of Håkon Willoch has kindly been made available by his son Kåre Willoch and is referred to as the 'Willoch Papers'.

44 Heradstveit, *Kongen som sa nei*; Koht, *For Fred og Fridom i Krigstid 1939-1940*; Koht, *Norsk Utanrikspolitikk fram til 9. April 1940*; Lie, *Leve eller dø*; and *Innstilling fra Undersøkelseskomiteen av 1945*, appendix, vol.2. Not until 1941 in London did the ministers become aware of the full set of incoming documents.

45 Kjølsen, *Optakten til den 9. april*; see also *Betænkning til Folketinget*.

Chapter 4

1   RM 48/176.

2   De Laporte's mission to Norway around 22 March and meeting with Quisling upset Schreiber and he flew to Berlin to protest. The Abwehr was consequently instructed to sever links with Norway.

3   From mid-January, Quisling had been ill and then underwent an operation for a jaw inflammation. He was only back on his feet by mid-March, still not fully restored.

4   RM 7/11; RM 7/180; N 172/14, *Nachlass Boehm*; Hartmann, *Spillet om Norge*; Hartmann, *Quislings konferanse med den tyske overkommando*; and Jodl's diary, in Hubatsch, *Weserübung*. During his trials after the war, Quisling denied any recollection of meeting Piekenbrock, claiming he only met Frits Clausen, the Danish NS party foreman. There is, however, no doubt that the meeting took place.

5   Pruck, *Abwehraussenstelle Norwegen*; and Hartmann, *Spillet om Norge*.

6   Bicycle Squadron of the 169th Reconnaissance Unit. Rittmeister is a rank equivalent to captain.

7   Most of the knowledge of the German side of the occupation of Egersund stems from the correspondence between Friedrich Rudolf Eickhorn and the local historian Ingvald Rødland in 1962. These documents have kindly been made available by Jostein Berglyd of Dalane Folkemuseum and collectively referred to as the 'Eickhorn Papers'.

8   Kammeraden-Echo No. 2, Erinnerungen und Informasjon für Angehörige des ehemaligen Grenadier-Regiments 193.

9   Jodl's diary, in Hubatsch, *Weserübung*.

10 Similar notes (in both English and French), were delivered to the Swedish Foreign Office in Stockholm as well as to the Norwegian and Swedish Embassies in London and Paris.

11 FO 371/24815; and Koht, *For Fred og Fridom i Krigstid 1939–1940*.

12 FO 371/24815; and Koht, *For Fred og Fridom i Krigstid 1939–1940*.

13 Harriman, *Mission to the North*.

14 Koht, *Norge neutralt och överfallet*; and Kjølsen, *Optakten til den 9. April*. The film was also shown to an assembly of diplomats in Berlin as well as in the German embassies in Copenhagen and Stockholm the same day.

15 Koht, *For Fred og Fridom i Krigstid 1939–1940*. The existence of the note was known in Berlin during 6 April.

16 Lie, *Leve eller dø*. Nygaardsvold had called Hambro, informing him of the Allied note. Both agreed a meeting was appropriate, but Koht saw no need to rush things and only agreed to meet on the following Tuesday, 9 April.

17 RM 7/11. The emphases appear in the original document.

18 ADM 199/474 and ADM 199/393.

19 Some sources give the seaman's name as Ricky, others as Gillo.

20 ADM 199/473. The trawlers *Friesland*, *Blankenburg* and *Nordland* were captured. Due to the rising seas on the morning of 7 April, only few British sailors got onboard the latter and *Hostile* was ordered to escort her to Kirkwall.

21 ADM 223/126; and ADM 199/474. The same signal was also sent to *Birmingham*.

22 *Jan Wellem* had been deployed as a U-boat supply depot at Basis Nord.

23 RA II-C-11-2150/52; RA II-C-11-1200/10; RM 7/11; and RM 35/II-35. Between 5 and 7 April, *Alster*, *Kattegat*, *Rauenfels*, *Levante*, *Main*, *Bärenfels* and *Skagerrak* arrived in Kopervik. The British vice-consul Bernardes in Haugesund reported to his superiors in Bergen on 5 April that German ships were passing through the Leads with light loads and tons of coke on deck. The significance of this was not realised, and the information was forwarded to London.

24 KTB SKL A March40; RM 7/891; and RM 98/22.

25 ADM 199/288.

26 The B-Dienst or Beobachtungsdienst (observation service) was the German cryptanalyst service. Most large ships had B-Dienst units onboard, which in addition to reading enemy signals were also experts in jamming and fake signals.

27 ADM 234/380; RM 7/11; and RM 35/II-35.

28 *Eckholdt* was reserve for Group II and when *Hermann Schoemann* reported engine problems she was included.

29 RM 92/5267. To maintain security, Heye handed the orders to his commanders in person, adding comments.
30 Realising that he would be depending on the Luftwaffe for reconnaissance and defence in Trondheim, Heye had, on his own initiative, arranged with X Fliegerkorps to include fifty men and two trucks with equipment to set up an airbase.
31 RM 92/5267; and RM 92/5078.
32 Wesermünde was renamed Bremerhaven after the war.
33 Kommodore was an honorary title, not a formal rank.
34 Weserübung naval command was split between Marinegruppenkommando West (Naval Group West) in Wilhelmshaven and Marinegruppenkommando Ost (Naval Group East) in Kiel. Head of Group West, Generaladmiral Alfred Saalwächter, was on leave but returned on 6 April while Admiral Rolf Carls returned to Group East in Kiel.
35 Not that their lives would be long. Few of the Gebirgsjägers (mountain rangers) landing in Norway survived the war.
36 RM 35/I-39; RM 35/II-35; RM 48/176; RM 7/11; RM 54/30; and Busch, *Narvik*.
37 RM 48/176; RM 7/92; KTB SKL A March40; RM 92/5267; RM 92/5097; RM 92/5223; RM 35/I-39; and RM 35/II-35. In all, there were 450 men onboard *Lützow*, (400 Jägers and 50 Luftwaffe ground crew) in addition to twenty-three tons of stores, ammunition and equipment, including three motorcycles with sidecars.
38 The Royal Navy referred to *Scharnhorst* and *Gneisenau* as 'battlecruisers', because of their 28-cm guns, high speed and official displacement of 26,000 tons. The intention of the German Navy was for them to be battleships, even if they were seriously under-gunned in their initial version – which was meant to be temporary.
39 RM 7/11; RM 92/5178; and KTB SKL A March40. Raeder held Lütjens in high regard and when the Flottenchef Admiral Marschall went on sick leave in March 1940, he was chosen as his temporary replacement.
40 Jodl's diary, in Hubatsch, *Weserübung*.
41 The port cool-water pump of *Georg Thiele* fell out. It was not possible to make the pump work and the port engine could only run when the ship was moving at fifteen knots or more, giving natural cooling. It was decided she could continue.
42 Bf110 fighters arrived over the fleet at dawn. Later, long-range He111s took over while Do18 flying boats were scouting further ahead. The ships had large swastikas painted on the deck and blue standards were flying from the top of the main mast north of 56° N to facilitate identification by own U-boats and aircraft.
43 '. . . einen schwächlichen Eindruck', RM 92/5245. The attack was lead by Wing Commander Basil Embry. All returned.
44 RM 7/11; RM 92/5267; RM 92/5178; RM 48/176; RM 54/30; RM 35/II-35; ADM 116/447; ADM 223/82; AIR 41/73; AIR 14/172; AIR 20/6260; AIR 14/3413; AIR 14/666; AIR 24/216 and Heye, *Z 13 von Kiel bis Narvik*. Both Lütjens and Heye trusted the new radar (DeTe-Gerät), even if the operators often were confused by waves and land.
45 Three weather ships were deployed prior to Operation Weserübung: *WBS 3 Fritz Homann* and *WBS 5 Adolf Vinnen* operated north of Iceland, while *WBS 4 Hinrich Freese* was in a position off Bergen.
46 The German word 'Zerstörer' is equivalent to the British destroyer. The Zerstörers operated by the German Navy in 1940 belonged to two groups commissioned in 1934 and 1936, respectively.
47 RM 54/30; RM 48/176; RM 7/92; RM 92/5178; RM 92/5267; Heye, *Z 13 von Kiel bis Narvik*; and Dietl and Herrmann, *General Dietl, das Leben eines Soldaten*
48 Schmundt was acting Befehlshaber der Aufklärungsstreitkrefte (BdA) when Lütjens was acting Flottenchef.
49 Based on the poor weather forecast, Schmundt decided that Kapitänleutnant Heinz Birnbacher's 1st S-Boot Flottilla should proceed independently, but the storm never came as far south as predicted. *S18, S19, S20, S21, S22* and *S24* left Wilhelmshaven on 7 April. *S18* and *S20* collided off Helgoland and had to be towed to Sylt by tugs.
50 *Carl Peters* developed engine troubles and had to slow down for repairs, but Korvettenkapitän Marks had left early, anticipating just such an event and there was time to spare, even if *Peters* could only do twelve knots for a while.
51 *Unity* was probably the only submarine east of the German declared area at this time; she was off Horns Reef.
52 RM 50/87; RM 35/II-35; RM 92/5255; and RM 92/5258.
53 RM 92/5257.

54 Eickhorn Papers and RM 96/667. Group X for Denmark consisted of 2nd Minesweeper Flotilla and *Königin Luise*, plus the minelayers *Roland, Cobra, Preussen*, which were to reinforce the minefields off Denmark.

55 RM 92/5087; RM 92/5088; RM 35 I/32; and KTB SKL A March40.

56 RM 7/194. Whereas the other groups are mostly designated by Roman numerals in the German documents, Group V is often referred to as Gruppe Oldenburg, using the code-name for Oslo.

57 One Arado 196 aircraft was in the hangar, un-fuelled. The second aircraft was on the catapult, partly fuelled and operational. Four 50-kg aircraft bombs were stored in the hangar.

58 Landser was an affectionate name for German soldiers, referring to medieval mercenaries carrying a lance.

59 RM 92/5088; RM 92/5087; RH 24-21/30; BA-MA III M 35/; RA 57/93; and RM 92/5088.

60 Treuhaupt diaries, in Aspheim and Hjeltnes, *Tokt ved neste nymåne*. To avoid observation, the hotel was emptied, the area was closed off and armed guards kept all unwanted persons off limits.

61 AIR 22/8; ADM 223/126; ADM 223/82; AIR 14/669; and ADM 199/393. Communication between the Air Ministry and Admiralty must, on this day, have been slow and incomplete. *Gneisenau* and *Scharnhorst* had been sighted at anchor off Wilhelmshaven by a Blenheim in the Helgoland Bight. It was unusual for the battleships to be at such an exposed position but no efforts were made by Bomber Command to bring this observation up with the navy.

62 AT 1259/7 – FO 371/24815; and ADM 199/3.

63 Denham, *Inside the Nazi Ring*; and Roskill, *Churchill and the Admirals*. Captain Edwards noted in his diary on 4 April that he was 'sure we ought to cancel Operation Wilfred. Winston however, is obsessed with the idea of forcing enemy ships out of the fjords into the open waters and I fear we shall be compelled to continue.'

64 Squadron Leader Embry radioed a report just after the attack, but on incorrect wavelengths and the report was not delivered until after he landed shortly before 17:00. The B-Dienst onboard *Hipper* and *Gneisenau* both intercepted the signal and reported to Lütjens, who took it for granted they were being chased.

65 ADM 199/361; ADM 199/2202; ADM 223/126; ADM 199/388; and ADM 199/474. The French cruiser *Emile Bertin* also took to sea with the two destroyers *Tartu* and *Maillé-Brézé*, but lost contact during the night and turned back.

66 *Glasgow* had temporarily been detailed from 18th to 1st Cruiser Squadron to replace the damaged *Norfolk*. Forbes was informed from Rosyth in the afternoon that the embarkation of stores and troops on to the ships of 1st Cruiser Squadron continued according to plan and the ships would be at two hours' notice from midnight.

67 ADM 199/393; ADM 199/385; ADM 223/126; ADM 267/126; ADM 199/479; and Roskill, S. *The war at sea*.

68 Further signals from *Syrian* were received at 08:40 and 09:51. *Syrian* guarded the minefield until news of the invasion was heard on the radio and Kaaveland decided to go to Bodø, where he arrived at 02:00 on the 10th.

69 ADM 223/126; ADM 199/474; RA II-C-11-52; RA II-C-11-940; AE 2913/2; FO 419/34; and Willoch Papers.

70 ADM 199/474.

71 A brief signal was sent at first after having identified the destroyers as British, followed by a second with more details. The first signal arrived at the Admiral Staff at 07:30, the second at 09:38.

72 RA II-C-11-52, diary of Kaptein Ullring; and ADM 199/474. The British destroyers stayed off Bjørnsund Lighthouse until nightfall. Ullring was not aware of other events until listening to the news on the radio in the morning of 9 April.

73 RM 35/II-35; and Halder, *Kriegstagebuch*.

74 ADM 199/361.

75 Onboard *Lüdemann*, *Glowworm* was at first identified as the Canadian destroyer *Restigouche*.

76 There is some discrepancy between the German reports and war diaries as to the timing of the events this morning.

77 RM 92/5267; RM 48/176; and RM 54/30.

78 ADM 199/2202; ADM 53/113071; ADM 199/474; ADM 199/323; and ADM 223/126. *Glowworm*'s last signal was 'Enemy course is 090 —' These signals were apparently not received directly onboard *Renown*, but retransmitted from Scapa Flow, delaying them by thirty to forty minutes. From Scapa Flow they were also forwarded to the Admiralty.

79 ADM 199/361.

80 RM 92/5078. British sources state that *Glowworm* fired two torpedo salvoes, but *Hipper*'s log reports only one.

81 RM 7/486; RM 92/5267; and RM 92/5078. Heye was later criticised by his superiors for having got too close to *Glowworm* and above all for having gone through the smokescreen without knowing what lurked behind.

82 Counter-flooding later reduced the list to 4°. Part of the double bottom was opened resulting in the loss of 253 m³ fuel.

83 RM 92/5267; and RM 92/5078. In one of Heye's reports he mentions a white flag being seen onboard *Glowworm*.

84 RM 35/II-35; RM 92/5267; and RM 54/30. Eight men were later transferred to hospital in Trondheim, while thirty were kept onboard during the return to Wilhelmshaven. Six of the perished sailors from *Glowworm* are buried at Stavne churchyard outside Trondheim.The British sailors' lack of appreciation of the tactical situation and knowledge of where they were has been confirmed by several veterans. The German sailors on the other hand were generally well informed.

85 RM 48/176.

86 ADM 199/473. *Erich Giese* also briefly sighted what was presumably *Hero*, seeking to catch up with the fleet after leaving the dummy minefield at Bud, in the morning of 8 April. She was not sighted herself, though, and Korvettenkapitän Smidt decided not to pursue (RM 54/30).

87 RM 100/125.

88 RM 48/176; and RM 35/II-35.

89 One hundred and seven army soldiers came from I/IR 159 and fifty-six pioneers came from 169th Pioneer Battalion. The rest were Luftwaffe men from 13th and 33rd A/A Regiment and administrative personnel.

90 Thirty-five dead from *Rio de Janeiro* were buried at Kristiansand churchyard on 12 April and another fifteen on the 13th.

91 ADM 199/285; and Steen, *Norges Sjøkrig 1940–45*, vol. 2.

92 'Army this side! Navy this side!' Lieutenant Voss was from the regimental staff of IR 159.

93 RA II-C-11-52; and RA FKA Ec, 0125. Eventually, soldiers were ordered to Lillesand, where they arrived around 20:30.

94 ADM 223/126; and ADM 199/278. Reuter's news agency reported the sinking at 20:30 and a low-priority signal was sent to the Home Fleet at 22:55, received onboard *Rodney* at 02:58 the next day. *Orzel* was lost in the North Sea with sixty Polish and three British sailors in May. The wreck has never been found.

95 ADM 199/286.

96 RA-II-C-11/52; RA-FKA-II-C-11/1103; AE 2958/41; and RM 35/II-35. *Stedingen* was a civilian tanker, requisitioned by the Luftwaffe shortly after completion. She carried the name *Posidonia* for a while before being enrolled. When stopped by *Trident*, she had the name *Posidonia* on the hull, but used *Stedingen* in her SOS.

97 RA II-C-11-1100.

98 RM 57/93; and RM 92/5257.

99 RM 7/11; and RM 35/I 39: 'Keine britischen Kriegsflaggen setzen.' At the Nuremberg Trials, Raeder stated the reason for this change of orders to be fear of complications after the British mine-laying.

100 Oberleutnant Peters had orders from Schmundt to take the crew of *S19* onboard *Wolf* and sink the S-boat if she became unseaworthy. Temporary repairs were completed during the night though, and *S19* arrived in Bergen on 10 April.

101 RM 50/87; and RM 57/125.

102 Bartels, *Tigerflagge Heiss Vor!*; and Eickhorn Papers.

103 *Erich Giese* was lagging some forty to fifty miles behind due to gyrocompass failure and a faulty fuel pump. In addition, Korvettenkapitän Karl Smidt decided to stop and rescue a Gebirgsjäger NCO, who went overboard. In a remarkable feat of seamanship, the man was saved after six minutes in the icy water. RM 54/30.

104 RM 48/176; RM 92/5178; RM 54/30; and Busch, *Narvik*.

105 Diary of Major Lessing, in Kurowski, *Seekrieg aus der luft*.

106 RM 7/92; RM 7/11; RM 35/II-35; KTB SKL A April40; and RM 12/II-167.

107 'Tag höchster Spannungen' – Springenschmid, *Die Männer von Narvik*.

108 AT 1007/8; AT 1100/8 – ADM 199/474; and ADM 199/393. Admiral Forbes generally received these orders on the bridge of the *Rodney* some fifteen to forty-five minutes after they had been sent from Whitehall.

109 ADM 199/474. The upper strake of the port bulge started to peel away from thrusting into the heavy seas.

110 AIR 20/6260; AIR 22/8; ADM 199/474; and ADM 199/361. The initial signal from Hyde's Sunderland was picked up onboard *Rodney* and delivered to Admiral Forbes at 14:29. The complete version was

forwarded from C-in-C Rosyth at 15:12. A second Sunderland from No. 204 Squadron, patrolling off the Norwegian coast, was shot down in a running dogfight with a He111 of 1(F)./122 and never sent any reports. Flight Lieutenant RP Harrison and his ten-man crew were lost.

111   AIR 22/8. Due to the extreme weather, the two pilots (Lieutenants Bateman and Bush) were instructed to fly towards Norway. The Walrus landed near Kristiansund and the aircraft served with the Norwegian forces after the invasion.

112   After giving up searching for *Glowworm*, *Birmingham* and *Fearless* turned north again, *Hostile* having been detached with the prize *Nordland*. At 21:00 on 8 April, Captain Madden decided to heave-to because of a very heavy north-westerly sea and did not continue until 04:30 on the 9th. By the time *Renown* was eventually discovered, the fuel reserves of *Birmingham* and *Fearless* were such that they were ordered to proceed to Scapa Flow.

113   ADM 199/474; ADM 199/361; ADM 199/2202; and ADM 199/393.

114   ADM 199/388. Vice Admiral Cunningham received verbal orders from C-in-C Rosyth to disembark troops at 11:30, confirmed by AT 1216/8 an hour later.

115   ADM 234/17; ADM 199/393; ADM 199/379; and ADM 199/388.

116   A mistaken interpretation of Group V on a zigzag course.

117   ADM 199/361; ADM 199/393; ADM 223/126; ADM 199/388; ADM 199/2202; and ADM 199/385.

118   ADM 199/388; and Roskill, *Churchill and the Admirals*.

119   From Rosyth to Stavanger is some 350 miles, i.e. eighteen hours at twenty knots or fourteen hours at twenty-five knots. Cunningham, receiving news of German ships at sea, warned the captains under his command to be 'prepared to disembark troops'.

120   Koht, *Frå skanse til skanse*; and RA II-C-11-1200-1210. It is notable that Diesen called Koht and not Ljungberg.

121   RA II-C-11-1200-1210; Hambro, *7.Juni – 9.April – 7.Juni Historiske Dokumenter*; and Lie, *Leve eller dø*.

122   *Förspelet till det Tyska angreppet på Danmark och Norge den 9 April 1940*.

123   Koht, *Frå skanse til skanse*; and Koht, *Norsk Utanrikspolitikk fram til 9. April 1940*.

124   Hambro, *De første måneder*; and *Innstilling fra Undersøkelseskommisjonen av 1945*.

125   RA 1256-3/10; and RA II-C-11-51.

126   *Innstilling fra Undersøkelseskomiteen av 1945*, appendix, vol. 2. Nygaardsvold, Koht and Ljungberg all requested the meeting to end several times so they could return to their ministries.

127   RA 1256-3/10; and Jervell, *Scener fra en ambassades liv*.

128   RA II-C-11-1200/186; RA II-C-11-51; RA II-C-11-52; RA II-C-11-1100; and ADM 223/126.

129   Fjeld, *Klar til strid*.

130   RA II-C-11-1200-1210; RA II-C-11-52; Willoch Papers; and *Oscarsborg Sambandsjournal*. Orders for some of the forts to draft further personnel were issued around 18:30, but implied no urgency. After the war, Diesen held he had given orders to lay mines in the Oslofjord before midnight, but it has not been possible to find any record of this.

131   RA II-C-11-52.2/52.6; ADM 223/126; ADM 199/2159; Willoch, *Minner og meninger*; *Innstilling fra Undersøkelseskommisjonen av 1945*, appendix, vol. 2; and Diesen, *Kvinne i Krig*.

132   Kaptein Rolstad has a note in his diary saying 'Commanding general waved the reports [of the German moves] aside.'

133   RA II-C-11-51. Ljungberg most likely did not know of the Allied notes from the day before at this stage, so strictly speaking his answer appears to have been correct – though Hatledal probably asked in a more general sense.

134   RA II-C-11-51.

135   RA II-C-11-1200/1210; *Innstilling fra Undersøkelseskommisjonen av 1945*, appendix, vol. 2; and Lie, *Leve eller dø*.

136   Fjørtoft, *Mot stupet*; and Heradstveit, *Kongen som sa nei*.

137   Skard, *Mennesket Halvdan Koht*.

138   Koht, *For Fred og Fridom i Krigstid 1939–1940*; and Koht, *Norsk Utanrikspolitikk fram til 9.April 1940*.

139   The two men left Berlin in the company of Major-General Himer, Chief of Staff of General Kaupisch. The latter and his secretary parted company in Copenhagen with a similar task there.

140   It appears that at the legation, only the attachés Spiller and Schreiber and the Abwehr men Pruck and Benecke had any knowledge of Operation Weserübung. After the war, Bräuer told the Norwegian historian Nøkleby that he guessed what was happening when he heard of *Rio de Janeiro*.

141   'Der Bevollmächtigte des Deutschen Reiches bei der Norwegischen Regierung' or 'Plenipotentiary of the Reich'.

142   GFM 33/1111; N 172/14; Pruck, *Abwehraussenstelle Norwegen*; *Innstilling fra Undersøkelseskommisjonen av 1945*; Hartmann, *Spillet om Norge*; Nøkleby, *Da krigen kom*; Steen, *Norges Sjøkrig 1940–45*, vol. 2; Guhnfeldt, *Fornebu 9. April*; and Hubatsch, *Weserübung*.

143   Guhnfeldt, *Fornebu 9. April.*
144   RM 7/92; RM 12/II/167; and Steen, *Norges Sjøkrig 1940–45*, vol. 2.
145   GFM 33/1111. The information regarding the mines was forwarded to Vizeadmiral Lütjens shortly after 20:00. The reference to further mines at Halten was wrong; it is not known where this information came from.
146   Kempf was an Abwehr officer. He had been withdrawn from Norway during March as the Norwegian Police had identified him as an agent and were waiting for an excuse to arrest him. Upon his return in April, he had a new identity.
147   RM 12/II/167; GFM 33/1111; Hartmann, *Spillet om Norge*; and Pruck, *Abwehraussenstelle Norwegen.*
148   NS Generalsekretærens protokoll 1934–45, www.arkivverket.no.
149   *Straffesak mot Vidkun Abraham Quisling*; Knudsen, *Jeg var Quislings sekretær*; and N 172/14, *Nachlass Boehm.* Stortingspresident Hambro actually discussed with Nygaardsvold during the night whether it was necessary to take 'certain persons' into custody, but the issue was overtaken by events.
150   ADM 223/126; ADM 199/288; ADM 199/1847; ADM 199/361; and ADM 234/380. Larvik had good landing facilities, railway connections and no defences. Landings there would be a good alternative to forcing the forts of the Oslofjord.
151   Behrens was part of the group detailed to take over the Norwegian broadcasting after the occupation.
152   According to *Lützow's* war diary, the contents of this signal, in line with orders from the SKL, had been suggested by Thiele hours before, when things looked rather more optimistic.
153   RM 92/5223; RM 92/5259; RM 92/5097; RM 92/5088; RM 57/93; and RH 24-21/30. From now times given are Norwegian.
154   The auxiliary *Farm* patrolled the eastern side of the fjord while *Skudd II* was to the west of *Pol III.*
155   *Pol III* usually had a seventeen-man crew, but on this night, two were sick.
156   RA II-C-11-1102.
157   RM 57/93; and RA II-C-11-1100. The survivors were transferred to *Emden*, and later released in Oslo. The wreck of *Pol III* was taken over by the Germans and after repairs in Oslo, renamed *Samoa* and assigned to Hafenschultzflotile Oslo as *NO 05*. Later, she was transferred to Tromsø. After the war, she was extensively rebuilt and still served as a fishing vessel in the 1990s.

Chapter 5

1   RA II-C-11-1100.
2   1st Minelayer Division consisted of the ancient ships *Laugen, Glommen, Nor* and *Vidar*. The barrage was planned as three to four rows of contact mines, 8,000 metres long. It would take at least twelve hours to load the mines and for the vessels to be in position to start laying them.
3   There is an unsolved controversy in the reports of the commanding admiral, the Admiral Staff and SDD1 over orders given or not regarding the mines in outer Oslofjord and at Oscarsborg. Whatever the reasons, no mines were laid.
4   RA-II-C-11-1100; and RA-II-C-11-1103. At 22:31, a copy of the telegram from the embassy in London warning that German ships were heading for Narvik was also received from the Admiral Staff – without any comments.
5   RA II-C-11-1100.
6   RM 92/5087. Since all documents from *Blücher*, including war diary, log and signals book, were lost, Heymann re-recorded the events assisted by some of the surviving officers, Senior Gunnery Officer Korvettenkapitän Kurt-Eduard Engelmann in particular. The senior engineering officer, Fregattenkapitän (Ing) Karl Thannemann, later lost with *Bismarck*, made a similar record of events for the engine room area.
7   RM 92/5223; RM 92/5087; and Kummetz's report, in Koop, and Schmolke, *Heavy Cruisers of the Admiral Hipper Class.*
8   The signal only arrived at Oscarsborg after fire had been opened.
9   RA II-C-11-1100; RA II-C-11-1102; and RM 57/93. The crew eventually abandoned *Otra* at Filtvet and during the morning men from *Kondor* came onboard, immobilising her and making the guns unserviceable.
10   Enger had a week earlier been relieved as commander of the landside batteries by Kaptein Hjelvik, but due to the seriousness of the situation, Oberst Eriksen ordered him back in command.
11   The mines planned for the Drøbak Narrows were remote-controlled cable mines. These were ready in nearby magazines, but would have taken days to prepare and lay.
12   Kommandørkaptein Anderssen had been commander of the torpedo battery at Oscarsborg for a generation. In 1927, however, he had moved to the reserve and settled as a businessman and pilot in Drøbak.

13 RA II-C-11-1100.
14 ADM 234/427; RM 70/1; RM 92/5259; RM 92/5087; RM 92/5088; RM 92/VM855/47900-910; RM 92/5223; and Pruck, *Abwehraussenstelle Norwegen*. On midday of 8 April, a radio signal from Naval Attaché Schreiber, forwarded by Group East to *Blücher*, stated that there in all likelihood were no mines at Drøbak.
15 Bøhmer's report, in Omberg, A., *Blücher's undergang, Kampen om Oslofjorden*; and Steen, *Norges Sjøkrig 1940–45*, vol. 2.
16 RM 92/5223; and RM 92/5097. Kapitän Thiele had been CO of one of the forts in the Baltic for six months in 1939 and knew the potential of land-based guns well.
17 RM 92/5088; RM 92/5087; and RA-FKA-II-C-11-1103. The aircraft was one of the MF11s, evacuated from Horten.
18 RA II-C-11-1100; and *Oscarsborg sambandsjournal*. The emphasised word is underlined in the journal.
19 RA II-C-11-1100; RA II-C-11-1102/1110; and RH 24-21/30. In other reports, time varies between 04:19 and 04:25.
20 RM 92/5087. The companionway was destroyed and the wounded were lowered in hammocks.
21 Norwegian sources report the hits in the opposite order, but all reports from *Blücher* have the hit in the foretop first.
22 BA-MA III M 35/1.
23 RA II-C-11-1100; RM 92/5087; and RM 92/5088. A few soldiers were lightly wounded by splinters from shells bursting in the trees. Some houses in the Drøbak area were hit, killing two women, Anette Hansen and Olaug Nyhus.
24 RM 92/5087; BA-MA III M 35/1; and RM 92/5088.
25 RA II-C-11-1100. In his time of service, Anderssen had fired several hundred torpedoes during exercises and he was recognised as one of the navy's foremost experts on this weapon.
26 RH 24-21/30.
27 RM 92/5087; RM 92/5088; BA-MA III M 35/1; and SKL 25908/41.
28 RM 92/5223. At the time, it was thought that the hits were '24-cm shells' from the Kaholm battery, but there is no doubt they were 15-cm shells coming from the Kopås battery.
29 RM 7/11; RM 92/5088; RM 92/5259; RM 92/5223; and RM 92/VM855/47900-910.
30 No. 1 gun (manned by cadets) ran out of ammunition after firing the ten shells that had initially been brought up from the magazine. No. 2 had one or two left, while no. 3 gun encountered temporary problems and stopped firing after three or four shells.
31 RM 70/1; and Steen, *Norges Sjøkrig 1940-45*, vol. 2.
32 At least three packages of floating documents were found by Norwegians. One (or possibly two) by civilians, one by the guardsmen who came to intern the survivors and one at Oscarsborg by Anderssen and his men. The Germans searched for the documents, but they were well hidden and not found. Neither, however, did they reach Norwegian authorities in time to make any difference.
33 The floats arrived a few days before departure and few knew how to handle them properly.
34 BA-MA III M 35/1; SKL 23685/41; RM 92/5223; SKL 23685/41; RM 92/5087; RM 92/5088; RH 24-21/30; and Hase, *Die Kriegsmarine erobert Norwegens Fjorde*. The time given for *Blücher's* sinking varies between 06:22 and 06:32.
35 Before he went into the water, Generalmajor Engelbrecht was given a lifebelt and a sailor rolled up his leather coat with his riding boots inside for him to use as an extra float and bring him dry to shore. SKL 23685/41.
36 The wounded were given priority indoors. Otherwise the men took turns cramming inside as best they could. During the night, the survivors had their first and only meal of the day: a potato each and some milk.
37 The order to withdraw the company came from Generalmajor Haug, the commander of 2nd Division via Oberstløytnant Graff-Wang, presumably due to reports of Spiller and the paratroopers heading into the Norwegian lines.
38 RM 92/5087; RM 92/5088; and RH 24-21/30.
39 RH 24-21/30.
40 RM 92/5087; RM 92/5088; and RH 24-21/30. Some two hundred survivors were brought onboard *Lützow* by *Norden* and the R-boats during the night. The wounded were forwarded to *Emden* as *Lützow's* hospital had been damaged.
41 Herzog, *Drei Kriegsschiffe Blücher*.
42 The naval historian Erik Steen categorically held that in a meeting with him in 1950 Briseid had confirmed Smith-Johannsen's version.

43 As the two sweepers were not subordinated to SDD1, the orders for preparedness were not issued to them and both captains allowed shore leave for parts of their crew.
44 RA II-C-11-1100; RA II-C-11/1102; Hovdenak's report; and Steen, *Norges Sjøkrig 1940–45*, vol. 2.
45 RA II-C-11-1102; and RA II-C-11-1100. The mines were eventually disarmed and offloaded at Melsomvik.
46 In general, the orders to each group consisted of a series of tactical goals with rules of engagement and a timetable, but otherwise left matters of detail to the commander. Detailed alternatives were sometimes outlined, but the execution of the attack always rested with the senior commander at the scene, making room for both success and failure.
47 RA II-C-11-1102. *Otra's* report, 'Enemy off Karljohansvern', was in code, and by the time it had been forwarded to *Olav Tryggvason*, decoded and brought to the bridge, events were already unfolding.
48 RM 7/486; and RM 70/1.
49 RM 70/1. These soldiers were landed quite some distance away and did not reach Horten until it was all over.
50 RM 57/93; RA II-C-11-1102; and Steen, *Norges Sjøkrig 1940–45*, vol. 2. The crew from *Pol III* were still onboard *Albatros* and could feel the hits. Later they saw several wounded being brought below.
51 RM 70/1; and RM 92/5223. There was at least one dead and several wounded onboard *R21*.
52 RA II-C-11-1100; and RM 92/5259.
53 Grundmann had the statement drafted in a notebook and it was typed while he waited.
54 RM 70/1; RA II-C-11-1100; RA II-C-11-1102; and Hovdenak's report.
55 RA II-C-11-1100. Smith-Johannsen tried to call the commander in Kristiansand to give him the correct version in person, but connection was not possible.
56 Legend later had it that Briseid was so angered by this order that 'his swearing was heard all over the yard'.
57 *Olav Tryggvason* was within a few days taken into German service by the crew from *Albatros*, first named *Albatros* and later *Brummer*. She was eventually destroyed in Kiel harbour in 1945. *Rauma* and *Otra* were also taken over.
58 RA II-C-11-1100. Kapitänleutnant(Ing.) Erich Grundmann, Oberleutnant Kurt Budäus and Stabsobersteuermann Arthur Godenau were awarded the Knight's Cross for their achievements in Horten.
59 RA II-C-11-1100.
60 This was according to the German backup plans, which listed Sandefjord, Larvik, Leira, Larkollen and Son as alternative landing sites from where it would be possible to move towards Oslo by railroad and car.
61 RM 92/5223; RM 92/5097; RM 92/5259; RM 57/93; RM 70/1; and RH 24-21/17. At one stage, Kapitänleutnant Neuss of *Möwe* felt obliged to ask: 'Which order applies, land troops or attempt to reach *Blücher*?'
62 As soon as the railway line was secured, trains were commandeered to facilitate the transport.
63 It appears the first attacks on the fortress were largely on the initiative of the pilots seeing the smoke from *Blücher* and the rest of the German ships still south of the Narrows. The radio frequencies assigned to the aircraft for communications with the navy did not function and the pilots could not communicate with Gruppe Oldenburg. A large number of the bombs did not explode and had to be defused in the months to come. In one instance, three bombs landed just a few metres away from one of the tunnel entrances, protected only by a thin door. Colonel Eriksen and several men were just inside and would probably not have survived had they exploded.
64 There were two L/60 Bofors 40-mm guns and three machine guns at Seiersten under the command of Løytnant Hans Sollie. One of the 40-mm guns malfunctioned after some twenty shots, the other fired as long as there was ammunition, damaging several aircraft and shooting down one. As long as the aircraft stayed high, the machine guns had little effect.
65 Evensen, *Oscarsborg forteller historie*.
66 RA II-C-11-1100.
67 RM 92/5097; RM 92/5223; RM 92/5259; and RA II-C-11-1100. Kontreadmiral Smith-Johannsen remained at Karljohansvern until the end of April, when he was released upon signing a declaration of no resistance. His son was killed fighting the Germans north of Oslo.
68 RA II-C-11-1100; and RM 92/5259.
69 RA II-C-11-1100; RM 57/93; RM 92/5097; and RM 92/5223. Most men and junior officers at Oscarsborg were released within a week. The officers from the mainland forts had, according to the Germans, offered resistance and were kept in PoW camps for several weeks.
70 The SKL insisted that navy personnel should be given 'naval tasks' and not subordinated to the army.
71 RM 92/522; RM 92/5259; and RM 57/93.
72 RH 24-21/30; and RM 92/5088. No aircraft is listed as missing in the Oslofjord region on 17 April. On the 16th, however, a Ju52 from KGzbV 105 vanished during a flight to Oslo. The three crewmembers are listed as lost by Luftwaffe, but there is no mention of any passenger. Jochen Woldag later wrote that

the widow of one of the crewmembers had been informed that her husband had vanished, without any further details. All investigations, according to Jochen Woldag, had been 'stopped from high up' (Herzog, *Drei Kriegsschiffe Blücher*).

73   Kummetz was back at his torpedo inspectorate. Heymann was in charge of the torpedo depot in Lorient. Many officers served somewhere in the U-boat branch. Woldag and Thannemann were dead.

74   RM 92/VM855/47900-910; SKL 23685/41, in Herzog, *Drei Kriegsschiffe Blücher* N300/5; *Bericht und Vernehmung des Generalobersten von Falkenhorst*; and KTB SKL A April40.

75   The wreck of *Blücher* today lies upside down at sixty to ninety metres depth outside Drøbak. Corrosion has taken its toll on the damaged hull and there is a constant leakage of oil.

76   The bodies were recovered from the sea and buried at Rauøy on 10 April.

77   RA II-C-11-1100; RM 70/1; and RM 92/5332.

78   A2 had one 76-mm gun, the R-boats two 20-mm cannons each.

79   RA II-C-11-1100; and RM 70/1. A2 was later towed into Teie, but left as a wreck. She is supposedly the oldest submarine ever to have been in battle. A3 and A4 returned to Teie after darkness and were sunk on the 15th. The Military Investigation Committee of 1946 found the conduct of Bruusgaard and Haga at fault and recommended that they were charged with neglect of duty.

80   RM 70/1; and RA II-C-11-1100. Stabsobersteuermann Karl Rixecker was later awarded the Knight's Cross.

81   RM 57/93; and RA FKA 2B.072.42(194). While hoisting the white flag, Private Hans Furuseth was attacked by an aircraft and killed.

82   Håøy and Måkerøy forts surrendered on 13 April, as did most other isolated units around Oslofjorden.

83   Twelve Gloster Gladiators had been purchased from Britain. Three had crashed, of which two were being rebuilt.

84   The identity of these aircraft remains uncertain, but they may have come from Long Range Reconnaissance Group 120 or 122 (Fernaufklärungsgruppe), the only units involved in Operation Weserübung flying Do17s.

85   1. Fallschirmjäger Regiment of General Kurt Student's 7th Airborne Division. 1st Company was led by Oberleutnant Schmidt and 2nd Company by Hauptmann Gröschke. 3rd Company under Oberleutnant von Brandis captured Sola-Stavanger. 4th Company under Hauptmann Gericke captured Aalborg airfield and the Storstrøm bridge in Denmark.

86   2./ZG 76 escorted the Ju52s taking the paratroopers to Aalborg while 3./ZG 76 covered Stavanger.

87   KGzbV: Kampfgeschwader zum Besondere Verwendung – Special Purpose Wing. KGzbV 1 had flown the paratroopers into exercise and battle since 1937. It consisted of well-trained, but young pilots without experience in instrument flying.

88   From Guhnfeldt, *Fornebu 9. April*. Other German reports vividly describe how Walther continued to argue with Drewes also after having landed in Aalborg.

89   I/ZG 76 later claimed and had approved destruction of four Gladiators, but this is wrong.

90   Guhnfeldt, *Fornebu 9. April*. Cato Guhnfeldt is one of those who have studied the air war in Norway to the greatest detail and in his book gives the following list of victories for the Norwegian pilots: Løytnant Tradin most likely shot down Leutnant Kort's Bf110 of 1./ZG 76. Sarsjant Schye probably downed the Bf110 of Unteroffizier Mütschele from 1./ZG 76. Sarsjant Waaler most likely shot down a He111 from 9./KG 26 over the Oslofjord. Løytnant Krohn and Løytnant Braathen probably damaged a He111 from III/KG 26, crash landing at Asker.

91   Leutnant Helmut Lent continued to fly the Bf110 in Norway, shooting down at least two British Gladiators over Bodø. Transferring to night fighters in September 1940, Lent continued to score and eventually received the Knight's Cross with Oak Leaves, Sword and Diamonds for his 110 credited victories (102 in night fighters). He died in a crash landing in 1944, by then C-in-C of NJG 3. Walter Kubisch stayed as Lent's backseat man and was killed with him. He was awarded the Knight's Cross in 1943, one of very few non-pilots to receive such an honour.

92   Hauptmann Ingenhoven was later awarded the Knight's Cross for this.

93   Guhnfeldt, *Fornebu 9. April*. The next day, III/IR 159, originally intended for Bergen, was flown in, as was III/IR 307 and III/IR 324. There was less chaos, but several aircraft crashed and far from all the soldiers arrived safely.

94   Hubatsch, *Weserübung*.

95   RA II-C-11-2150/52. Not until late morning of 10 April was the extended perimeter of Fornebu fully secured.

96   Landing through trees in deep snow, Sergeant George survived and spent the rest of the war as a PoW. The remaining crewmen rest in Sylling churchyard, west of Oslo.

97   I/StG 1 was equipped with the extended-range version of the Stuka dive-bomber. These had two 240-litre drop tanks on the underwing bomb racks, restricting the bomb load to a single 500-kg bomb on the centre-line rack.

98 Buschenhagen and Krancke arrived earlier in the morning and their aircraft almost crashed on landing.

99 Stevens, *Trial of Nikolaus von Falkenhorst*. Boehm was recalled from Norway when Dönitz succeeded Raeder in 1943. Von Falkenhorst remained in Norway until December 1944.

100 Pruck, *Abwehraussenstelle Norwegen*. Besides organising intelligence, PoW handling and communication control in the occupied areas, one of Pruck's tasks was to monitor the development of the political situation in Sweden.

101 RM 92/5259; RM 7/92; RM 12/II/167; and RM 48/176.

Chapter 6

1 RA II-C-11-1100; ADM 223/126; AIR 22/8; and Steen, *Norges Sjøkrig 1940–45*, vol. 2. Boyes received a signal from the Admiralty at 23:12 regarding the German activity in the Skagerrak. The signal alleged that two groups of warships were at sea, one led by *Gneisenau*, the other by *Blücher*, both heading west. There was no conclusion to the signal and no indication that any of the ships were heading for Oslo or any other Norwegian port. It is unclear if Boyes was instructed to forward this to the Norwegian Navy or went on his own initiative.

2 RA II-C-11-52,2/52,6; and RA II-C-11-1100. By April 1940, plans had been made in case of war to merge the commanding admiral, the Admiral Staff, the naval general inspector, the command of the coastal artillery and the naval air force, including all staff functions, into the Supreme Command of the Sea Defence Forces – Sjøforsvarets Overkommando or SOK. This would free up many officers for active service who were otherwise occupied in Oslo.

3 RA II-C-11-1100; and Steen, *Norges Sjøkrig 1940–45*, vol. 2.

4 RA II-C-11-51. Generalmajor Laake usually used the train to and from Oslo. Hatledal arrived at the General Staff offices at Akershus around 01:00; Laake close to 02:00.

5 Statsråd – Council of State – the formal meetings of the Norwegian government led by the king. Besides the eleven members of the government, Undersecretary Jens Bull of the Foreign Office was also present at Victoria Terrasse.

6 Nygaardsvold, *Norge i krig 9. April–7. Juni 1940*. Nygaardsvold on several occasions expressed annoyance at the British inability to halt or even fight the Germans after the invasion.

7 FO 419/34; FO 371/24829; IWM 67/25/1; Koht, *Frå skanse til skanse*; and Lie, *Leve eller dø*. Koht initially did not wish to call Dormer as he felt he had declined previous offers for British help, but eventually, after pressure from Nygaardsvold and Lie, agreed to make a call to 'inform him of the events'. Later, Koht wrote that he 'believed in Oscarsborg' and never considered it would be possible to transport sufficient troops by aircraft to threaten Oslo.

8 Borgersrud, *Konspirasjon og kapitulasjon*. How this could be maintained during the Neutrality Watch has never been explained.

9 During the 1930s, a 'partial mobilisation' had been combined with 'quiet mobilisation', where the men were called by personal letter or telegram.

10 RA II-C-11-51; *Innstilling fra Undersøkelseskommisjonen av 1945*; and *Krigen i Norge 1940, Operasjonene i kristiansand-Setesdals-avsnittet*. In all, there were six field brigades. Ljungberg and the government appear to have intended only the southern four to be mobilised, but Hatledal included the 5th Brigade when the orders were issued, as for him this was included in 'southern Norway', showing how casual the instructions were. Koht later held that the term 'the four brigades' for the government meant 'all of southern Norway'. At the railroad station a few hours later he told a journalist that a 'full mobilisation' had been ordered and at the first Parliament meeting at Hamar Koht told the assembly that a 'full mobilisation of 1st, 2nd, 3rd and 4th Brigade' had commenced.

11 RA II-C-11-51; *Innstilling fra Undersøkelseskommisjonen av 1945*; Koht, *Frå skanse til skanse*; Lie, *Leve eller dø*; Hjelmtveit, *Vekstår og vargtid*; and Munthe-Kaas, *Aprildagene 1940*. Parts of 5th and 6th Brigade had already been mobilised and deployed in the north.

12 Bräuer was late. It appears he assumed the government would meet with the king at the castle, and went there first.

13 RA FKA-Ya II-C-11-00; Koht, *For Fred og Fridom i Krigstid 1939–1940*; Koht, *Frå skanse til skanse*; and Lie, *Leve eller dø*. At this stage, none of the ministers knew that the German attack on Oslo had actually been halted at Oscarsborg.

14 Hubatsch, *Weserübung*. An hour later at 06:17 GeT, Group III in Bergen received a signal from Kiel: 'To all. Norwegian government has decided full resistance.'

15 Carl Joachim Hambro was born in 1885. He was one of the most distinguished Norwegian politicians of his time and one of those who first recognised the threats from the new dictatorships in Europe. As Stortingspresident, Hambro was formally the second most important man in the kingdom, next to the

king, ranking above the prime minister. After a career as journalist and editor, he was elected to the Parliament for Høyre, the Conservatives, in 1919. He was also chairman of Høyre's central committee for many years and was elected Parliamentary president in 1926; a position he held until the invasion. He was also leader of the Parliamentary Committee for Foreign Affairs (Utenrikskomiteen), to which the foreign minister formally reported. In 1939, he was elected president of the League of Nations. He was distantly related to Charles Hambro of the British MEW.

16 Hambro, *De første måneder*; and FKA-Ya II-C-11-00. Hambro travelled to Hamar by car ahead of the train to prepare for its arrival. Nygaardsvold wanted to bring his family and also used a car, picking them up on the way. For those MPs who could not make it in time, a convoy of buses was set up, leaving Parliament some hours later.

17 Koht was later criticised for revealing the whereabouts of the government, and excused himself by saying there was at this time no indication the Germans would be bombing indiscriminately to eliminate the Norwegian administration. The fact that the Norwegian government had moved to Hamar was reported by the BBC at 13:00. ADM 116/4471.

18 Øksendal, *Gulltransporten*. In all, some 818 large crates, 685 small crates and thirty-nine kegs with bullion were loaded onto the trucks. It all arrived safely at Lillehammer, where it was stowed into the vault of Norges Bank, as was about 10 million NoK in cash. The gold eventually ended up in Britain, from where it was transported to the USA and Canada.

19 Margaret Reid's diary. On 28 August 1939, Francis Edward Foley arrived in Oslo with his personal secretary Margaret Grant Reid. The staff at the German Embassy did actually observe the burning of papers with some satisfaction – as well as the hurried departure of the personnel. RM 12/II/167.

20 FO 371/24834. The answer to this request was an instruction to try to stay with the Norwegian government, while 'all redundant staff' should head for Sweden as soon as convenient.

21 Commandante Bertrand-Vigne was French military attaché, Capitaine de Frégate d'Arzur was naval attaché.

22 FO 371/24832; and FO 419/34. Mr Easton, the US consul, sealed off the doors to the British Legation, and Dormer's servant and butler, both 'over military age', were left behind to help look after matters. As the US minister, Mrs Harriman, and her staff also left Oslo, however, the practicality of these arrangements were minimal.

23 RA II-C-11-51; RA II-C-11-52; Willoch Papers; and Normann, *Uheldig generalstab*. At this stage, the SOK consisted of Commanding Admiral Diesen, Kommandør Corneliussen, Major Hoel, Kaptein Scheen, Kaptein Øgland, Kaptein Herseth and Løytnants Stup and Grimsgaard. After 12 April, Diesen's main strategy was to resist where possible, demolish equipment when opposition had no purpose, and conserve anything that could be used to fight the invaders once Allied help arrived. As opposition in south Norway ceased, Diesen ordered all ships capable of fighting on to leave Norway for British bases. Diesen and most of his staff travelled on British ships to Tromsø via Scapa Flow in early May and continued their work there until the final evacuation to Britain. In Britain he held the post until late 1941, when he was succeeded by Corneliussen.

24 Scheidt had been in Berlin the week before and knew something was going on, but not the extent nor the date. He returned to Oslo on 5 or 6 April. Schreiber had been informed through a coded telegram on the 5th.

25 Hubatsch, *Weserübung*.

26 Philler was told *Blücher* had been sunk with a great loss of lives, including most of the divisional staff. There was no knowledge of the fate of Generalmajor Engelbrecht at this stage.

27 GFM 33/1111; N 172/14, *Nachlass Boehm*; N 300/5, *Bericht und Vernehmung des Generalobersten von Falkenhorst*; RM 12/II/167; RM 7/92; RM 48/176; RA II-C-11-2150/52; Pruck, *Abwehraussenstelle Norwegen*; and Skodvin, *Striden om okkupasjonsstyret i Norge*.

28 Ismay, L., *Memoirs of General the Lord Ismay*.

29 ADM 234/380; ADM 116/4471; FO 419/34; and Churchill, *The Second World War*, vol. 1.

30 Danish casualties on 9 April mounted to eleven soldiers, three frontier guards and two airmen killed. Twenty soldiers were wounded. German losses are unknown, but were probably somewhat larger.

31 Hambro, *De første måneder*; Hambro, *CJ Hambro, liv og drøm*; and Lie, *Leve eller dø*.

32 By midday, most of the British and French embassy personnel had arrived, as had the US Ambassador Mrs Harriman. She had originally planned to stay in Oslo, but was encouraged by Koht to follow the government, which was also her instruction from Washington.

33 Oberst Gulliksen was one of the few high-ranking officers who was a member of the Labour Party and probably chosen by Koht and Nygaardsvold to become involved in the events because of this, as they knew and trusted him.

34 FO 419/34; FO 371/24832; FO 371/24834; and FO 371/24829. Minister Wold later wrote that he found it ironic that the British minister offered assistance by way of an illegal radio transmitter, the existence of which he had previously denied.

35 RH24-21/24.

36 In the meeting, Nygaardsvold brought up the issue of a coalition government. Hambro and the opposition leaders held that this was not the time for major changes and suggested instead that the government was enlarged by consultative ministers from the other parties. This was agreed.

37 Characteristically for the chaotic situation, Prime Minister Nygaardsvold missed the train, and he would have been left behind had it not been for a helpful businessman who placed his car at the prime minister's disposal.

38 FO 419/34; Nygaardsvold, *Norge i krig 9. April–7. Juni 1940*; Lie, *Leve eller dø*; Hjelmtveit, *Vekstår og vargtid*; and Margaret Reid's diary.

39 'Privatkrieg von Spiller'. N 300/5, *Bericht und Vernehmung des Generalobersten von Falkenhorst*.

40 Mrs Spiller later held that the expedition had been approved by Bräuer 'to convince the king to return'.

41 At Grorud, the Germans ran into Kaptein Øivinn Øi of the HOK on his way south to investigate the situation in Oslo. Being ordered out of his car, Kaptein Øi pulled his gun and was promptly shot and killed by the nervous paratroopers.

42 RH 24-21/24; Heradstveit, *Kongen som sa nei*; Ruge, *Felttoget, erindringer fra kampene April–Juni 1940*; and Munthe-Kaas, *Aprildagene 1940*. Walther and most of his paratroopers returned to Germany on 18 April.

43 RH 24-21/17.

44 Hubatsch, *Weserübung*.

45 N 172/14, *Nachlass Boehm*; *Innstilling fra Undersøkelseskommisjonen av 1945*, appendix, vol. 1; *Straffesak mot Vidkun Abraham Quisling*; Knudsen, *Jeg var Quislings sekretær*; and Heradstveit, *Quisling hvem var han?*

46 Grimnes, *Norge i Krig*, vol. 1. Nygaardsvold later claimed the news of Quisling's coup 'stiffened him up'.

47 Nygaardsvold, *Beretning om den Norske Regjerings virksomhet fra 9. April 1940 til 25. Juni 1945*; Hambro, *De første måneder*; and Lie, *Leve eller dø*. The legal basis of the *prokura* has been questioned as there was no formal vote, just a common consent. The Investigation Committee concluded after the war that the *prokura* made clarity in a situation that was not covered in the constitution. It certainly gave the government the authority needed in the days and weeks to come, and above all later in the war, after moving to London.

48 Princess Märtha and her three children also crossed into Sweden during 10 April.

49 In a conversation with the journalist and author Per Øyvind Heradstveit in 1979, Prince Olav, by then king of Norway, explained that King Haakon had decided Olav should stay behind, and be prepared to take over, in case there was foul play involved and the Germans planned to kill or kidnap him. Heradstveit, *Kongen som sa nei*.

50 Nothing had been agreed, though, and the Germans had certainly not ceased firing, far less halted their advance.

51 Hjelmtveit, *Vekstår og vargtid*.

52 Koht, *Frå skanse til skanse*; and Heradstveit, *Kongen som sa nei*. Quisling also sent a representative to King Haakon asking him to approve the new government and return to Oslo. The messenger was received at Nybergsund in the morning of 11 April, but was met by a short, courteous 'no'.

53 RH 24-21/24.

54 While waiting, Laake and Hatledal had a brief meeting with King Haakon, updating him on the situation.

55 RA II-C-11-51.

56 RA II-C-11-51; RA Ya-II-C-11-00; Nygaardsvold, *Norge i krig 9. April–7. Juni 1940*; Lie, *Leve eller dø*; Ruge, *Felttoget, erindringer fra kampene April–Juni 1940*; and Munthe-Kaas, *Aprildagene 1940*. The accounts of what was actually said and discussed at Rena vary as nobody took notes. Several of the officers later held they never realised the importance of the meeting, which they referred to as 'informal conversations' and, being tired, saw no need to make any comments or clarify Laake's statements. He, however, insisted he had only advised negotiations 'to be held open', to gain time while preparing a defence, waiting for Allied help.

57 It was conveniently forgotten that commanding general had an official retirement age of 68. Laake was hospitalised not long after. He died in 1950.

58 RA 0064-2B 023 2/1 927.9; RA II-C-11-51; and Reid, and Rolstad, *April 1940, En Krigsdagbok*. Otto Ruge, inspector general of the infantry, was on his way from northern Norway to Oslo through Sweden during 7–8 April. He passed into Norway during the night on the night-sleeper from Stockholm. After searching in vain for the army command in Oslo, he went to Elverum, where he took command of whatever troops

could be mustered and started arranging a defence line between the government and the Germans. The force at Midtskogen originated from these hastily gathered troops.

59   RA II-C-11-51; *Aftenposten*, 9 April 1990; and RA 0064-2B 023 2/1 927.9. Rasmus Hatledal did not recover in time to rejoin the HOK. He was arrested in 1943, and spent the last part of the war as a PoW in Germany. He died in 1963.

60   RH 24-21/24. Elverum was also heavily bombed on this day, fifty-four people were killed and over a hundred wounded.

61   Lie, *Leve eller dø*; and VGNett, 22 November 2005. Koht, Torp and Hjelmtveit crossed into Sweden on 13 April. Koht and Torp returned the next day whereas Hjelmtveit continued to Stockholm.

62   RA II-C-11-51; and Lie *Leve eller dø*. At first Dormer was rather ill-informed and for a period during 10 April he maintained that Bergen and Trondheim had been recaptured by Allied forces.

63   FO 419/34.

64   FO 419/34.

65   It appears that his diseases reappeared during those stressful days, and in some of the very few photographs of him, Quisling appears ill.

66   Hartmann, *Spillet om Norge*; Høidal, *Quisling – En studie i landssvik*; and Dahl, *Vidkun Quisling, en fører for fall*. Adding to the humiliation, he had to leave his offices in the Parliament as well as his room at the Continental. To make his retreat look more honorable, he was given responsibility for the demobilisation of the surrendered Norwegian soldiers and sailors, but he did not take the task on and it became a total failure.

67   RM/6-87. Bräuer and Benecke were made scapegoats for the things that went wrong in Norway. On 16 April Bräuer was ordered to Berlin, where he was given the choice of a court martial or a transfer to active duty in the army. Bräuer chose the second and eventually ended up on the Eastern Front where he was taken prisoner and only returned to Germany in 1954. He died in 1969. Benecke was court martialled and sentenced to two weeks' in confinement, after which he was given a minor position in Wiesbaden.

68   RM/6-87.

69   There has been a curious debate at times whether Norway was at war with Germany or not. Already at 13:25 on 9 April, however, there is a note in the war diary of Admiral Boehm, designated commanding admiral, Norway: 'Group XXI reports to Group East and West: Norway is at war with Germany.'

Chapter 7

1   Kristiansand was known as the 'Pearl of the South'. It was a neat little city of 23,000 inhabitants with many parks and wooded areas and surrounded by sandy beaches and a multitude of islands. The winters could be hard, but the summers were mild and it was (and is) considered a perfect place for a summer holiday.

2   Oberstløytnant Fosby was well qualified in all matters technical and well suited for the task of maintaining operational readiness while the fort was kept in reserve. He should have been retired, but it was convenient for both him and the coastal artillery that he stayed on, looking after the batteries. Handling the Neutrality Watch was apparently challenging for the ageing officer and there are reports of personnel problems among the officers at the fort.

3   2nd Division under Lieutenant F Halvorsen consisted of *Kjell*, *Skarv* and *Teist*. In the evening of 8 April the latter was in Farsund, *Skarv* in Egersund while *Kjell* was at the yard in Marvika. 3rd Division under Lieutenant Tor Holte was equally spread: *Jo* in Arendal, *Grib* in Risør and *Ravn* in Langesund; *Ørn* and *Lom* were at the yard in Horten.

4   RA 1256/310; RA II-C-11-2020-2040; Steen, *Norges Sjøkrig 1940–45*, vol. 2; and Fjørtoft, *Kanonene ved Skagerrak*.

5   RA II-C-11-1100; RM 8/1152.

6   RM 7/11.

7   RA II-C-11-1100. It is unclear to what extent this information was actually believed, far less forwarded.

8   RA II-C-11-2020/2040; and RA II-C-11-1100.

9   *Karlsruhe* had 600 soldiers, *Tsingtau* 270, *Luchs* and *Seeadler* 50 each. *Greif* had an additional 100 men for Arendal. Some 200 of the troops were naval artillerymen under the command of Kapitänleutnant Ernst Michaelsen with orders to ensure that the batteries at Odderøya and Gleodden were operational as soon as possible after being taken over.

10   When the warships entered the krigshavn, Kaptein Johansen fired two red rockets and pulled away, as instructed.

11   Later he was taken below, but released once *Karlsruhe* had anchored. Berge, *Fra Nøytralitet til Krig*.

12 The crew of the forward turret was largely new to the job and for most of them it was the first time they fired live, full-calibre ammunition. Their drill was good, though, and the rate of fire was high.

13 Pilot Aanundsen claimed in a newspaper interview in 1960 that *Karlsruhe* was hit in the bow just before Rieve decided to turn but there is no German report of this. Kapitänleutnant Kohlauf of *Seeadler* was not impressed by the Norwegian fire and characterised it as 'poorly led', indirectly criticising Rieve's early decision to turn away.

14 RM 92/5257; and RM 57/125.

15 RA II-C-11-2020/2040; RA II-C-11-1100; and Steen, *Norges Sjøkrig 1940–45*, vol. 2.

16 RM 57/125; and Herrmann, *Eagle's Wings*. Eight aircraft had taken off from Westerland on the island of Sylt, but some lost their bearings in the fog over the Skagerrak; only six made it to Kristiansand.

17 RA II-C-11-2020-2040. The He111s had a fair amount of armour around the cockpit and part of the fuselage and the low-calibre Norwegian machine-gun bullets did not penetrate this. In addition, the self-sealing mechanism of the fuel tanks was very efficient and even tracer bullets rarely ignited the petrol.

18 Rieve ordered the ship's seaplane to be flown off to spot for his artillery. Once up, however, the radio of the Arado did not work. It eventually landed west of Flekkerøy, rejoining the cruiser in the afternoon.

19 The Norwegian reports state that fire was opened at about 6,000 metres when the ships were off Dvergsøy. The German largely hold that fire was opened both times as they were just inside Grønningen–Oksøy at some 7,000 metres.

20 Robert Eichinger became engaged in the Resistance. His cell was blown in 1942 and he was subjected to horrific torture by the Gestapo. He was eventually sentenced to death but pardoned to the labour camps. Eichinger survived and after recovering his health, joined the Norwegian post-war navy, from which he retired in 1983 as Kontreadmiral.

21 In all, 262 buildings were damaged, forty-seven of them badly. Thirteen civilians were killed and at least seventeen seriously wounded. All available reports indicate that the damage caused to Kristiansand city by the Germans on 9 April was accidental.

22 RA II-C-11-2020/2040; RA II-C-11-1100; RM 92/5257; RM 92/5257; RM 57/125; Mæsel, *Kristiansand i krig – 9. April 1940*; Berge, *Fra Nøytralitet til Krig*; and Steen, *Norges Sjøkrig 1940–45*, vol. 2.

23 RM 57/125. The timing of the hits on *Seattle* varies: some say just after the first run. Most agree, however, that she was set ablaze after the second run. She burned for several days before drifting into the fjord, sinking on 13 April.

24 AIR 27/1365; Mæsel, *Kristiansand i krig – 9. April 1940*; and Berge, *Fra Nøytralitet til Krig*.

25 RA II-C-11-1130; RA II-C-11-2020/2040; RA II-C-11-1100; and Steen, *Norges Sjøkrig 1940–45*, vol. 2.

26 RM 92/5257.

27 RA II-C-11-1130; RA II-C-11-1100; and RA II-C-11-2020-2040. The origins of these orders have been very difficult to trace. Both commanding admiral and commanding general were on their way out of Oslo with their staffs at the time and signals and orders were often forwarded through public telephone lines – without proper identification.

28 RM 92/5257; and RM 57/125.

29 Berge, *Fra Nøytralitet til Krig*; and Steen, *Norges Sjøkrig 1940–45*, vol. 2.

30 RA II-C-11-2020/2040; and RA II-C-11-1100.

31 RA II-C-11/1130; RM 92/5257; Berge, *Fra Nøytralitet til Krig*; Mæsel, *Kristiansand i krig – 9. April 1940*; and Steen, *Norges Sjøkrig 1940–45*, vol. 2.

32 RM 92/5257.

33 RA II-C-11-1100. Wigers later wrote that he at this stage believed 'Oslo, Horten and possibly Bergen' to be in German hands. His surrender, he wrote, only applied to the ships and – in his mind – not the fort. Later, Wigers drove to Marvika, from where he informed Generalmajor Liljedahl of the events while his officers destroyed files and codebooks.

34 Norwegians soldiers were unarmed while they manned the guns.

35 RA II-C-11-2020/2040; RA II-C-11-1100; RM 92/5257; Michaelsen, 'Die Einnahme der Festung Odderö', in Hase, *Die Kriegsmarine erobert Norwegens Fjorde*; Berge, *Fra Nøytralitet til Krig*; and Mæsel, *Kristiansand i krig – 9. April 1940*. The issue of how and by whom Kristiansand Fortress was captured created a serious controversy between the Kriegsmarine and the army when various accounts started to be published about a year later. An investigation committee in 1941 ruled that it was a joint conquest, but neither side ever really accepted this.

36 AIR 14/666; AIR 22/8; and Berge, *Fra Nøytralitet til Krig*.

37 RM 57/93.

38 The distance between *Jo* and *Greif* was about 1,000 metres.

39   RA II-C-11-1120-1180; RM 57/93; Steen, *Norges Sjøkrig 1940–45*, vol. 2; and Frognes, *Fyrbøteren på Jo*. Later, Løytnant Holthe left for Shetland in a requisitioned fishing vessel. He served on several Norwegian ships during the war, among them the destroyer *Stord* during the sinking of *Scharnhorst*. He remained in the RNN and served in several high positions until his death in 1966.

40   *Odin* and *Gyller* had three 10-cm guns versus three 10.5-cm guns on *Luchs* and *Seeadler*; one 20-mm Oerlikon gun versus four and two torpedo tubes each, versus six on the German boats.

41   RA II-C-11-2020-2040.

42   After the events, there was significant disagreement between Wigers and Bro about what had been agreed at this meeting.

43   Sunrise on 9 April in Kristiansand was 05:35. 'First light' was at least forty to fifty minutes before this.

44   RA II-C-11-1100; and Steen, *Norges Sjøkrig 1940–45*, vol. 2.

45   RA II-C-11-1100; RA II-C-11-1120-1180; and Steen, *Norges Sjøkrig 1940–45*, vol. 2.

46   RM 45-III/12.1. From 11 April, some thirty Messerschmitt Bf109 fighters from II/JG 77 were stationed at Kjevik.

47   RM 96/667. *M9* and *M13* brought the fifty-five crewmen from *Seattle* back to Germany.

48   RM 45III/122. The auxiliaries *Kvik*, *Blink*, *Lyn*, *Lyngdal*, *Hval IV*, *Hval VI*, *Hval VII* and *William Barents* soldiered on with German crews as harbour protection vessels or escorts throughout the war, after which most of them were scrapped. *Odin* and *Gyller* were renamed *Panther* and *Löwe* respectively, and commissioned as escorts and torpedo-recovery vessels with 27th U-boat Flotilla in the Baltic until the end of the war. Both were returned to the RNN in 1945 and served until decommissioned in 1959.

49   RA II-C-11-1100.

50   RM 8/1152; and *Rapport fra den Militære undersøkeskommisjon av 1946. Nou 1979:47*. Several officers in Kristiansand were criticised in the report of the Military Investigation Committee of 1946. Kommandør Wigers was given the overall responsibility for the German entry to Kristiansand and particularly criticised for not controlling properly the reports of a French fleet approaching and for not having ordered the destroyers to attack the intruders. Kapteins Holck of *Gyller*, Gunvaldsen of *Odin*, Bro of *B2* and Brekke of *B5* were all criticised for being too passive and for surrendering their ships intact. Oberstløytnant Fosby was not mentioned at all, probably as he died in 1946. Generalmajor Liljedahl was also strongly criticised.

Chapter 8

1   Günther Capito's personal account, in Mæsel, *Ni dager i April*. The officers of the FschJgRgt only learned of their targets in the late morning of 8 April, just before they moved from the barracks at Stendal.

2   In January 1940, British airlines commenced weekly civilian flights between Perth in Scotland and Sola.

3   In the late nineteenth century, when the coastal defences of Norway were planned, Stavanger was just too small to be considered for a fort. Things had changed by 1940 and after the invasion, the Germans built extensive defences.

4   A telephone call from the German Consulate in Stavanger was made around this time to the German Embassy in Oslo. The call was misconnected to the Swedish Embassy. Before the caller realised this, he had made reference to Wesertag and asked for instructions regarding *Roda*. The Swedish Embassy immediately reported the incident to the Norwegian Foreign Office, where it was filed and forgotten. *Innstilling fra Undersøkelseskommisjonen av 1945*, appendix, Bind II.

5   Why *Æger* was equipped with a large number of 'cold' grenades (without exploding warheads) is puzzling. Most likely it must have been related to the anticipated need to fire warning shots during the Neutrality Watch.

6   RA II-C-11-1204; RM 45/III-136; and Steen, *Norges Sjøkrig 1940–45*, vol. 3. *Roda* sank slowly and only in the afternoon did she vanish in about fifty metres of water, in spite of German attempts to salvage her. She was raised in 1956 and emptied of eighty-five tons of ammunition, before being towed to Holland and scrapped.

7   RA II-C-11-1204; Steen, *Norges Sjøkrig 1940–45*, vol. 3; and Mæsel, *Ni dager i April*.

8   RM 96/667. The wreck of *Æger* was cut up where it had been beached. Part of it was used as a barge for many years until eventually sunk in 1985. Nils Bruun served in the RNN until 1957, when he retired with the rank of Kontreadmiral.

9   A company of engineers had been stationed at Sola from early February to build bunkers and other defences.

10   The Italian-built Capronis were unsuited for rugged offensive operations, in spite of their modern appearance, and spent more time with the mechanics than with the pilots. Only three of them were operational in the evening of 8 April.

11 During 8 April the ground and service personnel of the Bomber Wing left Sola, heading east via Bergen.
12 RA II-C-11-1203/188. The usual CO, Løytnant Fraser was on leave and Stansberg was acting senior officer.
13 Sola airfield had two runways, 850 and 920 metres long and 40 metres wide.
14 The navigator was Fenrik Stein Abildsø and the radio operator was Airman Grasskjær.
15 RA II-C-11-1203/188; Hafsten et al, *Flyalarm*; and Wyller and Stahl, *Aprildagene 1940*. This order, as well as the cold answer earlier in the night, stemmed from an issue between the navy and the army over who should attack targets at sea. Løytnant Hansen had argued for a pragmatic attitude and as a result was considered quarrelsome and disloyal. Who actually gave the order was never ascertained, partly as neither Hansen nor Jean-Hansen survived the war. Halfdan Hansen fell a week later, fighting German paratroopers at Dovre. Christian Jean-Hansen was one of the few survivors from the carrier *Glorious*. He fell over France in 1943, as a pilot in the RAF.
16 The He111s and Ju88s of KG 26 and KG 4 appear to have had fewer problems, probably as they flew above the fog.
17 Günther Capito's personal account, in Mæsel, *Ni dager i April*
18 The twelfth aircraft eventually landed at Aalborg.
19 RH 24-21/24; RM 45/III-136; *Kammeraden-Echo* No. 2; Mæsel, *Ni dager i April*; and Hafsten et al, *Flyalarm*. The pilots of KGzbV 104 and 106 had been instructed to fly at wavetop height to avoid enemy fighters. The more experienced pilots ignored this due to the heavily loaded aircraft, some even ordering equipment to be thrown overboard to be able to climb and keep their machines airborne. One of the Ju52s vanished with crew and eleven soldiers.
20 One other Caproni and one of the Fokkers were damaged and had to make forced landings after a while. The other Fokkers and the last Caproni made it to Kjevik-Kristiansand and eventually reached Norwegian forces.
21 Günther Capito's personal account, in Mæsel, *Ni dager i April*. All eleven Ju52s landed in Aalborg with empty fuel tanks. Capito served with distinction on many fronts throughout the war and survived to tell his story.
22 The bunker was camouflaged as a farm shed. Apparently, the Germans had no knowledge of its existence.
23 According to Wyller, one of the rangers' sub-lieutenants was 'a Nazi' and sabotaged Tangvald's order to attack.
24 RM 45/III-136. Two of the wounded were injured during the jump. The dead were Obergefreiter Ludwig Benedikt and Jägers Georg Woch and Karl Cypers. They were flown back during the day and buried in Germany.
25 3rd Company was dropped into battle again in the morning of 10 May at Dordrecht in Holland to capture the Alte Maas-Brücke. This time the resistance was even harder and Oberleutnant Otto von Brandis fell, together with several of his men, while most of those surviving were taken prisoner and spent the rest of the war in British PoW camps.
26 The remaining MF11 and the He115, still at their moorings, were both captured intact.
27 *Kammeraden-Echo* No. 2.
28 RA II-C-11-1204; RH 24-21/24; RM 45/III-136; Wyller and Stahl, *Aprildagene 1940, Kammeraden-Echo* No. 2; Hafsten et al, *Flyalarm*.
29 Platt and Olsson were British consular shipping advisers, but there is no doubt they had intelligence-related tasks.
30 Wyller and Stahl, *Aprildagene 1940*; Munthe, *Sweet is War*; Cruickshank, *SOE in Scandinavia*. Unfortunately, Munthe's narration of the events in Norway in 1940 (published in 1954) is rather colourful and to some extent unreliable. Munthe eventually ended up in Sweden, where he was appointed assistant military attaché.
31 *Draug* consumed coal in large quantities at anything but idle speed. To reach twenty-five knots, all three boilers had to be used and six tons of coal would be needed per hour.
32 Horve never fully realised what kind of ship he had seized. The closed and covered hatches were suspicious and the behaviour of her captain made it likely she was under military command, but he had of course no knowledge of the Ausfuhrstaffel and that *Main* was carrying supplies for the invasion troops.
33 One German sailor fell into the sea and drowned.
34 Horve embarked on the destroyer *Somali*. Later in the war he served as captain on the RNN destroyers *Sleipner* and *Glaisdaile*, mostly on convoy escort in the Atlantic and around the British Isles. From July 1943 he was C-in-C of the 54th Motor Torpedo Boat Flotilla at Shetland, operating Norwegian manned MTBs against occupied Norway. *Draug*'s first officer, Løytnant Østervold, embarked on *Afridi*, where Captain (D)4 Vian of *Altmark* fame greeted the Norwegian officer warmly and said, 'I intend to go into

one of your fjords, I hope you have no objections.' A somewhat puzzled Løytnant Østervold answered, 'No, sir, of course not.' Captain Vian laughed: 'Well, you had last time.'

35   RA II-C-11-1202/188, Letter 23.10.46 from Rear Admiral Horve to the Military Investigation Committee; Steen, *Norges Sjøkrig 1940–45*, vol. 3; and Sivertsen, *Sjøforsvaret i Rogaland*.

36   The troops belonged to Radfahrschwadron des Aufklärungs-Abteilung 169 (Bicycle Squadron of Reconnaissance Unit 169). The rest of 69th ID, including the commander Generalmajor Tittel, would land in Bergen and Stavanger.

37   The main lighthouses had been shut down in the evening of 8 April.

38   Eickhorn Papers; and Bartels, *Tigerflagge, Heiss Vor!* In 1962, the historian Ingvald Rødland initiated an extensive correspondence with Friedrich Eickhorn. This correspondence has kindly been made available by Jostein Berglyd of Dalane Folkemuseum and is collectively referred to as 'the Eickhorn Papers'.

39   In his book *Tigerflagge, Heiss Vor!* Bartels claims he himself led the people that captured *Skarv*, but this does not agree with other accounts and is probably another of the many colourful modifications in his book.

40   Radio connection with IR 193 in Stavanger could not be established because of faulty equipment and telephone lines that were quickly cut by the Norwegians. A German officer dressed as a civilian drove a motorbike to Stavanger to report.

41   RA II-C-11-1100; Bartels, *Tigerflagge, Heiss Vor!* and Eickhorn Papers. After his release from capture, Fenrik Svae tried to escape to England but was caught and sentenced to death. He escaped again, however, and finally succeeded in reaching Britain, where he served with the RNN. He died in 1960. Rittmeister Friedrich Eickhorn survived the war and after a short time as PoW returned to his factory in Solingen. Kapitänleutnant Hans Bartels and *M1* remained in Norway. He was awarded the Knight's Cross on 16 May 1940, a decision that has become no less controversial with investigation of what really happened during the events for which the decoration was awarded.

42   The defence of Stavanger had long been a subject of controversy between Oberst Spørck, General Liljedahl and the commanding general. Liljedahl advised Spørck 'to act as he considered best' – which he interpreted as being given a free hand.

43   Den Krigshistoriske Avdeling – *Krigen i Norge*; Wyller and Stahl, *Aprildagene 1940*; and Torgersen, *Kampene i Rogaland – Stavanger Aftenblad*. In all, some thirty-six Germans fell in Rogaland and seventy were wounded.

44   Oberfeldwebel Fleishmann and Feldwebel Gröning were both killed in their Bf110s within a month.

45   Norwegians working for the German occupants were heavily condemned during and after the war. Obviously there were as many reasons for doing this as there were individuals and many did so as a result of threats or otherwise being called by force or because their employer found it opportune to sign an attractive contract. It is, however, also true that many came because the Germans paid well and had good supplies of food, cigarettes and alcohol.

46   On the way home, Sergeant Rose encountered an He111 of II/KG 26 returning from an attack on Scapa Flow, damaging it so badly that although it staggered back to Sola it crashed on landing and was written off.

47   AIR 14/2595; AIR 20/6260; and AIR 14/669. DHO refers to Air Ministry, Directorate of Home Operations. In a revised signal of 14 April, 'guerrilla' was replaced by 'operations using cloud or other stratagem for evasion'.

48   9 Sqn moved to Lossiemouth and 115 Sqn to Kinloss on 2 April to operate against German shipping. While in Scotland, the Wellingtons operated under the orders of AOC-in-C Coastal Command.

49   254 Sqn had recently been transferred from Fighter Command to Coastal Command, converting to Blenheim IV-Fs and transferred to Lossiemouth to extend the range of its North Sea patrols covering the Norwegian coast.

50   AIR 14/666. Four of the six British airmen were recovered and buried at Eiganes churchyard on 14 April with full military honours, including a wreath from the German military command commemorating 'four brave opponents'.

51   Trondheim was out of range for most land-based RAF aircraft, except the Whitleys at Kinloss, and so was left to the FAA.

52   Few aircraft could carry more than two 500-lb bombs, partly due to the quality of the runways in Scotland; the chance of actually hitting the runways with a stick of only two bombs was limited.

53   Portal introduced a ban on approaching the Norwegian coast closer than sixty miles unless cloud cover was adequate – except for Blenheim attacks on Sola.

54   AIR 14/666; and AIR 14/669.

55   ADM 199/1840.

56   There was abnormally high atmospheric activity this morning. In addition, the navy was not aware that the chosen frequency, 6650 kc/s, was unreliable at dawn in the North Sea and not used by Coastal Command. AIR 15/202.

57   ADM 199/475; RM 7/295; and Edwards, *Norwegian Patrol*

58   This change of plan was apparently made by Churchill, Pound and Phillips during the evening of 16 April.

59   RM 7/295.

60   For his leadership of this raid, Wing Commander Embry received a bar to his DSO. Flight Lieutenant Clayton received a DFC, and his air gunner, Corporal Yeomans, a DFM for fighting off repeated attacks from Bf110s.

61   A Do18 from 1./KüFlGr 406 shadowing the ships was shot down by three Skuas from 801 Sqn. Other Skua pilots claimed a Do17. This is not recorded in the German files.

62   IWM PP/MRC/C10; AIR 15/202; ADM 199/475; and ADM 186/798.

Chapter 9

1   The Heinkels were powerful, modern aircraft delivered during the autumn of 1939. They had a large operational radius and could carry three 250-kg bombs – even if the bombsights were poor. There were no torpedoes. The MF11s were also relatively new and in spite of an old-fashioned design well suited to the task for which they were designed – scouting and surveillance. They could carry four 50-kg bombs.

2   Some mobile mid-calibre guns were available, but not manned. In December 1939, three 12-cm guns from Kongsvinger Fort north of Oslo had been moved to Bergen, intended to be used in a new fort at the southern entry to the Leads and in March 1940 three 15-cm guns originally intended for Narvik had been brought south. These guns were still in store in spite of several requests from Tank-Nielsen for them to be installed, at least provisionally.

3   RA II-C-11-2040/2046; and Willoch, *Bergen Festning falt 9.april 1940*. Both remote-controlled mines and standard mechanical mines were available in the depots in large quantities.

4   Ie that they were heading for somewhere other than Norway. In Norwegian, Danielsen's answer is also firm advice to Tank-Nielsen to focus his attention on the district and leave the strategic issues to the staff.

5   The transport ships left at Kopervik were by now so much delayed that many were redirected.

6   RA II-C-11-52; RA II-C-11-1200/18; RA II-C-11-1200/187; and Willoch Papers.

7   This was not official Norwegian policy; Tank-Nielsen was expressing his private pro-Allied sympathies – as he did on several occasions.

8   Not long after, the General Staff in Oslo also called Generalmajor Steffens, informing him that a decision to mobilise would not be taken by the government until the next day. Steffens was not comfortable with this and issued orders to Major Stenersen at Ulven to post guard units at three potential landing sites south of Bergen. He was also to organise buses and trucks for transport and keep the battalion ready to move on short notice.

9   AE 2988/71. The radio navigation beacons were also shut down as well as the sailing and anchor lights in the harbour. Some of the unmanned sailing lights inside the Lead remained burning, as they were not remotely controlled and would have to be shut down manually one by one.

10   RA II-C-11-1200/186; RA II-C-11-1200/187; RA II-C-11-2040/2046; and report of Løytnant Thorleif Pettersen, at www.9april1940.org. In his report of February 1941, Willoch holds he was only 'told to do his best'.

11   RM 50/87; RM 92/5255; and RM 35/II-35.

12   The signalman onboard *Manger* probably did not understand the meaning of the letters HMS; with limited knowledge of both English and German, pronouncing the word *Cairo* in his own Norwegian dialect, he, or one of those hearing his pronunciation, jumped to the conclusion that the signal sent was 'Sei ruhig'. In the pre-Americanised Norwegian language of 1940, C was very often pronounced S, making the words phonetically close. *Lindaas* reported intruders of unknown nationality by radio. This signal was intercepted by the radio operators of *Königsberg*, giving the German command hope the ruse was working.

13   RA II-C-11-1200/186. On the original signal is scribbled by hand 'sent Kvarven 01:35'. Signals reporting the intruders were forwarded to Oslo at 01:50 and to Trondheim at 02:50, both noting that the intruders were German.

14   Due to their slow speed (twelve knots), the trawlers had left Wilhelmshaven on 5 April, disguised as neutral Estonian vessels. *Schiff9* was the 437-GRT *Koblenz* and *Schiff18* the 419-GRT *Alteland*.

15   RA II-C-11-1200/186. From the discussions at the afternoon conference it is very likely that fire would *not* have been opened on British ships – had they been firmly identified as such.

16 During the morning Kaptein Eriksen took *B6* into Bergen harbour, submerged. Very little was seen except for numerous merchant ships and he returned to Flatøy.

17 The German plans specified three additional emergency landing sites in case it was impossible to pass the forts and enter the harbour. Two were in the south (Grimstadfjord and Fanafjord – as expected in exercises) and one was in the north near Arna. The latter would require an extensive rerouting of several hours.

18 BB A.2848.002/y/0002/01; RA II-C-11-1200/1210; and RA II-C-11-51.

19 BBA.2848.002/y/0002/04; and RA II-C-11-2040/2046. The observation posts at Store Kongshaug and Lyderhorn both reported seeing the ships (Willoch's report) and even if they could not use their rangefinders properly, should have been able to direct fire from Kvarven. A rough distance and direction could have been calculated from any number of maps available at the fort. During exercises in 1921, indirect fire had been practised with acceptable results and on the maps at Marineholmen the area was marked as within range of the guns at Kvarven.

20 Willoch, *Bergen Festning falt 9.april 1940. Hvorfor?* ; and www.9april1940.org. Willoch wrote that one of the battery commanders asked for confirmation that he should load with live ammunition and that one of the gunners asked him directly if it was true that they planned to fire live rounds on human targets.

21 The regular commander of the torpedo battery (Kaptein Simensen) had been transferred to naval service and an NCO was in charge of the reduced manning. Four torpedoes were at the battery, while warheads and firing charges were in nearby depots and gyroscopes at Marineholmen.

22 The fort's own emergency power supply was steam driven and would take hours to start.

23 Report of Løytnant Thorleif Pettersen, at www.9april1940.org.

24 The Norwegian torpedo boats used explosives to launch their torpedoes and the flames were very visible from some angles when the torpedo left its tube.

25 Later in the morning, Løytnant Pettersen took *Storm* back and found the torpedo floating near where the German ships had passed. He had anticipated that they would come at a much higher speed than they did and the torpedo probably passed ahead of the target. The warhead was damaged and the ignition mechanism activated, so it was demolished.

26 RM 50/87; RM 92/5255; and RM 57/125. At this stage *Leopard* was so far ahead of the cruisers that Schmundt sent an order for her to wait.

27 Steen, *Norges Sjøkrig 1940-45*, vol. 3. By this time, Group III was long passed Vatlestraumen, but the mines would later cause serious trouble.

28 Stangen Light was being shut down manually just as Group III approached, about 03:40–03:45.

29 The exact timing of the events at this stage has been difficult to reconstruct as there are discrepancies between the Norwegian and German reports and between individual reports on both sides.

30 There have been suggestions that the ships confusing Willoch were *Schiff9* and *Schiff18*, but considering the time and distance involved, this is virtually impossible, Most likely they were the freighters sighted by Group III turning back at Lerøyosen. It has not been possible to identify them with certainty, but they were probably two of the many merchant ships lying in Bergen harbour the evening before, seeking an early start.

31 It is notable in most Norwegian reports that the number and types of ship are very inconsistent and not in accordance with the actual composition of Group III; the commanders probably lost the ships repeatedly due to the poor visibility and fired at whatever ship they had in sight.

32 Signals mate Olav Aarekol was called from the communication central and he spelled it out letter by letter, after which it was translated by one of the officers who knew some English. Willoch later quoted 'Stop firing, good friends,' and 'Stop shooting,' in various reports. The signalling made him hesitate, but the firing continued.

33 RM 50/87; RM 92/5255; and RM 57/125.

34 Four soldiers from 8./IR 159 were killed in the forecastle and eight seriously wounded, four of whom later died.

35 BBA.2848.002/y/0002/04; RA II-C-11-2040/2046; RA II-C-11-1200; RM 57/125; RM 92/5255; Willoch, *Bergen Festning falt 9.april 1940*; and Steen, *Norges Sjøkrig 1940–45*, vol. 3.

36 RA II-C-11-2040/2046; RA II-C-11-1200; RM 92/5255; RM 57/125; RM 50/87; Willoch, *Bergen Festning falt 9.april 1940*; and Steen, *Norges Sjøkrig 1940–45*, vol. 3. The auxiliary was *Uller,* returning for more mines, but she did not actually come into the fjord until much later.

37 RA II-C-11-2040/2046; and letter from Fenrik Midtland to the Military Investigation Committee in 1946, in RA II-C-11-1202. *Brand* was damaged by British bombs on 16 April while in German service but repaired and operated as a guard vessel and escort under the name *Tarantel* (later NB.19 and V.5519). She was scrapped in 1946.

38 After Bugge returned, Flatøy was evacuated, and by 08:00 all aircraft were in Sognefjord or Hardangerfjord.

39   RA II-C-11-1203/188; and Steen, *Norges Sjøkrig 1940–45*, vol. 3.

40   RM 92/5258; RA II-C-11-2040 II; and personal account of Fregattenkapitän (Ing) aD Nonn. Three were dead and seventeen wounded, nine seriously. The hole in the side was eventually patched up and intake of water halted.

41   RA II-C-11-2040/2046. Kaptein Haugstad later held he was unable to open fire within the time available due to blocked telephone lines.

42   RM 92/5258; and personal account of Fregattenkapitän (Ing) aD Nonn. When the anchor caught bottom, *Königsberg* swayed towards the Swedish merchantman *Canadia*, but there was no damage.

43   Kaptein Årstad received concurrence from the Admiral Staff in Oslo before giving this order.

44   RA II-C-11-2040/2046; RM 92/5255; RM 57/125; and RM 50/87.

45   RA II-C-11-2040/2046; RA II-C-11-1200-1210; and Willoch, *Bergen Festning falt 9.april 1940*.

46   Tank-Nielsen left Voss for Sognefjord on 12 April, nominally hoisting his flag onboard *Garm*. He was very distressed by the events and reported sick from over-exertion by a naval doctor on 16 April.

47   While nearing Kvarven, the company was attacked by aircraft and went into defensive positions. After a brief exchange of fire with German troops, the company commander learned that Kvarven Fort had surrendered and decided to also lay down his arms, after which the entire company was taken prisoner.

48   RA II-C-11-1200-1210.

49   Each machine gun had about five hundred shots, sufficient for a couple of minutes of continuous firing.

50   Most accounts from the soldiers participating in the defence describe themselves as poorly prepared with unfamiliar guns and limited ammunition. The Germans soldiers, however, created awe when they were seen with steel helmets, hand grenades in their boots and heavy harness, looking very professional. When the word spread that attackers were seen to have mortars and flamethrowers the willingness of the artillerymen to stand firm became limited. There are no reports of the flamethrowers being used.

51   RA II-C-11-2040/2046; Steen, *Norges Sjøkrig 1940–45*, vol. 3; and Willoch, *Bergen Festning falt 9.april 1940*. From Kvarven, twenty-four shots had been fired from the 21-cm battery and ten from the howitzers. From Hellen, eleven shots had been fired.

52   During the evening of 9 April von Schrader moved from *Carl Peters* to Hotel Terminus near the railway station. Generalmajor Tittel followed to ensure a smooth co-operation. They left most of their staffs at the depot ship and at Bergenhus respectively. During the 11th, separate navy and army administration offices were established in requisitioned buildings above the harbour, but still close to each other.

53   The Flugsicherungsschiffe or 'aircraft maintenance vessels' *Rolshoven* and *Tschirschky*, which had proceeded independently from Germany, were an integrated part of the operation of the Luftwaffe's naval aircraft, used for rescue, salvage and supply duties as well as communication and navigation aid. They had low afterdecks onto which aircraft could be hoisted. Originally, *Tschirschky* was intended for Trondheim, but redirected to Bergen.

54   Eleven Norwegian, thirteen Danish, nine Estonian, ten Finnish, sixteen Swedish, one US (*Flying Fish*) and one German. The German *Theresia LM Russ* was not involved with Weserübung in any way. After the war, it was claimed that one or two of the Estonian ships carried mines and other military merchandise, but this is probably a mix-up with the auxiliaries that arrived during the morning of 9 April, some disguised as Estonian.

55   BB A.2848.002/y/0052/04; and RM 45/III/209. The 5295-ton German freighter *Claire Hugo Stinnes* ventured into Bergen harbour in the afternoon of 9 April. She was in ballast and had no connections to the invasion forces. To the surprise of Vizeadmiral von Schrader she left shortly after on her own accord as if nothing was the matter.

56   ADM 1/10964; and Cruickshank, *SOE in Scandinavia*. The staff at the British shipping office in Bergen was substantial, but the records of these officers and their tasks remain elusive.

57   BB A.2848.002/y/0052/09; RM 50/8; RA II-C-11-2150/52; RA II-C-11-2040/2046. By evening 72 officers, 44 NCOs and 635 men were interned at Marineholmen.

58   Eifert, *69 ID*.

59   RM 50/87; and RM 92/5258.

60   The use of the antiquated London flyingboat over enemy territory demonstrates the desperate situation of British air power. The Blenheim of 254 Sqn had Lieutenant Commander G Hare onboard as a naval observer and when encountering the Home Fleet in the North Sea on the way home, details of the reconnaissance were passed direct to the C-in-C by Aldis lamp. AIR 24/372; and AIR 14/666.

61   AIR 14/666; RM 92/5255; and RM 50/87. On the way home Squadron Leader Peacock encountered a Do18 flyingboat from 2./KüFlGr 406 that was shot up and forced to emergency land south-west of Bergen.

62 In fact they were not and it seems not to have been conceived by anyone on the British side that the ships were actually on their way home.

63 AIR 14/3413; AIR 14/666; AIR 41/73; AIR 22/8; AIR 27/485; RM 50/87; and RM 57/125.

64 RM 92/5255; and RM 50/87.

65 Two of the S-boats had propellers and rudder damaged during the the morning and had limited manoeuvrability until repairs could be completed at the yard where *S21* also needed to attend to her collision damage. *S19*, which had been damaged in the collision with *S21*, arrived on 10 April.

66 Kapitänleutnant Borcherdt bluffed his way through the auxiliaries on patrol in Korsfjorden and Lerøyosen with *Schiff111* flying the Estonian flag and neutrality markings. The neutrality markings were overpainted and the Estonian flag replaced with the swastika when she dropped anchor off Hestviken. *Schiff111* was pressed into commission on 2 April in spite of being 'very dirty' and in poor technical condition.

67 Some of the Norwegian gunners had removed the firing mechanisms of the guns when surrendering. The missing parts were retrieved, some say with the help of a willing officer, but the guns were unfamiliar to the German artillerymen and virtually all needed repair. The batteries would be declared 'partly combat ready' on 10 April.

68 RA II-C-11/2040II; RM 92/5258; RM 7/1476; and RM45/III/209.

69 The Blackburn Skua was designed as a two-seater 'fighter/dive-bomber' – a virtually impossible combination to fulfil, being too slow for a fighter and carrying too small a load for a bomber. The two squadrons had operated as fighters for many months and the dive-bombing skills of the otherwise experienced pilots were rusty.

70 The nominal maximum range of the Skua was seven hundred miles and Bergen would be at their maximum. Aircraft with less than 225 litres (50 gallons) of petrol left after the attack were instructed not to attempt recrossing the North Sea but to land in Norway as it was assumed Norwegian forces would still be in control clear of the city. If the aircraft was serviceable after landing, Norwegian authorities should be contacted to see if it would be possible to obtain fuel for a return flight. If not, the aircraft was to be destroyed. ADM 199/479.

71 According to Richard Partridge, in his biography, *Operation Skua*, the raid was conceived by William Lucy, while Partridge played the role of the 'non-fire-eater' and devil's advocate. This may well be overly modest, though, and a tribute to Lucy. Lieutenant Commander Geoffrey Hare was observer/navigator in Partridge's aircraft. He had been on secondment to Coastal Command as an observer and had been onboard the aircraft that first sighted the cruisers in Bergen harbour in the forenoon of 9 April. Anticipating an air attack on the ships, he hitched a lift with a transport aircraft from Lossiemouth to Hatston during the night and made it just in time to join the attack.

72 Partridge, *Operation Skua*.

73 AIR 14/669; and Partridge, *Operation Skua*.

74 There are some myths surrounding this aircraft, and some sources even claim it was a 'captured He111 still carrying German crosses'. There is no doubt though that it was a Hudson of 233 Sqn – appropriately marked with roundels – taking some excellent photographs of the harbour. Some German reports (eg RM48/176 and RM 45/III/209) later held the Skuas attacking *Königsberg* had crudely painted German markings, but there is no evidence to support this.

75 Partridge, *Operation Skua*.

76 What happened to Smeeton's aircraft has never been ascertained. Most likely it, or its crew, was hit by the flak.

77 ADM 199/479; RM 45/III/209; and Partridge, *Operation Skua*.

78 RM 92/5258, RM 45/III/209; and RA II-C-11-2040II. Most of the survivors had little apart from the clothes they wore and groups were organised to search for uniforms and provisions in Norwegian depots, as well as accommodation.

79 The first officer was appointed commander of the 'Naval A/A unit'. In his war diary von Schrader comments that even if the sinking of *Königsberg* was lamentable, the availability of her crews for the defence of the harbour was a bonus.

80 The wreck of *Königsberg* was refloated in July 1942 and eventually righted. Too damaged to repair, she was used as a floating barge and mooring for U-boats. After the war the *Königsberg* was scrapped in Stavanger.

81 Anticipating British retaliatory attacks from sea or air, many people decided to leave the city during the morning. Rumours were rife and at times the situation became almost panicky. In all, some thirty to forty thousand people fled the town, but most did not go far; feeling safe enough once out of the city, they settled in schools, barns and summerhouses or wherever there was a space to be found. Several

trains also left the railway station packed with civilians, particularly women and children. They were taken further into the mountains and it would be longer before they eventually returned.

82 *Sao Paulo* was one of three transport ships heading for Trondheim. She entered Kristiansand harbour on 7 April to pick up a pilot and did not leave until the morning of the 8th. Due to the delay, she was redirected to Bergen. Her cargo consisted of a large number of A/A guns – badly needed in both Bergen and Trondheim.

83 *Cremon* was a civilian German fishing vessel, promptly pressed into service when appearing in Bergen by chance.

84 RM 45/III/209. Eighteen men were dead or missing from the three vessels. On 27 April, the transport *Liege* also struck a mine in Lerøyosen. The captain managed to beach her before she sank and she was eventually towed to Bergen.

85 Vizeadmiral von Schrader recognised the services of her captain to be beyond his duty and awarded him the Iron Cross. He was later made commander of a fleet of auxiliaries (Vorpostenflottille) operating out of Bergen.

86 RM 48/176. During the morning of 14 April the U-boats *U7*, *U9*, *U14*, *U60* and *U62* arrived in Bergen to refuel and resupply in food and other basics. The supplies were largely taken from *Bremse* and *Carl Peters* but their stocks were limited and local depots were confiscated.

87 *Marie Leonhard* carried 111 horses and large amounts of stores and equipment, but no heavy weapons.

88 RM 45/III/209; and ADM 199/479. The US freighter *Flying Fish* was also strafed on this occasion but there was only light damage and no casualties.

89 The aircraft of Captain Eric D McIver and Leading Airman Albert A Barnard crashed in the harbour without survivors. Later, the body of one of the men was recovered.

90 Some of the Norwegian PoWs at Marineholmen were commandeered to the offloading. Willoch protested, but was overruled. *Bärenfels* was back in service in May 1942 after extensive repairs. On 14 April 1944, *Bärenfels* was again sunk in Bergen harbour, this time by the British midget submarine *X24*, which left two time-delayed mines at the seabed under what they believed was the great floating dock at Laksevåg. After the war, the wreck was salvaged but sank for good south of Bergen while under tow.

91 ADM 199/479; and AIR 199/480. Some 19 million litres of oil and petrol was ignited during these operations, burning for almost a week.

92 Of the Germans buried, nine were army and ten navy. There were some fifty dead Germans to be buried, but somebody found it inappropriate to bury that many compared to the seven Norwegians; the others were quietly laid to rest or cremated in the following days.

Chapter 10

1 ADM 199/393.

2 On the other hand, four destroyers were lost to the Home Fleet in the morning as *Kelvin* and *Kashmir* collided and had to be escorted back to Lerwick by *Zulu* and *Cossack*.

3 *Furious* had been ordered to leave Clyde in the afternoon of 8 April to join the fleet, screened by *Maori*, *Ashanti* and *Fortune*. It would be another twenty-four hours, though, before her two Swordfish Squadrons (816 and 818) had been landed onboard and she could cast off. The carrier joined the fleet at 07:45 on 10 April. The departure of *Furious* from Clyde was duly registered by the German *B-dienst*, RM 7/486.

4 ADM 199/2202; ADM 199/393; ADM 116/4471; and ADM 199/36. Convoy HN25 had departed Bergen on 7 April, but was recalled. During the morning of the 9th, while at anchor near Hovden, Captain JS Pinkney, acting convoy commodore and master of steamer *Fylingdale* decided something untoward was going on in Norway and decided to leave unescorted. Twelve of the ships were British, nine Norwegian, eight Swedish, five Danish, two Finnish and three Estonian.

5 ADM 199/385; and Vian, *Action this Day.*

6 ADM 116/4471; and Churchill, *The Second World War*, vol. 1.

7 ADM 186/798; and ADM 199/385.

8 ADM 199/474. The mention of a four-engine bomber by Commander Buzzard is somewhat puzzling. Neither KG 26 nor KG 30 were operating such aircraft and the only option is that one of the Fw200 Condors of 1./KG 40 ventured into the attack more or less by chance. It has not been possible to find any documents to this effect so far, though.

9 ADM 199/474; and Vian, *Action this Day.* Admiral Forbes concluded that he did not 'consider either a Board of Inquiry or a Court Martial necessary' following the incident. In April 2000 a memorial was unveiled near the museum at Telavåg outside Bergen, commemorating the sinking of *Gurkha*. At least three of those perished are buried in Norway.

10 Three officers and seven ratings were injured.
11 *Faulknor, Foxhound, Forester, Hyperion, Hero, Ashanti, Inglefield, Imogen, Ilex, Isis, Maori, Zulu, Escort, Eclipse, Cossack, Javelin, Janus* and *Juno.*
12 ADM 199/2202; ADM 186/798; ADM 116/447; and ADM 199/393.
13 ADM 199/393; ADM 199/385; and ADM 199/361. A signal from C-in-C to Captain Pegram of *Glasgow* to sweep south to Obrestad east of Stavanger, sent 18:37 on 9 April, was not received until 01:45 on 10 April, too late to comply.
14 ADM 199/385.
15 ADM 199/2063; and ADM 199/474. The engine officer and two ratings were killed, while eleven men were wounded.
16 ADM 199/388 and ADM 199/474.

Chapter 11

1 RA II-C-11-2050; and Steen, *Norges Sjøkrig 1940–45*, vol. 3. Oberstløytnant Jacobsen held in his report that the minimal manning put an extra strain on him and that he was 'exhausted from the inhuman pressure of work exerted on him from higher authorities'.
2 RA II-C-11-1200/186; and RA II-C-11-2050-2060. Jacobsen was an experienced officer with only a year left before retirement. Apparently he did not appreciate being subordinated to the younger Bergersen.
3 AE 614/11A. A supplementary order at 18:40 from the commanding admiral via SDD2 resulted in an attempt to accelerate the manning of Hambåra but this had no practical effect on events.
4 Some mortar, machine-gun and reconnaissance units of the 3rd Dragonregiment also initiated mobilising at Leveanger during 8 April but were not ready for combat by nightfall.
5 RA II-C-11-1200/186; and RA II-C-11-2050-2060.
6 RA II-C-11-1340; and Steen, *Norges Sjøkrig 1940–45*, vol. 3.
7 MMU 55708; RA II-C-11-1200/186; RA II-C-11-1340; and RA II-C-11-2050-2060.
8 RM 92/5267. The Arado was observed from Vevang coastguard station when landing and a MF11 was sent from Hitra to investigate, as was the torpedo boat *Sild*. Techam and Polzin claimed they had flown all the way from Germany and been forced to make an emergency landing due to the poor weather. The Arado was towed to Kristiansund and used by the Norwegian forces before being flown to Britain. The pilots were held as PoWs for some time until liberated.
9 In the operational order for Group II, the batteries at Brettingen and Hysnes were reported to have more guns than was the case and a battery was also (falsely) reported on the Agdenes peninsula.
10 MMU 55708 – Kaptein Bryhn's report of 13.04.40.
11 In addition to several coastguard stations in the region, there were five signal stations connected by telephone to Agdenes. These were in contact with the auxiliaries through signal lamp.
12 Electrical power was taken to the fort from the public network through unprotected lines. The fort's own system was steam operated and needed a long time, and crews, to be activated.
13 Korvettenkapitän Alberts of *Z8* held back his own fire in contempt at the inefficiency of the defences.
14 RA II-C-11-2050; RM 35/I/34; RM 92/5267; RM 7/1476; Steen, *Norges Sjøkrig 1940–45*, vol. 3; and Heye, Die Unternehmung gegen Drontheim', in Hase, *Die Kriegsmarine erobertNorwegens Fjorde.*
15 The commander, Oberstløytnant Jacobsen, had at this time arrived at Hysnes and it is possible that Lange felt his position somewhat invaded. He was anyway of the opinion that it was his responsibility as fort commander to defend his fort, while the battery commanders handled the guns.
16 Some Norwegian reports claim the aircraft was seen to crash but this appears not to be the case.
17 At one stage *Hipper* also moved out from Trondheim and lobbed a few salvoes onto the area. The explosions were impressive but made no damage.
18 RA II-C-11-2050. Obrstløytnant Jacobsen gave his word on behalf of all the officers that they would not carry arms against German forces, but few considered the promise valid. Many of the officers and men from Agdenes eventually reported for service with the Norwegian forces and served with distinction in Norway and later abroad. After the war, Jacobsen was sentenced to sixty days' detainment for failing to open fire on targets within range until it was too late. His argument that he did not wish to provoke a German attack before Allied help had arrived was not accepted by the court.
19 The guns of the 3rd Artillery Regiment were stored in magazines near the town, but there was nobody available to move them and an order was given to destroy the firing mechanisms. Due to a misunderstanding, this was not done and the guns were captured intact, as were the magazines, and later used in battles against Norwegian and Allied forces.

20 The British MIR agent Palmer had arrived in Trondheim only a few days earlier to establish himself as liaison officer to the Norwegian Army in preparation for Plan R4. He was surprised in bed by the Germans and taken as a PoW. French Consul Decrespidny was also captured, while the British Captain Rainer escaped to Sweden.

21 This actually happened for several days in Trondheim.

22 *Sao Paulo* was delayed and redirected to Bergen where she struck a mine and sank. *Main* was captured by *Draug* off Haugesund. *Moonsund* was sunk in Oslofjord on 12 April by *Snapper*. *Skagerrak* was redirected to a position offshore but intercepted by *Suffolk* on the 14th and scuttled by her own crew. *Levante* was chased by Wellingtons of 9 Sqn off Bergen in the afternoon of 11 April, but she was not located and escaped unhurt.

23 An American ship was allowed to sail according to the instructions issued by the SKL before the attack. Three German ships, *Trautenfels*, *Frankenwald* and *Frauenfels*, were all unrelated to Weserübung.

24 Five infantry and one pioneer battalion were airlifted in as well as field guns and additional personnel to man the forts.

25 *Jacobi*, *Riedel* and *Heinemann* were suffering engine problems as result of the storm during the crossing. *Riedel* was in bad straits, having one engine completely shut down in addition to the grounding during the morning.

26 It is obvious from the documents that both Group West and Heye (like Bonte in Narvik) believed that a few U-boats in the fjord would be a major obstacle for a British fleet trying to intervene, not realising the difficulties of operating the boats in the confined environment.

27 The fuel situation was so critical that for a long time it would not be possible to manoeuvre to avoid British ships and Heye counted on a good portion of luck to reach home. He at one stage considered heading north-west for the supply ship *Nordmark* already in the Atlantic designated to operate with *Lützow*. Failing to meet up with her, he would then only have Russia as an alternative.

28 RM 92/5267. Contrary to Kriegsmarine practice, Heye delivered an 'after the battle' report, much like in the Royal Navy, rather than a minute-by-minute war diary. For this he was criticised and to some extent ridiculed as he also included his uncertainties and fears of not being able to return safely to Germany.

29 RM 7/486; RM 48/176; RM 92/5267; RM 92/5078; and RM 92/5178. Some 250 m³ was still onboard but unavailable because of the damage from the encounter with *Glowworm*.

30 The 45-year-old Heye received a Knight's Cross and remained as captain of *Hipper* until September 1940, when he was transferred ashore and served as Chief of Staff in various positions until 1944 when he was appointed C-in-C for the Kleinkampf-Verbände, a unit experimenting with suicide torpedoes. At the end of the war, Heye ended up as a PoW with the British, co-operating actively with Allied naval history researchers. In 1953, he became a member of the German Parliament for over ten years. He died in 1970.

31 Luck ran out for *Eckholdt* on 31 December 1942 when she came under fire from *Sheffield*'s guns during the Battle of the Barents Sea. There were no survivors. *Heinemann* operated mostly in the Channel area until she struck two mines and sank in Dover Narrows on 25 January 1942. *Riedel* and *Jacobi* spent large parts of the war in various yards. After the war, they were taken over by the French Navy and served as *Kléber* and *Desaix*, respectively, until the mid-1950s.

32 The mines were laid in shallow water near land for easy retrieval.

33 The new German Naval Command in Trondheim approached Kommandørkaptein Bergersen, who remained in his offices, to order *Frøya* to Trondheim. He flatly declined this, saying he could only assist in passing a signal to the minelayer but without any comments or recommendations. The signal was ignored by Schrøder-Nielsen.

34 RA II-C-11-1340; and Steen, *Norges Sjøkrig 1940–45*, vol. 3.

35 Steen, *Norges Sjøkrig 1940–45*, vol. 3. Rangvald Tamber escaped to Britain to become one of the most distinguished officers in the Norwegian flotillas in Shetland.

36 AIR 14/669; and AIR 14/2595.

37 ADM 199/393.

38 Lieutenant Commander H Gardner and Lieutenant Commander P Sydney-Turner were in charge of 816 Sqn and 818 Sqn, respectively.

39 One of the torpedoes was later recovered by a unit from *Jacobi*, the first British magnetically fused torpedo to fall into German hands.

40 RM 48/176. The fact that the attacking aircrafts were 'light landplanes' (*Leichte Landflugzeuge*) was taken as evidence of an aircraft carrier offshore and the He115s of 1./106 at Sola-Stavanger were ordered to search for her.

41 ADM 199/393; and ADM 199/474.

Chapter 12

1   RM 92/5178; and RM 92/5245. All times in this chapter are British times.
2   Personal communicatio from Albert Goodey, HMS *Havock*.
3   Sunrise was around 04:25.
4   ADM 199/474. The Royal Navy always classified *Scharnhorst* and *Gneisenau* as 'battlecruisers'. The strong similarity of the silhouettes of the German ships rendered their identification difficult and when reported to the C-in-C and the Admiralty as 'a *Scharnhorst*' and 'a *Hipper*', this created some uncertainty as to where the second battlecruiser was.
5   *Impulsive* had been damaged in the bow during the night and was ordered back to Scapa Flow.
6   ADM 199/474; and ADM 199/473 110057.
7   Dezimeter-Telegraphie-Gerät, or the FuMO equipment. This was the first German shipborne radar; its antenna was the mattress-like aerial on top of the cupola of the foretop rangefinder.
8   RM 92/5245; and RM 92/5178.
9   ADM 199/474; RM 92/5178; and RM 92/5245.
10 Why *Gneisenau* fired high-explosive shells at an armoured target is unclear. Netzbandt describes seeing a hit on the enemy foreship, approximately half-way between her bridge and bow: 'There was a longish, oval black tongue of flame, which rose obliquely upwards, quite distinct through the mist and spray from the round, yellow specks of the gunfire.' RM 92/5245.
11 The A turret was not operable again until the afternoon of 10 April.
12 RM 48/176. At least at this stage, there was no question of more than one adversary.
13 Although in considerable pain, Evans refused to leave the bridge; two of his toes were later amputated.
14 *Penelope*, *Bedouin*, *Punjabi*, *Eskimo* and *Kimberley* were in *Repulse*'s company.
15 ADM 199/474; ADM 199/361; and RM 92/5245.
16 RM 48/176; RM 92/5178; and RM 92/5245.
17 RM 48/176.
18 'Die Operationen im Süden stoßen somit an den <u>nicht</u> erwarteten norwegischen Waffenwiederstand.' The underlining of the word *nicht* was made in the original war diary.
19 RM 48/176.
20 RM 48/176. Lütjens wanted to send two aircraft, but none of *Gneisenau*'s were operable, due to blast damage.
21 RM 48/176. The tanker *Nordmark* was ordered to proceed to a line between 67°23' and 67°53'N at 04°05'E and be prepared for refuelling operations in the morning of 11 April. The tanker *Skagerrak* was ordered to 64°30'N between 00°30' and 02°E with similar orders and *Kattegat* at 67°N between 04°30' and 06°E.
22 By the time this signal reached Bey, he had already turned back.
23 RM 48/176; RM 92/5178; and RM 92/5245. As it turned out, it would be June before they would sail again.
24 Admiral Sir William Whitworth KCB, CB, DSO was awarded the St Olav's Medal by King Haakon in 1946 for the operations at Narvik on 13 April 1940.

Chapter 13

1   Two old guns had temporarily been placed at the northern shore during WWI, but were later removed.
2   Steen, *Sjøforsvarets kamper og virke i Nord-Norge i 1940*. In March 1940 the Ministry of Defence decided, despite the protests of the local commanders, to ship the 15-cm guns south and install them as a supplementary battery at the northern entrance to the harbour of Bergen.
3   RA 1256.3/10-970.
4   ADM 223/82; ADM 1/10517; Steen, *Sjøforsvarets kamper og virke i Nord-Norge i 1940*; and Bjørnsen, *Narvik 1940*. Commander MP Vavasour was Naval Control of Shipping (NCS)officer in Narvik.
5   RA II-C-11-1350. *Norge* and *Eidsvold* were by 1939 the oldest ironclads in service anywhere in the world. Kommandørkaptein Per Askim was a fine officer and well liked by his men.
6   Generalmajor Fleischer would in case of an emergency be designated Supreme Commander North, in charge of all naval and army forces in northern Norway, due to the poor communications with Oslo.
7   Sivertsen. *Vår ære og vår avmakt – Panserskipet Norges kamp I Narvik 9. april 1940*. Askim was convinced that most British ships in the harbour had radio contact with the Royal Navy and he assumed the presence of many German vessels in Narvik was well known by the destroyers at the mouth of the fjord.
8   Askim, *Det Tyske angrep på Narvik*.

9   RA II-C-11-1350/192; and ADM 223/126. The Admiralty in London was informed of *Jan Wellem*'s arrival and the submarine departure around 17:20 BrT from an unknown source in Narvik. *Jan Wellem* had spent the winter at the German supply base near Murmansk. Just before her departure, the Russians had indicated to the German naval attaché in Moscow that they did not appreciate her presence any longer.

10 The pennant 'P' was also hoisted in the main mast with a searchlight shining at it to tell all on leave in town to return to the ships, but in the heavy snow it was difficult to see.

11 There were actually ten German freighters, including *Jan Wellem*.

12 It is unclear with what authority Diesen issued these orders. Most likely he had consulted Foreign Minister Koht.

13 Communication with Oslo and Bergen was challenging at the best of times and this night both connections failed, making the link to Trondheim the only reliable one.

14 RA II-C-1100; RA II-C-1152; RA II-C-11-1350; and Askim, *Det Tyske angrep på Narvik*. It is notable that Diesen once again bypassed his own defence minister and went directly to Koht.

15 Fleischer and Sundlo disagreed significantly on how to defend Narvik city. Overruling Sundlo, the generalmajor had, among other measures, initiated the building of six wooden bunkers around the harbour. In April, one at each end of the harbour were complete and manned.

16 RA II-C-11-1350.

17 RA II-C-11-1350.

18 Sunrise at Narvik on 9 April was 04:25. The civil twilight, when the sun is 6° below the horizon, occurred at 03:23. At this time of the year sunrise was about five minutes earlier each day. Sunset on the 8th was at 19:05.

19 RM 54/30.

20 RA II-C-11-1350. The signal was received at Lødingen signal station, but they never considered forwarding it.

21 IWM 04/35/1.

22 This was standard procedure under such conditions; 1,400 metres being so-called 'levelling range'.

23 Action stations was still sounded by drums onboard the panserships.

24 Askim, *Det Tyske angrep på Narvik*.

25 All guns confirmed target and orders were given from Kaptein Thorkelsen, the gunnery officer, to stay on the destroyer as the relative bearing of the two ships changed.

26 The administrative officer, Leutnant Kraft, acted as interpreter.

27 RA II-C-11-1350.

28 'Nå skal vi sloss, gutter.' RA II-C-11-1350, and Ludolf Holstad, *Ofotens Tidende*, 2 October 1945.

29 RM 54/30. The torpedoes were set to run at four metres depth and all appear to have run well.

30 *Eidsvold* was probably doing some ten to twelve knots when the torpedoes hit.

31 According to the survivor Ludolf Holstad, orders had not been given for the cartouches to be brought up from the magazines but Askim dismissed this as highly unlikely. He also dismissed the thought of ramming as 'rubbish'.

32 www.bjerkvik.gs.nl.no.

33 The fourth torpedo was later found ashore, unexploded.

34 RA II-C-11-1350; and Ludolf Holstad, *Ofotens Tidende*, 2 October 1945. Lieutenant H Opstad and the ratings A Inderbø, K Johannesen and Karl Nielsen were rescued by the boat from *Fisser*. Petty officers Ludolf Holstad and Henry Backe managed to save themselves on a float, while the two men in the boat aft were K Pettersen and B Torp. Few identifiable bodies were recovered from *Eidsvold*. The explosions were so powerful that parts of the armour plating were later found five hundred metres inland. The remains of the wreck were removed after the war and little is left today.

35 According to Captain Nicholas of *Blythmoor*, at least one shell hit one of the German freighters, probably *Hein Hoyer*.

36 RM 54/30; and RM 6/102. The first torpedo missed as the firing was disrupted by a snow squall. The second did not run because of ice in the firing mechanism but was set off by the firing of the third, resulting in both torpedoes running wild. The fourth and fifth grounded, possibly due to ice in the depth-keeping mechanism, and had their detonators destroyed.

37 The wreck of *Norge* is still on the bottom of Narvik harbour at about twenty-five metres depth; eroded by time but largely intact.

38 Kommandørkaptein Askim was not seriously wounded and escaped from the hospital on 15 April. Later, he sailed from Tromsø on the hospital ship *Ariadne*, which was attacked and sunk by German aircraft. Askim was eventually rescued by the British destroyer *Arrow*. During most of the war, he was naval attaché in Washington. He died in 1963.

39 RA II-C-11-1350; RM 54/30; and Askim, *Det Tyske angrep på Narvik*.

40 After the war, Oberst Sundlo was acquitted of any claims of misconduct during the surrender of Narvik by the Military Court as well as the Supreme Court. Both concluded he could have done nothing else without exposing the town to shelling from the destroyers with severe loss of life as a result. He was, however, found guilty of treason during the occupation as he continued his membership of the NS, becoming a close associate of Quisling.

41 Generalmajor Fleischer was in Finmark on a tour of inspection and did not arrive in Tromsø until the afternoon of 10 April.

42 RA II-C-11-1350; Hauge, *Kampene i Norge 1940*; and Skogheim, and Westrheim, *Alarm, Krigen i Nordland 1940*.

43 Cruickshank, *SOE in Scandinavia*. Torrance remained at the hut until 8 May, when hunger forced him to return to Narvik. He was well looked after by Mayor Brock and billeted in a private house until Norwegian troops arrived on 28 May. He then went north to Harstad to join the evacuation of the Allied force back to Britain.

44 RM 54/30.

45 RM 54/30.

46 The lack of knowledge regarding the guns in effect proves that Sundlo, contrary to some post-war Norwegian claims, did not forward any information to Germany. He would have certainly known the true position.

47 *Stråssa* had left Narvik already on 6 April, but anchored in Ofotfjorden to mend a minor engine defect.

48 RA II-C-11-1350/192; RA II-C-11-1350; and Petterøe, *Fem år på banjeren*.

49 RM 54/30; and Hauge, *Kampene i Norge 1940*. Eight thousand rifles, three hundred light and fifteen heavy machine guns with ammunition were captured at Elvegårdsmoen.

50 RA II-C-11-1350. Brekke eventually got in touch with the British forces and agreed to keep *B3* out of the area to avoid misidentification and moved to Tromsø. The boat was scuttled during the evacuation.

51 RA II-C-11-1350. Melsom and his crew went north to Tromsø. *B1* was retrieved when the Allied forces recaptured the area and later sailed to Britain where she was used as a training vessel until 1944.

52 *Bärenfels* was diverted to Bergen. *Rauenfels* reached Ofotfjorden on 10 April, but came across *Hostile* and *Havock* who were retiring from the first battle and was destroyed. *Alster* was stopped off Bodø by the Norwegian auxiliary *Syrian* on 11 April. Her captain abandoned ship but a boarding party from *Icarus* managed to secure her before she could be scuttled.

53 Armed merchant ships were in violation of the Neutrality Act, but apparently overlooked by Norwegian authorities. None of the German ships were armed; at least, there were no guns on deck.

54 Thirty-four men were taken prisoner, while five escaped into the mountains.

55 *Arnim* and *Thiele* both needed repair and probably would not have been able to depart anyway on 9 April.

56 It was considered necessary to give the older Type-34 destroyers maximum fuel load for stability reasons prior to departure, while the Type-36 could manage with less. The Type-34 ships would therefore be fuelled last.

57 This was 4th and 6th Destroyer Flotillas receiving orders to attack Bergen, but Bonte did not know this, of course.

58 RM 54/30; RM 8113/26; and RM 48/176.

59 ADM 199/474.

60 ADM 199/474.

61 *Hardy* was a flotilla leader and at 1,505 tons larger than the other H-class destroyers. She also had a larger complement (175 men) and carried a fifth 4.7-inch gun aft. *Hotspur*, Commander Herbert FH Layman, *Hunter*, Lieutenant Commander Lindsay de Villiers and *Havock*, Lieutenant Commander Rafe E 'Nutty' Courage. *Hunter* was the junior ship of the flotilla; 'Nutty' Courage was highly cherished by his men and *Havock* was a happy ship.

62 *Impulsive* had left for home in the morning due to storm damage.

63 ADM 199/474; and ADM 199/473 110057.

64 A cable length is one-thenth of a nautical mile or 185.3 metres.

65 ADM 199/474.

66 ADM 199/361; and ADM 199/474.

67 ADM 199/474; ADM 199/361; and ADM 199/473, Barnett, *Engage the Enemy More Closely*; Dickens, *Narvik, Battles of the Fjords*; and report of Commander Layman of 25 April in *London Gazette*, 1 July 1947.

68 RM 54/30; and Springenschmid, *Die Männer von Narvik*.

69 Due to a miscommunication between Heppel on the bridge and his leading torpedo man on the mounting, one torpedo remained in the forward tube, unknown to Heppel. Not knowing what to expect, *Hardy*'s aft torpedo tubes were trained to port and had to be swung round to starboard before they could be fired.

70 *Heidkamp* would capsize and sink in the early morning of the next day, but not before one 3.7-cm twin-flak gun, several smaller guns, four torpedoes and substantial ammunition had been salvaged.

71 Two merchant ships were also hit by *Havock*'s torpedoes. Being fired at from the British freighter *North Cornwall* by the German crew that had taken command of her, *Havock* fired back with a Lewis gun, 'silencing' the culprit.

72 Personal communication from Albert Goodey (stoker on HMS *Havock*). He was feeding shells to the X gun during action stations.

73 One or two torpedoes passed under the bridge of *Hardy* and at least two torpedoes passed underneath *Hunter*.

74 ADM 199/474; ADM 199/473; RM 54/30; RM 6/102; and Dickens, *Narvik, Battles of the Fjords*. Report of Lieutenant Commander RE Courage of 27 April in *London Gazette*, 1 July 1947.

75 Having just dropped anchor, there was no device in place to slip the cable and it could not be weighed because the power to the electrically operated capstan was severed.

76 ADM 199/473 110057; and RM 54/30.

77 After the event, rumours of one or two torpedoes striking the side of the huge tanker without exploding spread, but it is difficult to put any confidence in this and it is not found in any first-hand sources.

78 The forty-six British sailors managed to escape from their guards and, joining the survivors from *Hardy* in Ballangen, they were repatriated by British destroyers a few days later.

79 ADM 199/473 110057; and ADM 199/474. Why the signal was addressed to (D)20, Captain Bickford onboard *Esk*, is unclear, but Warburton-Lee must have been sure it would be read by *Renown* as well. It was also intercepted by the Home Fleet, off Trondheim at the time, and was the first news for the C-in-C of the attack on Narvik. None of the survivors could explain the cruiser, or who identified it.

80 Report of Commander HFH Layman of 25 April in *London Gazette*, 1 July 1947; RM 54/30; and Heye, *Z 13 von Kiel bis Narvik*.

81 RM 54/30; RM 6/102; RM 8/1326; ADM 199/473 110057; and Heye, *Z 13 von Kiel bis Narvik*.

82 ADM 199/473 110057. Paymasters were non-executive officers not trained or expected to take part in fighting, far less take command of a ship. Stanning, like all captains' secretaries was actually nicknamed 'Scratch'. There is little doubt that his initiatives that morning saved a large number of his shipmates.

83 It took Stanning more than a year to recover from Narvik, for which he was awarded the DSO. He died in 1997.

84 Able Seaman LJ Smale wrote in a letter to Narvik Museum in 1989: 'We owe special thanks to Mrs Christiansen and her daughter who took us into their home . . . They gave us everything they had to replace our wet, freezing clothes and to bring back warmth to our bodies.'

85 Warburton-Lee and some of the other dead were temporarily buried in the deep snow and later moved to the cemetery at Ballangen, where their graves can still be found today.

86 ADM 199/474; and ADM 199/473. The events for which Lieutenant Commander Roope of *Glowworm* was awarded his VC took place two days earlier, but the full story did not become known until after the war and the award was announced in 1946.

87 It is noteworthy that the German ships used their secondary guns with good effect due to the short distances involved whereas the British destroyers, according to the German reports, did not employ their 'pom-poms', according to some reports, as they were frozen.

88 ADM 199/473 110057. *Hotspur* was hit by seven 12.7-cm shells and innumerable splinters and small-calibre bullets.

89 All damage inflicted on the British destroyers was credited to *Arnim* and *Thiele*.

90 RM 54/30; and RM 6/102. Wreckage was later found near Tjeldsund, some of which was marked with *Hotspur*, leading the Germans to believe that she had also been sunk in addition to *Hardy* and *Hunter*.

91 Albert Goodey (stoker on HMS *Havock*) many years later claimed that his ship achieved thirty-six knots when withdrawing, 'being very low on fuel, shells and torpedoes and very high on adrenalin'.

92 Commander Layman of *Hotspur* was senior British officer, but as his ship was severely damaged, being conned from aft with no signalling arrangement, he wisely passed command to Wright.

93 Forty-six men were later released by the Germans and repatriated via Sweden. One hundred and eight men, including de Villiers, perished, many through exposure in the icy water after she sank. The wreck of *Hunter* was found in 2008 and commemorated by the British and Norwegian navies in a ceremony at the site.

94 RM 54/30. In spite of the efforts to dispose of confidential material, the Germans found some things of interest, including the orders from the Admiralty to attack Narvik and other signals of the last couple of days.

95 *U46* and *U25* heard gunfire from the direction of Narvik at dawn but never realised what it signified.

96 *Georg Thiele* lay at anchor outside the harbour for a while fighting the many fires burning before entering.

97   RM 54/30; RM 6/102; RM 8/1326; ADM 199/473; ADM 199/474; reports of Commander Herbert FH Layman of 25 April and Lieutenant Commander Rafe E Courage of 27 April, in *London Gazette*, 1 July 1947; Heye, *Z 13 von Kiel bis Narvik*; and Dickens, *Narvik, Battles of the Fjords*.

98   ADM 199/474. It is a bit surprising that this is what he believed they had been up against, but it probably reflects the extreme confusion of the engagement during the escape westward.

99   *U51* fired at least one torpedo at an H-class destroyer in the small hours of 11 April without result.

100 RM 98/155; and ADM 199/474.

101 ADM 199/474.

102 ADM 199/474.

103 *Alster* was later taken to Tromsø to unload her valuable load of guns and vehicles and later still taken over by the British merchant navy. She then carried the name *Empire Endurance* and was sunk on 20 April 1941 in the Atlantic by *U73*.

104 ADM 199/473; and ADM 199/474. At one stage after the second British attack *Hotspur, Hostile, Eskimo, Penelope, Punjabi* and *Cossack* were all attended to at Skjelfjord.

105 It is noteworthy that Bey in his report includes a 'heavy cruiser' in the forces that attacked Narvik. RM 54/30.

106 It does not appear from any British source that Bey's destroyers were observed from the British ships. Neither were they seen from *U46*. *U25* sighted them both and correctly identified them as friendly.

107 RM 48/176; RM 98/155; RM 54/30; and Heye, *Z 13 von Kiel bis Narvik*.

108 RM 48/176. At 12:30 on 11 April, three torpedoes were launched at a 'Cumberland Three-stacker' and 21:15 another three at a 'York-class cruiser'. All torpedoes missed or exploded prematurely.

109 The issue of the torpedo failure was to persist during the entire Norwegian campaign.

110 RA II-C-11-1350. Both ships were later raised and taken into German service.

111 ADM 267/126; and ADM 199/479. Lieutenant Commander Sydney-Turner of 818 Sqn later wrote: 'This attack was carried out in conditions of which the squadron had had no previous experience and without a reconnaissance, which would have been extremely valuable in deciding tactics of approach. The only maps available were photographic reproductions of Admiralty charts, which showed no contours.'

112 RM 54/30; and Heye, *Z 13 von Kiel bis Narvik*.

113 RM 54/30.

114 *Warspite* had temporarily been transferred from the Mediterranean to reinforce the Home Fleet, but with the growing threat that Italy would enter the war on the German side it was decided she would have to go back. *Warspite* had been released on 4 April, sailing for the Clyde to prepare for her return to the Mediterranean but recalled a few days later.

115 The German B-dienst intercepted this signal, but missed the vital part – where the attack would be aimed at. This was not decoded and reported until later on the 13th, when it was too late. RM 7/486.

116 Diary of Commander PD Hoare, IWM 96/6/1. On a regular Sunday mass, about twenty men would normally turn up.

117 *U64* arrived in Narvik to refuel in the afternoon of 12 April. Kapitänleutnant Schulz reported having been attacked off Værøy and he had dived away from groups of destroyers several times during the way in, so there was no doubt that the Germans were well and truly trapped.

118 *Forester* was to have been among the sweepers too, but her paravanes capsized and one was subsequently lost, so she joined the screen. IWM P.186.

119 Blair, *Hitler's U-boat War*, vol. 1. Later in the day *U48* was in position for another attack on two other destroyers – but again with no result. *U48* served as a front boat until July 1941 and was one of the most successful U-boats of the war, being involved in the sinking of fifty-two ships of over 300,000 tons. Herbert Schultze served in various staff positions from July 1942 and survived the war. He died in 1987.

120 ADM 199/473. Rice later wrote that 'Flying in the fjords – particularly in the narrow ones – resembled flying in a tunnel between the steep sides of the fjord and the low cloud ceiling.'

121 ADM 199/473; IWM 96/6/1; report of Captain Micklethwait, Narvik Museum; report of Admiral Whitworth of 25 April, in *London Gazette*, 1 July 1947; Commander Sherbooke's report of 19 April, Narvik Museum; Brown, *Naval Operations of the Campaign in Norway*; and Blair, *Hitler's U-boat War*, vol. 1.

122 *U51* was lost with all hands, including Kapitänleutnant Knorr, four months later in the Bay of Biscay, torpedoed by the submarine *Cachalot*.

123 RM 98/155. Some of the survivors were trapped inside the sunken boat and had to escape through a free-ascent to surface (three of the casualties occurred during this). The crew was employed for a while as gaolers and ammunition handlers before being repatriated to Germany by train through Sweden.

124 Brown had the highest rank of the two and was technically in charge of the flight. As pilot, Rice decided the details of how to fly and matters regarding the safety of the crew and aircraft.

125 ADM 199/473; RM 54/30; and RM 98/155.

126 RM 54/30. The Germans were taken to a PoW camp near Vardø but eventually liberated by their own troops and repatriated at the end of June via Sweden. Thirty-three of the men were wounded, fifteen seriously.

127 The red standard Z 'an den Feind' – 'advance on the enemy' – was a traditional signal used by German destroyers and torpedo boats going into battle.

128 In theory the guns of a destroyer should have been efficient to 8,000–10.000 metres.

129 RM 54/30; ADM 199/473; and Commander Sherbooke's report of 19 April, Narvik Museum. Unlike the British, who used largely SAP shells, the Germans used high-explosive grenades that exploded on impact with the water, generating a hail of splinters.

130 RM 6/102; and ADM 199/473. In the morning of 13 April *Zenker* had reported a maximum speed of twenty knots due to the propeller damage, but it seems that she was capable of much more during the action, probably as the tolerance of both her captain and engineering officer in terms of vibrations and noise was much increased when under fire.

131 ADM 199/473; Signalman Ron Maynard's unpublished memoirs; IWM 95/3/1; and Dickens, *Narvik, Battles of the Fjords*. At least twice, explosions were heard and shocks felt onboard *Warspite*; one of these was definitely a torpedo striking rocks after narrowly missing the ship.

132 At 13:31, some eleven miles west of Narvik, 'three or four bumps' were felt onboard *Cossack*, 'as if striking a submerged object'. We cannot know if these really were hits by faulty torpedoes from a *U25*.

133 Commander Sherbooke's report of 19 April, Narvik Museum; and Dickens, *Narvik, Battles of the Fjords*.

134 As the forward turrets were firing almost dead ahead, the blast from B turret damaged the blast bags of A turret, covering the points where the guns protrude from the armour. A turret thus filled with choking cordite smoke, adding to the discomfort of the turret crew from having the B guns blasting deafeningly just above their heads. ADM 199/473.

135 ADM 267/126. One of the crew was later rescued; the other was lost.

136 RM 54/30. The stern drifted in the fjord for several days.

137 Thanks to excellent damage-control procedure, *Punjabi* was back in action again about an hour later. The Y magazine was intentionally flooded because of the fires aft.

138 One of the survivors was the first officer, Kapitänleutnant Burkhard von Müllenheim-Rechberg. In May 1941, he was the senior surviving officer from *Bismarck*.

139 ADM 199/473; IWM 95/3/1; RM 54/30; and Dickens, *Narvik, Battles of the Fjords*. German sources later held persistently that British ships had used their machine guns on the sailors in the water, killing several.

140 IWM 95/3/1; ADM 199/473; and Signalman Ron Maynard's unpublished memoirs.

141 A short while after the grounding, two teenage cousins, Torstein and Leif Hansen, hailed the ship. The pair brought a captured German flag they had brazenly taken from a merchantman. The flag hangs in the Imperial War Museum in London today.

142 RM 54/30; Commander Sherbooke's report of 19 April; and Signalman Ron Maynard's unpublished memoirs.

143 ADM 199/473; Dickens, *Narvik, Battles of the Fjords*; and Brice, *The Tribals*.

144 The German torpedoes that missed all ran ashore on the snowy rocks near Straumen (one actually passed underneath *Forester*). None of them exploded and were later examined by engineers from *Hero*.

145 RM 8/1326; and RM 54/30. *Thiele* had several torpedoes left. One was lost when a wounded man accidentally fell on the firing mechanism, setting it off, but according to local sources there are still torpedoes onboard the wreck.

146 The Germans onboard *Thiele* saw the spectacular damage made by their torpedo and assumed the opponent to have been lost. The destroyer had been identified as *Cossack* and the next day, German radio reported her sunk.

147 Korvettenkapitän Max-Eckart Wolff later held firmly that many of his men had been killed or wounded after they had come ashore by British guns, which kept firing at the men scrambling off.

148 RM 8/1326; RM 54/30; ADM 199/473; diary of Vice Admiral Sir John Parker; IWM P.186; and IWM 96/22/1.

149 Rice was later awarded the DSM, Brown the DSC and Pacey was mentioned in dispatches.

150 Diary of Commander PD Hoare; IWM 96/6/1.

151 Munthe-Kaas, *Krigen i Narvikavsnittet 1940*.

152 ADM 199/473; and report of Admiral Whitworth of 25 April, *London Gazette*, 1 July 1947. None of the aircraft approached to attack.

153 *Punjabi* embarked several wounded from *Cossack* and *Eskimo* first, and only followed later. The repairs made after the hits on 13 April did not hold and the next day, *Punjabi* went to Skjelfjord, where she was

patched up sufficiently to make the trip back to Britain on the 20th in the company of *Hotspur* and *Jupiter*.

154 Later *Ivanhoe* was also fired at but still without result.
155 ADM 199/473.
156 At 04:50 the following morning she was taken in tow by *Bedouin* off Barøy. Steering was difficult and progress slow and it would be dawn on 15 April before *Eskimo* arrived at Skjelfjord.
157 It appears that the tireless Schütze again attacked and again achieved nothing before he gave up and laid *U25* to rest on the bottom for the night. *U46* tried to attack some of the destroyers leaving but was discovered and depth charged so hard that she eventually had to be taken off patrol and recalled a few days later. On land, Heppel saw the British ships approaching and with three sailors rowed towards them in a small boat, catching the attention of the *Ivanhoe*. Some of the wounded had been taken to the local hospital in Ballangen where they were found by the Irish Guards some weeks later.
158 Heye, *Z 13 von Kiel bis Narvik*.
159 ADM 199/473. Whitworth knew that a reconstituted military force had sailed on 12 April from the Clyde under the command of Major-General Mackesy, escorted by a naval force led by Admiral of the Fleet the Earl of Cork and Orrery.
160 ADM 199/475; and ADM 199/473.
161 Onboard were also two British prisoners captured in Narvik. One of them was Giles Romilly, a war correspondent for the London *Daily Express* and Churchill's nephew. He was later taken to Colditz.
162 RM 54/30; and Heye, *Z 13 von Kiel bis Narvik*.

Chapter 14

1 'There is no room for mistakes in submarines, you are either alive or dead'– according to Vice Admiral Max Horton.
2 ADM 234/52; ADM 199/1843; SKL KTB A; and Chalmers, *Max Horton and the Western Approaches*.
3 ADM 199/288.
4 ADM 199/288; and ADM 234/380.
5 RM 57/93.
6 It appears that the torpedo boats were frequently misidentified as destroyers by British lookouts early in the war.
7 IWM 91/38/1.
8 IWM 91/38/1; ADM 173/16665; and ADM 199/1861. Hutchinson received the DSO on 9 May 1940 for the sinking of *Karlsruhe*. The depth charging had taken its toll, however, and after another eventful patrol he was given three months sick leave before being appointed Staff Officer Operations at Horton's headquarters, the Admiralty and later Malta.
9 RM 92/5257; RM 57/93; and IWM 91/38/1.
10 RM 92/5223.
11 RM 57/93; and RM 7/1475. Kapitänleutnant Strelow and his crew took over *Olav Tryggvason* on 15 April. She was renamed *Albatros II* and later *Brummer*. Strelow took command of *U435*, which was lost in Biscay in 1943.
12 RM 92/5223.
13 *Lützow*'s sister-ship was actually in dock.
14 RNSM A1994/95; ADM 199/184;3 and ADM 199/294. Four days later, the upper conning tower hatch fell back after opening, hitting Lieutenant Commander Forbes hard on the head. The counterweight had fallen off, probably as a result of the depth charging. Forbes perished when *Spearfish* was torpedoed by *U34* off Stavanger in August.
15 The starboard propeller was gone. The port was still attached to the shaft but all bearings and gears were destroyed.
16 RM 57/93. *Kondor* had damaged a propeller on wreckage from *Blücher* and, capable of only twenty knots, lagged behind. *Jaguar* and *Falke* were eventually ordered back to Kristiansand.
17 RM 48/176; RM 6/87.
18 Allegedly phrased by Rear Admiral AK Wilson VC, regarding submarines in general.
19 For some reason, the Admiralty believed there was a German destroyer at Stavanger. ADM 116/4471.
20 ADM 199/1848; and RM 98/4. *Thistle* sank in position 59° 06'N, 05° 05'E, south-west of Karmøy in some two hundred metres of water; fifty-three men perished.
21 ADM 186/798.
22 The convoy consisted of *Scharhörn, Tucuman, Itauri, Espana, Fridenau, Hamm, Antares, Muansa* and *Wigbert*, escorted by *V1501, V1505, V1506, V1507, V1508, V1509* and some T-boats.

23   ADM 199/1847; and RM 72/169. *Triton* was lost with all hands in the Adriatic in December 1940, by then under the command of Lieutenant Commander GC Watkins.
24   ADM 199/288.
25   ADM 199/288; and ADM 199/1847.
26   ADM 199/288. *Moonsund* was under way from Germany to Trondheim with aviation spirit, though the master and second mate both maintained they were heading for Oslo where they would receive orders. The two dead were buried at sea.
27   ADM 199/288; and ADM 199/1843.
28   ADM 199/288; and RM 74/7.
29   The two torpedo boats had left Kristiansand on 13 April for Fredrikshavn, where each embarked some 150 soldiers. *F5* had about a hundred men onboard.
30   RM 57/93; and RM 102/3622.
31   Lieutenant Cowell was unconscious for quite some time and the first lieutenant took over command.
32   RNSM A1994/95; ADM 199/1843; RM 74/7; ADM 199/1840; and ADM 199/1877.
33   One officer and three ratings did not manage to escape.
34   ADM 234/380.

Chapter 15

1   Hubatsch, *Weserübung*.
2   Müllern, *Sveriges järnmalm och de krigförandes planer 1939–1940*.
3   Erdmenger, *Der Einsatz der Kriegsmarine bei der Bestezung Dänemarks und Norwegens in Frühjahr 1940*.
4   www.ca.nizcor.org.

Appendices

1   *B4* was at yard in Horten.
2   *Kjell* was at yard in Kristiansand, *Ørn* and *Lom* in the Horten yard.
3   *Olav Tryggvason* was at the naval depot in Horten for repairs on 9 April.
4   Compiled from ADM 187/7; ADM 234/380 and other sources.
5   *Warspite* from Mediterranean Fleet. *Nelson* and *Barham* were both at yards during this period.
6   *Hood* at Plymouth for refit.
7   *Sussex* and *Norfolk* at yards.
8   *Edinburgh* and *Newcastle* at yards.
9   *Hereward* and *Hasty* at yards. *Hereward* released 17 April.
10   *Imperial* and *Diana* at yards; both released during April.
11   *Nubian* at yard; released 12 April.
12   *Kelly, Kipling, Kandahar, Khartoum* and *Kingston* at yards. *Kipling* released 16 April, *Kelly* on 27 April.
13   *Jarvis, Jersey, Jackal* and *Jaguar* at yards.
14   *Fame, Foresight* and *Firedrake* at yards. *Fame* released 10 April.
15   Nore Command (Harwich) temporarily attached to Home Fleet. *Gallant* and *Grafton* at yards; *Grafton* released 15 April.
16   Rosyth Command, temporarily attached to Home Fleet. *Echo* and *Escort* at yards.
17   *Intrepid* and *Express* at yards.
18   *Triumph, Tribune* and *Wilk* at yards.
19   *Salmon* at yard.
20   *Sturgeon* at yard.
21   On 29 April, while heading out for her second Norwegian patrol, under her new commander, Lieutenant FJ Brooks, *Unity* collided off Blyth in dense fog with the Norwegian steamer *Atle Jarl* and sank shortly after. Four men were lost.
22   Lütjens was acting Commander-in-Chief of the Fleet because Admiral Marschall was on sick leave.
23   The destroyer *Richard Beitzen* (Korvettenkapitän von Davidson) was in reserve, but was eventually not needed and did not participate in Operation Weserübung.
24   RM 35/I/36.
25   RM 8/1152.
26   RM 7/797.
27   *Forsvarets Forum, Spesialutgave 1990*.

References

Primary Documents from Public Archives

The National Archives, Kew

ADM 1/10517, ADM 1/10680, ADM 116/447, ADM 116/4471, ADM 173/16665, ADM 186/798, ADM 199/1840, ADM 199/1843, ADM 199/1847, ADM 199/1848, ADM 199/1861, ADM 199/1877, ADM 199/2063, ADM 199/2159, ADM 199/2202, ADM 199/278, ADM 199/285, ADM 199/286, ADM 199/288, ADM 199/294, ADM 199/3, ADM 199/323, ADM 199/36, ADM 199/361, ADM 199/379, ADM 199/385, ADM 199/388, ADM 199/393, ADM 199/473, ADM 199/474, ADM 99/475, ADM 99/479, ADM 199/892, ADM 205/2, ADM 223/126, ADM 223/82, ADM 234/17, ADM 234/380, ADM 234/427, ADM 234/52, ADM 267/126, ADM 53/113071

AIR 14/172, AIR 14/2595, AIR 14/3413, AIR 14/666, AIR 14/669, AIR 15/202, AIR 199/480, AIR 20/6260, AIR 22/8, AIR 24/216, AIR 27/1365, AIR 27/485, AIR 41/73

CAB 65/1, CAB 65/11, CAB 65/12, CAB 65/2, CAB 65/4, CAB 66/1, CAB 66/3, CAB 66/4, CAB 66/5, CAB 66/6, CAB 66/7, CAB 80/105

FO 371/21087, FO 371/21088, FO 371/22276, FO 371/22283, FO 371/23658, FO 371/23667, FO 371/23674, FO 371/24815, FO 371/24818, FO 371/24819, FO 371/24820, FO 371/24821, FO 371/24829, FO 371/24832, FO 371/24834, FO 419/34

DM 199/2063, GFM 33/1111, PREM 1/419, WO 106/1840, WO 106/1969, WO 193/773

Imperial War Museum, London

IWM 04/35/1, IWM 67/25/1, IWM 89/3/1, IWM 90/23/1, IWM 91/38/1, IWM 95/56/1, IWM 95/3/1, IWM 96/22/1, IWM 96/6/1, IWM P.186, IWM PP/MRC/C10

Riksarkivet, Oslo

RA 0064-2B 023 2/1 927.9, RA 1256/310, RA FKA 2B.072.42 (194), RA FKA Ec, 0125, RA FKA II-C-11/1103, RA FKA Ya II-C-11-00, RA II-C-11-1100, RA II-C-11-1102, RA II-C-11-1103, RA II-C-11-1120/1180, RA II-C-11-1130, RA II-C-11-1200, RA II-C-11-1202, RA II-C-11-1204, RA II-C-11-1350, RA II-C-11-2020/2040, RA II-C-11-2040, RA II-C-11-2040 II, RA II-C-11-2150, RA II-C-11-5, RA II-C-11-51, RA II-C-11-52, RA II-C-11-940

Bergen Byarkiv, Bergen

BB A.2848.002/y/0002/01, BB A.2848.002/y/0052/04, BB A.2848.002/y/0052/09

Bundesarchiv, Freiburg

BA-MA III M 35/1, KTB SKL A April40, KTB SKL A Feb40, KTB SKL A Jan40, KTB SKL A March40, KTB SKL A Oct39, MSg 2/1882, N 172/14, N 172/16, N300/5, RH 24-21/17, RH 24-21/23,

RH 24-21/24, RH 24-21/30, RM 100/125, RM 102/3622, RM 12/II/167, RM 35/I-31, RM 35/I-32, RM 35/I-35, RM 35/I-39, RM 35/II-35, RM 45/III-12, RM 45/III-122, RM 45/III-136, RM 45/III-209, RM 48/176, RM 50/8, RM 50/87, RM 54/30, RM 57/125, RM 57/93, RM 6/102, RM 6/87, RM 7/11, RM 7/124, RM 7/1475, RM 7/1476, RM 7/177, RM 7/180, RM 7/194, RM 7/295, RM 7/486, RM 7/797, RM 7/891, RM 7/9, RM 7/92, RM 70/1, RM 72/169, RM 74/7, RM 8/1152, RM 8/1326, RM 8113/26, RM 92/5078, RM 92/5087, RM 92/5088, RM 92/5097, RM 92/5178, RM 92/522, RM 92/5223, RM 92/5245, RM 92/5255, RM 92/5257, RM 92/5258, RM 92/5259, RM 92/5267, RM 92/5332, RM 92/VM855/47900-910, RM 96/667, RM 98/155, RM 98/22, RM 98/4, RM 98/89, RNSM A1994/95, RNSM A1995/312, SKL 23685/41, SKL 25908/41

Miscellaneous

Eickhorn Papers (unpublished)
Willoch Papers (unpublished)
Goodey Papers (unpublished)
Law Papers (unpublished)
Oscarsborg Sambandsjournal
3.Gebigsjäger Div., Kriegstagebuch No. 2
Eifert, JD, '69 ID' (unpublished)
Munthe-Kaas, O, 'Aprildagene 1940' (unpublished)
Report of Admiral Whitworth of 25 April, *London Gazette*, 1 July 1947
Report of Commander Layman of 25 April, *London Gazette*, 1 July 1947
Report of Lieutenant Commander Courage of 27 April, *London Gazette*, 1 July 1947
Report of Commander Sherbooke, Narvik Museum
Report of Captain Micklethwait, Narvik Museum
Personal account of Fregattenkapitän (Ing) a.D. Anton Nonn (unpublished)
Signalman Ron Maynard's memories (unpublished)
Margaret Reid's diary (unpublished)
Diary of Kaptein Ullring (unpublished)
Aftenposten, 9 April 1990, 20 June 2005
Ofotens Tidende, 2 October 1945
Forsvarets Forum, Spesialutgave 1990
www.9april1940.org
www.bjerkvik.gs.nl.no
www.vrakdykking.com
www.nuav.net
www.uboat.net.de
www.hmsglowworm.org.uk
www.hmscossack.org.uk
www.scharnhorst-class.dk/index.html
www.world-war.co.uk/index.php3
http://freespace.virgin.net/john.dell/sinking_of_the_konigsberg.htm
http://members.aol.com/rkolmorgen/index.html

Published Books and Reports

Betænkning til Folketinget, Copenhagen, JH Schultz, 1945
Förspelet till det Tyska angreppet på Danmark och Norge den 9 April 1940, Stockholm, PA Norstedt, 1947

Innstilling fra Undersøkelseskommisjonen av 1945, Oslo, Stortinget, 1946
Innstilling fra Undersøkelseskommisjonen av 1945, appendix, vol. 1, Oslo, Stortinget, 1946
Innstilling fra Undersøkelseskommisjonen av 1945, appendix, vol. 2, Oslo, Stortinget, 1947
Rapport fra den Militære undersøkelseskommisjon av 1946, Oslo, Nou, 1979
Straffesak mot Vidkun Abraham Quisling, Oslo, 1946
Den Krigshistoriske Avdeling – Krigen i Norge, Oslo, 1952
Krigen i Norge 1940, Operasjonene i kristiansand-Setesdals-avsnittet, Oslo, Gyldendal, 1953
Lagevorträge des Oberbefehlshabers der Kriegsmarine vor Hitler 1939-1945, G Wagner (ed.), Munich, Lehmann, 1972
Kammeraden-Echo No. 2, *Erinnerungen und Informasjon für Angehörige des ehemaligen GR 193*, Dortmund, 1975

Askim, P, *Det Tyske angrep på Narvik*, Oslo, Grøndahl & Søns Forlag, 1947
Aspheim, O and Hjeltnes, G, *Tokt ved neste nymåne*, Oslo, Cappelen, 1990
Barnett, C, *Engage the Enemy More Closely*, London, Norton, 1991
Bartels, H, *Tigerflagge Heiss Vor!*, Bielefeld, Giesking, 1943
Beesly, P, *Very Special Intelligence*, London, Greenhill, 2000
Berge, W, *Fra Nøytralitet til Krig*, Tvedestrand, Tvedestrand Boktrykkeri, 1995
Binder, F and Schlünz, H, *Schwerer Kreuzer Blücher*, Hamburg, Koehlers Verlagsgesellschaft, 1991
Bjørnsen, B, *Narvik 1940*, Oslo, Gyldendal, 1980
Blair, C, *Hitler's U-Boat War*, vol. 1, London, Random House, 1996
Borgersrud, L, *Konspirasjon og kapitulasjon*, Oslo, Oktober, 2000
Brice, MH, *The Tribals*, London, Ian Allan, 1971
Brown, D (ed.), *Naval Operations of the Campaign in Norway*, Oxford, Frank Cass, 2000
Bröyn, P, *Den svenske malmeksport fram til besetingen av Narvik i April 1940*, Oslo, Hovedfags-oppgave i historie, Universitet i Oslo, 1964
Busch, FO, *Narvik*, Gütersloh, Bertelsmann, 1940
Butler, JRM, *Grand Strategy*, vol. 2, London, HMSO, 1970
Chalmers, W, *Max Horton and the Western Approaches: A Biography*, London, Hodder & Stoughton, 1954
Churchill, WS, *The Second World War*, vol. 1, London, Cassell, 1949
Colban, E, *Femti år*, Oslo, Aschehoug, 1952
Cruickshank, C, *SOE in Scandinavia*, Oxford, Oxford University Press, 1986
Dahl, HF, *Vidkun Quisling, en fører for fall*, Oslo, Aschehoug, 1992
Denham, H, *Inside the Nazi Ring*, London, John Murray, 1984
Derry, TK, *The Campaign in Norway*, London, HMSO, 1952
Dickens, P, *Narvik, Battles of the Fjords*, Annapolis, Naval Institute Press, 1974
Diesen, U, *Kvinne i Krig*, Oslo, 1965
Dietl, G-L and Herrmann, K, *General Dietl, das Leben eines Soldaten*, Vienna, Franz Hain, 1951
Dilks, D (ed.), *The Diaries of Sir Alexander Cadogan*, London, Cassell, 1971
——, 'Great Britain and Scandinavia in the Phoney War', *Scandinavian Journal of History*, 2: 1–2 (1977)
Dönitz, K, *Zehn Jahre und zwanzig Tage*, Munich, Bernard & Graefe Verlag, 1981
Edwards, G, *Norwegian Patrol*, Shrewsbury, Airlife, 1985
Erdmenger, H, 'Der Einsatz der Kriegsmarine bei der Besetzung Dänemarks und Norwegens im Frühjahr 1940', in *Jahrbuch für Deutschlands Seeinteressen 1942*, Berlin, Mittler & Sohn, 1942
Evensen, K, *Oscarsborg forteller historie*, Drøbak, Boksenteret, 1992
Fjeld, OT (ed.), *Klar til strid*, Oslo, Kystartilleriets Offisersforening, 1999
Fjørtoft, JE, *Kanonene ved Skagerrak*, Arendal, Agdin, 1985
Fjørtoft, K, *Mot stupet*, Oslo, Gyldendal, 1989

Frognes, K, *Fyrbøteren på Jo*, Tvedestrand, Tvedestrand Boktrykkeri, 1994

Gemzell, C-A, *Raeder, Hitler und Skandinavien*, Lund, Gleerup, 1965

Grieg Smith, S-E, *Ingen fiendtlige hensikter*, Arendal, Agder, 1989

Grimnes, OK, *Norge i Krig*, vol. 1, Oslo, Aschehoug, 1984

Guhnfeldt, C, *Fornebu 9. April*, Oslo, Wings, 1990

Hafsten, B, Olsen, B, Larsstuvold, U and Stenersen, S, *Flyalarm*, Oslo, Sem & Stenersen, 2005

Halder, F, *Kriegstagebuch*, Stuttgart, Kohlhammer, 1962

Hambro, CJ, *De første måneder*, Oslo, Aschehoug, 1945

—— (ed.), *9.April–7.Juni Historiske Dokumenter*, Oslo, Gyldendal, 1956

Hambro, J, *CJ Hambro, liv og drøm*, Oslo, Aschehoug, 1984

Harriman, FJ, *Mission to the North*, New York, Lippincott, 1941

Hartmann, S, *Quislings konferanse med den tyske overkommando*, Samtiden, vol. 5, Oslo, 1956

——, *Spillet om Norge*, Oslo, Mortensen, 1958

——, *Varslene til de Nordiske Legasjoner før den 9. april 1940*, Aarhus, Univeritetsforlaget, 1958

——, *Nytt lys over kritiske faser i Norges historie under annen verdenskrig*, Oslo, Fabritius, 1965

Hase, G, *Die Kriegsmarine erobert Norwegens Fjorde*, Leipzig, Hase & Köhler verlag, 1940

Hauge, A, *Kampene i Norge 1940*, vols 1 and 2, Oslo, Dreyer, 1978

Heradstveit, PØ, *Quisling hvem var han?*, Oslo, Hjemmets Forlag, 1976

——, *Kongen som sa nei*, Oslo, Hjemmenes Forlag, 1979

Herrmann, H, *Eagle's Wings*, Shrewsbury, Guild/Airlife, 1991

Herzog, P, *Drei Kriegsschiffe Blücher*, Marinekameradschaft SKrz. Blücher im Deutschen Marinebund

Heye, AW, *Z 13 von Kiel bis Narvik*, Berlin, Mittler, 1942

Hinsley, FH, *British Intelligence in the Second World War*, London, HMSO, 1993

Hjelmtveit, N, *Vekstår og Vargtid* Oslo, Aschehoug, 1969

Holst, JJ, 'Surprise, Signals and Reaction', *Cooperation and Conflict*, 1:3 (1965)

Hobson, R and Kristiansen, T, *Norsk Forsvarshistorie*, vol. 3, Bergen, Eide, 2001

Høidal, O, *Quisling – En studie i landssvik*, Oslo, Orion, 2002

Hubatsch, W, *Weserübung, Die deutsche Besetzung von Dänemark und Norwegen 1940*, Göttingen, Musterschmidt-Verlag, 1960

Ismay, L, *The Memoirs of General the Lord Ismay*, London, Heinemann, 1960

Jervell, S, *Scener fra en ambassades liv. Berlin 1905–2002*, Kartonisert utgave, Deichmanske bibliotek

Karlbom, R, 'Sweden's Iron Ore Exports to Germany 1933–1944', *Scandinavian Economic History Review*, 13:1–2 (1965)

Kersaudy, F, *Norway 1940*, London, Collins, 1990

Kjølsen, FH, *Optakten til den 9. April*, Copenhagen, Hagerup, 1945

——, *Mit livs logbog*, Copenhagen, Berlingske, 1957

Knudsen, HF, *Jeg var Quislings sekretær*, Copenhagen, Eget Forlag, 1951

Koht, H, *Norge neutralt och överfallet*, Stockholm, Natur och Kultur, 1941

——, *Frå skanse til skanse*, Oslo, Tiden, 1947

——, *Norsk Utanrikspolitikk fram til 9. april 1940*, Oslo, Tiden, 1947

——, *For Fred og Fridom i Krigstid 1939–1940*, Oslo, Tiden, 1957

Koop, G and Schmolke, K-P, *Battleships of the Scharnhorst Class*, London, Greenhill, 1999

—— and ——, *Heavy Cruisers of the Admiral Hipper Class*, London, Greenhill, 2001

Krancke, T, *Norwegen Unternehmen* AW 5(1965) 6

Kristiansen, T, *Krigsplaner og politikk i mellomkrigstiden*, Oslo, Forsvarets skolesenter/Institutt for forsvarsstudier, 2004

Kurowski, F, *Seekrieg aus der Luft*, Herford, Mittler, 1979

Lie, T, *Leve eller dø*, Oslo, Tiden, 1955

Lochner, RK, *Als das Eis brach*, Munich, Heyne Verlag, 1983

Macleod, R (ed.), *Time Unguarded, The Ironside Diaries 1937–1939*, New York, McKay, 1963

Mæsel, K, *Ni dager i April*, Oslo, Ex Libris, 1990

——, *Kristiansand i krig – 9. April 1940*, Kristiansand, Fædrelandsvennen, 1995

Mannerheim, G, *Minnen*, vol. 2, Stockholm, Schildts, 1952

Müllern, H, *Sveriges järnmalm och de krigförandes planer 1939–1940, Aktuellt och historiskt*, Årg 1/1953

Munthe, M, *Sweet is War*, London, Duckworth, 1954

Munthe-Kaas, O, *Krigen i Narvikavsnittet 1940*, Oslo, 1968

Nøkleby, B, 'Fra November til April – sendemann Bräuers personlige politikk', in Paulsen, H (ed.), *1940: fra nøytral til okkupert*, Oslo, Universitetsforlaget, 1969

——, *Da krigen kom*, Oslo, Gyldendal, 1989

Normann, H, *Uheldig generalstab*, Oslo, Pax, 1978

Nygaardsvold, J, *Beretning om den Norske Regjerings virksomhet fra 9. April 1940 til 25. Juni 1945*, Oslo, Stortinget, 1946–7

——, *Norge i krig 9. April–7. Juni 1940*, Oslo, Tiden, 1982

Øksendal, A, *Gulltransporten*, Oslo, Aschehoug, 1974

Omberg, A, *Blüchers undergang, Kampen om Oslofjorden*, Oslo, Alb. Cammermeyer , 1946

Ottmer, HM, *Weserübung*, Munich, Oldenbourg Verlag, 1994

Partridge, RT, *Operation Skua*, Yeovilton, FAA Museum, 1983

Petterøe, A, *Fem år på banjeren*, Fredrikstad, Delfinen, 1995

Pruck, E, *Abwehraussenstelle Norwegen*, Marine Rundschau no. 4, 1956

Raeder, E, *Mein Leben*, vol. 2, Thübingen, Verlag Fritz Schlichtenmayer, 1957

Ræder, G, *De uunnværlig flinke*, Oslo, Gyldendal, 1975

Reid, M and Rolstad, LC, *April 1940, En Krigsdagbok*, Oslo, Gyldendal, 1980

Reynaud, P, *La France a sauvé l'Europe*, Paris, Editions Flammarion, 1947

Riste, O, *Weserübung, det perfekte strategiske overfall?*, Forsvarsstudier, 4/94

Rødland, I, *Det tyske angrepet på Egersund og Dalane 1940*, Egersund, Dalane Folkemuseum, 1974

Roskill, S, *The War at Sea*, London, HMSO, 1954

——, *Churchill and the Admirals*, London, Pen & Sword, 2004

Ruge, O, *Felttoget, erindringer fra kampene April–Juni 1940*, Oslo, Aschehoug, 1989

Salmon, P, 'Churchill, the Admiralty and the Narvik Traffic, September–November 1939', *Scandinavian Journal of History*, 4 (1979)

——, 'British Strategy and Norway 1939–40', in Salmon, P (ed.), *Britain and Norway in the Second World War*, London, HMSO, 1995

Seraphim, HG, *Das Politische Tagebuch Alfred Rosenbergs*, Munich, Deutscher Taschenbuch Verlag, 1964

Sivertsen, J, *Vår ære og vår avmakt – Panserskipet Norges kamp I Narvik 9. april 1940*, Stavanger, Norsk Tidsskrift for Sjøvesen, 1996

Sivertsen, SC, *Sjøforsvaret i Rogaland*, Stavanger, Norsk Tidsskrift for Sjøvesen, 1995

——, *Viseadmiral Thore Horve fra Stavanger*, Stavanger, Norsk Tidsskrift for Sjøvesen, 2000

Skard, S, *Mennesket Halvdan Koht*, Oslo, Det Norske Samlaget, 1982

Skodvin, M, *Striden om okkupasjonsstyret i Norge*, Oslo, Det Norske Samlaget, 1956

——, *Bakgrunnen for 9. april*, Syn og Segn no. 3, 1961

——, *Norge i Stormaktsstrategien*, Oslo, Universitetsforlaget, 1969

——, 'Norwegian Neutrality and the Question of Credibility', *Scandinavian Journal of History*, 2 (1977)

Skogheim, D and Westrheim, H, *Alarm, Krigen i Nordland 1940*, Oslo, Tiden, 1984

Sørensen, J, *Panserskipene 1895–1940*, Stavanger, Norsk Tidsskrift for Sjøvesen, 2000

Springenschmid, K, *Die Männer von Narvik*, Gratz, Leopold Stocker, 1970

Steen, EA, *Norges Sjøkrig 1940–45*, vol. 1, Oslo, Gyldendal, 1954

——, *Norges Sjøkrig 1940–45*, vol. 2, Oslo, Gyldendal, 1954

——, *Norges Sjøkrig 1940–45*, vol. 3, Oslo, Gyldendal, 1956

——, *Sjøforsvarets kamper og virke i Nord-Norge i 1940*, Oslo, Gyldendal, 1958

Stevens, EH (ed.), *Trial of Nikolaus von Falkenhorst*, London, William Hodge, 1949

Torgersen, M, *Kampene i Rogaland*, Stavanger, Stavanger Aftenblad, 1980

Vian, P, *Action this Day*, London, Muller, 1960

Whitley, MJ, *German Cruisers of World War Two*, London, Arms and Armour Press, 1985

——, *German Capital Ships of World War Two*, London, Arms and Armour Press, 1989

Willoch, GI, *Bergen Festning falt 9.april 1940. Hvorfor?*, NMT 136/1 1966

Willoch. K, *Minner og meninger*, Oslo, Schibsted, 1988

Wyller, T and Stahl, K, *Aprildagene 1940*, Stavanger, Stabenfeldt, 1959

Index

Names

Ships

Br	–	British
Fr	–	French
G	–	German
N	–	Norwegian
Pl	–	Polish
US	–	American